C000050711

Journal of the American Revolution

EDITORIAL BOARD

TODD ANDRLIK, EDITOR-IN-CHIEF

DON N. HAGIST, EDITOR

HUGH T. HARRINGTON, EDITOR EMERITUS

J. L. BELL, ASSOCIATE EDITOR

JIM PIECUCH, ASSOCIATE EDITOR

RAY RAPHAEL, ASSOCIATE EDITOR

JOURNAL

OF THE

AMERICAN
REVOLUTION

Annual Volume 2017

WESTHOLME
Yardley

Compilation © 2017 The Journal of the American Revolution

All articles © 2017 by their respective authors

Images are from the Library of Congress unless otherwise indicated.

All rights reserved under International and Pan-American Copyright Conventions. No part of this book may be reproduced in any form or by any electronic or mechanical means, including information storage and retrieval systems, without permission in writing from the publisher, except by a reviewer who may quote brief passages in a review.

Westholme Publishing, LLC
904 Edgewood Road
Yardley, Pennsylvania 19067
Visit our Web site at www.westholmepublishing.com

ISBN: 978-1-59416-278-7

Printed in the United States of America.

CONTENTS

EDITORS' INTRODUCTION

We all learned the story of the American Revolution: colonists protest unjust taxation by throwing tea into Boston harbor, fighting breaks out, independence is declared, the British surrender at Yorktown, and the Constitution is ratified. Of course, a single good book will reveal that there's more to it than that, but even the best studies of the quarter-century between the Stamp Act and the ratification of the Constitution can give no more than an overview of the critical events. A lot happened in twenty-five years. Every piece of legislation, every military action, every event involved much activity by many people, including decisions, wrangling, ponderings, conflicts, progress and setbacks of all sorts. One need only to look at current events to realize the complexity of historical events, that twenty-five years in the life of an individual means hundreds of individual experiences and stories. Compound that over several million people, and there's a lot of history to be explored.

Exploring this history is what *Journal of the American Revolution* is about. With several new articles every week, we bring out the details that other venues cannot. In this, our fourth annual compilation of selected articles, our contributors showcase many things. We see the political maneuvering that took place to get single pieces of controversial legislation passed, revealing that policies concerning the American colonies were contentious within the British government as well as in America. We learn that many soldiers followed paths of self-preservation rather than unwavering dedication to a cause. We look at global aspects of the conflict such as the influence and involvement of Holland and India. We see how war was waged at sea as well as on land, and in the media as well as on the battlefield. We dissect the diverse religious, cultural, national, social and economic influences that were active in different ways in every community, affecting every citizen at least as much as politics did. We explore fascinating facets of major figures such as Washington, Jefferson, Hamilton and Arnold. Just as important, we follow the lives of individual soldiers and civilians confronted with disruption of political upheaval and war, telling their unheralded stories of courage and sacrifice.

Above all, we see that the American Revolution was not just a simple series of deterministic events, but a complex web of individual experiences, challenges, choices, actions and fates. Story after story. And there are lots more where these came from.

Henry McCulloh: The Unknown Co-Architect of the Stamp Act

❧ BOB RUPPERT ☙

The Stamp Act of 1765 is closely associated with Lord George Grenville, First Lord of the Treasury and the Prime Minister of England. However, there were other members of the British Government who played a roll in the direct construction and enactment of the Act. Some of them were Charles Jenkinson, Senior Secretary of the Treasury; Thomas Whately, Junior Secretary of the Treasury; Thomas Townshend, Lord of the Treasury under Rockingham, and Thomas Cruwys, Solicitor to the Stamp Office. There is one name, however, that should be part of the list, but history has been unclear as to the exact role that he played. His name is Henry McCulloh. His story has two distinct parts. The first spans from his time in the Plantations Office to his return to England from North Carolina in 1747; these years are about him as merchant and land speculator. The second part begins with his return to England and ends in the fall of 1765; these years are about his role in designing the Stamp Act, and are focus of this article.

Henry McCulloh, having viewed the situation and conditions in North Carolina firsthand and having been part of Gov. Gabriel Johnston's inner circle for six years, considered himself knowledgeable about colonial problems. Upon his return to England in 1747 he made himself available to the government as an advisor. McCulloh believed that four issues would continue to dog England's imperial administration if not remedied. They were the need for a stable colonial currency, royal officials' refusal to follow their instructions, accurate records of their proceedings being sent back to the Board of Trade, and an effective and efficient manner of collecting revenues. In 1751, he submitted to the Earl of Halifax, then President of the Board of Trade, a proposal for creating and issuing bills of credit under the denomination of Exchequer Bills of Union. He also recommended:

all Writings, Deeds, Instruments or other matters relating to the law in the said Provinces should be on Stamp Paper or Parchment and . . . the Money arising therefrom should be applied only to the Security and Advantage of the Colonies under the Management of the said Council of Trade , it is conceived that a very large Sum would arise . . . thereby the colonies would not be much Burthensome to this Kingdom in advancing money for their Security and enlargement.[1]

Unfortunately, the proposal was given little attention. Not to be deterred, over the next six years he wrote four pamphlets that focused on the same issues.

His first pamphlet, written in 1754, was entitled *General Thoughts on the Construction, Use and Abuse of the Great Offices*. He argued that,

> The Prerogative of the Crown and the Inspection of a Sovereign, is altogether formed for the Benefit of the Subject . . . But when the order of the great Offices . . . doth not open to the View of the Crown every Matter and Act of Importance, the wrong Frame of them will become a Snare to the Subject; remove all kind of Emulation in serving the Crown; . . . and draw Lines of Distinction between the Subjects, so as to make it impossible for any Person, however qualified, to attain the Favor of the Prince, unless he hath some Connections with Men of Power.[2]

His second pamphlet, written in 1755, was entitled *The Wisdom and Policy of the French in the Construction of their Great Offices*. McCulloh began by quickly referencing the previous pamphlet as a segue:

> when . . . private Interest is preferred to the public Good, and Stratagems are employed to deceive the People, it destroys Society . . . when the Channels of Information are obstructed, the Crown cannot either punish the Guilty, nor reward the Virtuous, nor in any respect exercise those Powers which are lodged in it for the Safety and Benefit of the Subject.

He then went on to contrast the procedures employed by the France's Imperial Administration with those of England:

> in order to keep all the Channels of Information open to the View of the Crown, all the Great Boards in France do report to the King in

---

1. British Museum and Library, Additional Manuscripts: 32874, *f.* 310.
2. Henry McCulloh, *General Thoughts on the Construction, Use and Abuse of the Great Offices* . . . (London: R. Baldwin, 1754), 1–4.

his Council of State the Course of the Officers belonging to the respective Boards [this did not occur in England on any regular basis].

At the Accession of every King, the Arrets of the former King in Council are renewed [this did not occur in England].

the Council of Commerce are under absolute Necessity, and even subject to great Penalties . . . if they do not examine and discuss all the Propositions and Memorials sent to them [this did not occur in England].

the [colonial] records are so regularly formed, kept, and transmitted, that the French Council of Commerce depend principally upon the Records in Matters of Information [this seldom occurred in England].

All the Revenues arising in the Colonies are accounted for in the Chamber of Accompts . . . by this means, there is a constant Fund of Supply for the Use of the Colonies [this was not established].[3]

McCulloh's third pamphlet, also written in 1755, *A Miscellaneous Essay Concerning the Courses pursued by Great Britain in the Affairs of her Colonies,* argued that,

In all well-regulated Governments there ought to be fixed and certain Measures which are not to be departed from, and that the Order and Subserviency of the Parts of all lesser Systems ought to concur to the Good of the general system, or else every Thing must run into Anarchy and Confusion . . . the principal Object in View is so to regulate our Offices in America, as to have a mutual Relation or Dependence upon the general System, or Plan of Government established.

He then cited the problems that result when this does not occur:

Governors . . . do many Acts of Government without the . . . Advice of their Council, and consequently no Entry thereof is made; At other Times, when Matters have been determined in Council, by the Governor's great Influence at the Board . . . Matters have been imperfectly entered; They keep back Records and do not transmit them to the proper Boards at Home; Governors have frequently formed Connections with particular Parties or Factions in the Assemblies . . . [and so pass laws] suited to their private Views and Interest.[4]

3. Henry McCulloh, *The Wisdom and Policy of the French in the Construction of their Great Offices* . . . (London: R. Baldwin, 1755), 4, 14, 19, 35, 55, 66, 72, 124.
4. Henry McCulloh, *A Miscellaneous Essay Concerning the Courses pursued by Great Britain in the Affairs of her Colonies* . . . (London: R. Baldwin, 1955), 10, 15, 19–20, 61–63, 67–68.

His final pamphlet, written in 1757, was entitled *Proposals for Uniting the English Colonies on the Continent of America*. It was in this work that he tied all of his ideas together.

> We entered into a War [the Seven Years' War], without regulating our Affairs, and establishing a Plan or System of Action; we have been thereby liable to an infinite Number of Mistakes and Inadvertencies . . . this ought to induce us, before we proceed further, to establish some invariable and fixed Plan of Action; for without it, private Interest will, for the most part, be preferred to the public Good.

He outlined what needed to be done:

> the Charter Governments are entitled to make Bye Laws for the better ordering their own Domestic Affairs, yet they are not entitled . . . in obstructing the Trade of this Kingdom; Bills of Credit . . . should be lent out on Land Security, at Legal Interest and as such persons possessed of the said Bills, should be entitled to pay their. . . . Provincial Taxes, in the Payment of the Quit-rents to the Crown, and of the Customs, and also in the Payment of such provincial troops, as are raised for the mutual Defense of the Colonies; . . . [and finally in order to create a Fund of Supply for the Use of the Colonies there should be] introduce[d] "a Stamped Duty on Vellum and paper in America, and to lower the Duty upon foreign Rum, Sugar, and Molasses, imported into our Colonies to one Penny Sterling per Gallon; which Duties, if Justly collected, would amount together to upwards of £60,000 Sterling per Annum.[5]

In 1761, after returning to the Plantation Office in England, McCulloh sent a

> discourse to the Earl of Bute, Secretary of State for the Northern Department, entitled *Miscellaneous Representations Relative to Our Concerns in America*. He continued to maintain that the whole colonial system of administration needed to be reorganized. He stressed the need for a fund in the colonies. It would be created "by a Stamp Duty on Vellum and Paper . . . and also by regulating and lowering the Duties upon French Rum and Molasses." To protect the value of the fund, he believed "colonial currency must be regulated and made uniform."[6]

5. Henry McCulloh, *Proposals for Uniting the English Colonies on the Continent of America* . . . (London: J. Wilkie, 1757), 11–12, 15–16, 18–19, 23–24, 31–32.
6. Henry McCulloh, *Miscellaneous Representations Relative to Our Concerns in America* (London: George Harding, 1761), 6–8, 11–12.

It is important to mention that Henry McCulloh was not the first government official to recommend a colonial stamp duty to the Board of Trade, but he was the most persistent. The notion of levying a duty upon the colonies was first proposed in 1722 by Archibald Cummings, a surveyor and customs official in Boston, and again in 1742 by Sir William Keith, the deputy governor of Pennsylvania.[7] Keith outlined his plan in *Two Papers on the Subject of Taxing the British Colonies in America.*[8] The duties, Keith believed, were the means of putting "an entire stop to all those Complaints and disputes, daily arising between the people of the Colonies, and their Respective Governours [and of reducing] the immediate Quantity of Paper Bills Struck in many of the colonies to the discouragement of Fair Trade."[9]

On July 5, 1763, Henry McCulloh sent a general proposal to Charles Jenkinson, Senior Secretary of the Treasury and former private secretary to Lord Bute, who was investigating ways to raise revenue in the colonies. In his proposal he outlined a plan for curbing the smuggling of rum and molasses as well as a plan for a

> stamp duty on vellum and paper in America, at sixpence, twelvepence and eighteenpence per sheet, would at moderate computation, amount to sixty thousand sterling per annum; or, if extended to the West Indies, would produce double that sum.[10]

On July 29, the Lords of the Treasury wrote to the Commissioners of Customs requesting what "further checks and restraints to be imposed by Parliament . . . will most contribute" to the collection of revenues in the colonies.[11]

On September 8, Jenkinson instructed Thomas Cruwys, the solicitor to the Stamp Office, to work with McCulloh on the plan for addressing the concerns of the Lords of the Treasury; McCulloh was to provide the knowledge of the colonial conditions and the ways to raise revenue—Cruwys was to provide the legal and technical style to the plan.

7. Lawrence H. Gipson, *Jared Ingersoll: A Study of American Loyalism in Relation to British Colonial Government* (New Haven CT: Yale University Press, 1920), 116–117.
8. Sir William Keith, *Two Papers on the Subject of Taxing the British Colonies in America* (London: J. Almon, 1767).
9. William Keith, "Reasons Humbly Offered in Support of a Proposal Lately Made to Extend the Duties of Stampt paper and Parchment all Over the British Plantations, December 17, 1742," British Museum and Library, *Newcastle Papers* in Additional Manuscripts: 33028, 376–77.
10. William J. Smith, ed., *The Grenville Papers: Being the Correspondence of Richard Grenville Earl Temple, K.G. and the Right Hon. George Grenville* (London: John Murray, 1852), 2:373–74.
11. Treasury Minute, July 29, 1763, Treasury Papers, XXIX, 35, *f.* 135.

Three days later, the Commissioners wrote back to the Lords and stated that the Molasses Act of 1733 had been "for the most part either wholly evaded or fraudulently compounded."[12] They proceeded to recommend the same duty reduction that McCulloh had recommended in 1757.

On September 14, McCulloh and Cruwys met for three hours. The next day Cruwys presented to Sir James Calder, one of the Commissioners of Stamp Duties, a comprehensive set of notes from the previous day's meeting. After receiving Calder's approval, Cruwys took the notes to Grenville.[13]

On September 23, the Lords of the Treasury sent instructions to the Commissioners of Customs to prepare a bill that outlined a plan for dealing with colonial smuggling.[14]

That same day Grenville directed Jenkinson to "write to the Commissioners of Stamp Duties to prepare a draft of a bill to be presented to Parliament for extending the stamp duties to the colonies."

On October 10, McCulloh was interviewed by an official from the Treasury. The *Minutes and Observations* of the conference, included:

a state of the several articles proposed by Mr. McCulloh to be stamped, and the duties thereon; likewise a state of all the different articles which are now stamped in Great Britain, in order to fix upon the articles which are to be inserted in the law intended for imposing Stamp duties in America and the West Indies.

On the back of the last sheet of the *Minutes* is the following endorsement, "10th October 1763, was presented to Mr. Greenvill, who approved it."[15]

On November 19, two drafts were submitted to the Treasury. One was by McCulloh and the other by Cruwys and Thomas Whately, Junior Secretary of the Treasury. It is not exactly clear why but Cruwys's draft was the one accepted.

On March 9, Grenville, in his budget speech in Parliament, proposed a new tax bill that had been submitted to him by the Lords of the Treas-

---

12. Commissioners of the Customs to the Lords of the Treasury, September 11, 1763, Treasury Papers, I 430, *ff.* 339–342.

13. List of Articles proposed by McCulloh to be Taxes, October 10, 1763, in the British Museum and Library, Hardwicke Manuscripts, Additional Manuscripts, 35910, *ff.* 136–159.

14. Thomas Whately to the Commissioners of the Customs, September 23, 1763, Treasury Papers, XI, 22, *ff.* 319–320.

15. *Minutes and Observations taken in Conference with Mr. McCulloh.* British Museum and Library, Additional Manuscripts: 36226, 357.

ury and the Commissioners of the Customs; it was a revision of the Molasses Act and came to be known as Sugar bill. Molasses was being smuggled into the colonies from the French West Indies because it was cheaper than that sold in the British West Indies. The colonies were importing as much as 8,000,000 gallons of molasses annually.[16] By lowering the duties on British molasses from six-pence to three-pence per gallon, Grenville was undercutting French sales and increasing British sales. The Act also gave wider authority to Vice-Admiralty Courts in order to reduce smuggling. This temporarily put a halt to the work of Cruwys and Jenkinson. The Sugar bill was officially approved on April 5.

At this point McCulloh disappears from any further account of the Stamp bill's preparation.

On July 2, Jenkinson wrote to Grenville,

> In the last Session of Parliament you assigned as a reason for not going on with the Stamp Act, that you waited only for further information on that subject. This having been said, should not Government appear to take some step for that purpose? I mentioned this to you soon after the Parliament was up. I remember your objections to it; but I think the information mat be procured in a manner to obviate those objections.[17]

On August 11, the Earl of Halifax, now the Secretary of State for the Southern Department and the person to whom McCulloh had sent his 1751 proposal, issued a circular letter to all of the colonial governors asking for "a list of all instruments made use of in public transactions, law proceedings, grants, conveyances, [and] securities of land or money"[18] that could be required to bear a stamp.

Grenville and Jenkinson quickly realized that the Sugar Act was costing more to operate than it brought in. A new source of revenue was needed to cover the shortfall between the cost of maintaining British troops in the colonies and the revenue generated by the Sugar Act. Work was ordered to resume on the Stamp bill. Jenkinson wrote:

> The people of the Colonies have done themselves much hurt by their resistance to the legislature of this kingdom in general . . . The economical spirit which has been introduced in consequence of the late law [the Sugar Act], if it should continue, will do no hurt to the

16. Public Records Office, Treasury, 1/434:119.
17. Smith, ed., *The Grenville Papers*, 2:373.
18. John Russell Bartlett, ed., *Records of the Colony of Rhode Island and providence Plantations, in New England* (Providence: Knowles, Anthony & Co., 1861), 6: 404.

public in general, though it might in a small degree diminish the revenue.[19]

Shortly after the governors' lists that had been requested by Halifax arrived in England, Thomas Whately, Junior Secretary of the Treasury and the person who had taken over the role of Thomas Cruwys, drew up a detailed list of duties and presented it to the Lords of the Treasury in mid-December. In January of 1765, he presented the final draft of the bill to the Lords of Trade. Whately was concerned about generating revenue, but he was more concerned that the evasion of the Laws of Trade struck at the heart of Great Britain's interests.

The contraband trade that is carried on there is a subject of the most serious consideration; and is become a much more alarming circumstance, than that increase in wealth, people, and territory, which raises apprehensions in many persons that the colonies may break off their connection with Great Britain.

He believed the Laws of Trade, properly applied and executed, would regulate and secure the colonies to the mother-country. He believed that an increase in customs duties would not only prove burdensome to trade, but also difficult to collect. The colonies, however, could afford a nominal tax that could prove equitable in its distribution.[20]

On February 13, the Stamp Bill was given a first reading and on February 15, its second reading. Five weeks later, on March 22, the bill became law; it passed by a vote of 205 to 49 in the House of Commons.

On July 13, Henry McCulloh reappears with an assessment of the recently approved Act entitled, *General Thoughts* . . . He predicted that the Act would encounter opposition in the colonies because it did not address "several . . . matters" that "ought to have been taken into Consideration" and contained several "very Exceptionable" clauses that were unnecessary. [21] His work, an appeal for revision of the Act, was addressed to the Honourable Thomas Townshend who had been appointed Lord of the Treasury just the day before.

---

19. "Letter from Charles Jenkinson, Senior Sec'y of Treasury, to Richard Wolters, Jan. 18, 1765," in the British Museum and Library, Liverpool Papers, Additional Manuscript, 38,304, folder 114.

20. Thomas Whately, *The Regulations Lately made Concerning the Colonies and the Taxes Imposed upon them, Considered* (London: J. Wilkie, 1765), 91–92, 87, 53, 76.

21. Henry McCulloh, *General Thoughts, endeavouring to demonstrate that the Legislature here, in all Cases of a public and General Concern, have a Right to Tax the British Colonies; But that, with respect to the late American Stamp Duty Bill, there are several Clauses inserted therein which are very Exceptionable, and have, as humbly Conceived, passed upon wrong Information*, Huntington Manuscripts, Townshend Collection (San Marino, CA: Henry E. Huntington Library and Art Gallery), 1480.

McCulloh did not believe the Act, as constructed, was going to succeed because it neglected to take into consideration the most basic problem: the medium of exchange. All stamped documents required payment in specie of which there was very little in the colonies. To require this "without Substituting any thing as a Medium in the Course of Payment" made it "impossible for many of the Colonists to pay Obedience to the said Law."

There also were some clauses that were inappropriate to the colonial conditions were considered "very Obnoxious":

> One, the Act required a stamp on all "Monitions, Libels, Answers, Allegations, Inventories, or Renunciations in Courts Exercising Ecclesiastical Jurisdiction." McCulloh stated, "There is not in America any Ecclesiastical Courts, but the people Settled there, who are mostly Dissenters or Sectuarys of various other Denominations, look upon the above Clause as a prelude to the Establishment of such Courts; and many of them would sooner Forfeit their Lives than pay Obedience to such Establishment."
>
> Two, violations of the Stamp Duty would be addressed in Vice-Admiralty courts instead of common law courts where guilt or innocence was determined by a judge and not by a jury of one's peers. "The Colonies [will] insist that, by the above Clause, they are denied their privileges they are entitled to as Free born Subjects of England . . . [that is] to the benefits of the Common Law of England, and to the Privileges Granted by Magna Charta."
>
> Three, duties would be placed upon "donation, presentation, collation, or institution of or to any benefice or any writ or instrument for the like purpose, or any register, entry, testimonial, or certificate of any degree taken in any university, academy, college, or seminary of learning." McCulloh believed "Their Seminaries of Learning are most of them of a very late date, and have been Encouraged by his Majesty's Bounty, and from the Contributions of well Disposed persons here. Therefore any Discouragements given to them, will be looked upon as a great hardship."[22]

It was clear to McCulloh that the final architects of the Act had no understanding of conditions in the American colonies. He ended his appeal with "I was desired to assist . . . in drawing the Stamp Duty Bill, but I left out the above, and several other Clauses that are now incerted therein, however that Affair was taken out of my Hands, and the Bill was afterwards drawn upon the plan of Business in use here which is

22. Ibid.

very different from what ought to have been observed in America." He believed the Act would " be another great means of introducing much disturbance and confusion in the . . . Colonies." He knew that to attempt to enforce the Act was useless. He believed that "There could not be a more effectual Method taken to render the said Colonies in Process of time, independent of their Mother Country."[23]

23. Ibid.

How Britain Tried to Intimidate Colonial Taxpayers into Compliance

❧ NEAL NUSHOLTZ ❧

The Fourth Amendment: The right of the people to be secure in their persons, houses, papers, and effects, against unreasonable searches and seizures, shall not be violated, and no Warrants shall issue, but upon probable cause, supported by Oath or affirmation, and particularly describing the place to be searched, and the persons or things to be seized.

During 1767, England enacted a few laws to generate more revenue in the American Colonies. One of those laws created a Board of Customs Commissioners to supervise revenue collection in America.[1]

THE BOARD OF CUSTOMS COMMISSIONERS

The Board located itself in Boston on November 5, 1767.[2] Their report home on February 12, 1768 sounded desperate. There was a shortage of seizures:

> . . . our Officers in these northern parts have been greatly discouraged for want of support from Government.
>
> Tho' smugling has been carried to a very great height, yet six seizures only have been made in the New England Provinces, within the course of two years and a half; and only one prosecuted to effect. a second· was rescued out of the custody of our Officers at Falmouth who were at the same time attacked by a Mob; A third was rescued at Newbury, and the Officers greatly abused, A fourth was carried off clandestinely at New-London, while, under prosecution; the fifth and sixth were acquitted at Rhode Island, thro' the combination and influence of the people. The Officers of this Port were resisted in the

---

1. Oliver Morton Dickerson, *The Navigation Acts and the American Revolution* (Philadelphia, PA: University of Pennsylvania Press, 1974), 195–196, 208.
2. G.G. Wolkins, "Hancock's Sloop Liberty," *Massachusetts Historical Journal*, March 1922," Vol. 55, 241.

Summer 1766, at noonday, when endeavouring to enter the house of one Malcolm, and finding themselves unsupported against a numerous mob that was assembled, they were obliged to retire without making the seizure . . .

At present, there is not a Ship of War in the province, nor a company of Soldiers nearer than New York, which is two hundred and fifty miles distant from this place.[3]

Three months later, the navy's commander in chief of the North American station, Samuel Hood, responded. On May 2, he ordered Capt. John Corner "to proceed without loss of time with His Majesty's ship *Romney* under your command to Boston . . . to be aiding and assisting unto the Commissioner of the Customs."[4] On June 10, two revenue officers went on board John Hancock's sloop, the *Liberty,* at the end of Hancock's wharf. They seized the ship and turned it over to the custody of the *Romney.*

When they saw the *Liberty* being taken, a mob came running onto the wharf. They threatened to throw the *Romney's* people overboard. They pelted the officers with rocks and grabbed the mooring lines of the *Liberty* in a tug of war with the *Romney.* After the *Romney* towed the *Liberty* away, the mob beat up the two seizing revenue officers. Members of the Board of Customs Commissioners hid for the night. The Commissioners fled to Castle William on the *Romney* the following morning. They dispatched a missive to England covering the events.[5]

THE COMING OF THE TROOPS

After September of 1768, an anonymous newspaper column about events in Boston began to appear in Boston, New York, Philadelphia, other parts of the country and in England.[6] It was titled *A Journal of the Times.* It started with a report of the arrival of troops on September 28, 1768: "Advice received that the men of war and transports from Halifax, with about 900 troops from several parts of America were safe arrived at Nantasket Harbor."[7] Nantasket Peninsula is about 11 miles from Boston as the crow flies.

On October 1, 1768, 700 troops landed in Boston and marched through town to camp out in the Commons.[8] An October 16, 1768 entry reported:

3. Ibid., 264, 267.
4. Ibid., 271.
5. Ibid., 274–275.
6. Oliver Morton Dickerson, *Boston under Military Rule 1768–1769* (Da Capo Press, New York, 1970), i-xiii.
7. Ibid., 1.
8. Ibid., 2.

This day Capt. Jenkins arrived from London, who brought a print of August 13th, in which there is the following article,—"There are 4000 troops ordered for Boston, which it is thought will sufficiently intimidate those people to comply with the laws enacted in England; especially as the other colonies seem to have deserted them.[9]

Another 2,000 troops arrived on October 24, 1768.[10] A November 18, 1768 entry reported twelve ships of war plying the waters of Boston when the 64th and 65th Regiments landed with 500 men each.[11] A December 26, 1768 *Journal* entry reported:

This morning a vessel from Salem or Marblehead, having a cask of sugar on board, which it was supposed had not been properly cleared out, was seized by one of the custom-house officers, who brought a number of SOLDIERS! to assist and keep possession of said vessel, but upon discovery that the sugar had been reported at the Custom-House, she was soon released. It is very extraordinary that soldiers should be called in upon such occasions: It seems calculated to lead the Administration to conceive that the quartering of troops in this town is necessary to enable the customhouse officers to discharge their duty.[12]

THE BRITISH NAVIGATION ACTS

The British Navy was called to Boston to enforce the British Navigation Acts. The Navigation Acts were a mercantile system enforced by the British Navy. The Acts were designed to raise revenue, increase economic production, expand markets and prevent home producers from being driven out of their occupations by cheaper, foreign competition.[13] Enumerated colonial goods could only be exported to other ports within the Empire or to other countries after they were shipped to England first.[14] Duties were imposed on importation of various goods such as, tea, British grown coffee, sugars, molasses, various wines and various cloths.[15]

The Navigation Acts relied on voluntary compliance by shipping merchants. Any voluntary system of taxation must include three essential features of enforcement. Government must probe for violations, as-

9. Ibid., 6.
10. Ibid., 18.
11. Ibid., 23.
12. Ibid., 40.
13. Ibid., 12 n1, 10 n17.
14. Ibid., 10–11.
15. Ibid., 172–173; 195–197.

sert penalties for non-compliance and establish rules that throw the task of proving compliance with the law upon the individual.[16] The ease of proving was solved with a strict system of cockets and bonds.

Cockets were an inventory of the taxable cargo on board a ship upon which duties were paid. Cockets were required on all ships beyond two leagues (7 miles) from the coast of the colonies. They were stamped for a fee[17] by a customs officer called a searcher.[18] Under Section 29 of the 1764 Sugar Act, goods found on board that were not listed on the cocket were confiscated.

Bonds guaranteed payment of treble penalties in the event that those colonial goods which were supposed to go to England (or other ports in the Empire) ended up going somewhere else. Bonds had to be approved by the collector and were required to be obtained prior to each time goods were placed on board a ship. After the Sugar Act of 1764, loading without a bond was subject to forfeiture of ship and cargo. [19]

When a ship with bonded goods arrived at its destination, the export bond would be shown and a certificate of delivery to discharge the bond would be given by a customs official. The discharge certificate needed to be provided to Customs within 18 months from the date of the bond[20] or the bond would be prosecuted for payment.[21]

Upon arrival at a destination, the master of a ship was obligated to go ashore to make entry in the Custom House, provide the cocket, answer any questions and provide evidence of required bonds.[22] Merchants notified of pending delivery would prepare a bill of entry that was submitted to the collector to calculate duties to be paid. Paperwork would be issued to permit the inspection and unloading of the shipped goods.

When ships were unloaded it was under the watchful eyes of customs officials. On the way to London, ships anchored at Gravesend and a tidesman was put on board to search the vessel. No person could go ashore unless they also had been searched. The goods were listed by the tidesman and checked off as they were loaded onto a small shallow draft boat or barge, called a lighter. The lighter took the goods and the tidewaiter to a loading platform jutting out into the water called a

---

16. Lawrence A. Harper, *The English Navigation Laws* (Octagon Books, Inc. New York), 85.
17. Ibid.
18. Ibid., 90 n18.
19. Ibid., 181 n19.
20. Section XII of the 1764 Sugar Act.
21. Harper, *The English Navigation Laws*, 165 n19.
22. Harper, *The English Navigation Laws*, 179 n1.

quay where the goods were turned over to a landwaiter. The landwaiter unpacked, searched and weighed the imported goods (or sniffed and tasted in the case of wine; or felt by hand in the case of fine cloths).

Any questionable or undeclared items would be sent to the King's Storehouse. After inspection and payment of duties, the unloaded goods were released to the merchants.[23] In the case of a dispute over a confiscation of a ship or goods, the burden of proof was on the owner to prove no violation had occurred.[24]

In the American colonies, the above rules were used to bludgeon the Boston colonists with confiscations during 1768–1769. The regular sightings by the Boston colonists of vessels seized under military escort and turned over to the control of customs officials was a source of great distress. Enforcement of the Navigation Acts was the topic of forty-six *Journal* newspaper stories from September of 1768 through August of 1769. It was characterized as an attack on trade.[25] Of those forty-six *Journal* newspaper stories, thirty-two of them involved seizures for picayune reasons unrelated to smuggling.[26]

One example was when a ship frozen in at the Vineyard was seized for breaking bulk by selling lemons before they spoiled but before entry at the customhouse.[27] Another example was when a seaman on the ship had his own private item for sale. That ship was seized because the item had not been declared on the ship's cocket.[28] One ship was seized for no current violations but on the allegation that it had "some time ago been employed in an illicit trade; and that they may oblige the owner to prove where and how she has been employed."[29] The seizure of John Hancock's sloop, the *Liberty*, on June 10, 1768 was for loading 20 barrels of tar and 200 barrels of oil without a prior bond (loading before bonding was a universal practice of convenience).[30]

The *Journal* complained that customs officers were threatening seizures for nonpayment of unnecessary and repetitious entry and clearance fees as ships traveled up and down the coast (despite an attorney general opinion that said intracoastal entry and clearance were not re-

---

23. Harper, *The English Navigation Laws*, 89–90, n19.
24. Section XLV of the 1764 Sugar Act.
25. Harper, *The English Navigation Laws*, 25 n8, 27, 48, 59, 63, 77, 84, 85, 102, 124–5.
26. Ibid., 9–113 n8.
27. Ibid., 77.
28. Ibid., 79.
29. Ibid., 9.
30. Oliver M. Dickerson, "John Hancock Notorious Smuggler or Near Victim of British Revenue Racketeers," *The Mississippi Valley Historical Review*, Vol. 22 No. 4 (Mar. 1946), 518–519.

quired).[31] A typical search of a ship by customs officials was reported as follows:

> [a customs officer] came on board, bringing a number of other officers as assistants, who with dark langthorns, gimblets, spears for the piercing of casks, spits and other implements of modern introduction made a thorough rummage and search of the hold and cabbin, when happening to find a small case which contained scarce six quarts of foreign spirits, part of the captains sea stores to carry off same to his employer.[32]

The *Journal* reports may have been sufficient to win the public relations battle. On June 21, 1769, the *Journal* reported that the troops would be leaving Boston over the protests of the Board of Customs Commissioners.[33]

SEARCH AND SEIZURE AND THE COLLECTION OF REVENUE UP TO 1768

Prior to 1768, protections against undue government intrusion from revenue enforcement existed in various forms. They were often abandoned, perhaps because they made it harder to collect revenue. One protection that was argued about during the American Revolution was whether searching customs agents could break into your home to look for smuggled goods.

SEYMAYNE'S CASE

The home search issue discussion starts with the 1604 *Seymayne's Case* written by celebrated jurist Lord Edward Coke. The case is often quoted for the phrase "a man's home is his castle." *Seymayne's Case* addressed whether and when government agents could break into your home. Lord Coke held that only a King's officer under a court issued warrant "may open the doors which are shut and break them." Lord Coke also wrote that warrants to search a home should be based on a written record of facts and not suppositions:

> One or more justice or justices of peace cannot make a warrant upon a bare surmise to break any mans house to search for a felon or for stolen goods, for their being created by act of parliament have no such authority granted unto them by any act of parliament. . . because justices of peace are judges of record, and ought to proceed upon record, and not upon surmises[34]

31. Ibid., 49, 59.
32. Ibid., 77.
33. Ibid., 111.
34. Edwardo Coke, *Coke's Institutes*, "The Fourth Part of the Institutes of the Laws of England, Concerning The Jurisdiction of Courts" (E. and R. Brooke, London, 1644), 176.

A warrant was not required to search a ship. Authority for that came from a July 26, 1660, statute which also included damages if ships were detained without just and reasonable cause:

XXII. The under Searcher or other Officers of Gravesend, having power to visite and search any Ship outward bound, shall not without just & reasonable cause deteyne any such ship under color of searching the goods therein laden above three tides after her arrival at Gravesend under paine of loss of their office & rendering damage to the Merchant & Owner of the Ship [an identical provision provided for "Searchers or other Officers of the Custome House in any of the out ports"][35]

In September of 1660, Parliament added a provision to the statute to allow customs officials to search homes for landed goods by warrant in the daytime. The prior provision for damages for unreasonable detention was removed. Damages were only allowed for false information used to obtain the warrant:

. . . [regarding] any Goods . . . to be landed or conveyed away without due entry thereof first made . . . it shall be lawfull to . . . issue out a Warrant to any person or persons thereby enableing him or them . . . to enter into any House in the day time where such Goods are suspected to be concealed, and in case of resistance to breake open such Houses, and to seize and secure the same goods soe concealed, ... if the Information whereupon any House shall come to be searched shall prove to be false, that then and in such case the party injured shall recover his full damages and costs against the Informer by Action of Trespasse to bee therefore brought against such Informer.[36]

A 1662 statute removed the warrant requirement and replaced it with what became known as a Writ of Assistance. The Writ was a perpetual general warrant that lasted for the lifetime of the King. The Writ allowed for limitless searches during daytime without any prior factual justification. Revenue officers could carry the Writ in their vest pockets while searching whatever vessels, buildings, trunks or packages they thought might contain smuggled goods.

35. Joseph Raphael Frese, *Early Parliamentary Legislation on Writs of Assistance*, Vol. 38 "Publications of the Colonial Society of Massachusetts," 321; see also Danby Pickering, *The Statutes at Large from the Thirty-ninth Year of Q. Elizabeth to the 12th year of K. Charles II. Inclusive Vol VII* (Cambridge 1763), 418.
36. Ibid.

The 1662 revisions also removed damages for trespass. Searching agents were free from liability as long as they were acting under the statute.[37]

> And it shall be lawfull to or for any person or persons authorized by Writt of Assistance under the Seale of his Majestyes Court of Exchequer to take a Constable Headborough or other Publique Officer inhabiting neare unto the place and in the day time to enter and go into any House Shop Cellar Ware-house or Room or other place and in case of resistance to breake open Doores Chests Trunks and other Package there to seize and from thence to bring any kind of Goods & Merchandize whatsoever prohibited and uncustomed and to put and secure the same in his Majesties Store house in the Port next to the place where such seizure shall be made.[38]

A 1736 statute allowed nighttime searches but only if there was probable cause to search:

> It shall and may be lawful for the Officers of the Duties by this Act granted, or any of them, from time to time, and at all Times by Day and by Night (but if in the Night-time in the Presence of a Constable or other Officer of the Peace, Oath being first made by any such Officer or other Person before any justice of the Peace dwelling in or near such Place, of a probable Cause of suspecting the Concealment of any such Spirituous Liquors therein) to enter into all and every of the said Warehouses, Storehouses, Shops, Cellars, Vaults, Rooms, or other Places made use of by any Retaler of any such Spirituous Liquors or Strong Waters.[39]

Under a 1745 Act, officers were protected from liability when illegally seized property was returned to the claimant if the judge certified there was probable cause to seize.[40]

THE WRIT OF ASSISTANCE ARGUMENTS

After King George II died on October 25, 1760, application was made to the Massachusetts Superior Court for new Writs of Assistance. Colonial attorney James Otis argued against the Writ on behalf of sixty-three merchants of Massachusetts Bay. While Otis argued on February 24,

---

37. Ibid.
38. Ibid., 80–81.
39. Vol. 6, *The Statutes at Large from the Third Year of the Reign of King George the Second to the Twentieth year of the Reign of King George the Second* (London 1764), 219.
40. *The Statutes at Large From the Fifth Year of the Reign of King George the Third to the Tenth Year of the Reign of King George the Third, inclusive* (London, 1771), 371–372.

1761, an excited twenty-six-year-old John Adams sat in and took notes.[41] According to Adams's notes, Otis asserted that the old 1660 statute should govern. That was the statute that had required a onetime warrant based on facts. Otis also argued that there was "the priviledge of House." A possibly innocent man should be as "secure in his house, as a Prince in his Castle."

Otis made a third argument. The 1662 law permitting general unlimited seizures was unreasonable. For that, Otis said, the Writ of Assistance should not be allowed. His legal argument was based on a 150-year-old case that had held that an unreasonable law should not be enforced. Otis lost the argument and the Writ was granted.[42] Adams wrote over fifty-five years later, "Then and there the child Independence was born."[43]

BOHNAM'S CASE

The 150 year old case Otis had relied upon to argue that an unreasonable law was unenforceable was *Bonham's Case* written by Lord Coke in 1610. Adam's notes had the *Bonham's Case* cite next to the statement "reason of ye common law to control an act of Parliament."

Bonham's Case involved the alleged false imprisonment of Thomas Bonham. Bonham was a London doctor who had been fined and imprisoned by the Royal College of Medicine for deficient medical practices. The fine was split one-half with the College and one-half with the King.

Bonham had sued the College for false imprisonment. To prevail, Bonham would have to prove he was imprisoned illegally and that meant the law under which Bonham had been imprisoned would have to be illegal. When a judge declares a statute illegal it is called judicial review. In today's world, when there is a constitutional issue to interpret, judicial review is derived from interpreting a higher law that is superior to the legislature. But, in 1610, Bonham was asking Lord Coke to throw out the King's statute based on general legal principles. Striking a law based on a judge's legal reasoning would place the judge above the King.

In his written opinion, Lord Coke reviewed three case precedents where courts had refused to enforce statutes. In one case, the statute

---

41. Josiah Quincy, Jr., *Reports of Cases Argued and Adjudged in the Superior Court of Judicature of the Providence of Massachusetts Bay Between 1761 and 1772* (Boston: Little, Brown and Company, 1865), 414, 471–476, 486.
42. Ibid.
43. Letter from John Adams to William Tudor, 29 March 1817. http://founders.archives.gov/documents/Adams/99-02-02-6735

was not enforced because, if enforced, it would upset too many settled principles of law. In another case there were two conflicting statutes and since only one could be enforced, the other was not enforced. In a third case, there was a penalty imposed upon the failure to perform a task which was impossible to be performed and that statute was not enforced. Coke concluded, following case precedent, that if a law was unreasonable or impossible to be performed, it was void.

Coke held that since the Royal College received one-half of the fines it had assessed, it was a party (i.e. someone who can benefit from the result) and a judge in the same case. Coke said it was impossible for a judge to be a party in a case in which the judge is ruling. Therefore, since the statute under which Bonham was imprisoned was impossible to be performed, it was void. When the King found out, he summoned Coke, removed Coke from the Bench and fired him as the official person who reported the holdings in cases.[44]

Otis's *Bonham's Case* argument was rejected by the widely respected jurist, Sir William Blackstone, in his 1765 *Commentaries on the laws of England*:

> I know it is generally laid down more largely, that acts of parliament contrary to reason are void. But if parliament will positively enact a thing to be done which is unreasonable, I know of no power that can control it . . . to set the judicial power above the legislature would be subversive of all government.[45]

After the American Revolution, state constitutions included prohibitions against general warrants. John Adams wrote the 1780 Massachusetts Constitution.[46] Article XIV appended the word "unreasonable" to searches and seizures for the first time:

> Art. XIV. Every subject has a right to be secure from all unreasonable searches, and seizures, of his person, his houses, his papers, and all his possessions. All warrants, therefore, are contrary to this right, if the cause or foundation of them be not previously supported by oath or affirmation, and if the order in the warrant to a civil officer, to make search in suspected places, or to arrest one or more suspected

---

44. Theodore F.T. Plucknett, "Bonham's Case and Judicial Review," 40 *Harvard Law Review* 30 (1926).

45. William Blackstone, *1 Blackstone's Commentaries* (Oxford Clarendon Press, 1st ed. 1765), 91.

46. John Adams to William D. Williamson, February 28, 1812, Maine Historical Society. See also, www.mass.gov/courts/court-info/sjc/edu-res-center/jn-adams/mass-constitution-1gen.html#JohnAdamsDraftstheMassachusettsConstitution.

persons, or to seize their property, be not accompanied with a special designation of the persons or objects of search, arrest, or seizure; and no warrant ought to be issued but in cases, and with the formalities, prescribed by the laws.[47]

The 1780 Massachusetts Constitution was published on October 30, 1779.[48] Before Sir William Blackstone passed away in February of 1780, he mysteriously left a handwritten note in the margin of his 1778 edition of his *Commentaries.* The note ended up as the following italicized language in the 1783 edition: "But if Parliament will positively enact a thing to be done which is unreasonable, I know of no power *in the ordinary forms of the Constitution* that is vested with authority to control it."[49]

No constitution existed to which Blackstone could have possibly referred other than the one written in 1779 by John Adams. A fair conclusion is that Adams had intended courts to have broad authority to review revenue enforcement for reasonableness.

When the debate over the Fourth Amendment started in the First Congress, the Amendment did not contain the phrase "unreasonable searches and seizures." That language was included after Adams's "faithful friend" Elbridge Gerry proposed adding Adams's phrase on August 17, 1789.[50] Gerry, along with John Adams, was one of the Massachusetts cosigners of the Declaration of Independence.

THE SLIPPERY SLOPE

The justification made for the Writ of Assistance was that if government did not have sudden searching power, people would escape tax collection by sneaking away. In other words, the end justifies the means. That argument was made in 1768 by the British Attorney General William De Grey:

> But it must be observed, that if such a General Writ of Assistants is not granted to the Officer, the true Intent of the Act may in almost every Case be evaded, for if he is obliged, every Time he knows, or has received information of prohibited or uncustomed Goods being

47. Francis Newton Thorpe, *The Federal and State Constitutions, Colonial Charters, and Organic Laws of the State Territories and Colonies Now or Heretofore Forming The United States of America* Vol. VI (Washington, DC: Government Printing Office, 1909), 3088.
48. www.mass.gov/courts/court-info/sjc/edu-res-center/jn-adams/mass-constitution-1gen.html.
49. Plucknett, "Bonham's Case and Judicial Review," 60.
50. *Annals of Congress,* 1st Congress, 783. Adams referred to Gerry as a "faithful friend" in his autobiography. www.masshist.org/digitaladams/archive/doc?id=A1_30&hi=1&query=faithful%20friend%20Elbridge%20Gerry&tag=text&archive=all&rec=13&start=10&numRecs=1082.

concealed, to apply to the Supreme Court of Judicature for a Writ of Assistants, such concealed Goods may be conveyed away before the Writ can be obtained.[51]

Justifying a government assertion of power by saying it will increase revenue is a slippery slope. Under that type of reasoning, an expansion of government power to collect revenue could be unlimited. John Adams created a limitation, reasonableness. For Adams, an assertion of government power to collect revenue was to be reasonable as determined by a particular judge.

Contrast the acceptance of general warrants in Boston with the rejection of general warrants in England when revenue was not involved. During the years 1763–1765, some British newspapers were critical of the government and the King. The Secretary of State issued general warrants allowing messengers to make surprise searches of the homes of three suspected men for seditious papers. The men sued for trespass and won because the warrants were illegal.[52]

CONCLUSION

When Adams wrote the Massachusetts Constitution, it was after Boston had experienced reviled exposure to abuses from tax searches and seizures. Nowadays, the Fourth Amendment has generally been a matter of protecting privacy, largely in the criminal context and mostly on the issue of whether evidence obtained by illegal search can be admitted at trial. Our Supreme Court has said that the Fourth Amendment has no reference to Internal Revenue Service "proceedings for the recovery of debts."[53] Whether you believe that Fourth Amendment reasonableness applies to tax collection depends on what you believe its original purpose was and whether you believe that purpose is obsolete.

The circumstances that existed in 1768 and which exist today is that the need for revenue puts pressure on government to either find new revenue sources or collect from existing sources in new ways. Those efforts can mean more drastic collection methods. If the government tries new harsher methods of collecting revenue, those unprecedented methods can bubble up through the court system where judges similarly concerned with federal revenues might approve those new methods along with a concomitant expansion of federal power. For instance, in

---

51. Josiah Quincy, Jr. *Reports of Cases Argued and Adjudged*, 452–454.
52. *Entick v. Carrington and Three Others*, 19 Howell's State Trials 1029; EWHC KB J98; 95 ER 807(1765); *Wilkes v. Wood*, 19 St. Tr. 1153, 98 ER 489 (1763) and *Money v. Leach*, 19 State Trial 1026 (1765).
53. *Den ex dem. Murray v. Hoboken Land & Imp. Co.*, 59 U.S. 272, 285 (1855).

1980, when presidential candidate Ronald Reagan was campaigning on a promise that he could balance the budget with top rate tax cuts, the Internal Revenue Service was trying to close the budget deficit by engaging in rampant nationwide seizures of property.[54] Three years later, an extraordinary case reached the Supreme Court wherein it was held that under the taxing power the government could force the sale of your home even if you did not owe taxes, as long as it helped the government to collect revenue from someone else who did owe taxes.[55]

The Fourth Amendment could militate against such drastic means of revenue collection by requiring reasonableness. Consider, however, that if harsh collection methods are expected to generate more revenue, then reasonable methods would be expected to yield less revenue. A reluctance to reduce revenue might explain why federal courts have abandoned a Fourth Amendment reasonableness standard for revenue collection. Ironically, the failure of a court to render a legal opinion that could reduce revenue was the event that prompted John Adams to impose a Fourth Amendment reasonableness requirement in the first place. For Adams, a reasonableness requirement was a counterweight to the natural pressure on government and the courts to expand the power of government to collect revenue. Today, that purpose is not obsolete.

---

54. U.S. Government Printing Office, *Internal Revenue Service Collection Practices; Impact on Small Businesses A Report prepared by the Subcommittee on Oversight of Government Management of the Committee on Governmental Affairs, United States Senate,* October 8, 1980.
55. *United States v. Rodgers,* 461 U.S. 677, 678 (1983).

Mount Vernon During the American Revolution

❧ MARY V. THOMPSON ❧

On June 18, 1775, soon after learning that he had been chosen to lead the Continental Army, George Washington sat down to write a difficult letter to his wife, Martha, who was back home at Mount Vernon, to tell her about this unexpected change in circumstances and what it would mean for her: "I therefore beg, that you will summon your whole fortitude, and pass your time as agreeably as possible. Nothing will give me so much sincere satisfaction as to hear this, and to hear it from your own pen."[1] Five days later, as he left Philadelphia to take command of the army near Boston, he wrote a quick note to his wife, assuring her of his love and noting his "full confidence of a happy Meeting with you sometime in the Fall."[2] Neither of them knew at that point that it would be more than eight years before the war was over, that his wife would spend half her time in those years in camp with her husband, and the other half helping to manage Mount Vernon, their beloved Virginia plantation. In the latter role, she and another relative, George Washington's distant cousin Lund Washington, who was the estate manager, would try to complete a building program started by her husband, while facing a multitude of problems, including shortages of basic supplies, escapes by both indentured and enslaved servants, a looming smallpox epidemic, and threats from British forces.

CAST OF CHARACTERS

The years of the American Revolution changed Martha Washington's life almost completely. When the war began in 1775, Martha Dandridge

1. George Washington to Martha Washington, June 18, 1775, *"Worthy Partner": The Papers of Martha Washington*, compiled by Joseph E. Fields (Westport, CT: Greenwood Press, 1994), 160.
2. George Washington to Martha Washington, June 23, 1775, *Ibid.*, 161.

Custis Washington was a forty-four-year-old wife and mother and the mistress of a large plantation. She had been given the standard education for a woman of her class and time period, which emphasized the skills needed to make her a good mother, capable of caring for and educating her children; a prudent steward of the resources provided by her husband; a fair and efficient manager of her household staff; and a graceful and charming companion in society. Unlike her husband, who, by his early twenties, was a figure of national importance and international reputation, however, she had never traveled outside of Virginia. She had always been rather sheltered and had very little experience with people from other parts of the country or other cultures. All that began to change with the coming of the war, an event which unknowingly prepared her for the role she would later play as first lady of the United States. Mrs. Washington spent fifty-two to fifty-four of the roughly 103 months from April 1775 to December 1783, or almost half of the time, either with her husband in camp, or nearby, in the hope that they could spend more time together.

Assisting with management of the Mount Vernon estate in George Washington's absence was his third-cousin, Lund Washington, who was five years younger than his employer. Having gained experience working at two other large Virginia plantations, Lund was hired to work at Mount Vernon in 1765, where he would remain for the next twenty years.[3] Many years after his death, a younger relative described Lund as "a stout man remarkable for his strength[,] activity and industry," as well as "close attention to business, . . . excellent management of plantation and household affairs, . . . and great frugality," but also noted that, while he was a "sensible well meaning man with a strong mind," Lund "had not much experience in the artifices of the World."[4] Although he was single when he arrived at Mount Vernon, according to a surviving prayer journal kept by Lund's wife, Elizabeth Foote Washington, it appears that she promised to marry him in the fall of 1779, and, following their wedding, she too moved to Mount Vernon, and remained there until they were able to finally acquire a home of their own, a nearby

3. *The Papers of George Washington, Colonial Series,* 10 volumes, edited by W. W. Abbot and Dorothy Twohig (Charlottesville: University of Virginia Press, 1983–1995), 7:376, 442, 515; 8:104, 220, 356, 479; 9:54, 238; 10:137; Lund Washington (1767–1853), "Lund Washington's History of His Family," *circa* 1849, and Bishop Frank M. Bristol, Copy of Lund Washington's Manuscript, circa 1900 (bound photostat, Fred W. Smith National Library for the Study of George Washington, Mount Vernon, Virginia, hereafter referenced as The Washington Library), 12–13 [14–15].
4. Washington and Bristol, "Lund Washington's History of His Family" and Copy of Lund Washington's Manuscript, 12–14 [14–16].

plantation called Hayfield, in 1785.[5] The couple had at least three children, but none survived childhood.[6]

George Washington's affection for Lund can be readily seen in their surviving correspondence. For example, at one point during the Revolution, Lund's salary (and that of other hired servants) was greatly devalued because of inflation. His employer tried to address the issue in a letter written in December of 1778, in which he noted that "The depreciation of Money, and the sudden rise in the price of produce in the course of this year . . . renders your present wages especially under short Crops, totally inadequate to your trouble and Services." George Washington's plan was that Lund "should receive a certain part of the last Crop, to be disposed of by you for your own benefit and so in future; this will give you the reward of your Industry without subjecting you to the peculiar hardship resulting from depreciation as it is presumable that the price of produce will rise in proportion to the fall of the other. I do not at this time ascertain what the part shall be, because I wish you to say what you think is just and right . . . it is my first wish that you should be satisfied."[7]

Other family members were frequently at Mount Vernon during the war years. Foremost among them were Martha Washington's only surviving child, John Parke Custis, and his wife, Eleanor Calvert Custis. The young couple had been married in early 1774, when he was only nineteen and she was sixteen. During the war, Jack and Nelly presented Mrs. Washington with seven grandchildren. While one little girl and a set of female twins died shortly after birth, of the four babies who sur-

---

5. Elizabeth's prayer journal is an amazing document, well worth reading, for anyone interested in Anglican household religion in eighteenth-century Virginia, or the relationships between women, free and enslaved, in those same homes (see Journal of Elizabeth Foote Washington, November 1779 to December 1796, (typescript, The Washington Library), 1). For more on this remarkable document, see Mary V. Thompson, *In the Hands of a Good Providence: Religion in the Life of George Washington* (Charlottesville: University of Virginia Press, 2008), 98–99, 103–106; and Lauren F. Winner, *A Cheerful & Comfortable Faith: Anglican Religious Practice in the Elite Households of Eighteenth-Century Virginia* (New Haven, CT: Yale University Press, 2010), 111–118.

6. For the birth of s stillborn baby girl in December 1782, and the deaths of two daughters as toddlers, in October 1785 and October 1788, see Journal of Elizabeth Foote Washington, 12, 13, 14, and 25, and Lund Washington to George Washington, December 11, 1782 (typescript, The Washington Library).

7. George Washington to Lund Washington, December 18, 1778, *The Writings of George Washington from the Original Manuscript Sources, 1745–1799*, 39 volumes (Washington, DC: United States Government Printing Office, 1931–1944), 13:428–429.

vived, their grandmother was away from home for the arrival of three.[8] Sadly, John Parke Custis succumbed to camp fever during a stint as his stepfather's volunteer aide at the siege of Yorktown. The young man died at the age of twenty-seven in the first week of November 1781, an event that turned what should have been a joyous period into utter heartbreak.

According to tax documents from Mount Vernon in 1774, there were also 134 workers on the plantation. They included fifteen hired and indentured men and 119 working adult slaves (sixty-eight men and fifty-one women). Of those who were enslaved, fifteen (six men and nine women) were domestics who worked in and around the mansion; thirteen men who were skilled craftsmen; and ninety-one people (forty-nine men and forty-two women), who did field work.[9] No records have been found to indicate the number of non-working adults and children there might have been among the enslaved population at this period, but Washington estimated later in the war that there were between 200 and 300 slaves in total. There are also records of about fifty-two births in the enslaved community during the war years.

Our knowledge about this period in Mount Vernon's history has been hampered by several factors, foremost the loss of two important sets of papers which were destroyed in the eighteenth and early nineteenth centuries, probably in the name of preserving the privacy of the correspondents involved. In the first instance, many of the letters between George Washington and his cousin Lund were burned by the latter's widow sometime after his death in 1796. We know from the let-

---

8. Mrs. Washington appears to have been present for the birth of Martha Parke Custis (1777–1854) on December 31, 1777; see Martha Washington to Burwell Bassett, December 22, 1777, *"Worthy Partner,"* 175, 176n. For the date of Nelly's birth, see David L. Ribblett, *Nelly Custis: Child of Mount Vernon* (Mount Vernon, VA: Mount Vernon Ladies' Association, 1993), 2. For the date of Washy's birth, see Arthur H. Quinn, "Custis, George Washington Parke," in *Dictionary of American Biography,* 20 volumes, edited by Allen Johnson & Dumas Malone (New York: Charles Scribner's Sons, 1928–1936), 5:9–10. For Mrs. Washington's whereabouts at the time Nelly and Washy were born, see Fields, *"Worthy Partner,"* 181–182 & 185–186. For the three other baby girls, who were born to John Parke Custis and Eleanor Calvert during these years, but died shortly after their births, see Christian Scott Blackburn to Martha Washington, September 26, 1775, and John Parke Custis to Martha Washington, August 21, 1776, in Fields, *"Worthy Partner,"* 162 & 162n, 170 & 171n; and Eliza Parke Custis [Law], "Self-Portrait: Eliza Custis, 1808," edited by William D. Hoyt, Jr., *Virginia Magazine of History and Biography* 53:89–100, 93.

9. *The Papers of George Washington, Colonial Series,* 10:135.

ters that do survive that Lund typically sent a long, chatty letter to his employer once a week to keep him apprized of conditions on the estate. Secondly, sometime between George Washington's death in 1799 and that of his wife Martha two-and-a-half years later, Mrs. Washington consigned forty years of correspondence between herself and her husband to the flames.[10] While it was not uncommon for the remaining spouse to destroy the correspondence of a deceased partner (both Thomas Jefferson and James Monroe, for example, did the same thing following the deaths of their wives), and the desire to maintain some degree of privacy is perfectly understandable, the loss to the historical record has been incalculable.

FEARS FOR SAFETY

Early in the war, there were concerns that both Martha Washington and Mount Vernon might be targeted by the British. Throughout the late summer and early fall of 1775, Mrs. Washington's safety was the subject of much of the surviving family correspondence. General Washington wrote in late August that he could "hardly think that Lord Dunmore [John Murray, fourth Earl of Dunmore and royal governor of Virginia] can act so low, so unmanly a part, as to think of seizing Mrs. Washington by way of revenge upon me." He was comforted by the thought that for the next couple of months she would be visiting away from home and so would "be out of his [Dunmore's] reach for 2 or 3 months to come," after which he hoped events would play out in such a way "as to render her removal either absolutely necessary, or quite useless." He asked that, should Lund believe there was "any sort of reason to suspect" that she was in imminent danger, to "provide a Kitchen for her in Alexandria, or some other place of safety elsewhere for her and my Papers."[11]

Martha Washington does not appear to have been worried for herself until she received several letters from her husband mentioning that Dunmore might try to capture and imprison her.[12] It probably added to the couple's anxiety that about this same time, George Washington's younger brother, John Augustine, tried to persuade his sister-in-law to

10. *"Worthy Partner,"* 464–465.
11. George Washington to Lund Washington, August 20, 1775, *The Writings of George Washington*, 3:432–433.
12. Lund Washington to George Washington, October 15, 1775, *The Papers of George Washington, Revolutionary War Series*, 23 volumes to date, edited by W. W. Abbot, Dorothy Twohig, Philander D. Chase, Theodore J. Crackel, and Edward O. Lengel (Charlottesville: University of Virginia Press, 1985–present), 2:174–175.

leave Mount Vernon for her own safety.[13] Early in October, Lund sought to calm Washington's fears about the safety of his wife:

> Tis true many people have made a Stir about Mrs Washingtons Continuing at Mt Vernon but I cannot think her in any Sort of danger—the thought I believe first originated in Alexandria—from thence it got to Loudon [Loudoun County, Virginia], I am told the people of Loudon talkd of sendg a Guard to Conduct her up into Berkeley with some of their principle men to persuade her to leave this & accept their offer—Mr John Agst. Washington wrote to her pressg her to leave Mt Vernon—she does not believe herself in danger, nor do I. without they attempt to take her in the dead of Night they woud fail, for 10 minutes notice woud be Sufficient for her to get out of the way . . . I have never Advise'd her to stay nor Indeed to go . . . you may depend I will be watchfull, & upon the least Alarm persuade her to move.[14]

Before going south to visit her family, Martha Washington put many valuables, especially her husband's papers, into trunks that could be easily moved if that became necessary, and Lund made plans to send the trunk containing papers to a neighbor for safekeeping.[15] Lund had asked, presumably upon the General's orders, that Mrs. Washington carefully tie the papers in bundles, so that "they might not be in any great confusion hereafter when they come to be open'd." She insisted on packing the trunk herself, although when she set off to visit her relatives in New Kent County she left the key to Washington's study with Lund, who assured his cousin that he would not "look into any part of [the desk], or in any other part of the Studdy, without her being present." He also stated quite strongly that the General had nothing to worry about while the estate was in Lund's hands, because "I will do every thing in my powr to, not only secure your papers, but every other Valuable thing that can be save'd even at the risque of my Life, if necessary."[16]

---

13. George Washington to John Augustine Washington, October 13, 1775, *The Writings of George Washington*, 4:28.
14. Lund Washington to George Washington, October 5, 1775, *The Papers of George Washington, Revolutionary War Series*, 2:116.
15. Lund Washington to George Washington, October 15, 1775, *Ibid.*, 2:172–175.
16. Lund Washington to George Washington, October 29, 1775, *Ibid.*, 2:257.

CONSTRUCTION AND DESTRUCTION

Two years before the American Revolution began, George Washington started making plans to enlarge the mansion house and re-do the nearby outbuildings. Major additions would be made to both ends of the house, with a wing containing a study and master bedroom suite on the south end and a second wing featuring a grand, two-story room for entertaining on the north. The overall plan included the "replacement of existing outbuildings with larger structures, creation of service lanes, development of the bowling green, and enlargement of the formal gardens."[17] Washington left for the Second Continental Congress in May of 1775, when all these plans had barely been started. It would be six years before he was able to see his home again and the project was left primarily in the hands of Lund and Martha Washington.[18]

When George Washington next saw the estate, he was on the way to Yorktown, in 1781. On the way to that fateful encounter, Washington, his generals, and several of his French allies were able to spend a few days at Mount Vernon. He arrived on the evening of September 9 along with one of his aides, Lt. Col. David Humphreys, making the sixty-mile journey from Baltimore in a single day, while, in the words of another aide, "The rest of the family jogg on easily."[19] Although there is no record of the reunion, the two men probably received an enthusiastic welcome from Martha Washington, her son and daughter-in-law, and Lund Washington. This was also George Washington's first opportunity to meet several new additions to the family: Lund Washington's bride of two years, Elizabeth Foote Washington and, more importantly, the four young Custis grandchildren, Eliza (age five), Patty (four), Nelly (two), and George Washington Parke Custis (four months), all born after George Washington left for the war. Mrs. Washington and the household staff would have spent much of the next day getting ready for their guests: the rest of Washington's military aides, who reached Mount Vernon on the afternoon of the tenth, just as the family was sitting down to dinner; and the two French generals—Jean Baptiste Donatien de Vimeur, Comte de Rochambeau, who arrived that same evening, and François Jean de Beauvoir, Chevalier de Chastellux, who arrived on the eleventh. The Frenchmen were each accompanied by

---

17. *Mount Vernon Commemorative Guidebook 1999: George Washington Bicentennial Edition* (Mount Vernon, VA: Mount Vernon Ladies' Association, 1998), 28.
18. *Ibid.*, 29.
19. For the quote from aide Jonathan Trumbull, see page 333 of "Minutes of Occurrences Respecting the Siege and Capture of Yorktown," in *Proceedings of the Massachusetts Historical Society* (1875–1876), 331–338 (downloaded from Google Books, September 13, 2011).

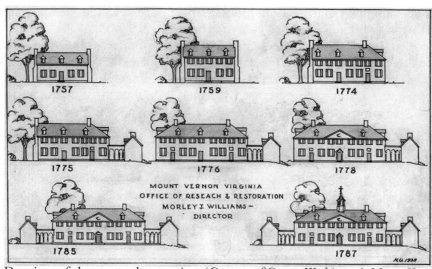

Drawings of changes to the mansion. (*Courtesy of George Washington's Mount Vernon*)

four to six aides.[20] The French generals' later arrival may have been because they "wanted to spare their horses, or perhaps Rochambeau with his usual tact may have guessed that Washington might well enjoy a day alone at Mount Vernon before his guests arrived. It was over six years since Washington had set foot in his own home, and Rocham-

20 See *The Diaries of George Washington*, 6 volumes, edited by Donald Jackson and Dorothy Twohig (Charlottesville: University Press of Virginia, 1976–1979), 3:419n1. For the fact that the French generals were accompanied by 4–6 aides, see George Washington to Brigadier General George Weedon or Alexander Spotswood, September 9, 1781, *The Writings of George Washington*, 23:111. For the arrival of the rest of Washington's aides at dinner time, see Trumbull, "Minutes of Occurrences Respecting the Siege and Capture of Yorktown," 333. For the arrival times of the French generals, see George Washington to the Marquis de Lafayette, September 10, 1781, and George Washington to Brigadier General George Weedon or Alexander Spotswood, September 10, 1781, *The Writings of George Washington*, 23:110 & 111; and Trumbull, "Minutes of Occurrences Respecting the Siege and Capture of Yorktown," 333. For the fact that an important element of Rochambeau's army was traveling more slowly and would not pass the road to Mount Vernon until September 26,1781, see "Itinerary of the Wagon Train of the Army From the Camp at Annapolis to Williamsburg, 1781," in *The American Campaigns of Rochambeau's Army, 1780, 1781, 1782, 1783*, 2 volumes, translated and edited by Howard C. Rice, Jr., and Anne S. K. Brown (Princeton, NJ, and Providence, RI: Jointly published by Princeton University Press and Brown University Press, 1972), 2: 89.

beau, a happily married man himself, knew what it would mean to the Washington family to have a day to themselves."[21]

Unfortunately, neither George Washington nor the other generals wrote anything substantive about their brief time at Mount Vernon. Chastellux had met Martha Washington in Philadelphia at the end of November 1780, when he described her as "about forty or forty-five [she was then forty-nine], rather plump, but fresh and with an agreeable face." He also expressed the opinion that she "looks like a German princess."[22]

They would have seen that the wing on the south end of the mansion was completed and the one on the north end, although not finished, was framed out and enclosed but still needed a lot of work. Graceful colonnades at each end linked the mansion to two new outbuildings, including a new kitchen building on the south (or right). They would also have noticed a new decorative plaster ceiling and graceful plasterwork surrounding the mantel in the dining room, completed in the fall of 1775.[23]

Another of Washington's aides, Connecticut native Lt. Col. Jonathan Trumbull, was quite impressed by his reception at the Washingtons' home, writing that, even though there was "A numerous family now present," they were "All accommodated." Trumbull found at Mount Vernon an "elegant seat and situation, great appearance of oppulence and real exhibitions of hospitality and princely entertainment," a testimony to Mrs. Washington's skills at household organization and entertaining.[24] Given the size of the group, the dinner may well have taken place either in the central passage, on the piazza, or on the east lawn overlooking the Potomac.[25]

21. Arnold Whitridge, *Rochambeau: America's Neglected Founding Father* (New York: Collier Books, 1965), 196.

22. Marquis de Chastellux, *Travels in North America in the Years 1780, 1781 and 1782*, 2 volumes, translated and edited by Howard C. Rice, Jr. (Chapel Hill, NC: Published for the Institute of Early American History and Culture at Williamsburg, Virginia, by The University of North Carolina Press, 1963), 1:134, 298n18.

23. *Mount Vernon Commemorative Guidebook 1999*, 56.

24. See the entry for September 11, 1781, in Trumbull, "Minutes of Occurrences Respecting the Siege and Capture of Yorktown," 333.

25. For many years, it was thought that a planning meeting was held in the New Room (variously referred to by later generations as the Banquet Hall or the Large Dining Room), but research for the restoration of the New Room in 2013 & 2014 showed that the floor in the room had not been installed until after the end of the Revolution, so neither that meeting nor the dinner could have been held there (presentation by architectural conservator Tom Reinhart, Mount Vernon, VA, March 11, 2013).

Washington and Rochambeau left Mount Vernon at five o'clock on the morning of September 12, 1781, leaving Mrs. Washington safely at home on the estate.[26] George Washington's risky plan to trap the British proved successful, effectively ending the active military phase of this very long war.[27] The new construction and improvements at Mount Vernon would not be completed until about the time of the Constitutional Convention.

In addition to new projects, some construction had to be undertaken during the war because of damage, although whether it was caused by accident or was deliberate is unknown. The first inkling that something had happened came in a letter to George Washington from the Comte de Rochambeau in Williamsburg, two days before Christmas in 1781: "I have learnt . . . that your Excellency's seat has suffered by the fire."[28] Although Washington downplayed the losses, the fire had been tremendous. He responded to Rochambeau a few weeks later from Philadelphia, where he had taken Martha Washington to help take her mind off the death of her son and only remaining child: "My loss at Mount Vernon [of the stable] was not very considerable, but I was in the greatest danger of having my House and all the adjacent Buildings consumed," which would have meant the destruction of all the improvements made during his absence.[29] More details emerged about a year-and-a-half later, as a new stable was under construction to replace the original. On a visit to Mount Vernon, Ludwig, Baron von Closen, noted that, "While I was there, a stable that had burned down some time previously was being rebuilt; the general lost 10 of his best horses in this unfortunate occurrence."[30]

---

26. For the time of the departure on September 12, 1781, see Whitridge, *Rochambeau*, 200.

27. Not everyone left with Washington and Rochambeau on the morning of the twelfth: according to Jonathan Trumbull, he—and presumably others—rested at Mount Vernon on that day and resumed their journey south on the following day (see Trumbull, "Minutes of Occurrences Respecting the Siege and Capture of Yorktown," 333).

28. Comte de Rochambeau to George Washington, December 23, 1781, translated by John C. Fitzpatrick, Library of Congress, Washington, D.C., June 19, 1936, *William and Mary Quarterly*, 2nd ser., 17, no. 2 (April, 1937): 235.

29. George Washington to Comte de Rochambeau, January 8, 1782, *The Writings of George Washington*, 23:435–436.

30. Baron von Closen, July 18, 1782, "The Journal of Baron von Closen," edited by Evelyn M. Acomb, *William and Mary Quarterly*, 3rd ser., 10, no. 2 (April 1953): 229.

RUNAWAYS

Very early in the war, the Royal Governor of Virginia, Lord Dunmore, issued a "much dreaded proclamation," offering "Freedom to All Indented Servts & Slaves (the Property of Rebels) that will repair to his majestys Standard—being able to bear Arms." As Lund Washington discussed this hated policy in a letter to his employer, he reassured George Washington that "if there were no white Servts in this family I shoud be under no apprehension about the Slaves," indicating that he suspected that the indentured servants would try to leave, but trusted the slaves. He went on to relate that one of the hired men, "[William Bernard] Sears who is at [work] here says there is not a man of them [the indentured servants], but [would] leave us, if they [believed] they [could] make [their] Escape . . . .& yet they have no fault to find[.] Liberty is sweet."[31]

In the spring of 1781, the largest slave escape in Mount Vernon's history took place while George and Martha Washington were at his military headquarters at New Windsor, New York. A British frigate had landed men on the Maryland side of the Potomac, where they burned a number of "gentlemen's houses . . . in sight of Mount Vernon." Capt. Thomas Graves of the *Savage* then sent a message to Mount Vernon, threatening the same treatment unless he and his crew were given "a large supply of provisions." According to Lund, several years after the fact, his initial response to the British demand was that General Washington "had given him orders by no means to comply with any such demands, for that he would make no unworthy compromise with the enemy, and was ready to meet the fate of his neighbors."

Furious at this reply, Captain Graves brought the ship closer to the shore in readiness to burn the estate, but offered Lund the chance to come aboard to talk. Lund did so, taking "a small present of poultry" for the ship's commanding officer. During their pleasant chat, Graves "expressed his personal respect for the character of the General," commended Lund's conduct, and "assured him nothing but his having misconceived the terms of the first answer could have induced him . . . to entertain the idea of taking the smallest measure offensive to so illustrious a character as the General." He also explained that some "real or

31. Lund Washington to George Washington, December 3, 1775, *The Papers of George Washington, Revolutionary War Series*, 2:479–480.

supposed provocations . . . had compelled his severity on the other side of the river." Lund went back to shore and "instantly despatched sheep, hogs, and an abundant supply of other articles as a present to the English frigate."[32] At some point before Lund went on board the *Savage* a group of slaves, fourteen men and three women, made their way to the ship, hoping to be emancipated on the basis of Lord Dunmore's proclamation.[33]

George Washington was extremely disturbed by Lund's actions, writing to his cousin on April 30 that he was "very sorry to hear of your loss; I am a little sorry to hear of my own; but that which gives me most concern, is, that you should go on board the enemys Vessels, and furnish them with refreshments." He went on to say that,

> It would have been a less painful circumstance to me, to have heard, that in consequence of your non-compliance with their request, they had burnt my House, and laid the Plantation in ruins. You ought to have considered yourself as my representative, and should have reflected on the bad example of communicating with the enemy, and making a voluntary offer of refreshments to them with a view to prevent a conflagration . . . . I am thoroughly perswaded that you acted from your best judgment . . . But to go on board their Vessels; carry them refreshments; commune with a parcel of plundering Scoundrels, and request a favor by asking the surrender of my Negroes, was exceedingly ill-judged.[34]

Of the people who left with the British at that time, seven were eventually returned to Mount Vernon sometime after the siege at Yorktown. One of them, Thomas, had managed to get as far as Philadelphia and

32. George Grieve, Notes on Conversation with Lund Washington, in Chastellux, *Travels in North America,* 2:597.
33. Lund Washington, List of Runaways, April 1781, *The Writings of George Washington,* 22:14n; for another published version of this list, which differs a bit from that in the *The Writings of George Washington,* see [Ellen McCallister Clark], "A Wartime Incident," *Annual Report 1986* (Mount Vernon, VA: Mount Vernon Ladies' Association, 1987), 25. According to historian Fritz Hirschfeld, John C. Fitzpatrick, the editor of *The Writings of George Washington,* was mistaken when he identified the commander of the *Savage* as Richard Graves, a prominent British naval officer, rather than his brother, Capt. Thomas Graves (see Fritz Hirschfeld, *George Washington and Slavery: A Documentary Portrayal* (Columbia: University of Missouri Press, 1997), 23n8).
34. George Washington to Lund Washington, April 30, 1781, *The Writings of George Washington,* 22:14.

Washington had to pay an unspecified amount for his "salvage." His travel expenses back to Virginia cost another twelve dollars.[35]

About six months after the incident with the *Savage*, Martha Washington's son, John Parke Custis, wrote to his mother from the camp outside Yorktown with news about some slaves who had run away, which suggests that many more enslaved people left than can be confirmed through surviving documentation. Although he had been making inquiries to learn if any of these slaves were nearby, Custis had not actually seen any of them, but he had heard rumors about the whereabouts of two or three. He offered that he was afraid "most who left Us are not existing," meaning that they were dead: "the mortality that has taken place among the Wretches is really incredible. I have seen numbers lying dead in the Woods, and many so exhausted that they cannot walk."[36]

LOSS OF MARKETS AND WARTIME SHORTAGES

Civilians faced many shortages during the American Revolution, as in all wars. Supplies were requisitioned for military use; manpower and draft animals used by the military were not producing agricultural or industrial products; and trade and transportation were disrupted. Some of these issues touched the people living at Mount Vernon.

In his search for new products and markets to replace others lost by the war, Lund Washington learned that people in Massachusetts were

35. See *Ibid.*, 22:14n; [Clark], "A Wartime Incident," 25. These two published sources conflicted in regard to whether all the men were captured in Philadelphia and the women were picked up after Yorktown, or if only Tom was found in Philadelphia. Examination of the original manuscript, which is in the Mount Vernon collections, suggests that all of the returned slaves were taken up after the siege at Yorktown, but that Tom is the only one who got as far as Philadelphia. Many thanks to Michele Lee, the Special Collections Librarian, and my delightful colleague, for helping to work out that conundrum. A second, as yet unsolved, problem concerns the identities of three Mount Vernon slaves who appear in the British records, at the end of the Revolution, when they were transported to Nova Scotia: Henry Washington, 43 years old, who is said to have escaped in 1776; Daniel Payne, age 22; and Deborah Squash, 20 years old, who ran away in 1779. The given names of these people match three of those from Lund's 1781 list. Are they the same people? Was Lund providing a comprehensive list of everyone who left in the war, or just those who escaped in 1781? For the work of other historians on the Mount Vernon slaves who escaped during the war, see Cassandra Pybus, *Epic Journeys of Freedom: Runaway Slaves of the American Revolution and Their Global Quest for Liberty* (Boston, MA: Beacon Press, 2006), 218; Simon Schama, *Rough Crossings: Britain, the Slaves and the American Revolution* (London: BBC Books, 2005), 16–17, 81, 232, 281, 381, 383; and Ruth Holmes Whitehead, *Black Loyalists: Southern Settlers of Nova Scotia's First Free Black Communities* (Nimbus, CA: Nimbus Publishing, 2013), 74, 139–140, 149.

36. John Parke Custis to Martha Washington, October 12, 1781, *"Worthy Partner,"* 187.

making rum, sugar, and molasses—important commodities from the West Indies which were in short supply—out of cornstalks. Just before Christmas in 1777, he told General Washington that, "If they make it, surely we may, and if I was sure it could be done to as great advantage as we are told it may, it would be much better for us to attempt it than to endeavor to make tobacco, under the disadvantages that we shall have . . . . In short, I am really uneasy that we should have no crops that will bring money, and for the year to come am anxious to fix upon something that will be profitable . . . . "[37] We don't know if Lund ever tried making rum or molasses from cornstalks, but it appears from other sources that this experiment was not as successful as early reports suggested. A New Jersey man had "constructed a mill for grinding the common Indian corn stalks," because he knew they contained "a considerable quantity of saccharine matter." Unfortunately, when the juice from the stalks was "converted into molasses, was found to possess an acrid and unpleasant taste, which he was not chemist enough to correct, and the experiment, after one year's trial, was abandoned."[38]

The most common methods of preserving meat and fish at Mount Vernon were salting and smoking, the most widely used methods at the time. Prior to the war, George Washington freely used Potomac fish as a source of both food and income, most frequently selling the catch in salted form. Some idea of the size of his fishing operation can be gained from his account books: in May of 1774, Washington sold 905 barrels of herrings averaging 800 per barrel to a Mrs. William Milnor of Philadelphia; that works out to 724,000 fish for £108.12.0.[39] Later that same year he sent 650 barrels of herrings to a gentleman in Jamaica.[40] This was in addition to local sales and fish kept for use on his own estate.

The salt needed to preserve foodstuffs was typically "made" by evaporating sea water, but could vary widely in quality. Very little salt was produced in America, primarily because of the low salinity in the bays where people tried making it. Salt was generally imported from Europe, with Lisbon in Portugal being the source of the most prized table salt, while cheaper salt from Liverpool in England served for preserving

---

37. Lund Washington to George Washington, December 24, 1777 (typescript, The Washington Library).
38. Ashbel Green and Joseph N. Jones, *The Life of Ashbel Green, V. D. M.* (New York: Robet Carter and Brothers, 1849), 52–53.
39. "Mrs. Willm. Milnor. . .Philada. . . ," May 1774, in Ledger B (bound photostat, The Washington Library), 123.
40. "Robt. McMickan Esqr. . . . Jamaica," August 3, 1774, in Ledger B, 127.

meat.[41] Shortages of this vital commodity caused Lund Washington considerable worry about whether there would be enough salt to preserve fish for the support of the Mount Vernon slaves (for whom it was the primary source of protein), much less to sell. British control of the seas meant that salt from Portugal and England was particularly hard to come by. In 1776 Lund noted that he had on hand, in several locations, about 350 or 400 barrels of salt, which he refused to sell, "knowg we cou'd not get more & our people must have Fish—therefore told the [prospective buyers] I had none."[42] Two years later he informed George Washington of the tenuous situation: "I have but very little salt, of which we must make the most. I mean to make a brine and after cutting off the head and bellys dipping them in the brine for but a short time, then hang them up and cure them by smoke, or dry them in the sun; for our people being so long accustomed to have fish whenever they wanted, would think it very hard to have none at all."[43] Lund Washington also made money for the estate by selling both brined beef and pork.[44]

It wasn't just salt that became hard to obtain. Beer and hard liquor were also in short supply, again due to the loss of access to European markets. Surviving Washington papers indicate that throughout the eighteenth century, beer was both made at Mount Vernon and purchased for use at the family's table. On the last page of a manuscript notebook kept by Washington in the late 1750s is a recipe for small beer, which, according to one source, was the type of weak beer usually consumed by servants and children. With an alcohol content between two and three percent and about 150–200 calories per pint, small beer provided calcium and a few vitamins. The most interesting aspect of Washington's recipe is that it used molasses, which helped the brewing process but, being a product of the West Indies, was hard to get during the war.[45] George Washington also purchased large quantities of beer

41. *Nelly Custis Lewis's Housekeeping Book*, edited and with an introduction by Patricia Brady Schmit (New Orleans, LA: The Historic New Orleans Collection, 1982), 23–24.
42. Lund Washington to George Washington, February 8, 1776, *The Papers of George Washington, Revolutionary War Series*, 3:271.
43. Lund Washington to George Washington, April 1, 1778 (typescript, The Washington Library).
44. Lund Washington to George Washington, March 11, 1778 (typescript, The Washington Library).
45. For George Washington's recipe for small beer, see George Washington, "To make Small Beer," [1757–1760] (typescript, The Washington Library). For the properties of small beer, see Sara Paston-Williams, *The Art of Dining: A History of Cooking and Eating* (London: National Trust Enterprises Limited, 1993), 156, 219–220.

and porter from good quality breweries in both England and America prior to the Revolution for use at his own table. Not surprisingly, both making and purchasing beer proved to be problematic during the war.[46]

While to modern ears a beer shortage might not seem like a major issue, it is important to remember that few people drank water during this period because of concerns that it could cause illness. Virtually everybody, of all ages and social classes, drank beer as a matter of course. George Washington once noted that his white servants customarily received a quart bottle of beer a day.[47] These workers were very likely not happy about losing access to one of the favorite perks provided for them. Beer was also considered a very healthful beverage.[48] In fact, alcoholic beverages, in general, were thought to be particularly beneficial to people doing hard physical labor. For example, George Washington wrote about his fears concerning the dangerous consequences of a shortage of rum in the army: "Not a drop of Rum has yet come on, and the Physicians report that the Artificers (who labour exceedingly hard) are falling sick for want of it."[49] Two months later, the army had received very little rum and Washington wrote another reminder: "This Article is so necessary for the Health as well as comfort of the Soldiery at this Season, that I wish it might be particularly attended to."[50]

Faced with a lack of beer and other spirits, Lund Washington had to get creative. He wrote in March 1778, "I find from experience there is a fine spirit to be made from persimmons, but neglected to gather them for that purpose, only got some for the purpose of makeg Beer."[51] Persimmon seeds were the largest category of botanical materials found during excavations of the cellar of a Mount Vernon slave quarter in the

46. For George Washington's purchases of beer prior to the Revolution, see Ledger A (bound photostat, The Washington Library), May 12, 1757, September 1760, April 5, 1768, January 10, 1769, on pages 34a, 105a, 269a, 287a; Orders and Invoices (bound photostats, The Washington Library), September 1757, August 1758, March 1759, March 1760, March 1761, October 1761, April 1762, November 15, 1762, April 1763, February 1764, February 1765, and June 1766; Ledger B, December 22, 1772 & April 16, 1777, 148a.

47. George Washington to William Pearce, December 22, 1793, *The Writings of George Washington,* 33:201.

48. Louise Conway Belden, *The Festive Tradition: Table Decoration and Desserts in America, 1650–1690* (New York: W.W. Norton, 1983), 232.

49. George Washington to Major General William Heath, June 8, 1781, *The Writings of George Washington,* 22:182.

50. George Washington to President Meshech Weare, August 5, 1781, *Ibid.,* 22:467.

51. Lund Washington to George Washington, March 4, 1778, *The Papers of George Washington, Revolutionary War Series,* 14:60.

1980s and 1990s, interesting because slaves in North America used persimmons and honey locust pods for making a type of beer which came to be associated with Christmas (probably because persimmons ripen after the first frost, so they were in season at that time of year).[52]

DISEASE

Throughout history, armies have tended to spread disease as they move from one front to another during a war. The same was true during the Revolution, especially with smallpox. This dreaded disease, which had been relatively rare in the American colonies, suddenly became a problem when large numbers of soldiers arrived from England and Germany where it was endemic, and introduced the disease to an American public which was largely unexposed to it. George Washington is credited with preventing an out-of-control epidemic by setting up an incremental plan to inoculate the soldiers in his army. The inoculation procedure involved taking infectious matter from the pustules of someone suffering from smallpox and placing it within a cut in the skin of the person being inoculated, resulting in their contracting a much milder case of the disease than if it had been caught naturally. It generally took about a month to recover from inoculation, during which they had to be quar-

52. For the fact that persimmon remains were so common, see Laura A. Shick, "An Analysis of Archaeobotanical Evidence from the House for Families Slave Quarter, Mount Vernon Plantation, Virginia" (unpublished master's thesis prepared for American University, 2004), 56; and email communication, Esther White to Christine Messing and others, April 17, 2007 (The Washington Library). For references to slaves and persimmon beer, as well as to recipes for making this beverage, see Catherine Ann Devereux Edmonston, *"Journal of a Secesh Lady": The Diary of Catherine Ann Devereux Edmonston, 1860–1866*, edited by Beth G. Crabtree and James W. Patton (Raleigh, NC: Division of Archives and History, Department of Cultural Resources, 1979), 22; Mrs. A. P. Hill, *Mrs. Hill's New Cook Book: A Practical System for Private Families, in Town and Country* (New York: Carleton, 1872), 342; Linda Garland Page and Eliot Wigginton, editors, *Foxfire Book of Appalachian Cookery* (Chapel Hill: University of North Carolina Press, 1992), 55; Charles L. Perdue, Jr., editor, *"Pigsfoot Jelly & Persimmon Beer:Foodways from the Virginia Writers' Project* (Santa Fe, NM: Ancient City Press, 1992), 33–34; "Persimmon Beer," (accessed December 16, 2002), http://cogs.dsustan/~gcrawford/beer-files/history.html; "Persimmon Recipes," (accessed December 16, 2002), www.eat-it.com/recipe.htm. According to African-American foodways specialist, Michael Twitty, persimmons that slaves found growing in America would have reminded them of the fruit of the ebony or jackalberry tree in West and Central Africa, known as the "alom" to the Wolof and "kuku" to the Fula peoples, who are known to have used it as a medicine, a dried fruit, an ingredient in bread, and a source for making beer (see Michael Twitty, *Fighting Old Nep: The Foodways of Enslaved Afro-Marylanders, 1634–1864* [(No publication location given]: Michael Twitty, 2008), 19; and "Sample Recipes," (accessed January 12, 2010), www.afrofoodways.com/Pages/recipes.html.

antined to prevent the disease from spreading.[53] This does not mean, however, that the civilian population was out of danger.

In early May of 1777, shortly before his wife's annual return to Mount Vernon, George Washington wrote that the latest news from home was that "the Small Pox . . . has got into my Family." He asked Doctor William Shippen to ensure that medical supplies he had promised for Mount Vernon would be sent. Those items were imperative because Washington was taking steps to have all the slaves on the plantation inoculated and these drugs were considered necessary during the patients' recovery. The two medicines specifically mentioned were calomel (mercurous chloride) and jalop (the dried and powdered roots of the plants *Exogonium purge* or *Ipomoea purge*); both served as purgatives.[54]

Martha Washington's summer at Mount Vernon that year would hardly have been a respite. Having seen the favorable results of the inoculation on his stepson, his wife, and his army's soldiers, Washington was pretty confident of its efficacy and wrote to his younger brother, John Augustine: "the Small Pox by Inoculation appears to me to be nothing; my whole Family [the term he often used for his slaves], I understand, are likely to get well through the disorder with no other assistance than that of Doctr Lund [a humorous reference to Lund Washington] . . . in general neither Physicians nor Physic is necessary except a few purgatives . . . that this is truely the case, I firmly believe, and my own People (not less I suppose than between two & three hundred) getting happily through it by following these directions is no inconsiderable proof of it."[55]

53. For more on George Washington's role in preventing a full-blown epidemic, see Mary V. Thompson, "More to dread. . .than from the Sword of the Enemy": Smallpox, the Unseen Killer," in *The Annual Report of the Mount Vernon Ladies' Association of the Union 2000* (Mount Vernon, VA: The Mount Vernon Ladies' Association of the Union, 2001), 22–27.

54. George Washington to Doctor William Shippen, May 3, 1777, *The Papers of George Washington, Revolutionary War Series*, 9:340. For information on the use of jalop and calomel, see"jalap . . . or jalop," "The Free Dictionary," (accessed May 12, 2016), www.thefreedictionary.com/jalop and "Evidence Based Science,"(accessed May 12, 2016), http://evidence-based-science.blogspot.com/2008/02/calomel-they-used-to-give-it-to.html.

55. George Washington to John Augustine Washington, June [1], 1777, *The Papers of George Washington, Revolutionary War Series*, 9:587.

Given the length of the recovery period, it is probable that the inoc-
ulations at Mount Vernon were spaced out through the summer, with
one group being done, quarantined, and allowed to recover before
doing the next, in order to keep a viable workforce in the fields. It is
entirely possible that much of Mrs. Washington's time at home that
year was taken up with helping to look after the slaves as they recuper-
ated.

Martha Washington was also helping relatives recover from the same
procedure. While smallpox inoculation was much less dangerous than
contracting the disease naturally, it could still result in death. Before
Martha had returned to Mount Vernon that year, George Washington's
younger brother Samuel's family was inoculated; unfortunately, his wife,
Anne Steptoe Allerton Washington, died from the procedure.[56] George
Washington wrote of his sister-in-law's death that he was sure it was a
terrible blow to Samuel and believed that "some mismanagement must
surely" have occurred while she was recovering. Brother John Augustine's entire family came through the inoculation process well, as did
Martha's nine-month old granddaughter, Eliza Parke Custis, and many
other residents in the neighborhood around Mount Vernon.[57] Two of
her nephews, Burwell and John Bassett (ages fourteen and eleven, re-
spectively) came to Mount Vernon to go through inoculation and recovery. When she sent them back to their mother in mid-November,
Martha Washington assured her sister that they were "as well as they
were" when she brought them from home, that they "have had the
small pox exceeding light and have been perfectly well this fortnight
past." Before packing them off for home, Martha "had all thare clothes
washed and rinsed several days—and do veryly believe that they can
bring no infection home with them." If her sister was still afraid of contracting smallpox from their clothes, however, Martha recommended
that she "let some one who has had the small pox put out thare cloths
to air for a day or two in the sun."[58]

Efforts to protect family members from smallpox continued throughout the war. While Martha was at Valley Forge, she would probably
have been alarmed to learn that her son had made several unsuccessful
attempts to inoculate her newest granddaughter. While the procedure
had taken place three times, the baby, a little over three months old,

56. George Washington to Samuel Washington, April 5, 1777, *Ibid.*, 9:71 & 72, 73n1.

57. Doctor James Craik to George Washington, May 13, 1777, and George Washington
to John Augustine Washington, June [1], 1777, *Ibid.*, 9:400, 410n2 & 410n3; and 9:587
& 588n4.

58. Martha Washington to Anna Maria Dandridge Bassett, November 18, 1777, *"Worthy
Partner,"* 174.

had not contracted the disease. As John Parke Custis noted, "This leaves Us in a very disagreable Suspence, as We shall be very uneasy lest She get the Disorder in the natural Way, the Doctor is much at a loss how to account for her not taking the Infection, unless Nelly [the child's mother, Eleanor Calver Custis] was with child when she was innocu-lated, and this can hardly be the Case. I shall wait some Time before I try a fourth time. I sincerely hope no Accident will happen to the dear Child. She has grown the finest Girl I ever saw and the most Good na-tured Quiet little Creature in the World."[59]

CONCLUSION

As George Washington prepared to return home after the Revolution—at the end of an eight-year period during which he had received no salary—he was surprised to find that he was deeply in debt. From cor-respondence with several relatives he learned, for example, that his cousin Lund, to whom he had entrusted the care of the estate, had not followed up on hiring British prisoners of war, a cheap form of labor, to supply a lack of skilled artisans during the conflict. This meant that there were many repairs that needed to be made at Mount Vernon. Washington complained further that Lund's "aversion to going from home" meant rents had not been collected from tenants, resulting in "many years arrears of rent" being due. And there was more: "But if your own [Lund's] wages, since the charge of them in the Acct. ren-dered at Valley Forge, has not been received by you in the specific ar-ticles of the Crop; which does not appear by the Accots. you have lately rendered to me; I shall be more hurt, than at any thing else, to think that an Estate, which I have drawn nothing from, for eight years, and which always enabled me to make any purchase I had in view, should not have been able for the last five years, to pay the manager: And that, worse than going home to empty coffers, and expensive living, I shall be encumbered with debt."[60] The fact that Washington began to require incredibly detailed weekly reports from his farm managers after the Revolution is likely a direct result of his shock at the condition of his farms upon his return from the war, and his consequent lack of trust in anyone but himself to stay on top of the situation at Mount Vernon. It would take years to repair the damage to the estate.

59. John Parke Custis to Martha Washington, April 3, 1778, *Ibid.*, 178–179.
60. George Washington to Lund Washington, June 11, 1783, *The Writings of George Washington*, 27:2–3.

In many ways, the Washingtons were also starting over in their private lives. The death of Martha's son in late 1781 and the consequent remarriage of his widow two years later, resulted in the youngest two Custis grandchildren being raised at Mount Vernon by the older couple. Once again there were little people who needed to be cared for, fussed over, educated, and raised to be productive members of society. Home at last, it was an exciting time, but, even as they tried to settle into civilian life once again, the country was already trying to draw the Washingtons back into the public arena—and away from Mount Vernon.

Religious Liberty and its Virginia Roots

ALEX COLVIN

Virginia's role in helping to spearhead disestablishment and religious freedom has not received the treatment it deserves although it was, itself, a moving force behind Virginia's entry into the revolution. It was, in fact, Virginia which ultimately spearheaded and codified separation of church and state, after a reform movement which itself played a significant role in Virginia's joining the independence movement.

That assessment has been eclipsed by other factors such as Dunmore's War of 1774, or the various British Acts of Parliament such as the Stamp Act of 1775. Among the few scholars who have taken up its examination, for example, has been John Rogasta in his *Wellspring of Liberty*, who recognizes dissenters' struggles as being of prime importance to understanding Virginians then laboring under the dominance of Anglican authority as they moved inexorably into the independence movement. That struggle, burnished by a sense of defiance, helped lead them into the Revolution and beyond. Thus, that struggle deserves a rightful place among the major factors helping to fuel Virginia's entrance into the war. That requires some explanation.

Among recruiters' greatest challenges in 1776, following the Siege of Boston and the resultant melting away of the *rage militaire*, was finding men who would enlist to continue the fight for American Independence. In Virginia that challenge was particularly vexing not only because of the imposed quotas of the Continental Congress—which were never met by any colony—but because of Virginia's religious composition and the omnipresence of the Anglican church.

In colonial Virginia, the power and influence of the Church of England was sewn into the very fabric of everyday life, not least because so many members of the House of Burgesses were its most stalwart supporters and members. Yet, by the time of the Revolution estimates show that "dissenters"—that is, non-Anglican colonists who were either Baptist, Presbyterian, or some other sect—had become a sizeable portion of the population, the Baptists being the most vilified.[1] Aside from their obnoxious, noisome gatherings and their lack of educational refinements (Anglican ministers were typically educated in Westminster College than shipped to America to fill posts; many Baptist ministers typically had no education other than knowing their Bible), there was the odious Baptist habit of preaching to the enslaved, having no compunction about ministering to them and calling them "brother" at their open-air meetings.[2] These open-air sermons, particularly those by evangelicals of the Separatist strain, stood in sharp and offensive contrast to their Anglican counterparts whose sermons were restricted to church pulpits.[3]

This social clash defined much of colonial Virginia life. While taxes and other fees supported Anglican priests' salaries, their glebe lands and their churches, dissenters often gathered secretly in individual homes and were fined for not attending mandatory Anglican services. Anglican marriages were performed by numerous Anglican priests, marriages between dissenters, however, required either finding a minister of their faith (usually only one dissident minister was permitted per county), or paying a substantially higher fee than an Anglican would to an Anglican priest for the same service. Worse, county clerks were under no obligation to record such ceremonies in county marriage registries, although

1 John A. Ragosta, *Wellspring of Liberty: How Virginia's Religious Dissenters Helped Win the American Revolution & Secure Religious Liberty* (New York: Oxford University Press, 2010), 20–21. Ragosta estimates the dissident population at one-fifth to one third of the population. He also notes that Thomas Jefferson's estimates of "two-thirds" while promoting his Religious Freedom bill in 1781–82, was likely an exaggeration. James Madison, in writing to Baptist separatist leader William Bradford in 1774, showed a considerable repugnance for what he called the "diabolical" persecution of dissidents in Virginia, especially since it was occurring near his plantation. See James Madison to William Bradford, January 24, 1774, *The Papers of James Madison* (Chicago: University of Chicago Press, 1962–1977), I: 106.
2 Keith E. Durso, *No Armor for the Back: Baptist Prison Writings, 1600s–1700s* (Macon: Mercer University Press, 2007), 224–226.
3 Monica Najar, Sectarians and Strategies of Dissent in Colonial Virginia," *From Jamestown to Jefferson: The Evolution of Religious Freedom in Virginia* (Charlottesville: University of Virginia Press, 2011), 108–133.

marriage license applicants were nevertheless required to pay the filing fee for a license.[4] And those were just a few of the civil abuses.

Among the catalog of physical abuses suffered by dissidents were physical assaults, imprisonment for preaching without a license; imprisonment for preaching to the enslaved, assaults upon their churches by fire or disruption, and assaults upon their congregations, to which their petitions to the General Assembly as well as other documents give legions of evidence. At least six Baptist ministers, for example, were in Culpeper County's jail, according to a letter written by James Madison, writing from his home in adjoining Orange County.[5] Theses dissidents were, in reality, an oppressed class both socially and politically, yet comprised a sizeable portion of the poor white population—the same population from which enlistments would be drawn by the states.

From this divided set of religious classes, recruitment efforts were expected to play out according to the terms of the Second Continental Congress's "eighty-eight battalion resolve," passed in September 1776, which introduced military quotas based on perceived population figures. Virginia had an estimated population of 500,000 and therefore was assigned a quota of fifteen battalions—some 5,700 men—at a time when one battalion equaled roughly ten companies of thirty-eight men each by British standards (although as an organizing concept it was used sloppily by colonists) for the coming fighting season of 1777.[6]

4. Evidence for this discriminatory practice is found throughout early Virginia marriage records where one finds recordings in clerk's records of many marriage bonds and notes of parental consent but a conspicuous dearth of ministers' returns. A sample can be obtained by examining Fauquier Co., Virginia Marriage Bonds & Returns Volume 1, 1759–1800. This dearth has often left genealogists, for example, with the erroneous impression that a marriage being investigated never occurred.

5. Lewis Peyton, *Imprisoned preachers and religious liberty in Virginia, a narrative drawn largely from the official records of Virginia counties, unpublished manuscripts, letters, and other original sources* (Lynchburg: J. P. Bell, 1938), 419.

6. Robert K. Wright, Jr., *The Continental Army* (Washington, D.C.: Center of Military History, 1983), 5:91, full text online at www.history.army.mil/books/RevWar/ContArmy/CAfm.htm For a table regarding Revolutionary-era unit definitions see Worchester Polytech Institute, Department of Military Science website, "British and Colonial Unit Definitions for the Revolutionary War," www.wpi.edu/academics/military/units.html. For the colonists, there was no standard description for a battalion size until 1778 when these numbers were introduced by Baron Von Steuben in his efforts to organize the Continental Army. Among Steuben's chief complaints was the sloppy way in which the divisional concepts were used, about which he wrote bitterly shortly after his arrival at Washington's winter encampment at Valley Forge: "the words company, regiment, brigade, and division were so vague that they did not convey any idea upon which to form a calculation, either of a particular corps or of the army in general. They were so unequal in numbers that it would have been impossible to execute any maneuver." See United States Congressional serial set, Issue 6486 (University of California, 1914), 143.

Military historians such as James Kirby Martin and Mark E. Lender, have made it clear that those who served in the non-officer corps of these battalions, particularly from 1777 onward, were mostly from the lower classes.[7] Other historians have found compelling evidence that this trend continued into the later war years by surveying extant draftee class lists. Benjamin Colvin, for example, a draftee from Culpeper County, Virginia, was among the poorest of his class, not even in pos-session of a horse.[8] Yet he served in the final battles of the Southern Campaign in 1781 at Yorktown, according to his service records and pension files.[9] In 1774 (the same year as Dunmore's War), Benjamin, like many "lower sorts," was among those who often made up the bulk of dissenters in the Virginia religious landscape. In Benjamin's case, this name appears along with his son's on the largest Baptist petition ever sent to the Virginia Assembly asking it to do something about the An-glican abuses—the so-called "Ten-thousand names" petition sent in Oc-tober 1776.[10] This is the same year Washington became desperate to increase troop strength. Those at the forefront of the struggle for dis-senter's religious liberty, however, sensed an emerging political oppor-tunity, and took their stance publically in the *Virginia Gazette*:

7. James Kirby Martin, Mark E. Lender, *A Respectable Army: The Military Origins of the Republic 1763–1789* (Arlington: Harlan Davidson, 2006), 89–92. See also Charles Niemeyer, *America Goes to War: A Social History of the Continental Army* (New York: NYU Press, 1996), 159–160. See also Michael A. McDonnell, "Popular Mobilization and Political Culture in Revolutionary Virginia: The Failure of the Minutemen and the Revolution from Below," *The Journal of American History*, Vol. 85, No. 3 (Dec., 1998): 946–981.

8. John R. Atta, "Conscription in Revolutionary Virginia: The case of Culpeper County, 1780–1781," *The Virginia Magazine of History and Biography*, 92:3 (July 1984), 263–281. According to Atta, despite quotas in place, they were typically not filled. Virginia, for example, in 1777 sent only 5,744 of its required 10,200, soldiers and even though its percentages improved slightly with each successive war year, like most states, it never satisfied its actual quotas. There are numerous reasons for this, including how the draft was itself designed and later executed. However, what intrigued Atta more, was how personal wealth (or a lack of it) played a role in draftee selection, and particularly how his economic standing impacted a draftee's ability to use substitutes. Atta also hoped to extract from the records what might motivate someone to serve as a substitute.

9. Pension application of Benjamin Colvin, July 22, 1833 (1–9), fold3.com. A faithful transcription is available at C. Leon Harris's online database, *Southern Campaign Revo-lutionary War Pension Statements & Rosters*, http://revwarapps.org/index.htm.

10. "Ten-thousand names" petition, October 16, 1776, Library of Congress American Memory webpage http://memory.loc.gov/cgibin/ampage?collId=relpet&fileName= 000/013/013page.db&recNum=0 . At least one estimate by Ragosta finds that no less than ten percent of the adult white male population in Virginia was represented on the petition. See Ragosta, *Wellspring of Liberty*, 56.

In these distressed times, in which our American rights, both civil and religious, are invaded, it is well to adopt that late maxim among politicians, 'United we stand, divided we fall.' To that end, the dissenters, (equally attached to America's liberty,) ought to petition their rulers for the removal of that yoke, that in these fearce [sic] times, it becomes more grievous, in paying the established clergy, and being still obliged to have the solemnization of matrimony performed by them. A word to the wise is enough.—a Dissenter of the Church of England.[11]

The sentiments of this anonymous writer in 1776 served as a bellwether of eventual dissident actions as non-Anglicans began to stake their claim to religious liberty. Ultimately that growing awareness of entitlement to the same rights enjoyed by Anglicans served as a strong enticement for delegates that year at the 5th Virginia Convention in Williamsburg to adopt Article 16 in its draft of its Declaration of Rights.[12] Its most striking language, however, not only granted religious tolerance, but conferred a moral obligation on the colony's inhabitants to do so: "therefore all men are equally entitled to the free exercise of religion, according to the dictates of conscience; and that it is the mutual duty of all to practice Christian forbearance, love, and charity toward each other."[13]

Although that clause signaled unheard of tolerance for dissenters, it hardly provided an end to Anglican monopoly and oppression. Prince William County dissenters in particular saw this, and took the opportunity to call to delegates' attention how religious freedom and the ongoing effort to recruit for Washington's Army, (desperate now for draftees) were inexorably tied together. In their petition, sent to Williamsburg on the heels of the new Declaration of Rights, petitioners were explicit, telling their delegates, "we will gladly unite with our Brethren of other denominations, and to the utmost of our ability, promote the common cause of Freedom."[14] In one sense, the petitioners were calling the delegates' bluff, even as they provided themselves with a bargaining chip. It was, in some ways, a masterstroke. They would fight in the independence movement to free the colonies from Imperial

11. *Virginia Gazette* (Purdie), April 26,1776.
12. "Virginia Declaration of Rights," transcription, final draft, adopted June 12, 1776, Virginia Convention, George Mason & Historic Human Rights Documents Collection, www.gunstonhall.org/index.php/george-mason/rights-documents.
13. www.archives.gov/exhibits/charters/virginia_declaration_of_rights.html.
14. "Prince William County petition", June 20, 1776, Library of Congress, American Memory, http://memory.loc.gov/cgibin/ampage?collId=relpet&fileName=000/010/010page.db&recNum=0&itemLink=P?relpet:1:./t emp/~ammem_u4n3.

rule; the ministers would even join in efforts for recruitment using their public pulpits to rally draftees for the cause. Their price? Religious liberty. Why? For dissenters, British tyranny and Anglican religious monopoly in Virginia were indistinguishable.

To fulfill their end of the bargain, dissenter ministers mobilized enlistment among their own on an impressive scale in Virginia. Their numbers were unmatched by Anglicans there and unparalleled elsewhere in the southern colonies by any religious group.[15] In 1776, for example, for the fifteen needed battalions, Baptists alone raised more than 800 men compared to Anglicans who raised fewer than 500.[16] It is difficult to imagine that as these enlistees mustered into their respective companies, the idea of their own religious liberty, bundled up as it was with their greater yearning for freedom from British tyranny, was not part of their motivation, given what they had endured up to this point. It is difficult to imagine, moreover, that such motivations, overall were not part of what drove Virginia into the Revolution and what kept her enlistees there until its conclusion in 1781. Unfortunately, but for a few recent attempts to more closely examine this aspect of Virginia and her entrance into the Revolution, many scholars have given minimal attention to this driving force.

Moreover, although many historical assessments include key elements to explain Virginia's entrance into the Revolution they exclude others that are just as significant. Neoprogressive historians have begun exploring these new elements, some with mixed results. Nevertheless, clearly Virginia was in the vanguard among the colonies in recognizing religious liberties, just as it was in the forefront of recognizing and codifying others.

---

15. County Response to Mobilization in 1776, Table 4.1, Ragosta, *Wellspring of Liberty*, 99–101.
16. Ibid, 99–102.

The Great Awakening and the American Revolution

DANIEL N. GULLOTTA

AMERICA'S COLONIAL ODD COUPLE

Scholars of Jonathan Edwards have continually compared him with Benjamin Franklin. Both were born in the early eighteenth century (Edwards in 1703, only three years earlier than Franklin), and both distinguished themselves as bright young thinkers. Yet the similarities stop there, as the two have come to embody very different kinds of American spirits. It is argued that, in Edwards, we can see a return to the Puritan roots of colonial New England, while in Franklin, we can observe the manifestation of Enlightenment thought within the New World. Due to these dynamics, they have become America's colonial odd couple. Franklin is seen as the dawning of the new and Edwards as the setting of the old.

Due to Franklin's role within the American Revolution, he is remembered as a revolutionary, while Edwards is remembered as the so-called "last Puritan."[1] But Franklin lived through the Revolutionary War (1775–1783), while Edwards died in 1758, so it must be asked whether this is a fair assessment. After all, much of our conception of Franklin is based on his life during and after the Revolution. If Franklin had died around the same time as Edwards (which he nearly did crossing the Atlantic in 1757), he would have died a fierce loyalist to the British crown.[2]

So what if the tables had been turned? Seated as the president of the College of New Jersey (now Princeton University), how would Edwards

---

1. For the "last Puritan" conception of Edwards, see David C. Brand, *Profile of the Last Puritan: Jonathan Edwards, Self-love, and the Dawn of the Beatific* (Atlanta: Scholars' Press, 1991).
2. This point is echoed by George M. Marsden; see George M. Marsden, *A Short Life of Life of Jonathan Edwards* (Grand Rapids: William B. Eerdmans Publishing Co., 2008), 3.

have reacted to the revolutionary motto, "Rebellion to tyrants is obedience to God?" In order to understand how men like Edwards would have felt about the American Revolution, we need to look at the deeper religious, political, and military background of colonial American history, particularly the First Great Awakening.

While revivals also took place in Germany and England, the American experience of the Great Awakening tended to cross class lines and take place in urban as well as rural areas. It was the first experience shared by large numbers of people throughout the American colonies, and helped shape the formulating American identity. Revivalists partook in large public meetings, openly criticized the elites of society, and prayed for the hastened arrival of Christ's Second Coming and the establishment of his kingdom on Earth. Because of these factors and more, some scholars have come to see the First Great Awakening as a kind of "dress rehearsal" for the War of Independence.[3]

To be sure, the Revolution itself was not conceived during the revivals, but the Great Awakening did cause a shift that historians must take seriously. Revivals did contribute to the coming Revolution in important ideological, sociological, and religious ways. The revivals shattered the social order of church hierarchy, rejecting the existing power structures of the day and focusing instead on the individual. People who had normally had their voices marginalized or silenced were suddenly able to speak freely about God's grace in their lives. It provided a millennial hope of a new age and promised damnation to those who imposed the tyranny of "popery."[4] As John Adams would later write, "The Revolution was effected before the war commenced. The Revolution was in the minds and hearts of the people; a change in their religious sentiments of their duties and obligations."[5] If we are to take this change of "religious sentiments" from before and after the Revolution seriously, we must take the phenomenon of the revivals seriously.

THE (UN)SURPRISING WORK OF GOD

The Great Awakening was America's first major religious revival and was the most important religious event within the colonial period.

3. Susan Juster, "The Evangelical Ascendency in Revolutionary America," in *The Oxford Handbook of the American Revolution*, eds. Edward G. Gray and Jane Kamensky (Oxford: Oxford University Press, 2013), 407.
4. For more on the definition of popery during the eighteenth century, see Thomas S. Kidd, *God of Liberty: A Religious History of the American Revolution* (New York: Basic Books, 2010), 16–19.
5. John Adams to Hezekiah Niles, February 13, 1818, *The Works of John Adams*, vol. X, ed. Charles Francis (Boston: Little, Brown, and Company, 1850–6). 282.

While reporting on the revivals being experienced within New England, an astonished Edwards described the events as a "surprising work of God."[6] But the First Great Awakening did not drop from heaven; rather, it sprang forth from a turbulent and formative time within the American colonials' history. British colonial power had begun to shift following the defeat of the Spanish Armada in 1588, and in 1727, another war with the Spanish had broken out in Panama.[7]

Inter-colonial conflict had continued to brew which would culminate with the coming French and Indian War (1754–1763).[8] Less than one hundred years prior, the English Civil War had broken out and climaxed with the execution of King Charles I in 1649.[9] Additionally, with the Glorious Revolution of 1688–1689 and the succession of William and Mary in favor of James II, the fear of royal persecution was resurrected among the Puritan colonies in America.[10] While the 1689 Act of Toleration granted Protestant dissenters the right of private religious conscience, its actual effectiveness remained ambiguous.[11] Yet in Massachusetts, a new charter in 1692 declared that "there shall be a liberty of Conscience allowed in the Worship of God to all Christians (except Paptists)."[12] With this more inclusive shift to extend further rights to Anglicans, Quakers, and Baptists within the New England colonies, "the age of exclusionary Puritanism had come to an end."[13]

---

6. Jonathan Edwards, *A Faithful Narrative of the Surprising Work of God in the conversion of many hundred souls in Northampton, and the neighbouring towns and villages of New-Hampshire and New-England in a letter to the Rev. Dr. Benjamin Colman of Boston* (Elizabeth-Town: Printed by Shepard Kollock, 1791).

7. See James McDermott, *England and the Spanish Armada: The Necessary Quarrel* (New Haven: Yale University Press, 2005).

8. For more on the precursors to the French and Indian War (or the Seven Years' War), see Fred Anderson, *Crucible of War: The Seven Years' War and the Fate of Empire in British North America, 1754–1766* (New York: First Vintage Books, 2000), 11–66.

9. See Michael Braddick, *God's Fury, England's Fire: A New History of the English Civil Wars* (New York: Penguin, 2009); Christopher Hill, *The Century of Revolution: 1603–1714* (New York: W. W. Norton, 1982).

10. See Owen Stanwood, *The Empire Reformed: English America in the Age of the Glorious Revolution* (Philadelphia: University of Pennsylvania Press, 2011).

11. Scott Sowerby, "Toleration and Tolerance in Early Modern England," in *The Lively Experiment: Religious Toleration in America from Roger Williams to the Present* (Lanham: Rowman & Littlefield, 2015), 53–64.

12. *The charter granted by Their Majesties King William and Queen Mary, to the inhabitants of the province of the Massachusetts-Bay, in New-England* (London, and re-printed at Boston: In New-England, by Benjamin Harris, over-against the Old-Meeting-House, 1692), 9.

13. Kidd, *God of Liberty*, 44.

Traditionally, the revivals that make up the Great Awakening have been understood as a series of religious events that took place in the 1730s and 1740s. The revivals were the result of the colonial importation of Pietism, a German movement of the late seventeenth and early eighteenth centuries that emphasized intense, personal, and experiential contact with God. Pietism influenced British and Dutch religious cultures and crossed the Atlantic between the 1680s and the 1730s due to German, Scottish, and Scotch-Irish immigration.[14] Championed by Jonathan Edwards in Northampton and typified by the preaching tours of George Whitefield, Theodore Jacob Frelinghuysen, James Davenport, Samuel Davies, and Gilbert Tennent, the revivals emphasized the focus on "spiritual rebirth." Those who had been "reborn" or "awakened" were called "New Lights," and stressed the individual and emotional experiences of conversion brought about by the workings of the Holy Spirit. They rejected any sort of understanding that included good works as integral to salvation. The "Old Lights," most notably Charles Chauncy, saw the revivals as a dangerous display of religious "enthusiasm" (by which they meant excess and delusion).

While some scholars have characterized the period of the First Great Awakening as a sort of "waiting period" before the Revolution, Richard Bushman's studies have revealed that revivals affected the economic ambitions of the time period. Given that the revivals centered on the transformation of the individual, this self-consciousness and self-focus profoundly affected the social and communal aspects of day-to-day life within colonial America. Rather than operating through covenants and contracts, God acted through the heart and commitment of each individual, and therefore, the individual need not look beyond himself for any source of authority. This meant that God did not work exclusively through kings or bishops, the clergy or the magistrates, but through the people themselves. This did not only have religious implications, but also economic ones. As Bushman puts it, "in the expanding economy of the eighteenth century, merchants and farmers felt free to pursue wealth with an avidity dangerously close to avarice, the energies released exerted irresistible pressure against traditional bounds. When the Great Awakening added its measure of opposition, the old institutions began to crumble."[15]

---

14. Hartmut Lehmann, "Pietism in the World of Transatlantic Religious Revivals," in *Pietism in Germany and North America*, eds. Jonathan Strom, Hartmut Lehmann, & James Van Horn Melton *1680–1820* (London: Ashgate, 2009), 13–22.

15. Richard L. Bushman, *From Puritan to Yankee Character and the Social Order in Connecticut, 1690–1765* (Cambridge: Harvard University Press, 1890), v.

SPEAKING OUT AGAINST "DEAD MEN"

While the First Great Awakening occurred during the age of Enlightenment, it was also the age of the commonwealth man. The assumption at the time was that God did "ordain orders of superiority and inferiority among men."[16] From the pulpit of Samuel Willard in Boston to the streets of London, "all-wise God . . . required all honor to be paid accordingly." In its simplest expression, the colonial hierarchy was constructed on the godly subordination of women to men, of men to the ministers, and of the people to their magistrates. This pre-ordained hierarchy was clearest during congregational meetings. Seating arrangements reflected the rank of every person within the community, being assigned by wealth, age, and standing within the community.[17] While some might try and advance to more prominent seats within the church, this progress was slow and normally depended on the death of a superior. Despite being communal, worship reflected and played out the hierarchical "social drama" found within the colonial communities.[18] Or to borrow Stephen Foster's reflection, "mutuality, subordination, and public service constituted a kind of sacred trinity of all respectable societies, Puritan or otherwise."[19]

The revivals dramatically changed the landscape of hierarchal order and assumed respect for one's betters. It was this higher class of commonwealth men and clerics that Gilbert Tennent and George Whitefield would openly criticize as "dead men" leading "lifeless" congregations.[20]

---

16. Samuel Willard, *The Character of a Good Ruler: As it was recommended in a Sermon Preached before His Excellency the Governour, and the Honourable Counsellors, and Assembly of the Representatives of the Province of Massachusetts-Bay in New-England.* May 30, 1694 (Boston: Printed by Benjamin Harris for Michael Perry, 1694), 2.

17. For more on the politics of Puritan seating arrangements, see Kevin Dillow, "The Social and Ecclesiastical Significance of Church Seating Arrangements and Power Disputes, 1500–1740," (Oxford University, D.Phil., 1990).

18. Joseph A. Conforti, *Saints and Strangers: New England in British North America* (Baltimore: John Hopkins University Press, 2006), 59.

19. Stephen Foster, *Their Solitary Way: The Puritan Social Ethic in the First Century of Settlement in New England* (New Haven: Yale University Press, 1971), 18.

20. Gilbert Tennent, *The querists, part III, or, An extract of sundry passages taken out of Mr. G. Tennent's sermon preached at Nottingham of the danger of an unconverted ministry: together with some scruples propos'd in proper queries raised on each remark / by the same hands with the former* (Philadelphia: Printed by B. Franklin in Market-street, 1740), 5; George Whitefield, *A continuation of the Reverend Mr. Whitefield's journal, from a few days after his return to Georgia to his arrival at Falmouth, on the 11th of March, 1741, containing an account of the work of God at Georgia, Rhode-Island, New-England, New-York, Pennsylvania and South-Carolina. The seventh journal.* London: Printed by W. Strahan; and sold by J. Robinson, in Ludgate-Street; at the Tabernacle, near Upper Moorfields; and by Mr. John Sims, near Hoxton, 1744), 38, 48.

This is not to say congregations had never complained about their religious leaders before; far from it, but this was typically done in a more local and privatized fashion. Ministers were dismissed over economic disputes and the like, but rarely was the authenticity of their faith and ministry questioned. Preachers like Tennent and Whitefield shamed these ministers in front of crowds of thousands. The revivalists channeled the rhetoric of the gospels and called out "unconverted" ministers who behaved like "Pharisees," "foxes," and "wolves."[21] The faculty of Harvard College, who looked at the effects of Whitefield in dismay and exclaimed that "the People have been thence ready to despise their own Ministers, and their usefulness among them, in too many Places, hath been almost destroy'd."[22]

In observing and partaking in these public and damning criticisms of their so-called betters, the same generation that partook in the Great Awakening was already mentally prepared to defy the British crown. In other words, when the Revolution was ignited, many of its leading participants and advocates had already transgressed the bounds of the social order. Benjamin Franklin supported Whitefield's revivalist endeavors. While a senior at Harvard, Samuel Adams heard Whitefield declare that the college's favorite theologian, the Archbishop of Canterbury John Tillotson, "knew less of Christianity than Mahomet."[23] Patrick Henry and James Madison studied the sermons of Samuel Davies, one of the Awakening's greatest contributors and preachers in support of the Revolution.[24]

---

21. Tennent, *The Danger of an Unconverted Ministry*, 72. Also see Michał Choi ski, *The Rhetoric of the Revival: The Language of the Great Awakening Preachers* (Göttingen: Vandenhoeck & Ruprecht, 2016),150–5.

22. Harvard University, *The Testimony of the president, professors, tutors and Hebrew instructor of Harvard College in Cambridge, against the Reverend Mr. George Whitefield, and his conduct* (Boston: Printed and sold by T. Fleet, at the Heart and Crown in Cornhill, 1744).

23. See Alexander Garden, *Six letters to the Rev. Mr. George Whitefield: The first, second, and third, on the subject of justification. The fourth containing remarks on a pamphlet, entitled, The case between Mr. Whitefield and Dr. Stebbing stated, &c. The fifth containing remarks on Mr. Whitefield's two letters concerning Archbishop Tillotson, and the book entitled, The whole duty of man. The sixth, containing remarks on Mr. Whitefield's second letter, concerning Archbishop Tillotson, and on his letter concerning the Negroes. / By Alexander Garden, M.A. Rector of St. Philip's, Charlestown, and commissary in South-Carolina, ; Together with, Mr. Whitefield's answer to the first letter* (Boston: Re-printed, and sold by T. Fleet, at the Heart and Crown in Cornhill, 1740).

24. See Gary B. Nash, *The Unknown American Revolution:The Unruly Birth of Democracy and the Struggle to Create America* (New York: Penguin Books, 2006), 9–10; Andy G. Olree, "'Pride Ignorance and Knavery': James Madison's Formative Experiences with Religious Establishments," *Harvard Journal of Law & Public Policy* 36.1 (2013): 211–76.

In addition to the Revolution's leaders, its older patriots would have recalled the Great Awakening and transferred their rebellious spirit against the clergy to the king. Of course, other factors contributed to the individualism found within the Revolution, such as the increased use of print and the cooperate ideology within republicanism. But through the condemnation of the social hierarchy, the Great Awakening assisted in formulating the ideology that would spring forth in following years. What resulted from the Great Awakening was nothing short of the first widespread popular "yell of rebellion" against the established authorities in the history of British American colonies.[25] As some of Whitefield's concerned critics articulated, "When Men strive so hard to dissolve the solemn Tye of the sacred Relation between Ministers and People under the Notion of Liberty, why may not they plead for the same Liberty in other Relations?"[26]

THE PLAIN STYLE AND THE PUBLIC SPACE

Beyond the rhetoric of public criticism, the gatherings themselves manifested a new social order. While traditional congregational meetings reflected God's supposed preordained hierarchy, the revivals altered this system due to their practice of open and public preaching. Whitefield could draw in a crowd of thousands, bringing in people from every socio-economic walk of life. Young and old, men and women, rich and poor, educated and unlettered shared common ground and undistinguishable space.[27] Additionally, the language of the revivals was encompassed by the "plain style." "The revivals sought to transcend both the rational manner of polite Liberal preaching and the plain style of orthodox preaching in order to speak directly to the people at large."[28] Overturning the conventions of the classical jeremiad and other ecclesiastical formalities, the revivalists spoke in everyday language among a large mixture of everyday people.

Preachers of the revivals also operated within a new dynamic framework. Because these preachers were neither employed by or in author-

25. See Kidd, *God of Liberty*, 21–3.

26. *A short reply to Mr. Whitefield's letter which he wrote in answer to the Querists: wherein the said Querists testify their satisfaction with some of the amendments Mr. Whitefield proposes to make of some of the exceptionable expressions in his writings. Together with som farther remarks upon what seems exceptionable in the present letter; which seem to occur to the Querists* (Philadelphia: Printed by Benjamin Franklin for the Querists, 1741).

27. Kidd, *God of Liberty*, 135. Also see Susan Juster, *Disorderly Women: Sexual Politics & Evangelicalism in Revolutionary New England* (Ithaca: Cornell University Press, 1994), 24–5.

28. Stout, "Religion, Communication, and the Revolution," *William and Mary Quarterly* 34 (1977):526–7.

ity over any particular congregation, the ways in which the gospel message was communicated could be free from ministerial politics and local dramas.[29] Not only this, but the same preacher could move from town to town with the same message, and due to the fact that they would be preaching to strangers, their message would always appear exciting and unexpected. Even at the familiar local level, ministers began leaving their regular congregations to preach in neighboring towns.

The best example of this was Jonathan Edwards and his famous sermon "Sinners in the Hands of an Angry God."[30] While it is known today as the defining sermon of the Great Awakening, it was originally preached to Edwards' home congregation of Northampton, Massachusetts, to limited effect. This was because they had heard all of this before and they knew Edwards' style intimately. Yet in Enfield, near the Massachusetts-Connecticut border, Edwards had been invited as a guest.[31] The reception of Edwards' preaching was so intense that he had to ask for silence in order that he could be heard. But the congregation's enthusiasm only increased as the "shrieks and cries were piercing and amazing."[32] Later, it was reported that "souls were hopefully wrought upon that night and oh the cheerfulness and pleasantness of their countenances that received comfort."[33] "Whitefield changed Edwards' conceptions of how [preaching] was best to be done."[34] Edwards was not alone: Whitefield's influence on the clergy was felt far and wide in how they began to preach and present themselves.[35] After the revivals, what was expected of the clergy and their sermons was never the same.

In the years following the Great Awakening, the plain style would gain more traction within the literature produced by the British American colonies.[36] It was no accident that Thomas Paine wrote his most famous pamphlet, *Common Sense*, in the language of the plain style. Like

29. Harry S. Stout, *The New England Soul: Preaching and Religious Culture in Colonial New England* (Oxford: Oxford University Press, 2012), 199.

30. See Jonathan Edwards, *Sinners in the Hands of an Angry God: A sermon, preached at Enfield, July 8, 1741, at a time of great awakenings; and attended with remarkable impressions on many of the hearers* (New York: Printed by G. Forman for C. Davis, 1741).

31. See George Marsden, *Jonathan Edwards: A Life* (New Haven: Yale University Press, 2003), 219–21.

32. Stephen Williams Diary, Entry for the July 8, 1741, Storrs Library, Longmeadow, MA.

33. Ibid.

34. Marsden, *Edwards: A Life*, 219.

35. John Howard Smith, *The First Great Awakening: Redefining Religion in British America, 1725–1775* (Madison: Fairleigh Dickinson University Press, 2015), 1–3.

36. See John Howe, *Language and Political Meaning in Revolutionary America* (Amherst and Boston: University of Massachusetts Press, 2004), 101–5.

Whitefield and the revivalist preachers of the Awakening, Paine sought to have his message read and understood as far and wide as possible.[37] *Common Sense* was such a success because it was a "kind of secular sermon, an extraordinarily adroit mingling of religion and politics."[38] While Paine's *Common Sense* marked the invention of a new mode of American political discourse, his use of common language and understandable prose can be traced back to the revivalist traditions of plain style preaching.

Not only did this change the pattern and behaviors of the clergy, but Evangelicalism presented a new challenge to social harmony. On average, New England meetinghouses only held up to 750 people.[39] Prior to the revivals, the largest forms of social assembly had been executions. While these grim events filled up the meetinghouses to capacity, they were few and far between.[40] One notable exception was the execution of the murderer James Morgan in 1686. Morgan's execution drew in a crowd of nearly 5,000, according to London bookseller John Dutton.[41] This was an impressive turnout, given that the entire popular of Boston was 7,000 at the time.[42]

The revivals, on the other hand, regularly drew crowds of thousands. Nathan Cole's description of the crowds gathering to hear Whitefield's preaching in Middletown, Connecticut, best captures the size and excitement of the people:

> . . . as I came nearer the Road, I heard a noise something like a low rumbling thunder and presently found it was the noise of horses feet coming down the road and this Cloud was a Cloud of dust made by the Horses feet. It arose some Rods into the air over the tops of the hills and trees and when I came within about 20 rods of the Road, I could see men and horses Sliping along in the Cloud like

---

37. Stout, "Religion, Communications, and the Revolution," 536–7.

38. Christine Leigh Heyrman, "Religion and the American Revolution," Divining America, TeacherServe©, National Humanities Center: http://nationalhumanitiescenter.org/tserve/eighteen/ekeyinfo/erelrev.htm.

39. For more on the volume of congregations during the eighteenth century, see Harry Knerr, "The Election Sermon: Primer for Revolutionaries," *Speech Monographs* 29 (1962):15–6.

40. See Scott D. Seay, *Hanging Between Heaven and Earth: Capital Crime, Execution Preaching, and Theology in Early New England* (DeKalb: Northern Illinois University Press, 2009), 21–27.

41. John Dutton, "Letter to George Larkin," March 25, 1686 in *The Puritans: A Sourcebook of Their Writings*, rev. ed., ed. Perry Miller and Thomas H. Johnson (New York: Harper Torchbooks, 1963), 414–20.

42. See Lawrence Kennedy, *Planning the City Upon a Hill: Boston Since 1630* (Amherst: University Massachusetts Press, 1992), 254.

shadows, and as I drew nearer it seemed like a steady stream of horses and their riders, scarcely a horse more than his length behind another, all of a lather and foam with sweat, their breath rolling out of their nostrils in the cloud of dust every jump; every horse seemed to go with all his might to carry his rider to hear news from heaven for the saving of Souls. It made me tremble to see the Sight, how the world was in a Struggle, I found a vacance between two horses to Slip in my horse; and my wife said law our cloaths will be all spoiled see how they look, for they were so covered with dust, that they looked almost all of a colour coats, hats, and shirts and horses.

We went down in the Stream; I heard no man speak a word all the way three miles but every one pressing forward in great haste and when we got to the old meeting house there was a great multitude; it was said to be 3 or 4000 of people assembled together.[43]

Whitefield's celebrity status during this period cannot be overstated. During his preaching tour of Boston, Whitefield drew crowds up to 8,000. Fifty-thousand people assembled to see him preach at Hyde Park. Cole commented that Whitefield's preaching tour in Philadelphia had "many thousands flocking to hear him preach the Gospel, and great numbers were converted to Christ."[44] By 1740, Whitefield had inspired thirty percent of the printed works published by the American colonies.[45] He preached in virtually every major town on the eastern seaboard of the North American colonies. Whitefield was so influential that before him "there was no unifying intercolonial person or event . . . . But by 1750 virtually every American loved and admired Whitefield and saw him as their champion."[46] On Whitefield's impact Franklin commented, "It was wonderful to see the Change soon made in the Manners of our Inhabitants; from being thoughtless or indifferent about Religion, it seem'd as if all the World were growing Religious; so that one could not walk thro' the Town in an Evening without Hearing Psalms sung in different Families of every Street."[47]

---

43. Nathan Cole, "The Spiritual Travels of Nathan Cole," Thursday, October 23, 1740, ed. Michael J. Crawford, *William and Mary Quarterly* 33.1 (1976): 93.
44. Cole, "The Spiritual Travels of Nathan Cole," 93.
45. Frank Lambert, *Pedlar in Divinity: George Whitefield and the Transatlantic Revivals, 1737–1770* (Princeton: Princeton University, 1994), 128.
46. Harry S. Stout, "Heavenly Comet," *Christian History* 38.2 (1993): 13–4.
47. Benjamin Franklin, *The Autobiography of Benjamin Franklin* (Philadelphia: J. B. Lippincott & Co, 1869), 253.

"ENTHUSIASM FOR LIBERTY"

Looking at these large and wide spectacles of "enthusiasm" displayed by the supporters of Whitefield and those like it, Chauncy bitterly preached against the revivals in favor of rational obedience to the Scriptures, humility before God, and respect for church order.[48] Chauncy argued that the revivals' lust for enthusiasm merely encouraged grand delusions, undignified displays of bodily convulsions, and the usurpation of ministerial privilege. What is noteworthy about Chauncy's writings is that they reveal that enthusiasm was not just a religious affront but also a political one. To be an "enthusiast" was to be "inspired" or "possessed," and it was usually an insult to call someone delusional or accuse them of being influenced by the devil.[49] Typically, those who refused to operate within the hierarchal norms of society were accused of "enthusiasm" and faced banishment, jail, or (albeit rarely) hanging. Roger Williams, Anne Hutchinson, those accused of witchcraft in Salem, the Quakers, and the early Baptists, were all charged with enthusiasm and were not tolerated by the wider social order.[50]

During the Awakening, the Old Lights used the slur of enthusiasm not just against those whom they saw as delusional, but also against those who broke social norms.[51] James Davenport would be labelled *non compos mentis* (not sound of mind) in 1742 and was banished from Connecticut and Massachusetts, after inciting a public burning of books, clothing, and other "worldly" materials. Future Princeton College president Samuel Finley would also be banished from Connecticut after he preached to a church in Milford, after which he was arrested and "transported as a vagrant."[52]

48. See Charles Chauncy, *Enthusiasm described and caution'd against: A sermon preach'd at the Old Brick Meeting-House in Boston, the Lord's Day after the commencement, 1742. With a letter to the Reverend Mr. James Davenport* (Boston: Printed by J. Draper, for S. Eliot in Cornhill, and J. Blanchard at the Bible and Crown on Dock Square, 1742).
49. See Ann Taves, *Fits, Trances, and Visions: Experiencing Religion and Explaining Experience from Wesley to James* (Princeton: Princeton University Press, 1999), 13–9.
50. Ibid., 20–46.
51. William G. McLoughlin, *New England Dissent, 1630–1833: The Baptists and the Separation of Church and State,* vol. 1 (Cambridge: Harvard University Press, 1971), 360–98.
52. Richard Webster, *A History of the Presbyterian Church in America: From its Origin until the Year 1760, with Biographical Sketches of its Early Ministers* (Philadelphia: Printed by Joseph M. Wilson in 27 South Tenth Street, Below Chestnut St., 1875), 489.

It was these extreme revivalists that inspired what was dubbed a "zenith of fanaticism," causing further anxiety to the colonies' social harmony. In an unsuccessful attempt to quell revivalists' enthusiasm, the Connecticut General Assembly (controlled by the Old Lights) passed a law in 1742, "An Act for regulating Abuses and correcting Disorder in Ecclesiastical Affairs," over the growing amount of "literate" men exhorting in public.[53] It is important to note that men were not the only participants in the First Great Awakening. Women, children, and the poor began to publically speak about their experiences of God's grace and express their opinions about correct Christian theology.[54] "Educated white men listened to these usually silent or silenced folks and concluded that they were filled with the Spirit."[55] During the Revolutionary war, in strikingly familiar language, a Philadelphia Lutheran pastor would complain that, "The whole country is in perfect enthusiasm for liberty. Would to God that men would become as zealous and unanimous in asserting their spiritual liberty, as they are in vindicating their political freedom."[56]

AN ALL-AMERICAN APOCALYPSE

Along with anti-authoritarian principles, the First Great Awakening fostered strong millennial hopes across the entirety of the colonies. Seeing themselves as actors on the stage of salvation history, revivalists understood themselves to be playing a pivotal role in bringing about the Second Coming of Christ.[57] Like most apocalyptic thinkers, revivalists envisioned themselves as a part of an epic and age-old battle between Christ and Satan, the forces of light and the forces of darkness. Jonathan Edwards was optimistic that the revivals were the dawning of God's final plans for the earth, a defining moment for America within salvation history. According to Edwards, "we can't reasonably think otherwise, than that the beginning of this great work of God must be near. And there are many things that make it probable that this work will begin

---

53. See Charles J. Hoadly, ed., "An Act for regulating Abuses and correcting Disorder in Ecclesiastical Affairs," in *The Public Record of the Colony of Connecticut,* vol. 7 (Hartford: Press of the Case, 1874), 454–7.

54. Kidd, *The Great Awakening,* 66.

55. Kidd, *God of Liberty,* 22.

56. Quoted in: Samuel Simon Schmucker, *Retrospect of Lutheranism in the United States: A Discourse* (Baltimore: Public Rooms, 1841), 14.

57. See Ruth H. Block, *Visionary Republic: Millennial Themes in American Thought, 1756–1800* (Cambridge: Cambridge University Press, 1985), 22–53.

in America."[58] Likewise, Rev. Josiah Smith boasted in a sermon in 1740 from Charleston, South Carolina, "Behold! . . . Some great things seem to be upon the anvil, some big prophecy at the birth; God give it strength to bring forth!"[59]

Related to these millennial hopes was also a deeply rooted anti-Catholicism. At this time, the Protestant faith had become intrinsically linked to the ideas of spiritual and political freedom, whereas Catholicism had become associated with tyranny and bondage. In the words of the Massachusetts minister, Peter Thacher, Catholicism is "excellently calculated to make men slaves."[60] Catholic influence or practice was typically decried as "the spirit of popery," and the Pope and the Catholic Church were also almost universally named as "antichrist."[61] Even though the excitement of the revivals began to die down by the mid-1740s, the millennial enthusiasm against Catholic tyranny did not fade away. The onset of the Seven Years' War furthered speculation about the coming of Christ's Kingdom, with many colonists reading the conflict as an apocalyptic struggle between Catholics and Protestants. Boston pastor Isaac Watts wrote to his colleague, Benjamin Coleman, that "if a French war should arise," it might hasten the arrival of Christ.[62] Watts theorized that "it is by the convulsion of nations that Antichrist must be destroy'd, and the glorious kingdom of Christ appear."[63]

58. Jonathan Edwards, *Some thoughts concerning the present revival of religion in New-England, and the way in which it ought to be acknowledged and promoted: humbly offered to the publick, in a treatise on that subject. : In five parts; Part I. Shewing that the work that has of late been going on in this land, is a glorious work of God. Part II. Shewing the obligations that all are under, to acknowlege [sic], rejoice in and promote this work, and the great danger of the contrary. Part III. Shewing in many instances, wherein the subjects, or zealous promoters, of this work have been injuriously blamed. Part IV. Shewing what things are to be corrected or avoided, in promoting this work, or in our behaviour under it. Part V. shewing positively what ought to be done to promote this work* (Boston: Printed and sold by S. Kneeland and T. Green in Queen-Street, 1742), 353.

59. Josiah Smith, *The character, preaching, &c. of the Reverend Mr. George Whitefield, impartially represented and supported in a sermon, preach'd in Charlestown, South Carolina, March 26th, Anno Domini 1740* (Boston: Printed by G. Rogers, for J. Edwards and H. Foster in Cornhill, 1740), 19–20.

60. Quoted in James Byrd, *Sacred Scripture, Sacred War: The Bible and the American Revolution* (Oxford: Oxford University Press, 2013), 5.

61. See Thomas S. Kidd, "'Let Hell and Rome Do Their Worst': World News, Anti-Catholicism, and International Protestantism in Early-eighteenth-century Boston," *The New England Quarterly* 76.2 (2003): 265–90.

62. Isaac Watts, "Isaac Watts to Benjamin Colman," in *Proceedings of the Massachusetts Historical Society* (Boston: Published by the Massachusetts Historical Society), 382.

63. Ibid, 382.

As American chaplain Theodorus Frelinghuysen told his troops, "Antichrist must fall before the end comes . . . The French now adhere and belong to Antichrist, wherefore it is be hoped, that when Antichrist falls, they shall fall with him."[64] The British's victory over the French was seen as another sign of God's favor upon the American colonies. During the Revolution, this anti-Catholic rhetoric would be applied to the British Crown. The Stamp Act would be decried as "Infernal, atheistical, Popish" by the *Boston Gazette*, later the king's supporters would be labelled "papists," and King George III called a "popish Pharaoh."[65] The anti-Catholicism that was fostered in the revivals within the colonies would come in full force during the American Revolution.

Additionally, the attempts by the British crown to place an Anglican bishop within the American colonies blended this anti-authoritarian spirit and the anxieties of popery. In 1749–1750 and 1760–1770, the Anglican Church made moves to establish an episcopal authority within the American colonies. These moves aroused fear among the non-Anglican colonists that they would be persecuted for their religious beliefs and that such an authority would inspire popish tyranny.[66] An infamous cartoon immortalized the reaction of Boston Congregationalists to the idea of a bishop arriving on their shore featuring the banner, "No Lords, Spiritual or Temporal in New England."[67] John Adams would later recall that "the apprehension of Episcopacy, contributed 50 years ago, as much as any other cause, to arouse the attention, not only of the enquiring mind but of the common people."[68]

THE FIRST AMERICAN REVOLUTION

In conclusion, I would agree that it would be an overstated to claim that without the Awakening there would have been no Revolution. The Awakening, however, is a historical reality that more historians need to grapple with in understanding the Revolution's origins. After the First Great Awakening, the so-called preordained order of society was com-

---

64. Theodorus Frelinghuysen, *Wars and Rumors of Wars, Heavens decree over the World: A Sermon preached in the camp of the New-England forces. On occasion of the expedition to remove the encroachments of the French, on His Majesty's dominions in North-America* (New York: Published by H. Gaine, 1755), 36.

65. See Francis D. Cogliano, *No King, No Popery: Anti-Catholicism and Revolutionary New England* (Westport: Greenwood Press, 1995).

66. See Carl Bridenbaugh, *Mitre and Sceptre: Transatlantic Faiths, Ideas, Personalities, and Politics, 1689–1775* (New York: Oxford University Press, 1962).

67. *An Attempt to Land a Bishop in America*. Engraving from the Political Register. London: September, 1769. John Carter Brown Library at Brown University, Providence, RI (86).

68. John Adams, *John Adams to Jedidiah Morse*, December 2, 1815.

pletely turned upside down. It was during the revivals that the colonists began to view themselves as capable of interpreting the will of God for themselves. While John Winthrop may have promised that the Massachusetts Bay Colony would be like "a city upon a hill," it was the First Great Awakening that truly provided the ground for the American colonists to begin to see themselves as a chosen people. They believed that God was working within the American colonies in a special way. Not only this, but the Awakening provided the means by which colonists could communicate this revolutionary ideology. The First Great Awakening was not *the* American Revolution, but it was an American revolution.

"An Attempt to land a Bishop in America," 1769.
(*John Carter Brown Library*)

I would like to express my thanks to Dr. Harry S. Stout and Dr. Kenneth P. Minkema for their guidance in the formulation of this paper. A debt of gratitude is also owed to the Jonathan Edwards Center at Yale University, as well as Dr. David J. Gary (previously at the Sterling Memorial Library at Yale University and now at the American Philosophical Society) for all his help during the research process. I would also like to thank Koray Er, Nicholas Patler, Catherine Treesh, James M. Duffin III, and John T. Lowe for their insights. This paper is dedicated to the loving memory of Brex Wayne Whalen (August 21, 2010–December 27, 2016).

How John Adams Won the Hancock Trial

❧ NEAL NUSHOLTZ ❧

Historian Oliver Morton Dickerson was studying American colonial newspapers when he noticed identical articles appearing in newspapers in New York, Pennsylvania, Boston, elsewhere in the colonies and in England. It was an anonymous column called *A Journal of the Times*. The *Journal* covered daily events in Boston from September of 1768 through August of 1769 when Boston was under military occupation by the British. The last column was published in the *New York Journal* on November 30, 1769. Dickerson published the *Journal* in a book.[1]

Frequent topics in the *Journal* included outrageous tax enforcement through zero tolerance searches and seizures in Boston Harbor (as orchestrated by the Treasury Board of Commissioners) and abuses by the occupying British soldiers who were robbing and beating the townspeople or raping an old woman and stealing her laundry.[2] A third frequent topic in the *Journal* was the John Hancock Admiralty Court smuggling trial. Hancock was one of the wealthiest shipping merchants in the country.[3] He had been accused by the British Empire of conspiring to unload goods from his commercial vessel without payment of duties. His trial attorney was John Adams. At the time, Adams was a thirty-three-year-old married attorney with two young kids and a third born shortly after the trial started.

The series of events that led up to Hancock's Admiralty Court trial and his arrest in November of 1768 began to unfold when the Board of Customs Commissioners arrived in Boston to manage revenue collec-

---

1. Oliver Morton Dickerson, *Boston Under Military Rule* (Boston: Chapman & Grimes, 1936; reprinted New York: Da Capo Press, 1970), vii-xii, 1, 123–127.
2. Ibid., 93.
3. Oliver Morton Dickerson, *The Navigation Acts and the American Revolution* (University of Pennsylvania Press, 1974), 232.

tion for the American Colonies. They picked a fight with John Hancock and he with them.[4] The Hancock trial was not their first attempt to make an example out of Hancock.

Seven months before Hancock's arrest, the Board of Commissioners had wanted the local prosecutor to convict Hancock on a different matter—the manhandling of a tidesman named Owen Richards. A tidesman was a customs official stationed on deck to make sure goods were not smuggled ashore before clearance and payment of duties; and it was someone who would collect a third of the financial results as an informer. On April 8, 1768, Hancock and his men had discovered Richards standing on the upper deck of the brig *Lydia*. Richards did not have a Writ of Assistance, which was a court document necessary for Richards to search below deck. Richards told Hancock that he did not intend to search the *Lydia*. Hancock admonished his men not to let Richards go below deck. Richards was found below deck twice. The second time, Hancock's men grabbed Richards and carried him above deck. For that, the Commissioners referred the matter to the local prosecutor, Jonathan Sewall.

Sewall declined to prosecute for two reasons. First, prosecution for forceful resistance to revenue collection required clubs or other weapons which were not present. Second, under the statute, the tidesman only had the authority "freely to go and remain on Board until the Vessel is discharged of her Lading." Sewall decided that to be "on Board" meant to be "on deck" and Richards, without a Writ of Assistance, did not have authority to go below deck.[5]

The Commissioners wrote home to the Treasury Board, who also refused to authorize prosecution of Hancock. One reason the Commissioners gave in favor of prosecution was that Hancock and the members of his battalion had refused to attend a party because the Commissioners would be on the guest list:

> We cannot omit mentioning to your Lordships that Mr. Hancock before named is one of the leaders of the Disaffected in this town, that early in the Winter he declared in the General Assembly that he would not suffer our officers to go even on board any of his London Ships and now he carries his opposition to Government to even a higher pitch. Being Major of his company of Cadets which distin-

---

4. Ibid., 208.

5. *Opinion of Attorney General Jonathan Sewall in the Case of the Lydia, Given to the Commissioners of Customs at Boston, April 23, 1768.* Oliver Morton Dickerson, "Opinion of Attorney General Jonathan Sewall of Massachusetts in the Case of the Lydia," *The William and Mary Quarterly*, Third Series, Vol. 4, No. 4 (Oct., 1947), 499–504.

guished itself in the year 1766 by putting a stop to the riots, and it being usual for the Governor to invite all the servants of the Crown to Dine with him on the Day of their general election, which happens on the 25th instant, a Majority of his Corps met together a few days ago and came to a resolution to acquaint the Governor, that they would not attend him on that occasion as usual if he invited the Commissioners of the Customs to dine with him, and this being signified to His Excellency, he answered that he would enter into no stipulation with them, and positively required their attendance. Mr. Hancock thereupon tore the seal off his Commission, and all the rest of the Company except nine Declared they would not continue any longer in the service. This infatuated man now gives out in public that if we are not recalled, he will get rid of us before Christmas.[6]

The charges against Hancock in the Admiralty Court were based on events occurring a month after the *Lydia* incident on the night of May 9, 1768 on Hancock's sloop, the *Liberty*. When the *Liberty* unloaded the following day, the tidesman Thomas Kirk gave the sloop proper clearance. But a month later (on June 10) Kirk changed his mind. He swore out a new affidavit saying goods had been unshipped off the *Liberty* without payment of duties.

The new affidavit recited that on the night of May 9, a Captain Marshall and five or six men arrived asking Kirk "to consent to the hoisting out several Casks of Wine." Kirk refused and was forced below deck, and the cabin door was nailed shut. Kirk said he could hear the tackle moving. Kirk also said that Marshall had threatened his life, but Marshall had died thereafter and his subsequent death explained the new affidavit. A second tidesman, who was supposed to be present, was examined but he said he was asleep at the time. Kirk said the other tidesman "was drunk and had gone home to Bed."[7] The British Attorney General, William De Grey, approved prosecution to be "brought against persons concern'd in unshipping the Goods" from Hancock's Sloop *Liberty*."[8]

By the time the prosecution of Hancock had been approved by De Grey, the *Liberty* had already been seized. It was seized on the night of June 10, the same date as Kirk's revised affidavit. The seizure provoked

---

6. Memorial of the Customs Commissioners to the Treasury Board in London, May 12, 1768 Treasury 1:465.

7. G. G. Wolkins, "Hancock's Sloop Liberty," *Massachusetts Historical Journal*, March 1922", Vol. 55; Opinion of Attorney General, William De Grey July 15, 1768, 252–276.

8. Ibid.

a mob riot of about 4 or 500 persons. The Commissioners fled and wrote home about the riot.[9]

According to Oliver Dickerson, the *Liberty* was not seized on June 10 for anything having to do with the events on the 9th of May. The charge against Hancock in the Admiralty Court trial was that on March 9, Hancock had been "willfully and unlawfully aiding and assisting in unshipping and landing one hundred Pipes of Wine."[10] But, according to the filed seizure paperwork, the *Liberty* was seized for loading 20 barrels of tar and 200 barrels of oil without a permit on June 10. Loading without a permit, although illegal, was an unfair technicality that could have led to the seizure of every ship anchored in Boston Harbor. The universal practice in Boston Harbor was to load goods first and then proceed to the nearest customhouse to complete the paperwork.[11]

After the June 10 riot, Britain sent troops to occupy Boston. The *Journal* reported on October 1, 1768:

> At about 1 o'clock, all the troops landed under cover of the cannon of the ships of war, and marched into the Common, with muskets charged, bayonets fixed, colours flying, drums beating and fifes, &c. playing, making with the train of artillery upwards of 700 men.[12]

Paul Revere made an engraving of the Landing of the Troops. In it are the longboats unloading sailors from the British military vessels and the sailors lining up on the Long Wharf to march through town.

The *Journal* later reported:

> 26 December 1768. This morning a vessel from Salem or Marble-head, having a cask of sugar on board, which it was supposed had not been properly cleared out, was seized by one of the custom-house officers, who brought a number of SOLDIERS! to assist and keep possession of said vessel, but upon discovery that the sugar had been reported at the Custom-House, she was soon released. It is very extraordinary that soldiers should be called in upon such occasions: It seems calculated to lead Administration to conceive that the quartering of troops in this town is necessary to enable the customhouse officers to discharge their duty.[13]

9. Ibid., 274–275.
10. Massachusetts Historical Society, *Legal Papers of John Adams, Vol. 2,* 194–195; www.masshist.org/publications/apde2/index.php/view?mode=p&vol=LJA02&page=1 94#194.
11. Oliver Morton Dickerson. "John Hancock Notorious Smuggler or Near Victim of British Revenue Racketeers," *The Mississippi Valley Historical Review,* Vol. 22 No. 4 (Mar. 1946), 518–519.
12. Dickerson, *Boston Under Military Rule,* 2.
13. Dickerson, *Boston Under Military Rule,* 40.

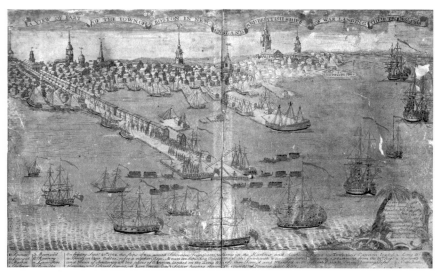

"A view of Part of the Town of Boston in New-England and the British Ships of War landing their Troops! 1768." Paul Revere engraving.
(*New York Public Library*)

The American colonies were introduced to the John Hancock trial on November 3, 1768:

> November 3, 1768 We can now account for the orders of the last night. This morning Mr. Arodi Thayer, marshal of the Court of Admiralty for three provinces, with a hanger at his side, came to the house of John Hancock, Esq; to serve him with a precept for £9000 sterling, and having arrested his person, demanded bail for £3000 sterling. Mr. Hancock offered him divers estates to the value thereof, which were absolutely refused; he then made him an offer of £3000 in money, and afterwards of £9000, which were also refused Mr. Thayer alledging that such were his directions.[14]

THE ADMIRALTY COURT

At this juncture, a short explanation of Admiralty Court procedures and English common law may help understand the legal situation. The initiating document in Admiralty Court is called a libel and the proceeding is initiated with the arrest of the person charged and their posting

---

14. Dickerson, *Boston Under Military Rule*, 18.

bond.[15] The verdict is rendered by the judge.[16] Procedural rules in Admiralty Court came from Roman civil law where judges rendered verdicts in non-criminal Roman civil law trials.[17] Judge verdicts in Admiralty Court proceedings were a departure from English common law jury trials to which English subjects were accustomed.

Juries under English common law grew out of a Norman procedure called an "inquest" that was imported into England during the Norman Conquest. The inquest consisted of men in the neighborhood with knowledge of the pertinent events being summoned to reply under oath to any inquiries that might be addressed to them. That inquest evolved into English jury trials.[18] In contrast, Roman civil law developed in a class society where judgeships were dispensed to upper class patricians as a kind of compensation.[19]

Civil law and common law trials differ in certain procedural respects that pertain to the Hancock trial. Civil law verdicts required at least two qualified witnesses or at least one witness with strong corroborating circumstances.[20] Common law jury verdicts did not have that requirement.[21] Decisions by judges under civil law rules could be based entirely on written answers to interrogatories that had been given to the judge (and without any oral testimony).[22]

Originally, Admiralty Courts were a forum for resolving commercial disputes in the sea trade and that was the case for hundreds of years before the American Revolution.[23] When the British suspected that American colonial jury trials were too sympathetic to smugglers, they transferred jurisdiction of customs violations to the Admiralty Court where the King's judges would be sympathetic to the Crown. That sus-

15. Charles Sumner, Luther S. Cushing and George S. Hillard, "On the Effect of an Answer Upon Oath in Admiralty" *The American Jurist and Law Magazine Vol XVIII* (Boston: Weeks Jordan and Company, January 1838), 298.

16. *The Solicitors' Journal and Reporter Vol. XXXIX*, 1894–95 (London: 27 Chancery Lane, W.C. 1895), 760.

17. Sumner et al., "On the Effect of an Answer," 297–298.

18. Leonard W. Levy, *Origins of the Fifth Amendment* (New York: Macmillan Publishing Company, 1986), 7–9.

19. Alexander Adam, *Roman Antiquities or an Account of The Manner and Customs of The Romans* (Philadelphia: J.B. Lippincott & Co., 1872), 83.

20. Sumner et al., "On the Effect of an Answer," 296.

21. John H. Wigmore, "Required Numbers of Witnesses; A Brief History of the Numerical System in England," *Harvard Law Review*, Vol. 15, No. 2 (June 1901), 83.

22. Jerome Frank, "Civil Law Influence on the Common Law—Some Reflections on 'comparative' and '"Contrastive Law'," *University of Pennsylvania Law Review* Vol. 104 (May 1956) No. 7, 887.

23. *The Solicitors' Journal*, 759, 778.

picion of juries developed sometime before 1696. Surveyor General Edward Randolph had written in 1695: "The illegal trade of the plantations
was supported and encouraged by the Generall partiality of Courts and
Jurys (byassed by private Interest) in causes relating to the Crown."[24]

It was Randolph who suggested transferring jurisdiction of customs
violations to non-jury Admiralty courts where judges could be picked
by the King.[25] That suggestion was enacted in 1696[26] after which seven
Admiralty Court jurisdictions were created in the colonies.[27]

The Colonies fought back. In Rhode Island, the governor refused to
administer the new Admiralty Court Judge oath of office.[28] The Governor of Connecticut refused to recognize the commission of the judge,
holding that it was a violation of the colonial charter.[29] A judge in South
Carolina complained of mistreatment by the colony. The governor and
council in the Bahamas denounced the commission and the judge fled
for fear of his life. Pennsylvania passed a law providing that all breaches
of the trade laws should be tried before juries in common law courts.[30]

Eventually, under the Sugar Act of 1763, a new single Vice Admiralty
Court was created in Halifax where prosecutors or informers could sue
regardless of the location of the infraction.[31] But a single Vice Admiralty
Court covering the entire expanse of America did not work well geographically. So, the Vice Admiralty Court Act of July 6, 1768, amended
the law to provide for four territorial Vice Admiralty Courts in Halifax,
Boston, Philadelphia and Charles Town.[32]

One other issue relates to the Hancock trial. Hancock was charged
with treble damages of the value of the goods unshipped without payment of customs duties.[33] Admiralty Court judge compensation was
customarily paid out of the proceeds from the sale of condemned property[34] creating a financial incentive for the judge to condemn property

---

24. Winfred Drexler Root, *The Relations of Pennsylvania with British Government 1696–
1765* (Philadelphia: University of Pennsylvania, 1912), 91.

25. Ibid., 92.

26. Danby Pickering, *Statutes at Large from the First year of K. William and Q. Mary to the
Eighth year of K. William III, Vol. IX* (Cambridge, 1764), "An Act for preventing frauds,
and regulating abuses in the plantation Trade" section VII:432.

27. Root, *The Relations of Pennsylvania*, 94.

28. Ibid., 97.

29. Ibid.

30. Ibid.

31. King George the III, *Statutes at Large, Vol. 9*, 1764, Geo III c. 15 XLI, 126.

32. www.revolutionary-war-and-beyond.com/vice-admiralty-court-act-of-1768–text.
html.

33. Massachusetts Historical Society, *Legal Papers of John Adams, Vol. 2*, 194–195.

34. Root, *The Relations of Pennsylvania*, 119–120.

in order to get paid. Governor Bernard of Massachusetts had written in 1764: "the objection to the Judge of the Admiralty being paid by the poundage of condemnation is very forcible; for thereby it is his interest to condemn, rather than to acquit."[35]

In response to a concern about a judicial compensation bias, the 1768 Vice Admiralty Court Act also provided for a set salary paid from the King's share of fines and forfeitures. Theoretically, judgeships could be terminated under the Act if the judge should "take any Fee or Gratuity whatsoever for any Judgment given or business done in their respective Courts."[36] That salary change in the law was mentioned in the *Journal of the Times*:

> January 28, 1769 . . . this pay of former judges, was a commission on condemnations; It was viewed in the light of a bribe; the grievance has been redressed, by substituting a greater; the present judges salaries are to be paid out of fines and forfeitures, and is six times more upon an average than has been received by all former judges thro' the continent.[37]

THE HANCOCK LEGAL ARGUMENTS

The Hancock Admiralty Court trial was reported in the *Journal of the Times* on eighteen occasions. The critical legal question in the Hancock trial was whether there was any evidence to show that Hancock was aiding and assisting Captain Marshall. According to Adams: "That even if Captain Marshall had landed the wines before the duties were paid, (of which there was evidence,) Mr. Hancock, if he 'neither consented to this Frollick, nor knew of it' could not be held to be 'assisting or otherwise concerned in the unshipping or landing inwards.'"[38]

One important witness of unknown testimony may have provided a crucial conspiracy link between Hancock and Marshall. That man was Maysel (at times spelled Muzzele). Maysel was indicted for perjury by a Massachusetts county grand jury on March 27, 1769,[39] and convicted *in absentia* on April 22.[40] Maysel was absent from the proceedings apparently because, according to the *Journal*, he had been given a job by

---

35. Root, *The Relations of Pennsylvania*, 126 n135.

36. www.revolutionary-war-and-beyond.com/vice-admiralty-court-act-of-1768-text. html.

37. Dickerson, *Boston Under Military Rule*, 56–57.

38. Josiah Quincy, *Reports of Cases Argued and Adjudged in the Superior Court of Judicature of the Province of Massachusetts Bay* (Boston: Little, Brown and Company, 1865), 459.

39. Dickerson, *Boston Under Military Rule*, 84.

40. Ibid., 92.

the Commissioners outside of the jurisdiction "on board the *Liberty*, late Mr. Hancock's, now a guarda costa."[41]

In his court arguments, Adams insisted that the introduction into evidence of Maysel's written answers to interrogatories should not happen without a cross examination of Maysel.[42] To make sense of Adams's argument, suppose that Maysel gave written testimony quoting Captain Marshall (who had since died) to the effect that Marshall had conspired with Hancock to unload without paying duties. Based on *Journal* reporting, Maysel was to be indicted by the local colonists for perjury and had been moved outside of the jurisdiction by the British.

> February 24 The advocates for Mr. Hancock, offered evidence to prove that a witness, who had been before examined for the proponent, [the crown] was a fugitive from his native country, to avoid the punishment due to a very heinous crime.—The advocates for the crown objected to this evidence as improper, urging that by common law, nothing could be proved against a witness, but his general character for falsehood. The advocates for the respondent, [Adams] replied, that the Court of Admiralty proceed according to the civil law, whereby a witnesses whole life and conversation ought to be examined . . . If therefore the court is to adopt the common law, because the jurisdiction was created by act of Parliament; it ought to adopt it as a system, and summon a jury . . . But if the court is to proceed by the civil law, the respondent ought to have the advantage of all the beneficial rules of that law, particularly to examine into the whole life and conversation of the witnesses, to except peremptorily to all persons, who are related to him, within the degrees mentioned in the civil law, and to all persons under 20 years of age, and finally to be convicted only on the testimony of two unexceptionable witnesses.[43]

The Admiralty Court ruled that it would not change its procedures and decreed Adam's question withdrawn.

> March 2 A Court of Admiralty relative to Mr. Hancock's libels, sat yesterday.—It is said the judge has given his decree upon the question mentioned, in our last Journal.—And it is said that the purport of it is, that considering the usage of the court, and the inconveniences that would attend the introduction of the rules of civil law, in cases of this nature, he decreed the question to be withdrawn . . . As

---

41. Ibid., 68.
42. Root, *The Relations of Pennsylvania.*
43. Dickerson, *Boston Under Military Rule*, 68.

to the inconveniencies; these have not been sufficient to deter the court from introducing interrogatories into such cases, which are unknown to the common law. . . It is reported that the advocates for Mr. Hancock, had no solicitude about the question they put to the witness, but they thought that if the court would proceed by such rules of the civil law, as pleased the officers of revenue, they had a right to such rules of the same law, as made in favour of Mr. Hancock.[44]

On March 26, 1769, England dropped its case against Hancock. Adams won.

March 26 . . . upon a motion made by the King's advocate, the prosecutions which have for many months past been carrying on against John Hancock, Esq; and other gentlemen of this town were dropt— We cannot help remarking at present, that one of the witnesses summoned on the part of the crown in these vexatious prosecutions, stands presented by the grand jury of the county for perjury, in this very instance; but we shall defer a full narration of the infamous steps taken by the C—m—rs without the least shadow of proof, to harass and if possible, to ruin the fortunes, as well as reputations, of gentlemen of the most distinguished and unblemished character; until we shall have leisure to make it the particular object of our attention.[45]

As for the eventual fate of the *Liberty*, that was reported in the *Journal* on August 1, 1769:

The sloop *Liberty*, lately owned by Mr. Hancock, and by way of insult to the merchant, fitted out by the C—m—rs, at a most enormous expence to the crown, as a guarda costa, having for some time past greatly distressed the fair trader, has at length come to an untimely end, in the harbor of New-Port Rhode Island, where a number of persons exasperated at the imprudent behavior of the captain and some of his people, went on board her as she lay at anchor, cut the cable, let her drift ashore and then set her on fire.—It is unhappy both for the mother country and colonies that the power of stopping, seizing vessels &c. in our several harbours, has been committed to little injudicious officers of petty guarda costas.[46]

44. Ibid., 72.
45. Ibid., 83.
46. Ibid., 125.

CONCLUSION

England dropped its case against Hancock after having prevailed on the main issue of the admission of Maysel's written testimony. A likely explanation was the (pending) indictment of Maysel and the embarrassing mass media implications of a Hancock conviction based on the testimony of a convicted perjurer. If so, the *Journal* deserves some credit.

Perhaps Adams was one of the *Journal's* anonymous authors. This is suggested by the technical nature of the Hancock trial reporting and it is also suggested by this entry in Adams's diary dated in September of 1769:

> sept 3d. sunday. SEPT 3D. SUNDAY. Heard Dr. Cooper in the forenoon, Mr. Champion of Connecticutt in the Afternoon and Mr. Pemberton in the Evening at the Charity Lecture. Spent the Remainder of the Evening and supped with Mr. Otis, in Company with Mr. [Sam] Adams, Mr. Wm. Davis, and Mr. Jno. Gill. The Evening spent in preparing for the Next Days Newspaper—a curious Employment. Cooking up Paragraphs, Articles, Occurences, &c.—working the political Engine.[47]

The reason that nobody to date has identified the authors of the Journal may be because at least one of its authors intended their identities to be a carefully guarded secret. This is suggested by John Adams's letter to William Tudor in June of 1817.

> Without the character of Samuel Adams, the true history of the American Revolution can never be written. For fifty years his pen, his tongue, his activity were constantly exerted for his country, without fee or reward. During all that time he was an almost incessant writer. But where are his writings? Who can collect them? And if collected, who will ever read them? The letters he wrote and received, where are they? I have seen him at Mrs. Yard's in Philadelphia, when he was about to leave Congress, cut up with his scissors whole bundles of letters, into atoms that could never be reunited, and throw them out at the window, to be scattered by the winds. This was in summer, when he had no fire. In winter he threw whole

47. Butterfield, Series I Diaries, *Diary and Autobiography of John Adams Volume 1, Diary 1755–1770* (Cambridge MA: The Belknap Press of Harvard University Press, , 1962), 342–343; Massachusetts Historical Society "Diary of John Adams" https://www.masshist.org/publications/apde2/view?id=ADMS-01-01-02-0013-0002-0002.

handfuls into the fire. As we were on terms of perfect intimacy, I have joked him, perhaps rudely, upon his anxious caution. His answer was, "Whatever becomes of me, my friends shall never suffer by my negligence."[48]

The authors of the *Journal* are not the only mystery here. One has to wonder how much widespread colonial reading of the British abuses in the Journal contributed to the antipathy that led the colonists to break off from their mother country. One also has to wonder if the *Journal* made Adams into a celebrity attorney with enough fame to vault him into becoming our first Vice President and our second President.

The real lesson here, about which there is no mystery, is the British effort to subvert the courts to suit the purposes of government. We still have that same fear, the one that we cannot afford to have courts that are sympathetic to taxpayers. This was explained by our Supreme Court in 1875: "If there existed in the courts, State or National, any general power of impeding or controlling the collection of taxes, or relieving the hardship incident to taxation, the very existence of the government might be placed in the power of a hostile judiciary."[49]

One has to ask, hostile to whom?

48. John Adams to William Tudor, June 5, 1817, in Charles Francis Adams, *The Works of John Adams* (Boston Little Brown and Company, 1856), 262, 264.
49. Cheatham v. United States, 92 U.S. 85 (1875).

Manipulation of the Minutes of a Privy Council Meeting

❦ BOB RUPPERT ❦

On May 10, 1769, Parliament had voted to repeal all of the Townshend Acts except one—the tax on tea. It was another four years before this law became a catalyst for open rebellion. Why was this Act left in place when the others were repealed?

In the 1760s, the United Company of Merchants of England Trading to the East Indies, better known as the East India Company, was a monopoly trading company in India and the Far East. On December 31, 1600, it had been granted its charter and monopoly privileges by Queen Elizabeth.[1] She hoped that the company would be able to break the Dutch East India Company's monopoly on the spice trade. Eventually, it would do that as well as create scattered trading settlements and secure vast territory through conquest or treaty.

The company paid a 24 percent *ad valorem* tax on all of the tea that it imported into England and was forbidden to sell it directly to the retail merchants in the colonies.[2] The tax was £23 18s 7.5d on every £100 of the gross price.[3] The tea was "sold at auction to English wholesale merchants, who then sold to American wholesale merchants who in turn sold to [colonial] retail merchants."[4] After purchasing the tea, the English merchants were subject to a second tax called the inland tax; it was one shilling per pound. Because the government of Holland did

1. Panchanandas Mukherji, ed., *Indian Constitutional Documents (1600–1918)*. Vol. 1 (Calcutta: Thacker, Spink & Co., 1918), 1–20.
2. Peter David Garner Thomas, *The Townshend Duties Crisis: The Second Phase of the American Revolution, 1767–1773* (Oxford: Oxford University Press, 1987), 18.
3. Samuel Baldwin, *Surveys of the British Customs* (London: J. Nourse, 1770), Second Part: 26, 91.
4. Edmund S. Morgan, *The Birth of the Republic, 1763–89,* 3rd edition (Chicago: University of Chicago Press, 1992), 58.

not tax the tea it imported (it is not known if the tea was subject to an inland tax), the tea was sold in the colonies at a much lower price. By 1767, ninety percent of the tea that the colonists drank was purchased from the Dutch.

The company was also required to pay to the government £400,000 a year to maintain its monopoly. Unfortunately, in order to pay its dividend of 12.5 percent to its shareholders in 1768,[5] it was forced to miss its payment to the government.

By 1773, the company was on the verge of bankruptcy predominantly due to corruption and mismanagement but also due to the colonial non-importation agreement and the smuggling of Dutch tea. Its debt was £8 million.[6] It was forced to cut its dividend to 6.0%, a share of the company on the London Stock Exchange had dropped from £280 to £160, and millions of pounds of unsold tea was rotting in the West India warehouses in London.[7] The company claimed that if they were allowed to sell their tea in the colonies without paying an export tax, they might become solvent. With the Tea Act still in place even though the other Townsend Acts had been repealed, on April 27, 1773, Parliament granted the East India Company the right to export its tea without paying the export tax, without paying the inland tax, and to sell it directly to colonial retail merchants.

With everything that unfolded between May 10, 1769, and December 16, 1773, the question remains, why didn't Parliament repeal all of the Townshend Acts? The answer may lie in three documents. They are the Minutes of the May 1, 1769, Privy Council Meeting, the list of shareholders in the East India Company as of May 10, 1769, and a letter written by George III to Lord North on September 11, 1774.

On May 1, 1769, the Privy Council met at Lord Weymouth's Office. Those present included Lord Camden, Lord Chief Justice of the King's Bench and Lord Chancellor; The Duke of Grafton, First Lord of the Admiralty and Acting Prime Minister; and Lord Hillsborough, Secre-

5. Narendra Krishna Sinha, ed., *Fort William India House Correspondence and Other Contemporary Papers relating thereto*, (Public Series) Vol. V (Delhi: Manager of Publications Government of India, 1949), 7.

6. William Cobbett, *The Parliamentary History of England from the Earliest Period to the Year 1803*, Vol. XXIII (London: T.C. Hansard, 1814), 1194.

7. East India Company: Trade and Domestic Financial Statistics, 1755–1838," United Kingdom Data Archive, Study Number 5690; Alfred Thomas Story, *The Building of the British Empire: 1689–1895* (London: G.P. Putnam's Sons, 1898), 157.

tary-of-State for the American Colonies.[8] A discussion took place as to whether their recommendation at the beginning of the next session of Parliament should be a partial or total repeal of the Townshend Acts. Each opinion was taken down by Lord Hillsborough. A vote was taken and the decision was five to four in favor of a partial repeal. Later, Lord Grafton would write, "Sir Edward Hawke [First Lord of the Admiralty] was absent from including the Teas in the repeal: I think he would have agreed with those, who voted for including the Teas in the repeal."[9] If Hawke had been present and if he voted as Grafton assumed, the vote would have been tied and under such situations the Prime Minister's opinion would have prevailed. It is possible that Grafton was anticipating Lord Rochford to vote for a total repeal since he, Grafton, was the person who nominated Rochford for his position. The minority, however, was able to prevail upon the majority by assuring them that when the circular to Colonial Governors announcing their decision was written, it would be "amend[ed] by words as kind and lenient as could be proposed . . . and not without encouraging expressions."[10] Instead of running the circular by the council before it was sent, Hillsborough sent it off in a dispatch as quickly after the meeting as he could. This was discovered by the councilors when they were later given a copy of it. They quickly realized that the circular was not in the words or form of the last corrections agreed to by the cabinet. "It was drawn up in harsh and ungracious terms, and omitted all those softening expressions which the minority in the Cabinet had, as they thought, prevailed in introducing."[11]

On June 9 Lord Camden wrote to Hillsborough,

> Lord Chancellor presents his compliments to Lord Hillsborough and begs leave to know, whether the circular letter to the governors of America, explaining the conduct of the King's servants in respect to the dispute between Great Britain and the colonies is dispatched,

8. The other attendees were Lord Gower, Lord President; Lord Granby, Commander-in-Chief of the Forces; Lord Rochford, Secretary-of-State for the Northern Department, Lord Weymouth, Secretary-of State for the Southern Department, Lord North, Second Lord of the Treasury and Chancellor of the Exchequer; and General Conway, Minister without Portfolio who remained in the Cabinet at the King's desire. Philip Henry Stanhope, The Earl of Stanhope, *History of England from the Peace of Utrecht to the Peace of Versailles, 1713–1783* (London: J. Murray, 1851), 5: Appendix xxxi.
9. Sir William R. Anson, ed., *Autobiography and Political Correspondence of Augustus Henry Third Duke of Grafton K. G. from hitherto Unpublished Documents on the Possession of his Family* (London: John Murray, 1898), 230.
10. Ibid.
11. Stanhope, *History of England*, 243.

or not: because Lord Chancellor has material objections to the draught which came first to his hands the day before yesterday.[12]

Hillsborough wrote back the same day,

Lord Hillsborough presents his compliments to Lord Chancellor, and is sorry the circular letter has long been dispatched. He wrote and sent it immediately after the Cabinet, nor can he conceive what can be his lordship's objections to it, as it is exactly conformable to the Minute[s], and as near as possible in the same words.[13]

Hillsborough claimed he spent half the day looking for the rough draught of the minutes but could not find it. He then claimed that he probably did not keep the original after he had constructed the "fair draught" from which he wrote the circular. He sent a copy of both to Camden. The "Fair Draught" read:

It is the unanimous opinion of the lords present to submit to His Majesty as their advice that no measure should be taken which can any way derogate from the legislative authority of Great Britain over the colonies. But that the Secretary of State in his correspondence and conversation be permitted to state it as the opinion of the king's servants that it is by no means the intention of Administration nor do they think it expedient or for the interest of Great Britain or America to propose or consent to the laying any further taxes upon America for the purpose of raising a revenue, and that it is at present their intention to propose in the next session of Parliament to take off the duties upon paper, glass, and colours, imported into America, upon consideration of such duties having been laid contrary to the true principles of commerce.

The circular, on the other hand, read:

Whitehall May 13, 1769

Inclosed I send you the gracious speech made by the king to his Parliament at the close of the session on Tuesday last.

What His Majesty is pleased to say, in relation to the measures which have been pursued in North America will not escape your notice, as the satisfaction His Majesty expresses in the approbation his Parliament has given to them, and the assurances of their firm sup-

---

12. Sir William R. Anson, ed., *Autobiography and Political Correspondence of Augustus Henry Third Duke of Grafton K. G.*, 231. This endnote and the three that follow reference copies made from the records of Lord Camden by the Duke of Grafton's son.
13. Ibid.

port in the prosecution of them, together with his royal opinion of the great advantages that will probably accrue from the concurrence of every branch of the legislature, in the resolution of maintaining a due execution of the laws, cannot fail to produce the most salutary effects. From hence it will be understood that the whole legislature concur in the opinion adopted by His Majesty's servants, that no measure ought to be taken which can any way derogate from the legislative authority of Great Britain over the colonies; but I can take upon me to assure you notwithstanding insinuations to the contrary from men with factious and seditious views, that His Majesty's present Administration have at no time entertained a design to propose to Parliament to lay any further taxes upon America for the purpose of raising a revenue, and that it is at present their intention to propose in the next session of Parliament: to take off the duties upon glass, paper and colours upon consideration of such duties having been laid contrary to the true principles of commerce.

These, sir, have always been and still are the sentiments of His Majesty's present servants, and the principles by which their conduct in respect to America have been governed, and His Majesty relies upon your prudence and fidelity for such an explanation of his measures, as may tend to remove the prejudices which have been excited by the misrepresentations of those who are enemies to the peace and prosperity of Great Britain and her colonies, and to reestablish that mutual confidence and affection upon which the safety and glory of the British Empire depend. I am &c.

(Signed) Hillsborough.[14]

A day or two later, Camden wrote back,

I had the honor or receiving your lordship's note with copies of the Minute and the Circular Letter, and am very sorry to say that I cannot bring myself to approve the letter, though I have considered and reconsidered it, with the utmost attention. I wish your Lordship had not mislaid the original minute, because I do not remember the first sentence of the fair draught to have been part of that original, and so I told your lordship when you was pleased to shew me the

14. Ibid., 233; Colin Nicolson, ed., *The Papers of Francis Bernard, Governor of Colonial Massachusetts, 1760–1769* (Boston: Colonial Society of America, 2015), 5:263–63; William S. Powell, ed., *The Correspondence of William Tryon and Other Selected Papers* (Raleigh: Division of Archives and History, Department of Cultural Affairs, 1981), n:334.

draught a day or two after the meeting. All that I mean to observe
to your lordship upon that subject is, that this sentence was not a
part of the original minute, nor in my poor judgment necessary to
have been made a part of it.

But the principal objection wherein I possibly may be mistaken, is
to the letter, which ought to have been founded on the minute, and
it is this, that the letter does not communicate that opinion, which
is expressed in the second paragraph of the minute, and which the
Secretary of State is authorized to impart both by his conversation
and correspondence.

The communication of that opinion was the measure; if that has
not been made, the measure has not been pursued, and therefore
your lordship will forgive me for saying that though I am responsible
for the minute as it was taken down, I am not for the letter. I confess
that I do not expect this letter will give much satisfaction to America,
perhaps the minute might: but as the opportunity of trying what effect that might have produced, is lost, I can only say, that I am sorry
it was not in my power to submit my sentiments to your lordship
before the letter was sent.[15]

Grafton's minority was angry and beside themselves; both documents were inaccurate depictions of what was decided in the Council
on May 1. Grafton believed "the circular was calculated to do all mischief." Frustrated, he quickly realized that any weight that he might
have carried in the cabinet was now all but gone, especially since under
his leadership his group could not carry a proposal on a matter belonging to his department. On January 13, 1770 Lord Granby resigned; on
the 17th, Lord Camden resigned; and on the 20th, Lord Grafton resigned. Grafton's greatest fear had occurred:

I shall ever consider Lord Chatham's long illness, together with his
resignation [Oct. 14, 1768], as the most unhappy event that could
have befallen out political state. Without entering into many other
consequences at that time, which called for his assistance; I must think
that the separation from America might have been avoided ... [with]
his effectual support in the Cabinet ... There can be no doubt, that
the favor would have been gladly received by the colonies; especially,
if it was held out to them, that their former constitutions, with their

15. Ibid., 231–2.

different charters, were no longer suited to their condition; and that Great Britain was ready to confer with them on establishing a free Government, dependent on the mother country, and exclusively possessed of the full right of taxing themselves.[16]

Six days after Chatham's resignation, another pro-colonies member of the Privy Council tended his resignation—it was Lord Shelburne. It was his position that was filled by Lord Rochford.

Going back to the question asked earlier, "Why didn't Parliament repeal all of the Townshend Acts?," there were four apparent reasons. First, twenty-three percent of all the members of Parliament, that is, 118 sitting members of the House of Commons and 34 peers in the House of Lords, held stock in the East India Company between 1768 and 1774.[17] When the dividend was cut to 6 percent and the value of a share dropped from £280 to £160, then almost one quarter of the policy makers in Parliament suffered a 50% drop in the dividend income and 35% drop in the value of their investment. In today's market, a stockholder would have dumped his shares quickly. The company was also deeply in debt with no apparent solution on the horizon. Any shareholder had to be concerned of a total collapse of the company and a 100% loss of his investment. The members of Parliament had a vested interest in finding a solution.

The second reason was that a total collapse of the East India Company would cause an end to British trading settlements along the coasts of India and allow France to become the major European trader in the East Indies.

Another reason had to do with budget problems caused by earlier legislation. Parliament needed to find a way of offsetting a property tax cut it had given the farmers. It also needed to pay governors' salaries in the colonies, and also appease the English merchants and manufacturers that were losing money due to non-importation agreements. The solution was to repeal all of the taxes on the *manufactured* goods but retain the tax on the *non-manufactured* goods. This kept a tax in place that had the potential to bring considerable revenue.

Those three reasons were above all economic reasons; the final reason was political. It was expressed in a letter from King George III to Lord North, the prime minister, on September 11, 1774: "I do not wish to come to severer measures, but we must not retreat; by coolness and

16. Ibid., 225–6.
17. Huw V. Bowen, "'Dipped in the Traffic': East India Stockholders in the House of Commons, 1768–1774," *Parliamentary History*, Vol. 5 (1986), 40–2.

an unremitted pursuit of the measures that have been adopted I trust they will come to submit; I have no objection afterwards of their seeing that there is no inclination for the present to lay fresh taxes on them, but I am clear *there must always be one tax to keep up the right*, and as such I approve of the Tea Duty."[18]

18. "King George III to Lord North, 11 September, 1774" in William Bodham Donne, *Correspondence of King George III with Lord North* (London: John Murray, 1867), 1:202.

The Seizure of the *Virginia Gazette,* or *Norfolk Intelligencer*

❧ GERALD HOLLAND ❧

On April 20, 1775, John Hunter Holt announced to the public his recent acquisition of the Norfolk newspaper, the *Virginia Gazette or Norfolk Intellingencer*. For a newspaper that had only been in print since 1774, this sudden change in ownership was more than just a business venture, it would serve as an open act of rebellion against Virginia's royal governor, Lord Dunmore. Continuing in his announcement, Holt insinuated that those from whom he purchased the press, William Duncan and Robert Gilmour, had caused "many difficulties with which the business of this press has hitherto been obstructed."[1] As his father, John Holt, recognized in a letter to Samuel Adams on January 29, 1776, "it was by means of newspapers that we received and spread the notice of the tyrannical designs formed against America and kindled a spirit that has been sufficient to repel them."[2] It was by means of the newspaper that the seizure of his son's press by Lord Dunmore was brought about at the end of September 1775.

John Hunter Holt's father, John Holt, was the patriot printer who published the *New York Journal* in New York City. The elder Holt had formerly been a resident and mayor of Williamsburg, where he learned the printing business from his brother-in-law, William Hunter, printer of the *Virginia Gazette* from 1751–61 and 1775–78. Relocating to New England in 1754 due to financial difficulties, John Holt forged a business relationship with James Parker and eventually purchased Parker's New York paper, the *New York Gazette*, in 1762, changing the name to the

1. *Virginia Gazette, or Norfolk Intelligencer*, April 20, 1775, available from https://digitalarchive.wm.edu/handle/10288/15430.
2. Victor Hugo Paltsits, *John Holt, Printer and Postmaster: Some Facts and Documents Relating to His Career* (New York: New York Public Library, 1920), 24.

New York Journal.[3] During the Stamp Act crisis, the elder Holt openly opposed British rule by continuing to print his newspapers without the British mandated stamps, stating that "he had no choice; he could not order stamped paper from the crown without certain destruction to his person and property from the general resentment of his countrymen."[4] As a printer, the elder Holt developed a reputation for being a strong Whig who advocated for the rights of the colonies. Outside of Boston, he became one of the most important printers due to his coverage of the struggle between the colonies and England. His publication of the *Journal of Occurrences* in 1768 and 1769 allowed news of the struggles in New England against British rule to reach a much wider audience as the journals made their way to the other colonies.[5]

In April 1775, the three newspapers being published from the capitol in Williamsburg and the sole version out of Norfolk all carried the name *Virginia Gazette*, the Norfolk version adding the subtitle of *Norfolk Intelligencer.* There was no real difference in the various versions aside from the mottos that adorned the top of each paper as all carried similar news and advertisements. Colonial assemblies, like the Virginia House of Burgesses, utilized the "Gazettes" as part of their official record and mandated that resolutions and proclamations be printed in the "Gazettes" allowed for some sort of government oversight of the press.[6]

The younger Holt no doubt was influenced by his father's patriot connections and stern stance against Parliamentary rule when he took over the *Norfolk Intelligencer* in April 1775. Through these connections, the purchase of the Norfolk newspaper by the younger Holt was certainly made possible. As an ardent patriot and son of a patriot printer himself, it is no surprise that John Hunter Holt spoke in tones that echoed his father, both at the beginning of his venture and for the remainder of his time at the press. In his first issue, Holt let it be known that "the subscriber enters upon the office encumbered with the bad effects of those difficulties, which, however, he will make it his study to

---

3. Ibid, 2.
4. Eric Burns, *Infamous Scribblers: The Founding Fathers and the Rowdy Beginnings of American Journalism* (New York: Public Affairs, 2006), 126.
5. The *Journal of Occurrences*, attributed to Samuel Adams and William Cooper, first appeared in the October 13, 1768 edition of the *New York Journal*. Written from the American perspective, the *Journals* were a series of articles that chronicled Boston's occupation by the British Army and were often exaggerated to add to the propaganda effect. Martin J. Manning and Clarence R Wyatt, eds., *Encyclopedia of Media and Propaganda in Wartime America, Volume 1* (Santa Barbara, CA: ABC-CLIO, 2011), 71–72.
6. A History of the Virginia Gazette, www.vagazette.com/services/va-services_gazhistory-story.html.

remove and flatters himself with the prospect of success."[7] Only thirty when he took over the press, John Hunter Holt had a sneaking suspicion that he would only be in business six months, a suspicion that would prove true.

Two months after taking over the press in Norfolk, Virginia's colonial government took a drastic turn. Governor Dunmore fled Williamsburg, fearing for his and his family's safety as the result of his growing dispute with the Williamsburg citizens in regards to the gunpowder incident from the previous April. As was printed in the June 15, 1775 issue of the *Norfolk Intelligencer*, Dunmore stated that he was "fully persuaded that my person and those of my family likewise, are in constant danger of falling sacrifices to the blind and unmeasurable fury which has so unaccountably seized upon the minds and understanding of great numbers of the people."[8]

From his new station aboard the H.M.S. *Fowey*, now removed from Yorktown to the Elizabeth River near Norfolk and reinforced by a detachment of soldiers from Florida, Dunmore began ordering raids of Tidewater plantations for supplies and stores to provide for his small naval force. With these raids came protests from the four regional newspapers, each echoing the other in their challenge against the policies of the British government, and more specifically, the activities of Dunmore and his fleet commanded by Capt. Matthew Squire.

The first report of Dunmore's tenders seizing Virginia goods was published in Holt's paper on July 5, 1775. In it, Holt reported that "a brig lately loaded by Gibson, Donaldson and Hamilton of Suffolk with a large quantity of provisions, was lately seized by some of the tenders, and taken to Boston for the supply of the navy and army." On August 16, Holt called out the commander of the H.M.S. *Otter*, Captain Squire, stating that "last week several slaves, the property of gentlemen in this town and neighborhood, were discharged from on board the Otter, where it is now shamefully notorious, many of them for weeks past have been concealed and their owners in some instances ill-treated for making application for them."[9] The squabble with Captain Squire would only increase in its magnitude in the coming weeks.

A week later in the August 23 issue of the *Norfolk Intelligencer*, Holt published an account of the quartering of British troops by Dunmore in a warehouse owned by Andrew Sprowle. In this report, it was stated that Mr. Sprowle had protested against the quartering of troops in his

7. *Virginia Gazette, or Norfolk Intelligencer*, April 20, 1775.
8. *Virginia Gazette, or Norfolk Intelligencer*, June 15, 1775.
9. *Virginia Gazette, or Norfolk Intelligencer*, July 5, 1775; August 16, 1775.

property but "Lord Dunmore paid no attention to his repeated solicitations, but still continued to keep forcible possession, for the space of ten or twelve days." Holt continued his attacks against Dunmore and Squire by recommending "to the inhabitants of this county that they have no connections or dealings with Lord Dunmore or Capt. Squires, and the other officers of the Otter sloop of war, as they have evinced on many occasions the most unfriendly disposition to the liberties of this continent, in promoting a defection among the slaves, and concealing some of them for a considerable time on board their vessels."[10]

The unremitting attacks by Holt against Dunmore and Squire came to a head beginning with the September 9 issue of the *Norfolk Intelligencer*. A week prior, on September 2, the Tidewater region had been struck by a hurricane that caused great damage throughout the area. On reporting the hurricane, Holt printed, "on Saturday last between 12 and 1pm came on one of the severest gales within the memory of man, and continued with unabated violence for eight hours."[11]

The hurricane brought great embarrassment towards Squire and his fleet as the *Mercury* man-of-war went aground in the Elizabeth River. But it was the grounding of Squire's own ship, the tender *Liberty* in Back River in Elizabeth City County, that brought forth the fury of Captain Squire upon both the town of Hampton and the press of John Hunter Holt. When the grounding of his vessel occurred, Squire abandoned the ship, only to escape the Hampton citizenry by taking "shelter under the trees . . . and in the morning under disguise to some negro's cabin, from whom he borrowed a canoe, by which means he got off," according to Pinkney's *Virginia Gazette* of September 7. Further insulting to Squire was Holt's September 6 issue where he wrote "is it not a melancholy reflection that men, who affect on all occasions to style themselves 'his majesty's servant' should think the service of their sovereign consists in plundering his subjects, and in committing such pitiful acts of rapine as would entitle other people to the character of robbers?" Pinkney, in his *Virginia Gazette* on September 14, regaled his readers with a rumored story: "Lord Dunmore, it seems, fared but poorly in this hurricane, as, by some accident or other, occasioned by the confusion in which the sailors were, his lordship fell overboard and was severely ducked. But according to the old saying, those who are born to be hanged will never be drowned."[12]

10. *Virginia Gazette, or Norfolk Intelligencer*, August 2, 1775.
11. *Virginia Gazette, or Norfolk Intelligencer*, September 9, 1775.
12. Pinkney, *Virginia Gazette*, September 7 and September 14, 1775; *Virginia Gazette, or Norfolk Intelligencer*, September 6, 1775.

Sure to be angered by the grounding and subsequent loss of his vessel to the town of Hampton, Squire now had to face personal attacks from the newspapers. In the same issue as the story of Dunmore falling in the water, Pinkney reported that Squire had "taken two or three vessels belonging to gentlemen in either Norfolk or Hampton. What a saucy coward! How miraculous it is, that men-of-war can overcome and be the terror of oyster boats and canoes." In their September 16 edition of the *Virginia Gazette*, Dixon and Hunter referred to him as a sheep stealer, but it was the words of Holt that struck a chord.[13]

On September 9, as printed in the September 13 issue of the *Norfolk Intelligencer*, Squire wrote to Holt, "Sir, you have in many papers lately taken the freedom to mention my name, and thereto added many falsities, I now declare, if I am ever again mentioned therein with any reflections on my character I will most assuredly seize your person and take you on board the Otter." The disrespectful response from Holt must have certainly continued the build-up of anger within Squire: "it needs no comment but the printer cannot forbear to say, that he has always endeavored to keep an open and liberal press, as free for Captain Squire as for anyone else, if there have been any mistakes, they have been the result of the popular voice, and although it would always have given the printer pleasure, to be in any degree instrumental to the strictest harmony between his majesty's subjects in this colony and the gentlemen of the navy, yet he does not conceive that his press is to be under the direction of any one but himself, and while he has the sanction of the law, he shall always pride himself in the reflection that the liberty of the press is one of the grand bulwarks of the English constitution."[14]

Adding further to Squire's anger was his disagreement with the Hampton Town Committee regarding the return of his tender's materiel. In Pinkney's September 14 *Virginia Gazette*, Squire had published his demand to the city of Hampton, composed on September 10, that "the king's sloop, with all belonging to her be immediately returned, or the people of Hampton who committed the outrage must be answerable for the consequence." In response, the town committee of Hampton had their rebuttal published in Dixon and Hunter's September 23 *Virginia Gazette*, which, like Holt's response on the 13th, proved to be less than flattering towards Squire's demands. The town committee ac-

---

13. Pinkney, *Virginia Gazette*, September 14, 1775; Dixon and Hunter, *Virginia Gazette*, September 16, 1775.
14. Mathew Squire to John Hunter Holt, September 9, 1775, and Holt to Squire, *Virginia Gazette, or Norfolk Intelligencer*, September 13, 1775.

cused Squire and his vessels of engaging in "pillaging and pleasuring" rather than "His majesty's service." They also demanded the return of a slave named Joseph Harris and other slaves who had been stolen and used against the town in the act of pillaging, the return of all vessels Squire had seized, and that he "shall not, by your own arbitrary authority, undertake to insult, molest interrupt, or detain the persons or property of any one passing to and from this town." With adherence to these demands, the Hampton town committee agreed to return the tender's materiel, which they claimed was not stolen, but procured from an abandoned vessel.

Through all the insulting language over the course of the summer, it was the September 20 issue of the *Norfolk Intelligencer* that forced the hand of Dunmore and Squire to bring an end to the insolent words of Holt. In this second to last issue of his paper Holt published:

> we are informed from good authority that a system of justice similar to that adopted against the devoted town of Boston, is likely to be established in this colony, by the renowned Commodore of the Virginia fleet. He has, in the course of this week, as a reprisal for the loss of his tender, seized every vessel belonging to Hampton that came within his reach, and thereby rendered himself the terror of all the small craft and fishing boats in this river; especially the latter, having brought some of them under his stern, by a discharge of his cannon at them. He has likewise seized a vessel belonging to the Eastern Shore, and having honored the passengers so far with his notice, as to receive them on board his own vessel, took the liberty of sending one of their horses to Lord Dunmore. This act of generosity we not doubt will gain him considerable interest with his Lordship, it being an instance of his industry in distressing a people who have of late become so obnoxious to his Excellency for their spirited behavior. We hope that those who have lived under and enjoyed the blessings of the British constitution will not continue tame spectators of such flagrant violations of its most salutary laws in defense of private property. The crimes daily committed by this plunderer we would not willingly brand with the odious name of piracy, but we are confident they come under those offenses to which the English laws have denied the benefit of clergy.[15]

The September 27 issue of the *Norfolk Intelligencer*, which would be the paper's last issue, published personal attacks against Dunmore's fam-

---

15. *Virginia Gazette, or Norfolk Intelligencer*, September 20, 1775.

ily, especially the actions of his father during the Jacobite Rebellion in 1745. Along with the attacks against Dunmore's family, Holt took one more chance to insult Squire by implying that the British captain had engaged in some form of bestiality by being "too free with people sheep & hoggs" during a recent seizure of a vessel off of Hampton.[16]

The result of this final tirade by Holt against Squire was the seizure of his printing press on September 30. It was reported in Dixon and Hunter's Gazette on October 7:

> Yesterday came ashore about 15 of the King's soldiers, and marched up to the printing office, out of which they took all the types and part of the press, and carried them on board the new ship Eilbeck, in presence, I suppose, of between two and three hundred spectators, without meeting the least molestation; and upon the drums beating up and down the town, there were only about 35 men to arms. They say they want to print a few papers themselves; that they looked upon the press not to be free, and had a mind to publish something in vindication of their own characters. But as they have only part of the press, and no ink as yet, it is out of their power to do anything in the printing business. They have got neither of the compositors, but I understand there is a printer on board the Otter. Mr. Cumming, the bookbinder, was pressed on board, but is admitted ashore at times. He says Captain Squire was very angry they did not get Mr. Holt, who happened to be in the house the whole time they were searching, but luckily made his escape, notwithstanding the office was guarded all round. Mr. Cumming also informs, that the captain says he will return everything in safe order to the office, after he answers his ends, which, he says will be in about three weeks.[17]

Dunmore defended the action when he wrote to Lord Dartmouth on October 4, "The public prints of this little dirty borough of Norfolk, has for some time past been wholly employed in exciting, in the minds of all ranks of people the spirit of sedition and rebellion by the grossest misrepresentations of facts, both public and private; that they might do no further mischief I sent a small party on shore on Saturday last [Sept 30] at noon and brought off their press type, paper, ink, two of the printers and all the utensils and am now going to have a press for the king on board on of the ships I have lately taken into his majesty's service."[18]

16. Lord Dunmore to Lord Dartmouth, October 4, 1775, in William Bell Clark, ed. *Naval Documents of the American Revolution, volume 2* (Washington, DC: U. S. Government Printing Office, 1966), 167.

17. Dixon and Hunter, *Virginia Gazette*, October 7, 1775.

18. Lord Dunmore to Lord Dartmouth, October 4, 1775, in Clark, *Naval Document*, 167.

Protests abounded from all corners, both against the actions of Dunmore and Squire and against the lack of action from the citizens and militia in Norfolk. In a letter to Thomas Jefferson, John Page wrote that the citizens of Norfolk "are under a dreadful apprehension of having the town burnt . . . many of them deserve to be ruined and hanged but others again have acted dastardly for want of protection." While in session at the Continental Congress, Richard Henry Lee yearned to hear "the disgraceful conduct" of Norfolk. The Norfolk town council reacted by calling the raid "a gross violation of all that men and freemen can hold dear." In their letter of protest, published in Purdie's October 13 *Virginia Gazette*, they demanded Dunmore to return the seized materials and punish Squire.[19]

Dunmore responded several days later, writing, "if any individual shall behave himself as your printer has done, by aspersing the characters of his majesty's servants and others, in the most scurrilous, false, and scandalous manner, and by being the instigator of treason and rebellion against his majesty's crown government, and you do not take such steps as the law directs to restrain such offenders, I do then expect you will not be surprised if the military power interposes to prevent the total dissolution of all decency, order, and good government."[20]

For his part, Holt promised his readers a return of his press. In Dixon and Hunter's *Virginia Gazette*, along with Pinkney's, he published the following:

The subscriber having been prevented from continuing his business, by a most unjustifiable stretch of arbitrary power, begs leave to inform the public that he has some expectations of procuring a new set of materials, which, if he should be so fortunate to succeed in, will enable him once more to apprize his countrymen of the danger they may be in from the machinations and black designs of their common enemy; the particular place where the office will be erected is not yet fixed, but it will be so near Norfolk as to give him an opportunity of receiving the earliest and most authentic information of the proceedings of the gentleman of the army and navy and of sounding the alarm whenever danger approaches; as his paper has hitherto been free and open to all parties, he intends to observe the same caution and impartiality in his future publications and cannot

19. John Page to Thomas Jefferson, November 11, 1775, ibid, 991; "Address of the Common Hall of the Borough of Norfolk to His Excellency Lord Dunmore, Sept. 30, 1775," *Virginia Gazette* (Purdie), October, 13, 1775.
20. Lord Dunmore to the Common Hall of the Borough of Norfolk, October 3, 1775, *Virginia Gazette* (Purdie), October 13, 1775.

but flatter himself that his conduct has been such as will entitle him to the future encouragement of his subscribers and the public.

Unlike his father, however, the younger Holt did not reenter the printing business until after the Revolution when he continued the trade in Richmond until his death on May 16, 1787. While his father continued spreading the word of the Revolution in New York and New England, Holt served as a 1st lieutenant and captain in the 1st Virginia Regiment. Dunmore took the seized press and began publication of his own paper from on board the ship *William*. From here, he published his proclamation which offered freedom to slaves and indentured servants of masters who were found to be in rebellion. The first issue of Dunmore's version of the *Virginia Gazette* was be printed on November 25, 1775; the paper ran for approximately six months. In December 1775 Dunmore was defeated at Great Bridge, Norfolk would was burned on New Year's Day 1776, and the British would not return to Virginia until May 1779.

The Battle of Gwynn's Island:
Lord Dunmore's Last Stand
in Virginia

❦ MIKE CECERE ❦

With the Revolutionary War entering its second year in May 1776, the focus of most Virginians was not on events to the north in Massachusetts, but rather, in Williamsburg and Norfolk. On May 15, the 5th Virginia Convention in Williamsburg (comprised of delegates from all the counties) voted unanimously to support independence from Great Britain for Virginia and instructed Virginia's delegates at the Continental Congress is Philadelphia to propose a resolution on independence before the entire Congress.

Meanwhile, the deposed British royal governor, John Murray, the Earl of Dunmore, sat threateningly among a ragtag fleet of ships off Norfolk, a town which lay in ruins from a massive fire that was set on New Year's Day by "rebel" troops. Dunmore's assorted force of British regulars (around 100), sailors from several British warships, loyal Tories and armed runaway slaves, had engaged Virginia's "rebel" forces several times in 1775, the most bloody and significant occurring at Great Bridge in early December. Dunmore suffered a decisive defeat at Great Bridge and was forced to abandon Norfolk, which was subsequently torched by the rebels.

Months had passed since then and although Dunmore had remained largely passive, his presence in southeastern Virginia remained a threat to the colony, so much so that nearly all of the troops raised in Virginia by "rebel" authorities remained in the colony to defend it. The exceptions to this included a regiment of troops sent to South Carolina (the 8th Virginia) to help defend Charlestown in the spring of 1776, two companies of riflemen that marched to Boston in the summer of 1775, and, of course, Gen. George Washington, who went to Boston ahead of the riflemen to assume command of the continental army. Washington was now in the process of preparing the defense of New York, the presumed next target of the British, and he eagerly awaited reinforcements from all of the colonies. Yet, Dunmore's continued presence in Virginia prevented its leaders from sending any troops north. The threat from Dunmore, which even General Washington recognized, was still too great. Washington expressed his concern about Dunmore at the end of 1775:

> If, my Dear Sir, that Man is not crushed before Spring, he will become the most formidable Enemy America has—his strength will Increase as a Snow ball by Rolling; and faster, if some expedient cannot be hit upon to convince the Slaves and Servants of the Impotencey of His designs. . . I do not think that forcing his Lordship on Ship board is sufficient; nothing less than depriving him of life or liberty will secure peace to Virginia.[1]

Unable to pry Dunmore and his supporters from Norfolk harbor and Portsmouth, much less crush him as Washington advocated, Virginia's leaders found themselves stuck waiting for Dunmore to make a move. He did so in late May when he suddenly sailed down the Elizabeth River with his fleet. The hope among most Virginians was that Dunmore and his flotilla of nearly 100 vessels would sail to New York or Nova Scotia, but his destination proved to be much closer, only thirty miles up the Chesapeake Bay at Gwynn's Island.

Gwynn's Island was a sparsely populated body of land just a few hundred yards off the coast of Gloucester County.[2] A narrow channel less than 200 yards wide separated the island from the mainland at its closest point and the flat, roughly four square mile island rose just a few feet about sea level.

Although Gwynn's Island was certainly not an ideal location to establish a new base of operations, the island offered safe ground free from rebel attack (or so Dunmore thought) on which his supporters and troops could recover from their long stay aboard their overcrowded, unhealthy ships. Gwynn's Island also possessed an abundant supply of livestock as well as plenty of fresh water (again, so Dunmore thought). Most importantly, the island allowed Lord Dunmore to main-

---

1. "George Washington to Richard Henry Lee, December 26, 1775," in Philander Chase and Beverly Runge, *The Papers of George Washington,* Vol. 2, (Charlottesville, VA: University Press of Virginia, 1986), 611.
2. Today Gwynn's Island is part of Mathews County, which split from Gloucester after the American Revolution.

tain the royal standard (and the illusion of royal authority in Virginia) while he awaited reinforcements and assistance from Great Britain.

Dunmore's fleet arrived off Gwynn's Island on May 26 and anchored in Hills Bay at the mouth of the Piankatank River. A detachment from the 7th Virginia Regiment posted at Burton's Point (overlooking Hill's Bay) observed the ships and sent an express to Gloucester Courthouse, approximately twenty miles to the west. The 7th Regiment, under the command of Col. William Daingerfield of Spotsylvania County, had mustered at Gloucester Courthouse in early April. Half of the regiment (five of its ten companies) was then posted in Williamsburg to help defend the capital and the other half was posted throughout Gloucester County to guard against possible raids by Dunmore or the British navy. When the dispatch from Burton Point announcing Dunmore's arrival reached the courthouse at 3:00 p.m., the ranking officer at headquarters was Capt. Thomas Posey. Captain Posey, whose father John was a neighbor and friend of General Washington, had moved to the Virginia frontier as a young man and commanded a company of Botetourt County riflemen in the 7th Virginia. Captain Posey immediately alerted Colonel Daingerfield (whose quarters were a few miles from town) of Dunmore's arrival and then rushed to New Point Comfort to collect the rest of his company and march to Gwynn's Island.[3]

While troops from the 7th Virginia Regiment and local militia converged on Gwynn's Island, Governor Dunmore landed troops on the island's north shore. British marines from the H.M.S. *Roebuck, Fowey* and *Otter* spearheaded the landing. Capt. Andrew Hamond, the commander of the *Roebuck*, noted that, "At day break [of May 27] we landed & took possession of the Island, with our whole force, which with the Marines of the Squadron, did not amount to more than 200 effective men, so great had been the mortality among the Negroes while at [Norfolk]."[4]

Dunmore's small force spread quickly across the island. Finding no opposition, the troops re-assembled on the narrow strip of land closest to the mainland. Separated by a channel of water only 200 yards wide, Lord Dunmore believed that this spot was most vulnerable to rebel attack, so he ordered the construction of earthworks and established his main camp behind them. The redoubt that protected the camp was dubbed Fort Hamond, after the captain of the *Roebuck*.

3. Thomas Posey's Revolutionary War Journal, May 27, 1776, Thomas Posey Papers, Indiana Historical Society Library, Indianapolis, IN (hereafter called Posey's Journal).
4. "Narrative of Captain Andrew Snape Hamond," in William J. Morgan, ed., *Naval Documents of the American Revolution*, Vol. 5 (Washington, D.C., 1970), 322.

While Dunmore's troops searched the island and established a fort and camp on the narrow strip of land, Captain Posey and his company arrived on the scene ahead of the rest of the 7th Regiment. They joined detachments of local militia who were perplexed on what they should do. Posey recorded in his diary that, "I found a number of the militia assembled, which appear'd to be in the utmost consternation, some running one way, and some another, under no kind of control or regularity."[5]

Colonel Daingerfield soon arrived with four more companies of his regiment (the other five companies in Williamsburg would arrive a few days later with reinforcements). As the ranking officer on the scene, Daingerfield assumed command. He ordered all of the troops closer to shore to prevent Dunmore's troops from landing on the mainland. Captain Posey observed:

> The whole were put in motion, (though I must confess the militia were in very great motion before the orders were given). However, these orders served to put them in something grator; for as soon as we came neare enough for the grape[shot], and cannon shot to whistle over our heads, numbers of the militia put themselves in much quicker motion, and never stopped. . .to look behind them until they had made the best of their way home.[6]

Captain Posey candidly admitted that it was not just the militia that was spooked by the enemy gun fire: "I cant say that our regulars deserved any great degree of credit for after two or three getting a little blood drawn, they began to skulk and fall flat upon there faces."[7]

Despite their apprehension, Colonel Daingerfield's troops and most of the militia held their ground and endured enemy cannon fire and heavy rain into the evening. As the hours passed, they grew more determined to face the enemy. Posey recalled, "We began to grow very firm and only wish them to come into the bushes, where we are certain of beating them."[8]

Rather than attack the mainland, however, Lord Dunmore was content to stay on the island and harass the Virginians with the navy's cannon. Captain Hamond seemed to agree with this strategy, noting that

> We have taken possession of this Island which is about three or four Miles in length and one in breadth. Seperated from the Main

5. Posey's Journal, May 27, 1776.
6. Ibid.
7. Ibid.
8. Ibid.

1/2 a mile, except on one place (which is that where Lord Dunmore has his Camp) this is not above the reach of [enemy] Musquet Shot, However this part is defended by the Guns from the Ships.[9]

As the days passed and Dunmore's hold on the island strengthened, Gen. Andrew Lewis in Williamsburg, the commander of Virginia's continental troops, realized that without artillery of his own his troops were powerless to effectively challenge Dunmore. He took measures to mount several cannon and carriages and transport them to the encampment opposite Gwynn's Island, but the process took time.[10] While the Virginians waited, they guarded the mainland from incursions by Dunmore's forces (who sought provisions and forage) and occasionally fired at Dunmore's camp and at several small vessels that had sailed into Milford Haven (the body of water that separated Gwynn's Island from the mainland). In one incident, the Virginians were able to seize a small sloop loaded with liquor that had run aground.[11] The loss of this sloop did not particularly concern Lord Dunmore; he was confident that his position on Gwynn's Island was secure. Dunmore was more concerned about his fresh water supply, which was inadequate for the hundreds of people who were with him on the island. The rampant illness and death (largely to smallpox and fever) that ravaged his troops, particularly his black soldiers, also was a concern for Dunmore. A report in one Virginia newspaper claimed that, "there are not above 200 blacks now alive, 75 at least having died within six days after they left Norfolk, and that the number of whites on shore is very inconsiderable."[12]

Lord Dunmore privately acknowledged his losses to Lord George Germain, his superior in London, in late June:

> I am extreamly sorry to inform your Lordship that the Fever of which I informed you in my Letter No. 1, has proved a very Malignant one and has carried off an incredible Number of our People, especially the Blacks, had it not been for this horrid disorder, I am Satisfied I should have had two thousand Blacks, with whom I should have no doubt of penetrating into the heart of the Colony . . . There was not a ship in the fleet that did not throw one, two, or three or more dead overboard every night.[13]

9. "Captain Hamond to Commodore Parker, June 10, 1781," in Morgan, *Naval Documents*, 5:460.
10. "General Andrew Lewis to General Charles Lee, June 12, 1776," in *The Lee Papers*, Vol. 1, (Collections of the New York Historical Society, 1871), 63.
11. "General Lewis to General Lee, June 12, 1776," *Lee Papers*, 1:64.
12. Dixon and Hunter, *Virginia Gazette*, June 15, 1776.
13. "Lord Dunmore to Lord Germain, June 26, 1776," in Morgan, ed., *Naval Documents*, 5:756.

Captain Hamond, the commander of the *Roebuck*, confirmed the significant toll smallpox and fever had inflicted on Dunmore's force:

> The Negro Troops, which had been inoculated before they left Norfolk, got thro' the disorder with great success, but the Fever which had been so fatal to them there, followed them also to the Island; so that notwithstanding the Corps was recruited with Six or eight fresh Men every day, yet the mortality among them was so great, that they did not now amount to above 150 effective Men. The detachment of the 14th Regt also became very weak, and the few Men of the New raised Corps [Queen's Own Loyal Virginians] were all down with the small Pox: so that we were still under the necessity of keeping the Marines on Shore to do the Common duty.[14]

Frequent sightings of bodies afloat and washed ashore gave the Virginians facing Gwynn's Island a clue of the enemy's struggles and condition, as well as giving many rebels satisfaction and bolstering their morale.[15]

Despite all of the suffering that Dunmore's troops and supporters endured on Gwynn's Island, they seemingly remained secure from attack, protected by the cannon of Fort Hamond, several British warships, and additional land batteries placed along the western shore of the island. Unfortunately for Dunmore and his men, this sense of security was about to end.

THE ATTACK

The morning of July 9, 1776, dawned hot and humid, a typical summer day in Virginia. Six weeks had passed since Dunmore's arrival at Gwynn's Island and he and his supporters felt relatively secure, confident that the guns of the British navy and the artillery batteries erected along the southwestern shore of Gwynn's Island could repulse any attempt of the rebels to land.

Unbeknownst to Dunmore, Gen. Andrew Lewis had arrived in the rebel camp the evening before from Williamsburg to break the stalemate. A patriot battery of two eighteen-pound cannon, positioned directly across from Fort Hamond and within point blank range of Lord Dunmore's ship (the *Dunmore*) was finally ready to commence fire. Four nine-pound cannon formed another artillery battery a few hundred yards south of the eighteen-pounders. They were in range of the *Dun-*

---

14. "Narrative of Captain Andrew Snape Hamond, June 10, 1781," in Morgan, ed., *Naval Documents,* 5:840.
15. "General Lewis to General Lee, June 12, 1776," *Lee Papers,* 2:64.

more as well, but their main focus was on Fort Hamond, Dunmore's encampment, and the three British tenders (service ships to larger warships) that were in Milford Haven to prevent the rebels from crossing to the island.

At some point in the morning (reports differ on the start of the bombardment) the eighteen-pound rebel cannon opened fire on the *Dunmore*, which was anchored close to the mainland. The first shot reportedly crashed through the stern of the ship, slightly wounding Governor Dunmore with a large splinter in his leg.[16] The other eighteen-pound gun quickly followed and also struck the *Dunmore*. The four nine-pound cannon joined the bombardment, directing their fire upon the camp and earthworks. Captain Hamond on the *Roebuck* reported that it was not long before the *Dunmore* realized it was overmatched.

> [The rebels] directed their Fire principally upon Lord Dunmore's Ship. . . . The Dunmore returned the Fire, but seeing that her small Guns had no effect upon either of the Batterys, and that every shot from the Enemy struck the Ship she cut her Cable, and being Calm, [was] towed off out of reach of the Guns.[17]

Lord Dunmore provided a similar account of the start of the battle:

> The Enemy brought down Ten Pieces of Ordnance, and on the 9th Instant began to play on my Ship from two Batteries; She was laid very near the Shore in order to prevent the Rebels from Landing on the Island. We were so near one of their Batteries (which consisted of an Eighteen and a Twenty four Pounder) that they Struck the Ship every Shott. I got our raw and weak Crew to fire a few Shott at them, but I soon perceived that our Six Pounders made no impression on their Batteries, our Boatswain being killed and several of the People Wounded, I found it impracticable to make them stand any longer to their Guns, we were therefore obliged to cut our Cable, tho' there was not a breath of Air Stirring, but the little Tide there was drifted us from the Shore.[18]

Claims in the Virginia newspapers after the engagement that the *Dunmore* was damaged beyond repair were contradicted by Captain Hamond, who reported that despite the many hits upon the ship, it ac-

16. Purdie, *Virginia Gazette*, July 12, 1776.
17. "Narrative of Captain Snape Hamond, July 9, 1776," in Morgan, ed., *Naval Documents,* 5:1078.
18. "Lord Dunmore to Lord George Germain, July 31, 1776," in Morgan, ed., *Naval Documents,* 5:1312.

tually did not suffer significant damage.[19] Whatever the case, the fire from the rebel batteries proved too hot for the ships anchored within range of the guns and they scrambled to tow them further away from the mainland.

While the patriot eighteen-pound cannon focused on the *Dunmore*, the four patriot nine-pound cannon concentrated their fire on Fort Hamond and Dunmore's encampment. Dunmore's troops replied with cannon fire of their own, but the accuracy of the rebel nine-pounders quickly silenced Fort Hamond's cannon and raked the encampment, throwing Dunmore's troops into confusion.[20] Capt. Thomas Posey witnessed the barrage and reported that

> The fireing was kept up in a very regular manner from the whole of our works for near two hours; during which time [the enemy] received great damage . . . Upon the enemies receiving this very unexpected [bombardment], they gave immediate orders to evacuate the Island.[21]

The patriot fire came to an abrupt end when the commander of the two eighteen-pound cannon, Capt. Dohickey Arundel, unwisely experimented with a wooden mortar that exploded on its first shot, killing Arundel instantly. This tragic episode was the one sour note to an otherwise immensely successful morning for the rebels. With Dunmore's fleet drawn off deeper into the bay and his troops withdrawn from Fort Hamond and their camp, the rebels had little to fire at by the afternoon.

Governor Dunmore and Captain Hamond agreed that the presence of rebel artillery made Gwynn's Island untenable and they prepared to evacuate the island in the evening. Under cover of darkness, the cannon, tents and other military stores were loaded onto ships. Guards were posted along the shore to watch for a surprise rebel landing, but a shortage of boats prevented any such move by General Lewis.

During the evening of July 9, Lewis's troops gathered a number of canoes and other small boats in anticipation of crossing Milford Haven and landing on Gwynn's Island in the morning. At dawn on July 10, the patriot batteries opened fire on the three British tenders that had remained in Milford Haven. A rebel observer noted that

19. "Narrative of Captain Snape Hamond, July 9, 1776," in Morgan, ed., *Naval Documents*, 5:1078.
20. "Extract of a letter from Williamsburg, July 13, printed in the *Pennsylvania Packet*, July 22, 1776," in Morgan, ed., *Naval Documents*, 5:1068.
21. Posey Journal, July 9, 1776.

There were three tenders in the haven, which attempted to prevent our passage. Their works were still manned as if they meant to dispute their ground, but as soon as our soldiers put off in a few canoes, they retreated precipitately to their ships [on the other side of the island]. The tenders fell into our hands, one they set on fire, but our people boarded it and extinguished the flames.[22]

With the tenders eliminated and enemy batteries abandoned, a detachment of troops from the 7th Regiment embarked on canoes to cross over to the island. Captain Posey was one of the first to reach Gwynn's Island and described the landing in his diary:

> Crossed into the Island but no fighting ensued except a few shot. By one o'clock the whole of the enemy had evacuated and embarked ... I cannot help observing, that I never saw more distress in my life, than what I found among some of the poor deluded Negroes which they could not take time, or did not chuse to cary off with them, they being sick. Those that I saw, some were dying, and many calling out for help; and throughout the whole Island we found them strew'd about, many of them torn to pieces by wild beasts—great numbers of the bodies having never been buried.[23]

British losses at Gwynn's Island are difficult to ascertain. Captain Posey estimated "that at least 4 or 500 negroes lost their lives," during the six week occupation of the island.[24] Posey added that another 150 [white] soldiers were also lost. The vast majority of these deaths occurred prior to the attack as a result of illness. Such losses significantly hampered the effectiveness of Dunmore's force and explained his feeble response to the attack.

The events at Gwynn's Island exasperated Lord Dunmore. His men were weak from disease and demoralized by defeat, and there was little hope of assistance from Britain. Discouraged and frustrated by the lack of British support, Dunmore made preparations to leave Virginia and join Gen. William Howe's large invasion force off of New York. Ships were sent up the Chesapeake to the Potomac River to obtain badly needed fresh water. They sailed as far as Stafford County, where they skirmished with a party of local militia and burned the plantation of

---

22. "Extract of a letter from Williamsburg, July 13, printed in the *Pennsylvania Packet*, July 22, 1776," in Morgan, ed., *Naval Documents*, 5:1068.
23. Posey Journal, July 10, 1777.
24. Ibid.
25. John Selby, *The Revolution in Virginia: 1775–1783* (Colonial Williamsburg Foundation, 1988), 126.

William Brent before they filled their water casks and returned to Dunmore's fleet.

By early August Dunmore was ready to depart. Half of his force sailed to New York, the other half to St. Augustine, Florida.[25] British authority in Virginia had finally vanished.

Dunmore's departure was a significant development that ushered in three years of relative peace in eastern and central Virginia. Perhaps more importantly, it allowed Virginia authorities to send thousands of troops north to reinforce General Washington's continental army in New York. These troops would play a crucial role in the battles to come, namely, Harlem Heights, White Plains, Trenton, and Princeton in the fall and winter of 1776–77 as well at Brandywine, Germantown, Saratoga, and Monmouth in 1777 and 1778. Had they not been available to General Washington, it is possible that the battles at Trenton and Princeton, as well as those that followed, could have ended quite differently. It is for this reason that the events at Gwynn's Island are so significant.

The Southern Expedition of 1776: The American Revolution's Best Kept Secret

❈ ROGER SMITH ❈

One of the most enjoyable aspects of researching the history of the American Revolution is the process of looking beneath and/or beyond those events and factoids that survive simply because they are a "given." "Givens" are the greatest indicators of opportunities to search for missing pieces to any historical puzzle and new questions are the primary tools of discovery. For instance, one of the more common notions about the American Revolution is that the southern colonies were not significant until after General Burgoyne's defeat at Saratoga in 1777, and the war would not "turn south" until the siege of Charleston in 1780. Why, then, did Henry Clinton sail an invasion fleet into Charleston Harbor in the summer of 1776? For that matter, as Washington was pounded across Long Island and down through New Jersey in 1776, why were there no southern regiments in his army when he was so desperately short of men and munitions? Why is there so little information concerning the southern colonies during the first five years of the war? Why is there no discussion on East Florida and West Florida? Since neither of those colonies, acquired from Spain in 1763, chose to rebel against king and country, would they not have created the same concerns for Washington's southern defenses that Canada triggered in the north?[1] If put to an unannounced pop quiz and asked to name the battles that

---

1. To understand Washington's concerns for the political loyalties of East Florida, for example, consider that once news of the Declaration of Independence reached St. Augustine, an angry crowd gathered in the city plaza on August 11, 1776, and hung effigies of Samuel Adams and John Hancock before setting fire to them. Martha Condray Searcy, *The Georgia-Florida Contest in the American Revolution* (Tuscaloosa: University of Alabama Press, 1985), 54.

occurred in the southern colonies prior to the siege of Charleston in 1780, most would answer with Clinton's aforementioned blunder at Charleston in June 1776, and perhaps the Battle of Moore's Creek Bridge, North Carolina, on February 27, 1776.

The tendency to geographically compartmentalize the chronology of events of the American Revolution is a primary example of one of the "givens" that need review. It is generally accepted that in 1775 and 1776, the war was primarily fought in New England, then shifted to the mid-Atlantic colonies from 1776 through 1777, and did not concern the southern colonies until 1780 and 1781.[2] Such an uncomplicated view makes for wonderful, albeit inaccurate, history class discussions that are more legend than fact. So the question begs, what were southern troops doing from early 1775 through 1779? Is it not possible that simultaneous, equally significant events south of the Chesapeake Bay precluded the contribution of southern troops to Washington's northern defenses and campaigns during that time frame? If so, we must then reconsider the widely accepted timelines of events, especially as they involve the southern colonies.[3]

Part of the problem with the traditional American perspective of the Revolutionary War is that while our nation's fight for existence is the stuff of heroes and legends here in the United States, this distant colonial struggle was far from the center of the then-known universe. The British Empire was much larger than just thirteen colonies and a motherland, and held overall political concerns that reached global proportions. Many noted historians have recognized the value of viewing the American Revolution from a British perspective and have extended the

---

2. For just a few examples of esteemed scholars who have advocated this school of thought concerning the dearth of Revolutionary events in the southern colonies prior to 1780, see Robert Middlekauff, *The Glorious Cause: The American Revolution, 1763–1789* (New York: Oxford University Press, 1982); Bernard Bailyn, *The Ideological Origins of the American Revolution* (Cambridge, MA: Harvard University Press, 1967); Gordon S. Wood, *The American Revolution: A History* (New York: Random House, 2002); Edward Countryman, *The American Revolution* (New York: Hill and Wang, 1985—Revised Edition 2003); John Pancake, *This Destructive War: The British Campaign in the Carolinas, 1780–1782* (Tuscaloosa: University of Alabama Press, 1985); Simon Schama, *Rough Crossings: The Slaves, the British, and the American Revolution* (New York: HarperCollins Publishing, 2006).

3. Examples of timelines constructed by sources that are highly regarded by the general public: http://memory.loc.gov/ammem/gwhtml/gwtimear.html www.nps.gov/rev war/about_the_revolution/timeline_of_events_06_10.html www.pbs.org/ktca/liberty/chronicle_timeline.html (January 2008).

historical lens to view the war from that vantage point.[4] Unfortunately, while widening the lens to consider the impact of imperial needs and decrees globally, it is often in regards to how they affected American colonists from New Hampshire to Georgia. The lens, therefore, needs to be adjusted a little further, as the British Americas were comprised of thirty-three colonies that stretched from Nova Scotia in the north to Grenada in the southern Caribbean. There were seventeen colonies in North America alone: the thirteen of Revolutionary fame along with the aforementioned East Florida and West Florida, as well as Nova Scotia and Quebec, which were also brought into the empire (along with Grenada) as the result of the 1763 Treaty of Paris.[5]

Much more significant to imperial finances were the British West Indies. Simply put, the production of sugar, indigo, coffee, and cocoa in these islands afforded empire.[6] The impact of sugar alone on eighteen-century imperial coffers might even be compared to the relevance of crude oil on global economics today. The primary interest that the British Empire had in North America was easy access to inexpensive supplies needed to support the industry of West Indian agriculture.[7] To Parliament, the North American colonies held little more economic value than that of a factory/warehouse for inexpensive supplies for their interests in the Caribbean.[8] John Adams went so far as to write that it was common belief that the imperial significance of the North American colonies had been forsaken in favor of the production of sugar.[9]

---

4. For just a few examples of esteemed scholars who have advocated this position, see Andrew Jackson O'Shaughnessy, *An Empire Divided: The American Revolution and the British Caribbean* (Philadelphia: University of Pennsylvania Press, 2000); Eliga H. Gould, *The Persistence of Empire: British Political Culture in the Age of the American Revolution* (Chapel Hill: The University of North Carolina, 2000); Lester D. Langley, *The Americas in the Age of Revolution, 1750–1850* (New Haven: Yale University Press, 1996); Eliga Gould, "Revolution and Counterrevolution," in David Armitage, Michael Braddick, ed., *The British Atlantic World, 1500–1800* (New York: Palgrave Macmillan, 2002—Second Edition 2009); Richard B. Sheridan, "The Crisis of Slave Subsistence in the British West Indies during the American Revolution," *William and Mary Quarterly*, 3rd ser., 33, no.4 (October 1976): 615–641; Gary B. Nash, *The Unknown American Revolution: The Unruly Birth of Democracy and the Struggle to Create America* (New York: Viking Penguin, 2005); Peter Linebaugh and Marcus Rediker, *The Many-Headed Hydra: Sailors, Slaves, Commoners, and the Hidden History of the Revolutionary Atlantic* (Boston: Beacon Press, 2000).

5. http://avalon.law.yale.edu/18th_century/paris763.asp

6. Jan Rogoziński, *A Brief History of the Caribbean: From the Arawak and Carib to the Present* (New York: Plume Group, 1999), 108.

7. Philip D. Curtin, *The Rise and Fall of the Plantation Complex: Essays in Atlantic History*, 2nd ed. (Cambridge, UK: Cambridge University Press, 1998), 153.

8. Philip D. Curtin, *The Rise and Fall of the Plantation Complex*, 153.

9. Andrew Jackson O'Shaughnessy, *An Empire Divided*, 66.

Therefore, political stability in the southern colonies of North America meant consistency of supplies for the British West Indies, particularly foodstuffs and flax, which was used to make simple clothing for the slave population that produced the sugar. When the British colonies from Virginia to Georgia fell in domino-fashion to the rebellion in 1775, the delivery of much-needed supplies to West Indian sugar factories faced an immeasurable threat.[10] The Continental Congress was quick to impose a trade embargo on Great Britain, Ireland, and the British West Indies to cut them off from American goods and food supplies.[11] Adding to West Indian woes, hurricanes, famine, drought, and disease ravaged the islands throughout the Caribbean.[12] As death tolls reached the thousands from natural disasters the region became a hotbed of slave revolts.[13] The impact of an embargo of such basic necessities of life as food and clothing would be unfathomable on the production of Caribbean agriculture and, as a result, imperial economics.

To shake up our view of the British Americas even further, when the distance between the capitals of Nova Scotia and Grenada is measured, the geographic center of George III's American holdings is just a few miles north of the St. Johns River in present-day Jacksonville, Florida. Taking that information into account with the fact that St. Augustine, the capital of East Florida, possessed the only tandem of masonry fortresses south of the Chesapeake Bay, it becomes indefensible to assume that the ministers of Whitehall had no military, political, or eco-

---

10. Britain lost the southern colonies of Virginia, the Carolinas, and Georgia as follows: 1: North Carolina: May 31, 1775. North Carolina History Project. www.northcarolinahistory.org/encyclopedia/812/entry (August 2012); 2: Virginia: June 8, 1775. Encyclopedia Virginia. www.encyclopediavirginia.org/Governors_of_Virginia#start_entry (August 2012); 3: Georgia: June 9, 1775 (though the royal governor was allowed to remain in the colony in a lame duck role until January, 1776). *Collections of the Georgia Historical Society* (Vol. 1–21; Savannah: Georgia Historical Society, 1840–2010), 3:183–185, 195, 218–220, 226–227.; 4: South Carolina: September 1775. Preservation Society of Charleston. www.halsey map.com/Flash/governors.asp (August 2012)

11. Sherry Johnson, *Climate and Catastrophe in Cuba and the Atlantic World in the Age of Revolution* (Chapel Hill: University of North Carolina, 2011), 132–134, 136; see also Richard B. Sheridan, "The Crisis of Slave Subsistence," 615–641; Andrew Jackson O'Shaughnessy, *An Empire Divided*, 143, 161–162.

12. For a full study of the ecological disasters and ensuing calamities brought to the Caribbean region from the El Niño/La Niña cycles of the Revolutionary War era see Johnson, *Climate and Catastrophe*, 92–153; see also Sheridan "Crisis of Slave Subsistence," 615–641; O'Shaughnessy, *An Empire Divided*, 143, 152.

13. Johnson, *Climate and Catastrophe*, 133; see also O'Shaughnessy, *An Empire Divided*, 145, 151, 161–162.

nomic interests in the southern colonies. The same may be said of George Washington, for on December 18, 1775—while personally involved in the extensive siege of Boston and simultaneously concerned with an army invading Canada—he requested Congress to authorize an invasion of East Florida. This would be the first of five such requests from 1775 to 1780.[14]

In order to avoid the devastating effects of a North American trade embargo against the British West Indies by the Continental Congress, the monarchy needed to act swiftly. A series of counterstrikes was devised in the fall of 1775, calling for the British military, Loyalist militias, and Native American allies in the region to participate in the active reclamation of the southern colonies. The first stage began on September 12, 1775, with an order from Gen. Thomas Gage, commander of all British troops in North America, to John Stuart, Indian Superintendent to the Southern Region, for Native Americans allies to attack all disloyal colonists.[15] On October 16, King George III authorized a full-scale military invasion of the South, dubbing it the "Southern Expedition," with Savannah the primary target.[16]

14. The George Washington Papers, "George Washington to Continental Congress, Cambridge, December 18, 1775." http://memory.loc.gov/ammem/gwhtml/ (gw070293); see also Kathryn T. Abbey, "Florida as an Issue During the American Revolution" (Ph.D. dissertation, University of Illinois, 1926), 184–85; the George Washington Papers, "George Washington to Robert Howe, Edward Rutledge, and Jonathan Bryan, Morris Town in Jersey, March 17, 1777;" "George Washington to Robert Howe, Head Quts., Camp at Morris Town, July 4, 1777;" "George Washington to John Rutledge, Head Quarters, Morris Town, July 5, 1777;" "George Washington to Benjamin Lincoln, Head Quarters, Morris Town, April 15, 1780;" "George Washington to Jean B. Donatien de Vimeur, Comte de Rochambeau, and Charles Louis d'Arsac, Chevalier de Ternay, New Windsor, December 15, 1780;" "George Washington to Nathaniel Greene, Head Quarters, Verplanks Point, September 23, 1782." http://memory.loc.gov/ammem/gw html/(gw080298); http://memory.loc.gov/ammem/gwhtml/ (gw070292); http:// memory.loc.gov/ammem/gwhtml/ (gw080305); http://memory.loc.gov/ammem/gw html/ (gw180288); http://memory.loc.gov/ammem/gwhtml/ (gw200526); http:// memory.loc.gov/ammem/gwhtml/ (gw250217)

15. Thomas Gage to John Stuart, September 12, 1775," Gage Papers, William L. Clements Library, University of Michigan (hereafter WLCL), in Edward J. Cashin, *William Bartram and the American Revolution on the Southern Frontier* (Columbia: University of South Carolina Press, 2000), 189.

16. Lord Dartmouth to General William Howe, October 22, 1775, PRO 30/55/1, doc. 83, p. 1; see also Ira D. Gruber, "Britain's Southern Strategy," in Robert W. Higgins, *The Revolutionary War in the South: Power, Conflict, and Leadership*; Essays in Honor of John Richard Alden (Durham: Duke University Press, 1979), 210; see also Lord George Germain to Henry Clinton, December 6, 1775, CO 5/92, f. 375–82, p. 759–84.

The first attack fleet sailed from Ireland for the Cape Fear River, North Carolina, around December 1, 1775, under the command of the Gen. Charles, Earl Cornwallis, where it was to rendezvous with a second fleet carrying Gen. Henry Clinton and his troops—about 2,500 redcoats total.[17] In addition, Lord George Germain, Secretary of State of the American Colonies, specified that Adm. Sir Peter Parker was to command the fleet and provide naval reinforcements to the expedition, which included "a squadron of warships (two 50–gun two-decker 'fourth rates,' four 28–gun frigates and a half dozen other vessels of substantial potency) plus transports . . . fifty sail in all."[18] In addition, based upon the promise of ten thousand volunteers by North Carolina's deposed governor Josiah Martin, Cornwallis came equipped with an additional ten thousand stands of arms.[19] Once ships were provisioned and the North Carolinians armed, the combined fleet was to carry Clinton and Cornwallis south to Savannah. Germain was under orders by George III to allow Clinton the option of where to strike first, but His Lordship would encourage Clinton in every way imaginable—over the length of seven pages of text—to strike first at Savannah. Germain went so far as to pinpoint the landing site for the army at Cockspur Inlet in the mouth of the Savannah River.[20]

17. In this correspondence, Lord Germain specified that the seven regiments involved were the 15th, 37th, 53rd, 54th, and 57th Regiments of Foot, with the 53rd being replaced by the 33rd for the actual expedition; the king added the 28th and 46th Regiments of Foot after they were blown off course by a storm on their way to Quebec. "Lord George Germain to Sir William Howe, November 8, 1775," PRO 30/55/1, doc. 80, p. 1–8; "Lord George Germain to Henry Clinton, December 6, 1775," CO 5/92, f. 375–82, p. 759–84; see also John W. Gordon, *South Carolina and the American Revolution: A Battlefield History* (Columbia: University of South Carolina Press, 2003), 37.

18. The warships ships listed in this letter were the "*Bristol, Acteon, Solebay, Syren, Sphinx,* and *Deal Castle,* the *Hawk* Sloop, and *Thunder* Bomb." "Lord George Germain to Henry Clinton, December 6, 1775," CO 5/592, f. 375–82, p. 759–84; see also Gordon, *South Carolina and the American Revolution,* 37. For a full detailed account of battles at Moore's Creek Bridge and Fort Sullivan (first British assault on Charleston Harbor) see John S. Pancake, *1777: The Year of the Hangman* (Tuscaloosa: The University of Alabama Press, 1977), 22–25; Gordon, *South Carolina and the American Revolution,* 36–46; see also "May 31," in William Moultrie, *Memoirs of the American Revolution, so far as it related to the States of North and South Carolina, and Georgia* (Vol. 1 and 2; New York: Printed by David Longworth, for the Author, 1802; reprinted New York: Arno Press, Inc., 1968), 1:140.

19. "Lord Dartmouth to General William Howe, October 22, 1775," PRO 30/55/1, doc. 83, p. 1; see also Gruber, "Britain's Southern Strategy," in Higgins, *The Revolutionary War in the South,* 210.

20. "Lord George Germain to Henry Clinton, December 6, 1775," CO 5/92, f. 375–82, p. 759–84.

From East Florida, Gen. Augustine A. Prevost would augment the assault with approximately eleven hundred British regulars stationed in St. Augustine.[21] An unexpected addition to the invasion came when a brash, young Yorkshireman named Thomas Brown claimed to have the names of four thousand Loyalists sworn to secure the Carolina and Georgia backcountries for the Crown.[22] Though Brown had no real military experience, John Stuart agreed to secure the enlistment of Creek warriors into Brown's frontier army. Stuart was a master political tactician and Brown the great-grandson of Sir Isaac Newton and the son of an immensely wealthy shipping magnate. Such an alliance would no doubt be a feather in Stuart's cap. Brown's plan was to haul powder and shot from Pensacola into the southern backcountries, gathering his army as he went. He would then strike at Augusta, the western hub of the southern Indian trade routes, which would "distress the rebels beyond measure."[23] Once Augusta was secured Brown's army could either hold fast to allow Loyalists a firm base in the backcountry or proceed down the Savannah River to join Clinton's assault on the Georgia capital.

Thomas Brown was not your average militia leader. He was driven by revenge after refusing an "invitation" on August 2, 1775, by Augusta's Sons of Liberty to sign an oath of loyalty to the rebellion. Though there were several reports of the incident, all agree that after suffering a fractured skull from a rifle-butt blow Brown was severely beaten, stripped naked to his boots, and tied to a tree. There he was scalped at least three times then tarred and feathered. Reports are mixed as to whether it was the hot tar collecting in Brown's boots that burned off two or more of his toes or if that occurred when his boots were pulled off and hot brands or lighted sticks put to his feet. He was then tossed into the

21. While there are no records available concerning deployment of troops to East Florida to support the expedition from St. Augustine, there is a budgetary item found in the Treasury Papers that documents the need for funds to "victualize" fifteen hundred British regulars in St. Augustine on March 28, 1776. That is approximately eleven hundred more troops than St. Augustine normally garrisoned. "John Robinson to John Pownall, Treasury Chamber, March 28, 1776," PRO 30/55/2, doc. 148, p. 1–2.
22. Thomas Brown to Jonas Brown, November 10, 1775, in possession of Joan Leggett, descendant of Thomas Brown," in Cashin, *William Bartram*, 209.
23. Thomas Brown to Patrick Tonyn, February 24, 1776, in Patrick Tonyn to Sir Henry Clinton, June 10, 1776, Sir Henry Clinton Papers, WLCL, in Edward J. Cashin, *The King's Ranger: Thomas Brown and the American Revolution on the Southern Frontier* (Athens: University of Georgia Press, 1989), 44.

back of a cart and paraded through the streets of Augusta.[24] Amazingly, Brown survived and by December made his way to St. Augustine. Gov. Patrick Tonyn took a special liking to the bitter young man and listened intently to Brown's plan for a Loyalist uprising. Tonyn was in a position to help Brown coordinate this action with the impending Southern Expedition.[25]

So why have these valuable pieces of the southern puzzle gone missing? Unfortunately, the Southern Expedition was so poorly orchestrated that while bits of the event are well known, a full composite of the invasion is absent from virtually every history text. We should look at the events as they occurred chronologically, beginning with (you guessed it) the Battle of Moore's Creek Bridge on February 27, 1776. As mentioned, Gov. Josiah Martin guaranteed an army of ten thousand Loyalists to assist British regulars in reclaiming North Carolina. Only sixteen hundred men, however, answered the call and they were in need of the arms that Cornwallis carried from Ireland. The rendezvous at the Cape Fear River with the invasion fleets was scheduled for March 1, but the Loyalists were intercepted by a well-informed, well-armed rebel militia of one thousand men at Moore's Creek Bridge, terminating this phase of the Southern Expedition.[26]

Clinton's fleet from New York appeared at the Cape Fear on March 12—nearly two weeks late, which is not bad timetabling for the age of wind and sail. Three days later John Stuart arrived to announce that his Creek warriors would not be joining Brown's frontier army.[27] In spite of Clinton's furious protests, Stuart claimed that was not safe for the Creek men to travel so far to the east and leave their homes unprotected against a serious Choctaw threat to the west.[28] Governor Tonyn believed this was nothing more than Stuart's rethinking of his alliance with Brown.[29] Victories on distant battlefields brought much glory in London. Stuart fancied himself in that role instead of Brown, a twenty-

---

24. Patrick Tonyn to Lord Germain, November 23, 1776, CO 5/557, p. 20–21. For the collective account of multiple reports concerning Thomas Brown's assault see also Cashin, *William Bartram*, 134; Cashin, *The King's Ranger*, 27–29; Searcy, *The Georgia-Florida Conflict*, 13; Charles B. Reynolds, *Old St. Augustine: A Story of Three Centuries* (St. Augustine, FL: E.H. Reynolds, 1884), 92–93.
25. "Governor Patrick Tonyn to Sir Henry Clinton, February 15, 1776," Sir Henry Clinton Papers, WLCL, in Cashin, *William Bartram*, 215.
26. Gordon, *South Carolina and the American Revolution*, 37.
27. Gruber, "Britain's Southern Strategy," in Higgins, *The Revolutionary War in the South*, 213; see also Cashin, *William Bartram*, 215.
28. Cashin, *William Bartram*, 215.
29. Patrick Tonyn to General Henry Clinton, May 8, 1776, CO 5/556, 172.

five year old aristocrat who had not been in the southern region very long.[30] Stuart went to such lengths to guarantee the failure of Brown's backcountry uprising that he called a congress in Pensacola to draw Native American headmen in the opposite direction of Augusta and Savannah.[31] Stuart's actions confused American leaders such as Gen. William Moultrie, who would later command the defenses at Fort Sullivan in Charleston Harbor. Moultrie wrote in his memoirs

> If the British had set their Indian allies upon us a few months before Sir Henry Clinton and Sir Peter Parker made their descent on South-Carolina, they would have disconnected us very much, by keeping thousands of our back country people from coming down; because they must have staid at home to protect their families from the savages.[32]

Thomas Brown roamed the backcountry of West Florida and Georgia in search of a Creek army that was never to materialize.[33] General Clinton was of the understanding that Brown's western pincer actions were not canceled, just postponed until Lord Germain could be consulted.[34] He was wrong. An embittered Brown would not make his way back to St. Augustine until September. Tonyn compensated Brown with a commission of lieutenant colonel of militia and command of the East Florida Rangers, the governor's personal contribution to the war.[35]

To add to the calamity that befell the Southern Expedition, Cornwallis had been blown out to sea by a hurricane and would not arrive at the Cape Fear River until May 3.[36] The next debacle came later in

---

30. Cashin, *The King's Ranger*, 45.
31. Cashin, *The King's Ranger*, 54–55.
32. Moultrie, *Memoirs*, 1:185.
33. Searcy, *The Georgia–Florida Contest*, 28.
34. Cashin, *The King's Ranger*, 45. On May 5, 1776, Brown stated that he could raise 2,000–3,000 Loyalists in just one month's time. Letter from Thomas Brown Concerning Indian Issues, May 5, 1776, CO 5/556, f. 172–180.
35. CO 5/556, 173–180, in the "Lawson Files" at the P.K. Yonge Library of Florida History and Special Collections at the University of Florida. The East Florida Rangers were a military unit drawn from former Georgia and South Carolina backwoodsmen and small planters. Many of these refugees from revolutionary upheaval in their home colonies were hand-picked by Governor Tonyn and he saw them as his personal army, over which he claimed "absolute authority." Patrick Tonyn to Augustine Prevost, July 5, 1777, CO 5/557, 148–49; see also Colin G. Calloway, *The American Revolution in Indian Country: Crisis and Diversity in Native American Communities* (Cambridge: Press Syndicate of the University of Cambridge, 1995), 259; Cashin, *The King's Ranger*, 59, 61–62, 64–65, 74, 78–79, 89–90.
36. Gruber, "Britain's Southern Strategy," in Higgins, *The Revolutionary War in the South*, 213.

May when Georgia militia drove into East Florida, digging in on the banks of the St. Johns River, just thirty miles north of St. Augustine. While holding that line, Continental regulars encamped on the north banks of the St. Marys River on the Georgia-East Florida border. Prevost, concerned for the safety of his own colony, withdrew from the attack on Savannah to bolster St. Augustine's defenses. As Clinton sat brooding at the Cape Fear River it became obvious that the Southern Expedition was a fiasco. Clinton then called an audible in the field and determined that if he must strike at a rebel port city with no cover from Prevost or Brown then he might as well make that effort at Charleston for greater spoils and glory. Sir Peter Parker voiced extreme concerns and insisted that the invasion be cancelled. Clinton chose otherwise. The rest, as they say, is history. The British attack on Charleston was soundly defeated, providing an unnecessary boost in moral for the rebellion. Clinton's ego would bear this humiliation for the next four years and he and Sir Peter Parker would incessantly blame the other for this humiliating defeat.[37]

In 1775, the British ministry and George III expressed their intentions "to proceed upon an Expedition for reducing to Obedience the Southern Provinces of North America, now in Rebellion."[38] This was a calculated plan in which the "Object & purpose of this Expedition is to endeavour, with the Assistance of the well affected Inhabitants in the Southern Colonies, to effect the Restoration of legal government."[39] From this correspondence from Lord Germain to Henry Clinton we find evidence that the restoration of a "legal government"—a British government—in all of the southern colonies was the focus of the Southern Expedition. That could not have occurred simply from a random attack on Charleston in 1776, but only from a coordinated, full-scale campaign of conquest. There is no tone in this document that speaks of southern interests being secondary to events in the North, refuting the misconception that the southern colonies were insignificant during the first five years of the American Revolution. So many new pieces to the puzzle simply because we looked beyond the "given" and asked new questions.

---

37. Frances Reece Kepner, "A British View of the Siege of Charleston, 1776," *Journal of Southern History* 11, no. 1 (February 1945), 94.
38. Lord George Germain to Henry Clinton, Dec. 6, 1775, CO 5/92, f. 375, p. 759.
39. Ibid.; see also Gruber, "Britain's Southern Strategy," in Higgins, *The Revolutionary War in the South*, 211.

Why the British Lost the Battle of Sullivan's Island

❦ C. L. BRAGG ❦

"What say you now, Sir Peter Parker!"[1]

The high and mighty will sometimes do seemingly odd things in order to make a point. Like, for instance, having oneself rowed into a channel in front of Fort Moultrie to see if the water's depth was sufficient to accommodate an attacking ship. The date was May 27, 1780, and after four years Fort Moultrie on Sullivan's Island was finally in British hands.[2]

Lt. Gen. Sir Henry Clinton was among the high and mighty. Born about 1730 in Newfoundland, he was the only son of George Clinton, an admiral in the Royal Navy who served as governor of colonial Newfoundland in 1731 and governor of New York from 1743 to 1753. Little is known of Henry's early life. His wife Harriet bore him five children in five years of marriage until her death in 1772, a loss that left him emotionally devastated. He was an able soldier but known to be prickly and quarrelsome, often aloof, insensitive, and at times petulant. After studying his voluminous writings and consulting with his biographer, a psychologist inferred that Clinton, who once referred to himself as a "shy bitch," was compulsive, neurotic, blame-shifting, self-defeating, and guilt-ridden. In reality he was a paradox; he resented authority while under it, was greedy for it, yet he was uncomfortable when wielding it. During his career he proved himself to be a troublesome subordinate, a trying colleague, and a vexing superior.[3]

---

1. Henry Clinton and William T. Bulger, "Sir Henry Clinton's Journal of the Siege of Charleston, 1780," *South Carolina Historical Magazine* 66, no. 3 (1965): 174.
2. Ibid.
3. Leslie Stephen and Sidney Lee, eds., *Dictionary of National Biography*, vol. 4 (New York: MacMillan Co., 1908), 550–51; Henry Clinton, *The American Rebellion: Sir Henry Clinton's Narrative of His Campaigns, 1775–1782, with an Appendix of Original Documents*,

Clinton became a provincial army officer in New York in 1745 and a regular British army officer in 1751. Because of his distinguished service in Germany during the Seven Years' War he ascended through the ranks of the officer corps so that by the time he landed in Boston in 1775 he had attained the rank of major general. He exhibited coolness and initiative under fire at Bunker Hill on June 17, 1775. A year later, however, he played little more than a spectator's role in South Carolina where he and his army command watched a Royal Navy squadron of warships fail to reduce a small unfinished fort constructed of palmetto logs and sand on Sullivan's Island at the entrance of Charleston harbor on June 28, 1776.[4]

Commanding the Royal Navy at Sullivan's Island on June 28, 1776, was Cde. Sir Peter Parker. His father was Rear Admiral Christopher Parker and consequently Peter, born in 1823, was practically raised in the Royal Navy. He began his sea service at a young age and by 1743 had advanced to the rank of lieutenant. A series of promotions rewarded his ability which was particularly on display during the Seven Years' War after which he retired in 1763 at the rank of captain. He received the honor of knighthood in 1772, returned to active service in 1773, and was elevated to the rank of commodore in 1775. Parker sailed across the Atlantic aboard his flagship *Bristol*, at the head of a squadron that transported troops to the North American theater from Cork, Ireland.[5]

Parker was nearly a decade older than his joint commander Henry Clinton and seems to have been Clinton's personality polar opposite. Perhaps not the most brilliant officer in the Royal Navy, Parker nevertheless had broad experience with independent command. He was usually polite and affable, occasionally stubborn, but confidant and certainly long-suffering with Clinton. And he was generally a good tactician.[6]

Clinton and Parker had come to South Carolina as a consequence of an ill-conceived British strategy designed to restore royal government in the southern colonies. North Carolina had been the campaign's pri-

ed. William B. Willcox (New Haven: Yale University Press, 1954), xvii; Frederick Wyatt and William Bradford Willcox, "Sir Henry Clinton: A Psychological Exploration in History," *William and Mary Quarterly* 3rd ser., vol. 16, no. 1 (1959): 3–26.

4. Stephen and Lee, *Dictionary of National Biography* 4: 550–51.

5. George Godfrey Cunningham, ed., *Lives of Eminent and Illustrious Englishmen from Alfred, the Great to the Present Time, On an Original Plan* (Glasgow, Scotland: A. Fullerton & Co., 1840), 113–16.

6. William B. Willcox, *Portrait of a General: Sir Henry Clinton in the War of Independence* (New York: Knopf, 1964), 90, 124, 512; Wyatt and Willcox, "Sir Henry Clinton: A Psychological Exploration in History," 26.

mary objective but circumstances shifted attention to Charleston, the region's center of commerce and a favored discretionary target. If the British could seize an uncompleted fort on Sullivan's Island, they could control Charleston harbor, capture the city, and establish a base for future operations inland. A victory here could bring the war to a speedier conclusion, at least in theory. Practically speaking, the fort on Sullivan's Island was an attainable prize, but Clinton and Parker had not the manpower, artillery, or time necessary to capture and hold Charleston. And if they did succeed, any loyalists who flocked to the king's standard would be abandoned to face the fury of the rebels when British regulars returned north from whence they came.[7]

Parker settled his fleet in Five Fathom Hole, a broad anchorage off Morris Island at the southern entrance of Charleston harbor. He and Clinton worked to come up with a viable plan that would accomplish their mission. Instead, through a series of communications delivered in writing or verbally through intermediaries that fostered general misunderstanding between the co-commanders, they formulated an incoherent strategy that was doomed to tactical failure. They originally envisioned a reduction of the fort on Sullivan's Island by way of a sudden and rapid stroke consisting of a amphibious assault on the north end of Sullivan's Island that would be launched simultaneously with a naval bombardment of the fort—a coup de main. But when Clinton reconnoitered the islands in a small sloop he was disappointed to find that the violent surf that pounded the shore of Sullivan's Island, combined with an entrenched patriot force ashore, made a landing there too hazardous. Alternatively, Long Island would be considerably easier to occupy and he decided that cooperation with the movements of the fleet against Sullivan's Island could be best managed if the army established a base there. This decision would prove fatal.[8]

The Battle of Sullivan's Island on June 28, 1776, could have and probably should have been a decisive British victory. Maj. Gen. Charles Lee, who was the most experienced officer on the Continental side, considered Col. William Moultrie's position on the island a veritable slaughter

---

7. Eric Robson, "The Expedition to the Southern Colonies, 1775–1776," *English Historical Review* 66, no. 261 (1951): 538–41; Clinton, *American Rebellion*, 23–28; Willcox, *Portrait of a General*, 81–86.

8. Clinton, *American Rebellion*, 28–30, 29n22; Robson, "The Expedition to the Southern Colonies," 540–41, 551–55; William James Morgan, ed., *Naval Documents of the American Revolution*, vol.5 (Washington: U.S. Government Printing Office, 1970), 573, 609; Edward S. Farrow, *A Dictionary of Military Terms* (New York: Thomas Y. Crowell Co., 1918), 147; Willcox, *Portrait of a General*, 87.

pen that would not hold against the British for half an hour. Lee predicted that the garrison would be inevitably and needlessly sacrificed and it was beyond his comprehension just why the island had been occupied and fortified in the first place. To prevent such a calamity he ordered the construction of a narrow pontoon bridge, a rickety affair not completed by the time of the battle, which extended precariously from Sullivan's Island to the mainland. Lee was not alone in his opinion of the island's indefensibility but Moultrie, who had the support of South Carolina's chief executive, President John Rutledge, would not be persuaded to abandon the post. He and his inexperienced but brave and determined men, about 435 in all, would hold their fort come what may, a shortage of gunpowder notwithstanding.[9]

Covering Moultrie's rear at the northeast end of Sullivan's Island— a fortified position known as the Advance Guard—was his old friend Lt. Col. William "Danger" Thomson. Thomson led 780 North Carolina and South Carolina troops who were determined to thwart any attempt by Clinton's 3,000 or so British soldiers encamped on Long Island should they try to cross the channel that separated the two islands and attack the fort from behind.

The channel that separated Long Island (now Isle of Palms) from Sullivan's Island, known as Breach Inlet, would be forever linked with the name of Henry Clinton after the battle. He would not be ashore very long before he discovered to his horror— "unspeakable mortification" were his words—that reports of the channel between Long Island and Sullivan's Island being passable on foot at low tide were absolutely false. Breach Inlet, said to be only eighteen inches deep at low tide, was in fact seven feet deep. Clinton had only fifteen lightly-armed flatboats, enough to put 600 or 700 men across the inlet at a time. Across the inlet, Thomson's North and South Carolinians with their breastworks and cannon rendered a landing on Sullivan's Island impossible without great sacrifice.[10]

Having been "enticed by delusive information," Clinton notified Parker that he could not attack across Breach Inlet as planned; the army could offer no more than a diversion in concert with Parker's naval attack on the fort. As an alternative, Clinton proposed to transport troops

---

9. Charles Lee, *The Lee Papers, 1754–1811. Vol. 2, 1776–1778*, edited by Henry Edward Bunbury, *Collections of the New York Historical Society for the Year 1872* (1872), 80– 81; William Moultrie, *Memoirs of the American Revolution so far as it Related to the States of North and South-Carolina, and Georgia*, vol. 1 (New York: David Longworth, 1802), 141.
10. Morgan, *Naval Documents* 5:573, 608, 609, 653, 782; Clinton, *American Rebellion*, 30– 31.

from Long Island by boat and land near Haddrell's Point to attack the rebel battery and capture Mount Pleasant. This scheme depended on the support of the Royal Navy and Parker agreed in principle to send frigates flank the rebel position. This plan, however, was never positively developed.[11]

After a week or so of weather delays, on the morning of June 28, 1776, nine ships from Parker's squadron loosened their sails, cruised from their anchorage in Five Fathom Hole off Morris Island, and dropped anchors in two parallel battle lines abreast of the fort and approximately 400 yards off Sullivan's Island. Parker's signal from the *Bristol* unleashed a furious cannonade that lasted nearly ten hours. Joining the *Bristol* in the center of the first line of ships was the 50–gun Experiment, and on the flanks were the 28–gun frigates *Active* and *Solebay*. The 20–gun corvette *Sphynx* accompanied by the 28–gun frigates *Acteon* and *Syren* formed a second parallel line behind the first, filling the intervals between the ships of the first line. The bomb-ketch *Thunder* with 8 guns that included a large mortar, protected by the armed transport *Friendship*'s 22 guns, was anchored to the east and behind the line about a mile and a half from the fort.[12]

The South Carolinians in the fort replied slowly and methodically, taking careful aim with their cannons to conserve their powder. Aside from what amounted to demonstrations on Long Island, Clinton watched impotently. At one point, from Parker's perspective, it appeared that his gunners were having success but this proved to be an illusion. Back in Charleston the townspeople crowded the wharves and waited in prayerful but dreadful anticipation for news of the battle's outcome. As darkness fell on Charleston, the view of the battle took on the appearance of a heavy thunderstorm with its repeated flashes of lightning and peals of thunder.

To Charleston's relief, a dispatch boat sent by Moultrie finally appeared through the darkness bringing news that the British ships had retired and that the South Carolinians were victorious. More than victorious, actually. The brave but outnumbered, outgunned, and undersupplied Americans had decimated their British foes. Despite the long hours of bombardment, only twelve men inside the fort were killed. Twenty-five were wounded, five so grievously that they subsequently died of their injuries, raising the fort's final death toll to seventeen. By Parker's count the British suffered 205 sailors and marines killed and

---

11. Clinton, *American Rebellion*, 31–32 (quoted),32–33n29; Morgan, *Naval Documents* 5:608, 745.
12. Morgan, *Naval Documents* 5:999.

wounded. He was among the wounded and the Bristol was so riddled that her seaworthiness was questionable. The loss of men and damage to the ships rendered a renewal of the attack on the next morning unfeasible. The Battle of Sullivan's Island was America's first absolute victory.[13]

Undoubtedly the construction of the fort was an important factor in the Americans' success. Clinton would write that "the Materials with which Fort Sullivan is constructed form no inconsiderable part of its strength. The Piemento Tree, of a spungy substance, is used in framing the Parapet & the interstices fill'd with sand. We have found by experience that this construction will resist the heaviest Fire." Maj. Charles Cotesworth Pinckney observed on the day after the battle that "the Fort, though well peppered with shot, has received scarcely any damage, not a single breach being made in it, nor did the Palmetto logs, of which it is built, at all splinter."[14]

The fortunate use of the Sabal palmetto, commonly known as the Cabbage Palmetto, in no way diminishes the determination of the men inside the fort and stationed at the advance guard. The American strategy had been relatively simple: hold two perilous positions on an island against overwhelming odds, while lacking a secure escape route. And without adequate munitions, inflict as much damage on the enemy as possible. In this they were surprisingly successful. Had the fort been breached by naval gunfire or had the British crossed Breach Inlet the Americans on the island would have been trapped. But the South Carolinians did not operate in a vacuum. The British tactical plan was confused, poorly communicated, flawed at its core, and herein germinated the seeds of British failure and American success.

Setting aside American valor and the palmetto tree, the British defeat can be distilled down to two main factors, British mistakes that initiated a cascade of consequences of their own. First chronologically but arguably of secondary importance was the landing and continued presence of General Clinton and his British army troops on Long Island after it was discovered that the depth of Breach Inlet at low water rendered the British army tactically impotent. Clinton being on Long Island also adversely affected the two commanders' ability to devise a plan. They never communicated very well in the first place, causing

---

13. Moultrie, *Memoirs* 1:177n; John Drayton, *Memoirs of the American Revolution, from its Commencement to the Year 1776, Inclusive*, vol. 2 (Charleston: A. E. Miller, 1821), 326n; Robert Wilson Gibbes, *Documentary History of the American Revolution* (New York: D. Appleton, 1857), 17; Morgan, *Naval Documents* 5:1001.
14. Morgan, *Naval Documents* 5:802 (first quote); Gibbes, *Documentary History*, 9–10 (second quote).

Parker to later remark to Clinton that "in Our private Conversations, we have often misunderstood Each Other." With Clinton ashore on Long Island their ability to communicate, either by written word or through intermediaries, completely broke down.[15]

Clinton's alternative proposals aside, Parker considered the reduction of Fort Sullivan to be a primarily a naval operation. Once a naval bombardment silenced the batteries in the fort, Parker planned to land seamen and marines under the guns to storm the embrasures. A union flag would be hoisted at the fort as a signal for Clinton to bring over troops to help the sailors and marines retain possession of the fort in case of a counterattack. That Clinton's force was in no position to assist beyond creating a diversion at Breach Inlet would be a matter of long discussion afterwards, but for now, Parker meant to continue the Royal Navy's long record of success against land fortifications.[16]

The second main contributory factor to the British defeat was the closing distance between the two opponents, a factor over which the Americans in the fort had no control but from which they certainly benefited. Combatants and eyewitnesses representing both sides generally and consistently agreed that the distance from which the ships engaged the fort was roughly 350 to 500 yards. The most notable outlier was Henry Clinton who placed the ships about 900 yards offshore. Parker estimated "450 yards or less," while Generals Moultrie and Lee and Capt. Barnard Elliott, inside the fort, estimated 400 yards. *Bristol's* master Capt. John Morris gauged the distance to be "two Cables in 7 fm [fathoms] Water" which is congruent with the estimates of Parker, Moultrie, and Elliott.[17]

Even though Clinton badly overestimated the distance between ships and fort, he considered Parker's failure to get close to the fort to be the foremost factor in the British defeat. In his opinion, his and Parker's joint efforts would have been successful only "if the Ships should bring up as near the Fort *as the pilots assured Sir Peter Parker in my hearing Presence was possible* (about 70 yards) [emphasis added]; as the fire from the Ships Tops being so much above the Enemys Works would probably at that distance soon drive raw Troops (such as those assembled there were certainly at that time) from their guns, and it was

15. Peter Parker to Henry Clinton, January 4, 1777, Henry Clinton Papers, 1736–1850, volume 20:6, William L. Clements Library, University of Michigan, Ann Arbor, Mich.
16. Clinton, *American Rebellion*, 32–34; Morgan, *Naval Documents* 5:745, 999.
17. Moultrie, *Memoirs* 1:180; Clinton, *American Rebellion*, 35, 35n33 (first quote); Gibbes, *Documentary History*, 6, 8; Morgan, *Naval Documents* 5:796 (second quote)–99, 800, 801n3, 825, 841, 864; Clinton and Bulger, "Sir Henry Clinton's Journal of the Siege of Charleston, 1780," 157.

not unlikely that our moving into their rear at that critical Moment might cause them suddenly to evacuate the Island." In a July 8 letter to colonial secretary Lord George Germain he expressed his disappointment that when the fleet attacked the fort, "they did not appear to be within such a distance, as to avail themselves of the fire from their tops, grape Shot, or Musquetry." For this reason he was most apprehensive that "no impression would be made upon the Battery."[18]

Col. Christopher Gadsden, who viewed the battle from Fort Johnson across the harbor on James Island, later forwarded information gleaned from five deserters from the British fleet, two men from the *Bristol* and three from the *Acteon*, who were all former American seamen who had been impressed into His Majesty's service when their ships were stopped at sea. The sailors reported that one of the first shots from the fort aimed at the *Bristol* killed a man in the rigging, causing Parker to order all of his men out of the tops and depriving the British of a vantage point from which to attempt to pick off Americans in the fort. They said that in the unlikely event of a second British attempt to take the palmetto fort, Parker would surely bring his ships as close as possible in order to rake the fort with musketry from the ships' tops.[19]

Parker himself agreed with the premise that the ships had been too distant from the fort but he tried to absolve himself of responsibility by arguing that it was his harbor pilots who refused to move in closer. He offered for an excuse that as the *Bristol* approached the fort a cannonball grazed his left knee, sending him aft to have it examined. When he returned to the forepart of the quarterdeck he was astonished to discover that the ship had just dropped anchor. His protestations and expressed desire to close the distance proved futile—the pilot would not go nearer. Resigned to the situation, Parker then hailed the *Experiment* and conveyed to Capt. Alexander Scott his opinion that they were at too great a distance and that he wanted Scott to take his ship in as close as possible. *Experiment*'s pilot not only refused, but imagining the *Bristol* to be as near as they ought to venture, anchored the *Experiment* on an outboard quarter.[20]

The man aboard *Bristol* upon whom Parker placed the blame was a freed black man named Sampson, a pilot with more than fifteen years experience in South Carolina waters. It was Sampson who, whether cajoled or threatened, obstinately refused to take the *Bristol* to within the

18. Morgan, *Naval Documents* 5:784 (first quote), 984 (second and third quotes); Henry Clinton to Edward Harvey, November 26, 1776, Henry Clinton Papers, volume 18:55.
19. Moultrie, *Memoirs* 1:170–71; Clinton, *American Rebellion*, 34–35.
20. Clinton, *American Rebellion*, 35, 35n33; Moultrie, *Memoirs* 1:171; Parker to Clinton, January 4, 1777, Henry Clinton Papers.

desired distance of 150 yards of the shoreline. The pilots of the other ships apparently followed suit. Sampson's rationale is difficult to discern. He had been in British service since July 1775 when he was taken aboard the *Scorpion*. Both deposed royal governor William Campbell and the current patriot governor John Rutledge considered him to be Charleston's best harbor pilot, but perhaps he was unfamiliar with the water immediately off Sullivan's Island, particularly the depth. Or maybe he was unaccustomed to piloting such a large, heavy man-of-war like the *Bristol*. Nor is it inconceivable that he was intimidated by the cannon fire from the fort and lost his nerve. In any event he was neither punished nor removed. Instead, so valuable was he to the Royal Navy that he was sent below deck and "put down with the Doctor out of Harm's Way" for safety's sake. Unlike Parker, Sampson came through the battle physically unscathed and with usefulness undiminished. He continued to guide British warships along the Georgia and South Carolina coast until he was captured aboard the *Experiment* by the French in 1779.[21]

Standing too far offshore had further negative consequences for the British attack. In accordance with Parker's plan, about an hour into the bombardment the 20–gun corvette *Sphynx* and two 28–gun frigates *Acteon* and *Syren*, all comprising the second line-of-battle, set a westerly course for a new position off the fort's right flank that would allow them to enfilade the patriot position and cut off the only possible avenue of retreat from the island to the mainland if the rebels were driven from their works and tried to escape. Moultrie's position in the fort would become untenable and surrender would be inevitable since retreat would be virtually impossible.[22]

Instead of sealing the Americans' doom the British would-be flankers, deprived of full use of the channel by the first battle line, ran aground on a sandbar that projected outward from James Island. The *Acteon* and the *Sphynx* ran afoul of each other as all three ships became stranded on the shoals (where Fort Sumter would later be built) southwest of the main line, rendering them not only incapable of accomplishing their mission, but completely useless for the rest of the fight.

21. Kevin Dawson, "Enslaved Ship Pilots in the Age of Revolutions: Challenging Notions of Race and Slavery along the Peripheries of the Revolutionary Atlantic World," in Jeffrey A. Fortin and Mark Meuwese, *Atlantic Biographies: Individuals and Peoples in the Atlantic World* (Boston: Brill, 2014), 170; Morgan, *Naval Documents* 3:539; Kevin Dawson, "Enslaved Ship Pilots in the Age of Revolutions: Challenging Notions of Race and Slavery between the Boundaries of Land and Sea," *Journal of Social History* 47, no. 1 (2013): 87–88; Morgan, *Naval Documents* 5:861 (quoted).
22. Morgan, *Naval Documents* 5:999.

There just wasn't room to maneuver. Their pilots, whoever they were, had failed miserably and bear the burden of responsibility for the misadventure. This British mistake was providential for the South Carolinians on Sullivan's Island. Moultrie noted that "had these three ships effected their purpose, they would have enfiladed us in such a manner, as to have driven us from our guns."[23]

If Henry Clinton ever viewed English artist Nicholas Pocock's 1783 painting *A View of the Attack Made by the British Fleet Under the Command of Sir Peter Parker against Fort Moultrie on Sullivan's Island, June 28th, 1776*, he would surely have vehemently objected to Pocock's depiction of the attacking British ships closely engaged with the fort and firing their broadsides from near point-blank range. It is likewise improbable that Clinton ever saw a watercolor executed by Lt. Henry Gray soon after the battle. Had he done so he certainly would have appreciated Gray's historical accuracy. Gray was present on the fort's parapets on the day of the battle and his painting *The Unsuccessful Attack on the Fort on Sullivan's Island, the 28th of June, 1776*, is a fairly accurate-to-scale rendition showing the ships firing on the fort from a distance.

Clinton was enraged to learn that a report in the *London Gazette* implied that he was at fault for the disaster, that he had offered no alternative plan, and that he had remained idle on Long Island after finding Breach Inlet impassable at Sullivan's Island. He blamed Lord George Germain and Sir Peter Parker for what he considered to be a cruel injustice and he spent almost a decade trying to set the record straight. For his part Parker, who was patient and conciliatory, tried to appease his aggrieved comrade, a task he found to be virtually impossible. Parker had concluded that the whole matter "best be consigned to Oblivion . . . . My wish is that not a syllable be ever mentioned in Publick about the expedition which is an affair now forgot and a Subject not pleasing to Revive."[24]

Notwithstanding the abortive British campaign in the South, for conspicuous gallantry during the capture of New York in later in 1776 Clinton was promoted to lieutenant general and knighted by George III. In 1778 he succeeded Lt. Gen. Sir William Howe as commander-in-chief

---

23. Moultrie, *Memoirs* 1:178.
24. *London Gazette*, August 24, 1776; Morgan, *Naval Documents* 5:999–1001; Willcox, *Portrait of a General*, 91–93, 124–25, 130; Clinton, *American Rebellion*, 36–37, 36n34, 376–79; Henry Clinton, *A Narrative of Sir Henry Clinton's Co-Operations with Sir Peter Parker, On the Attack of Sullivan's Island, in South Carolina, in the Year 1776*. ([New York: Printed by James Rivington (?),] 1780), 1–20; Clinton to Harvey, November 26, 1776, Henry Clinton Papers, 1736–1850; Parker to Clinton, January 4, 1777, Henry Clinton Papers, 1736–1850 (quoted).

Top: Nicholas Pocock, *A View of the Attack Made by the British Fleet Under the Command of Sir Peter Parker against Fort Moultrie on Sullivan's Island, June 28th, 1776,* 1783 (*South Caroliniana Library, University of South Carolina, Columbia, S.C.*); bottom: Henry Gray, *The Unsuccessful Attack on the Fort on Sullivan's Island, the 28th of June, 1776,* [1776], (*Gibbes Museum of Art, Charleston, S.C.*)

of British forces in North America. While moving his army from Philadelphia to New York, Clinton fought Washington to a stalemate at Monmouth Court House on June 28, 1778, exactly two years after the British defeat in Charleston. It was his first and only pitched battle against the Continental Army.[25]

25. George Athan Billias, ed., *George Washington's Generals and Opponents: Their Exploits and Leadership,* vol. 2 (New York: Da Capo Press, 1994), 73–76; Stephen and Lee, *Dictionary of National Biography,* 4:550–51.

In March 1780 Clinton returned to Charleston with more than eighty-seven hundred British, provincial, and Hessian soldiers—the flower of the British army in North America. This time he would not be denied. Employing formal siege operations, by the end of April he had invested the town. Maj. Gen. Benjamin Lincoln, commanding the Southern Department of the Continental Army, refused to evacuate his troops before Clinton's forces severed all avenues of escape and thus Charleston became the greatest disaster to befall an American army during the war. Lincoln surrendered his 5,600 Continentals and militiamen to the British on May 12, 1780. Timidity on the part of the Continental navy during the siege of Charleston had resulted in Fort Moultrie being tamely given up without a contest. Eight British warships and a small assortment of other vessels sailed past on April 8, each man-of-war pausing only long enough to unleash a single broadside at the fort. The British subsequently landed five hundred sailors and marines on Sullivan's Island during the night of May 4. They were preparing to take the fort by storm on May 6 when its commander, Col. William Scott, realized the futility of his situation and negotiated the fort's surrender. Scott and his garrison relinquished the stronghold the next day. When the British victors marched into the fort, they "leveled the thirteen Stripes with the Dust, and the triumphant English Flag was raised on the Staff." From his vantage in town looking across the harbor General Moultrie could see the British flag flying from Fort Moultrie's flagstaff. Even though he was not surprised that the fort was lost, he was disgusted that it surrendered without firing a shot in its own defense, a vast contrast to the gallant stand he had made nearly four years earlier.[27]

On May 27 Clinton visited Sullivan's Island for the first time. He concluded that if British marines and sailors had tried to storm Fort Moultrie they would have been repulsed with great loss even though the fort was only lightly manned. However he had interest beyond inspecting

---

27. Moultrie, *Memoirs* 2:60–61, 63, 84–85, 84 n [†]; Clinton, *American Rebellion*, 169; Uhlendorf, *Siege of Charleston*, 283, 285; Banastre Tarleton, *A History of the Campaigns of 1780 and 1781, In the Southern Provinces of North America* (Dublin, Ireland: Colles, Exshaw, White, H. Whitestone, Burton, Byrne, Moore, Jones, and Dornin, 1787), 53, 55– 57; Richard K. Murdoch, "A French Account of the Siege of Charleston, 1780," *South Carolina Historical Magazine* 67, no. 3 (1966): 152, 152n53; Franklin Benjamin Hough, *The Siege of Charleston, by the British Fleet and Army Under the Command of Admiral Arbuthnot and Sir Henry Clinton, which Terminated with the Surrender of that Place* (Albany, N.Y.: J. Munsell, 1867), 166–69 (quoted); Lachlan McIntosh, *Lachlan McIntosh Papers in the University of Georgia Libraries*, edited by Lilla Mills Hawes (Athens: University of Georgia Press, 1968), 118.

the captured fort—his ulterior motive when he went to the island was to prove to himself right about the navy's ability to bring ships into close proximity with the fort during the 1776 battle. He reported in his journal that he "sounded the anchorage within 50 yards of Sullivan's Island Fort at low water and found 5 fathoms and a quarter [31.5 feet]!!!" The channel was indeed deep enough for the fourth-rate 50-gun *Bristol* and the other ships-of-the-line to have engaged the fort at close range with the tide rising as it was at the time of the battle on June 28, 1776. *Bristol* was the largest and drew less than eighteen feet.[28]

Brimming with self-vindication, he wrote in a journal, if only for himself, "What say you now, S[ir] P[eter] Parker!" The remark is intriguing in light of Parker's 1777 acknowledgment to Clinton that he would have very much liked to bring his battle line closer to the fort. One can only wonder if a disagreement remained between the general and the commodore concerning the depth of the channel. No documentation of such a discussion has been found and Clinton mentioned nary a word about channel depth in a detailed narrative that he published in 1780. Nonetheless he seems to have remained neurotically obsessed with the possibility of being blamed for the 1776 debacle, hence his compulsion to have himself rowed out into the water so he could personally sound the channel.[29]

Portions of this article have been extracted or adapted from C. L. Bragg, *Crescent Moon over Carolina: William Moultrie and American Liberty* (Columbia: University of South Carolina Press, 2013) and C. L. Bragg, *Martyr of the American Revolution: The Execution of Isaac Hayne, South Carolinian* (Columbia: University of South Carolina Press, 2016).

28. Clinton and Bulger, "Sir Henry Clinton's Journal of the Siege of Charleston, 1780," 174 (quoted); Clinton to Harvey, November 26, 1776, Henry Clinton Papers; Angus Konstam, *British Napoleonic Ship-of-the-Line* (Botley, Oxford, U.K.: Osprey Pub., 2001), 45; Morgan, *Naval Documents* 5:827–28; C. Leon Harris, "An Estimate of Tides During the Battle of Sullivan's Island, S.C., 28 June 1776," November 12, 2010, https://thomsonpark.files.wordpress.com/2010/06/tides-12xi10.pdf, accessed on March 28, 2016.
29. Clinton and Bulger, "Sir Henry Clinton's Journal of the Siege of Charleston, 1780," 174; Parker to Clinton, January 4, 1777, Henry Clinton Papers, 1736–1850; Clinton, *A Narrative*, 1–20.

Understanding Continental Generals

JEFF DACUS

On the pages of the *Journal of the American Revolution* there have been articles on the best and worst generals of the Revolutionary War. It is not a question of the best or worst but rather how could a group of amateur generals leading a force of civilians abruptly turned into fighting men defeat a professional army led by professional officers? This leads to a further question, who were these generals and what were the backgrounds that allowed them to lead the successful military effort against Great Britain? Where were they from? How old were they? What did they do before their Continental service? What was their educational background? What was their fate as an officer in the army?

There were eighty-six general officers commissioned in the Continental Army, including three that were brevetted, a military commission rewarding outstanding service by which an officer was temporarily promoted to a higher rank without the corresponding pay. This does not include twenty-six brevetted in September, one in October and four in November of 1783, too late to serve as general officers in the field. Initially, there were four major generals, nine brigadier generals, and George Washington, the "Commander in Chief" or "Commanding General." During the course of the conflict, additional officers were selected as brigadier generals and some brigadier generals were promoted to major general. Five officers skipped the initial rank of brigadier general and were promoted directly to the rank of major general: Benjamin Lincoln, Marquis de Lafayette, Baron de Kalb, Philippe DuCoudray, and Baron Von Steuben.

The average age of these men was forty-two. The youngest was the "boy general," Marquis De Lafayette, who was nineteen when given a commission by Silas Deane in France. The youngest general born in the thirteen colonies was Henry Knox, twenty-six when commissioned in December of 1776. The oldest was Seth Pomeroy, commissioned at age sixty-nine, who declined the honor and remained an officer in the Massachusetts militia. Four others were over sixty when they made brigadier general. James Hogun is a mystery, his date of birth unknown.

The generals chosen by Congress were not total amateurs; forty-seven served during the French and Indian War or Seven Years War. Two served in the Cherokee War. Nine served in the French Army, primarily the volunteers from France who joined the Continental Army after the Revolution began. Two served in the Regulators War in North Carolina. Despite the large number who served during wartime, some had minimal combat service. Benedict Arnold served only thirteen days with his militia before it was disbanded, or he deserted, depending on the source. Philip Schuyler served in the French and Indian War as a staff officer, an asset in the Revolution as his combat career was checkered but his experience in logistics paved the way for other generals' success in battle. The generals appointed later in the war gained their experience commanding companies, battalions, and regiments in the early engagements of the war. By the time men like Enoch Poor and Anthony Wayne were appointed in February of 1777, they had fought the British throughout the colonies and in Canada.

Identifying the occupations of generals before the war is complicated by the times when men had several occupations or skills. Most of them, including skilled tradesmen and physicians, owned land but at least twenty-three lived primarily as planters or farmers. Nine were lawyers. Six were in the medical field. Thirteen were merchants of some kind. Five were surveyors. One was a bookseller and another a gunsmith. Thirteen, mostly the foreign volunteers, were soldiers before the Revolution. Horatio Gates and Charles Lee both purchased farms before the war but were more soldiers than planters. Among the more unusual occupations was that of Peter Muhlenberg, a minister.

Most of the generals, nineteen, were born in Massachusetts, which is no surprise as Massachusetts had one of the largest free populations. The next most numerous by state were eight from Virginia, and six from Connecticut. Many were foreign born, nine from Ireland, five from Scotland, seven from France and three from different parts of Germany.

When the generals commissioned by Congress are broken down by place of residence at the start of the war, it is still Massachusetts that gave us the majority of generals, fifteen. Twelve lived in Pennsylvania. Eleven resided in Virginia, including the recent immigrants Charles Lee and Horatio Gates. Six were from Connecticut and five each were living in New York and North Carolina. Of those residing in Europe, ten were in France, two in parts of Germany, and one in Poland. Moses Hazen was living in Canada.

Nineteen of the officers attended college or a military school. Three attended Harvard in Cambridge, Massachusetts and the same number attended Trinity College in Dublin, Ireland. Many of the college attendees were those who had medical backgrounds, including Arthur St. Clair who went to Edinburgh in Scotland.

Many of the Continental Army's general officers became casualties, paying the price for the young army to learn its lessons. Six generals were killed in action, the first Richard Montgomery in 1776 and the last Baron De Kalb in 1780. Ten generals were wounded; Benedict Arnold and Isaac Huger were each wounded twice. Twelve generals died during the war from various other causes, mostly disease. The most inglorious was the death of Frenchman Philipe Tronson du Coudray, who drowned crossing the Schuylkill River. Sixteen generals were captured but most were exchanged, with the notable exceptions of Virginian William Woodford, who died aboard a British prison hulk in New York Harbor, and James Hogun, fatally maltreated in captivity.

Not all of the officers commissioned by Congress served throughout the war. Of the four major generals commissioned at the start of the conflict, none were serving at the end. Three other men, John Cadwalader, Seth Pomeroy, and John Whitcomb, were never actually general officers as they refused to accept their commissions. Nineteen officers resigned before the war ended. Benedict Arnold deserted, Adam Stephen and Charles Lee were dismissed from the service. John Glover and Otho Williams retired before the war ended.

In the end, some general officers proved incompetent, some took to the service and performed admirably. Whatever their military experience, age, or educational background, most of the men commissioned by the Continental Congress performed well enough, with the help of France, a little luck, and Divine Providence, to defeat the British Empire.

Name	Age	Job	Service	Education	Birthplace	Residence
George Washington	43	Planter	F&I War		Virginia	Virginia
Artemas Ward	57	Storekeeper	F&I War	Harvard	Massachusetts	Massachusetts
Charles Lee	43	Soldier	F&I War, Europe	Switzerland	England	Virginia
John Philip Schuyler	41	Landowner	F&I War		New York	New York
Israel Putnam	57	Farmer	F&I War		Massachusetts	Connecticut
Richard Montgomery	38	Farmer	F&I War	Dublin	Ireland	New York
John Thomas	51	Physician	F&I War		Massachusetts	Massachusetts
Horatio Gates	47	Soldier	F&I War, Europe		England	Virginia
William Heath	38	Farmer			Massachusetts	Massachusetts
Joseph Spencer	61	Lawyer	F&I War		Connecticut	Connecticut
John Sullivan	35	Lawyer			Massachusetts	New Hampshire
Nathaniel Greene	32	Iron Monger			Rhode Island	Rhode Island
William Alexander/ Lord Stirling	50	Landowner/ Mining	F&I War		New York	New Jersey
Thomas Mifflin	32	Merchant		Edinburgh	Pennsylvania	Pennsylvania
Arthur St. Clair	39	Landowner	F&I War	Scotland	Scotland	Pennsylvania
Adam Stephen	58	Physician	F&I War	Scotland	Scotland	Virginia
Benjamin Lincoln	43	Farmer	F&I War		Massachusetts	Massachusetts
Benedict Arnold	35	Merchant	F&I War		Connecticut	Connecticut
Marquis de Lafayette	19	Nobleman	French Army		France	France
Johan de Kalb	55	Soldier	Seven Year's War		Bavaria	France
Philip du Coudray	38	Soldier	French Army		France	France
Robert Howe	44	Planter	F&I War		North Carolina	North Carolina

Name	Age	Job	Service	Education	Birthplace	Residence
Alexander McDougall	44	Merchant	F&I War		Scotland	New York
Thomas Conway	44	Soldier	French Army		Ireland	France
Baron von Steuben	47	Soldier	Seven Year's War		Prussia	Germany
William Smallwood	44	Planter	F&I War	Eton	Maryland	Maryland
Samuel Parsons	39	Lawyer		Harvard	Connecticut	Connecticut
Chevalier DuPortail	34	Soldier	French Army	Mezieres	France	France
Henry Knox	26	Bookseller			Massachusetts	Massachusetts
William Moultrie	45	Planter	Cherokee War		South Carolina	South Carolina
Seth Pomeroy	69	Gunsmith	F&I Wars		Massachusetts	Massachusetts
David Wooster	65	Customs Collector/Merchant	F&I War	Yale	Connecticut	Connecticut
Joseph Frye	64	Storekeeper	F&I War		Massachusetts	Massachusetts
John Armstrong	58	Surveyor	F&I War		Pennsylvania	Pennsylvania
William Thompson	39	Surveyor	F&I War		Ireland	Pennsylvania
Andrew Lewis	55	Landowner/Surveyor	F&I War		Ireland	Virginia
James Moore	39	Landowner	F&I War		North Carolina	North Carolina
Baron de Woedtke	36	Soldier	Prussian Army		Prussia	Prussia
John Whitcomb	65		F&I War		Massachusetts	Massachusetts
Hugh Mercer	50	Physician	F&I War	Aberdeen	Scotland	Virginia
James Reed	54	Tailor/Tavernkeeper	F&I War		Massachusetts	New Hampshire
John Nixon	49	Farmer	F&I War		Massachusetts	Massachusetts
James Clinton	39	Landowner	F&I War		New York	New York

Name	Age	Occupation	Military Experience	Education	Birthplace	State
Christopher Gadsen	52	Merchant			South Carolina	South Carolina
Lachlan McIntosh	51	Planter			Scotland	Georgia
William Maxwell	43	Soldier	F&I War		Ireland	New Jersey
Roche de Fermoy	39	Soldier	French Army		Martinique	France
Enoch Poor	40	Merchant	F&I War		Massachusetts	New Hampshire
John Glover	44	Sailor/Merchant			Massachusetts	Massachusetts
John Paterson	33	Lawyer		Yale	Connecticut	Massachusetts
James Varnum	28	Lawyer		Rhode Island College	Massachusetts	Massachusetts
Anthony Wayne	32	Surveyor			Pennsylvania	Pennsylvania
John de Haas	41	Merchant	F&I War		Netherlands	Pennsylvania
Peter Muehlenburg	30	Minister	F&I War		Pennsylvania	Pennsylvania
Francis Nash	56	Lawyer	War of the Regulators		Virginia	North Carolina
George Weedon	43	Innkeeper			Virginia	Virginia
John Cadwaladar	34	Merchant			New Jersey	Pennsylvania
William Woodford	42	Planter	F&I War		Virginia	Virginia
George Clinton	37	Lawyer	F&I War		New York	New York
Edward Hand	32	Physician		Trinity	Ireland	Pennsylvania
Charles Scott	38	Farmer	F&I War		Virginia	Virginia
Ebenezer Learned	48	Tavernkeeper/ Farmer	F&I War		Massachusetts	Massachusetts
Chevalier de Borre	59	Soldier	War of Austrian Succession		France	France
Jedediah Huntington	33	Merchant		Harvard/ Yale	Connecticut	Connecticut
Joseph Reed	34	Lawyer		Temple	New Jersey	Pennsylvania

Name	Age	Job	Service	Education	Birthplace	Residence
Count Pulaski	29	Nobleman	Europe		Poland	Poland
John Stark	49	Farmer	F&I War		New Hampshire	New Hampshire
James Wilkinson	20	Medical Student			Maryland	Maryland
Chevalier de la Neuville	34	Soldier	Seven Year's War		France	France
Jethro Sumner	46	Planter	F&I War		Virginia	North Carolina
James Hogun	?	?			Ireland	North Carolina
Isaac Huger	36	Planter	Cherokee War		Ireland	North Carolina
Mordecai Gist	36	Merchant			Maryland	Maryland
William Irvine	37	Physician	Navy Surgeon	Trinity	Ireland	Pennsylvania
Daniel Morgan	44	Farmer	F&I War		New Jersey	Virginia
Moses Hazen	48	Farmer	F&I War		Massachusetts	Canada
Otho Williams	33	Merchant			Maryland	Maryland
John Greaton	41	Merchant/Innkeeper			Massachusetts	Massachusetts
Rufus Putnam	44	Surveyor/Miller	F&I War		Massachusetts	Massachusetts
Elias Dayton	45	Merchant	F&I War		New Jersey	New Jersey
Charles Armand Tuffin	26	Soldier	France		France	France
Thaddeus Kosciusko	37	Soldier	Poland	Mezieres	Poland (Lithuania)	France
Stephen Moylan	46	Merchant			Ireland	Pennsylvania
Samuel Elbert	43	Merchant			South Carolina	Georgia
Charles C. Pinckney	37	Lawyer			South Carolina	South Carolina
William Russell	48	Landowner	F&I War		Virginia	Virginia

KILLED (6):

Richard Mongomery, December 31, 1776
Baron de Kalb, August 16, 1780
David Wooster, May 2, 1777
Hugh Mercer, January 12, 1777 Francis Nash October 4, 1777
Casimir Pulaski, October 9, 1779

WOUNDED (10):

Anthony Wayne, July 16, 1779
Benjamin Lincoln, October 8, 1777
Isaac Huger June 20, 1779, March 15, 1781
James Clinton October 6, 1777
Marquis de Lafayette, September 11, 1777
Benedict Arnold, December 31, 1775; October 7, 1777
John Nixon, October 7, 1777
Otho Williams, November 16, 1776
Samuel Elbert, March 3, 1779
William Woodford, September 11, 1777

CAPTURED (16):

John Sullivan, August 27, 1776
William Alexander, Lord Stirling, August 27, 1776
Charles Lee, December13, 1776
Benjamin Lincoln May 12, 1780
William Thompson, June 8, 1776
James Hogun, May 12, 1780
Otho William, November 16, 1776
William Russell, May 12, 1780
William Woodford, May 12, 1777
Charles C. Pinckney, May 12, 1777
Louis Lebique Duportail, May 12, 1780
William Moultrie, May 12, 1780
Lachlan McIntosh, May 12, 1780
Charles Scott, May 12, 1780
Daniel Morgan December 31, 1775
William Irvine, June 8, 1776

DIED BEFORE END OF WAR OTHER THAN BATTLEFIELD (12):

Charles Lee, October 2, 1782
John Thomas, smallpox, June 2, 1776
Lord Stirling, January 13, 1783
Philipe Tronson du Coudray, drowned, September 15, 1777
Seth Pomeroy, pleurisy, February 19, 1777
William Thompson, September 3, 1781
Enoch Poor, typhus, September 8, 1780
William Woodford, in prison hulk, November 13, 1780

Baron de Woedtke, exposure, July 28, 1776
James Hogun, in captivity. January 4, 1781
James Moore, April 9, 1777
Baron de Woedtke, July 28, 1776

RESIGNED, DISMISSED, DECLINED OR QUIT (27):

Benedict Arnold, deserted September 25, 1780
Artemas Ward resigned April 23, 1776
Charles Lee, dismissed January 10, 1780
Philip Schuyler, resigned April 19, 1779
Joseph Spencer, resigned January 13, 1778
John Sullivan, resigned November 30, 1779
Thomas Mifflin, resigned February 25, 1779
Adam Stephen, dismissed November 20, 1777
Thomas Conway, resigned April 28, 1778
Seth Pomeroy, declined commission July 19, 1775
John Whitcomb, declined commission June 26, 1776
Joseph Frye, resigned April 23,1777
John Armstrong, resigned April 4, 1777
Andrew Lewis, resigned April 5, 1777
James Reed, resigned September, 1776
John Nixon, resigned September 12, 1780
William Maxwell, resigned July 25, 1780
Alexis de Fermoy, resigned January 31, 1778
John Glover, retired July 22, 1782
John de Haas, resigned about June 19, 1777
John Cadwalader, refused commission
Ebenezar Learned, resigned March 24, 1778
Chevalier de Borre, resigned September 14, 1777
Joseph Reed, resigned, June 7, 1777
James Wilkinson, resigned March 6, 1778
Daniel Morgan, resigned February 10, 1781
Otho Williams, retired January 16, 1783

CENSURED BY CONGRESS (1)

William Thompson, November 23, 1778

SOURCES

Mark Boatner, *Cassell's Biographical Dictionary of the American War of Independence, 1763–1783* (London: Cassell & Company LTD, 1966) Francis B. Heitman, *Historical Register of Officers of the Continental Army during the War of the Revolution, April, 1775, to December, 1783* (Genealogical Publishing Co.Inc., 1982) Mary Theresa Leiter, *Biographical Sketches of the Generals of the Continental Army of the Revolution* (Cambridge: Cambridge University Press, 1889). Lynn Montross, *Rag, Tag and Bobtail: The Story of The Continental Army, 1775–1783* (New York: Harper & Brothers Publishers, 1952)

George Washington Convenes a Firing Squad

❄ JOSHUA SHEPHERD ❄

In an army where men died as a matter of course, there was nonetheless something peculiarly unsettling about the business scheduled for the morning of September 23, 1776. The grim verdict of a court-martial four days before had, at least in the opinion of Connecticut's Joseph Plumb Martin, left the troops "greatly exasperated."[1] For his part, Pennsylvania Lt. James McMichael blandly described the prelude to the unpleasant affair. "At 11 o'clock," he recorded in his diary, "the whole army at Mount Washington met on the grand parade in order to see a man shot."[2]

It was a stark exhibition of force that was nonetheless deemed unavoidable. From the outset of his tenure as commander in chief, George Washington was unambiguous in his expectations for the appropriate submission of the troops under his command. For the general, who clearly entertained hopes that his own men would eventually be capable of challenging the British toe-to-toe, subjection to military authority was imperative to the fighting trim of the army. In the first general orders which he issued after his arrival outside of Boston, Washington explained that "it is required and expected that exact discipline be observed, and due Subordination prevail thro' the whole Army, as a Failure in these most essential points must necessarily produce extreme Hazard, Disorder and Confusion; and end in shameful disappointment and disgrace."[3]

1. Joseph Plumb Martin, *Memoir of a Revolutionary Soldier: The Narrative of Joseph Plumb Martin* (Mineola, New York: Dover Publications, 2006), 27.
2. Diary of Lt. of the Pennsylvania Line, 1776–1778, in William Henry Egle, ed., *Journals and Diaries of the War of the Revolution with Lists of Officers and Soldiers* (Harrisburg: E.K. Meyers, 1893), 199–200.
3. General Orders, July 4, 1775, in John C. Fitzpatrick, ed., *The Writings of George Washington from the Original Manuscript Sources, 1745–1799* (Washington: Government Printing Office, 1931), 3:309.

The Continental Congress had already adopted a basic framework for the discipline of the army. On June 30, 1775, delegates adopted a body of regulations known as the sixty-nine Articles of War which governed the behavior of American troops. One article addressed an obviously intolerable infraction: physical assaults, or even threats, against superior officers. Any soldier "who shall strike his superior officer, or draw, or offer to draw, or shall lift up any weapon, or offer any violence against him," would be subject to the highest form of military adjudication, a general court-martial.[4] Any soldier who abandoned his post in action would receive little mercy and "suffer death immediately."[5]

The first conspicuous test of such infractions, and Washington's willingness to punish them, came on September 16, 1776. From the army's position at Harlem Heights on Manhattan Island, Washington had ordered out a morning scouting party to probe British positions further south. The American detachment, a New England outfit known as Knowlton's Rangers, tangled with enemy light infantry pickets and was then forced to give ground in the face of a counterattack. When Washington formulated plans to strike at exposed British troops, he directed a staff officer, Col. Joseph Reed, to bring up reinforcements.

Reed was a highly valued member of the general's staff. A Philadelphia attorney and something of a self-made man, Reed entered the military world the previous year with the rather plum assignment as Washington's first military secretary. After barely a year of service, he received a marked promotion, which had been announced in the army's general orders on June 18. "Joseph Reed Esqr: is appointed Adjutant General of all the Continental Forces with the Rank of Colonel, and is to be regarded and obeyed accordingly."[6]

Unfortunately, not everyone heeded that counsel on the morning of September 16. Following Washington's instructions, Reed located the 3rd Virginia Regiment, ordered up reinforcements for the planned attack, and then headed back for the front. Before he reached Knowlton's troops, the colonel encountered a skulking soldier, who, at least by Reed's description, was "running away from where the firing was, with every mark of fear and trepidation."[7] It was Ebenezer Leffingwell, a sol-

4. Worthington Chauncey Ford, ed., *Journals of the Continental Congress, 1774–1789* (Washington: Government Printing Office, 1905), 2:113.
5. Ford, *Journals of the Continental Congress,* 2:116.
6. General Orders, June 18, 1776, in Fitzpatrick, *The Writings of George Washington,* 5:156.
7. Peter Force, ed., *American Archives* (Washington, D.C.: 1843), 5th series, 2:500.

dier from Col. John Durkee's Connecticut regiment, who had been on detached duty with Knowlton's Rangers during the morning's skirmish.[8]

The encounter between the two men proved less than cordial. Reed struck Leffingwell with his sword—presumably using the flat of the blade—and barked orders for him to return to his post. Leffingwell agreed, and, seeming to comply, scampered into the underbrush toward the direction of the fighting. Soon thereafter, Reed again noticed Leffingwell making a dash for the rear. It was a classic case of no more Mr. Nice Guy. Although Reed had previously swatted at Leffingwell with his sword, the frustrated adjutant immediately set out in pursuit, he later explained, "with a determination to mark him."[9]

Thereafter, the ugly confrontation degenerated to a wildly confused fracas.[10] Reed, with drawn sword, thrashed away at Leffingwell's head and shoulders. Leffingwell exclaimed that he would kill Reed if he didn't back off. From the distance of about sixteen feet, he then pointed his musket at Reed and appeared to pull the trigger. Much to the latter's relief, the cock snapped but the gun failed to go off. While a furious Reed seized a musket from a passing soldier, Leffingwell apparently attempted to gain the cover of a ditch.

Reed was far from giving up the chase. When Leffingwell saw Reed approaching, the hysterical soldier "fell to bellowing out." Reed angrily leveled his musket and pulled the trigger; miraculously, his piece likewise snapped but failed to fire. Whether due to dull flints, bad powder or improper loading, both men had narrowly escaped death. "I should have shot him," claimed Reed, "could I have got my gun off."[11] Reed possibly took a few more swings at Leffingwell. It had not been a bloodless argument. At some point during the melee, Leffingwell's scalp was laid open by a sword blow and one of his thumbs was severed.

---

8. Henry P. Johnston, ed., *The Record of Connecticut Men in the Military and Naval Service During the War of the Revolution, 1775–1783* (Hartford: Case, Lockwood & Brainerd Company, 1889), 106. Johnston, who cites "incomplete" rolls for Durkee's Regiment, lists Leffingwell as a private in 1776. Court-martial proceedings fail to indicate any rank. Leffingwell had previously served a twenty-three day stint during the Lexington alarm, and as a sergeant in Huntington's Regiment during 1775. Johnston, *The Record of Connecticut Men*, 19, 86. Joseph Plumb Martin, who did not serve in Leffingwell's regiment, recollected decades after the fact that Leffingwell was a sergeant.

9. Force, *American Archives*, 2:500.

10. Reed left two accounts of the incident: in testimony before the court-martial and in a letter to his wife. Although the pertinent facts are identical, the precise chronology of the confrontation varies slightly between the two accounts.

11. Force, *American Archives*, 2:500.

That was the least of the hapless soldier's difficulties. By so much as lifting his weapon against Reed, Leffingwell had crossed the line from mere insubordination to outright mutiny. After he was taken into custody, the Connecticut soldier seems to have committed yet another egregious error. "He has since confessed to me," Reed later testified, "that he was running away at the time I met him."[12]

There was, not surprisingly, another side to the story. Fellow Connecticut soldier Joseph Plumb Martin later penned his recollections of campfire gossip. According to Martin, Leffingwell was not only the innocent victim of a gross misunderstanding but a selfless hero. Leffingwell, so the story went, had been directed to bring up more ammunition and was simply obeying orders when he was accosted by Reed, who refused to believe his explanation and threatened him with a sword. "Fired with just indignation at hearing and seeing his life threatened," Leffingwell simply "cocked his musket and stood in his own defence."[13]

Such grandiose scuttlebutt did little to help Leffingwell. On September 19, he was brought before a general court-martial and charged with "cowardice and misbehaviour before the enemy, and of presenting and snapping a musket at Colonel Reed." Leffingwell plead not guilty, but there is no record that he offered further testimony. There was certainly no evidence that he was acting under orders, or that he was engaged in securing ammunition for his comrades. Lieutenant Benoni Shipman offered the only testimony on Leffingwell's behalf, claiming that the soldier had performed well during the early morning skirmish at Harlem Heights. But subsequent to the initial stages of the fighting, Shipman admitted that "I know nothing of the prisoner, or where he was."[14] Reed provided the most lengthy testimony, but came just short of claiming that Leffingwell had pulled the trigger on his musket. "He presented his piece at me," said Reed, "and I think snapped his piece at me." That minor detail, in any event, was somewhat immaterial. The evidence was clear enough to the officers that composed the court, who reached a verdict in short order. Leffingwell was found guilty of "'misbehaving before the enemy, and of presenting his musket at Colonel Reed', and of a breach of the twenty-seventh article of the rules and regulations for the government of the Continental forces."[15] The sen-

12. Ibid.
13. Martin, *Memoir of a Revolutionary Soldier*, 27.
14. Force, *American Archives*, 2:500.
15. Congress adopted the original sixty-nine Articles on June 30, 1775, but revised the code with the passage of sixteen additional articles on November 7, 1775. The articles were further updated as the "Code of 1776" on September 20, 1776. John Henry Wigmore, *A Source-Book of Military Law and War-Time Legislation* (St. Paul, Minnesota: West Publishing Company, 1919), 9.

tence was short and grim: Leffingwell would "suffer death for said crime."[16]

As the date of the pending execution approached, the Connecticut troops, in the words of Joseph Plumb Martin, were "greatly exasperated" by the whole affair. Leffingwell's version of events was clearly believed by a good number of the soldiers, who manifested their displeasure by voicing "secret and open threats" against their superiors.[17] Joseph Reed never expressed doubt of Leffingwell's guilt, but on further reflection decided to intercede on the condemned soldier's behalf. In a letter to his wife, Reed explained that although "one of our own rascals" had made an attempt on his life, "I believe I must beg him off." The colonel indicated that the loss of Leffingwell's thumb was punishment enough.[18]

On September 22, Washington announced his approval of the sentence, and set the date of the execution for the following morning at 11 o'clock. The entire affair was orchestrated as a sobering object lesson in the dangers of quitting one's post in action and threatening a superior officer. "The men of the several Regiments below Kingsbridge," Washington ordered, "not upon Fatigue or Guard are to march down at that hour." Leffingwell was "to be shot at the head of the Army, on the Grand-Parade."[19]

One can only imagine Leffingwell's terror as the scene unfolded on Monday morning, September 23.

An earthen embankment was thrown up, and although eyewitness accounts fail to mention it, a grave had likely been dug. The Connecticut regiments were formed up around the parade ground but remained outraged by the entire business. The prisoner was escorted to the site, publicly bound and blindfolded, and forced to kneel. A firing squad lined up in front of Leffingwell and prepared for "the fatal word of command."[20]

In an astounding eleventh hour reversal, Leffingwell abruptly received a pardon. The reprieve, recalled Joseph Plumb Martin, was read by a chaplain, who seems to have annoyed the troops. The clergyman, Martin recalled, delivered a lengthy harangue in which he described "the enormity of the crime charged upon the prisoner, repeatedly using this sentence, 'crimes for which men ought to die,'—which did much

16. Force, *American Archives*, 2:500.
17. Martin, *Memoir of a Revolutionary Soldier*, 27.
18. William B. Reed, ed., *Life and Correspondence of Joseph Reed* (Philadelphia: Lindsay and Blakiston, 1847), 1:238.
19. General Orders, September 22, 1776, in Fitzpatrick, *The Writings of George Washington*, 6:90–91.
20. Martin, *Memoir of a Revolutionary Soldier*, 27.

to further the resentment of the troops already raised to a high pitch." When the actual pardon was announced, the troops erupted in wild cheering. The reprieve was well timed, thought Martin, as Leffingwell's blood "would not have been the only blood that would have been spilt."[21]

Joseph Reed's good graces were no doubt crucial in securing mercy. In his general orders for that day, Washington explained that Leffingwell had been pardoned on account of "his former good Character and upon the intercession of the Adjutant General, against whom he presented his firelock." Despite the pardon, the commander in chief remained eager to instill rigid discipline in the Continental Army, and coolly announced that "the next offender shall suffer death without mercy."[22] As Washington would prove on subsequent occasions, it was no hollow threat.

For Ebenezer Leffingwell, the entire experience was, no doubt, horrifically bittersweet.

21. Ibid.
22. General Orders, September 23, 1776, Fitzpatrick, *The Writings of George Washington*, 6:102–103.

Arnold, Hazen, and the Mysterious Major Scott

❧ ENNIS DULING ☙

In July 1776, Brig. Gen. Benedict Arnold brought charges against Col. Moses Hazen for disobeying orders and neglecting merchandise seized in Montréal. Hazen was a Massachusetts-born Québec landowner and merchant who commanded a small regiment of Canadians in the Continental army. In April when Arnold took command in Montréal, he called Hazen "a sensible judicious officer, and well acquainted with this country," but soon the two men despised each other.[1]

In the French and Indian War, Hazen had been a lieutenant and captain in Roger's Rangers and then a lieutenant in the 44th Regiment of Foot. As a ranger, he led brutal raids against the Acadians in present-day New Brunswick. He fought in the major battles along the St. Lawrence River, and Gen. James Murray commented that he had seen so much "bravery and good conduct" in Hazen "as would justly entitle him to every military reward he could ask or demand." At the start of the American invasion of Canada in the late summer and fall of 1775, Hazen was caught between the warring sides: his property along the Richelieu River was plundered by the Americans, who considered him an enemy, and then he was imprisoned by the British. With the fall of Montréal in November, he committed wholeheartedly to the American cause. He was forty-three in the summer of 1776, eight years older than Arnold.[2]

---

1. Benedict Arnold to Philip Schuyler, April 20, 1776, in Peter Force, ed. *American Archives* (Washington, D.C.: 1837–1853), Ser. 4, 5:1099. Abbreviated below as *AA*.
2. Allan S. Everest, *Moses Hazen and the Canadian Refugees in the American Revolution* (Syracuse University Press, 1976), 1–45, quote on 13.

Although historians argue about details, as a teenager Arnold had only limited experience in the French and Indian War.[3] He became a rising star in the first year of the Revolutionary War, helping to seize Fort Ticonderoga, leading an expedition through the Maine wilderness to Québec, and maintaining the siege through the harsh winter. Arnold and Hazen may have had more in common than they might have admitted to. Both were ambitious, aggressive, mercenary in business, and quick to take offense if they believed their honor was at stake.

Their dispute began as the American invasion of Canada was collapsing. On May 26, 1776, following the American surrender at the Cedars west of Montréal, Arnold wanted to lead a relief expedition to cross the Ottawa River and attack the Natives and British from the rear at dawn. Citing his "long experience with the Indian character," Hazen argued that the Indians would not be surprised and would quickly kill their American captives. Col. John Phillip De Haas of the 1st Pennsylvania Battalion, who had fought on the western frontier in the earlier war, supported Hazen's view. Arnold was "highly irritated" when the council of officers agreed with the colonels and voted not to attack. "Some reproachful language . . . passed between Arnold and Hazen," observed young Cap. James Wilkinson.[4]

Arnold returned to Montréal certain that the invasion of Canada was a lost cause. With the agreement of the Commissioners from Congress, Samuel Chase and Charles Carroll, he ordered goods and provisions seized in the city, but always with a promise of payment. The merchandise was tagged with the owner's name as if Arnold and the commissioners expected the debt to be repaid when the Continental treasury was full.[5]

Arnold entrusted the goods to a Major Scott for transport to Fort Chambly where Scott tried to turn them over to Hazen, who was the commander on the upper Richelieu River. "Colonel Hazen refused taking the goods into store, or taking charge of them; they were heaped in piles on the banks of the river," wrote Arnold to Maj. Gen. Philip Schuyler on June 13. Even after Hazen placed guards, the goods were "neglected in such a manner that [a] great part were stolen or plundered." [6]

3. James Kirby Martin, *Benedict Arnold, Revolutionary Hero: An American Warrior Revisited* (New York University Press: 1997), 28–29 discusses other possibilities and concludes the future general served for only a few weeks in 1757.

4. James Wilkinson, *Memoirs of My Own Times* (Philadelphia: Abraham Small, 1816), 1:45–46.

5. Commissioners in Canada to President of Congress, May 27, 1776, *AA*, Ser. 4, 6:590.

6. Arnold to Schuyler, June 13, 1776, *AA*, Ser. 4, 6:1038.

Arnold told Brig. Gen. John Sullivan, "It is impossible for me to distinguish each man's goods, or ever settle with the proprietors . . . . This is not the first or last order Colonel Hazen has disobeyed. I think him a man of too much consequence for the post he is in."[7]

In response, Hazen called for a court of inquiry or a court-martial. "I am very conscious of having done my duty in every respect; but if otherwise, I am equally unworthy the honour which the Congress conferred on me, as unfit for the service of my country."[8]

No statement from Maj. Scott survives. Although he is central to the incident and to the court-martial that followed, no historian seems to have identified Scott's first name, regiment, or state, let alone to have found details that might allow for an evaluation of his trustworthiness as an officer or a witness.[9] The difficulty is understandable. Francis Bernard Heitman's *Historical Register of Officers of the Continental Army during the War of the Revolution, April, 1775, to December, 1783* lists twenty-two Scotts, but none at first glance meets the criteria. The only *Major* Scott did not serve in Canada or on Lake Champlain and was promoted to the rank in the fall of 1777. Only one Continental officer named Scott served in the north, *Captain* John Budd Scott of Col. William Maxwell's Second New Jersey Regiment.[10]

Packed into one hundred fifty bateaux, the retreating American army reached the Crown Point narrows on Lake Champlain during the night of July 1–2, 1776. Within a few days, Hazen was arrested.[11] Arnold wanted an immediate trial, but Hazen protested to Maj. Gen. Horatio Gates, who was in command at Ticonderoga, arguing that the men on

7. Arnold to John Sullivan, June 10, 1776, *AA*, Ser. 4, 6:797.

8. Arnold to Schuyler, June 13, 1776; Arnold to Sullivan and Moses Hazen to Sullivan, June 13, 1776, *AA*, Ser. 4, 6:1105.

9. A sampling: Mark R. Anderson, *The Battle for the Fourteenth Colony* (Hanover, N.H.: University Press of New England, 2013), 325; Isaac N. Arnold, *The Life of Benedict Arnold: His Life and Treason* (Chicago: Jansen, McClurg & Company, 1880), 97–99; Douglas R. Cubbison, *The American Northern Theater Army in 1776: The Ruin and Reconstruction of the Continental Force* (Jefferson, N.C.: McFarland & Company, 2010), 165; Everest, 42, 44; Robert McConnell Hatch, *Thrust for Canada: The American Attempt on Quebec in 1775–1776* (Boston: Houghton Mifflin Company, 1979), 219; Martin, 218–219, 239–240. Alone among primary or secondary accounts, Wilkinson identifies *Captain* Scott as having charge of the plundered goods. Wilkinson also knows Scott's future career. (Wilkinson, 1:70.)

10. Francis Bernard Heitman, *Historical Register of Officers of the Continental Army during the War of the Revolution, April, 1775, to December, 1783* (Washington, D.C., 1893), 358–359.

11. Lewis Beebe, "Journal of a Physician on the Expedition against Canada, 1776," *The Pennsylvania Magazine of History and Biography* 59 (October 1935), 4:341–342.

the court-martial panel were not all field officers, meaning colonels, lieutenant colonels, and majors. Gates agreed that Hazen had a right to be tried by his peers. Hazen contended as well that the panel had been "named by his accuser." "This (if a fact) is also very irregular," Gates commented in a letter to Arnold.[12]

A new panel consisting of thirteen field officers was announced on July 18. *Captain* Scott, no first name given, was appointed judge advocate.[13] This Scott was unquestionably John Budd Scott, a young attorney from Sussex County, New Jersey. He had served in the New Jersey Provincial Congress and was chosen as "First Major" of the county's First Regiment of Militia. The Sussex County Committee of Safety objected to that appointment for reasons they did not record, but the Provincial Congress confirmed it. Then Scott took a captain's commission in the 2nd New Jersey under Maxwell, but continued to use his loftier militia rank when he could.[14]

The trial opened on July 20, but was adjourned quickly because Arnold was busy with the construction of the fleet to defend Lake Champlain. For about five days he was in Skenesborough (present-day Whitehall), New York, giving—as Gates told Continental Congress president John Hancock—"life and spirit to our dock-yard."[15]

Col. Enoch Poor, a merchant and shipbuilder from Exeter, New Hampshire, presided over the panel of twelve other officers. Impartiality based on a lack of knowledge of events and people was impossible. There were only about forty regimental field officers in the camps at Ticonderoga and across Lake Champlain on Mount Independence. They knew each other, Arnold and Hazen, and the gossip in the army. Four officers on the panel were part Arnold's First Brigade, located on the high ground on Mount Independence. Two men had recent disagreements with him; another was soon to write a savage characterization.

Two months earlier, Colonel De Haas, who had already sided with Hazen against Arnold's proposed surprise attack after the Cedars, re-

12. Horatio Gates to Arnold, July 15, 1776, *AA*, Ser. 5, 1:358.
13. Doyen Salsig, ed., *Parole: Quebec ; Countersign: Ticonderoga: Second New Jersey Regimental Orderly Book 1776* (Rutherford, N.J.: Fairleigh Dickinson University Press, 1980), 173–174; "The Wayne Orderly Book," *Bulletin of the Fort Ticonderoga Museum*, vol. 11, no. 2, (Sept. 1963), 98.
14. New-Jersey Provincial Congress, List of Deputies, *AA* Ser. 4, 3: 41; New-Jersey Provincial Congress, October 26–27, 1775, *AA*, Ser. 4, 3:1234–1235. Scott's exact age is unknown, but his parents were married in October 1750. Florence E. Youngs, ed., *Genealogical Record: Saint Nicholas Society of the City of New York* (New York: Saint Nicholas Society, 1905), 249.
15. Gates to Hancock, July 29, 1776, *AA*, Ser. 5, 1:649.

sisted written orders from Arnold, received May 30, to "burn and destroy the town and inhabitants of Canassadaga [present-day Kanesatake]," a Mohawk settlement forty miles northwest of Montréal. De Haas called a council of officers, which agreed not to attack. A false rumor went through camp in early July that De Haas, like Hazen, had been arrested.[16]

Col. Elisha Porter, an attorney from Hadley, Massachusetts, clashed with Arnold just a few days before the trial reconvened. Porter's militia regiment, which was part of Arnold's brigade, had cleared ground on Mount Independence and had nearly completed their camp of log huts when a staff officer ordered Porter to "remove ye officers' houses, &c., and alter the front of my encampment." Porter protested to Arnold, but he agreed with the alterations, and grudgingly Porter complied.[17]

And Col. William Maxwell, whose regiment had joined the siege of Québec in March, had seen as much of Arnold's leadership as anyone in the army. Like Hazen and De Haas, Maxwell was older than Arnold and had extensive experience as an officer in the French and Indian War. After the defeat of Arnold's fleet on Lake Champlain in October, 1776, he told New Jersey governor William Livingston that Arnold was "our evil genius to the north." This opinion was likely formed before the court-martial.[18]

In Arnold's absence, the court met from July 22 through July 28, bringing discipline to an army that had been devastated by the disaster in Canada. Scott facilitated the trials as judge advocate. He was prosecutor and legal adviser, but he was also expected to be so impartial that he could be a "friend" to the accused. Usually judge advocates coordinated trials, walking witnesses through their testimony without engaging in aggressive questioning.[19]

Hazen's trial reconvened on Wednesday, July 31. "Nothing extraordinary," noted Colonel Porter, who must have expected something else.[20] By August 1, the trial was not going as Arnold or Scott wanted. "Divers[e] witnesses" testified that the goods had been damaged or lost

16. Wilkinson, 1: 47; Arnold to Commissioners, June 2, 1776, *AA*, Ser. 5, 1:16; Beebe, 342.

17. Elisha Porter, "The Diary of Colonel Elisha Porter, of Hadley, Massachusetts," Appleton Morgan, ed., *The Magazine of American History with Notes and Queries* (New York: A.S. Barnes, 1893), 202.

18. William Maxwell to Governor Livingston, October 20, 1776, *AA*, Ser. 5, 2:1143.

19. "The Army Lawyer: A History of the Judge Advocate General's Corps, 1775–1975," (Washington: Government Printing Office, 1975), 16.

20. Porter, "The Diary of Colonel Elisha Porter ," 203.

under Scott's care, not Hazen's, and Scott himself admitted he never gave Hazen written orders from Arnold. The court was told Hazen never took control of the goods and had no place to store them if he had.

According to Arnold, during the trial Hazen offered the "grossest abuse," and the court allowed him to speak without reprimand. Historians have suggested that Hazen, who knew the Montréal merchants personally, accused Arnold of seizing property for personal gain. In fact, there were rumors of packages of select goods being labeled with Arnold's initials.[21]

Scott's role in the court-martial is confusing. A few days later, Poor told Gates that the court saw in Scott a man with an "overstrained zeal to serve as Judge Advocate during the course of the trial," who was "extremely solicitous to give evidence in the cause." Some historians have interpreted Poor's comment as meaning that Scott was not judge advocate but acted "as if" he were. But while it is hard to believe that any court would rely on a legal adviser so personally involved in a case, Scott unquestionably had been appointed to the position. Perhaps Poor meant that Scott had stopped presenting evidence dispassionately and had become an aggressive prosecutor. Once Scott asked the court for permission to cross-examine a witness who was favorable to Hazen, but it is unclear whether his request reveals he was no longer judge advocate or if it shows him wanting to confront a witness whose statement he found objectionable (Poor did not note the court's response.) At some point in the proceedings, Scott was replaced as judge advocate by Maj. William D'Hart of the 1st New Jersey Regiment.[22]

Finally, when Scott himself was called to testify, presumably by Arnold, Hazen objected, and after hearing arguments, the court agreed. Scott was viewed as "so far interested in the event of Colonel Hazen's trial, as to render his testimony inadmissible."[23]

Arnold objected, saying he would enter a formal protest if Scott was not permitted to testify. In his written objection, Arnold told the court that Scott was "my principal evidence." He had "punctually obeyed" orders and "of course is not the least interested in the event of Colonel Hazen's trial." Arnold concluded, "I do solemnly protest against their

---

21. Papers of the Continental Congress, R71 i58, p 385, 397. Or Fold3: Continental Congress Papers / Papers of John Hancock, 385, 397.
22. Poor to Gates, Aug. 6, 1776, *AA*, Ser. 5, 1:1273; Martin, 240; "Arnold and a General Court-Martial," *The American Historical Record*, vol. 3, no. 34 (October 1874), 448.
23. Poor to Gates, Aug. 6, 1776, ibid.

[the court's] proceedings and refusal as unprecedented, and I think unjust."[24]

The panel of officers believed that Arnold had questioned the integrity of the court and directed Colonel Poor to demand an apology. He told Arnold, "You have drawn upon yourself their just resentment, and that nothing but an open acknowledgment of your error will be conceived as satisfactory."

Poor explained to Gates that Arnold's protest was "couched, as we think, in indecent terms, and directly impeaching the justice of the Court." If a superior officer could "blast" a court-martial with a protest, then an honorable acquittal would be impossible and an accused officer would always be sent "back to his room a melancholy prisoner." Poor assured Gates that the protest was not the only affront: "The whole of the General's conduct during the course of the trial was marked with contempt and disrespect towards the Court."[25]

Asked for an apology, Arnold refused to back down and in a written response delivered on August 2, he told the officers, "Your demand I shall not comply with." The directions of the court and the "extraordinary demand" of the President were "ungenteel and indecent reflections on a superior officer." Then Arnold issued a challenge to any and all members of the panel: "As your very nice and delicate honour, in your apprehension, is injured, you may depend, as soon as this disagreeable service is at an end (which God grant may soon be the case,) I will by no means withhold from any gentleman of the Court the satisfaction his nice honour may require."

With that, the court exonerated Hazen and in a few days sent Gates a forty-two-page record of the trial, which suspiciously does not survive, along with copies of letters filled with outrage. Gates accepted the dismissal of the charges against Hazen. On August 10, in celebration of his vindication, Porter and the other members of the court dined with Hazen. Then on August 12, they ordered Arnold arrested for "conducting himself in a contemptuous, disorderly manner, in the presence of said Court; by using profane oaths and execrations; by charging the court with injustice in the course of the proceedings; and by using menacing words before them." Gates promptly dissolved the court. [26]

24. "Arnold's Protest," *AA*, Ser. 5, 1:1272.
25. Poor to Arnold, Aug. 1, 1776, Ser. 5, 1:1272; Porter, 203; Court to Gates, Aug. 6, 1776, *AA*, Ser. 5, 1:1273–1274.
26. Porter, "The Diary of Colonel Elisha Porter ," 204; "Arnold and a General Court-Martial," 448.

Finally on September 2, Gates wrote Congress about the trial. He told President Hancock that Arnold might have crossed the "precise line of decorum" and that he, Gates, had been "obliged to act dictatorially, and dissolve the Court-Martial," since "the United States must not be deprived of that excellent Officer's Service, at this important Moment." By then, the fleet under Arnold's command was sailing north to battle.[27]

For the most part, historians have taken Arnold's side in the court-martial, seeing jealous, lesser men trying to bring down the most talented and active officer on Lake Champlain.[28] Arnold insisted that he was the victim of "their private resentment." In a letter to Schuyler on September 11, 1776, Gates wrote: "To be a man of honour, and in an exalted station, will ever excite envy in the mean and undeserving. I am confident the Congress will view whatever is whispered against General Arnold as the foul stream of that poisonous fountain, detraction."[29]

But critics of the panel miss how seriously the officers tried to do their job. "We had nothing but the good of our country and the discipline of the army in view," they told President Hancock. If they erred, they believed, it was in giving Arnold too much leeway in the hope that he would "become sensible of the impropriety of his conduct."[30] Some men on the panel were petty and undeserving, but others were rock-solid.

Col. William Bond died of bilious fever within a month of the court-martial and was greatly mourned. Maxwell, De Haas, and Poor were soon promoted to the rank of Continental brigadier general. Historian David Hackett Fischer has called Maxwell "a combat leader of true genius" for his conduct of the New Jersey winter war of 1777. At Saratoga, Poor worked for reconciliation between Arnold and Gates, who had lost all respect for each other, and helped to keep Arnold in camp for the decisive battle on October 7, 1777. De Haas soon resigned from the Continental army, but in July 1778 following the raid on the Wyoming Valley in northeast Pennsylvania, he rallied the settlers and militia on the frontier, winning praise for his actions.[31]

---

27. Gates to Hancock, Sept. 2, 1776, *AA*, Ser. 5, 1:1268.

28. For examples, Isaac Arnold, *The Life of Benedict Arnold*, 99; Martin, *Benedict Arnold, Revolutionary Hero*, 242.

29. Arnold to Gates, Aug. 7, 1776, *AA*, Ser. 5, 1:1274; Gates to Schuyler, Sept. 11, 1776, *AA*, Ser. 5, 2:294–295.

30. Field Officers to Hancock, Aug. 19, 1776, *AA*, Ser. 5, 1:1072.

31. David Hackett Fischer, *Washington's Crossing* (New York: Oxford University Press, 2004), 348–349; Henry B. Livingston to Schuyler," Sept. 24, 1777, in Isaac Arnold, *The Life of Benedict Arnold*, 182; "Disposition of Jeremiah Fogg," New-Hampshire Gazette; or State Journal, and General Advertiser, January 15, 1781, *The New England Historical*

At the other end of the spectrum, Maj. Nicholas Haussegger, by then colonel of the Pennsylvania German Battalion, was captured (or perhaps he deserted) at Assunpink Creek on January 2, 1777, dined happily with Hessian officers in New York, and was eventually declared a traitor.[32] In the summer of 1779, Maj. Jotham Loring, by then a lieutenant colonel, was tried on numerous charges, including defrauding his regiment, and was dismissed.[33]

Hazen's career after the court-martial had a few constants. He worked for a second invasion of Canada, launched from the upper Connecticut River. He petitioned for compensation for his financial losses and for promotion. And he was never far from the courtroom, facing or bringing charges. In June 1781, he was breveted as a brigadier general. He and substitute judge advocate D'Hart were the only men from the court-martial on Lake Champlain still in the Continental army when Cornwallis surrendered at Yorktown.

For Arnold, the controversies of the spring and summer of 1776 never went away. In December 1776, Lt. Col. John Brown of Pittsfield, Massachusetts, presented Gates with thirteen charges against Arnold for incompetent, dishonorable, cruel, illegal, and traitorous activity.[34] Brown expected to have nearly thirty witnesses testify against Arnold, including Hazen, De Haas, and Maj. John Sedgwick, a member of the court-martial panel from Burrall's Connecticut State Regiment. In May 1777, the Congress's War Board met with Arnold and reported that Brown had "cruelly and groundlessly aspersed" his character.[35]

By the winter 1778–1779, Arnold was facing new charges from the Pennsylvania Council, which claimed that, among other crimes, he was

and Genealogical Register 60 (July 1906), 311; Abram Hess, "The Life and Services of General John Philip de Haas, 17351786," *Paper Read before the Lebanon County Historical Society, February 10, 1916* (Lebanon, Pa.: Lebanon Historical Society), 87; Jeff Dacus, "Brigadier General John de Haas: A Bad Example to Others," *Journal of the American Revolution,* allthingsliberty.com/2015/04/brigadier-general-john-de-haas-a-bad-example-to-others/.

32. Fischer, *Washington's Crossing,* 300, 528; Ethan Allen, *The Narrative of Colonel Ethan Allen* (Bedford, MA: Applewood Books), 88–89.

33. General Orders, Aug. 12, 1779, George Washington Papers at the Library of Congress, online at http://memory.loc.gov

34. Brown to Gates, Dec. 1, 1776, *AA,* Ser. 5, 3: 1158–1159; Brown to Theodore Sedgwick, Dec. 6, 1776, Massachusetts Historical Society.

35. Brown to Gates, Dec. 1, 1776, *AA,* Ser. 5, 3:1158–1159; May 23, 1777, *Journals of the Continental Congress, 1774–1789,* ed. Worthington C. Ford et al. (Washington, D.C., 1904–37), 8: 382; John to Abigail Adams, May 22, 1777, *Letters of Delegates to Congress, 1774–1789,* Smith, Paul H., et al., eds., (Washington, D.C.: Library of Congress, 1976–2000), 7:103.

profiteering from his position as military governor of Philadelphia. In the *Pennsylvania Packet*, Arnold engaged in a war of words with secretary of the council Timothy Matlack. Arnold defended himself by taking the patriotic high ground, writing that he had "served my country faithfully for near four years, without once having my public conduct impeach'd." In response, the *Packet* published Brown's thirteen charges, and Matlack commented, "When I meet your carriage in the street, and think of the splendour in which you live and revel . . . and compare these things with the decent frugality necessarily used by other officers in the army, it is impossible to avoid the question: From whence have these riches flowed if you did not plunder Montreal?" Within two months Arnold made his first offers to the British through a Loyalist merchant.[36]

And what of Captain/Major Scott, the forgotten man at the heart of Hazen's court-martial?[37]

Scott was soon back in court. Early in October 1776 he was arrested by Col. Maxwell and charged with embezzling from the regiment's payroll. Scott asked Gates to discharge him from arrest so he could help defend the Lake Champlain forts, and then he tried to resign his commission before a court-martial could be held. But Gates would not allow him an easy way out. He was found guilty and cashiered for "defrauding the Continent, by presenting a full payroll, drawing the pay accordingly, and also of ungentlemanlike behaviour in extorting extraordinary prices for some articles purchased for his men."

---

36. *Pennsylvania Packet*, Feb. 9 and March 6, 1779, Readex Microprint.
37. There is a second mystery involving a Captain Scott. On September 23, 1776, two hundred fifty Americans attacked Montresor's Island (present-day Randalls Island now joined to Ward Island) in the East River off Manhattan (*AA*, Ser. 5, 2:523–524). Captain John Wisner of Isaac Nichols' New York militia regiment and a Captain Scott (no first name or regiment given) failed to land their boats, setting up a disaster for those who did. Both were charged with cowardice. Wisner was tried and cashiered (*AA*, Ser. 5, 2:610–613), but Scott was never brought to court-martial and seems to have vanished from the record. Historian John C. Fitzpatrick, the 1930s editor of *The Writings of George Washington from the Original Manuscript Sources, 1745–1799*, identified the Montresor's Island Scott as John Budd Scott of the 2nd New Jersey Regiment, basing his view on Heitman's information that Scott was cashiered on November 2, 1776 ("General Orders, September 29, 1776," note 50, The George Washington Papers, Library of Congress: American Memory at http://memory.loc.gov; Heitman, 359). However, there seem to be no primary sources that identify the Montresor's Island Scott, and it is unlikely that John Budd Scott left Lake Champlain at a time when the forts were daily expecting attack, embarrassed himself at Montresor's Island two hundred fifty miles away, and then hurried back to Ticonderoga to be dismissed on other charges.

Soon afterwards Scott attempted to join a Loyalist regiment, the 5th Battalion of the New Jersey Volunteers, but officers objected. In May 1778, he became a captain in another Loyalist corps, the Royal American Reformees, led by Rudolphus Ritzema, who had also served in Canada on the American side. The regiment was short-lived before it merged into the British Legion. In the fall of 1778, a John Scott, apparently the same man, was a captain in the British Legion. Six months later, he retired before the regiment was sent south. In May 1779 John Budd Scott was married in British-held New York.[38]

38. Scott to Gates, Oct. 17, 1776, *AA*, Ser. 5, 2:1103–1104; Scott to Gates, Oct. 27, 1776, *AA*, Ser. 5, 2:1267; Orderly Book, Nov. 2, 1776, *AA*, Ser. 5, 3:534; "A History of the 5th Battalion, New Jersey Volunteers," The Online Institute for Advanced Loyalist Studies, www.royalprovincial.com/; "Roll of Officers in the British American or Loyalist Corps," *Collections of the New Brunswick Historical Society* (Saint John, N.B.: Sun Printing Company, 1899), 2:246; *Genealogical Record: Saint Nicholas Society of the City of New York*, 249.

Was Richard Stockton a Hero?

❖ CHRISTIAN MCBURNEY ❖

With helpful research from two stalwart *Journal of the American Revolution* authors, Todd Braisted and J. L. Bell, I have concluded that Richard Stockton, a signer of the Declaration of Independence for New Jersey, while not a traitor to the Patriot cause, should not be celebrated as a great Whig hero. New Jersey treats Stockton not only as one of its greatest Patriots from the American Revolution, but as one of the greatest New Jerseyans in its history. Each of the fifty U.S. states is entitled to place two statues of its greatest heroes in the U.S. Capitol in Washington, D.C. One of New Jersey's two statues is of Richard Stockton. After reading this article, you may agree with me that New Jersey may want to reconsider its selection.

After occupying New York City, the British army rolled through New Jersey and seized all of Long Island, New York, in late November and early December of 1776. Loyalists, able to call on nearby British soldiers, had the chance to even scores by trying to kidnap them. It was not a good place and time for signers of the Declaration of Independence.

It is difficult to imagine now, but when delegates to the Continental Congress strode up to affix their names on the Declaration, it was with some trepidation. While waiting to sign, Benjamin Harrison, a Virginia planter and a large man, told the diminutive delegate from Massachusetts, Elbridge Gerry, "I will have a great advantage over you, Mr. Gerry, when we are all hung for what we are now doing. From the size and weight of my body I shall die in a few minutes, but from the lightness of your body you will dance in the air an hour or two before you are dead."[1] Many years later, Pennsylvania's Dr. Benjamin Rush remem-

---

1. Quoted in Howard W. Smith, *Benjamin Harrison and the American Revolution* (Williamsburg, VA: Virginia Independence Bicentennial Commission, 1978), 42.

bered the solemnness of the proceedings in a letter he wrote to John Adams of Massachusetts: "Do you recollect the pensive and awful silence which pervaded the house when we were called up, one after another, to the table of the president of Congress to subscribe what was believed by many at the time to be our own death warrants?"[2]

Francis Lewis, a member of the Continental Congress representing New York from 1774 to 1779, after accumulating wealth as a New York City merchant, had purchased a country estate at Whitestone on Long Island. Due to the influence of Tories in New York, Lewis was instructed not to vote for independence on July 1 or July 2. But, patriotic as he was, he signed the Declaration of Independence on August 2. Following the Battle of Brooklyn on August 27, 1776, Long Island was held by the British. Shortly thereafter, while still in Philadelphia serving in Congress, Lewis's Whitestone house was burned and his farm destroyed, amounting to a loss of some £12,000, on orders of Lt. Col. Samuel Birch of the 17th Light Dragoons. In addition, his wife was taken prisoner and held for eight months before being exchanged for the wives of British officials captured by the Americans.[3] Her health reportedly was ruined while in captivity, and she died in 1779. The grief-stricken Lewis immediately left Congress, but continued to serve on the Board of Admiralty until 1781. He died in 1802 and was buried in an unmarked grave in the yard at Trinity Church in New York City.[4]

John Hart of Hunterdon County, New Jersey, about seventy years old in 1776 and the only Baptist to sign the Declaration, was described by Benjamin Rush as a "plain, honest, well-meaning Jersey farmer, with but little education but with good sense enough to discover and pursue the true interests of his country." Hart had earned the trust of his neighbors and had been elected several times to the New Jersey Assembly and had served as the Speaker of the House before the legislature disbanded on December 2 in the face of Gen. Charles Cornwallis's invasion. As British and Hessian troops swept through the Hopewell area, Hart fled to the woods, hiding for a short time in caves and in the Sour-

2. B. Rush to J. Adams, July 20, 1811, in L. H. Butterfield, ed., *Letters of Benjamin Rush* (Princeton, NJ: Princeton University Press, 1951), 2:1089–90.
3. F. Lewis to S. Sayre, September 4, 1779, in Paul H. Smith, ed., *Letters of Delegates to Congress, 1774–1789* (Washington, D.C.: 1977–1987), 13:451; Philander D. Chase, et al. eds., *The Papers of George Washington. Revolutionary War Series* (Charlottesville, VA: University of Virginia Press, 1996), 7:115, n. 1; Mark M. Boatner, *Encyclopedia of the American Revolution* (New York, NY: D. McKay Co., 1974), 2619.
4. Robert G. Ferris, ed., *Signers of the Declaration. Historic Places Commemorating the Signing of the Declaration of Independence* (Washington, D.C.: U.S. Department of the Interior, 1973), 95–96.

wood Mountains. While enemy troops plundered his farm, they did not entirely destroy his house.[5]

Richard Stockton of Princeton, New Jersey, was the only signer taken prisoner specifically because of his status as a signatory to the Declaration. The son of a wealthy landowner, he was born in 1730 at Morven, the family estate and his lifelong home in Princeton. He graduated from the College of New Jersey, later named Princeton University, and then practiced law, becoming one of New Jersey's best attorneys. He was appointed to the Royal Council of New Jersey and as a justice to the New Jersey Supreme Court. With Benjamin Rush of Philadelphia, who later would marry Stockton's daughter Julia, Stockton sailed to Scotland in 1766 and the two men successfully recruited the Rev. John Witherspoon to become the next president of the college. Witherspoon would become a strong Whig and also become a signer of the Declaration.

As the Revolutionary movement grew, Stockton associated with the Whig cause, although he was a moderate and dreaded the prospect of war. After he was elected to the Continental Congress on June 22, 1776, and had his credentials presented to Congress six days later, he voted for independence and signed the Declaration. Its adoption sparked celebrations at Princeton, centered at the college's main building. "Nassau Hall," the *Philadelphia Evening Post* reported, "was grandly illuminated, and independency proclaimed under a triple volley of musketry."[6] When Stockton lost his bid for the governorship of New Jersey to William Livingston in a close and bitter vote by the state's legislature, he remained in Congress.

In late September of 1776, Stockton and fellow delegate George Clymer left Philadelphia to inspect American troops at Fort Ticonderoga and other parts of the Northern Department in upper New York State. After filing helpful reports and recommendations with Congress on November 27,[7] Stockton hurried home, worried about the ongoing British invasion of New Jersey. He removed his family from his beloved Morven to Federal Hall, the country estate of John Covenhoven at Hopewell

---

5. John Hart Hammond, *The Biography of a Signer of the Declaration of Independence* (Newfane, VT: Pioneer Press, 1977), 61–62; Boatner, *Encyclopedia,* 493; Norman H. Maring, *Baptists in New Jersey* (Valley Forge, PA: The Judson Press, 1964), 73; Benjamin Rush Recollections in Benjamin Rush, *The Autobiography of Benjamin Rush. His "Travels Through Life" Together with His "Commonplace Books" for 1789–1813* (Princeton, NJ: Princeton University Press, 1948), 148.

6. Quoted in Alfred Hoyt Bill, *A House Called Morven. Its Role in American History* (Princeton, NJ: Princeton University Press, 1954), 38.

7. Smith, *Letters of Delegates* 5:256, n. 4.

in Monmouth County. As this county was known for harboring some strong Tories, Stockton would have done better to flee across the Delaware River to Pennsylvania, as did many of his neighbors.

On December 2, Stockton submitted a claim to Congress for his travel expenses.[8] Perhaps that very night, militant Loyalists who had discovered he was staying at Hopewell, seized him as well as Covenhoven. It appears that Stockton's captors were not simply local Tory civilians, as most histories of the event suggest, but instead were from the New Jersey Volunteers, a Loyalist brigade in the British army.[9] The man who informed the soldiers of the location of Stockton was a local, Cyrenus Van Mater. According to one letter writer from Philadelphia, Stockton's captors "treated him with the greatest barbarity, driving him, on foot, through rivers and creeks, with the greatest precipitation, to Amboy, where we hear he lies dangerously ill."[10] Even prominent Loyalist William Smith recorded in his journal that Stockton's captors had "apprehended and forced [him] away naked to Amboy, in a most distressed condition."[11]

The New Jersey Volunteer captors turned Stockton over to the British, who reportedly imprisoned him under harsh conditions at Perth Amboy, New Jersey. Transferred to New York City, he was imprisoned in the infamous Provost Jail like a common criminal. He reportedly was put in irons, kept without food for twenty-four hours, and then given only the coarsest fare.[12] Dr. Benjamin Rush, a fellow signer, wrote to Richard Henry Lee on December 30, "I have heard from good authority that my much honored father-in-law, who is now a prisoner with General Howe, suffers many indignities and hardships from the enemy,

---

8. Ibid., 465, n. 4.

9. The December 29, 1776 orders issued by Lt. Col, James Webster, cited in the main text accompanying note 14 below, indicate that Stockton's captors were from the New Jersey Volunteers.

10. Extract of a letter from Philadelphia, December 30, 1776, in *Massachusetts Spy,* January 30, 1777, and *Norwich Packet,* February 3, 1777.

11. W. Smith Diary Entry, January 16, 1777, in William H. W. Sabine, ed., *Historical Memoirs of William Smith* (New York, NY: W. H. W. Sabine, 1956), 2:66. Most sources state that Stockton was captured on November 29 or 30, and a few state it occurred as late as December 1; but given that Stockton dated a letter December 2, the author has selected December 2 as the date of his capture. The December date is supported by the July 8, 1778 edition of *The New Jersey Gazette,* which reported that Richard Stockton and John Covenhoven were seized in "the month of December, 1776." For the most complete discussion of Richard Stockton's capture, release, and taking General Howe's protection, see a series of 2008 and 2009 stories by J. L. Bell in his website at boston1775.blogspot.com (search for "Richard Stockton").

12. Bill, *A House Called Morven,* 40.

from which not only his rank, but his being a man, ought to exempt
him."[13] However, there are no eyewitness reports of Stockton being
treated cruelly in New York City. Because Stockton was a gentleman
and respected jurist, it is unlikely that General Howe would have treated
his harshly.

On November 30, General Howe had issued a proclamation offering
a "full pardon" to anyone who, within sixty days, swore an oath of loyalty to the king. Within a month of his captivity, Stockton apparently
signed a declaration of allegiance to the king, giving his word of honor
that he would not oppose the Crown. It is not known if Stockton
cracked under the pressure of imprisonment or honestly believed that
the country should return to Crown rule.

The following document, discovered only recently by Loyalist historian Todd Braisted, indicates the extent to which Stockton had been
pardoned by the two British commanders, Adm. Lord Richard Howe
and Gen. William Howe:

> Lord and General Howe having granted a full pardon to Richard
> Stockton, Esq., by which he is entitled to all his property, and he
> having informed that his horse, bridle and saddle were taken from
> the ferry by some of the people under your command, you will upon
> receipt of this restore the same horse and such other of his effects as
> shall come within your department to the said Mr. Stockton at the
> house of John Covenhoven in Monmouth. I am sir yours, etc.
> James Webster
> Lt. Col. 33d Regt.
> Perth Amboy
> December 29, 1776
> To Col. Elisha Lawrence of the New Jersey Volunteers[14]

Lieutenant Colonel James Webster's use of the term "full pardon"
strongly indicates that Stockton had sworn an oath of loyalty to King
George III or had promised not to oppose Crown efforts to defeat the
rebellion.

Congress finally passed a resolution to file a formal remonstrance
with General Howe about the conditions of Stockton's confinement on
January 3, 1777, complaining that the signer had "been ignominiously

13. B. Rush to R. H. Lee, December 30, 1776, in Smith, *Letters of Delegates,* 5:706.
14. New Jersey State Archives, Dept. of Defense Manuscripts, Loyalist Mss. No. 192–
L (found by Todd Braisted and set forth in J. L. Bell, "Richard Stockton's Release Date,"
July 28, 2009, at boston1775.blogspot.com (search for "Richard Stockton")).

thrown into a common goal [jail] and there detained."[15] Three days later John Hancock, President of the Congress, wrote to General Washington that while negotiating with the British over military prisoners he should "make enquiry whether the report which Congress have heard of Mr. Stockton's being confined in a common jail by the enemy, has any truth in it, or not."[16] But by then Stockton, after having spent only about one month in captivity, was on his way home or may have arrived there already. It appears General Howe allowed the signer to be released and did not wait for him to be exchanged (most histories incorrectly state that he was exchanged). Lord Richard Howe and Gen. William Howe typically allowed gentlemen civilians who had sought the Crown's protection to be granted paroles and immediately permitted them to return to their homes.[17]

When he returned to Morven, Stockton was in poor health. He found that his home had been occupied by some dragoons under Lt. Col. William Harcourt, the captor of Maj. Gen. Charles Lee at Basking Ridge, New Jersey, and that they had plundered some of his furniture and other possessions. Stockton's son-in-law, Dr. Benjamin Rush, wrote that "The whole of Mr. Stockton's furniture, apparel, and even valuable writings have been burnt. All his cattle, horses, hogs, sheep, grain, and forage have been carried away by them. His losses cannot amount to less than £5,000."[18] Elias Boudinot, an important New Jersey Patriot and a brother-in-law to Stockton, later reported that Harcourt's dragoons had taken away bonds, notes and other personal property worth about £4,000 to £5,000 pounds.[19]

Back in Congress, a rumor began to circulate that Stockton had claimed the King's protection. On December 23, 1776, Congressional delegate Elbridge Gerry wrote to James Warren in Massachusetts, "Judge Stockton of the Jerseys who was also a member of Congress has sued for pardon. I wish every timid Whig or pretended Whig in America would pursue the same plan, as their weak & ineffectual system of

15. Congressional Resolution, January 3, 1777, in Worthington Chauncey Ford, ed., *Journals of the Continental Congress, 1774–1789* (Washington, D.C.: Government Printing Office, 1907), 7:12–13.

16. J. Hancock to G. Washington, January 6, 1777, in Smith, *Letters of Delegates,* 6:40.

17. Bell, "Primary Sources on Richard Stockton," September 8, 2008, at boston1775. blogspot.com (search "Richard Stockton").

18. B. Rush to R. H. Lee, January 7, 1777, in Butterfield, *Letters of Benjamin Rush,* 1:126.

19. E. Boudinot to G. Carlton, October 2, 1783, in Smith, *Letters of Delegates,* 21:10; see also Bill, *A House Called Morven,* 40.

politics has been the cause of every misfortune that we have suffered."[20] On February 8, Congressional delegate Abraham Clark wrote to signer John Hart that New Jersey was seeking a replacement for Stockton in Congress because "Mr. Stockton by his late procedure cannot act" (meaning he could not serve in Congress and oppose the Crown without violating his recent oath).[21] The next day, Hancock informed Robert Treat Paine, "Stockton it is said, & truly, has received General Howe's protection."[22] On February 15, the New Jersey legislature received the judge's formal resignation as delegate to the Continental Congress.

Writing about the period just after Stockton's return to Princeton, the Rev. John Witherspoon on March 17 wrote, "Judge Stockton is not very well in health & much spoken against for his conduct. He signed Howe's declaration & also gave his word of honor that he would not meddle in the least in American affairs during the war."[23]

There is also some evidence that Stockton did not sign the oath of allegiance to the Crown. In favorably commenting on the number of Americans who had signed Howe's proclamation in early 1777, the cabinet official overseeing American affairs, Lord George German, added that they did not include "the leaders nor principal instigators and abettors of the rebellion."[24] Had Stockton signed Howe's proclamation, Germain presumably would have mentioned him. It is possible that Stockton simply signed a special parole promising not to support any efforts to oppose the Crown. Most paroles permitted the prisoner to be exchanged for a prisoner held by the enemy of equal rank, but that apparently was not part of Stockton's arrangement with Howe. He had to sit out the rest of the war, and that is what he did.

Because he had spent time behind enemy lines, or perhaps due to the rumors of his taking the Crown's protection, on December 22, 1777, Stockton was called before the New Jersey Council of Safety, then meeting at nearby Princeton, and requested to sign an oath of allegiance to the Continental Congress, "which he took and subscribed the same, and was thereupon dismissed."[25] Stockton did not turn in any papers related to his oath of allegiance to the Crown, as was required.

20. E. Gerry to J. Warren, December 23, 1776, in Smith, *Letters of Delegates,* 5:641.
21. A. Clark to J. Hart, February 8, 1777, in ibid., 6:240.
22. J. Hancock to R. T. Paine, February 9, 1777, in ibid., 247.
23. J. Witherspoon to D. Witherspoon, March 17, 1777, in ibid, 6:454–56.
24. G. Germain to R. Howe and W. Howe, May 20, 1777, in *Sixth Report of the Royal Commission on Historical Manuscripts* (London: 1877), 402.
25. *Minutes of the Council of Safety of the State of New Jersey* (Jersey City, NJ: John H. Lyon, 1872), 178.

Loyalist Judge William Smith of New York kept tabs on Stockton and his journal entries suggest that Stockton harbored some Loyalist views. In July of 1779, Stockton asked Miss E. Livingston to inform Judge Smith that "he dare no longer appear as counsel for the persecuted Loyalists, that they [the Whigs] threaten to mob him, and he finds a tyranny in the Country instead of liberty and law."[26] This reference likely refers to Stockton's representing Loyalists whose property was ordered to be confiscated by the state. His son-in-law, Benjamin Rush, alluded to this episode when he remembered Stockton as a man who was "sincerely devoted to the liberties of his country" but who "loved law and order, and once offended his constituents by opposing the seizure of private property in an illegal manner by an officer of the army."[27]

According to Dr. Rush, it took almost two years after his release from his captivity for Stockton to regain his health, but he did recover.[28] As indicated in the above paragraph, he had recovered enough by 1779 to begin practicing law again. Two years later he died at his beloved Morven estate in Princeton at the age of fifty on February 28, 1781, of a cancer in his neck, after suffering from cancer for more than a year.[29]

Stockton was the only signer of the Declaration of Independence to sign an oath of allegiance to the Crown or promise not to oppose Crown efforts to suppress the rebellion. It appears that Stockton was neither a Loyalist nor a fully committed Patriot, and that after his capture, he decided to remain neutral and not to actively favor either side in the war.

Stockton had voluntarily signed the Declaration and prior to his capture had worked diligently for the Patriot cause in Congress. Had he not been captured, he would have likely never had his patriotism questioned. But once captured, it appears that he was not so strongly attached to the Whig cause that he was willing to suffer discomfort in jail and risk death from a disease caught in confinement. In this limited sense, Stockton sacrificed for the American cause; but he was no great hero either. He may, however, have faced harsher treatment than other gentlemen captives since he was a signer.

26. W. Smith Diary Entry, July 10, 1779, in Sabine, *Historical Memoirs of William Smith*, 2:130.

27. Benjamin Rush Recollection, in Rush, *Autobiography,* 147.

28. B. Rush to G. Morgan, November 8, 1779, in Butterfield, *Letters of Benjamin Rush*, 1:245.

29. B. Rush to J. Rush, April 21, 1784, in ibid., 327; see also ibid., 245, n. 3.

In my recent book, *Abductions in the American Revolution: Attempts to Kidnap George Washington, Benedict Arnold and Other Military and Civilian Leaders*, I explain that Patriot leaders who were kidnapped sometimes faced suspicions that they had been turned to the enemy's side. Usually, such suspicions were unwarranted. But in Stockton's case, the concerns were warranted.

By the 1820s, as explained by historian J. L. Bell, Stockton's family had created a myth about Stockton's patriotism, which many Revolutionary War historians have bought into. The myth is that British treatment of the signer was so cruel that he became ill in captivity and after his release died of the illness before the war ended.[30] In 1888 the State of New Jersey even selected Stockton as one of two New Jersey heroes to have their statues placed in The National Statuary Hall Collection in the U.S. Capitol in Washington, D.C. The on-line description accompanying Stockton's statue indicates that those who selected Stockton were not privy to all of the facts: "Shortly after he signed the Declaration of Independence, he was taken prisoner by the British. Although he remained in prison for only a month, his health was broken. He became an invalid and died at Princeton on February 28, 1781."[31] While this item and several histories claim that Stockton never regained his health after his captivity, this claim is not accurate.

As mentioned at the beginning of this article, each of the fifty U.S. states is entitled to place two statues of its greatest heroes in the U.S. Capitol, and one of New Jersey's two statues is of Richard Stockton. A state, if approved by its governor and legislature, is permitted to request the Architect of the Capitol to withdraw a state's statue from the National Statuary Hall Collection and accept a new one.[32] The State of New Jersey should consider replacing the statue of Richard Stockton. It appears that the state originally chose a statue of Stockton based on a history of his life that was inaccurate.

To summarize, I believe Richard Stockton showed great courage in signing the Declaration of Independence. For that reason, and for other

---

30. Bell, "Richard Stockton and the Creation of a Legend," September 18, 2008, in boston1775.blogspot.com (search "Richard Stockton").

31. See online list of statues in The National Statuary Hall Collection at www.aoc.gov /the-national-statuary-hall-collection and search for Richard Stockton, accessed March 23, 2016.

32. See Public Law 106–554, Section 311; see also "Procedure and Guidelines for Replacement of Statues in the National Statuary Hall Collection," obtained by going to www.aoc.gov.the-national-statuary-hall-collection, clicking on "About the National Statuary Hall Collection," and clicking on the PDF at the bottom of the webpage where state's deciding to replace a statue is discussed. Accessed March 23, 2016.

work he performed as a Patriot, I believe he is a hero of the American Revolution. But because strong evidence indicates that he signed an oath of allegiance to the Crown or a promise not to oppose Crown efforts to crush the rebellion, I do not believe he should be celebrated as one of New Jersey's greatest heroes. I believe that George Washington, Benjamin Franklin, and other great heroes of the American Revolution would be surprised that New Jersey, out of all of its great contributors to the American Revolution, chose Richard Stockton as its top Revolutionary hero.

The American Vicars of Bray

TODD W. BRAISTED

Loyalists, those Americans who openly supported the British Government during the American Revolution, have been largely assumed to have had unchanging allegiance during the conflict; once a Loyalist, always a Loyalist. Similarly, those supporters of Congress and the new United States are assumed to have been constant in their beliefs throughout the war, with one famous general as the notable exception.

The reality was more complex than that. It is becoming clear that thousands of soldiers changed sides at one time or another, some more than once. This is not a fundamentally new revelation; recent research, however, shows that the numbers are greater than has been previously appreciated. The Philadelphia Campaign of 1777–1778 provides superb examples. Surviving records for a large portion of both the Continental Army and the Provincial (Loyalist) Corps during this period are much more complete than for most earlier or later periods, making it possible to quantify the phenomenon of switching sides during one stage of the war.

The most tantalizing piece of evidence in showing the extent of disaffection in Washington's Army during that campaign comes from Joseph Galloway, a former delegate to the Continental Congress. Galloway had come over to the British in December 1776, and joined Sir William Howe on the Philadelphia expedition. Upon the city's capture, Galloway was appointed by Howe as Superintendent of the Philadelphia Police. In this office he tendered oaths of allegiance to the city's inhabitants and all those seeking refuge within it. Galloway, assisted by Philadelphia merchant and Loyalist Enoch Story, were engaged in "making out weekly returns of all recruits attested, with the names of deserters from the Rebel Army and Navy, as well as the Inhabitants who had taken the Oaths of allegiance."[1] While their list of named deserters has not been located, we do have an abstract of some of its information.

Two documents by Galloway, one showing a month by month breakdown of oaths of allegiance tendered and another showing the nativity of deserters who arrived in Philadelphia, show the precarious situation of Washington's Army and underscore what might have been with a more active British commander in Philadelphia. Galloway was no fan of Sir William Howe, and would spend his later years in London penning newspaper pieces against the former British commander-in-chief. The first document shows deserters from the Continental Army on a monthly basis once the British entered Philadelphia on 26 September 1777:

October 1777	300
November 1777	187
December 1777	100
January 1778	152
February 1778	132
March 1778	180
April 1778	106
May 1778	104
June (to the 17th)	28
	1289 soldiers

Also on Galloway's list, but not included above, were 61 wagoners, 391 sailors and 603 militiamen, plus 2003 inhabitants.[2]

Galloway's second document breaks down the deserters by nationality, giving us an insight into the composition of Washington's Army at this time. Of the 1134 Continental Army deserters who had registered with the British, there were:

English	206
Scottish	56
Irish	492
German	88

1. "The Memorial of Enoch Story, late of the City of Philadelphia Merchant" London, March 16, 1784. Audit Office, Class 13, Volume 102, folios 1205–1206, Great Britain, The National Archives (hereafter cited as TNA).
2. "An account of the number of Persons who have taken the Oath of allegiance at Philadelphia from the 30th of September 1777 to the 17th June 1778. . ." George Germain Papers, Volume 7, item 46, University of Michigan, William L. Clements Library (hereafter cited as CL).

American	283
Canadian	4
French	5
	1134 soldiers

Nationalities for the 354 sailors that had registered were proportionally similar. Significantly, Galloway estimated that perhaps one-third more had come in and bypassed the registration process.[3]

What was to be done with all these deserters? Deserters tended to be doubly beneficial: while decreasing the strength of the army they deserted from, they often enlisted in the army they deserted to. British official policy, as ordered by Sir William Howe on July 3, 1777, stated: "The Provincial Troops (except Wemys's Corps) are not to enlist Deserters from the Rebels."[4] This prohibition, however, was not even casually enforced. Every Provincial unit raised, most from their inception, eagerly took in rebel deserters.

An examination of the rolls, in various states of completeness, of sixty-three Continental regiments, and scattered documents on some sixteen others, identifies by name some 2,953 deserters, prisoners and missing in action from the end of August 1777 until the end of June 1778. By cross-referencing the names of those men and the times of their desertion or capture against corresponding enlistments in Provincial units, a more detailed picture can be drawn of the men who served on both sides. Some common names make this process difficult, but even using a conservative approach, some 546 former Continental soldiers have been identified amongst the Provincials raised at Philadelphia. To put this into perspective, it is necessary to know how many men the British raised there at that time. Sir William Howe later testified the number was just under a thousand, while Galloway estimated sixteen hundred.[5] Neither figure is correct, as neither had access to the rolls kept in the muster master's office. Shortly after the Battle of Brandywine, there were 543 Provincials serving with Howe's Army, divided among the Queen's Rangers, 2nd Battalion New Jersey Volunteers, and Guides &

---

3. "An Account of the number of Deserted Soldiers, Gallymen &c from the Rebel Army and Fleet, who have come in to Philadelphia and taken the Oath of Allegiance, with a particular account of the places in which they were born. Philadelphia March 25th 1778." Germain Papers, 7:31, CL.

4. "Wemys's Corps" refers to the Queen's American Rangers, then commanded by Major James Wemyss. General Orders, Head Quarters, New York, July 3, 1777. "The Orderly Book of Lt. Col. Stephen Kemble, 1775–1778," *Collections of the New-York Historical Society for 1883* (New York: printed for the Society, 1884), 460.

5. Howe appears to have used a state of his army prepared on March 24, 1778 for his figure. Colonial Office, Class 5, Volume 95, folio 222, TNA.

Pioneers. By the time of the Battle of Monmouth, there were 2,016 Provincials with Clinton's force, not including detachments of recruits and baggage guards sent on ship to New York. In between there were deaths, desertions, prisoners captured and men discharged, amounting to several hundred men. Muster rolls and other documents show at least 1,947 men were raised at Philadelphia. 546 known Continental enlistments means that at least twenty eight percent of the new recruits were from Washington's Army. The actual figure was probably higher, given the incomplete state of Continental Army records and the ambiguities caused by common names and other factors.

These deserters present an interesting problem to those who feel the need to label groups of people: were these men considered Rebels or Loyalists? It was a puzzle then just as it is now. The question was actually asked in 1779 by Lt. Col. John Graves Simcoe, the commanding officer of the Queen's Rangers. Simcoe, since October 16, 1777, had under his command the colorful Capt. John Ferdinand Dalziel Smyth, who during the six preceding weeks had attempted to raise an independent corps, the Royal Hunters. On that date, however, his unit, the strength of two companies, was attached to the Queen's Rangers and fully incorporated into them by Simcoe. Smyth, in 1779, brought Simcoe to trial on a number of charges concerning this and other things. During his trial, Simcoe noted that Smyth's Company "being in general Rebel Deserters and not Loyalists as he had been ordered to raise was one reason of his being sent to the Rangers for they [the Queen's Rangers] having a General Order in their favor to enlist Rebel Deserters, and all other Corps being excluded, had a right to any men of that description that Captain Smyth had enlisted." The trial testimony of Captain Smyth provides an excellent description of recruiting at Philadelphia during that time:

> Q. You . . . had orders to enlist no men but of approved Loyalty and attachment to Government. Do rebel Deserters come under the denomination of approved Loyalists?
>
> A. I had orders to enlist any men that I thought good; but to be particular careful they were so. I conceive a great number of men, who have deserted from the Rebels, have been Loyalists from the beginning, and forced into their Service, and who have deserted from them the first opportunity: Instances of which I have in my own Company.
>
> Q. [Y]ou say you proposed to raise men who were well acquainted with the roads throughout the Country. Do rebel Deserters come under that description?

A. I conceive they do.

Q. What do you mean by saying you refused many men as improper persons, that other Corps must enlist?

A. A great number of men came to me at Philadelphia when having examined them, I conceived some only wished to enlist for the sake of Provision, Cloathing or some other Sinister purpose: on which suspicion tho their appearance was ever so good, I did not enlist them.[6]

While few deserters left behind written records of their actions, one appears to somewhat confirm Captain Smyth's opinion. Gersham Hilyard of Piscataway, New Jersey, entered the Philadelphia Campaign as a sergeant in Capt. William Piatt's Company of the 1st New Jersey Regiment. Muster rolls of that corps show he deserted sometime in October 1777.[7] After the war, applying to Parliament for compensation for property losses, Hilyard related that he joined the British "from Loyalty and Attachment to his King and Country." After serving some time in the secret service, Hilyard enlisted as a sergeant in Emmerick's Chasseurs, a Provincial corps in which he was later promoted to quartermaster.[8] He remained with the British for the remainder of the war, and was in London in 1784.[9]

The deserters from Valley Forge and other places around Philadelphia are only a part of the story. Another significant source of recruits, not mentioned by Galloway and possibly unknown to him, was the prisoners taken during the campaign. Battles such as Brandywine and Germantown yielded hundreds of prisoners for the British. Enlisting prisoners for the Provincial Forces began in 1776, when hundreds of those captured at Quebec and Brooklyn joined the Royal Highland Em-

6. Court Martial Proceedings of Lt. Col. John Graves Simcoe, Jamaica, Long Island, May 4–8, 1779. War Office, Class 71, Volume 88, Pages 448–496, TNA.
7. Hilyard enlisted on December 15, 1776 in the 1st New Jersey Regiment. Muster Roll of Capt. William Piatt's Company, 1st New Jersey Regiment, May 31, 1777. Record Group M246, Revolutionary War Rolls, RG 93, Reel 57, Folder 18–1, National Archives and Records Administration (hereafter cited as NARA).
8. Enlistment attestation of Gersham Hilyard, May 1 and 19, 1778. Misc. Manuscripts No. 3616, New York State Library. See also muster roll of Captain Benjamin Ogden's Troop of Emmerick's Chasseurs, June 1778. RG 8, "C" Series, Volume 1891, Library and Archives Canada (hereafter cited as LAC).
9. Memorial of Gersham Hilyard to the Commissioners for American Claims, March 24, 1784. Audit Office 13/96/492, TNA.

igrants.[10] Although officially prohibited by Congress and Washington, the practice had actually been started by the Americans in the very first weeks of the war when George McKay, a British private soldier of the 26th Regiment of Foot taken prisoner at Crown Point on May 11, 1775, immediately joined the American army.[11]

Richard Jesper was another person enlisted out of the prison. When on trial in July 1778, he related the story of his capture, his enlistment in the Pennsylvania Loyalists, his desertion from them, and his subsequent apprehension:

> he was a Servant to a Colonel Antill of the Congress's own Regt. and was taken prisoner at the Battle of Germantown, and put in the Provost Guard, where Captain [Thomas] Stephens found him; that upon Captain Stephens asking him what Countryman he was, and whether he would enlist, he reply'd that he would rather wait upon some Gentleman, & Captain Stephens said that he would enquire if any Gentleman wanted such a man, & that he afterwards took him out of Goal to wait upon himself, that Captain Stephens gave him small Sums of money at different times, which he thought he had earned, as a Servant, & not as a Soldier and never Signed any Pay Lists; that he had no thoughts of going off till Smith persuaded him to attempt to go home in some Ship, as there was a Slur lay upon his Character in the Regt. but Smith being apprehended, he could find no Opportunity of going off, & therefore went into the Jersies, where he lived as a servant with a Colonel Ogden, in which Capacity he was and not in Arms or Serving as a Soldier, when he was taken by a Party of the Guards.[12]

Jesper's story indicates that he was a non-combatant, but he was on trial for his life when he told it. His account does not bear scrutiny. If he had been a servant of Lt. Col. Edward Antill, he was not in that capacity at the battle of Germantown: Antill had been taken prisoner six weeks earlier during an American raid on Staten Island.[13] The muster

10. Robert William Walker of the 2nd Battalion Royal Highland Emigrants recruited 173 of the 1006 prisoners taken at the Battle of Brooklyn on August 27, 1776. "The Case of Robert William Walker a Loyalist Planter in Maryland." Audit Office 13/40/234–236, TNA.

11. Return of the Garrison of Ticonderoga, etc. made prisoners, May 10–11, 1775. Thomas Gage Papers, American Series, Volume 129, CL.

12. Court Martial of Richard Jesper, Pennsylvania Loyalists, held at Brooklyn between July 24 and August 1, 1778. War Office 71/83/181–183, TNA.

13. "Return of Prisoners received from Staten Island into New York August 25, 1777." Sir Henry Clinton Papers, Volume 23, item 19, CL.

rolls of the Pennsylvania Loyalists show that Jesper enlisted on October 20, 1777 as a soldier in the ranks of Captain Stephens's company, from which he deserted on February 7, 1778.[14] After deserting from the Pennsylvania Loyalists, he eventually enlisted in Capt. John Flahaven's Company of the 1st New Jersey Regiment, joining them on May 24, 1778; he is listed as having been taken prisoner the following month.[15] The muster rolls of the Pennsylvania Loyalists show he rejoined that corps on June 27, 1778, the day before the Battle of Monmouth, and was found lodged in the provost wearing a blue coat faced with red, the uniform of the 1st New Jersey. For the crime of desertion, the British found Jesper guilty and sentenced him to receive 1,000 lashes on the bare back with a cat o' nine tails. Whether he actually received all or part of the punishment is not recorded, but Jesper went on to become a useful soldier. He served with the Pennsylvania Loyalists in the garrison of Pensacola, the capital of West Florida, where he was killed on May 4, 1781, during the Spanish siege of the city.

The stories of Hilyard and Jesper raise the question of just how reliable or serviceable men were who had at least once deserted their cause. Parliament had similar thoughts when it inquired of Joseph Galloway, "What is the character that the Provincials serving in the British army bear? Are they good troops, and have they behaved well when employed?" To which Galloway replied "I have understood, as soon as they are disciplined, they are very good troops, and have always behaved well; I know of no instance to the contrary. That I know to be the opinion of many of the military gentlemen."[16] Galloway was right in general, but the deserter recruits ran the full spectrum of very good to very poor.

British Judge Advocate records provide several accounts of former deserters' troubles with their new army, none more serious than Edward Warren, a deserter from the 1st New York Regiment who enlisted in the Roman Catholic Volunteers. When this corps was drafted in 1778 (that is, its men transferred into other regiments), Warren entered into the Volunteers of Ireland, from whom he deserted on March 28, 1779.

14. "Muster Roll of Captain Stephens Company in the first Battalion of Pennsylvania Loyalists Commanded by Lieutenant Colonel Allen, Banks Skulkyll 24th February 1778." RG 8, "C" Series, Volume 1907, 6, LAC.

15. Pay Lists of Captain Flahaven's Company of the 1st New Jersey Regiment for May and June, 1778. Record Group M246, Revolutionary War Rolls, RG 93, Reel 56, Folder 10–2, NARA.

16. *The Examination of Joseph Galloway, Esq; Late Speaker of the House of Assembly of Pennsylvania, Before The House of Commons in a Committee of the American Papers with Exploratory Notes* (London: Printed for J. Wilkie, 1779), 20.

He was not seen again for several months, when he was brought back into New York City by HMS *Rainbow* among the crew of a captured rebel privateer.[17] Warren had the dubious distinction of being the only Provincial executed at New York during the command of Sir Henry Clinton.[18]

Some deserters had their new careers in the British Army cut short—literally, in the case of John Crawford. Crawford deserted from the 2nd Connecticut Regiment on June 10, 1778 and enlisted as a sergeant in Emmerick's Chasseurs four days later. In a severe action against a party of Stockbridge Indians in the Bronx on August 31, 1778, Crawford lost an arm, effectively ending his military career.[19] He continued on as an invalid until the corps was drafted exactly a year later, soon after which he was discharged from the army and sent to England in quest of a pension at the soldier's hospital of Chelsea.[20]

Some deserters not only maintained a new sense of loyalty to King George, but chose the British Army as a lifelong career. William Jackson, a soldier in the 2nd Pennsylvania Regiment, was captured on September 21, 1777, at Paoli.[21] Not choosing to remain a prisoner, he enlisted in the Queen's Rangers, with whom he served the remainder of the war. At the termination of the conflict, apparently enjoying a soldier's life, he enlisted in the British 3rd Regiment of Foot, serving until discharged because of wounds received at St. Vincent in 1798, almost twenty-one years to the day after his capture at Paoli.[22]

Some Continentals-turned-Provincials served faithfully for the remainder of the war and then settled on land grants in the Maritime provinces of Canada. Almost every Provincial regiment disbanded along the River Saint John or across the Bay of Fundy in Nova Scotia included Continental Army veterans from the Philadelphia Campaign. One interesting settler was John Bettle. Before deserting to the British in Jan-

17. Court Martial Proceedings of Private Edward Warren, New York, August 1779. War Office 71/90/90–92, TNA.
18. Warren was hanged at New York on August 30, 1779. "List of Executions, during the Command of His Excellency Lt. Genl. Sir Henry Clinton, in North America &c &c &c. New York 6th Mat 1782." Clinton Papers, 194:8, CL.
19. "Muster Roll of Capt. Muirsons Troop of Lt. Dragoons Commanded by Lieut. Col. Emmerick, October 24th 1778." RG 8, "C" Series, Volume 1891, LAC.
20. Discharge of John Crawford, New York, October 24, 1779. War Office 121/6/246, TNA.
21. Muster Roll of Captain Joseph Howell's Company, 2nd Pennsylvania Regiment, for September 1777. Record Group M246, Revolutionary War Rolls, RG 93, Reel 80, Folder 9–1, NARA.
22. Discharge of William Jackson, London, September 24, 1798. War Office 121/33/340, TNA.

uary 1778, Bettle was a surveyor and commissary for Pennsylvania. He apparently made a detailed survey of Washington's position at Valley Forge and headed straight to Philadelphia with it. Continental Congressman William Duer, upon learning of Bettle's desertion, wrote to George Washington that "before he [Bettle] went in he told a Person confidentially that he could put the Enemy in a way of investing it in such a Manner as to cut off your Communication with the Country, and thereby prevent the Supply of Provisions &ca."[23] For his daring, Bettle was rewarded with a lieutenant's commission in the West Jersey Volunteers, with whom he served until that corps was drafted in the fall of 1778. Thereafter he put his surveying talents to use in the Guides & Pioneers. He was captured and spent six months in 1781 confined as a prisoner in Philadelphia, but somehow escaped being hanged for desertion.[24] By 1786 Bettle was at Saint John, New Brunswick, petitioning the British for the retirement income due to British officers.[25]

Representative of the rank and file soldiers was James Dyer, a soldier who deserted from the 2nd Pennsylvania Regiment the day following the bloody defeat at Paoli.[26] About three weeks later, Dyer enlisted into Capt. John F.D. Smyth's Royal Hunters, which was almost immediately absorbed into the Queen's Rangers.[27] The thirty year old Irishman served with the Rangers throughout the war, surrendering with his corps at Yorktown in 1781. Because he was a deserter, he was able obtain passage to New York rather than remain in American incarceration; he remained there on parole until the final exchange of prisoners in May 1783. After the disbanding of his corps on October 10, Dyer eventually settled on Regimental Block 5 at Queensbury, New Brunswick.[28] He and his wife Margaret were living in Brighton Township, Carleton

23. Duer to Washington, Reading, February 16, 1778. George Washington Papers, Series 4, General Correspondence, January 25, 1778—March 16, 1778, Library of Congress.

24. Bettle (also spelled Biddle or Bittle) was never put on the half pay list like other reduced officers, the British claiming he 'having several times desired to resign." Memorial of John Biddle to Sir Henry Clinton, New York, September 21, 1780. Clinton Papers, 124:9, CL.

25. Memorial of John Bittle to the Commissioners for American Claims, Saint John, February 20, 1786. Audit Office 13/25/45, TNA.

26. Muster Roll of Captain John Patterson's Company, 2nd Pennsylvania Regiment, for October 1777. Record Group M246, Revolutionary War Rolls, RG 93, Reel 80, Folder 12–1, NARA.

27. Dyer enlisted in Smyth's Company on October 11, 1777. This company was permanently made a part of the Queen's Rangers five days later. Muster Roll of Captain John F.D. Smyth's Company, Queen's Rangers, Philadelphia, November 30, 1777. RG 8, "C" Series, Volume 1861, Page 4.

28. "Return of Settlers on Block No. 5 as Surveyed by Mr. Allan." F-50, Folio 13, No. 5, Collections of the New Brunswick Museum.

County in 1838 when he applied for a pension as an old soldier, being in "indigent circumstances."[29]

Piecing together a man's entire military career takes some effort, as shown by the case of Daniel Gill, a soldier of Hartley's Regiment. When he gave a deposition for his pension application, he stated succinctly that "at the battle of Iron hill, I was taken a prisoner by the enemy and was held by them nine months and made my escape from the enemy at Charleston, South Carolina and after having thus escaped again entered into the service of the United States."[30] At face value, this appears to be a patriotic soldier who served his country, was captured in battle, then escaped from the enemy far from home. But the events described need to be examined for their historical accuracy, then checked against the Provincial Forces for possible references. In Gill's case, it was not difficult. The Battle of Iron Hill, or Cooch's Bridge, was fought in Delaware on September 3, 1777. If Gill's deposition was truthful and accurate, he would have effected his escape in South Carolina around June 1778. The problem with this of course was that there were no British troops in South Carolina in 1778, and prisoners were not removed out of their district. Gill's tenure as a prisoner actually lasted no more than three months, when he enlisted in the Maryland Loyalists commanded by Lt. Col. James Chalmers.[31] Gill, promoted to corporal, sailed with his new corps for Pensacola, West Florida, stopping en route at Jamaica, where he deserted on December 16, 1778.[32] His subsequent whereabouts are unknown until he enlisted in the 2nd Battalion New Jersey Volunteers in New York on July 29, 1780.[33] The part of Gill's story that is true is that he left the British service in South Carolina. After joining the New Jersey Volunteers, Gill volunteered for service in the

29. Memorial of James Dyer to Gov. Sir John Harvey and the Legislative Council and Assembly, Brighton, January 26, 1838. RS 24, Provincial Secretary, Old Soldiers and Widows Pension Administration Records, 1838 Petition No. 149, Provincial Archives of New Brunswick.

30. Pension Application of Daniel Gill, July 25, 1820. Collection M-804, Pension and Bounty Land Application Files, No. S42745, Daniel Gill, Maryland, NARA.

31. His date of enlistment was either November 29 or December 10, 1777. "Muster Roll of Recruits in the First Battalion of Maryland Loyalists Commanded by Lieutenant Colonel James Chalmers Esqr. January 19th 1778." RG 8, "C" Series, Volume 1904, Page 10, LAC.

32. Muster Roll of Captain Walter Dulany's Company, Maryland Loyalists, Pensacola, February 22, 1779. RG 8, "C" Series, Volume 1904, Page 42, LAC.

33. Abstract of Pay for the 2nd Battalion, New Jersey Volunteers, August 25 to October 24, 1780. Dept. of Defense Manuscripts, Loyalist Manuscripts, Doc. No. 47, New Jersey State Archives.

battalion's newly-formed light infantry company, which was then at-tached to the corps of Provincial Light Infantry.[34] This unit embarked for Virginia in early October 1780 as part of Maj. Gen. Alexander Leslie's expedition, staying there but a month or so before moving on by sea to South Carolina.[35] The corps marched into the High Hills of Santee, where Gill indeed did desert on January 27, 1781. Whether or not he actually re-entered the service of the United States is anyone's guess.[36]

There are many similar cases among the thousands of depositions for Revolutionary War pensions, particularly for those Continentals who surrendered in 1780 at Charleston and Camden, many of whom later served at Jamaica as part of the Duke of Cumberland's Regiment or other similar corps.[37] They prove that single sources cannot be taken at face value, particularly things like pension applications and court tes-timony where the deponent was likely to put himself in the best light possible. Correlation of data from muster rolls and other sources is te-dious and time-consuming, but it reveals the complexity of the war and its many and varied participants. For thousands of soldiers and civilians, "patriotism" or "loyalism" were secondary concepts to personal safety and security.

34. Major John André to Colonel Beverley Robinson et al, New York, August 15, 1780. Clinton Papers, Volume 275, Letter Book of John André, CL.
35. The Provincial Light Infantry was described by Sir Henry Clinton as "well officered & commanded." Return of the corps commanded by Maj. Gen. Leslie embarked for Virginia, October 6, 1780. Clinton Papers, 125:18, CL.
36. Muster Roll of Captain Norman McLeod's Company, Provincial Light Infantry, High Hills of Santee, February 23, 1781. RG 8, "C" Series, Volume 1900, LAC.
37. Between the Duke of Cumberland's Regiment, Jamaica Corps, and the Loyal Amer-ican Rangers, some 1,200 or more Continental prisoners or deserters served from 1781–1783 at Jamaica or on the Spanish Main in Honduras and Nicaragua. Many settled in Nova Scotia after the war. See "Recruiting List of the Continental Prisoners of War, Taken at the Surrender of Charlestown, the 12th day of May 1780 and at Gates's defeat by Cambden, the 16th day of August 1780 Now inlisted in His Majesty's Service, since the 10th February 1781 For the West Indies, in His Royal Highness the Duke of Cum-berland's Regiment of Carolina Rangers; Commanded by the Right Honble Lord Charles Montagu. The within named Soldiers have been inlisted by me, William Löwe Captain in said Corps." State Papers, Class 41, Volume 29, TNA.

A Brief Publication History of the "Times That Try Men's Souls"

JETT CONNER

Thomas Paine's sensational pamphlet *Common Sense*, published anonymously in January of 1776, has a singular place of importance in the literature of the American Revolutionary era. So famous was the title that Paine would adopt it as a sobriquet when authoring future works. The publication history of that wildly successful pamphlet is well established.[1] But other than its famous opening lines, beginning with the words "These are the times that try men's souls," Paine's *American Crisis No. 1*, published in December, 1776, is less remembered today and its publication history has been somewhat cloudy. Still, it was a terribly important and timely piece that appeared at a most critical moment of the Revolutionary War, one described by Paine as the "very blackest of times."

Because the publication of *American Crisis No. 1* (hereafter *Crisis 1*) is intimately tied through legend to Washington's crossing of the Delaware and the first Battle of Trenton, it is time to put some light on the publication history of Paine's first *Crisis* paper, so that the role it supposedly played in those events can more accurately be portrayed.

Common Sense and *Crisis 1* serve as book ends for that remarkable year in American history, the first urging a declaration of independence and the second exhorting Americans to buckle down and achieve it.[2] As the title of *Crisis 1* makes clear, things were not going well for Washington toward the end of 1776. Paine saw his call for independence in *Common Sense* achieved in July, but he also witnessed first-hand the near collapse of Washington's army over the course of the late summer and

---

1. See, for example, Scott Liell, *46 Pages* (Philadelphia: Running Press, 2003), 16–92, *passim.*
2. Phillip Foner, *The Complete Writings of Thomas Paine,* 2 vols. (New York: The Citadel Press, 1969), 1:3–57.

through the fall. By early December, the army had been pushed west across New Jersey and the Delaware, and was encamped just beyond the reach of the pursuing British army on the west banks of the river.

Many biographies of Paine and historical accounts of his role at the time of Washington's crossing of the Delaware and the first Battle of Trenton—stating that *Crisis 1* either circulated among Washington's troops or was read to them on Washington's orders prior to the crossing— provide a limited publication history of the first *Crisis* paper. The most commonly repeated version of this history claims that *Crisis 1* appeared first in the *Pennsylvania Journal* newspaper on December 19, and was published as a pamphlet four days later on December 23.[3] This is incorrect, because the *Journal* had suspended publication from December 4, 1776, until January 22, 1777.[4] In fact, most newspapers in Philadelphia suspended publication during much of this time, fearing an imminent invasion of the city by the British.[5]

But support for the newspaper origin of *Crisis 1* gained traction over the years and was reinforced by descriptions adopted by several important library collections that repeat this version of the story, as we'll see.

Interestingly, the first newspaper known to have printed *Crisis 1* was the *Pennsylvania Packet*, which printed the first half of the piece on December 27, 1776, and the rest in its January 4, 1777, issue.[6] The *Packet* had resumed printing on December 18, 1776, sooner than the rest of the Philadelphia newspapers, but Paine's *Crisis 1* did not appear in that issue. That's important because there's no evidence that any newspaper printed *Crisis 1* prior to Christmas or Washington's crossing. If the piece circulated among the troops or was ordered by Washington to be read to the soldiers prior to crossing the Delaware, as is commonly claimed, then it had to have appeared first somewhere other than in the newspaper.

---

3. See, for example, David Hackett Fischer, *Washington's Crossing* (New York: Oxford, 2004), 141: ". . . the first number of *The American Crisis* appeared in the *Pennsylvania Journal* on December 19, 1776. Four days later it was published as a pamphlet."
4. Library of Congress, "Eighteenth-Century American Newspapers in the Library of Congress," (http://loc.gov/rr/news/18th/pennsylvania.html), accessed November14, 2015.
5. *Ibid.*
6. An example of the first part of *Crisis 1* as printed in the *Pennsylvania Packet* on December 27, 1776, can be found on Google books (https://books.google.com/; accessed November 15, 2015). I am indebted to Todd Andrlik, *Journal of the American Revolution*, and the staff at the Library Company of Philadelphia for helping me to determine that the first newspaper printing of *Crisis 1* likely was in the *Pennsylvania Packet* on December 27.

PUBLISHING THE FIRST *CRISIS* PAPER, PAINE'S OWN ACCOUNTS

So what did Paine have to say about all of this? He provided several accounts of the publication history of the first *American Crisis*. In a little over two months after Independence was declared, Paine was serving in the Continental army as a volunteer aide-de-camp to General Nathanael Greene and was sending dispatches, written on a drumhead in camp, to Philadelphia newspapers about events from the field.[7] He witnessed the fall of Fort Washington from across the Hudson at Fort Lee and soon after was retreating with Washington's despondent army across New Jersey and toward Pennsylvania with the British in pursuit. The following are several of Paine's accounts of publishing *Crisis 1*.

> I served as volunteer aid to General Greene at Fort Lee, and continued with him during the gloomy campaign of Seventy-Six. . . . The wretched and despairing condition of the Country occasioned me to publish the first number of the Crisis at a time when few would venture to speak and the printing presses had left off working. I began it at Newark on the retreat and got it printed in Philadelphia the 19th of Dec. 1776. But the printer did not choose to put his name to it.[8]

The last two sentences are revealing. They confirm that *Crisis 1* was printed on December 19 but not in one of Philadelphia's newspapers. This raises the question, who first published *Crisis 1*? There are several other accounts by Paine. One read that *Crisis 1* was "written while on the retreat with the army from Fort Lee to the Delaware and published in Philadelphia in the dark days of 1776 December the 19th, six days before the taking of the Hessians at Trenton."[9] And there is this statement:

> I began the first number of the Crisis, beginning with the well-known expression ('These are the times that try men's souls'), at Newark, upon the retreat from Fort Lee and had it printed at Philadelphia the 19th of December, six days before the taking the Hessians at Trenton, which, with the week after, put an end to the black times.[10]

---

7. Fischer, *Washington's Crossing*, 138–39.
8. Foner, *Collected Writings*, 2:1230.
9. *Ibid*, 1480.
10. Thomas Paine, "*Reply to Cheetham*," found on Google books (https://books.google.com/books; accessed November 15, 2015).

The following account by Paine is probably the most important of all, one that again shows that *Crisis 1* first appeared as a pamphlet and not in a newspaper:

> A few days after our army had crossed the Delaware on the 8th of December, 1776, I came to Philadelphia on public service, and, seeing the deplorable and melancholy condition the people were in, afraid to speak and almost to think, the public presses stopped, and nothing in circulation but fears and falsehoods, I sat down, and in what I may call a passion of patriotism wrote the first number of the Crisis. It was published on the 19th of December, which was the very blackest of times, being before the taking of the Hessians at Trenton. I gave that piece to the printer gratis, and confined him to the price of two coppers, which was sufficient to defray his charge.[11]

Paine continued: "I then published the second number, which, being as large again as the first number, I gave it to him on the condition of his taking only four coppers each. It contained sixteen pages. I then published the third number, containing thirty-two pages, and gave it to the printer, confining him to ninepence."[12]

Who was the "him" Paine mentioned? It was likely Melchoir Styner or Charles Cist.

THE PUBLISHERS OF *CRISIS 1*

Because the first number of Paine's *American Crisis* series lacked a date and publisher information, there has been uncertainty ever since about its publication history. The only thing certain about the first appearance of the piece is that it was written by "the Author of Common Sense," because that appears on the earliest known, undated copies of *Crisis 1*.

But there is no doubt that Philadelphia printers Styner (sometimes Steiner) and Cist printed the first issue of Thomas Paine's *Crisis 1*, as a pamphlet. The piece did not first appear in the *Pennsylvania Journal* and then as a stand-alone pamphlet, as is often claimed. On the contrary, the reverse is closer to the truth. *Crisis 1* appeared first in pamphlet form, undated and with no publisher information. Only later did it appear in newspapers, most likely for the first time in the *Pennsylvania Packet*, December 27, 1776, and, importantly, after the first Battle of Trenton. And while it is possible that other publishers pirated copies of the pamphlet soon after the first issue appeared, it is certain that

---

11. Foner, *Collected Writings*, 2:1164. (Eric Foner argues that this passage proves that *Crisis 1* appeared first as a pamphlet on December 19, and not first in a newspaper. See: www.loa.org/volume.jsp?RequestID=95&section=notes).
12. *Ibid.*

Styner and Cist continued to serve as Paine's primary publisher, at least for the first few numbers of the *American Crisis* series.

Interestingly, in 1956, the great-great-grandson of Charles Cist gave to the Library Company of Philadelphia a first edition of *The American Crisis, Numbers I-III,* published by Styner and Cist in 1776 and 1777. The Library Company of Philadelphia's annual report describes that gift:

> The first number of the *Crisis*, beginning with the famous sentence: "These are the times that try men's souls," is of the edition with the date December 19, 1776 at the end. We already had a copy of the different printing without the date. For the sake of the bibliographi-cally curious, we would like to point out that . . . this is the indication of edition, for the two variants represent completely different settings of the type.[13]

The donation to the Library Company of the copy mentioned here strongly indicates that Styner and Cist published the first *Crisis* without a date or publisher information, and then in subsequent editions began to include not only publisher and dates, but the date of the first *Crisis* as well, which it had first published on December 19, 1776.

AMERICAN HISTORY ON A LIBRARY CARD

A search of holdings at two key institutions, the Library of Congress and the Historical Society of Pennsylvania, shows that almost identical statements about the publication history of *Crisis 1* appear on their re-spective library caption cards, cards that describe their rare, undated, copies of the pamphlet.

At the Historical Society of Pennsylvania, a library caption card has this information: "[Philadelphia?: Styner and Cist?, 1776?]. Caption Title: without signature or date. First published in the Pennsylvania journal, Dec. 19, 1776, and reprinted as a pamphlet Dec. 23, 1776."[14]

The same statement about the printing history of *Crisis 1* appears on the library caption card at the Library of Congress, which can only be accessed at the library in the card catalog file drawers (yes, the wooden kind!). A note in their online catalog about their rare pamphlet version of *Crisis 1* states that the record contains "unverified, old data" on the caption card. The cover of the pamphlet and description of this

---

13. *The Annual Report of the Library Company of Philadelphia for the year 1956* (Philadel-phia: The Library Company of Philadelphia, 1957), 26: found on Google books (https://books.google .com/books; accessed November 15, 2015).

14. Paine, *American Crisis Number 1,* http://discover.hsp.org/Record/marc-270052, ac-cessed November 15, 2015.

holding can be viewed online.[15] I have reviewed the caption card in the card files in the Library of Congress. The staff cannot determine when the printing history was added to the card.

Though both institutions acknowledge Styner and Cist as publishers of the pamphlet *Crisis 1*, both include information on their library cards indicating that the pamphlet was published after it had first appeared in the *Pennsylvania Journal* on December 19. Both are wrong. There is no record of that newspaper having printed anything on that date. So, in spite of these library cards' caution that they may contain "unverified data" or questionable dates, statements of publishing history on those cards nevertheless go beyond mere descriptions of library holdings: they convey, sometimes mistakenly, a context for an important moment in American history.

CONCLUSION

To the extent that Paine is widely given credit to this day for penning the famous words that were supposedly instrumental to the success of Washington's crossing and the first Battle of Trenton. The publication history of "These are the times that try men's souls" is a critical piece of the story. How exactly Paine's words circulated among Washington's troops up and down the west bank of the Delaware, as some claim, and in what form if Washington indeed ordered them to be read to his soldiers prior to crossing the Delaware, as others assert, are necessary questions. And though some answers may remain elusive forever, inaccuracies in some accounts of the first appearance of *Crisis 1* can certainly be revealed.

15. Paine, *American Crisis Number 1*, www.loc.gov/pictures/item/2005694599/, accessed November 15, 2015.

Conrad Heyer Did Not Cross the Delaware

✻ DON N. HAGIST ✻

An internet search for Conrad Heyer will reveal that he was a Revolutionary War soldier who crossed the Delaware with George Washington. In fact, you'll find a variation of this sentence repeated on page after page almost word for word: "He served in the Continental Army under George Washington during the Revolutionary War, crossing the Delaware with him and fighting in other major battles."[1] Everyone, including some usually authoritative sources, apparently copied what someone else had already written without attempting to verify the information.[2]

The reason that Heyer draws so much attention is that he is one of the hundred or so Revolutionary War veterans to have been photographed.[3] By the 1840s, when photography was becoming widely available, veterans of the war were becoming scarce. Heyer, when his picture was taken in 1852, was among the oldest men ever photographed. The daguerreotype image eventually came into the possession of the Maine Historical Society where it remains today.

I recently wrote a book about six Revolutionary War veterans who'd had their pictures taken. *The Revolution's Last Men: The Soldiers Behind the Photographs* was originally intended to be a simple update of the

1. The earliest occurrence I've found dates to January 8, 2008: https://unitedcats.word-press.com/2008/01/08/the-worlds-first-eyewitness/
2. See, for example, www.smithsonianmag.com/smart-news/conrad-heyer-a-revolutionarywar-veteran-was-the-earliest-born-american-to-ever-be-photographed-180947660/
3. For the most extensive collection of images of Revolutionary War veterans, see Maureen Taylor, *The Last Muster: Images of the Revolutionary War Generation* (Kent, OH: Kent State University Press, 2010); *The Last Muster Volume 2: Faces of the American Revolution* (Kent, OH: Kent State University Press, 2013).

1864 book *Last Men of the Revolution* which included photographs and biographies of what were believed to be the last six surviving pensioners of the war.[4] As I researched the wartime service of the book's six subjects, however, I discovered that the book was filled with errors, dramatically overstating the service of some men while omitting significant wartime events in the lives of others. The biographies written in 1864 bear little resemblance to the men's actual service, determined from documents written much closer to the events including their own pension depositions. And yet, the flawed 1864 biographies, along with copies of the photographs, continue to be circulated and accepted without question.

Because I showed how wrong those six biographies were, people ask me about others. What about Conrad Heyer, who famously crossed the Delaware with Washington? Is anything amiss with his story?

To find out, I started in the same place that I did with the other six pensioners: their own pension depositions. The United States government passed legislation granting pensions to veterans of the Continental Army in 1818. Each applicant had to prove his military service using documents such as discharge papers, testimony of others with whom he had served, or a combination of the two. Most men applied in person at their local courthouse and gave a deposition that was witnessed by a judge or other official. Corroborating depositions by others were also sworn and recorded. Most of these records survive in the United States National Archives, and are readily available on microfilm at research facilities or through subscription internet services.

The purpose of the depositions was to prove service, not to tell war stories, so most of them are brief and focus on dates, titles of military units and names of officers. Because the first depositions were given thirty-five years after the war ended, and some long after that, discrepancies are common. But the very basic facts of how long a man served, and during what years, are usually not difficult to determine by comparing a deposition to other primary source information. The pension deposition of Conrad Heyer,"[5] dictated to a justice of the peace who spelled his name "Hyer" on July 14, 1819, reads:

4. Don N. Hagist, *The Revolution's Last Men: The Soldiers Behind the Photographs* (Yardley, PA: Westholme Publishing, 2015); E. B. Hillard, *The Last Men of the Revolution* (Hartford, CT: N. A. & R. A. Moore, 1864).

5. Conrad Heyer (Hyer) pension file, S35457, Revolutionary War Pension and Bounty Land Warrant Application Files, 1800–1900, Record Group 15; National Archives Building, Washington, DC, accessed through Fold3, Revolutionary War Rolls, www.fold3.com, accessed January 30, 2016.

I Conrad Hyer of Waldoboro in the County of Lincoln & State of Massachusetts testify & declare that about the middle of December AD 1775 I enlisted to serve as a private in the army of the American Revolutionary War in the Massachusetts Line and Continental establishment to serve against the common enemy for the term of one year and that in pursuance of paid inlistment I did actually serve said term of one year in the army aforesaid and the line aforesaid & Continental establishment and against the common enemy; that the first of said year I was under Capt. Fuller in Colonel Bond's Regiment, but that I was afterwards transferr'd to Captain Smith's company in said Regiment and that after the death of said Colonel Bond the regiment was commanded by Colonel Alden who had the command of the same when I was discharged & that I was then in said Smith's company. I received my discharge which was an honorable discharge from Captain Agry who gave me a pass in writing including three or four others, but nothing else in writing & said pass is now lost. The place of my discharge was on the North River at Fish Kilns and the time I received it about the middle of December AD 1777. That I never have received any pension under the United States. And I further testify & declare that by reason of my reduced circumstances in life I am in need of subsistence from my country for support & therefore respectfully ask to be placed on the pension list of the United States by virtue of the Act of Congress of March 18 AD 1818, entitled "an Act to provide for certain persons engaged in the land & naval service of the United States in the Revolutionary War.

Conrad Hyer (X his mark)

Nothing about crossing the Delaware, but at a glance it seems plausible if Heyer served until December 1777. Looking more closely, though, there's an inconsistency: Heyer says that he enlisted in December 1775 and served for just one year. This sort of discrepancy turns up frequently in pension depositions, and can be resolved by learning about the regiment in which Heyer served, a Massachusetts regiment commanded initially by Colonel Bond and then by Colonel Alden. This was the 25th Continental Regiment, raised in January 1776 under Col. William Bond. When he died on August 31, 1776, Lt. Col. Ichabod Alden took over.[6] Company commanders included Capt. Nathan Fuller

6. Francis B. Heitman, *Historical Register of Officers of the Continental Army during the War of the Revolution* (Washington, DC: Rare Book Ship Publishing, 1914), 56, 110.

and Capt. Daniel Egery (spelled Agry in Heyer's deposition);[7] Lt. Nathan Smith, who started the year in Fuller's company, was promoted to captain and assumed command of a company on August 31.[8] All of the names given by Heyer, then, match contemporary information about the regiment.

The 25th Continental Regiment marched to the New York City area in April 1776 but was then sent to join the army in Canada. The regiment returned from that difficult campaign and was in Morristown, New Jersey, by November. The organization was disbanded in December 1776, its soldiers discharged from their year-long obligation.[9] Witnesses gave corroborating depositions, also in Heyer's pension file. Fellow soldier Valentine Mink deposed that he had served in Captain Fuller's and Captain Smith's companies, and "that I well knew Conrad Hyer in said service that he enter'd the same with me." Mink went on to say that Hyer "served from the middle of December AD 1775 to the middle of December AD 1776 at which time he was discharged honorably from said service at Fish Kilns on the North River by a pass in writing sign'd by Captain Agry." John Vanner, another soldier in the 25th, also "well knew Conrad Hyer" had served "from December AD 1775 to December AD 1776," and "was honorably discharged at Fish Kilns by a pass from Capt. Agry to himself and several others of whom I was one." It is clear that Conrad Heyer's service in the 25th Continental Regiment ended in December 1776, and that it was a slip of the writer's pen that put the year 1777 in his deposition.

No mention is made of any subsequent army service.[10] It is significant that Heyer was discharged in Fishkill, New York, a place along the Hudson River (called the North River during the American Revolution) in mid-December. Even if he had reenlisted, it is nearly impossible that he could have traveled from Fish Kill to join Washington's army in Pennsylvania by December 25, in time to participate in the crossing of the Delaware that night.

7. "A List of the Names & Rank of the Officers of the Twenty fifth Regiment," William Bond Papers, Mss. 80, Mandeville Special Collections Library, University of California San Diego.
8. Ibid.; Heitman, *Historical Register*, 506.
9. Robert K. Wright, *The Continental Army* (Washington, D.C.: United States Army Center of Military History, 1983), 206.
10. The most comprehensive source of information on Massachusetts militia service makes no mention of Conrad Heyer, or any likely name variations (Hyer, Higher, Hayer, etc.). *Massachusetts Soldiers and Sailors of the Revolutionary War* (Boston: Wright & Potter Printing Co., 1896).

Conrad Heyer was born in Waldoboro' (throughout the nineteenth century the name is usually spelled with an apostrophe, although it occasionally appears as Waldoborough), Maine in 1749, the son of German immigrants. At the time of the American Revolution, Maine was not a separate colony but part of Massachusetts, so Heyer was a Massachusetts soldier. He lived for an exceptionally long time, from 1749 until February 1856, all of it in Waldoboro'. His obituary read:

> Died, on the 18th inst., at Waldoboro', Conrad Heyer, at the advanced age of 106 years, 10 months and 9 days. His parents were from Germany, and he was the first child, of the white race, born in that town, in which he always continued to reside. Though of rather slender form, Mr. Heyer had great physical energies, with much power of enduring labor and fatigue. He possessed remarkable health, having never till this winter been confined a day by sickness. Mr. Heyer was from early life a respected and consistent member of the German Lutheran Church. For three years, he served in the war of the Revolution, and was a pensioner. He voted at every Presidential election since the establishment of our National Government. His employment was that of a farmer. For the last ten years, he attracted much attention, many strangers visited him, and always found him a source of much interest, not only as a relic of the past, but for the exactness of his memory, and the very clear accounts he loved to give of early occurrences within his own observation. His maxims of prudence and propriety deduced from his long observation of men, had weight with his neighbors. As he lived with mental powers wonderfully preserved, so he continued to hold the respect of his acquaintances, and the memory of his virtues and of his wisdom will, for a long time, exert useful influences in the circle where he was so well known.[11]

Notice that this memorial says three years of service in the Revolution, even though Heyer himself had claimed only one year when he applied for his pension in 1819. As indicated in the obituary, by the 1850s Heyer's advanced age and Revolutionary War service had brought him some popularity. He was mentioned in a Bangor newspaper in 1851: "The first child born of the German settlers who founded Waldoboro', is still living in that town (says Mr. Eaton, in the History of Warren.) His name is Conrad Heyer, born in 1749, now 102 years of age, and in the enjoyment of pretty good health."[12]

---

11. *Bath Tribune*, February 22, 1856; reprinted in a number of other newspapers.
12. *Bangor Whig & Courier*, November 22, 1851.

Also in 1851, local historian Cyrus Eaton published *Annals of the Town of Warren in Knox County* which included a paragraph about Heyer, saying he had "enlisted in the army in the fall of 1775, served upwards of two years."[13.] Eaton lauded him for having "ever been a hard-working, temperate man, and now, at the age of 102 years, is able to read fine print without glasses, though his hearing is somewhat impaired." After the 1852 presidential election, newspapers around the country mentioned that "Conrad Heyer, of Waldoboro', (Maine,) aged one hundred and three years the tenth of April last, notwithstanding a severe storm on the 2d instant, travelled six miles, and was at the polls as usual, and cast his vote for President."[14] Some of the newspapers that

13. Cyrus Eaton, *Annals of the Town of Warren in Knox County, Maine* (Hallowell, Maine: Masters, Smith & Co., 1851). In 1877 a second edition of this book was published by Emily Eaton, who added, "some authorities say three years, and that he was in the army at Cambridge when the battle of Bunker Hill was fought; was a member of the advance guard at the crossing of the Delaware, and in many of the battles under Washington." She also added this anecdote: "As Martin Heyer died from exposure and hunger after his arrival at Waldoboro' before his son Conrad was born, the popular belief that a man 'who never saw his father' has the gift of healing sore eyes and other ills by a look or touch, led to Mr. Heyer being sought after for that purpose; and tradition tells of a wonderful cure thus performed for the daughter of a rich Bostonian in early days, but of whom, according to rule, no reward was accepted for fear of annulling the cure."

Three months after Heyer died, it was announced that "The funeral obsequies of the old revolutionary soldier, Conrad Heyer, the oldest man known in this part of the United States, who died at Waldoboro' some months ago, are to be celebrated at that place on the coming anniversary of the Battle of Bunker Hill—the 17th of June. The Rockland City Guards have accepted an invitation to be present." *Bangor Whig & Courier*, May 27, 1856. The 1877 edition of *Annals of the Town of Warren* presented this as more than just a celebration: "This interesting man died Feb. 19, 1856. . . and the succeeding 17th of June was celebrated in Waldoboro' by the disinterment of his remains and their re-burial with public military honors in the German burying-ground at the village where his fellow citizens have erected a monument to his memory."

An 1869 news item about the Lutheran meeting house in Waldoborough noted that "Old Conrad Heyer acted as chorister in the old house for eighty years, and, although a hundred years old, would sing the highest notes with scarcely any of the tremulousness of age." *Boston Daily Advertiser*, December 27, 1869, quoting the *Rockland Free Press*.

14. *Daily National Intelligencer* (Washington, DC), November 16, 1852. Earlier that year a Bangor newspaper included a paragraph about Heyer due to his being a centenarian. It reported that he had served three years during the Revolution, and that "He has nine children living, the baby being nearly three score years old. His wife died ten years ago, after having lived with her 65 years. He is of German origin being the first person born in Waldoboro, and knows no language but the German. His German Bible is his constant companion, which he reads daily." This is the only indication that he spoke only German, and there is no evidence that he gave his pension deposition through a translator, suggesting that the statement is inaccurate. *Rockland Gazette*, February 27, 1852, quoting the *Bangor Jeffersonian*.

picked up this snippet, however, added, "He
served three years in the war of the Revolution."[15] Somehow, after Heyer's pension
claim in 1819 and before 1851, word had
spread that Heyer had served for longer than
he'd originally claimed.

On May 21, 1855, Heyer himself revised
his claim. In a statement reaffirming his pension claim, he stated that he'd been discharged in December 1778 rather than 1776.
The printed form with specifics handwritten
into blank spaces by a justice of the peace as-
serts that Heyer "was in the army when Burgoyne surrendered; for the details of his
service refer to his application & proofs on

Conrad Heyer (1749–1856)

which his Cert. of Pension was issued, dated July 14, 1819." It further
says that he "Enlisted first at Waldoboro State of Maine on or about
the first day of December 1775 for the term of three years . . . was honorably discharged in the state of New York on or about the fifteenth
day of December AD 1778 as will appear by the muster rolls of Capt.
Smiths Company & other rolls. That he was at one time one of Genl
Washington's body guard." At the time this document was prepared in
Lincoln County, Maine, the "application & proofs" and muster rolls that
it refers to were at the pension office in Washington, DC. Today, all of
these documents are together in Heyer's pension file, but in 1855 the
justice of the peace took the one-hundred-and-six-year-old veteran's
statements at face value. No one since has seemed to question the in-
consistencies.

It is possible that Heyer served in Washington's life guard, a corps
initially formed in March 1776 of men selected from each infantry regiment in Washington's army. But there is no record that he did; complete muster rolls for the life guard do not exist, and his name is not
among those known to have served in the corps. And once again there
is no mention of Heyer crossing the Delaware, even in the inflated claim
of service from 1855. Perhaps it arose from the assertion that he'd served
in Washington's guard, and therefore must have accompanied the commander-in-chief everywhere. A 1925 inquiry to the Pension Office
shows that the Delaware claim was already popular at that time.

When he was photographed in 1852, there was no way to make
copies of the daguerreotype picture. With the advent of the internet,

15. See, for example, *Milwaukee Daily Sentinel*, November 23, 1851.

however, images of the photograph have been widely circulated and acclaimed, along with the assertion that he was the only man who crossed the Delaware to be photographed, was the last survivor of that crossing, and so forth. Although a glance at his pension file seems to support the claims, a more detailed and discerning look indicates that they are simply not true. My work with the six aged veterans in *The Revolution's Last Men* revealed how the military service of centenarians was exaggerated through a combination of fading memories and wishful admiration. The same appears to be true for Conrad Heyer: he certainly spent a year in the Continental Army, service worthy of study and commemoration, but the available evidence indicates that his soldiering days ended before Washington's famous river crossing.

Arthur St. Clair's Decision to Abandon Fort Ticonderoga and Mount Independence

RON MORGAN

On the night of July 5–6, 1777, an American army under the command of Maj. Gen. Arthur St. Clair abruptly withdrew from the twin fortifications of Ticonderoga and Mount Independence, abandoning them (along with a massive quantity of supplies and ordnance) to an advancing British and German force from Canada under the command of L. Gen. John Burgoyne. News of the loss of the "Gibraltar of the North" was met with shock and dismay by Americans supporting the Revolution. George Washington expressed the prevailing sentiment in a letter to Philip Schuyler, St. Clair's superior in command of the Northern Department:

> The evacuation of Ticonderoga and Mount Independence is an event of chagrin and surprise not apprehended nor within the compass of my reasoning. I know not upon what principle it was founded. . . . This stroke is severe indeed, and has distressed us much.[1]

The shock and surprise were not confined to the American side. A junior officer in the Riedesel Regiment wrote of what he observed as his company reconnoitered the fortifications shortly after the Americans fled:

> We were astounded when we caught sight of the place. There was one earthwork after another, each rising above the previous one, eleven to twelve in number. On the beach there was also one trench after another, and [both] shores were studded with cannon. . . . The

1. George Washington to Phillip Schuyler, July 15, 1777, The George Washington Papers at the Library of Congress, 1741—1799.

artillery stretched all the way from the water's edge right up to both the [stone] citadel and Fort Independence, one gun protruding above the other. The magazines—crammed with flour, meat, coffee, wine, porter beer, sugar, medicines, etc.—held stock in superabundance. . . . If the enemy had made a truly determined effort to defend the post, we could not have taken it considering the fact that our army was too weak for the task of attacking so important a location.[2]

The American fortifications were formidable indeed. The Ticonderoga Peninsula on the west side of Lake Champlain, and Mount Independence on the east, contained nearly three and a half miles of defensive works, studded with multiple artillery batteries with interlocking fields of fire, covering the landward approaches as well as the lake. The two posts were connected across the lake by a floating bridge secured by twenty two massive wooden caissons and fronted by a log and chain boom designed to obstruct any attempt to penetrate the fortifications by water. In short, the place was virtually impregnable. How St. Clair came to his decision to abandon this strategic outpost, where so much treasure, and no small amount of blood,[3] had been invested, was and is more than a matter of idle curiosity; many have attempted to explain it, from the participants (on both sides) and their contemporaries, to subsequent generations of historians, making the study of how the history was written a worthy subject for closer examination. That story is one of competing tales, and of how one such tale came to be the prevailing one, with important consequences for our understanding of one of the Revolution's critical moments.

THE BRITISH VERSION OF EVENTS

From the British perspective, the events leading to the American retreat were straightforward.[4] On July 1, Burgoyne's army of 7,000 men deployed on both shores of Lake Champlain at a point three miles north of Ticonderoga, having travelled there by water from Canada. The eastern contingent, comprised of Britain's German allies under the com-

2. Thomas M. Barker, "The Battles of Saratoga and the Kinderhook Tea Party: The Campaign Diary of a Junior Officer in Baron Riedesel's Musketeer Regiment in the 1777 British Invasion of New York," *The Hessians: Journal of the Johannes Schwalm Historical Association*, 9:31.

3. It has been estimated that casualties from disease and exposure as the fortifications were being built in 1776 and early 1777 numbered in the dozens, if not hundreds.

4. See generally Douglas R. Cubbison, *Burgoyne and the Saratoga Campaign, His Papers* (The Arthur H. Clark Company, 2012), 51–64.

mand of Baron von Riedesel, advanced southward with the objective of cutting off the landward approaches to Mount Independence. At the same time, Burgoyne's British troops on the western shore moved to seal off the line of communication between the Ticonderoga fortifications and Lake George, the principal conduit to the Hudson River and thence to Albany and beyond. Over the next three days, the British force accomplished its objectives and began to construct artillery batteries overlooking the "French Lines" covering Ticonderoga, while Riedesel's men built batteries on the eastern shore to effectively bracket the Ticonderoga peninsula as they slowly advanced through dense marshland towards Mount Independence.

At this point an event occurred which, in Burgoyne's view, proved decisive:

> July 5th Lt. Twiss the commanding Engineer was ordered to reconnoiter Sugar Hill on the South west side of the Communication from Lake George into Lake Champlain. It had appear'd from the first to be a very advantageous post. And it is now known that the Enemy had a council some time ago upon the expediency of possessing it; but the Idea was rejected upon the Supposition that it was impossible for a Corps to be established there in force. Lt. Twiss reported this Hill to have the entire command of the Works and Buildings both of Ticonderoga and Mount Independence; that the ground might be levelled so as to receive cannon; and that a road to convey them, tho' difficult, might be made practicable in twenty-four hours. This Hill also entirely commanded in reverse the Bridge of communication, saw the exact situation of the Vessels, nor could the enemy during the day make any material movement or preparation without being discovered, and even having their numbers counted. It was immediately determined that a battery should be raised upon Sugar Hill for light twenty-four Pounders, medium twelve's, and eight inch Howitzers. This very arduous work was carried on so rapidly that the battery would have been ready the next day.[5]

As events transpired, the new battery never had the opportunity to open fire. The British preparations on Sugar Hill were observed by the Americans, and in the early afternoon of July 5, 1777, St. Clair convened a council of war with his brigade commanders, who unanimously resolved to retreat that night. In the aftermath of St. Clair's withdrawal, Burgoyne was convinced that his opponents had simply been outsmarted. In a letter dated July 11, he observed:

5. Ibid., 59–60.

The manner of taking up the ground at Ticonderoga convinces me that they have no men of military science. Without possessing Sugar Hill, from which I was proceeding to attack them, Ticonderoga is only what I once heard Montcalm expressed it to be—'une porte por un honnete homme de se deshonorer;'[6] they seem to have expended great treasure and the unwearied labour of more than a year to fortify, upon the supposition that we should only attack them upon the point where they were best prepared to resist.[7]

Thus, in Burgoyne's view, once his artillerists had occupied Sugar Hill, the "weak link" in the Americans' entire defensive position, St. Clair had no alternative but to conduct an ignominious retreat. The Americans' assessment was quite different, a point which has been obscured both by the passage of time and by subsequent generations of historians.

THE AMERICAN VERSION OF EVENTS

The American side of the story begins, as it necessarily must, with the written conclusions of the council of war called by St. Clair on July 5, attended by Maj.-Gen. St. Clair and his four brigade commanders:

General St. Clair represented to the Council, that there is every reason to believe that the batteries of the enemy are ready to open upon the Ticonderoga side, and that the camp is very much exposed to their fire, and to be enfiladed on all quarters; and as there is also reason to expect an attack upon Ticonderoga and Mount Independence at the same time, in which case neither could draw any support from the other; he desired their opinion, whether it would be most proper to remove the tents to the low ground, where they would be less exposed, and wait the attack at the Ticonderoga lines, or whether the whole of the troops should be drawn over to Mount Independence, the more effectually to provide for the defense of that post. At the same time the General begged leave to inform them that the whole of our force consisted of 2089 effectives, rank and file, including 124 artificers unarmed, besides the corps of artillery, and about 900 militia who have joined us, and cannot stay but a few days.

The Council were unanimously of opinion, that it is impossible with our force to defend Ticonderoga and Mount Independence, and that the troops, cannon and stores, should be removed this night, if possible, to Mount Independence.

6. "A means for an honest man to dishonor himself."
7. Edward Barrington De Fonblanque, *Political and Military Episodes in the Latter Half of the Eighteenth Century, Derived from the Life and Correspondence of the Right Hon. John Burgoyne, General, Statesman, Dramatist* (London: MacMillan & Co., 1876), 247.

Second. Whether, after the division of the army at Ticonderoga have retreated to Mount Independence, we shall be in a situation to defend that post; or, in case it cannot be defended, if a retreat into the country will be practicable.

The Council are unanimously of opinion, that, as the enemy have already nearly surrounded us, and there remains nothing more to invest us compleately but their occupying the neck of land betwixt the Lake and the East Creek, which is not more than three quarters of a mile over, and possessing themselves of the Narrows betwixt and Skeensborough, and thereby cutting off all communication with the country, a retreat ought to be undertaken as soon as possible, and that we shall be very fortunate to effect it.[8]

Although the questions put to the council were formulated by St. Clair, their structure was dictated by a council of war convened at Ticonderoga by Philip Schuyler, Commandant of the Northern Department and St. Clair's immediate superior, just fifteen days earlier. In that council, at which St. Clair and his general officers were all present, it had been determined that the available manpower was greatly insufficient to defend both Ticonderoga and Mount Independence, and that if the enemy arrived in force and it became necessary to evacuate one of the posts, the army was to withdraw from Ticonderoga and concentrate at Mount Independence.[9] Significantly, St. Clair was only authorized to retreat from Mount Independence in the event there were insufficient provisions to feed the army until relief could arrive.[10]

Given the plan of action laid out by Schuyler, which expressly took into account the numerical inferiority of the garrison, the council's decision to evacuate Ticonderoga is unsurprising and bound to have been made regardless of any particular actions taken by Burgoyne, other than that of making his appearance in the first place. Therefore, the critical question relating to the decision to retreat is the second one posed by St. Clair: could Mount Independence be defended on its own under siege until relief could arrive? St. Clair's council did not address that question at all, in glaring contrast to the specific determination the council made to abandon Ticonderoga. Applying Occam's razor, we could infer that the most likely reason for the omission was that while

---

8. "Proceedings of a General Court Martial, &c.", *Collections of the New-York Historical Society for the year 1880*, the John Watts De Peyster Publication Fund Series, Volume XIII (New York, Printed for the Society, 1881), 33–34. Hereinafter cited as "St. Clair Court Martial."
9. Ibid., 24–25.
10. Ibid., 25.

the members of the council were in agreement on the necessity of abandoning Mount Independence, there was a lack of unanimity concerning the reasons for doing so. The available evidence supports this conclusion. Correspondence written in the immediate aftermath of the retreat reveals two independent rationales for taking the decision to retreat, neither of which was grounded upon the threat presented by the British battery on Sugar Hill.

In the weeks following the retreat, an anonymous letter by a "General Officer of the Northern Army" was submitted to *The New York Gazette*, offering an "apology" (e.g., explanation) for the abandonment of Ticonderoga. The author, after pointing out that Burgoyne's force outnumbered the American troops by more than two to one, described the situation that the Northern Army was in:

> . . . two batteries were erected in front of our lines, on higher ground than ours, within half a mile; on our left, they had taken post on a very high hill overlooking all our works [Sugar Hill]; our right would have been commanded by their shipping and batteries they had erected on the other side of the lake, that our lines at Ticonderoga would have been of no service, and we must have inevitably abandoned them in a few days after their batteries opened, which would have been the next morning. We then should have been necessitated to retire to Fort Independence . . . we might have stayed at the Mount as long as our provisions would have supported us; we had flour for thirty days, and meat sufficient only for a week.[11]

Similarly, a letter by Lt. Col. George Reid, written to his brother a few weeks after the retreat, asserted that due to the "battries on all quarters," "in all probability we could not live on [the Ticonderoga] side any time, whether or not we might have stood a siege some time on the Mount I'm not alone to determine . . . it is very probable if we had Continued any considerable time longer without assistance we must have been made prisoners."[12]

To summarize, the foregoing narrative, while expressly acknowledging the threat to Ticonderoga presented by the Sugar Hill battery, jus-

11. *The Remembrancer; or, Impartial Repository of Public Events for the year 1777* (London: printed for J. Almon, 1778), 360. The most likely author of this document is General Enoch Poor, brigade commander, who had been making written reports to General Gates concerning the state of the posts prior to St. Clair's arrival. At St. Clair's court martial, Poor was asked no questions concerning the specifics of the deliberations of the council.
12. "Letter from George Reid to Mr. Jn. Neysmith, From Moses Creek about 5 miles below Fort Edward 22nd July, 1777," from the collection of Dr. Gary Milan.

tified the abandonment of Mount Independence based upon a lack of provisions necessary to withstand a siege, in stark contrast to Burgoyne's contention that his battery made the Mount Independence defenses as untenable as those at Ticonderoga. Burgoyne's contention is further undermined by the testimony at St. Clair's court martial, reinforcing the conclusion that the Sugar Hill battery did not impact the Americans' assessment of the viability of the Mount Independence defenses.[13]

Interestingly, St. Clair initially chose not to advance the central proposition of the foregoing account (the lack of provisions), thus muddying the waters considerably. St. Clair claimed that he did not guide the council in its deliberations,[14] and while he agreed with its conclusions, he pointedly refused to adopt its rationale with respect to abandoning Mount Independence. At his court martial, St. Clair asserted: "I have never pretended, for all this, that the want of provision obliged me to evacuate the posts."[15] The fact was that St. Clair had concluded weeks earlier that Mount Independence could not be held on its own, putting himself on a collision course with his superior, Philip Schuyler. On June 18, 1777, two days before Schuyler held his council of war, St.

13. Lt. Col. James Livingston, an Aide de Camp to St. Clair, testified that the Sugar Hill battery "caused the greatest alarm to the garrison" because it had "an entire command of Ticonderoga" but with respect to Mount Independence, Livingston simply noted that it was soon to be cut off from supply. St. Clair Court Martial, 116–117. Colonel Kosciuszko, the esteemed military engineer who supervised the construction of a portion of the works at Ticonderoga and Mount Independence, acknowledged the establishment of the Sugar Hill battery immediately prior to the retreat, but then responded to a series of questions from St. Clair regarding the viability of the Mount Independence defenses without mentioning the battery at all. Ibid., 59–61. St. Clair only made reference to Sugar Hill once in his closing argument, in passing, remarking that the enemy's possession of a "high hill on the opposite side of the Lake [from Mount Independence], from hence they could see our every movement" necessitated that the retreat be conducted at night. Ibid., 151.

14. "Letter from General St. Clair to John Hancock, President of Congress, Fort Edward, 14th July, 1777", ibid., 74–75: *Inclosed you will find a copy of the council of war, in which is contained the principles upon which the retreat was undertaken. As I found all the general officers so fully of opinion that it should be undertaken immediately, I forbore to mention to them many circumstances which might have influenced them, and which I should have laid before them had they been of different sentiments; for I was, and still am, so firmly convinced of the necessity as well as the propriety of it, that I believe I should have ventured upon it had they been every one against it.*

15. St. Clair Court Martial, 162. For a detailed analysis of St. Clair's court martial, see Ron R. Morgan, " *'Shamefully abandoning the posts of Ticonderoga and Mount Independence, in his charge'* The Court Martial of Major General Arthur St. Clair and the Verdict of History", http://035a6a2.netsolhost.com/wordpress1/historical-articles/reconsidering-the-retreat-frommount-independence/, accessed February 25, 2016.

Clair addressed a letter to him, saying: "I am making some improvement upon the Mount, but that and the Ticonderoga side have such dependence upon, and connection with, each other, that in my opinion it will be very dangerous to give up either, and yet it is certain we cannot with our present numbers hold both."[16]

Schuyler acknowledged, while testifying at St. Clair's court martial, that St. Clair had flatly told him that it would be impossible to hold Mount Independence if Ticonderoga were abandoned.[17] Nevertheless, Schuyler refused to authorize a retreat (provided that adequate provision could be laid in before the British arrived), saying that the Continental Congress expected the post to be held.[18]

St. Clair defended his admitted disregard of Schuyler's orders by addressing lengthy letters to Congress and General Washington in the immediate aftermath of the retreat, making the case that he had insufficient men and equipment to properly defend the extensive fortifications on both sides of the lake,[19] and he later called a parade of witnesses at his court martial to testify that a minimum of 10,000 men were required to hold the posts.[20] That testimony, combined with a belated adoption by St. Clair of the "lack of provisions" argument (albeit based on rather dubious factual grounds),[21] ultimately resulted in St. Clair's full acquittal by the court.

From St. Clair's point of view, the critical point was that his army had been preserved to fight another day. As he reported to Congress on July 14, 1777: "I have made good a retreat from under the nose of an army at least four times their numbers, and have them now betwixt the enemy and the country, ready to act against them."[22]

16. Ibid., 19.

17. Ibid., 108.

18. Ibid., 106.

19. "General St. Clair to John Hancock, President of Congress, Fort Edward, 14th July, 1777", ibid., 74–75; "General St. Clair to General Washington, Fort Edward, 17th July, 1777", *The St. Clair Papers* (Cincinnati, Robert Clarke & Co., 1882), 1:429–433.

20. Testimony of Major General Gates, 49–50; Testimony of Brigadier General Poor, 79; Testimony of Major General Schuyler, 103–106 (including an intriguingly muddled retraction of his previous representations to Congress that a force of 2,000 to 3,000 men would be sufficient to hold Mount Independence); St. Clair Court Martial. See also, Testimony of Colonel Kosciuszko, 58–61 (reflecting St. Clair's efforts, with limited success, to establish via his engineer's testimony that the Mount Independence defenses would be seriously compromised if the Ticonderoga peninsula was not held).

21. The provisions situation was not as dire as portrayed in the "apology" published in *The New York Gazette*, or as St. Clair argued at his Court Martial. Based upon the evidence, the supply of meat should have lasted at least thirty days, not merely a week to ten days, and there was sufficient flour for sixty days. *See* Ron R. Morgan, supra., 36–41.

22. St. Clair Court Martial, 75.

St. Clair was vindicated when Burgoyne was eventually forced to surrender at Saratoga, at the hands of many of the same troops who had escaped three months earlier. But historians have given St. Clair scant credit for executing a successful retreat, focusing instead on the disputed question of why he had felt compelled to do so.

HISTORIANS WEIGH IN

St. Clair's acquittal brought an official end to the inquiry into the circumstances of the retreat, but the controversy continued as historians struggled to reconcile the conflicting narratives that it had spawned. The stark differences between the British and American accounts presented significant challenges; in particular, Burgoyne's assertion that the Americans were forced to abandon one of their most important posts due to the gross incompetence of their leaders was highly embarrassing, resulting in a temptation to alter the historical record which, as we shall see, some American historians eventually found themselves unable to resist.

The earliest accounts of the Revolution, from the American point of view, reflected the divergent opinions which had arisen in the aftermath of the retreat and at St. Clair's court martial. The viewpoint of the New Englanders is well represented in Mercy Otis Warren's *History of the Rise, Progress, and Termination of the American Revolution*, published in 1805.[23] A redoubtable propagandist of the Revolution, Warren was an ardent detractor of St. Clair, whom she and her fellow New Englanders despised for his shameful action in abandoning the "Gibraltar of the North," leaving New England exposed to Burgoyne's depredations. Describing him as "an officer always unfortunate, and in no instance ever distinguished for bravery or judgment," Warren excoriated St. Clair for, on the one hand, hastily retreating with great loss of supplies and equipment when he had a healthy, recently reinforced and well supplied garrison, and on the other hand, for not retreating soon enough to minimize his losses.[24]

A far more charitable view of St. Clair can be found in Rev. William Gordon's *History of the Rise, Progress, and Establishment, of the Independence of the United States of America*, a four volume work published in 1788.[25] Gordon closely followed the evidence adduced at St. Clair's

23. Mercy Otis Warren, *History of the Rise, Progress, and Termination of the American Revolution*, Vol. II (Boston, 1805), https://archive.org/details/historyofrisepro01warr , accessed March 25, 2016.

24. Ibid., 6–7. This was one of the specific charges brought against St. Clair at the court martial.

25. William Gordon, *The History of the Rise, Progress, and Establishment, of the Independence of the United States of America: Including an Account of the Late War; and of the Thirteen Colonies, from Their Origin to That Period* (London, 1788), https://archive.org/details/historyofrisepro03gordrich, accessed March 25, 2016.

court martial,[26] but he deviated from the historical record in two significant (and not merely coincidental) ways. First, Gordon dodged the
question of whether there were sufficient provisions to withstand a
siege, which had been the subject of extensive testimony and argument
at the court martial. Instead, he simply noted that St. Clair had determined to evacuate as a result of "Schuyler not having force sufficient at
fort Edward to relieve him."[27] Second, Gordon claimed that St. Clair
was well aware of the Sugar Hill vulnerability, which "had been discovered months before upon trial, when a cannon had been drawn up and
fired from the top of it," but due to the smallness of the garrison, he
was unable to occupy it. [28] Thus, without further elaboration, Gordon
deftly disposed of two of the more troublesome issues with respect to
St. Clair's actions, taking the first steps to revise the American narrative
concerning the retreat.

THE FOCUS SHIFTS

As Warren's work demonstrated, long after the war's end many, particularly in New England, were unwilling to accept St. Clair's exoneration
at his court martial, and the controversy lingered. In 1817, James Wilkinson, St. Clair's adjutant general at the time of the retreat, published a
memoir of the Saratoga campaign containing a vigorous defense of St.
Clair's actions.[29] Using his personal recollections, supplemented by direct quotations from primary sources, Wilkinson contended that it was
obvious weeks before Burgoyne appeared on the scene that the situation of the garrison was hopeless if it had to face an enemy of any substantial force.[30] Wilkinson's arguments closely tracked those made by
St. Clair at his court martial, but then he went further, citing British authorities to support his contention that the posts were indefensible.
After quoting directly from Burgoyne's account concerning the decisive
effect of artillery on Sugar Hill, Wilkinson opined:

> Yet from the indolence natural to man, and his disposition to trust
> to appearances, this height had been previously neglected by the
> French, British, and American commanders . . . indeed such appears

26. Ibid., Vol. II, 476–482.
27. Ibid., 480.
28. Ibid., 479–480. Testimony given at St. Clair's court martial contradicts this claim.
See note 47 infra.
29. James Wilkinson, *Memoirs of My Own Times*, (Philadelphia, 1815), https://archive.
org/details/memoirsofmyownti01wilk , accessed March 27, 2016.
30. Ibid., Vol. I, 168–179. Wilkinson maintained that Schuyler and St. Clair both knew
that a withdrawal was advisable when they convened the June 20 council of war, but
that "they were governed more by respect for public opinion than their own understanding." Ibid., 176.

to have been the common error of the engineers in the early settlements of this continent, from Canada to Florida, from Michilimackinac to Natchez, and hence the principle, that a military commander
should determine, never to trust to appearances or the judgment of
any man, where it is practicable for him to examine and judge for
himself.[31]

Wilkinson did not explicitly state that St. Clair decided to retreat as
a direct result of the Sugar Hill debacle, but his critique opened the door
to that conclusion, thus taking a crucial step towards adopting the
British narrative and supplanting the original American one set forth
in painstaking detail in correspondence and court martial testimony
nearly forty years earlier. This seismic shift in focus was reinforced in a
memoir published in 1823[32] by James Thacher, a surgeon at Ticonderoga at the time of the retreat, who observed: "It must be universally
conceded, that when the enemy had effected their great object by hoisting cannon from tree to tree, till they reached the summit of Sugar-loaf
Hill, the situation of our garrison had become perilous in the extreme."[33]

Thus, by the 1820s, the temptation to accept Burgoyne's superficially
compelling and dramatic account of the reason for the retreat had
proven to be irresistible to historians. This prompted the emergence of
remarkable new narratives from two people who were only tangentially
connected to the event.

A MYTH EVOLVES

Once American historians began to accept the assertion that the failure
to fortify Sugar Hill (by this time called Mount Defiance) was a grievous
error that had made an ignominious retreat unavoidable, it was impossible to escape the question it begged: who was responsible for this
egregious oversight? That question undoubtedly put the spotlight on
Schuyler, who was commander of the Northern Department for most
of the year preceding the retreat, but it shown especially brightly on
Maj. Gen. Horatio Gates, who had been in direct command of Ticonderoga and Mount Independence during most of the non-winter

31. Ibid., 192.
32. Although Thacher structured his work as a military journal, it is generally accepted
that the published version contains substantial *post hoc* material grafted on to a less detailed contemporaneous journal. See, e.g., J. L. Bell, "The Harrison-Gerry Anecdote",
Boston 1775, February 29, 2012, http://boston1775.blogspot.com/search/label/Dr.%20
James%20Thacher , accessed March 27, 2016.
33. James Thacher, *Military Journal of the American Revolution, 1775–1783* (an
unabridged reprint)(Corner House Historical Publications, 1998), 85.

months of that period, and who would have been in the best position to recognize and to address the problem. In the 1830s, John Armstrong, Gates' aide de camp at that time, felt compelled to come to Gates' defense.

Writing to the renowned early American historian Jared Sparks,[34] Armstrong asserted that Gates, prior to being relieved of command in May 1777, had determined that Sugar Hill was the key to the entire defensive position at Ticonderoga and Mount Independence, and he had warned St. Clair and others of this fact. Armstrong's "documentation" of these facts consisted of two lengthy letters that he wrote to Sparks in 1831 and 1837.[35]

In 1831, Armstrong described a letter written by Gates to St. Clair, specifically to inform him of "a certain high mound of earth [called] the Sugar Loaf the occupation of which decides the fate of your campaign." In this letter, Gates allegedly states that he had thought of taking possession of the height when he commanded the garrison in 1776, but saw no necessity, because he had been advised that it would be impossible to carry heavy cannon up the sides. Then (in what was evidently a forehead-slapping moment), Gates confessed to St. Clair his realization that lighter howitzers "could easily be carried up [and] would completely answer the purpose of driving off an enemy from either Ti or the Mount." The letter was ostensibly written after Gates had arrived in Philadelphia following his relief from command of the Northern Department. This would place it in mid-June, 1777, when Gates was haranguing the Continental Congress about its decision to replace him with Schuyler.[36] Interestingly, Gates's written notes of his speech to Congress specifically make reference to the critical importance of maintaining the defense of a height of land covering the portage between Ticonderoga and Lake George—but Gates was referring to Mount Hope, not Sugar Hill.[37]

34. Owner and editor of the highly regarded *The North American Review* and author of several multi-volume histories (including *The Writings of George Washington*), Sparks was a pioneer in collecting historical manuscript material and he corresponded extensively with Armstrong in the 1830s.

35. Papers of Jared Sparks, 1820—1861, 1866, Call No. UAI 15.886, Armstrong, John, 1758—1843, "A.L.s to Jared Sparks [Red Hook, December 4, 1831] (8 p.)", Harvard University Archives at 2–4; Ibid. "A.L.s. to Jared Sparks [Red Hook, September 2, 1837] (7 p.) enclosing an account of Kosciuszko".

36. William Duer to Philip Schuyler, June 19, 1777 (relating that Gates had arrived in Philadelphia the day before) Letters of Delegates to Congress: Volume 7 May 1, 1777–September 18, 1777, Library of Congress, American Memory, https://memory.loc.gov/cgibin/query/r?ammem/hlaw:@field(DOCID+@lit(dg007T000)):(4/7/2016).

37. Ibid., Horatio Gates' Notes for a Speech to Congress.

Six years later Armstrong wrote another letter to Sparks, revealing that in the early spring of 1777—*prior to writing the June letter to St. Clair*—Gates had ordered his engineer, Thaddeus Kosciuszko, to determine "whether Sugar Loaf hill could be made practicable to the ascent of guns of large caliber," and that the latter found the hill "may, by the labor of strong fatigue parties, be so shaped as to permit the ascent of the heaviest cannon" and that "a battery so placed, from elevation and proximity, would completely cover the two forts, the bridge of communication and the adjoining boat harbor." Apparently, we are to believe that Gates chose not to convey this critical information to St. Clair in his June letter (favoring a discussion of howitzers instead), nor did he see fit to suggest that St. Clair discuss the matter with Kosciuszko, who was still at the posts and was now under St. Clair's command. Perhaps unsurprisingly, Kosciuszko's detailed report to Gates dated May 1777 is silent on the question of Sugar Hill,[38] and in his testimony at St. Clair's court martial, Kosciuszko said nothing about plans to fortify the hill or about any threat it might have posed to the Mount Independence defenses.[39] To put it bluntly, in the absence of direct evidence in the form of original correspondence from Gates or Kosciuszko with respect to these matters, it is difficult to escape the conclusion that Armstrong's narrative was fabricated, years after the fact, to defend the reputation of his former boss.

In 1841, a new claimant to prescience concerning the Sugar Hill debacle emerged when John Trumbull, the noted Revolutionary era artist, published his autobiography. Trumbull had served for a brief period as General Gates's deputy adjutant-general in the summer and fall of 1776, as the ragged remains of an American army gathered at Ticonderoga and Mount Independence to make a stand after a disastrous retreat from Canada. Trumbull had accompanied various officers as they inspected the terrain and determined the placement of defensive works, and he drew several maps of the fortifications in July and August as work progressed. Trumbull claimed to have become very concerned about "a lofty eminence, called Mount Defiance" which he regarded "as completely overruling our entire position."[40] In a colorful account, Trumbull described his insistence on conducting experiments involving firing cannon from the northern end of Mount Independence and from

38. Kosciuszko to Gates, May 18, 1777, Gates Papers, New York Historical Society (original in French).
39. St. Clair Court Martial, 59–61.
40. John Trumbull, *Autobiography, Reminiscences and Letters, 1756—1841* (New York & London: Wiley & Putnam. New Haven: B.L. Hamlen, 1841), 2–16, 30–31, https://archive.org/details/autobiographyre00trumgoog , accessed April 17.

a spot near Fort Ticonderoga, both aimed towards Mount Defiance, which demonstrated that artillery placed at the summit would be within range of the American fortifications. When some officers insisted that the height was inaccessible to an enemy, he formed a party, consisting of himself, Gen. Benedict Arnold, Col. Anthony Wayne, and other officers, who climbed to the summit, where "it was obvious to all, that there could be no difficulty in driving up a loaded carriage."[41]

Trumbull's account states that, following these experiments, he devised a detailed plan to build a "small but strong post" at the top of Mount Defiance to be held by 500 men and 25 heavy guns, which "would be a more effectual and essentially a less expensive defense of this pass, than all our present extended lines."[42] Trumbull claimed that he sent his proposal to Gates, Schuyler, and Congress, but he was unable to produce a copy for his autobiography, having vainly searched for one among Gates's and Schuyler's papers. Fortunately, according to Trumbull, he found among the papers of his father a drawing of the post that he had made in August, which "sufficiently explains and confirms all that has been said upon this subject."[43]

The drawing to which Trumbull refers, a print of which is included in his autobiography,[44] depicts the Ticonderoga and Mount Independence fortification complex and immediately surrounding area, including Sugar Hill, to which is annotated: "Mount Defiance, a very high Hill— supposed inaccessible for carriages," followed by the words "Proposed Work" and a small fortification symbol. The evidentiary value of this document as support for Trumbull's claims is, however, substantially undermined (if not utterly demolished) by previous scholarship which has shown that the original version of the map used in Trumbull's autobiography contained only the words "Very high Hill. Inaccessible to Carriages."[45] Moreover, it does not appear that the term "Mount Defiance" was in use prior to the retreat.

Testimony at St. Clair's court martial acknowledged that the issue of a Sugar Hill vulnerability was "in agitation" at the time Trumbull was at the posts,[46] and it is entirely possible that Trumbull was involved in,

41. Ibid., 31–32.
42. Ibid., 32–33.
43. Ibid.
44. Online copies of Trumbull's autobiography do not contain a complete copy of the map. For copies of it and related maps drawn by Trumbull, see Joseph R. Frese, "A Trumbull Map of Fort Ticonderoga Rediscovered," *The Bulletin of the Fort Ticonderoga Museum*, Vol. XIII June 1971, 129–136.
45. Ibid., 135.
46. Testimony of Lt. Col. Livingston, St. Clair Court Martial, 116: "to occupy that height with artillery . . . was judged to be impracticable."

if not at the center of, those discussions.[47] Nevertheless, the known evidence makes it highly unlikely that he had convinced other senior officers that placing artillery on Sugar Hill was feasible, as he claimed, or that he even believed so himself at the time.

Ultimately, regardless of their questionable veracity, the Armstrong and Trumbull accounts are non-sequiturs as far as the decision to retreat is concerned; they both presuppose a fact that has never been in evidence: that St. Clair's decision to abandon Mount Independence was compelled by the Sugar Hill/Mount Defiance battery. Nevertheless, the belief that St. Clair had no option but to retreat once he saw the British guns looming above him has become firmly embedded in American historiography. In his magnum opus, the *Pictorial Field Book of the Revolution*, published in 1850, Benson J. Lossing drew upon the transcript of St. Clair's court martial to describe the circumstances surrounding the retreat, but he made the Sugar Hill battery the centerpiece of his narrative,[48] and so it has been for historians ever since, with varying degrees of emphasis.

CONCLUSION

At this point, it is fair to ask: "why does any of this matter?" If St. Clair didn't need Burgoyne's Sugar Hill maneuver to convince him to retreat, the remainder of the historical record obviously demonstrates that St. Clair made the right decision, particularly in light of the subsequent surrender of Burgoyne's army. What else is there to discuss? The "what else?", as it happens, is a point that was emphatically made by St. Clair and many of his contemporaries in the aftermath of Burgoyne's defeat, but which has been almost completely obscured by the controversy surrounding the decision to retreat and historians' obsessive focus on Sugar Hill. The point was that St. Clair's army had escaped, against nearly impossible odds, thereby preserving the vital core of Continental troops that would make a decisive stand against Burgoyne at Saratoga three months later.

47. An appendix to Trumbull's autobiography contains the text of a letter to Trumbull dated November 13, 1837, from General Ebenezer Mattoon, former adjutant general of the Massachusetts militia, describing Mattoon's recollection of personally observing Trumbull conducting the artillery experiment at Mount Independence, concluding: "From this experiment, and subsequent facts, it was fully demonstrated that your opinion was correct and the posts untenable, for, when the enemy at length gained this height, we were actually driven from our encampment." Ibid., 306–307. Mattoon's analysis involves the same *post hoc, ergo propter hoc* reasoning employed by Burgoyne.
48. Benjamin Lossing, *Pictorial Field Book of the Revolution*, Volume I, Chapter VI, (1850), at notes 16–25, https://archive.org/details/pictorialfieldb00lossgoog , accessed April 17, 2016.

Perhaps because the evacuation was largely successful—despite some notable setbacks at Skenesborough and Hubbardton—historians have largely overlooked the circumstances surrounding the conduct of the retreat itself, and Burgoyne's energetic attempts to prevent it. The facts were that on the night of July 5–6, 1777, an American army of more than 4,000 men marched out from under the noses of a better trained and equipped enemy force nearly twice their number, a force determined to prevent their escape, much of which was encamped within a few hundred yards of the American lines. To accomplish this feat, St. Clair had to evacuate the bulk of his force, including a substantial contingent of poorly disciplined militia, via a rugged wilderness track so narrow that the men were obliged to march single file for the first several miles of it, a wilderness in which Burgoyne had more than 500 Indian allies available to harry them and a large German contingent capable of joining in the pursuit in short order. The survival of St. Clair's army under these circumstances was, as one might say, "a neat trick". And therein lies a story.

Benedict Arnold:
Natural Born Military Genius

❋ JAMES KIRBY MARTIN ❋

Denouncing the reputation of Benedict Arnold began immediately after he fled West Point and returned his allegiance to the British empire on September 25, 1780. Without hesitation, contemporaries castigated him as a nefarious human being, a devious villain suddenly well-known to everyone for his "barbarity," "avarice," "ingratitude," and "hypocrisy," in sum nothing more than "a mean toad eater." Stated General Nathanael Greene a week after Arnold's apostasy: "Never since the fall of Lucifer has a fall equaled his."

Since 1780, why Arnold committed treason has remained the focal point of interest about this general officer whom Washington once held high as his best fighting general. Was it insatiable greed, his beguiling second wife Peggy, or Satan himself that provoked Arnold's apostasy? Forgotten in these explorations and denunciations about his allegedly corrupt character is the reason why Arnold's contemporaries were so upset about his apparent treachery: Arnold's natural military genius in support of the Revolution.

Born in January 1741, Benedict Arnold grew up in Norwich, Connecticut, before establishing himself as an apothecary and sea going trading merchant in New Haven. His biggest childhood challenge involved a family crisis that started when a diphtheria epidemic struck his community. His father nearly died, and he lost two of his younger sisters. His father, also named Benedict, once a respected carrying merchant, began to lose his way after seeing his family devastated. He took to drink, became an alcoholic, and eventually succumbed to acute alcoholism.

As the sole surviving son, young Arnold had to step forward as a surrogate head of household, which fits with his only description of himself as a teenager. He portrayed himself as "a coward until he was fifteen years of age" and noted that his adult reputation for "courage" was an "acquired" trait. He was not the little hellion of fictional old wives' tales about his presumed dissolute youth, rather a lad who had to grow up quickly to help take care of his mother and surviving sister Hannah.

His mother, also named Hannah, secured an apprenticeship for him with her cousins, Daniel and Joshua Lathrop, who taught him the apothecary's trade. During these appriced years, the French and Indian War was engulfing the colonies. One set of misleading stories had young Benedict repeatedly enlisting in New York regiments, only to grab bounty money and desert, thereby demonstrating his self-serving, avaricious nature. Apparently, the Lathrop brothers never missed him, even when he was gone for weeks at a time.

In actuality, Arnold's lone military experience before 1775 was about two to three weeks of militia duty in 1757 when French and Indian forces captured and destroyed Fort William Henry at the southern end of Lake George. The Norwich militia unit he joined returned home when the French force withdrew north rather than invading New England.

Benedict Arnold, in sum, entered adulthood with no meaningful military training or experience, unless one counts parading around as a lowly private on militia muster days. At the outset of the Revolutionary War in April 1775, he was at best a military novice, a true amateur in arms. Yet within two years, Arnold had emerged as one of George Washington's most invaluable generals. Nathanael Greene found no hint of Lucifer in Arnold when he described him in late 1776 as "a fine spirited fellow, and active general." Nor did Washington foresee problems when he wrote in 1777 that "surely a more active, a more spirited, and sensible officer, fills no department" of the Continental army.

What was it about Arnold, then, that made him so useful a leader in the pre-treason eyes of Greene and Washington, among many others? Whether in his business dealings or in military operations, Arnold repeatedly demonstrated the inborn capacity to think in broad strategic terms while drawing upon tactical options that would ultimately yield positive results. At times, Arnold seemed to be channeling the precepts of the ancient Chinese military thinker Sun Tzu, sometimes rendered Sun Wu, in his classic volume entitled *The Art of War*. In other situations, the ideas of Sun Tzu would have been too constraining for the martial challenges Arnold faced. Regardless, his capacity to act decisively with well-reasoned boldness, with a fiery temperament thrown in, was Arnold's bountiful gift to the cause of American liberty during the initial phases of the Revolutionary War.

When Arnold first opened his apothecary's store in New Haven in the 1760s, he offered a variety of books for sale, including some military tracts. Even if he perused such volumes, his military acumen could not have radiated back to the Sun Tzu's teachings. The first modern translation of *The Art of War* appeared in the French language during the early 1770s. Apparently no English translation existed until the early twentieth century. Arnold, by his own temperament and instincts, as well as determination and vision, was actually his own teacher. In his seagoing trading ventures to the West Indies and Canada, he often served as the captain of his own vessels. He learned how to handle crews of mariners to get the best efforts from them in daily challenges. No evidence exists that he treated them harshly, rather that he was able to gain their respect by his even-handed leadership.

By 1774, Arnold could smell a civil war brewing within the British empire. An enthusiastic advocate of defending American rights, he organized some sixty-five New Havenites, including a few Yale College students, into what the Connecticut government recognized as the Governor's 2nd Company of Footguards in March 1775. Serving as the elected captain, Arnold prepared to lead the Footguards to the Boston area after learning about the battles of Lexington and Concord. The Footguards had uniforms, paid for by their captain, but they lacked muskets, powder, and ball. These martial necessities were available in New Haven's powder magazine. The cautious town fathers, fearing the spread of a shooting rebellion, refused them entrance. Arnold gave them a few minutes to rethink matters, then informed them that his company would force its way into the magazine unless the keys were forthcoming. Thoroughly intimidated by Arnold's threat, they finally handed over the keys, thereby avoiding a nastier confrontation.

Within a few days, the well-armed Footguards arrived in Cambridge, Massachusetts, where thousands of New Englanders were gathering to pin down Gen. Thomas Gage and his redcoats in Boston. Arnold, for his part, met with such local rebel leaders as Dr. Joseph Warren and spoke of the need to capture the valuable cache of artillery pieces at Fort Ticonderoga and Crown Point on Lake Champlain. In desperate need of such weaponry to help contend with possible British breakouts of Boston, the Massachusetts Committee of Safety gave Arnold a colonel's commission. His orders were to hasten west, recruit a regiment, and seize lightly defended Fort Ticonderoga, which he described as in "ruinous condition," so bad that it "could not hold out an hour against a vigorous onset."

Taking the fort was not a problem, but contending with Vermont's Ethan Allen and the Green Mountain Boys proved a vexing challenge.

Allen and the Boys, operating under apparent authority from Connecticut, were already in position to take Fort Ticonderoga when Arnold caught up with them on the east bank of Lake Champlain. Arnold displayed his commission, but the Boys, a roughhewn lot, laughed at him. Allen was their leader, and they would follow no other, especially since Arnold had no troops with him. Finally, after some shrewd negotiating on Arnold's part, Allen agreed to a joint command. Under cover of darkness, the two of them led a party of Green Mountain Boys across the lake and easily captured the fort with nary a lost life on May 10, 1775.

Too often, through the prism of treason, Arnold has been portrayed as an impulsive, needlessly confrontational military leader. In reality, he was often a master of patience and restraint, concentrating on the goals he wanted to achieve. Such was the case with Allen and the Boys. To him, they were not exactly enthusiastic patriots determined to secure valuable ordnance pieces for the cause of liberty. Rather, he viewed them as frontier ruffians mostly interested in plundering whatever goods they could find in the fort.

Once inside, the Boys rejoiced when they discovered ninety gallons of rum. Getting roaring drunk, they repeatedly belittled Arnold; and two of them apparently took pot shots at him. Still, these "wild people," as he called them, did not intimidate Arnold. Showing impressive forbearance, as he so often did during his military career, he kept his fiery temperament in check and waited out the Boys until they drifted back across the lake to Vermont territory with various forms of plunder in hand.

Arnold had shown wisdom in his dealings with Allen and the Boys, a key characteristic for successful commanders according to Sun Tzu. He had not let personal differences and insults divert him from the mission of gaining access to the much needed military ordnance. Once in charge, Arnold focused on pulling together his own regiment at Fort Ticonderoga. Tearing off his cautionary mask, he did something else that Sun Tzu would have commended. He went on the offensive and attacked when the enemy was not expecting a quick-hitting strike.

Concerned about a possible British counter stroke coming out of Canada to retake the fort, Arnold seized the initiative. In mid-May he led a small force north down Lake Champlain and twenty-five miles into Canada. They struck the British stronghold of St. Johns, completely surprising a handful of defenders there. He and his raiders seized small weapons and two 6–pounder cannons, destroyed any small craft they could find, and sailed away in a British sloop later named the *Enterprise*.

By this one aggressive stroke, Arnold had taken command of the lake. Nearly a year and a half would go by before the British attempted an invasion of their own out of Canada. As for Arnold, after many more adventures, he would be waiting to greet them, this time as the commodore of the hastily assembled rebel fleet on Lake Champlain.

In mid-June 1775, Arnold sent a letter to the Continental Congress in which he advocated the movement of a large patriot force into Canada to seize and secure Quebec Province as the fourteenth colony in rebellion. Why? Having sailed his own trading vessels into such Canadian ports as Quebec and Montreal, he understood the terrain. He could envision what would become British strategy in 1776: to surround New England and cut off the head of the rebellion. The British, as they would do, deployed masses of troops to New York City and Quebec Province in an effort to take control of the Lake Champlain/Hudson River corridor. Having cut off New England from the rest of the colonies, these forces were to sweep eastward while Royal Naval warships put pressure on such key port towns as Boston on the Atlantic Ocean side.

In his letter, Arnold stressed the need to "frustrate" a major portion of Britain's "cruel and unjust plan of operation" to squeeze life out of the rebellion in New England by sending one invading force south through Canada. Seizing Quebec Province would disrupt that move while also assuring "a free government" there fully dedicated to liberty. Furthermore, Canada could serve as "an inexhaustible granary in case we are reduced to want," should a long-term war eventuate. Arnold closed by laying out an operational plan to invade Quebec Province "without loss of time." He offered to take command of his proposed expeditionary force, confident that "the smiles of heaven" would soon be blessing the patriot cause.

Arnold instinctively appreciated the strategic maxim of Sun Tzu: "Thus the highest form of generalship is to balk the enemy's plans." Attack yes, Congress soon concluded, but not with the likes of Arnold in command, not initially. Congress was an unabashed political body, and Arnold had few insider connections. Further, the Massachusetts rebels, complaining of the costs they were mostly bearing in standing up to the British around Boston, got Connecticut to agree to pick up the expense tab in the Champlain region. Despite his highly meritorious effort there, Arnold found himself dumped from command after Connecticut agreed to send troops to garrison Fort Ticonderoga and Crown Point under the well-connected but uninspiring Col. Benjamin Hinman.

As events played themselves out, overall command of the invasion through Lake Champlain would go to Congress's designated Northern Department commander, wealthy Philip Schuyler of New York. He rated Arnold's performance at Fort Ticonderoga and Crown Point as fully meritorious. In August 1775 Schuyler and others brought Arnold to George Washington's attention. His Excellency had recently taken command of rebel forces encircling Boston. Meeting with Arnold, he too saw merit in the energetic patriot and the ideas he was sharing.

Arnold accepted Washington's offer of a Continental colonel's commission with the assignment to lead one of two patriot forces into Canada. Thus began a martial adventure that would culminate with the defeat and surrender of Gen. John Burgoyne's army at Saratoga in October 1777. One detachment under Schuyler, who fell ill and turned the command over to Brig. Gen. Richard Montgomery, headed north down Lake Champlain and captured Montreal in mid-November. Arnold's column, meanwhile, struggled through the backwoods of Maine and, after much suffering, reached the Plains of Abraham outside the injudicious city of Quebec, also in mid-November. Arnold's personal stamina and boundless energy during this death-defying trek through the wilderness earned him the epithet "America's Hannibal" and a brigadier generalship awarded him by Congress.

The two detachments rallied together as one before Quebec City in December but failed to gain a victory in a desperate attempt to breach the city's gates under cover of a driving blizzard on the last day of 1775. The plan of attack, Arnold knew, was impetuous and born of desperation, not the kind Sun Tzu would have approved for a military force much weaker than Quebec's defenders. Reality, however, dictated ill-advised action, since the enlistment periods of patriot soldiers were over at the end of that day. Arnold and Montgomery felt they had no choice but to attack before some portion of their force disappeared into the woods and returned to New England.

Montgomery, heading one column, was killed instantly from a cannon blast; Arnold, heading a second, sustained a nasty wound to his left leg that knocked him out of the assault. Before the fighting was over, dozens of patriots lay dead or wounded with over 400 taken prisoner by the defending British forces under the command of Gov. Guy Carleton.

What was amazing was that Arnold refused to quit. As his badly wounded leg began to heal, he drew on his boundless energy to maintain a paper siege of sorts around Quebec City with the few troops he had left. He spent the winter season, as he wrote, laboring "under almost as many difficulties as the *Israelites* of old, obliged to make brick without straw." Arnold drew up plans to break into the walled city but lacked the necessary resources to do so. In the end, despite an ennobling effort by Congress to send more troops to Canada, Quebec Province could not be held. As British strategy dictated, British and Hessian reinforcements began arriving at Quebec City during May 1776. By late June, they had driven the whole of patriot forces, now riddled with smallpox and other diseases, all the way back to Fort Ticonderoga.

Typical of his fighting character, Arnold was among the last rebels to leave Canadian soil. He was among the first to think through operational plans to block the British military invasion that was sure to come out of Quebec Province. By June 1776 a massive British land and sea invasion of the rebellious colonies was under way. Given the limited size of most eighteenth-century military forces, British numbers, including Hessians, were impressive. By early August some 45,000 soldiers and sailors were getting into position to capture and establish New York City as their main base of operations; another 8,000 were preparing to move out of Canada and crush patriot resisters in the northern theater. By mid-summer, Governor Carleton, with John Burgoyne serving as his second in command, was assembling a flotilla of vessels to move south with his army in tow across Lake Champlain.

From Arnold's perspective, the key step was to block or, better yet, drive Carleton's advancing force back into Canada. In doing so, he worked closely with Northern Department commander Philip Schuyler and former British field grade officer Horatio Gates, now a major general in the Continental army. Schuyler would operate as the key supply officer, and Gates would take charge of strengthening the rebel defensive line at Fort Ticonderoga. As for Arnold, he would demonstrate a kind of versatility never imagined by Sun Tzu. At the request of Schuyler, Arnold agreed to serve as commodore of the rebel fleet being assembled on Lake Champlain, a daunting assignment that involved constructing enough vessels to put on a show of defiance that might frighten off the expected British onslaught.

Readying the fleet was a major undertaking, but by mid-September enough vessels were in the water for Arnold to sail north toward the Canadian border. Nine of the craft were gundalows, really overgrown bateaux. They were flat-bottomed boats, each having a fixed sail and the capacity to carry a crew of up to forty-five men as well as a few ordnance pieces. They could sail with the wind but could not maneuver to the windward, so crew members had to be prepared to pull at oars when needed.

Arnold, for his part, pushed for the construction of row galleys, larger craft featuring two masts rigged with lateen sails that could swivel with the wind. Such rigging gave the row galleys much more maneuverability than the gundalows, regardless of the wind's direction. In addition, the fleet had a few other craft, including the sloop *Enterprise* that Arnold had captured when he and his raiders launched their surprise attack on

St. John's back in 1775. Three schooners were also available, including the *Royal Savage*, captured from the British during Montgomery's advance into Canada. This vessel served as Arnold's flagship until three row galleys—the *Congress*, *Trumbull*, and *Washington*—joined the flotilla. Arnold moved over to the *Congress* and designated this craft his flagship.

Assembling the fleet was one challenge being conquered, given the shortage of skilled ships' carpenters plus the lack of such essential supplies as cordage, sailcloth, and various kinds of cannon shot. A second was preparing orders to guide Arnold's actions on the lake. This assignment, wrote Gates, was "momentous" in the critical objective to secure "the northern entrance into this side of the continent." Arnold was to operate by conducting "defensive war." He was to take "no wanton risk" with the fleet, yet he was to display his "courage and abilities" in "preventing the enemy's invasion of our country." In other words, he was not to conduct such offensive operations as sailing into Canada and attacking the British fleet then being assembled at St. Johns. Rather, he was "to act with such cool, determined valor, as will give them [the enemy] reason to repent their temerity" in their movement up the lake toward the patriot defenders then gathering at Fort Ticonderoga.

By any reasonable measure, Arnold had accepted an impossible military assignment, once again not the kind that Sun Tzu would have endorsed. The ancient Chinese strategist had warned about the danger of a smaller force attempting "an obstinate fight" with a larger one, which in the end would result in its being "captured by the larger force." Arnold knew he was commanding the inferior fleet, made worse by crews of soldiers with no sailing experience. Sun Tzu had declared that "if slightly inferior in numbers, . . . avoid the enemy," and "if quite unequal in every way, . . . flee from him." Even on the defensive, Arnold could not flee. His only hope for retarding the British was to innovate, and innovate this natural military genius did.

Sun Tzu had declared that "all warfare is based on deception," a principle that Arnold instinctively understood. Even before the row galleys were available, he led his less than impressive fleet of about twelve vessels toward Canada, arriving near the border in mid-September. Once there he acted as if he might sail north down the Richelieu River to St. Johns where the British fleet was assembling. In reality, Arnold was just putting on a show with no intention of engaging in offensive operations. Rather, his purpose was to intimidate, if possible, Governor Carleton, who received scouting reports about the fleet's presence and seemingly readiness for combat.

The ruse worked. Even though the British governor already had Arnold's fleet outnumbered and outgunned, he hesitated. To assure complete superiority, Carleton refused to let his flotilla proceed south until the final assembly of a sloop of war, the *Inflexible*, a craft that mounted eighteen 12–pounder cannons and was superior in firepower to any vessel available to Arnold. On October 4, Carleton finally ordered his flotilla to move out. Having noted the presence of the "considerable naval force" waiting to defend Lake Champlain, his objective was to sweep aside that fleet and retake Crown Point and Fort Ticonderoga before early winter weather in this northern clime would halt further operations pointing toward New England.

Sun Tzu had advised to "learn the principle" of an opponent's capacity for "activity or inactivity." During the months when Arnold maintained a paper siege of Quebec City, he sized up his chief opponent Carleton as a cautiously calculating leader. The governor would not take unnecessary risks, even when he held the military advantage, unless he was sure he had totally superior military strength. As such, Arnold's brassy appearance near the Canadian border had caused Carleton to delay three critical weeks, which gave the patriots more time to strengthen defenses at Fort Ticonderoga. Pretending he would take aggressive action when committed to defensive maneuvers secured Arnold as a winner of the first round in the game of martial wits.

The Champlain commodore knew something else of critical importance. Despite the pleadings of General Schuyler, Fort Ticonderoga was short on supplies of powder and ball and could not stand up to a sustained British onslaught. As such, the patriot fleet could not just stand by and let Carleton and his minions move easily up the lake without significant resistance. Only a dramatic—and very real—show of force might convince the governor to return to Canada, despite his superior strength. Arnold could count on sixteen vessels, but Carleton had thirty-six, including twenty-eight gunboats, smaller craft that carried one sizable cannon (12 to 24 pounders) each. The British, with 417 artillery pieces, held a more than four-to-one advantage in firepower, since Arnold's fleet mounted only 91 cannons, including small swivel guns. Just as bad, Arnold's crews contained few sailors, whereas the British crews were full of experienced mariners.

What Arnold did have was the creative vision and energy to fight Carleton's fleet to a draw of sorts. Like Sun Tzu, the American commodore realized that understanding "the natural formation of the country is the soldier's best ally." Terrain mattered, especially if Arnold could find a location on Lake Champlain that would both surprise the enemy and neutralize Carleton's crew and firepower advantages. While cruising down the lake toward Canada, Arnold had spotted that location, a bay close to the New York shoreline hidden to any fleet moving south.

Blocking the view from the lake's main channel was Valcour Island, which rose to 180 feet in height. The bay itself was a half-mile wide, and by late September Arnold had his fleet nestled together in a half-moon formation, getting ready for combat.

Arnold explained that this defensive battle line would mean that only a "few vessels can attack us at the same time, and those will be exposed to the fire of the whole fleet." He was correct. On the morning of October 11, 1776, Carleton's fleet, riding a crisp northerly wind, cruised around the eastern side of Valcour Island intent on reaching Fort Ticonderoga some seventy miles away. About two miles south of the island the British finally spied the waiting Americans, but hauling into the wind broke up the fleet's formation. What ensued was a battle that fit Arnold's prediction. The whole of the British flotilla, trying to maneuver against the wind, could not get into an organized battle line. As a result, even though the patriot craft suffered serious damages with many casualties, the Champlain fleet was still functional when nightfall ended the battle.

For his part, Carleton was satisfied with the day's results. As soon as the wind started blowing from the south, his flotilla could move in and finish off the patriot fleet. Arnold realized the same. Now for all practical purposes trapped in the bay, his vessels were sitting ducks waiting for total obliteration. Up to this point, "the clever combatant" Arnold, in the words of Sun Tzu, had succeeded in imposing "his will on the enemy." Now the question was whether Arnold possessed the genius to "not allow the enemy's will to be imposed on him." What he and his captains observed as night approached was that the British had left a small opening for escape close to the New York shoreline; and escape they did. Taking advantage of a heavy fog, the patriot vessels formed into a single line and used muffled oars to row through that gap. When the fog lifted the next morning, an astonished Carleton could not believe what he beheld. Valcour Bay was empty of American craft.

Now the race up the lake was on. By October 13, the British were starting to overrun the damaged, slow moving American vessels near a land form called Split Rock. Arnold, conscious of munitions shortages at Fort Ticonderoga, had to act decisively to slow the enemy advance. He did so in one of the most unheralded fighting moments of the whole Revolutionary War. Aboard the *Congress*, he issued orders to have his craft turn northward to take on swarming enemy vessels. For something like two hours, he and his crew engaged in close quarter combat with three of Carleton's vessels having a five-fold advantage in firepower. Soon four more enemy craft joined in the pounding. It was like a fight to death in which one opponent kept landing knockout punches but with no referee calling the ten count. All but completely battered with "the sails, rigging, and hull of the *Congress* . . . shattered and torn to pieces," Arnold somehow maneuvered his foundering vessel, along with the four torn up gundalows that he was protecting, into a small bay in Vermont territory where the British could not reach them. To leave nothing for the enemy, he ordered all five vessels set on fire before he and his crew made their way overland, reaching Fort Ticonderoga the next day.

Arnold's courageously aggressive performance in defending Lake Champlain had significant consequences, both for the Revolution and for himself. Governor Carleton, amazed by the death-defying spirit of Arnold and the patriot fleet, moved his forces up to Crown Point but then hesitated. Burgoyne was ready to take on Fort Ticonderoga, but Carleton started to fret about supply lines back to Canada, especially with the winter season looming. In early November, the governor decided to withdraw his whole force back to Canada to wait out the winter before launching another invasion in 1777. Affecting the pullback decision was Arnold's bravado at the northern end of the lake that delayed the British flotilla from launching its invasion for three critical weeks. Also, the death-defying heroics of Arnold and his patriot fleet had intimidated Carleton. With such fighting prowess displayed by the rebels, certainly a reversal of what the governor had observed earlier that year when patriot forces pulled out of Canada, he was no longer sure he could capture Fort Ticonderoga without grave results, possibly even defeat.

Benedict Arnold's natural born military brilliance had helped save the patriot cause in the northern theater, at least for another year. Members of the Continental Congress called Arnold a true hero, but demeaning voices were also in play. Brig. Gen. William Maxwell, a former British field-grade officer devoid of martial accomplishments who was then at Ticonderoga, labeled Arnold "our evil genius to the north." According to Maxwell, Arnold's "pretty piece of admiralship" had wasted the Champlain fleet. He claimed nothing more than personal aggrandizement had motivated Arnold, just another self-serving showoff who in reality had actually outwitted and disrupted a major part of British military operations in 1776.

Sun Tzu called any general "a heaven-born captain" who could "modify his tactics in relation to his opponent and thereby succeed in winning." Through deceptive tactics and strategic vision, Arnold lost the fleet but won the northern campaign in 1776. More than a hundred years later, long after the Revolutionary generation was dead and gone, the famous naval historian Capt. Alfred Thayer Mahan wrote in his classic *The Influence of Sea Power upon History, 1660–1783* (1890): "The little American navy on Champlain was wiped out; but never had any force, big or small, lived to better purpose or died more gloriously, for it saved the Lake for that year."

During 1777 Arnold stepped forward again and provided invaluable service to the American cause. His vision and courage came through dramatically in the defeat and capture of General Burgoyne's invading army. That, however, is another story. Even before the momentous Saratoga campaign, Benedict Arnold had established himself as Washington's fighting general and commodore, an amateur in arms but also a natural military genius who tenaciously outwitted superior enemy forces in 1776. That Arnold turned against the cause of liberty he once so enthusiastically embraced was both a shock and an embarrassment to his contemporaries. To preserve the good name of the Revolution, he had to be stripped of his accomplishments and denounced as "a mean toad eater," misled by greed, Peggy, and the devil, or some depraved combination thereof. As a result, the natural born military genius Benedict Arnold remains to this day an accursed being, likely forever shunned from the pantheon of American heroes.

The Rhetoric and Practice of Scalping

⁂ ZACHARY BROWN ⁂

Scalping, the removal of the scalp from the head often for use as a trophy, is usually regarded as a uniquely sanguineous Indian practice confined to America's distant colonial past. However, little remembered today is the important role the practice played during the Revolutionary War. While traditionally seen by colonials as a symbol of Indian barbarity, the role of scalping was reimagined during the Revolution as "Englishmen scalped Englishmen in the name of liberty."[1] Throughout the war Patriots and Tories scalped to terrorize their foes while also claiming that their enemy's willingness to scalp proved that their cause embodied Indian savagery.

Accusations of scalping emerged as early as the first engagement of the war at Lexington and Concord. Ensign Jeremy Lister of the 10th Regiment of Foot, serving under Capt. Parsons, reported finding "4 men of the 4th company killd who [were] afterwards scap'd their Eyes goug'd their Noses and Ears cut of, such barbarity . . . could scarcely be paralelld by the most uncivilised Savages."[2] Gen. Thomas Gage, the royal governor of Massachusetts and commander in chief of British forces in North America, sought to capitalize on the rumors of atrocities committed by the minutemen at Concord in an attempt to swiftly turn public opinion against the Patriot cause. He reported his own version of the events in a broadside published by Loyalist printer John Howe,

---

1. James Axtell, "Scalping: The Ethnohistory of a Moral Question," in *The European and the Indian: Essays in the Ethnohistory of Colonial North America* (New York: Oxford University Press, 1981), 241.

2. Jeremy Lister, *The Concord Fight: Being So Much of the Narrative of Ensign Jeremy Lister of the 10th Regiment of Foot as Pertains to His Services on the 19th of April, 1775, and to His Experiences in Boston During the Early Months of the Siege* (Cambridge: Harvard University Press, 1931), 27.

claiming that the three companies commanded by Parsons "observed three Soldiers on the Ground one of them scalped, his Head much mangled, and his Ears cut off, tho' not quite dead; a Sight which struck the Soldiers with horror."[3]

While it remains unclear if the minutemen did in fact scalp British troops at Concord this mattered little in the ensuing controversy and press war that followed the battle. The British press lambasted American colonials for embracing the cruel tactics of Indian war, claiming that they used "savageness unknown to Europeans" and even declared sardonically "their humanity is written in the indelible characters with the blood of the soldiers scalped and googed [sic] at Lexington."[4] The Massachusetts Provincial Congress responded to the allegations of Indian savagery by claiming that Gage's account was fraudulent and meant only to "dishonor the Massachusetts people, and to make them appear to be savage and barbarous."[5] While the scalping incident at the North Bridge, whether real or not, would soon fade into obscurity, the British and Loyalist press's likening of Patriots to Indian savages due to their willingness to scalp set an important precedent which would persist until the end of the war.

Ironically, despite the incident at Concord, the most infamous reports of scalping from the Revolutionary period come from the Patriot press in accusations leveled against British and Loyalist forces. These accusations emerged as effective weapons to garner support for the Patriot cause by stimulating deep-seated racial fears as when "speaking of scalping, founding American citizens spoke meaningfully, making sense of their world, joining Indian barbarity to imperial cruelty."[6] Consequently, as the war progressed, British and Loyalist troops were often charged with encouraging their Indian allies to scalp Continentals and even civilians. Based mostly on hearsay, the Lieutenant Governor and Superintendent of Indian Affairs Henry Hamilton became a hated figure along the American frontier and was derisively named the "Hair-buyer General" following accusations that he incited "the Indians to perpetu-

3. Thomas Gage, *A Circumstantial Account of an Attack that Happened on the 19th of April 1775, on his Majesty's Troops* (Boston: Broadside Printed by John Howe, 1775).

4. John Moir, *Obedience the best charter, or, Law the only sanction of liberty: in a letter to the Rev. Dr. Price* (London: Published for Richardson and Urquhart, 1776), 55. "An Answer to the Declaration of Independence," in *The Scots Magazine*, 39 (1777), 237.

5. *A Narrative of the Excursion and Ravages of the King's Troops Under the Command of General Gage, On the nineteenth of April, 1775* (Worcester: Printed by Isaiah Thomas, by order of the Provincial Congress, 1775).

6 Gregory E. Dowd, *Groundless: Rumors, Legends, and Hoaxes on the Early American Frontier* (Baltimore: John Hopkins University Press, 2015), 170.

A Scene on the Frontiers as Practiced by the Humane British and Their Worthy Allies, 1812. British general Henry Hamilton was the most infamous practitioner of this policy, earning him the nickname "The Hair Buyer." (See page 363.)

ate their accustomed cruelties" including "the indiscriminate murther of men, Women and children with the usual circumstances of barbarity practised by the Indian savages" by providing "standing rewards for [white] scalps, but [offering] none for prisoners."[7] While most reports of scalping perpetrated against Patriots involved allied Indian groups, these accusations often extended to British and Loyalist troops themselves. The South Carolina Loyalist, and commander of the King's Rangers, Thomas Brown was vilified across the South for embracing the tactics of Indian war to instill terror in his Patriot enemies, particularly scalping the sick and wounded, an accusation he long denied.[8]

The best-known case of scalping during the Revolution is the tale of Jane McCrea, a women who was engaged to a Loyalist lieutenant when she was abducted, scalped, and shot by Indians under the command of British Lt. Gen. John Burgoyne. Continental commanders immediately

7. "Order of Virginia Council of State Placing Henry Hamilton and Others in Irons, 16 June 1779," in *The Papers of James Madison*, vol. 1, *16 March 1751–16 December 1779*, ed. William T. Hutchinson and William M. E. Rachal (Chicago: The University of Chicago Press, 1962), 288. "From Thomas Jefferson to Theodorick Bland, 8 June 1779," in *The Papers of Thomas Jefferson*, vol. 2, *1777–18 June 1779*, ed. Julian P. Boyd (Princeton: Princeton University Press, 1950), 286.
8. Maya Jasanoff, *Liberties Exiles: American Loyalists in the Revolutionary War* (New York: Vintage, 2012), 45.

realized that the incident could be used to garner greater popular support and military recruits for their cause. To this effect, Maj. Gen. Horatio Gates wrote a scathing letter to Burgoyne in September 1777, with copies sent to Congress and many Philadelphia newspaper presses, primarily blaming the British for the incident:[9]

> That the savages of America should in their warfare mangle and scalp the unhappy prisoners, who fall into their hands, is neither new nor extraordinary; but that the famous Lieut General. Burgoyne, in whom the fine gentleman is united with the soldier and the scholar should hire the Savages of America to scalp Europeans and the descendants of Europeans; nay more, that he should pay a price for each scalp so barbarously taken, is more than will be believed in England until authenticated facts shall in every Gazette, convince mankind of the truth of the horrid tale—Miss McCrea, a young lady lovely to the sight, of virtuous character and amiable disposition, engaged to be married to an officer in your army; [she] was . . . carried into the woods, and there scalped and mangled in the most shocking manner . . . [by] murderers employed by you.[10]

Once distributed throughout the colonies the tale of Jane McCrea led to an explosion of anti-British and anti-Loyalist literature, much of which contained rhetoric directly conflating the Tory cause with Indian cruelty.

This rhetoric of British and Indian convergence took many forms following the scalping of McCrea. A popular 1778 poem by Wheeler Case memorialized McCrea by blaming the British directly for supporting the atrocity and likened them to savages:

> Oh cruel savages! what hearts of steel!
> O cruel Britons! who no pity feel!
> Where did they get the knife, the cruel blade?
> From Britain it was sent, where it was made.
> The tom'hawk and the murdering knife were sent
> To barb'rous savages for this intent.[11]

9. Peter R. Silver, *Our Savage Neighbors: How Indian War Transformed Early America* (New York: W. W. Norton, 2009), 246.

10. William Digby, *The British invasion from the north: the campaigns of Generals Carleton and Burgoyne, from Canada, 1776–1777, with the journal of Lieut. William Digby, of the 53d, or Shropshire regiment of foot*, ed. James P. Baxter (Albany: J. Munsell's Sons, 1887), 262.

11. Rev. Wheeler Case, *Revolutionary memorials* (New York: M.W. Dodd, 1852), 39.

The strongest proponents of the Revolution used this new rhetoric of likening the British to Indian savages to great effect. Thomas Paine wrote to British military official Sir Guy Carleton claiming that the British and Loyalists did not differ from Indians in either their conduct or character. Paine even added that while the "history of the most savage Indians does not produce instances [of cruelty] exactly of this kind," as Indians at least had "formality in their punishment," there was not a more "detestable character, nor a meaner or more barbarous enemy, than the present British one."[12] These attacks on the British and Loyalists for supporting and enabling Indian cruelty eventually took on an explicitly racial tone. To this effect, an anonymous writer for the Philadelphia *Freeman's Journal* declared in 1781 that the British, despite all their achievements in the last centuries, were "the same brutes and savages they were when Julius Caesar invaded . . . for it is certain their mixture with the Saxons and other foreigners, has done very little toward their civilization," explaining why they were willing to scalp and become "so bloody, so barbarous a nation . . . whose hands *have been,* and *will yet* be dyed in [Americans'] blood."[13] As a result of this rhetoric, even some English writers began to question Britain's alliances with Indians. In his 1778 book *English Humanity No Paradox, or An Attempt to Prove that the English Are Not a Nation of Savages,* Edward Long harshly criticized British policy in the New World, writing that they had become "patrons and abettors of *Wanton Homicide,*" by inciting "Cannibal Indians to scalp, tomahawk, and torture, with undistinguishing fury . . . [leading to] killings in cool blood, rapes, torturing, rapines, and devastations."[14] Evidently, British cruelty and eagerness to scalp Americans was now understood by many as a natural product of their immutable racial and national character. Through their denouncements of scalping, Patriots now argued that Englishness, which they had celebrated just years prior, was a natural condition no better than that of savage Indians.

The great irony of this rhetoric is that at the very same time Patriots were also scalping for their own purposes, often using this racial rhetoric of British and Loyalist savagery to justify violence against these groups.

12. Thomas Paine, "A Supernumerary Crisis. To Sir Guy Carleton," in *Crisis Papers* (Philadelphia, 1782).
13. *The Philadelphia Freeman's Journal,* September 19, 1781.
14. Edward Long, *English humanity no paradox: or, an attempt to prove, that the English are not a nation of savages* (London: Printed for T. Lowndes, 1778), 81–82, 90.
15 Dowd, *Groundless: Rumors, Legends, and Hoaxes on the Early American Frontier,* 183.

This new readiness to scalp was a significant transformation, as in earlier American history colonials only approved when done through bounties so that the actual act of scalping remained out of sight and was carried out by allied Indians rather than whites.[15] However, this attitude began to change during the French and Indian War as colonial authorities began to offer scalping bounties advocating that whites should scalp as symmetrical retribution against the tactics of Indian warfare. The New English colonies issued scalping bounties by 1755, most famously the Phips Proclamation in Massachusetts which offered fifty pounds for the scalps of Penobscot Indians, while the Deputy Governor of Pennsylvania Robert Morris proclaimed a general bounty for Indian scalps in 1756.[16] The purpose for these bounties was explicitly racial and genocidal with Pennsylvania government official James Hamilton justifying the bounties as "the only way to clear our Frontiers of . . . Savages, & . . . infinitely cheapest in the end."[17]

Once regarded as a uniquely violent form of Indian cruelty, the practice was thus increasingly normalized among colonial whites. David Owens, a British deserter who had taken refuge with Indians and married a Delaware women, gained fame during Pontiac's Rebellion after he murdered his companions, shooting two, killing a third with a hatchet, and tomahawking to death the women and children. He then scalped the adults in an attempt to collect a scalping bounty and make peace with British authorities as he returned to Philadelphia.[18] Following the war the Paxton Boys, a vigilante group composed of Scottish and Irish frontiersmen from central Pennsylvania, were often accused of emulating Indian savagery in their attempts at retribution against Native Americans. These accusations included taking an "enemy Indian . . . examining him . . . [and as] the Indian begged for his life and promised to tell all what he know . . . they shott him in the midst of them, scalped him and threw his Body into the River."[19] Other colonial

16. Henry J. Young, "A Note on Scalp Bounties in Pennsylvania," *Pennsylvania History* 24 (1957), 207.
17. Silver, *Our Savage Neighbors,* 161.
18. "From Benjamin Franklin to [Peter Collinson?], 12 April 1764," *The Papers of Benjamin Franklin,* vol. 11, *January 1, through December 31, 1764,* ed. Leonard W. Labaree (New Haven and London: Yale University Press, 1967), 180. Stephen Brumwell, *Redcoats: The British Soldier and War in the Americas, 1755–1763* (Cambridge: Cambridge University Press, 2006), 175.
19. "Conrad Weiser to Governor Robert Morris, December 22, 1755," in *Colonial Records: Minutes of the Provincial Council of Pennsylvania from the organization to the termination of the proprietary government. v. 11–16 Minutes of the Supreme Executive Council of Pennsylvania from its organization to the termination of the revolution* (Philadelphia: J. Severns & Company, 1851), 763.

scalpers were primarily motivated by the potential profits from state sponsored bounties. During the French and Indian War freelance soldier James Cargill of Newcastle, Maine, led a scouting party which killed and scalped twelve peaceful Penobscot Indians to receive bounty payments, which he received after being arrested, put on trial, and found not guilty of murder.[20] While the actual effectiveness and profitability of these bounties is much debated it undoubtedly got numerous whites to scalp on an unprecedented scale.[21]

This transformation in colonial attitudes reemerged during the Revolutionary period as the war allowed Americans to find new justifications to scalp their foes. Indians still remained the most common targets. During the Sullivan Expedition in 1779, an offensive against frontier Loyalists and the British allied nations of the Iroquois Confederacy, Lt. William Barton reported that near the town of Canesaah, New York, Continentals captured, killed, and scalped fleeing Indians.[22] During the same expedition, celebrated Patriot sharpshooter Timothy Murphy reportedly scalped an "unsuspecting elder . . . [and] two innocents," and "bragged of killing and scalping every Native he happened across."[23] It is important to note that while independent soldiers preformed many if not most incidents of scalping by Continentals, high-ranking officers occasionally encouraged it. Following the siege of Fort Sackville in Indiana the American commander George Rogers Clark ordered that four Indian prisoners be executed with tomahawks and scalped before their bodies were thrown in the river and their scalped hair displayed on the fort's main gate.[24] While the claim is likely embellishment meant to sully his reputation, Clark's British enemies also asserted that he had performed the scalping himself. Henry Hamilton's aide Lt. Jacob Schieffelin reported that Clark led the ritualized execution, as he "took a tomahawk, and in cold blood knocked their brains

20. Robert Francis Seybolt, "Hunting Indians in Massachusetts: A Scouting Journal of 1758," *The New England Quarterly*, 3 (1930), 528–531. Michael Dekker, *French & Indian Wars in Maine* (Mount Pleasant: Arcadia Publishing, 2015), 120.

21. Silver, *Our Savage Neighbors*, 161–162.

22. Frederick Cook ed., *Journals of the military expedition of Major General John Sullivan against the Six nations of Indians in 1779; with records of centennial celebrations; prepared pursuant to chapter 361, laws of the state of New York, of 1885* (Auburn: Knapp, Peck & Thompson, Printers, 1887), 11.

23. Barbara A. Ann, *George Washington's War on Native America* (Reno: University of Nevada Press, 2008), 94, 95, 97.

24. Bernard W. Sheehan, "'The Famous Hair Buyer General': Henry Hamilton, George Rogers Clark, and the American Indian," *Indiana Magazine of History,* 79 (1983), 20. Theodore Savas, and J. David Dameron, *Guide to the Battles of the American Revolution* (New York: Savas Beatie, 2010), 202.

out, dipping his hands in blood, rubbing it several times on his cheeks, yelping as a Savage." Hamilton added that following the scalping Clark "spoke with rapture of his late achievement, while he washed of the blood from his hand's stain'd in this inhuman sacrifice."[25] Ironically, Clark had merely a few weeks prior denounced the savagery of British and Indian conduct on the frontier in a letter to then Virginia Governor Patrick Henry and singled out Hamilton, who was among the captured at Fort Sackville, as "The Famous Hair Buyer General."[26] Nevertheless, Patriots widely approved and often celebrated such atrocities openly when committed against Indians, like the Providence newspaper *American journal and general advertiser*, which in 1779 praised Continental Brig. Gen. Edward Hand for destroying the Iroquois capital of Onondaga and collecting a "great number of scalps" in the process.[27]

Evidently, like in the French and Indian War before it, the scalping of Indians by white Americans was an important, but largely uncontroversial, reality of fighting in the Revolutionary War, especially along the frontier. However, far more contentious was Patriots' newfound willingness to scalp other Englishmen, something that would have been unthinkable in earlier colonial history. A particularly interesting case is that of the aforementioned Loyalist militia leader Thomas Brown, who, in August 1775, was abducted from his home, tarred and feathered, and scalped by a Patriot mob. Brown later recounted the incident in a letter sent to British commander Lt. Gen. Charles Cornwallis:

> I was ordered to appear before a committee then sitting in Augusta, and on my refusal to attend, a party consisting of 130 armed men headed by the committee surrounded my house in South Carolina and ordered me to surrender myself a prisoner and subscribe a traitorous association. I told them my determination to defend myself if any person presumed to molest me. On their attempting to disarm me, I shot one of the ringleaders . . . Being o'erpowered, stabbed in many places, my skull fractured by a blow from a rifle, I was dragged in a state of insensibility to Augusta. My hair was then chiefly torn up by the roots; what remained, stripped off by knives; my head scalped in 3 or 4 different places; my legs tarred and burnt by lighted torches, from which I lost the use of two of my toes and rendered

---

25. Sheehan, "'The Famous Hair Buyer General'," 21.

26. "Clark to Patrick Henry, February 3 1779," in *George Rogers Clark Papers Volume VIII, 1771–1781*, ed. Clarence Walworth Alvord (Springfield: Trustees of the Illinois State Historical Library, 1912), 97.

27. *American journal and general advertiser*, May 7, 1779. Dowd, *Groundless: Rumors, Legends, and Hoaxes on the Early American Frontier*, 213.

incapable of setting my feet to the ground for 6 months. In this condition, after their laying waste a very considerable property, I was relieved by my friends and conveyed to the interior parts of South Carolina.[28]

Ironically, it was this public humiliation that inspired Brown to escape to Florida and form a Loyalist provincial unit, the King's Rangers, which would be plagued by accusations of scalping from Patriots throughout the war.[29] While the dramatic nature of Brown's scalping is unique, it was not an isolated incident. In fact, George Clark's men captured and scalped British subject Francis Maisonville. Hamilton once again claimed that Clark was directly responsible, testifying that he "orderd one of his people to take off [Maisonville's] scalp, the man hesitating he was threatened with violent imprecation, and had proceeded so far as to take off a small part when the Colonel thought proper to stop him."[30] While Hamilton's account should be read skeptically, it is important to note that Clark vigorously denied these allegations, blaming the scalping of the white Maisonville on two of his subordinates, while he had no such apprehension in admitting to directly ordering the scalping of Indians at Fort Sackville.[31]

During the American Revolution, scalping, while still ostensibly regarded as a savage Indian practice, emerged as a valuable tool for combatants. However, rather than solely expecting Indians to scalp, as had been the practice in most previous colonial wars, both Patriots and Loyalists were now willing to directly encourage allied Indians and even use scalping themselves as a means to terrorize their enemies, whether that enemy be an Indian or Englishman. At the same time, each side claimed that their enemy's use of scalping proved that the opposed cause embodied Indian savagery. This new understanding of scalping would remain a central tension in Anglo-American warfare until the end of the War of 1812 and would fundamentally shape American policy and conduct in Indian Wars throughout the nineteenth century.

28. "Brown to Cornwallis, 16 July 1780," in *The Cornwallis Papers Volume 1 The Campaigns of 1780 and 1781 in The Southern Theatre of the American Revolutionary War*, ed. Ian Saberton (East Sussex: Naval and Military Press, 2010), 278.
29. Wayne Lynch, "The Making of a Loyalist," *Journal of the American Revolution*, https://allthingsliberty.com/2014/01/making-loyalist/, accessed July 3, 2016.
30. John D. Barnhart, ed., "Lieutenant Governor Henry Hamilton's Apologia," *Indiana Magazine of History*, 52 (1956), 394.
31. Dowd, *Groundless: Rumors, Legends, and Hoaxes on the Early American Frontier*, 185.

General Israel Putnam— Reputation Revisited

嶺 GENE PROCKNOW 彬

Entering the American Revolution, Israel Putnam enjoyed an esteemed reputation as a fearless warrior and an accomplished military officer. Putnam earned this repute through over ten years of military experience including serving in the French and Indian War and with the Connecticut militia. During French and Indian War, he rose from a captain to a colonel in the Connecticut provincial ranks and fought alongside the famed Robert Rogers in battles around Lakes George and Champlain. Putnam effectively led many small unit clashes, survived Native American captivity and returned home with a reputation for battlefield valor and personal courage.

In the initial formation of the Continental Army in 1775, Congress appointed Putnam as one of four major generals to serve under George Washington. The achievements and failures of the other three major generals, Artemas Ward (Massachusetts), Charles Lee (Virginia) and Philip Schuyler (New York) were generally agreed upon by their contemporaries and are consistently viewed by historians. However, Israel Putnam is an enigma, with both numerous contemporary proponents and detractors and differing historian assessments of his generalship and character. Even some biographers present two sides: a fierce partisan warrior but weak general.[1] How can a senior general and highly experienced military leader with such a strong reputation entering the Revolution, end up with a checkered reputation and largely be ignored today?

1. For an example of how historians regard Israel Putnam see William M. Welsch, "The Ten Worst Continental Army Generals", *Journal of the American Revolution,* October 10, 2013, https://allthingsliberty.com/2013/10/10–worst-continental-army-generals/ , accessed May 21, 2016.

EARLY LIFE

Born in 1718, Putnam grew up on a Salem, Massachusetts farm and received only the basics of a formal education. In 1739, Putnam purchased 514 acres between the villages of Pomfret and Brooklyn in rural Connecticut in partnership with this brother-in-law. Well respected by his neighbors, he became a community leader and enjoyed success as a farmer. It was on the Connecticut frontier, where predators and dangers abounded, that Putnam's reputation for courage first emerged. Neighbors recounted a fabled story of Putnam tracking down a wolf that had killed seventy sheep. Cornering the wolf, Putnam crawled on his belly into its den to kill the dangerous predator. Some historians believe that Putnam's feat was not as daring as stated but greatly enhanced by latter historians to burnish Putnam's heroic reputation.[2] Whether or not embellished, the wolf-killing story created the impression among frontier residents that Putnam was a man of fortitude and courage.[3]

In 1755, Connecticut formed a provincial unit to assist the British army against the French in the French and Indian War and appointed Putnam to lead a company. Serving alongside a ranger unit led by Robert Rogers, the combined New Hampshire/Connecticut units conducted dangerous scouting missions and raids on French outposts. On one foray, Rogers and Putnam stopped to have a playful shooting contest. Unfortunately, the gunfire attracted a Native American raiding party who attacked and captured Putnam. Ironically, this careless episode enhanced Putnam's reputation as he survived two Native American attempts to burn him at the stake; first when a rainstorm intervened and second when a French officer came to his rescue. After an officer exchange, Putnam resumed combat with the Connecticut provincial unit. By war's end, Putnam rose to the rank of Colonel and returned to Connecticut as a celebrated warrior. His close association with Rogers's ranger unit further enhanced the public's view of his war service.

REVOLUTIONARY WAR EXPERIENCES

After the hostilities at Lexington and Concord on April 19, 1775, Putnam led his militia unit to the aid of Massachusetts, demonstrating his early support for independence from Britain. During the subsequent siege of Boston, Putnam participated in a notable skirmish near Nod-

---

2. John Fellows, *The Veil Removed; or, Reflections on David Humphrey's Essay on the Life of Israel Putnam* (New York: James D. Lockwood, 1843).
3. The purported site of the wolf den is preserved and can be visited. For directions, see www.ct.gov/deep/cwp/view.asp?a=2716&q=325238&deepNav_GID=1650.

dle's and Hog Islands designed to deny the British forage for their horses. While the extent and impact of his participation is debated,[4] Putnam garnered further acclaim for his warrior nature and heroism under fire.

However, the most disputed event in Putnam's military career is his participation in the battle of Bunker Hill on June 17, 1775. This battle occurred before the formation of the Continental Army, and the colonial militia units lacked effective, coordinated command and control. Serving as a general in the Connecticut militia, Putnam was the most senior military officer on the battlefield but exercised little command over the Massachusetts forces under Col. William Prescott and the New Hampshire forces under Col. John Stark. Subsequently, battle participants and historians have disputed Putnam's actions and overall effectiveness. During the retreat, Col. Prescott angrily questioned why Putnam did not send ammunition and reinforcements from the American position in the rear, the actual Bunker Hill, to where the fighting was taking place on Breed's Hill. And in a politically motivated account, Capt. (later Gen.) Henry Dearborn excoriated Putnam's performance, all but calling him a coward.[5]

On the positive side, former aide Col. David Humphreys' battle account depicted Putnam riding his horse from Charlestown Neck to Bunker Hill to Breed's Hill issuing orders and rallying the troops in a heroic fashion. In the most recent battle account, Nathaniel Philbrick characterizes Putnam's role as moving from distraction to distraction with ineffective command of the thousand militia soldiers milling behind the lines at Bunker Hill.[6] Contrary to some early accounts and not in dispute today is that Putnam did not issue the famous Bunker Hill order "Don't shoot until you see the whites of their eyes".[7]

No matter his exact role at Bunker Hill, the Continental Congress named Israel Putnam as one of the initial four Continental Army major generals serving under George Washington. Controversy ensued as Congress raised Putnam's rank over two Connecticut officers holding

4. Fellows, *The Veil Removed*, 99–164.
5. Henry Dearborn, "An Account of the Battle of Bunker Hill with De Berniere's map corrected by General Dearborn," *Portfolio*, March 1818. For background on Dearborn's political motivations see Elizabeth M. Covart, "Bunker Hill Monument and Memory," *Journal of the American Revolution*, June 28, 2013, https://allthingsliberty.com/2013/06/monuments-and-memory-the-battle-of-bunker-hilldebate/, accessed May 22, 2016.
6. Nathaniel Philbrick, *Bunker Hill: A City, A Siege, A Revolution* (New York: Viking, 2013), 212–214.
7. That is if such an order was really issued in this form.

more senior militia positions, David Wooster
and Joseph Spencer.[8] Connecticut Congressman Roger Sherman reported to Wooster
that Putnam's reputation after the skirmish
at Noddle's and Hog Islands convinced Congress of Putnam's generalship abilities.[9] As a
result of this Congressional slight, Spencer
left his command at the siege of Boston in a
huff. However, Congress soon commissioned both Wooster and Spencer as
brigadier generals, which ended the controversy but not the animosity towards Putnam.
George Washington was not pleased with
Congress creating discord within the senior
officer corps.[10]

Israel Putnam (1718–1790).

Controversy continued to follow Putnam.
At the disastrous August 27, 1776 Battle of Long Island, critics blamed
Putnam for leaving critical roads and passes unguarded, opening up the
Patriot army to a decisive surprise flanking maneuver.[11] There is even
controversy as to who was in charge—Gen. John Sullivan or Putnam.
In the end, Washington did not blame Putnam for the devastating loss.

In the summer of 1777, Washington entrusted Putnam with an important independent command to protect the strategically vital Hudson
Highlands that guarded river crossings critical to moving supplies and
communications between New England and the southern states. Patriot
Forts Clinton and Montgomery as well as artillery batteries on Constitution Island guarded the Hudson River to prevent British waterborne
passage to Albany and a junction with the invading Gen. John Burgoyne from Canada. In October 1777 with three thousand troops, Sir
Henry Clinton utterly befuddled Putnam's undermanned defenses. Clinton faked invasion on the east side of the river and then landed his main
army below Forts Clinton and Montgomery and executed a march to

8. On April 28, 1775 the Connecticut legislature appointed David Wooster major general
and Joseph Spencer 1st brigadier general for six regiments. See "Connecticut Units in
the Revolutionary War," www.revolutionarywar101.com/american-units/ct/ accessed
June 16, 2016.
9. Edmund C. Burnett, ed., *Letters of Members of the Continental Congress*, Volume 1
(Washington, DC: Carnegie Institution of Washington, 1921), 142.
10. W. W. Abbot, ed., *The Papers of George Washington: Revolutionary Series Volume 1
June-September 1775* (Charlottesville: University of Virginia Press, 1985), 89.
11. Linda Davis Reno, *The Maryland 400 in the Battle of Long Island, 1776* (Jefferson,
NC and London: McFarland & Co., 2008), 18–19.

attack the forts landward from the west. Clinton quickly overran the forts before Putnam could send reinforcements. To preserve his forces, Putnam retreated to the hills east of the river and left valuable stores in the Continental Village to be destroyed by the British.

While Putnam had only a small force to cover multiple strategic points and the British firmly controlled the river, detractors heavily criticized his judgment and strategic battlefield management. New York Governor George Clinton lobbied Washington and Congress to replace Putnam. Yielding to this pressure, Washington sent Gen. Alexander McDougal to relieve Putnam and ordered a court martial to determine his culpability for the defeat.

Assigning Putnam to a low-profile role, in April 1778 Washington ordered him to his home state of Connecticut on a recruiting mission. When General McDougal handed down an exonerating verdict, Washington reassigned Putnam to a main army command under his direct supervision, and never again would Putnam hold an independent command. Putnam's last notable military exploit came in February 1779. It was a close encounter with a raiding British unit and a mad dash down a steep Greenwich, Connecticut slope to freedom. Subsequent biographers have described his horse ride as a fearless descent down a precipitous hill that the timid British were unwilling to follow. However daring, this last military episode has been used to further establish Putnam as a fearless and intrepid warrior. In December 1779, on a road between military camps, Putnam was stricken by a paralysis of his right side. While the stroke effectively ended his military career, Putnam regained a measure of health and mobility before passing on May 29, 1790.

CONTEMPORARIES' VIEWS OF PUTNAM

As the Revolutionary War wound down, Washington wrote a laudatory letter to Putnam thanking him for his service.[12] Descendants point to this letter as proof of Putnam's exemplary Revolutionary contributions. Henry Laurens, a member of the Continental Congress from South Carolina, appears to have been of the same mind in writing Lafayette on October 10, 1777 about Putnam's ability to protect the Hudson Highlands. "He is a brave Officer in the field, cautious & timid only upon paper therefore I am not diffident of his success"[13]

12. George Washington to Israel Putnam, June 2, 1783, http://founders.archives.gov/documents/Washington/99–01–02–11360, accessed June 15, 2016.
13. Stanley J. Idzerda, Ed., *Lafayette in the Age of the American Revolution: Selected Letters and Papers, 1776–1790* (Ithaca and London: Cornell University Press, 1977), 1:120.

On the other hand, Lafayette penned a harsh evaluation of Putnam's later loss of the Hudson Highlands, writing that the British, "were hardly bothered by old Putnam, the man who, when the troubles first began, had left his plow and given the army more zeal than talent"[14]

In addition, there are curious signs that Putnam was not always firmly committed to American independence. In December 1776, the British *Middlesex Journal* reported about Putnam: "no man in either army will do his duty with greater bravery in the field. He never was a favorer of American Independence."[15]

In the fall of 1777, British spymaster and provincial officer Col. Beverly Robinson, who also attempted to turn Ethan Allen, may have sought to entice Putnam to defect to the British cause. Under the pretext of looking after the status of his property and under a flag of truce, Robinson visited his home that also served as Putnam's headquarters. Robinson relayed a turncoat offer to Putnam's wife and communicated with Putnam's son. With Burgoyne's surrender, these communications ceased.[16]

Further, some contemporaries, especially New Yorkers, viewed Putnam as too easy on Loyalists. He allowed Loyalist and Patriot newspapers to pass between lines, provided Tories with safe passage, and well-treated captured wounded British soldiers. These actions became issues at his court martial as well as a charge that he misappropriated army funds. However, none of these accusations were proved. And clearly demonstrating that he prosecuted Tories to the fullest extent, Putnam hanged British spy Edmund Parker with little remorse.[17]

Lastly, in a curious May 14, 1783 letter to American loyalist Beverly Robinson, Putnam seemed to waiver in his support of the Revolution. "There was a time when I firmly believed that a separation from the mother country would be the greatest blessing to this. But alas! Expe-

---

14. Idzerda, *Lafayette*, 1:99.
15. *Middlesex Journal*, December 21, 1776, quoted in Frank Moore, ed., *The Diary of the American Revolution 1775–1781* (New York: Washington Square Press, 1967), 176–9.
16. For information on British attempts to turn Putnam see, Carl Van Doren, *Secret History of the American Revolution* (New York: Viking Press, 1941), 3–6 and Dave Richard Palmer, *The River and the Rock: The History of Fortress West Point, 1775–1783* (New York: Hippocrene Books, 1969), 125–6.
17. In a curt letter to Sir Henry Clinton, Putnam wrote:
Headquarters August 7, 1777
Edmund Palmer, an officer in the enemy's service was taken as a spy lurking within our lines; he has been tried as a spy, condemned as a spy and shall be executed as a spy, and the Flag is order to depart immediately
Israel Putnam
P.S. He has been accordingly executed

rience—too late experience—has convinced me, as well as thousands of others, how very erroneous this opinion was."[18]

Whether or not this letter conclusively proves that Putnam had second thoughts, neither contemporaries nor subsequent historians have referenced it.

HISTORICAL ASSESSMENT OF PUTNAM'S MILITARY CONTRIBUTIONS

Historians in the first half of the nineteenth century hotly debated the effectiveness of Putnam's military career.[19] First to print, David Humphrey, an officer on Putnam's staff, published a flattering 1788 biography. The first part of Humphrey's biography was complied with the assistance of Dr. Albigence Waldo, a former army surgeon who interviewed Putnam about his French and Indian War experiences. Also Humphrey interviewed Putnam to corroborate Waldo and to fill in details about his Revolutionary War experiences. Humphrey's text remained the authoritative biographical source until the emergence of a political fight thirty years later.

During the 1818 election campaign, Henry Dearborn, a candidate for governor of Massachusetts and participant in the Battle of Bunker Hill, wrote an essay challenging Putnam's leadership role and labeling him as incompetent and a coward. This attack sparked rebuttals from Putnam's son and other supporters. In the end, Dearborn's attack on Putnam's character did not help him politically, and he was defeated. However, the controversy over Putnam's reputation continued to simmer.

In an 1843 book, John Fellows penned another attempt to debunk or downplay Putnam's Revolutionary War contributions as well as almost all of his pre-Revolutionary War accomplishments. Fellows, a member of the Massachusetts militia who served at Roxbury, Massachusetts during the Battle of Bunker Hill, was particularly critical of Putnam's warrior reputation and ability to command men under combat conditions.[20] In the mid-twentieth century, Howard Parker Moore espoused these same themes in his biography of Gen. John Stark who served with Putnam in many battles in the French and Indian War as

---

18. Original letter is in possession of the Robinson family. Quoted from C. W. Robinson, *Life of Sir John Beverly Robinson* (Edinburgh and London: William Blackwood and Sons, 1904), 14.

19. For an overview of the General Israel Putnam historiography, see https://geneprock.com/2016/06/24/general-israel-putnam-a-historiography/.

20. See www.fold3.com for pension application dated July 18, 1838. John Fellows should not be confused with his uncle Gen. John Fellows. For a genealogy of the Fellows family see, www.genealogy.com/ftm/f/e/l/Mark-D-Fellows/GENE-0021.html.

well as Bunker Hill. Stark was reputed to be highly critical of Putnam's battlefield performance at Bunker Hill, stating that with proper generalship the Patriots could have thoroughly defeated the British.[21]

In the next seventy years after the Fellows book, three biographers chronicled Putnam's life. Of these, William Livingston's biography written in 1901 is the most comprehensive and contains the highest supporting scholarship. Siding with Humphrey and Putnam's family, Livingston generally provides a positive view of Putnam's Revolutionary war performance and takes the side of Putnam and his family in the Dearborn-Fellows controversies. The four subsequent twentieth century biographies are written principally for young adults, relying mostly on secondary sources and containing fictionalized narratives. The last of these romanticized accounts was published in 1967.

Another measure of Putnam's reputation is the view of his reputation by the post-revolutionary public and the succeeding generation. The people of Connecticut, New York and numerous other states memorialized Putnam's reputation by naming counties, towns and geographical features after him. Connecticut citizens named a town after him, raised statues in prominent sites and placed his grave stone in the state capitol. Finally, the Greenwich, Connecticut scene of his fabled, madcap ride evading the British is now referred to as Putnam Hill.

Although highly critical during the war, New Yorkers also commemorated Putnam by naming a subdivided a portion of Dutchess County and a town in northern New York after him. In addition, seven other states honored Putnam's service by dubbing counties for him. By comparison, among the three other initial major generals, only Philip Schuyler had three counties named after him; Artemas Ward and Charles Lee had none.

CONCLUSION

Having served throughout the French and Indian War and the first four years of the Revolution, no detractor can dispute Putnam's personal commitment to military service. He willingly served in over ten years of military campaigns and numerous times risked his life in close-quarters combat.

His military strengths were as a small unit commander, rallying troops with his martial spirit and setting an example of courage under fire. However, he was less effective in exercising large-scale battlefield

21. Moore quotes a conversation between Stark and a Dr. Bentley on May 10, 1810: *"He was a poltroon. Had he done his duty, he would have decided the fate of his country in the first action."* Howard Parker Moore, *A Life of General John Stark of New Hampshire* (New York: Published by Howard Parker Moore, 1949), 151.

command and control and demonstrated limits in his strategic military thinking and brigade level decision-making. Further, he acted rashly, such as parading a small force before the British ships at Charlestown and advocating an attack on New York City with only a few troops from his Hudson Highlands command.

Personally, Putnam exhibited courage and fortitude on many battle-fields. However, he could not meld his bold, aggressive nature with sufficient political skills to garner widespread contemporary support from fellow military officers and political leaders. As to his patriotism, he was not a traitor and the hearsay aspersions on his wartime loyalties are unfounded. However, unlike many other Continental Army officers, he did not exhibit personal enmity toward Loyalists but likely expressed some political frustrations with several of them.

While receiving a checkered reputation from nineteenth century historians and being relatively unknown today, Putnam joined the rebellion at its earliest juncture, assumed senior leadership responsibilities and rallied his troops when necessary. Further, in battles against greater numbers and better-trained forces, he preserved his commands to fight another day. Finally, well-liked by his troops, Putnam "rose to the occasion" to competently serve his country in times of crises. And his countrymen memorialized his contributions with numerous place-names in nine states.

Drummer Fisher Hung from a Tree

DON N. HAGIST

John Fisher hung from a tree. "Near the high road" from Fostertown to Mount Holly, New Jersey, he was in plain sight to the soldiers who marched past.[1] He hung there as an example of what deserters could expect, especially if they were caught bearing arms for the enemy. The impact Fisher's dangling corpse had on the rank and file soldiers cannot be measured, but it made a strong enough impression on officers that several recorded the grizzly sight in their writings. Today the tree is gone, but a roadside marker commemorates the event that occurred on June 22, 1778, albeit with an error. Fisher's story, however, has been overlooked.

When war broke out in America in 1775, Englishman John Fisher was a private soldier in the 36th Regiment of Foot serving in Cork, Ireland.[2] The 36th Regiment spent the entire war in Ireland, but not all of the regiment's soldiers did. When the British army deployed regiments on overseas service, those regiments were brought up to strength using two methods: recruiting, of course, but also by drafting, or transferring, experienced men from other regiments into the deploying regiment. (The term draft, in this context, denoted pulling, as in draft horse or draft beer; the men were pulled from one regiment to another. The word did not refer to civilians pulled into military service, the way it is used today.) Drafting insured that the operational readiness of the deploying regiment was not compromised by having too many new recruits. The 36th Regiment provided over 225 drafts to other regiments in 1775 and 1776, and spent the next few years recruiting and training

1. F. A. Whinyates, ed., *The Services of Lieut.-Colonel Francis Downman* (Woolwich, England: The Royal Artillery Institution, 1898), 66.
2. Muster rolls, 36th Regiment of Foot, WO 12/5025/2, The National Archives of Great Britain (hereinafter cited as TNA).

new men in Ireland. This method of training and deployment worked well for the British army throughout the era. Drafting orders usually directed officers to seek volunteers first, then select men to be transferred if there were not enough volunteers. The regiment receiving the drafts had the right to refuse men deemed unfit, which prevented the giving regiment from dumping unsuitable men.[3]

In early 1776, John Fisher and twenty-eight of his fellow soldiers were drafted from the 36th Regiment into the 28th Regiment of Foot. There, he met up with Irishman John Fisher, a soldier who had joined the 28th Regiment about three years before. One regiment, two John Fishers. This sort of thing wasn't unusual.[4]

The 28th was one of six regiments on the abortive British expedition to the southern colonies in 1776. When the attempt to take Charleston, South Carolina failed, the troops sailed to New York where they joined General Howe's army in the campaign that took New York City. Fisher was put into the regiment's light infantry company and appointed drummer. This was an important assignment, particularly in the light infantry where drummers did not actually play drums, at least not on campaign. For the fast and fluid field maneuvers used by the British light infantry, the hunting horn was the signaling instrument of choice. Besides being easy to carry and having a sound that carried well, using the horn to sound the advance, retreat, and other commands stirred the spirits of British soldiers while humiliating their opponents. Through Manhattan, Westchester County, and into New Jersey, the hunting horn sounded the rout of American troops in the face of a British onslaught throughout the autumn of 1776.

Winter was different. Having established a string of posts stretching from Staten Island to Trenton, New Jersey, the British army stopped campaigning for the months when roads became impassible because of snow and mud.[5] The light infantry battalion that John Fisher served in was quartered in Piscataway. They had crude accommodations in whatever buildings were available, scarcely enough clothing because most of their belongings remained in storage in New York City, and relied heavily on foraging to procure food and firewood. Fortunately, New Jersey was a bountiful place, so food and fuel could be found reasonably easily. It was, nonetheless, dangerous. American soldiers were quartered

3. For more on drafting, see Don N. Hagist, *British Soldiers, American War* (Yardley, PA: Westholme Publishing, 2012), 51–59.

4. Muster rolls, 28th Regiment of Foot, WO 12/4416 and /4417, TNA. All subsequent information about the service records of these two men are from this source.

5. Linnea M. Bass, "Bloody Footprints in the Snow? January 1777 at Brunswick, New Jersey," *Military Collector & Historian* number 45 (Spring 1993), 9–10.

nearby, just over the Short Hills range to the west of the British posts. Patrols and parties from both sides frequently clashed, and straying far from quarters could be quite hazardous. On April 11, 1777, John Fisher disappeared.

Some months later the British withdrew from the interior of New Jersey, and instead went by sea to Head of Elk, Maryland, and then by land to Philadelphia. The light infantry battalion containing the 28th's company went on this campaign, as did the 28th Regiment itself. After a rigorous campaign that left Philadelphia in British hands but the surrounding countryside firmly in American control, another winter halted campaigning once more.

It was during this winter that an incident occurred which has confused John Fisher's story. The other John Fisher, who served in a different company, had been appointed corporal. On February 25, 1778, he was tried by a general court martial for raping a nine-year-old girl. She was the daughter of a sergeant and his wife in the 28th Regiment; they'd asked another soldier to take care of her while they went out for the evening, and that soldier, wishing to sleep instead, asked Corporal Fisher to look after the girl. He took very inappropriate advantage of the situation, and in spite of offering an eloquent defense was found guilty by the court.[6]

Cpl. John Fisher, the Irishman who had enlisted in the 28th Regiment in 1772 or 1773, was sentenced to be "hanged by the neck until he is dead." The execution was to take place on Monday, March 23, on the common in Philadelphia, "between the hours of ten and twelve in the forenoon."[7] But when the fatal time came, a pardon was granted "in consideration of his youth, and the very good character given of him by the field officers of his regiment."[8] Corporal Fisher was a free man, and by 1781 had advanced to sergeant in his regiment.

But this story is not about Cpl. John Fisher, it's about Drummer John Fisher. Because the general orders concerning Corporal Fisher's conviction and pardon have been published, many have assumed him to be the same man as Drummer Fisher even though the rank is clearly stated in the orders. They were two different men. While Cpl. John Fisher was on trial in Philadelphia in March of 1778, Drummer John Fisher, who had disappeared from the 28th Regiment's light infantry

6. Trial of Cpl. John Fisher, WO 71/85, 290–307, TNA.
7. General Orders, March 16, 1778, in "The Kemble Papers," *Collections of the New York Historical Society for the Year 1883* (New York: New York Historical Society, 1884), 1:556.
8. Ibid., 1:560.

company in April of 1777, was still nowhere to be found. Three months later, that changed.

The decision by France to join the American Revolution caused a dramatic change in British strategy. Instead of a war on the other side of an ocean, Great Britain was now faced with an age-old enemy just across the English Channel, an enemy with global interests similar to Britain's. In addition to defending the shores of England and Ireland, the British navy and army had to protect key interests in the West Indies from French invasion. The closest troops were in America, and expanding their responsibilities to include the West Indies meant redistributing those forces. The decision was made to evacuate Philadelphia, a move that was accomplished in June 1778. Lacking sufficient shipping to move everything by sea, the British army set out over land. The bulk of the American army was in Pennsylvania, behind the British route of march, but New Jersey teemed with small bodies of soldiers poised to harass the huge British force that filled dusty roads in the early summer heat.

On June 19, a party of Hessian Jägers, expert riflemen who probed the front and flanks of the British line of march, were fired upon from a clump of woods. The Jägers lost a man, but rushed into the woods and scattered some skulking militia men, most of whom fled. They found one man lying on the ground wounded, wearing a bayonet and cartridge box but with no musket. They took him up and brought him to the British column.

The man they had captured was John Fisher. He was quickly recognized as a deserter; his own regiment was, after all, part of the army moving across New Jersey. Less than forty-eight hours after his capture, when the army stopped in Mount Holly, Fisher sat before a hastily arranged general court martial, charged with the crime of "having deserted from the said Regiment and born Arms in the Rebel Service."[9] As the court of thirteen officers (none from the 28th Regiment, to insure impartiality) listened, an officer and a sergeant of the 28th testified to Fisher's service in the regiment, mentioning that he was a draft from the 36th Regiment and the date he went missing. They affirmed that he had "received Pay and Cloathing," a critical point because it affirmed that the army had upheld its obligations of the enlistment contract. The sergeant testified that Fisher had taken away only the clothing he wore when he disappeared, differentiating him from men who carefully planned to desert and absconded with extra clothing and other possessions.

9. Trial of Drummer John Fisher, WO 71/87, 202–208, TNA. Subsequent information about Fisher's trial is from this source unless otherwise cited.

Three of the Jägers who captured Fisher were called before the court. These men needed a translator, so a bilingual German serving in the 10th Regiment of Foot was sworn in for that purpose. Through the interpreter, the Jägers related that Fisher was among the five or six rebels who fired on them, after which "the prisoner then threw himself upon the Ground and was wounded and taken." All concurred that, although he had no musket, he wore the accoutrements of a soldier, a bayonet and a cartridge box.

British military justice was rigidly governed by law; discipline was harsh but not arbitrary. One of the privileges to which John Fisher was entitled was legal counsel from a deputy judge advocate, an officer well-versed in martial law who oversaw the court martial proceedings. By June 1778, many British prisoners of war had made their escape and returned to British service. Some even came in wearing American uniforms, claiming to have enlisted with the enemy in order get close to the front lines so that they could escape. Even if Fisher had not known about this, the judge advocate certainly did, and may have advised Fisher to use this defense.

Fisher claimed that he had not deserted, "but was cut off from his Quarters by a party which came between him and them" when he went to procure some spruce beer for a sick comrade. Unable to return to his quarters in Piscataway, he was "obliged to make his escape to Morris Town," over fifteen miles to the north and well inside American territory. There, he claimed, he found work as a laborer and also found a woman to marry, in what must have been a quick courtship given that he was gone for a total of only fourteen months. In spite of this secure-sounding situation, he professed "always a desire of returning to the British Army." He was unable to do so, however, because only soldiers were allowed to go more than a mile into the countryside without a pass. "He enlisted in order to get an opportunity of returning to his regiment," he said, but refused to go with the party that fired on the Jägers until his captain threatened his life. He asserted that he had not fired on the Jägers, but instead threw down his gun and tried to surrender to them.

Other soldiers had told similar stories in the past, but usually they were men who had come in voluntarily; that is, they had clearly deserted from American service to rejoin the British. Fisher needed a stronger case, because he was with the party that fired on the Jägers. He had something that few others before him had had, though: a witness. While he was in Morristown, he'd come to know another British soldier, a man of the 17th Regiment of Foot named John Hatter who had deserted in New Jersey exactly two weeks after Fisher had disappeared.[10] Hatter rejoined the British army in Philadelphia on February 1, 1778, and was on the march across New Jersey and available to testify on Fisher's behalf. Fisher told the court that, while in Morristown, he'd told Hatter of his desire to return to British service, and called Hatter before the court for questioning.

Fisher asked one question, hopeful of being exonerated by his old comrade: "Did he ever know the Prisoner to serve or do any thing against his Country?" Hatter, however, did not give the response that Fisher was hoping for; he said that Fisher had indeed served for a month in the militia, "as a Substitute for another Man." The court then took over the questioning, and asked Hatter if he'd ever heard Fisher "say that he wished to get back to the British Army?" Hatter's response: "He does not remember that he ever did." We can only wonder how Fisher reacted to this.

The court, still giving Fisher the benefit of the doubt, pursued another angle: given that Fisher had served as a substitute (that is, he took the place of someone else who was required to serve in the militia), the court asked Hatter if Fisher was "forced into the Army, or put into Goal because he would not serve?" Again, Hatter's response was incriminating: "No, they never force Deserters to enlist."

This left one more avenue for the court to probe. Fisher had said that he didn't desert, but fled to evade capture. What did Hatter know about this? The court asked him, "Did he ever hear him say how he had got away from his Regiment?" For the fourth time, Hatter gave a response that contradicted Fisher's account: "He heard him acknowledge that he had Deserted."

The court had heard enough. They found John Fisher guilty and sentenced him to death on June 21, 1778. The sentence was carried out the following morning, using a tree by the road on the army's route of march, where any soldiers contemplating desertion could ponder his fate. Today a sign marking the spot gives his name as "Corporal John Fisher," confusing the English drummer with the Irishman who was tried and pardoned four months earlier.[11]

10. Muster rolls, 17th Regiment of Foot, WO 12/3406/2, TNA.
11. The marker is on Burlington County Route 543, three-tenths of a mile east of the intersection with Petticoat Bridge Road, near Columbus, New Jersey (40° 4.33 N, 74° 43.854 W).

Fever

✺ KIM BURDICK ✺

"These are the times that try men's souls."—*Thomas Paine*

Throughout the American Revolution, opposing armies fought a common enemy. Primary documents on both sides are full of complaints, descriptions and responses to the attacks of a stubborn adversary; fever.

As the Declaration of Independence was being prepared, Joseph Hewes of North Carolina complained from Philadelphia on May 17, 1776, "An obstinate ague and Fever, or rather an Intermitting Fever, persecutes me continually; I have no way to remove it unless I retire from Congress and from public business; this I am determined not to do till N. Carolina sends a further delegation, provided I am able to crawl to the Congress Chamber."[1] The next day, Benedict Arnold and his men, who had left Montreal for the border area of St Johns, arrived at that "dirty, stinking place" in a camp which "echoed with execrations upon the musketoes."[2]

The following week, Nathanael Greene wrote George Washington from Bound Brook, New Jersey, pleading for vinegar for his feverish troops.[3] On May 27, 1776, Richard Hutson, South Carolina delegate to the Continental Congress, optimistically predicted that if the British did not move against Charleston soon, that city could breathe freely at least

1. Joseph Hewes to James Iredell, May 17, 1776, in *MS. Records in Office of Secretary of State. Volume 10*, 458, http://docsouth.unc.edu/csr/.
2. Mary Gillette, "The Army Medical Department 1775–1818," in *Office of Medical History in Army History Series*, edited by Maurice Matloff, 60, www.history.amedd.army.mil/booksdocs/rev/gillett1/ch3.html.
3. Nathanael Greene to George Washington, May 25, 1777, Bound Brook, NJ. http://founders.archives.gov/.

until November, "for it would be the height of madness and folly for them to come here during the sickly season."[4]

As far north as Fort Ticonderoga, fever was reported. In August of that year, Pvt. Simeon Walker of Woodbury, Connecticut, arrived with Hinman's Connecticut troops, remaining "at Ticonderoga until sometime in the fall being taken sick with fever and ague. Was permitted to return home."[5] Walker was one of the lucky ones. Generally, if a soldier had an "ague fit," complete with chills and shaking, he had no choice but to persevere and move on. A medical book of the day supported this stoic behavior: "the patient ought to take as much exercise between the fits as he can bear. . . . Nothing tends more to prolong an intermitting fever than indulging a lazy indolent disposition."[6]

The pension records of John Almy describe what having fever and ague was like for a boy who at age thirteen or fourteen "in Feby or March 1776" enlisted into a rifle company in the State service:

> Was taken with a fever and ague, and from that, a continual fever; and was left in the hospital at Trenton. After getting better in about two or three weeks, he set off for the regiment and travelled to Princeton. There he had a return of the fever and ague; and after remaining about as long as he did at Trenton, went on to Fort Lee, and crossed, as he thinks, to York Island, where he found his regiment encamped near Fort Washington. The same evening there came orders for all the sick that were able to walk, to make the best of their way in the direction that the baggage went. Fort Washington being taken[7] and the army obliged to retreat, declarant kept on with the sick, until he arrived at the White Plains, but could not keep so far ahead, but that they would bring the wounded to dress where he had stopped to shake with the ague . . . When he arrived at the White Plains, he found a few loads of baggage; no provision, or any kind of convenience for the sick; of consequence, the sick straggled out to the farm houses, and begged. Declarant continued to wander

4. Gillette, "The Army Medical Department," 60. See also Richard Hutson; *Hutson Letterbook, 1765–1777*, South Carolina Historical Society.

5. Simeon Walker, Revolutionary War Pension Application, 12 Jul 1832, Court of Probate for the District of Caledonia, in National Archives; "State of Vermont SS District and County of Caledonia.1832. Simeon Walker's compatriot, Aaron Barlow noted that he and his men were, "lodging among the fleas" during his brief stay at Ticonderoga. https://archive.org/stream/waroftherevolution00recorich/waroftherevolution00recorich_djvu.txt.

6. William Buchan, "Of Intermitting Fevers, Or Agues: Symptoms." *Domestic Medecine, Chapter IV*. London, 1769. www.Americanrevolution.Org/Medicine/Med14.Php,

7. This was in November, 1776.

about, but failed in his health, and could hear nothing of his regiment. He then wrote a letter to his father in Tiverton in the State of Rhode Island, with little hope that it would reach him, but he received it, came on, went to the encampment of the sick, there saw one of the company to which declarant belonged, who told him, he did not know where declarant was, or what had become of him. After making diligent search, declarant's father set off on his return; by accident, took a wrong road, where he found declarant in the road, and with some difficulty conveyed him home. Fever and ague grew worse, continual fever set in; and declarant did not get well in six months' time, nor does he think that he ever got over it.[8]

Fevers were, at that time, believed to be caused by "effluvia and miasma" and it is difficult to tell from most eighteenth-century documents what kind of fever was being discussed. Fevers were, and are, caused by mosquitos and by ticks, fleas, contaminated food and water, bacteria, and crowded conditions. Not every case of fever and ague was malaria, and mosquitos were not America's "secret weapon" as some secondary sources blithely report. In the fens and marshlands of England and in British holdings around the globe, malaria had been known for centuries."[9] Scottish physician William Buchan's explanation of the causes of these fevers applied to the swampy places and irrigation ditches of the New World as well as to the Old:

> Agues are occasioned by effluvia from putrid stagnating water. This is evident from their abounding in rainy seasons, and being most frequent in countries where the soil is marshy, as in Holland, the Fens of Cambridgeshire, the Hundreds of Essex, &c. This disease may also be occasioned by eating too much stone fruit, by a poor watery diet, damp houses, and evening dews, lying upon the damp ground, fatigue, depressing passions, and the like. When the inhabitants of a high country remove to a low one, they are generally seized with intermitting fevers, and to such the disease is most apt to prove fatal.

8. John Almy, Revolutionary War Pension Application in State of Rhode Island, Ss. County of Newport, Town of Little Compton, Sc Southern Campaign American Revolution Pension Statements & Rosters. Pension Application of John Almy W1531 Transcribed and annotated by C. Leon Harris. www.revwarapps.org/w1531.pdf.
9. Mary Dobson, "The History of Malaria in England," excerpted from *Contours of Death and Disease in Early Modern England* (Cambridge University Press, 1997), www.malaria.wellcome.ac.uk/doc_WTD023991.html accessed September 25, 2015.

In a word, whatever relaxes the solids, diminishes the perspiration, or obstructs the circulation in the capillary or small vessels, disposes the body to agues.[10]

As the Philadelphia Campaign began to take shape, army hospital personnel at Ephrata, Lititz, and Bethlehem, Reading, Trenton, Princeton and areas beyond began complaining. In December of 1777, Dr. Benjamin Rush wrote a long letter to General Washington insisting on a reorganization of the Medical Department, noting: "Too many sick are crouded together in One house. I have seen 20 sick men in One room ill with fevers & fluxes, large eno' to contain only 6 or 8 well men without danger to their health. Six of our Surgeons have died since the 1st of last may, from Attending the sick under these circumstances, and almost every Surgeon in the department has been ill in a greater or lesser degree with fevers caught in our hospitals."[11]

Robert Jackson, surgeon's mate with the 71st Regiment of Foot in the British army, similarly lamented, "It is unfortunate that the mode, too frequently pursued, of collecting sick soldiers into general hospitals, so multiplies the causes of disease, as defeats the purpose." "It is proved in innumerable instances, that sick men recover health sooner and better, in sheds, in huts, and barns, exposed occasionally to wind, and sometimes to rain, than in the most superb hospitals in Europe. Pure air, in this respect, is alone superior to all forms of care, and to all other remedies, without such aid. Where a number and variety of human beings are accumulated under the same roof, the air cannot long remain pure. It may not be positively impregnated with contagion; but it is not salutary."[12]

In the spring of 1778, Lt. James Morris of Connecticut was held prisoner by the British in Philadelphia. The situation in the prison was similar to the hospitals but worse: "At this time seven hundred prisoners of war were in the jail. The soldiers were soon seized with a jail fever and in the course of three months it swept off four hundred men, who were all buried in one continuous grave, without coffins. Such a scene of mor-

10. William Buchan, "Of Intermitting Fevers, Or Agues: Symptoms," *Domestic Medecine* (London, 1785), www.Americanrevolution.Org/Medicine/Med14.Php.

11. Benjamin Rush to George Washington, December 26, 1777, Princeton, N.J., National Archives, Founders Online, http://founders.archives.gov/documents/Washington/03–13-02-0006.

12. Tabitha Marshall, "Surgeons Reconsidered: Military Medical Men," 339–40, www.cbmh.ca/index.php/cbmh/article/viewFile/1363/1332.

tality I never witnessed before. Death was so frequent that it ceased to terrify; it ceased to warn; it ceased to alarm survivors."[13]

As the war effort moved south, reports of fever and ague increased. Rice irrigation ditches and pools of stagnant shallow water were the home of the anopheles mosquito. Mosquitos biting those who already suffered from the malaria parasite spread the disease to rich and poor alike. An eighteenth century saying, variously attributed to a German soldier, to Eliza Lucas Pinckney and to the ever-popular "anon," summed it up: "South Carolina is in the spring a paradise, in the summer a hell, and in the autumn a hospital."

According to surgeon's mate Robert Jackson, the most common illnesses the army suffered in 1780 were "intermittents," probably vivax malaria. It was reported that a Hessian regiment had lost "many men and some officers, and at present has not really above sixty men fit for duty,"[14] and, on July 17, 1780, Cornwallis received a letter from Lt. Col. Nisbet Balfour, commandant of Charleston: "We are turning sickly fast and our surgeon very ill."[15] On July 29, 1780, Cornwallis received a similar letter from Major James Wemyss writing from Georgetown, South Carolina, reporting that his men were "falling down very fast" with intermittent fevers. A few days later, he reported that six men had died of putrid fevers and thirty other men were ill. Cornwallis ordered Wemyss to move inland along the Black River, cautioning him not to stay long in any place along the river "which is a very sickly country" and to move by "short and easy marches" to encamp in the High Hills of Santee, an area reputedly much healthier.[16]

On the American side, things were no better. General Horatio Gates wrote to the Director of Hospitals, Southern Department from Hillsborough on July 19, 1780, "I find an Hospital under the Direction of a Regimental Surgeon — without medicines or Stores of any kind—I also learn from the Army that with it there's no Hospital Establishment whatever, and that the Sick are but illy accommodated—I have now to request that you will repair to my Head Quarters immediately—with

---

13. Rev. James Morris, US Army, www.history.amedd.army.mil/booksdocs/rev/Med-Men/MedMenCh08.html.

14. Alured Clarke to Cornwallis, July 10, 1780. PRO 30/11/2/258–61, Clarke to Cornwallis, August 30, 1780, PRO 30/11/63/83–84; Clarke to Cornwallis, October 5, 1780, PRO 30/11/3/86–87, British National Archives.

15. Nisbet Balfour to Cornwallis, in Peter McCandless, "Revolutionary Fever, Diseases and War in the Lower South 1776–1783," *Transactions of the Clinical and Climatological Association*, 2007, 118:225–249, http://europepmc.org/articles/PMC1863584 .

16. Cornwallis to Wemyss, July 30, 1780, (PRO) 30/11/78/61–64, British National Archives.

such other Gentlemen as fall within your Arrangement, and may be absent. Should any Accident prevent your complying with this order, you will give me as Early Notice of it as possible."[17]

The next day, he wrote to the President of the Board of War, Philadelphia, "As I have no answer to any Letter I have wrote you, since I recd the Orders of Congress to take command this way, I know not what is doing to supply the medical Department . . . I yesterday wrote to Doctor Rickman, who lives near Williamsburgh, and ordered him to come and reside here, when the First General Hospital must be fixed. The Board will do well to enforce this Order, or see that some otherwise properly provided with a Director to the General Hospital of the Southern Army."[18]

On August 23, British General Cornwallis wrote to Sir Henry Clinton: "I am at present so hurried with business, with everybody belonging to me sick. Our sickness is great and truly alarming. The officers are particularly affected; Doctor Hayes (John M. Hayes) and almost all the hospital surgeons are laid up. Every person of my family (official) and every Publick officer of the Army is now incapable of doing duty."[19]

At almost the same time, an American was writing a comparable letter to his commander:

Sir:
The great numbers of men that are down with the Ague, & fever prevents my even giving a Guess when it will be in my power to comply with yr. orders. I am truly unhappy for the unfortunate Event of the G. Army On the 16th Instant, and sorry that the Want of Horse should in so great a measure be the Cause of it.[20]

---

17. Horatio Gates to the Director of Hospitals in the Southern Department, Hillsborough, July 19, 1780, Letter #8, Southern Campaign Revolutionary War Pension Statements & Rosters, www.battleofcamden.org/documents.htm.

18. Gates to the Director of Hospitals in the Southern Department. Hillsborough, July 19, 1780, Letter #12, *Southern Campaign Revolutionary War Pension Statements & Rosters*, www.battleofcamden.org/documents.htm.

19. Cornwallis to Sir Henry Clinton, August 29, 1780. Office of Medical History. Chapter XII, 313, http://history.amedd.army.mil/booksdocs/rev/MedMen/MedMenCh12.html, 15:276–278. Cornwallis to Clinton. Received September 23, No. 3. in Sir Henry Clinton's, No. 107. Camden, August 29, 1780, http://docsouth.unc.edu/csr/index.html/document/csr15-0196.

20. Anthony White to Gates, Halifax, North Carolina, August 31, 1780, in The Colonial and State Records of North Carolina, 583. http://docsouth.unc.edu/csr/index.html/document/csr15-0193.

1781 was a busy year for battles; Cowpens, Guilford Courthouse, Hobkirk's Hill, the Siege of Ninety-Six, all took place before the "fever season" really began. By the late spring and summer of 1781, there were many cases of fever reported in Virginia and the Carolinas. Some soldiers, like John Ware, were not hospitalized. His pension papers state, "In the Summer of 1781, in the month of July . . . this deponent was taken sick with what was in those days called the Dumb ague or Slow fever and was left on the road . . . and owing to this circumstance he failed to get a fight as he expected."[21] Among those imprisoned at Charleston, a putrid fever caused by "the human miasma" was highly contagious. The sick brought into the general hospital from the prison ships generally died in the course of two or three days, with all the marks of a highly septic state.

In early August 1781, some of General Wayne's men were sent to a general hospital located in a private home at Hanover, Virginia. In September, as preparations for the siege of Yorktown increased, the physician at the Hanover hospital died and the responsibility for the care of his fellows fell entirely upon one of the patients.

Following the Battle of Eutaw Springs, South Carolina on September 8, 1781, reports of fever increased. Although most reports simply noted that a soldier suffered from "fever and ague," some pension records tell a story.

One soldier explained that "owing to sickness and fatigue, very near perishing before he reached the camp, when Adjutant Weathers . . . carrying him to a shade, gave him brandy and cheese, etc. and he was there sick about a month."[22]

British reports were no less dramatic. On the retreat from Eutaw Springs to Charleston, Maj. John Marjoribanks fell ill and was left at Wantoot Plantation where, racked by fever, he died in the hut of one of Daniel Ravenel's slaves. On September 20, 1780, Banastre Tarleton became violently ill and Maj. George Hanger filled in as commander of the British Legion. Hanger also became ill and was sent to Camden, South Carolina to recover. When Tarleton was well enough to resume command, Cornwallis came down with a fever, remaining severely ill until late October.

21. John Ware, Revolutionary War Pension Application, Caswell County Historical Association, September 20, 2010, http://ncccha.blogspot.com/2010/09/john-ware-revolutionary-warpension.html.
22. John Chaney, Revolutionary War Pension Application, Southern Campaign American Revolution Pension Statements & Rosters, Pension application S32177 fn42SC/NC, http://revwarapps.org/s32177.pdf.

General Nathanael Greene moved his Continental army to the Upper Coastal Plain's High Hills of Santee to gain relief from the heat, humidity, and diseases associated with the adjacent Middle Coastal Plain swamps. On September 27, Robert Kirkwood noted in his journal that he had gone to Headquarters "for Docts. Medecine for my men and returned the 30th, Inst. 40 miles."[23]

The siege of Yorktown, Virginia began on September 28. During course of the battle, Army surgeon James Thacher of the 16th Massachusetts Regiment, wrote, "Our New England troops have now become very sickly; the prevalent diseases are intermittent and remittent fevers, which are very prevalent in this climate during the autumnal months."[24] On October 19, Cornwallis surrendered 7,087 officers and men, 900 seamen, 144 cannons, 15 galleys, a frigate and 30 transport ships. Pleading illness, he did not attend the surrender ceremony. Cornwallis later estimated that only 3,800 of his 7,700 men were fit to fight.

In the minds of many people, the surrender at Yorktown in the fall of 1781 brought the Revolutionary War to an end, but it was not over. Delaware's Kirkwood simply noted in his Journal from South Carolina, "Received Intelligence of the Surrender of Lord Cornwallaces whole Army to his Excelency Genl. George Washington in York Town Virginia."[25] In November 1781, "This day was ordered to march by the way of Howell's Ferry to Col Thompson's and there to join the Army. The troops moved, but I went to Capt Howells having the ague & Fever where I stayed untill the 27th Inst."[26]

The letter Lt. Andrew Armstrong wrote to Gov. Thos. Burke from Camden, South Carolina on July 10, 1782, summed up the feeling of many by the end of the war:

Dear Sir:
I have a d—d fever and ague, but I do not believe that writing to a Doctor will cure me.
I am Sir, with my compliments to Mrs. Burke.
Andr. Armstrong.[27]

23. Robert Kirkwood, *Journal and Order Book of Captain Robert Kirkwood of the Delaware Regiment of the Continental Line*, Joseph Brown Turner, Ed. (Wilmington, DE: Historical Society of Delaware, 1910), 25.

24. James Thatcher, *Military Journal: The American Revolutionary War from 1776 to 1783; Describing the Events and Transactions of This Period with Numerous Historical Facts and Anecdotes* (Hartford, CT: Hurlbut, Williams & Co., 1862), 286.

25. Kirkwood, *Journal*, 26.

26. Kirkwood, *Journal*, 20–26.

27. Andrew Armstrong to Thomas Burke, July 10, 1782, *The Colonial and State Records of North Carolina*, 583. *Documenting the American South*, 16:629–630. sr/index.html/document/csr150193.

There were other hospitals, other diseases, other soldiers, and other documents pertaining to fever and ague in the Revolutionary era. This is only a glimpse of what transpired, told as much as possible by the voices of the past. Today's soldiers still suffer from malaria, yellow fever, typhus, and typhoid.[28] No matter the ideology, nationality, or cause, fever remains a leveling force.

28. Centers for Disease Control and Prevention. www.cdc.gov/malaria/about/faqs.html

Captain John Peck Rathburn:
As Audacious as John Paul Jones

❧ ERIC STERNER ❧

John Paul Jones tends to overshadow the study of the American Revolution at sea. While his accolades are well deserved, Jones earned many
of them with John Peck Rathbun at his side. An American-born merchant captain who joined the Continental Navy at its beginning, Rathbun's exploits are as daring as Jones's, but less well known.

Rathbun was born in Exeter, Rhode Island in 1746. Orphaned at an
early age, he likely grew up in Boston under the tutelage of his maternal
uncle, Thomas Peck, and went to sea as a ship's boy. By 1773, Rathbun
commanded a small schooner plying the coastal routes in New England
and Canada's maritime provinces. Peck was actively participating in the
patriot cause, likely involving Rathbun in Boston's political cauldron.
When the 1774 Intolerable Acts closed Boston's port, the young cargo
captain found himself beached. That winter and spring the restless skipper courted a much younger Polly Leigh, marrying her less than a
month after Lexington and Concord.[1]

The outbreak of fighting led Rathbun to leave Boston and head for
Rhode Island, where his last living sister resided. Conveniently, Rhode
Island's Esek Hopkins had just become Commander in Chief of the
new Continental Navy, leaving recruiting in the hands of Abraham
Whipple. By November, 1775 Rathbun had signed papers to join the
Navy of the United Colonies and departed for Philadelphia with a
handful of recruits aboard the sloop *Katy,* already in the service of

---

1. "Merchant Skipper Becomes Officer in Continental Navy," *Rathbun-Rathbone-Rath-
burne Family Historian*, Vol. 2, No. 4, October 1982, 52. Rathbun's last name is spelled
several ways in various documents: Rathbun, Rathburn, Rathbourne, Rathburne, etc.
The twentieth-century United States Navy named two ships after Rathbun, and mis-
spelled his name each time.

Rhode Island under Whipple's command as a warship defending the colony's interests.[2] *Katy* also bore John Trevett to Philadelphia as a new recruit in the Marines.[3] Arriving in Philadelphia, the Rhode Island sloop joined the Continental Navy as well, becoming *Providence*. Rathbun would enjoy a fruitful relationship with both the ship and the Marine.

During the winter of 1775–1776, Congress and its agents assembled a small squadron by buying and converting civilian ships and placing them under Hopkins' command. By February 1776, the *Alfred, Columbus, Cabot, Andrew Doria, Fly, Hornet, Wasp,* and *Providence* swung at anchor in the mouth of the Delaware Bay. Collectively they mounted just 114 guns, most of which were relatively small, 200 Marines, and 700 sailors and officers, the newly commissioned second lieutenant John Peck Rathbun among them aboard the *Providence*.[4]

Congress set Hopkins' eyes south, wishing his squadron to put a stop to water-borne raids in Virginia and the Carolinas.[5] Hopkins had other ideas. He led his little fleet toward the Bahamas in search of arms and ammunition. Only six ships, including *Providence*, arrived on March 1.[6] It was Rathburn's first cruise as a naval officer.

Hopkins hoped to surprise the British governor of the Bahamas, but word of his squadron's departure arrived in the islands ahead of him. Two dilapidated forts guarded the island's largest town, New Providence. Hopkins' initial attempt to seize Fort Nassau by sneaking *Providence,* two captured schooners, and a landing party into the harbor failed when his largest warships hove into sight before *Providence* could reach its target. The Continentals eventually landed some Marines and sailors east of town, from where they marched overland. The local mili-

2. "Providence I (Slp)," Dictionary of American Naval Fighting Ships (Washington, DC: Naval History and Heritage Command), Available at: www.history.navy.mil/research/histories/ship-histories/danfs/p/providence-i.html, accessed May 26, 2016.

3. "Journal of John Trevett," December 3, in William Bell Clark, ed., *Naval Documents of the American Revolution, American Theatre: Sept. 3–Oct. 31, 1775, European Theatre: Aug. 11, 1775–Oct. 31, 1775, American Theatre: Nov. 1, 1775–Dec. 7, 1775,* Volume 2 (Washington, DC: The U.S. Navy Department, 1966), 1255. The Navy Department has continuously assembled and published *Naval Documents of the American Revolution,* hereafter NDAR, since 1964. Future cites will refer to NDAR by year of publication, volume, and page.

4. James M. Volo, *Blue Water Patriots: The American Revolution Afloat* (Lanham, MD: Rowman & Littlefield Publishers, Inc., 2006), 105–106.

5. "Journal of the Continental Congress," December 2, 1775 in NDAR, 1966, 2:1231–1232. The Naval Committee's order to Hopkins is contained in NDAR, 1968, 3:637–638.

6. Nathan Miller, *Sea of Glory: A Naval History of the American Revolution* (Annapolis, MD: Naval Institute Press, rev. ed., 1992), 107.

tia garrisoning Forts Montagu and Nassau quickly abandoned them, leaving the Marines in control of the town and harbor. Hopkins occupied New Providence for two weeks to remove as much war materiel as he could, going so far as to charter a local ship to carry some of it back to the colonies.[7]

Because Hopkins's early plans relied so heavily on the *Providence*, Rathbun likely would have worked with the Marine contingent and reacquainted himself with Lt. John Trevett, who was assigned to the *Columbus* but was also a member of the landing party.

When Hopkins departed, he set sail for Rhode Island. A minor clash on the return tarnished the entire raid. After taking a few prizes off New England's coast, the fleet encountered HMS *Glasgow*, a 20–gun frigate. Though outnumbered, *Glasgow* out-sailed and out-fought the American squadron, retiring successfully after inflicting severe damage.[8] *Providence* proved the greatest disappointment. Though she was among the fastest ships in the fleet, Capt. John Hazard failed to engage *Glasgow*. Hazard was court-martialed and replaced with John Paul Jones in his first independent naval command.[9] Rathbun initially remained the second lieutenant, but eventually rose to first lieutenant, becoming Jones's executive officer.

Jones and Rathbun spent May to October of 1776 aboard *Providence* cruising familiar waters, convoying civilian ships and looking for British prizes. Jones biographer Evan Thomas argued that the two established a close working relationship. Jones was a foreign-born disciplinarian only recently arrived in the colonies. Rathbun, on the other hand, was a successful America-born merchant skipper who knew the waters *Providence* plied quite well. He seems also to have been more familiar with Providence as a ship type. Rigged as a single-masted sloop, she touted a vast amount of canvas for her size, making her fast and maneuverable, but tricky to handle.[10] Having served on the ship longer, Rathbun may also have enjoyed a better relationship with the crew than the prickly Jones.

As the British invasion of New York got underway that summer, Rathbun found himself anchored with Jones in the Delaware Bay while

7. Robert L. Tonsetic, *Special Operations in the American Revolution* (Philadelphia: Casemate, 2013), 52–63; See also Tim McGrath, *Give Me a Fast Ship: The Continental Navy and America's Revolution at Sea* (New York: NAL Caliber/The Penguin Group, 2014), 52–56.
8. Miller, *Sea of Glory*, 112–115.
9. Volo, *Blue Water Patriots*, 107–109.
10. Evan Thomas, *John Paul Jones: Sailor, Hero, Father of the American Navy* (New York: Simon and Schuster, 2003), 56–57.

the captain sought better orders. The Marine Committee eventually provided them, and *Providence* left Delaware for a prize cruise on August 21.[11] Armed with just twelve four-pounders and a seventy man crew, Jones and Rathbun set off. Not content with simply taking prizes and the wealth they promised, Jones struck targets on land and in port, including the harbor of Canso in Nova Scotia and two ports on the Island of Madame.[12] Jones also tempted fate twice, separately encountering the British frigates *Soleday* and *Milford*. In both instances, he out-sailed the much better-armed warships, seemingly taunting their captains by cutting across their paths or alternatively shortening sail to bring them in close before adding sail to pull away.[13]

Following his return to the colonies in October, Jones was promoted to command the *Alfred*. Rathbun went with him as first lieutenant. Clearly, both men valued their partnership. Jones's first assignment was to rescue American prisoners in Nova Scotia, but manpower shortages delayed his departure. While waiting, Jones presided over a court martial, Rathbun joining as a member of the court.[14] Finally *Alfred*, still short of men, started its mission with *Providence*. Within a day, Jones came across the American privateer *Eagle*, out of Providence, Rhode Island. Because privateering offered greater chance for financial reward than the Continental Navy, it was a popular destination for deserters. Consequently, Jones decided to board *Eagle* and search its crew to meet his own needs. He sent two boats across, Rathbun commanding one from *Alfred* and marine Lt. John Trevett aboard one from *Providence*.[15]

Rathbun commandeered *Eagle* and brought her under *Alfred's* stern to expedite his search. The next morning Rathbun re-boarded the privateer and began his search. The privateer's prize master complained of his crew's treatment at Rathbun's hands. According to the him, *Eagle's* captain acceded to Jones's order to remove any suspect crewmen, but Rathbun indicated that he planned to take all the men on board and removed twenty-four crewmen "by Force and Violence."

11. "Narrative of Captain John Paul Jones, August 21 to October 7," NDAR, 1972, 6:1148–1149.

12. Ibid., 1149. See also "Diary of Simeon Perkins, Liverpool, Nova Scotia, Friday, Oct. 11th," NDAR, 1972, 6:1211–1212.

13. Samuel Eliot Morison, *John Paul Jones* (New York: Time Incorporated, 1964 ed.), 61–62; Thomas, *John Paul Jones*, 59–61, 64–65.

14. "Court Martial of James Bryant, Gunner of the Continental Brig Hampden, October 23, 1776," NDAR, 1972, 6:1378–1380. Bryant was found guilty of mutiny, but only cashiered from the service.

15. "Captain John Paul Jones to Commodore Esek Hopkins, extract, 2nd November 1776," NDAR, 1976, 7:16–17.

Rathbun also ordered a search of the hold at sword point. Finding more men, Rathbun then heaved *Eagle's* first lieutenant on deck and committed "many other Acts of high insult."[16]

Foul weather ended Jones's rescue plans and sickened his crews. From time to time he still took prizes, typically supply ships supporting British forces in Canada. The normal procedure called for placing prize crews aboard and dispatching the ships to an American port, but one such ship, *John*, was an armed sloop. Jones placed Rathbun in command and ordered him to keep station with *Alfred*.[17] Rathbun's brief period in command hints at a charitable streak that the prickly Jones may have lacked. Jones sent word by a Marine lieutenant that *John's* master, Edward Watkins, had fomented some sort of unrest. Rathbun investigated and determined the reverse, that Watkins had sought to tamp it down, going so far as to take a cutlass from one rebellious crewman. He asked Jones for a personal favor, to let Watkins remain aboard *John* for the time being as Watkins was ill. One suspects he may also have sought to shield Watkins from Jones's wrath.[18]

Alfred returned to Boston in December, where authorities sought to arrest Jones over the *Eagle* affair. Involved in suits and counter-suits, he lost *Alfred* and was only offered an opportunity to return to the *Providence*. Jones and Rathbun were both dissatisfied with the state of affairs and decided to make their cases directly to the Marine Committee. Rathbun detoured to see Esek Hopkins in Rhode Island on the way. There, he secured a letter of recommendation from Hopkins, addressed to William Ellery, a member of the Committee. Hopkins praised Rathbun, explaining:

> he [Rathbun] has Served since the Fleet went from Philadelphia there being no Vacancy whereby I could promote him agreeable to his Merits—if there Should be any Vacancy with you I can recommend him as a man of Courage and I believe Conduct, and a man that is a Friend to his Country—and I believe the most of the Success Capt [John Paul] Jones has had is owing to his Valour and good Conduct, he likewise of a good Family in Boston—Any Service you may

16. "Deposition of Justin Jacobs," attached to Jones' report to Commodore Hopkins, extract, 2nd November 1776, NDAR, 1976, 7:16.
17. "Captain John Paul Jones to Lieutenant John Peck Rathbun, Novr 25th, 1776," NDAR, 1976, 7:270–271.
18. Lieutenant John Peck Rathbun to Captain John Paul Jones, Novr 25," NDAR, 1976, 7:71.

do him will be Serving the Cause—he able to give you some Account of Captn Jones's Conduct which you may give Credit to—[19]

Hopkins graciously allowed Rathbun to give a copy to John Hancock, president of the Committee.

While Rathbun was lobbying Hopkins and Hancock, the *Eagle* affair continued to plague Jones. By the end of April, Rathbun was given command of *Providence* and was on his way to Rhode Island to assume his new post.[20] To Rathbun's disappointment, Hopkins had already sent *Providence* on a cruise, which ended in June. Rathbun finally rendezvoused with his ship in Bedford, Massachusetts early that summer. His new captain of Marines was John Trevett.[21]

After completing repairs to *Providence*, Rathbun returned to sea, skirting past British-occupied New York. He quickly demonstrated a dash of Jones's aggressiveness. Spying a squadron of five ships convoying south off Sandy Hook, New Jersey, Rathbun mirrored their course from inshore, eventually attacking the largest, which proved to be a 16–gun ship, *Mary*. *Mary* and two of the vessels fought him off, but Rathbun still managed to capture a small schooner.[22] Unfortunately, the fight with *Mary* cost Rathbun his sailing master. The next day, *Providence* continued south, searching for *Mary*, but instead encountered a British privateer. The privateer's captain thought better of engaging *Providence* and managed to evade her. By August, Rathbun had returned, disappointed, to Bedford.

Rathbun's second cruise in command of *Providence* took him south. Departing Bedford in mid-November, he arrived near Charlestown (Charleston) in December and promptly captured a Loyalist privateer, the *Governour Tonyn*.[23] Rathbun took that ship into Georgetown, South

---

19. "Commodore Esek Hopkins to William Ellery, Providence March 13 1777," NDAR, 1980, 8:99–100. Errors in the original.

20. "Merchant Skipper Becomes Officer in Continental Navy," 55.

21. "A Muster Roll of All Officers Seamen & Marines Belonging to the Continental Armed Sloop Providence Commanded By John Peck Rathbun ESQR From June 19, 1777 to [August 28, 1777]" NDAR, 1986, 9:830. Trevett had also sailed aboard *Providence* on her cruise prior to Rathbun's arrival.

22. "John Peck Rathbun Takes Sloop Providence to Sea," *Rathbun-Rathbone-Rathburn Family Historian*, Vol. 2, No. 1, January 1983, 4–5; See also, "Providence Gazette," August 16, 1777, NDAR, 1986, 9:753; "New York Gazette," August 18, 1777, NDAR, 1986, 9:765–766; Journal of Marine Lieutenant John Trevett, Continental Navy Sloop Providence, August 31, NDAR, 1986, 9:853–854.

23. "The South Carolina and American General Gazette, December 25, 1777," NDAR, 1996, 10:809. The *Governour Tonyn* carried several African American fisherman who turned out to be slaves. Rathbun planned to return them to their owners. "Journal of Marine Captain John Trevett, November-December 1777," NDAR, 2005, 11:1169–1179.

Carolina, disembarked, and retired with Trevett and his prisoners to Charleston. There, Rathbun heard that *Mary* was in the port of New Providence for repairs and resolved to pay her, and the town, another visit.

He also encountered Capt. Nicholas Biddle, commanding the frigate *Randolph*. Biddle, well-acquainted with Trevett, pressed the Marine to join his crew, but Trevett informed him that he had already committed to sail for New Providence under Rathbun. *Mary* loomed too large for Trevett to abandon his promise.

As *Providence* returned to sea in January, 1778 bound for the Bahamas, Rathbun and Trevett marked the beginning of their third year of war. The Marine took a moment to contemplate the risks of raiding Nassau with a single ship, writing "I have had A Long time to think of What I am A Going to undertake but I am Very Well Satisfied that we Are in a Good Cause & we are fiting the Lords Battel."[24] *Providence* encountered three British vessels at first light the day after leaving Georgetown. They chased her and Rathbun could not shake them, despite tossing supplies overboard to lighten the ship. Fortunately, *Providence* stayed just far enough ahead to lose its pursuers that night by dousing its lights and dropping sail. Once the British passed by, Rathbun raised sail and altered course. His horizons were clear the next morning.

With fewer provisions, Rathbun made straight for New Providence. The Continental captain opted to give Hopkins' initial plan for sneaking into New Providence another try. After arriving offshore, he shipped the top sail mast and yard, housed the guns, and sent most of his men below to disguise *Providence* as a simple merchant vessel. Around midnight on January 27, *Providence* came abreast of the harbor under a light breeze while Trevett prepared his team of twenty-eight raiders below decks. No one in Nassau raised the alarm. In the distance, anchored near the wall of Fort Nassau, *Mary* beckoned.[25]

With *Providence* hanging off the harbor, Trevett loaded his men into a barge and took them ashore in two trips, landing a mile from Fort Nassau. They carried a scaling ladder, their weapons and ammunition, but no food or water. Drawing on his experience in the 1776 raid, Trevett went forward, discovered the fort lacked a picket, and entered alone through an embrasure. He hid and measured the march of two sentries. As the cry "all is well" from opposite corners of the fort died on the breeze, he slipped back out and brought his men forward with

24. "Journal of Marine Captain John Trevett," 1–31 January 1778, NDAR, 11:245. Errors in original.
25. Ibid.

their scaling ladder. They waited below the walls another thirty minutes until "all is well" carried over the wall again, then raised the ladder. Everyone followed Trevett back into the fort. Trevett ordered his men not to fire lest it alert the town. Just as the Marine captain turned a near corner around the barracks, he ran smack into one of the sentries and seized the initiative by grabbing the man's collar and forcing him into the nearest door. While the confused sentry stammered out his innocence of any transgression—"for God Sak What have I done"—the next man behind Trevett fired his pistol at the guard. He missed. Fortunately, the sound did not provoke a reaction. Trevett and his men quickly captured the other sentry. In the process, he discovered several of the fort's eighteen-pounders were loaded and lit matches were nearby. They were ready to signal the local militia, as the captured sentries informed him that 500 men would assemble to defend the fort ten minutes after a cannon discharge. Trevett opted to maintain appearances by putting out his own sentries and keeping up the cry "all is well," which was echoed from a ship in the harbor. Rathbun's landing force spent the rest of the night arming the cannon and training them down the streets of New Providence and at ships in the harbor.[26] Meanwhile, a nasty gale that blew all night forced Rathbun to weigh anchor and put out to sea.[27]

Dawn found a striped American flag flying over Fort Nassau. Trevett's first move in the morning was to send a note to a local merchant and American expatriate, James Gould, who arrived and climbed the ladder into Fort Nassau for a quick meeting. There, the Marine informed him that a landing party of 200 men and thirty officers came from Captain Biddle's squadron and was bound for Jamaica, would not molest civilian property, except war materiel, and would take the *Mary* as a prize. He further told Gould that he had provisions for all his men, but demanded breakfast just the same. Gould agreed and while Trevett waited for his morning meal, he sent a three-man detail through the town to the gates of Fort Montagu. They demanded, and received, the surrender of that fort as well.[28]

That task accomplished, Trevett next set his eyes on *Mary*, which lay within a pistol's shot of Fort Nassau. The captain was ashore ill and the executive officer initially declined to allow Trevett's party to board the vessel, but after some harsh and direct language, which no doubt

26. Ibid., 245–247.
27. Hope S. Rider, *Valour Fore and Aft: Being the Adventures of the Continental Sloop Providence, 1775–1779, Former Flagship Katy of Rhode Island's Navy*, (Annapolis, MD: Naval Institute Press, 1977), 142–143.
28. "Journal of Marine Captain John Trevett," 1–31 January 1778, NDAR, 11:247.

included reference to the shore-based cannon trained on her, Trevett took possession of the ship. Finally, with the town in confusion, Trevett and his men sat down to a hearty breakfast, going so far as to request, and get, cooked turtle for dinner.[29] That afternoon, *Providence* hove into sight, a British privateer of sixteen guns, *Gayton*, just two hours behind her. Trevett and Rathbun decided to haul down the American colors and maintain the ruse that all was well in New Providence. The trick failed as townsmen and women had already taken to the hills and were signaling alarm. *Gayton* passed back outside the bar, at which point Fort Nassau loosed three eighteen-pound rounds at her. The Continentals hit her in the main beam, but did not significantly damage her and she came to anchor within sight, but outside the range, of Fort Montagu. Trevett ordered his detail at Fort Montagu to spike the guns, break the rammers, and ruin the powder before abandoning the fort and returning to Fort Nassau. All in a day's work for one of the country's first Marines.[30] With Fort Montagu abandoned, *Gayton* moved deeper into the harbor, closer to *Providence*. Rathbun moored her abreast of the town and set her on her springs, which enabled the ship to pivot while anchored and expanded her field of fire. He resisted going ashore lest *Gayton* attack.[31]

January 28 dawned clear and pleasant. While Rathburn and his sailors set to work readying *Mary* for sea, Trevett and his party remained in Fort Nassau. Their force was too small to occupy New Providence and Trevett observed large numbers of armed men moving about the town and hills above the fort, making his Marines and accompanying sailors nervous. The island's governor and customs house collector approached the fort to ask about Trevett's intentions. He repeated the story he had told Gould: under Commodore Biddle's orders, they were to seize the fort, all armed vessels, and all American property they could find, while leaving civilian property undisturbed. Trevett later went into town in search of equipment from *Mary* around its captain's house, which he found and directed be delivered to *Providence* and *Mary*.[32]

Rathbun came ashore on the 30th and visited Trevett in the fort. He planned to depart the next day and required three pilots, one for *Providence*, one for *Mary*, and a third for a sloop. He also planned to take two schooners then in the harbor. Trevett proposed another ruse to get

29. Ibid., 247.
30. Ibid., 248.
31. Rider, *Valour Fore and Aft*, 50.
32. "Journal of Marine Captain John Trevett," 1–31 January 1778, NDAR, 11:249.

the required pilots, which Rathbun approved. Later in the day, someone Rathbun knew informed him that the locals planned to attack in company with men from *Gayton's* crew. Trevett did his best to keep up his bluff and disguise the Americans' imminent departure, inviting them to do so at dawn. As the night wore on, he and his landing party set about wrecking the fort and its guns.

Daylight on the 31st found *Providence* with her mainsail up and Trevett ready to go. His Marines towed the scaling ladder into the harbor before letting it drift and heading for *Providence*. When she finally passed the bar, her gaggle of charges included *Mary*, a brig, two schooners, and thirty Americans who had been held prisoner in New Providence.[33] The next day, Rathbun and Trevett parted company as the Marine boarded *Mary* to travel home. The two ships were separated when a British ship came upon *Providence* and its prize vessels, with *Mary* eventually making her way to New England.[34] After a passage troubled by inclement weather, she arrived at Bedford and a rendezvous with *Providence*. Rathbun left for home and directed Trevett to handle legal matters regarding *Mary's* disposition and his crew's prize money.

Rathbun captained the *Providence* on two more successful cruises before taking command of the 28–gun *Queen of France* in 1779. There, in July, his ship was sailing in heavy fog as part of a three-ship squadron and stumbled into the midst of a large British convoy escorted by a ship of the line and several frigates. Rather than doing the prudent thing and slinking away, Rathbun impersonated a British captain and tricked four merchantmen into surrendering to his boarding parties, again displaying the audacity he had demonstrated aboard *Providence*. Between them,

33. Ibid., 251. Trevett's memory, or his writing, did not serve him well here. Several of the prisoners rescued from New Providence participated in taking the *Mary* and two sloops, likely the *Washington* and *Tryal*. "Memorial of Captains Cornelius Anabil, John Cockrom, Nathan Moar, and Isaac Mackey to the Continental Congress," February 21, 1778, NDAR, 11:400. A family historian only credits Rathbun with two prizes on this raid. See "John Peck Rathbun Takes Sloop Providence to Sea," 6–7. British accounts, however, square more closely with Trevett's. One contemporary source credited the raid with five captures; a second with only four. See "Extract of a Letter from Rio Novo Bay, St. Mary's, in the Island of Jamaica, Feb, 21 1778," NDAR, 11:401 and, "Lieutenant Governor John Gambier to Lord George Germain, 25th Feb 1778," NDAR, 11:431. The smaller vessels appear to have been prizes of the *Gayton*. Modern histories indicate that Rathbun burned the schooners, which might explain some of the discrepancies. Rathburn may have captured five vessels, but having burned two, could only treat three as prizes. See, for example, Rider, *Valour Fore and Aft*, 155; McGrath, *Give Me a Fast Ship*, 207–208.

34. "Journal of Marine Captain John Trevett, 18–21 February 1778," NDAR, 11:395–396.

the other two Continental ships captured six more prizes. It was, perhaps, the Continental Navy's richest haul during the entire war.[35] 1780 found Rathbun and the Navy part of Charleston's defenses and he was captured when that city fell to British forces. Paroled, Rathbun bought the Kingston Inn in Little Rest, Rhode Island and settled down. Businessmen in the privateering business soon approached him to take command of the 34–gun brigantine *Wexford* and in August 1781, Rathbun went back to sea, bound for the British Isles. Damaged in a storm while crossing the Atlantic, *Wexford* encountered a swifter and more heavily-armed British frigate off the southern coast of Ireland. After a chase and desultory few rounds from his guns, Rathbun accepted the inevitable and hauled down his colors. He spent the rest of the war shuttling among English prisons before dying of illness in Old Mill Prison outside Plymouth in June, 1782.[36]

Rathbun left behind no great quotes or sea fights and his death during the Revolution precluded service under the flag of the United States. He did not go on to serve in the Quasi-War with France, the conflict with the Barbary Pirates, or the War of 1812, many of whose heroes began their naval careers in the Revolution. Yet, his audacity and aggressiveness easily match those of John Paul Jones, Nicholas Biddle, John Barry, or Gustavus Conyngham. Bloodlessly capturing New Providence and carrying away several prizes with nothing more than a small, lightly-armed sloop and James Trevett's bluffing skills is the stuff of legend.

---

35. "Capt. Rathbun Gets Command Of 28–Gun *Queen of France*," *Rathbun-Rathbone-Rathburn Family Historian*, Vol. 3, No. 2, April 1983, 20–21; Miller, *Sea of Glory*, 411–412.

36. "Rathbun is Captured Again, Dies at 36 in English Prison," *Rathbun-Rathbone-Rathburn Family Historian*, Vol. 3, No. 3, July 1983, 36–38, 46.

The Loyalist Exodus of 1778

JIM PIECUCH

In March 1778, several hundred South Carolina Loyalists began a march to the British province of East Florida to seek refuge from persecution and assist the British. Their successful effort threw the Whigs of South Carolina and Georgia into a panic and provided a valuable accession of military manpower to East Florida. The Loyalists' actions demonstrated that Britain had a substantial number of supporters in the southern backcountry, thus encouraging British officials in their expectation that a shift in military operations to the South would attract strong local support.

South Carolina Loyalists had first exerted themselves to support the British in November 1775, when some two thousand Loyalists surrounded a slightly smaller Whig force that occupied the backcountry town of Ninety Six. After several days of skirmishing, the two sides agreed to a truce and the combatants returned to their homes. The Whigs, however, then ignored the agreement and sent a militia force through the region, disarming the Loyalists and arresting their leaders in the "Snow Campaign" of November and December. Over the next two years, Whig leaders adopted a policy of harshly persecuting suspected Loyalists, causing many Loyalists to flee the state.[1]

This persecution undoubtedly was a factor in convincing many Loyalists to escape to St. Augustine in 1778, but the more immediate cause was the South Carolina legislature's passage of a loyalty act that spring. The law required all males sixteen and older to swear allegiance to the state. Those who refused to do so would forfeit their right to vote and to conduct business and legal transactions. Anyone who left the state

---

1. Jim Piecuch, *Three Peoples, One King: Loyalists, Indians, and Slaves in the Revolutionary South* (Columbia: University of South Carolina Press, 2008), Chapters 2 and 3.

to avoid taking the oath was subject to the death penalty if they re-turned. As a result, many wealthier Loyalists sold whatever property they could and sailed to Britain or the West Indies.[2] For many of the poorer Loyalists in the backcountry who were unwilling to pledge al-legiance to the Whig government and could neither afford the sanctions for refusal nor the cost of a sea voyage, escape to East Florida seemed the best solution to their dilemma.

As men formulated their plans and word began to circulate among the Loyalists, those willing to escape began gathering in the vicinity of Ninety Six early in the spring. Benjamin Gregory and John Murphy as-sumed leadership of the group, which numbered about four hundred, all mounted, by late March. They had intended to wait for another party to join them, but rebel militia leaders learned of the plan and the second group decided that it was too risky to attempt the proposed flight. Gregory and Murphy then led their followers on a rapid march southward toward the Savannah River.[3]

On first hearing that the Loyalists were in motion, Whig officials dismissed the group as "no more than a Plundering Party." A few militia units were dispatched to round them up, but the Loyalists eluded them.[4] Soon, however, the Whigs received more accurate reports of the Loy-alists' strength and panicked. "The back Country is all up in Arms; The Tories . . . have risen, and as if informed by the same spirit and moved by the same spring, have put themselves in motion at one and the same time throughout all parts of the State," Gov. Rawlins Lowndes reported with considerable exaggeration.[5]

To elude possible pursuit and make it easier to secure supplies, the Loyalists split into several parties, "plundering robbing and terrifying the Inhabitants" along their routes and gathering reinforcements. By the time they reached the Savannah River, Lowndes estimated that the Loyalists' numbers had increased to six hundred. They crossed the river into Georgia on April 3, putting "that Country in a very great Conster-nation."[6] Although Lowndes had ordered the Whig militia to take the

2. Robert S. Lambert, *South Carolina Loyalists in the American Revolution* (Columbia, University of South Carolina Press, 1987), 62–64.
3. Harry M. Ward, *Between the Lines: Banditti of the American Revolution* (Westport, CT: Praeger Publishers, 2002), 195.
4. Thomas Pinckney to Harriott Pinckney, April 7, 1778, in Jack L. Cross, ed., "Letters of Thomas Pinckney, 1775–1780," *South Carolina Historical Magazine*, Vol. 58, No. 3, July 1957, 148–149.
5. Rawlins Lowndes to Henry Laurens, April 14, 1778, in David R. Chesnutt, ed., *The Papers of Henry Laurens* (Columbia: University of South Carolina Press, 1993), 13:114.
6. Lowndes to Laurens, ibid.

field and halt the Loyalists, the Whigs only managed to kill and capture a handful of stragglers.[7]

Once the Loyalists entered Georgia, Maj. Gen. Robert Howe, commander of the Continental forces in the Southern Department, took charge of the effort to capture them. On April 6 he ordered Col. Samuel Elbert of the Georgia Continentals to assemble as many troops as possible "to prevent the Insurgents, now embodied & marching to East Florida, from joining the forces of that province." Elbert was to treat the Loyalists "as enemies to the united States" and use every method "consistent with the rules of war" to defeat them.[8] Elbert failed to halt the Loyalists, largely, Howe later explained, because the mounted Loyalists easily eluded and outdistanced Elbert's infantrymen; Howe believed that he could have stopped the refugees if he had had a sufficient force of cavalry. Growing conscious of their power, the Loyalists "Hoisted the British Kings standard, as they passed" with impunity across Georgia.[9] Along their route they attracted an additional two hundred Georgia Loyalists, including a party led by Col. John Thomas. Several deserters from the Whig forces also joined them.[10]

After the Loyalists successfully reached East Florida in mid-April, Whig leaders concluded that the exodus had not been spontaneous, but was instead part of a larger British plan to attack the southern states. Georgia Gov. John Houstoun believed that the Loyalists' escape presaged "the total Reduction" of Georgia.[11] Brig. Gen. William Moultrie agreed and predicted that an invasion from both St. Augustine and Pensacola in British West Florida was imminent; according to rumor, Loyalists and Indians would attack from West Florida while British regulars and Loyalists would advance from East Florida.[12] Robert Howe also expected "serious Consequences" to follow the Loyalists' junction with the British. Considering the weakness of the southern states and the "Disaffection among the People & that this Infection is still more preva-

---

7. William Moultrie to Robert Howe in William Moultrie, *Memoirs of the American Revolution, So Far As It Related to the States of North and South-Carolina, and Georgia*, Vol. 1 (New York: David Longworth, 1802), 205.

8. Robert Howe to Samuel Elbert, April 6, 1778, Robert Howe Papers, Georgia Historical Society.

9. Howe to unnamed, April 13, 1778, Robert Howe Papers.

10. Ward, *Between the Lines*, 195.

11. John Houstoun to Henry Laurens, April 16, 1778, in *Papers of Henry Laurens*, 13:121–122.

12. Moultrie to Laurens, April 20, 1778, ibid; Charles E. Bennett and Donald R. Lennon, *A Quest for Glory: Major General Robert Howe and the American Revolution* (Chapel Hill: University of North Carolina Press, 1991), 71–72.

lent in the Back parts of So Carolina," Howe thought it wise "to prepare for the worst."[13] Whig Joseph Clay of Georgia expressed concern at "the very great additional Strength" that the British were "daily receiving from the great Defection" of South Carolina's Loyalists.[14] He warned Henry Laurens that the influx of Loyalists was making the British in East Florida "so formidable" that they might soon overrun Georgia.[15]

Although the feared British invasion never materialized, other South Carolina Loyalists inspired by the exodus tried to replicate the escape. Many Loyalists from both Carolinas gathered along the Pee Dee River in northeastern South Carolina, probably with the intention of marching to St. Augustine, but Whig militia from North Carolina attacked them before they moved. A battle ensued in which several men were killed on each side, including a Whig colonel, but the Loyalists were dispersed.[16] Officials in the three southernmost states called out detachments of militia and kept them actively patrolling to discover and prevent Loyalist gatherings, effectively ending the exodus. In late April, "several other large parties of the disaffected attempted to cross Savannah River," however, the South Carolina militia prevented them from entering Georgia.[17] A few men who did manage to slip through the cordon informed Lt. Col. Thomas Brown, a South Carolina refugee who commanded the East Florida Rangers, that other South Carolina Loyalists had hoped to make their escape, but now "thought proper to postpone their insurrection to a more favourable opportunity, as the rebels upon receiving intelligence of the March of Murphy and Gregory's party had embodied themselves in every district." Because the Loyalists lacked sufficient arms and ammunition, they could not hope for success without the element of surprise. Brown's informants claimed that another 6,300 men across South Carolina were prepared to assist the British when opportunity offered.[18]

Some of the Loyalists decided to strike directly at their enemies rather than attempt to flee. Near Orangeburg, Loyalists launched a se-

13. Howe to Laurens, April 26, 1778, in *Papers of Henry Laurens*, 13:190–192.

14. Joseph Clay to Josiah Smith, undated c. March-May 1778, in *Letters of Joseph Clay, Merchant of Savannah, 1776–1783, Collections of the Georgia Historical Society*, Vol. 8 (Savannah: Morning News Printers and Binders, 1913), 70.

15. Clay to Laurens, May 30, 1778, in *Letters of Joseph Clay*, 76.

16. William Gipson, Pension Application, in John C. Dann, ed., *The Revolution Remembered: Eyewitness Accounts of the War for Independence* (Chicago: University of Chicago Press, 1980), 187.

17. James Whitefield to Laurens, May 6, 1778, in *Papers of Henry Laurens*, 13:261–262.

18. Thomas Brown to Augustine Prevost, April 10, 1778, in *Report on American Manuscripts in the Royal Institutions of Great Britain*, Vol. 1 (London: Mackie & Co., 1904), 227–228.

ries of attacks against area Whigs. They "cut off the ears of one Prichard a Magistrate, and another Man," beat a Whig militia captain, and burned the home of a member of the assembly. These acts, Lowndes noted, "have thrown all that part of the Country into a general Panick, and so intimidated the Inhabitants that those well affected, are deterred from taking any steps for their own Security least . . . they should bring upon themselves the resentment of these banditti." The governor ordered one hundred Continental troops to Orangeburg to reinforce the local militia, instructing the officers "to settle the point of Law, on the spot," if they captured the perpetrators.[19] The show of force put an end to the loyalists' attacks.

Meanwhile, Gov. Patrick Tonyn of East Florida, an aggressive former army officer, believed that the Loyalist reinforcements he had received, along with reports of Loyalist strength in the South Carolina backcountry, justified invading Georgia. With the provincial units at St. Augustine, the Rangers and South Carolina Royalists, greatly strengthened by the eight hundred refugees, Tonyn told Gen. Sir William Howe that "the province of Georgia may be taken in possession" with his British and Loyalist units, augmented by Indian auxiliaries. The conquest of Georgia "will give a fair opportunity for the loyalists in South Carolina to show themselves," and if they were as numerous as reports indicated, "I should apprehend that province would soon be compelled to subjection," Tonyn mused.[20]

Tonyn, however, never got the opportunity to try his plan. Before Howe could reply, the Whigs undertook their own offensive. For the third time in as many years, they launched an invasion of East Florida with the aim of capturing St. Augustine. The Loyalist exodus had convinced many Whigs that the invasion was necessary to prevent the British from being joined by even more refugees.[21] The Loyalists formed a large part of the force that opposed the Whigs; an estimated 350 South Carolinians, along with 150 of Brown's Rangers and 150 Indians, fought a series of delaying actions from north of the St. John's River to the St. Mary's River, where the Whig offensive came to a halt. Informants told the Whigs that a short time before, both Brown's troops and the South Carolina refugees had been "extremely discontented with

---

19. Lowndes to Laurens, Sept. 22, 1778, in *Papers of Henry Laurens*, Vol. 14 (1994), 343.

20. Patrick Tonyn to William Howe, April 6, 1778, Sir Guy Carleton Papers, Vol. 10, No. 1073.

21. John Faucherau Grimke, "Journal of a Campaign to the Southward. May 9th to July 14th, 1778," *South Carolina Historical and Genealogical Magazine*, Vol. 12, No. 2, April 1911, 63–64.

their Change of Situation & had expressed a wish to Return."[22] Prisoners captured by the Whigs on June 23 declared that some time earlier the Loyalists "had been very discontented & that some of them had threatened to return to Carolina & throw themselves upon the Mercy of their Country," but had since been "Reconciled."[23] About fifteen South Carolina Loyalists did desert during the campaign, as did some Whig soldiers, but the Loyalist troops showed no signs of demoralization in their encounters with the Whigs and fought well in the various skirmishes against the invaders. The Whigs began to withdraw on July 14.[24]

The Loyalist exodus had many short term benefits for the British. The refugees had spread panic throughout the South Carolina and Georgia backcountry, reinforced British forces in East Florida, and helped provoke the Whigs into a costly and unsuccessful invasion of that province. The refugees also provided the bulk of the forces that halted the invasion. In the longer term, their action and the reports they brought of thousands of other Loyalists eager to support the British encouraged Tonyn and other royal officials to advocate an offensive in the South. Loyalist support, they believed, would produce great results with a limited commitment of British forces.

The Whigs, despite the short term harm they suffered in terms of exposing their inability to control their own populations and the losses of manpower, money, and supplies in the invasion of East Florida, learned valuable lessons. When the British finally began their southern campaign with the capture of Savannah in December 1778, South Carolina officials acted promptly to prevent another exodus of refugees. The assembly passed an "Act to Prevent Persons Withdrawing from the Defense of the State to Join Its Enemies," which authorized Gov. John Rutledge to punish anyone who joined the British and did not surrender within forty days. The penalty was death and the confiscation of the offender's property.[25] Rutledge assembled a force of 2700 militia "to crush any Insurgents in our back Country."[26] Another detachment of militia commanded by Andrew Pickens pursued one group of Loyalists, numbering between seven and eight hundred men, into Georgia and

22. Grimke, "Journal," 65.
23. Grimke, "Journal," *South Carolina Historical and Genealogical Magazine*, Vol. 12, No. 3, July 1911, 130.
24. Brown to Tonyn, June 30, 1778, Carleton Papers, Vol. 11, No. 1247; Martha Condray Searcy, *The Georgia-Florida Contest in the American Revolution, 1776–1778* (University: University of Alabama Press, 1985), 142, 144, 145–147.
25. Lambert, *South Carolina Loyalists*, 83.
26. "John Rutledge to Benjamin Lincoln," February 28, 1779, *South Carolina Historical and Genealogical Magazine*, Vol. 25, No. 3, July 1924, 133–134.

defeated them at Kettle Creek on February 14, 1779. Only 270 survivors managed to reach British lines.[27] About twenty of the prisoners taken at Kettle Creek were among 150 Loyalist captives tried at Ninety Six between March 23 and April 12. More than twenty were sentenced to death for assisting the British, and five were eventually executed.[28] These measures intimidated the state's Loyalists from making any effort to join or otherwise assist the British.

Another long term consequence of the Loyalist exodus was that when the British finally occupied South Carolina in May 1780, their most committed supporters had already left the state and been incorporated into provincial units, or had been captured and executed. Those who remained had suffered through five years of repression, and in some cases violent persecution, at the hands of the Whigs. Less bold to begin with, they had been made even more timid by this treatment, and many of the men who could have provided the backbone of a reliable loyal militia were no longer available for that purpose. This was one of the most important reasons why the loyal militia in South Carolina never achieved the strength or effectiveness that the British had expected. Thus, in the end, the 1778 flight of the Loyalists may have done the British almost as much harm as good.

27. Robert S. Davis, Jr., and Kenneth H. Thomas, Jr., *Kettle Creek: The Battle of the Cane Brakes; Wilkes County, Georgia* (Atlanta: Georgia Department of Natural Resources, 1975), 33–34, 36–39, 43.
28. Robert Scott Davis, Jr., "The Loyalist Trials at Ninety Six in 1779," *South Carolina Historical Magazine*, Vol. 80, No. 2, April 1979, 174–175.

Temper, Temper: Officers and Gentlemen Go Berserk

JOSHUA SHEPHERD

"Civility is the cheapest, and yet the most profitable traffic."[1]

Put large numbers of men together for extended periods of time and they're bound to eventually get on each other's nerves. For armies in the eighteenth century, rowdy brawls were to be expected from the men in the ranks, who were generally drawn from the lower and middling classes of society. Far better behavior was expected of officers, who were, at least in theory, "gentlemen" possessed of better makings.

But all men, as Thomas Jefferson observed, "are created equal;" consequently, they can be equally obnoxious. American commanders were regularly bedeviled by controversies and courts-martial stemming from arguments and scuffles involving officers, who were just as prone as the enlisted men to run amok. Ready access to strong drink didn't help matters. Brig. Gen. Anthony Wayne, who could be pretty starchy in his own right, was nonetheless annoyed by quarrelling officers who persistently placed each other under arrest during fiery confrontations. Wayne enjoined his men to "Indeavor to Cultivate that harminey and friendship that ought to subsist . . . but should there be a misunderstanding among any of the officers in futer, he wishes them to settle it amicably or find some other mode than that of Court Martials."[2]

Even when Americans were held as prisoners of war, a condition that one would expect to occasion a sense of cooperation, ill manners could make things pretty unpleasant. When about 250 captured officers

1. Richard Lambart, Earl of Cavan, *A New System of Military Discipline, Founded Upon Principle* (Philadelphia: R. Aitken, 1776), 255.
2. Orderly Book of Captain Robert Gamble of the Second Virginia Regiment, in R.A. Brook, ed., *Proceedings of the Virginia Historical Society* (Richmond: Virginia Historical Society, 1892), 11: 242.

were placed in confinement subsequent to the fall of Charleston, South Carolina, discipline collapsed in a seething atmosphere of juvenile bickering. Maj. Gen. William Moultrie, who was left with the unpleasant task of refereeing the arguments, later observed that it was not surprising that there "should be continual disputes among them, and frequently duels," considering the fact that so many men were "huddled up together in the barracks, many of them of different dispositions." In an offhanded comment directed, no doubt, at officers who weren't South Carolinians, Moultrie noted that some of the men were "very uncouth gentlemen."[3]

Dismissive Britons occasionally offered commentary on the Rebels' penchant for turning average men into officers. The colorful diarist Nicholas Cresswell was confounded when he met "an Irish Tailor metamorphosed into a Captn. and an Irish Blacksmith his Lieutenant."[4] Even cultivated American officers bemoaned the caliber of men who had been granted commissions. After dealing with a frustrating string of petty disputes, Maj. Gen. Richard Montgomery carped that "I wish some method coud be fallen upon of engaging *Gentlemen* to serve—a point of honor and more knowledge of the world to be found in that Class of men woud greatly reform discipline and render the troops much more tractable."[5]

George Washington was ultimately exasperated by such incessantly childish bickering between men who were ostensibly on the same team. "Nothing gives me more pain," he wrote, "than the frequency of complaints that are made and difference of various kinds that happen among a set of Men embarked in the same great cause, who ought rather to cultivate harmony than break out into dissensions upon almost every occasion that offers."[6]

MAN'S BEST FRIEND

For the members of Seth Warner's Extra Continental Regiment, garrison duty at New York's Fort Edward, a post near Lake Champlain that saw little activity after 1777, could be painfully monotonous. But during

3. William Moultrie, *Memoirs of the American Revolution, So Far as it Related to the States of North and South Carolina, and Georgia* (New York: David Longworth, 1802), 2:119.
4. Lincoln MacVeagh, ed., *The Journal of Nicholas Cresswell, 1774–1777* (New York: The Dial Press, 1924), 160.
5. Michael P. Gabriel, *Major General Richard Montgomery: The Making of an American Hero* (Madison, New Jersey: Fairleigh Dickinson University Press, 2002), 140.
6. Letter, George Washington to Thomas Proctor, March 22, 1778, in John C. Fitzpatrick, ed., *The Writings of George Washington, From the Original Manuscript Sources* (Washington: Government Printing Office, 1934), 11:128.

the last week of June, 1779, the troops were treated to an ugly incident which no doubt relieved the tedium a bit.

It all started when Lt. David Bates stepped out the door of the post barracks and Private Doctor Prindle (his name, not his occupation), walked in the door after him. The two men didn't exactly care for each other to begin with; Bates, it would seem, was in the habit of hitting Prindle's dog. But Bates also had a dog, and with Bates out of the building, Prindle took his revenge, slapping Bates's dog in the ear. Bates, clearly infuriated when his dog yelped, stormed back into the barracks and demanded to know who had kicked his dog. "Nobody kicked him," replied a quick-thinking onlooker. When Bates persisted, Prindle confessed that he had hit the dog, and the lieutenant then demanded why he had done so. Obviously without choosing his words too carefully, Prindle shot back "For fun by God."

With that, tempers escalated quickly. Bates snapped, "struck" Prindle, and asked him "how he Liked that for fun" and "if he Struck for fun." "Yes by God, as you have my dog often," answered Prindle; for good measure, the private then "Cursd and damd" the lieutenant. Outraged by such insubordination, Bates then hit Prindle several more times and called out the guard. Regimental Surgeon Azel Washburn, who witnessed the nasty squabble, claimed that Prindle broke into hysterics when he knew he was under arrest. "Being very full of anger," recalled the good doctor, Prindle "raved and cursed every thing that came first into his head. Damd the dog and the rascal that owned him."[7]

Prindle, who had been struck by an officer during what amounted to little more than a private argument, was found guilty of "impertinent language" but elicited sympathy from the presiding officers of his court-martial. The fracas was "attended with Such Curcumstances" that Prindle was sentenced to no more than a severe reprimand.[8]

AND IN THIS CORNER . . .

If you're going to be cashiered from the service, you might as well leave a memorable impression. That was apparently the thinking of Lt.

---

7. "Rascal" was a much more insulting term than it is today; while Samuel Johnson's famous dictionary gave the definition as "A mean fellow; a scoundrel; a sorry wretch," a period dictionary of slang defined it as "a rogue or villain . . . a rascal originally meaning a lean or shabby deer, at the time of changing his horns, penis, &c. whence, in the vulgar acceptation, rascal is conceived to signify a man without genitals . . ." Samuel Johnson, *A Dictionary of the English Language* (London: W. Strachan, 1755); Francis Grose, *A Classical Dictionary of the Vulgar Tongue* (London: S. Hooper, 1785), 134.
8. "Fort Edward, in 1779 and 1780, Orderly Book of the Captain Commanding", in Henry B. Dawson, ed., *The Historical Magazine, and Notes and Queries* (Morrisania, New York: 1867), 2nd Series, 2:374.

William Horton, who gathered with a number of other officers at Mandival's Tavern in New York's Hudson Highlands. Drink flowed freely, senses dulled, and tempers flared. For reasons unrecorded, and likely unknown to the participants themselves, a noisy argument broke out. A witness to the ensuing theatrics explained that things really went awry when "Captain Graham came into the room to still the rout."

Lieutenant Horton didn't welcome the interference, and commenced arguing with Captain Graham. Horton "cursed, damned, and swore," and Graham gave him a push. It led to a shove. At some point during the altercation, an enraged Horton stripped off his shirt, and, bare-chested, got down to business. He seized the captain, "jammed" him up against the bar, and then threw him down in the chimney corner. Not satisfied, Horton leapt on top of Graham and commenced strangling him. Although witnesses failed to mention it, one suspects that there was more profanity during the grappling on the floor.

Horton was pulled off his victim and taken from the room, but still held a considerable grudge. Struggling to get back at Graham, an apoplectic Horton thundered, "Now I am under an arrest, damn you, I will give a flogging!" Whatever his failings may have been, Horton was bluntly honest at his court-martial on December 5, 1776. Captain Graham, he admitted, "told near the truth" about the unfortunate incident. Such forthrightness, however, failed to help him, and Horton was cashiered, sadly denying Patriot forces the services of an undeniably fierce, albeit terribly misguided, fighter.[9]

A FRENCHMAN BEHAVING BADLY

Col. Charles Armand, the former Marquis de la Rouerie, was a well respected officer but apparently not much of a house guest. In June of 1779 Armand, along with a handful of other officers, stopped at the home of James Vandeburgh, a well connected New Yorker and colonel of the Dutchess County militia. During the short two hour visit, the patrician Armand got into a spat with Vandeburgh's son, then Vandeburgh himself, and had the former locked up under guard.

Armand got himself worked up into quite a dander, took control of the home, and raved like an outraged nobleman. Vandeburgh claimed that he was "in bodily fear" during the incident, and the ruckus emanating from the home drew the attention of passersby. When Jeremiah Clarke attempted to intercede and requested that Armand release the young Vandeburgh, the colonel responded by slapping the hat off of Clarke's head and kicking him out of the room. To get his point across,

9. Peter Force, ed., *American Archives* (Washington, 1853), 5th Series, 3:1084–1085.

Armand then proceeded to knock the hat off the head of Jonas Adams. The spat ended with wounded feelings on all sides. By Armand's reckoning, the New Yorkers were guilty of anti-French bigotry, and he regretted that a court-martial would result from "the quarrel of a respectable officer with a rascal" like Vandeburgh.[10]

Ultimately, Armand was found guilty of confining Vandeburgh's son and slapping the hats off the heads of Clarke and Adams. "The Confinement of a Citizen by military authority," read Armand's reprimand, "was irregular and blamable, and there appears to have been an improper degree of warmth in Colonel Armand's conduct."[11]

ANOTHER FRENCHMAN BEHAVING EVEN WORSE

He was, arguably, the most violently erratic officer to serve in the Continental Army. JeanBernard-Bourg Gauthier de Murnan, a major in the corps of engineers, was apparently proficient in his official duties but utterly incapable of working and playing with others. A letter from George Washington in August 1780 detailed Murnan's first recorded brush with trouble. "I am sorry to find," wrote Washington, that a quartermaster sergeant in the 3rd Connecticut Regiment "has been stabbed by you in the Arm and Body."[12]

It was not the last of Murnan's shocking outbursts. That September he faced a court-martial subsequent to a confrontation with, of all people, the Reverend David Jones, who was serving as a chaplain. Murnan had occupied quarters which Jones considered his, and was tried for "unofficer and ungentlemanlike" behavior. Murnan was exonerated of the charges, but had clearly been a little rough on the hapless clergyman.[13]

Murnan's provocative behavior only got worse, and at Dobbs Ferry, New York, on July 25, 1781, he apparently took leave of his senses. The precise chronology of the day's chaotic events is difficult to piece together, but Murnan was a walking disaster. Attempting to seize a boat but confronted by the sentry tasked with guarding it, the infuriated Frenchman responded by spitting in the man's face, drawing a sword,

10. Armand's self-justification, in French, can be found in Harold C. Syrett, ed., *The Papers of Alexander Hamilton* (New York: Columbia University Press, 1961) 2:134–136.

11. General Orders, August 31, 1779, in Fitzpatrick, *The Writings of George Washington*, 16: 207–208.

12. Jean-Bernard-Bourg Gauthier de Murnan to George Washington, August 8, 1780, Founders Online, National Archives (http://founders.archives.gov/documents/washington/99–01–02–0263).

13. General Orders, September 21, 1780, in Fitzpatrick, *The Writings of George Washington*, 20:76.

and threatening to kill him. Murnan stirred up even more trouble when he interfered with a fatigue party of New Hampshiremen. Capt. Daniel Livermore, who was quite protective of his troops, didn't particularly care for the Frenchman's treatment of the work party, which included kicking the men.

When their dispute came to a head, it's remarkable that no one was killed. Murnan called Livermore a "damned rascal", threatened to cut off his nose, and then drew a sword and took a swing. Livermore fought back with his espontoon, striking Murnan so hard that the staff broke. He then grabbed another espontoon from a fellow officer and continued beating the Frenchman; for good measure, he kicked Murnan "in case he should again Kick any of the soldiers."

For his actions, Livermore was cashiered but reinstated when fellow officers interceded on his behalf. At Murnan's court-martial, accusations revealed a bizarre string of violent episodes that stretched back for several years. Murnan had supposedly stolen a fellow officer's horse at sword point, attacked a servant, stolen wood belonging to an officer's family, and badly clubbed an enlisted man. Not surprisingly, the presiding officers of the court sentenced the tempestuous Frenchman to be dismissed from the service.

George Washington confirmed the opinion of the court, but his final decision was no doubt disheartening to anyone who had ever served with Murnan. Because some of the testimony didn't appear to support the worst accusations, Washington reinstated Murnan, "notwithstanding the impropriety of his Conduct on the 25th. of July."[14]

YOU'RE NOT MY BOSS

When dinner conversation turns into an armed confrontation, it's bound to end up in a court-martial. Lt. Abner Bacon of Knowlton's Rangers explained how it all started. Entering the officers' quarters on the evening of September 26, 1776, Bacon observed a group of men dining and, apparently making a snide comment about the appetites of his fellow officers, quipped that "we must draw more rations." Ensigns Thomas Fosdick and Benoni Shipman took umbrage with the remark, and the evening's atmosphere turned stormy. Both of the ensigns, claimed Bacon, "came up and damned me, and abused me very much." The altercation grew ugly, and it was agreed to let lieutenants Lemuel Holmes and Jacob Pope settle the matter. Although Holmes was in nominal command of the detachment, both Fosdick and Shipman de-

14. Information for the events of July 25 come from Fitzpatrick, *The Writings of George Washington*, 22:482–483 and 23:63–65.

cided to take up an argument with him as well. Having stirred up a hornet's nest, Bacon quietly slipped out of the room.

The situation only got worse. Holmes ordered the ensigns to quiet down, and Fosdick responded that he would take no such orders as "he was as good as any of us, and would not be commanded by any of us." Shipman was of the same mind, and after cursing Holmes and every one else in the room, added that "There was no one more than another who had command of the detachment." Getting nowhere with the unruly ensigns, Holmes ordered them under arrest, but Fosdick shot back that "he would not go under arrest unless he pleased." Fosdick then lost control of himself and basically threatened a mutiny, shouting that "they would turn out their company against the rest of the party." Fosdick, apparently joined by Shipman, then went into a back room and emerged with a musket. After a brief scuffle, the other officers succeeded in disarming them, but Shipman remained defiant, shouting and cursing with wild abandon.

Their court-martial was short and to the point. Both Fosdick and Shipman plead not guilty to charges of abusive language, disobedience of orders, and mutiny. The official record of their defense was a little thin: "The prisoners produce no evidence." The duo was found guilty of the lesser charges, but let off of the charge of mutiny, and were sentenced to no more than a reprimand.[15]

15. Force, *American Archives*, 5th Series, 2:589–590.

Untangling British Army Ranks

❀᠅ DON N. HAGIST ᠅❀

After a few years of editing articles for this journal, it's become apparent that the ranks of British officers sometimes confuse people. By "sometimes" I mean "often." And not without reason. Although titles like colonel and captain are familiar to us all, the roles associated with these ranks, and the fact that an individual could have more than one rank, lead many a writer astray. So here's a primer that should help sort things out.

The British army that served in American during the Revolution was composed primarily of infantry regiments. The full, or established, strength of infantry regiments varied during the course of the war, and actual strength was almost invariably different from the established strength, but a good rule of thumb is to think of a regiment as consisting of about 500 soldiers. There were exceptions, but this is a good overall guideline. Regiments were typically divided into ten companies of equal size. In most regiments, each company had three officers, and the regiment also had five staff officers; this sounds simple enough, but there were a number of nuances.

In general, each company was commanded by a captain. Three of the company commanders, however, also held higher ranks in the regiment: the colonel, the lieutenant-colonel, and the major. These three officers were collectively called field officers. So a regiment of ten companies had three field officers and seven captains, each commanding one company. On regimental muster rolls we sometimes see the field officers referred to as, for example, "Major and Captain," but in common parlance only the senior of the two ranks was used. Companies were generally referred to by the name of the commanding officer, for example, "Captain Handfield's company" or "Lt. Col. Campbell's company," but the field officers' companies might be referred to only by the rank since there was only one of each field officer, for example, the major's company.

The next company officer was the lieutenant. This was true in all companies but one. The colonel's company had a specialized rank called captain-lieutenant. Although the colonel was the commander of the regiment, he usually also held other roles (more on that later), so he was seldom present with the regiment. This meant that the next officer of this company, normally a lieutenant, was almost invariably in sole charge of the company. To acknowledge this, his rank was called captain-lieutenant. For a long time this rank had the authority of a captain but the pay of a lieutenant, but in the early 1770s it had been declared equal to captain. It nonetheless retained the title of captain-lieutenant, and there was only one officer of this rank in a regiment. The colonel's company was always referred to by the name of the colonel, rather than of the captain-lieutenant.

The third officer in most companies was an ensign, the lowest-ranking commissioned officer in the army. Eight of the regiment's companies had ensigns, but a few regiments used a different name for this rank. The Royal Artillery used the term 2nd Lieutenant instead of Ensign. Three infantry regiments, the 7th, 21st and 23rd, had originally been created as fusilier regiments with the role of protecting the artillery. By the time of the American Revolution these regiments were functionally identical to other infantry regiments, but they retained the honorific of Fusiliers (spelled a variety of ways during the period) and maintained the tradition of calling their youngest officers 2nd lieutenants instead of ensigns. There was no difference in these ranks other than the name. Cavalry regiments used yet another name, cornet; same rank, different name.

Because fusilier regiments had the rank of 2nd lieutenant, the senior lieutenant in each of their companies was sometimes called a 1st lieutenant. But "1st lieutenant" and "lieutenant" were identical ranks, even though the terminology was slightly different. Most companies in an infantry regiment, therefore, contained a captain, a lieutenant and an ensign, whereas most companies in the 7th, 21st and 23rd regiments contained a captain, a 1st lieutenant and a 2nd lieutenant. Functionally they were the same even though the names of the ranks were different.

Two companies in each regiment were composed only of experienced men fit for especially active campaigning: the grenadier company and the light infantry company, collectively called flank companies. Called upon to be at the forefront in battle, these companies were no place for inexperienced officers. Instead of having ensigns, each of these companies had another lieutenant; in other words, a flank company had a captain and two lieutenants instead of a captain, a lieutenant and an ensign. The flank company lieutenants were not differentiated by "1st" and "2nd," though; they were both simply lieutenants, even in a fusilier regiment.

To summarize, infantry regiments typically had thirty company officers, nominally distributed among their ten companies like this:

Colonel's Company:
Colonel (seldom present), Captain-Lieutenant, Ensign

Lieutenant-Colonel's Company:
Lieutenant-Colonel, Lieutenant, Ensign

Major's Company:
Major, Lieutenant, Ensign

Grenadier Company:
Captain, two Lieutenants

Light Infantry Company:
Captain, two Lieutenants

Captains' Companies (5):
Captain, Lieutenant, Ensign

A few regiments were structured differently, with four officers per company, but that was rare enough that we'll leave it out of this discussion.

Besides the company officers, regiments had an adjutant, a quarter master, a surgeon, a surgeon's mate, and a chaplain. The latter three were highly specialized and were normally filled by men explicitly trained in their disciplines (British regimental chaplains seldom accompanied their regiments on overseas service, but that's another story). The offices of adjutant and quarter master, on the other hand, were usually held by the same type of men as company officers, but with some nuances.

Before the American Revolution began, the adjutancy was usually held by one of the regiment's lieutenants—one man filling two roles in the regiment. Less often, this was also true of the quarter master. While the war was in progress, it became common practice to promote deserving sergeants to the adjutancy and quarter master roles.

That completes the suite of regimental officers, but only lays the groundwork for the confusing aspects of ranks and positions in the British army during the American Revolution. The army needed a host of officers to fill all sorts of wartime posts: brigadier generals, aides-de-camp, deputy judge advocates, adjutant generals, quartermaster generals, brigade majors, and so forth. Almost all of these posts were filled by regimental company officers, detached from their regiments, leaving fewer officers behind to manage each regiment's affairs.

General officers provide the best example, because their case was typical of peace as well as war. Most regimental colonels were also general officers, and as such usually had little time for direct management of their regiments. Lt. Gen. Thomas Gage was appointed colonel of the 22nd Regiment of Foot in 1763, retained that rank throughout his service as commander in chief of British forces in America, and continued it thereafter; one man with more than one rank, general and colonel. William Howe was colonel of the 23rd Regiment of Foot in addition to being a major general, then a lieutenant general; John Burgoyne was colonel of the 16th Light Dragoons; Sir Henry Clinton was colonel of the 12th Regiment of Foot; Charles Cornwallis was colonel of the 33rd Regiment of Foot, and so on.

The rank of brigadier general, sometimes called just brigadier, was a temporary rank authorized only in wartime. For wartime operations, regiments were grouped into brigades, with each brigade consisting usually of two to four regiments. The brigade was commanded by a brigadier, who held the rank only in the theater of operations and only for the duration of the conflict. Most British brigadiers in America were regimental colonels or lieutenant colonels—mostly the latter, because colonels were usually also already more senior generals. A few examples in America were Brigadier General Francis Smith, who was lieutenant colonel of the 10th Regiment of Foot; Brigadier General James Agnew, who was the lieutenant colonel of the 44th Regiment of Foot; and Brigadier General Simon Fraser, lieutenant colonel of the 24th Regiment of Foot.

To handle administrative and other duties of a brigade, another staff officer was required, called the extra major of brigade. One of these men was appointed for each brigade, and the man who held the rank was usually a regimental company captain, not necessarily from a regiment in the brigade. The appointment was temporary, for the duration of the brigade's existence, but the officer who held it was entitled to be addressed as major while he held the appointment. An example was the famous diarist Frederick Mackenzie, a captain in the 23rd Regiment of Foot; from 1776 through 1779 he served as extra major of brigade in a brigade consisting of the 22nd, 43rd, and 54th Regiments (for some periods it also included the 38th and 63rd Regiments) commanded by Brig. Gen. Francis Smith. Although Mackenzie regimental rank was captain, he was Major Mackenzie to the troops in his brigade.

This was the case with many British staff officers. When John André was caught and charged with spying, he was adjutant general to the British army in New York, but he was also a company captain in the 54th Regiment of Foot. So why was he called Major André? We'll get to that . . .

Another temporary wartime formation was a battalion. This terminology is particularly confusing because the term battalion is used for several similar, but distinctly different, organizations. We noted above that British infantry regiments were composed of ten companies, including two flank companies. When the two flank companies were detached (more on that later), the remaining eight companies were referred to as the battalion (today we often call the individual companies battalion companies, but that phrase doesn't appear often during the American Revolution). Sometimes the entire regiment, including the flank companies, was called a battalion. A few regiments were twice the size of other regiments; a noteworthy example was the 71st Regiment of Foot, Fraser's Highlanders. Instead of having ten companies, the 71st had twenty, with two of every officer except the colonel. The 71st Regiment was divided into two battalions, called the 1st Battalion 71st Regiment and 2nd Battalion 71st Regiment. Decades after the American Revolution this structure became quite common, but in America only a very few regiments were organized in this manner.

For this discussion of British ranks, however, the interesting battalions were the flank battalions. During the war in America, the specialized grenadier and light infantry companies were detached from their regiments and formed together into grenadier battalions and light infantry battalions. Being composed of companies, these battalions operated very much like regiments. Battalions were raised and disbanded during the war as needed, and the composition of a given battalion might change, but the flank battalions usually contained eight to twelve companies. In places where there were only a few flank companies, such as Rhode Island in 1778, a single flank battalion might be formed consisting of both grenadier and light infantry companies (Rhode Island had only two companies each from the 38th and 54th Regiments, formed into one small battalion).

Flank battalions needed commanders, so a regimental lieutenant colonel or major was appointed to that role. This officer retained his current rank, but was detached from his regiment to command the flank battalion. A major or captain was appointed as second in command.

The upshot of all these brigade, battalion and staff appointments was that many British infantry regiments suffered from a shortage of officers. For the most part there were men appointed to each position in the regiment, but many of those men were detached on some other duty. Take, for example, the 22nd Regiment of Foot in late 1780. The eight companies that formed the battalion of the regiment (since the two flank companies were detached) should have included twenty-four officers (three per company). But due to staff assignments and other causes, only fifteen were actually present, not even two per company, to handle the regiment's day-to-day activities.

There's more. As in many professions, career advancement was important and sometimes competitive. There were only so many regimental officer positions available, and once a man reached the rank of captain, the path upwards became quite narrow; remember that regiments had seven captains but only one major, so there was a lot of competition for that next step in rank (officers often changed regiments, but in the entire army the proportion of captains to majors was roughly the same as within an individual regiment). To accommodate deserving officers in this competitive environment, the War Office sometimes bestowed a brevet rank, that is, a rank in the army even though there was no opening in a regiment. For this reason, an officer could have an army rank of major but a regimental rank of captain. Such an officer was addressed as Major, but performed the function of a company captain— he was a major and was in a regiment, but not the regiment's major. There were also lieutenant-colonels and colonels in this situation, holding an army rank that was above their regimental rank. Remember Major André? He was a captain in the 54th Regiment, but a major in the army, and he served in the role of deputy adjutant general.

As if there weren't already enough special cases, a large detachment of the Foot Guards served in America. The Foot Guards were household troops, administered differently than the rest of the army; each of the three regiments of Foot Guards was considerably larger than a regular army infantry regiment. For service in America, volunteers from each of the three Foot Guards regiments were formed into a brigade consisting of two battalions, each with five companies. Following a long-standing tradition, some officers in the Foot Guards held army ranks that were higher than their regimental ranks; Foot Guards captains were lieutenant-colonels in the army, and Foot Guards lieutenants were majors in the army. In the Brigade of Guards, then, companies were commanded by officers addressed as lieutenant-colonel, reflecting their army rank.

All of the information above applies to infantry regiments of the British regular army, unless otherwise specified. Cavalry regiments were similar in terms of officer ranks, except that they had cornets instead of ensigns, and most cavalry regiments were organized into six troops instead of ten companies (the term "troop" described a component of a cavalry regiment, while "troops" was the general term for a quantity of soldiers). The Royal Artillery, Engineers, and Marines used the same titles for ranks, but were organized differently than the infantry. Loyalist regiments generally included the same ranks as British regular regiments and the same caveats of staff positions, battalions and what have you. American regiments were organized in a variety of ways, depending upon the year and the state that raised them, so the number of companies and the number of officers in each company varied. The German, French and Spanish armies followed their own practices.

What does it all mean? It means that rank can be a confusing thing, and that an officer's rank alone often didn't describe his role. As if this weren't confusing enough, there was no way to distinguish a British regimental officer's rank by looking at his uniform. But that's another story.

FOR FURTHER READING:

J. A. Houlding, *Fit for Service: The Training of the British Army 1715–1795*. Oxford, England: Clarendon Press, 1981.

Edward R. Curtis, *The British Army in the American Revolution*. New Haven, CT: Yale University Press, 1926.

Steven M. Baule and Stephen Gilbert, *British Army Officers Who Served in the American Revolution*. Bowie, MD: Heritage Books, 2004.

The Carefree and Kindhearted George Washington

NANCY K. LOANE

"The most unhappy man in the world," wrote the Commissary General of Purchases at Valley Forge about Gen. George Washington.[1] On every portrait we examine, on every image we see, the commander in chief does appear burdened and preoccupied. Occasionally, though, hidden among the millions of words written by, and about, General Washington, we catch a glimpse of the kindhearted side of the man. Sometimes a rare view of the carefree general emerges, too.

Consider the dreary days of the Valley Forge encampment. Even then, General Washington joined in a game or two of "wicket," and he undoubtedly enjoyed the competition and exercise.[2] Although Washington looks stern and dour on the dollar bill, he did occasionally share a hearty laugh or two. The commander himself proposed to General Lafayette that the two meet at Mount Vernon after "we shall triumph over all our misfortunes," as he phrased it, to "laugh at our past difficulties and the folly of others."[3] And Mrs. Theodorick Bland found him to be charming and "chatty"—even "impudent."[4]

1. Ephraim Blaine to William Buchanan, February 18, 1778, in *My Last Shift Betwixt Us & Death: The Ephraim Blaine Letterbook 1777–1778*, ed. Joseph Lee Boyle (Bowie, MD: Heritage Books, 2001), 131.
2. *The Military Journal of George Ewing: A Soldier of Valley Forge,* transcribed by Thomas Ewing, Jr., 47. www.sandcastles.net
3. George Washington to the Marquis de Lafayette, December 31, 1777, in *George Washington* Papers at the Library of Congress, 1741–1799, Letterbook 1, 52. Library of Congress (LOC) website. See also James Thacher, M.D., *Military Journal of the American Revolution 1775–1783* (Gansevoort, NY: Corner House Historical Publications, 1998), 160. Thacher wrote of Washington that "a loud laugh, it is said, seldom, if ever, escapes him."
4. Martha Daingerfield Bland, "Life in Morristown in 1777," letter to Frances Bland Randolph, May 12, 1777, *Proceedings of the New Jersey Historical Society* 51:3 (July 1933): 150–53.

Martha Bland was well-acquainted with both General and Mrs. Washington. In 1777 she traveled from her plantation in Virginia to visit with her husband, Col. Theodorick Bland, quartered near the Morristown, New Jersey, camp. The vivacious, young Martha Bland revered General Washington, calling him "our noble and agreeable commander" with "excellent skills in military matters." She went to camp several times a week—"by particular invitation," she noted with pride to Fanny, her sister-in-law—and took horseback rides throughout the Morristown countryside with General and Mrs. Washington, his aides, and several others. These casual jaunts, it seems, took place between dinner (served mid-afternoon) and dusk. On such relaxed, social occasions, Mrs. Bland found that the commander displayed an "ability, politeness, and attention" that she found charming. Occasionally, too, Martha Bland confided in a May 12, 1777, letter to Fanny, General Washington "throws off the hero, and takes on the chatty, agreeable companion—he can be downright impudent sometimes."

Washington could also be an enthusiastic dancer, as Catharine (or Caty) Greene, the wife of Gen. Nathanael Greene, discovered at the fourth encampment of the Revolutionary War. In March 1779, the Greenes hosted a "pretty little frisk" at their Middlebrook, New Jersey quarters. That evening, General Greene proudly reported, General Washington whisked the beguiling Mrs. Greene around the dance floor "upwards of three hours without once sitting down."[5]

Two years later, Caty considered traveling from Rhode Island to South Carolina to visit her husband. Undecided about this arduous endeavor, she consulted General Washington about the propriety of her journey. Then, on October 6, 1781, the commander extended an invitation to Caty through his friend Nathanael Greene: "should she (Caty) persist in . . . undertaking so long a journey as that from New England to Carolina I hope she will make Mount Vernon . . . a stage of more than a day or two."[6] Sometime before December 15, 1781, the intrepid Mrs. Greene arrived at Philadelphia from Rhode Island "in perfect health, and in good spirits, and thinking no difficulties too great not to be surmounted." To further assist Caty's travels, Washington assured her husband that he would "endeavor to strew the way over with flowers." Washington followed up on his promise, subsequently requesting

5. Nathanael Greene to Col. Wadsworth, March 19, 1779, in *The Papers of General Nathanael Greene,* ed. Richard K. Showman (Chapel Hill: University of North Carolina Press) 3:354.
6. George Washington to Nathanael Greene, October 6, 1781, *The George Washington Papers at the Library of Congress, 1741–1799,* Letterbook 2, Image 266. LOC website.

all quartermasters and officers in the Continental service to "give Mrs. Greene every aid and assistance in their power in her journey to the State of South Carolina."[7] Undoubtedly the commander's kind letter, which Caty carried with her, did help to smooth her journey.

Washington also acted kindly towards another wife of one of his officers. After Maj. Daniel Neil, an artillery officer, was killed at Princeton, his widow turned to Washington for assistance. Writing to the commander on February 19, 1777, Mrs. Elizabeth Neil lamented that the recent "unhappy situation" had rendered her and her two small children "destitute of support:" they had lost a husband and father, an estate in England, and a farm in New Jersey that was now "rendered useless by the enemy." Relying on the general's "known benevolence," as Elizabeth Neil wrote, she inquired about Congress's rumored resolutions supporting the widows of fallen soldiers and officers.[8] Washington forwarded the letter to Congress soon after he received it, noting that, although he did not recall any such Congressional provision, he recommended some reparation be made to Mrs. Neil "for her great loss."[9]

Instead, on March 14, 1777, Congress informed General Washington that no provisions had yet been made to support widows whose husbands has been killed in battle.[10] Replying to Mrs. Neil himself on April 27, 1777, Washington enclosed a copy of the March 14 Congressional resolution, thanked her for sending him a piece of buff cloth, wrote that he could "sincerely feel for your distress," and included a "small testimony of my inclination to serve you upon any future occasion." This small testimony was a gift of fifty dollars.[11]

Washington also acted kindly towards his servants. Mrs. Elizabeth Thompson, described as a worthy Irish woman, loyally served as Washington's housekeeper and cook for five years of the Revolutionary War. She finally left his service at the age of seventy-seven; a letter said that age had "made it necessary for me to retire." Several years later, in October 1783, Washington received a letter signed "Your Excellency's Old Devoted Servant, Elizabeth Thompson" that had been written on her

7. George Washington to Nathanael Greene, December 15, 1781, *The George Washington Papers at the Library of Congress, 1741–1799*, Letterbook 14, Image 327. LOC website.

8. Elizabeth Neil to George Washington, February 19, 1777, *The George Washington Papers at the Library of Congress, 1741–1799*, Image 324. LOC website.

9. George Washington to Continental Congress, February 28, 1777, *The George Washington Papers at the Library of Congress, 1741–1799*, Letterbook 2, Image 198. LOC website.

10. *Journals of the Continental Congress*, A Century of Lawmaking for a New Nation: U.S. Congressional Documents and Debates, 1774–1875. 7: 177. LOC website.

11. George Washington to Elizabeth Neil, April 27, 1777, *The George Washington Papers at the Library of Congress, 1741–1799*, Letterbook 1, Image 94. LOC website.

behalf. (Mrs. Thompson could not write; her signature was an X.) The letter said that should I "ever want, which I hope will not be the case, I will look up to your Excellency for assistance, where I am sure I will not be disappointed."[12] Two months later Mrs. Thompson received the sum of $240.00 in full account for services with General Washington's family during the Revolutionary War.

But the commander did not stop there. It seems that Mrs. Thompson and the general continued to correspond, for a letter written for her to Congress dated two years later, on February 17, 1785, notes that "the General who was always kind to me, and whose countenance was a comfort to me when our affairs were at the worst" had invited her to spend her final days "in his own house"—which was, of course, Mount Vernon. This kind invitation, however, could not be accepted; at eighty-one, Mrs. Thompson was burdened with a "heap of infirmities" that made travel from New York to Virginia impossible.[13]

General Washington made unexpected kindly gestures to others under his command, too. At Valley Forge, after learning that Lt. Col. Leven Powell had been stricken with the debilitating St. Anthony's fire, he sent Powell three bottles of what the patient considered to be "excellent" wine.[14] On the occasion of the May 6, 1778, celebration of the French Alliance, Washington acquitted a French soldier condemned to death and also "availed himself of the opportunity to pardon all other criminals" in the camp provost.[15] On June 3, 1778, Capt. Allen McLane, also stationed at Valley Forge, received special permission to enter Philadelphia to care for his property after the British left the city. This "indulgence of his Excellency," however, was to be kept secret, "as it may give room for other applications of a similar nature."[16] It is no sur-

---

12. Elizabeth Thompson to George Washington, October 10, 1783. *The George Washington Papers at the Library of Congress, 1741–1799,* Image 373. LOC website. .
13. Elizabeth Thompson to Continental Congress. February 17, 1785. The Papers of the Continental Congress, 1774–1789. National Archives and Record Administration (NARA), microfilm publication M247. Roll 103, Vol. 22, item 78, p.297. In this same letter, Mrs. Thompson asked Congress to grant her "little something" to close her eyes in peace; the next day Congress voted to give her $100.00 immediately and $100.00 a year for life, to be paid quarterly. See also A Century of Lawmaking for a New Nation: U.S. Congressional Documents and Debates, 1774–1875. *Journals of the Continental Congress,* February 18, 1785. 28:85.
14. Levin Powell to Sarah Powell, January 21, 1778, in Joseph Lee Boyle, *Writings from the Valley Forge Encampment of the Continental Army, December 19, 1777–June 19, 1778* (Bowie, MD: Heritage Books, 2000), 1:35.
15. Johann de Kalb to Madame de Kalb, May 12, 1778, in ibid., 6:134.
16. James McHenry to Allen McLane, June 3, 1778. *The George Washington Papers at the Library of Congress, 1741–1799,* Letterbook 5, Images368, 369. LOC website.

prise that the soldiers at the encampment thought General Washington to be both "great" and "good" and "the friend and father of us all," although "the many embarrassments continually thrown in his way have rather made him look older."[17]

At times Washington also acted kindly towards the enemy. After the battle of Germantown he returned a dog that had wandered away from the British camp. "General Washington's compliments to General Howe," began Washington's October 6, 1777, note. "He [Washington] does himself the pleasure to return him [Howe] a dog, which accidentally fell into his hands, and by the inscription on the collar appears to belong to General Howe."[18] The commander also obliged Dr. Robert Boyes, a surgeon in the British army. Boyes had sent Washington a "very polite letter" asking for the return of valuable medical manuscripts confiscated by the Americans from the British brig *Symetry*. "I have no other view in doing this," the general wrote about returning the manuscripts to Dr. Boyes, "than showing our enemies that we do not war against the Sciences."[19]

Elias Boudinot wrote from Valley Forge that the "worthy" Washington has "both hands & heart full."[20] Yet, even during those dark days and throughout the Revolutionary War, the commander occasionally relaxed for a ball game, chatted a little, danced a lot. And, throughout the wartime years, the general's innate decency showed through in his kind gestures towards the wives of the officers, the soldiers themselves, his servants, and even the enemy.

17. Alexander Scammell to Timothy Pickering, February 6, 1778, *Writings from the Valley Forge Encampment*, 3:62; Samuel Ward to Phebe Ward, April 1778, in ibid., 1:127.
18. George Washington to William Howe, October 6, 1777, *The George Washington Papers at the Library of Congress, 1741–1799*, Letterbook 1, Image 85. LOC website.
19. George Washington to William Smallwood, January 23, 1778. *The George Washington Papers at the Library of Congress, 1741–1799*, Letterbook 5, Image 7. LOC website.
20. Elias Boudinot to Hannah Boudinot, April 20, 1778, *Writings from the Valley Forge Encampment*, 4:110.

Two Years Aboard the *Welcome*: The American Revolution on Lake Huron

❀❂ TYLER RUDD PUTMAN ❂❀

In the spring of 1775, the fur trading post at the junction of Lakes Michigan and Huron looked much as it had for years. Fort Michilimackinac, significantly larger than when the French founded the site in 1715, comprised a tall stockade wall surrounding streets of privately owned row houses, a church, a soldiers' barracks, officers' quarters, storehouses, privies, and workshops. The community, having long since outgrown the tight confines of the stockade, now included dirt streets with rows of small houses running eastward from the fort.[1] Everyone lived close to the water. The Great Lakes provided news, transportation, and livelihoods.

Past the village, near the beach of sand and pebbles, a small work crew clamored around the skeletal frame of a ship under construction.[2]

---

1. On Michilimackinac at this time, see David A. Armour and Keith R. Widder, *At the Crossroads: Michilimackinac During the American Revolution* (Mackinac Island, MI: Mackinac State Historic Parks, 1986), 8. This book and John E. McDowell, "When the Welcome Sailed the Great Lakes," in *A Wind Gone Down: Out of the Wilderness* (Lansing, MI: The Michigan History Division, Michigan Department of State, 1978) are the only secondary sources to discuss the *Welcome* in any detail.

2. Armour, a reliable Michilimackinac historian, believed the *Welcome* was constructed there in 1775, probably based on "List of Vessels," 1783, Michigan Pioneer and Historical Society (henceforth MPHS), ed., *Historical Collections: Collections and Researches Made by the Michigan Pioneer and Historical Society*, vol. XXIV (Lansing, MI: Robert Smith & Co., State Printers and Binders, 1895), 12. See David A. Armour, "Askin's WELCOME Will Sail Again," *Telescope* 22, no. 5 (October 1973): 139–41. There is no mention of the *Welcome*'s construction in Askin's published papers. In 1778, Askin wrote that Robertson had been "master of my Vessell," how he usually referred to the *Welcome*, " this several years past," suggesting that the ship was a few years old in 1778: Askin to McMurry, April 28, 1778, Milo M. Quaife, ed., *The John Askin Papers*, vol. 1: 1747–95 (Detroit: Detroit Library Commission, 1928), 70.

This was a peculiar sight. It was the first large sailing vessel ever built at Michilimackinac, and one of the largest seen in the Mackinac region since French explorer La Salle's *Le Griffon* almost a century before.[3] John Askin, who owned the unfinished vessel, had walked down to survey the work. A forty-five-year-old Irish-born British army veteran and fur trader, Askin settled at Michilimackinac in 1764 and by 1775 was one of the most prosperous merchants in the region.[4] Above all, he hoped that his latest investment would pay off. The vessel would be a small sloop, a type of single-masted vessel, and measure only 47 feet at the keel, the long timber at its base, but it was costly.[5] The following year, as the vessel wintered in the Cheboygan river east of Michilimackinac, Askin counted "the Sloop Welcome with everything belonging to her," worth £700, as the most valuable entry in the inventory of his real and personal property.[6]

The *Welcome* proved more valuable than Askin ever imagined, but for very different ends than he intended. Michilimackinac seemed placid in 1775, but war simmered in the east. By the end of the American Revolution in 1783, despite all their other losses, British authorities claimed success in Canada. Communities around the Lakes Huron, Michigan, and Superior remained loyal to the British throughout the war. The

3. Data on ship measurements in the Great Lakes before this period are sparse, so the precise relation of the *Welcome* to other, earlier Mackinac vessels is difficult to determine with certainty. The only larger ship preceding the *Welcome* was the schooner *Gladwin*, 80 tons burthen and carrying 8 guns, which made it to Michilimackinac in 1764, captained by Patrick Sinclair. See J. Carver, *Travels Through the Interior Parts of North-America, in the Years 1766, 1767, and 1768* (London: Printed for the Author, 1778), 149, a 1778 return in *The Canadian Institute, Transactions of the Canadian Institute*, vol. IV (Toronto: The Canadian Institute, 1895), 311, and Keith R. Widder, *Beyond Pontiac's Shadow: Michilimackinac and the Anglo-Indian War of 1763* (East Lansing and Mackinac Island, MI: Michigan State University Press and Mackinac State Historic Parks, 2013), 133 and 208. I am grateful to Keith R. Widder for bringing the *Gladwin* to my attention. On Le Griffon, see Great Lakes Exploration Group, "The Search for the Elusive Griffon," www.greatlakesexploration.org/.

4. Quaife, *Askin Papers*, 1: 1747–95:4–5. Recent dissertations on Askin include Elizabeth Sherburn Demers, "Keeping a Store: The Social and Commercial Worlds of John Askin in the Eighteenth-Century Great Lakes, 1763–1796" (PhD diss., Michigan State University, 2010) and Justin M. Carroll, "John Askin's Many Beneficial Binds: Family, Trade, and Empire in the Great Lakes" (PhD diss., Michigan State University, 2011).

5. Armour, "Askin's WELCOME Will Sail Again," 139. Brian Jaeschke, Registrar, Mackinac State Historic Parks, was able to locate an uncited photocopy in the Park files of a document, probably from the Haldimand Papers in the British Library, entitled "A General Return of His Majesty's Arm'd Vessels . . . 1st Jany. 1779," which gave this figure: email communication, April 1, 2013.

6. John Askin, "Inventery of my Estate Viz:," December 31, 1776, Armour and Widder, *At the Crossroads*, 209.

Welcome and other ships knit the region together, convincing individuals from diverse backgrounds that they had enough in common, politically and economically, to make British government worth maintaining.

This was no mean feat. British authority around the Great Lakes was little more than a decade old and far from absolute when the colonial rebellion broke out in 1775. Most Canadian towns, such as Detroit, Montréal, and Québec, still felt more French than British. Lake Huron seemed an ideal cargo route to Askin, but many British officers and administrators viewed it as a wide swath of undefended territory. With the profitable fur trade in the balance and the Revolution now in full swing in the East, the British in Canada warily eyed rebel incursions south and east of the Great Lakes.[7]

"It is dangerous to leave this post any longer without a vessel to winter at it," Maj. Arent Schuyler De Peyster, commander of the British garrison and head of the Fort Michilimackinac community, wrote in 1778, "& there is constant employment for one all the summer besides that the appearance of an armed vessel awes the Savages who are encamped where they can annoy the Fort without our being able to bring a gun to bear upon them unless it be from the water."[8] In May of that year, he took the *Welcome* into the "Kings Service," a phrase he used to describe what was, in essence, a temporary loan.[9] The arrangement held, and men such as Capt. Alexander Grant, in charge of the ships on the Upper Lakes, used the *Welcome* to reassure worrisome superiors. "I can stake my veracity and twenty one years knowledge of the Lakes," he wrote in 1780, "That the Sloop Welcome answers all the ends of a vessel of War at Mackina, as the Great Fleet of England would."[10]

7. On the Revolution in the Great Lakes, see Armour and Widder, *At the Crossroads*, Thomas Kurt Knoerl, "Empire in the Hold: The British Maritime Cultural Landscape in the Western Great Lakes 1759–1796" (Dissertation, George Mason University, 2012), David Curtis Skaggs and Larry L. Nelson, eds., *The Sixty Years' War for the Great Lakes, 1754–1814* (East Lansing, MI: Michigan State University Press, 2001), Nancy L. Woolworth, "Grand Portage in the Revolutionary War," *Minnesota History* 44, no. 6 (Summer 1975): 198–208, and Arthur Britton Smith, *Legend of the Lake: The 22–Gun Brig-Sloop Ontario, 1780, New Discovery Edition* (Kingston, Canada: Quarry Heritage Books, 2009).
8. De Peyster to Carleton, May 30, 1778, MPHS and Henry S. Bartholomew, eds., *Collections: Report of the Pioneer Society of the State of Michigan*, 2nd ed., vol. IX, Michigan Pioneer and Historical Collections (Lansing, MI: Wynkoop Hallenbeck Crawford Company, State Printers, 1908), 366.
9. De Peyster to Carleton, May 30, 1778, Ibid. On De Peyster, see Armour and Widder, *At the Crossroads*.
10. Grant to Bolton, undated [August 1780], MPHS, ed., *Historical Collections: Collections and Researches Made by the Michigan Pioneer and Historical Society*, vol. XIX, Michigan Pioneer and Historical Collections (Lansing, MI: Robert Smith & Co., State Printers and Binders, 1892), 556.

And so it did. In early August, 1779, De Peyster dispatched the *Welcome* in support of a large party of Indian warriors commanded by British officers.[11] This mixed force set off to confront Americans and Indians operating in the Illinois country south of the St. Joseph River who, De Peyster believed, aimed to capture Detroit.[12] When the rebels never appeared and the Indians wandered away in dissatisfaction, the expedition dissolved. But such actions at least gave the British some claims to authority and control, and they would have been impossible without British ships. De Peyster believed that the Indians were left "exposed to the impositions of designing people," and they seemed "in constant alarm, and are often much persuaded Detroit is taken."[13]

No less alarmed were the British themselves, as Indians in the Detroit region reported increasingly frequent and friendly contact with American rebels.[14] The *Welcome* offered a convenient solution, then, to several of De Peyster's problems. The cargo capacity of the vessel would supply some of the material needs of the Michilimackinac garrison, and the ship's speed would allow regular correspondence with Detroit, reassuring De Peyster as much as the Indians that the city remained firmly in British hands.

11. Lt. George Clowes, although an army officer, seems to have been in charge of the *Welcome* during this voyage. De Peyster to Haldimand, August 23, 1779, and Lt. Thomas Bennett's report, September 1, 1779, MPHS and Bartholomew, *Collections*, IX:394 and 396–397.

12. On this expedition, see De Peyster's letters of July 9 (two) and 21, August 9, 13, and 23, and September 4, 1779, and Bennett's letter and report, Ibid., IX:389–397. De Peyster had apparently been contemplating using the *Welcome* on Lake Michigan as early as October, 1778: De Peyster to Haldimand, October 24 and October 27, 1778, Ibid., IX:374–277. The St. Joseph region remained problematic for the British. On January 27, 1781, Harrow noted that "about Noon Two Traders with a Party of Canadians who had repuls'd + routed a Party of Rebells at St. Josephs, arriv'd here [Mackinac Island] bringing 3 Prisoners."

13. De Peyster to Haldimand, July 21, 1779, MPHS and Bartholomew, *Collections*, IX:391.

14. For examples of Indian reporting American encounters to the Detroit garrison, see William E. Evans and Elizabeth S. Sklar, eds., *Detroit to Fort Sackville, 1778–1779: The Journal of Normand MacLeod* (Detroit, MI: Wayne State University Press, 1978). On British responses at Michilimackinac, see Keith R. Widder, "Effects of the American Revolution on Fur-Trade Society at Michilimackinac," in *The Fur Trade Revisited: Selected Papers of the Sixth North American Fur Trade Conference, Mackinac Island, Michigan, 1991*, ed. Jennifer S. H. Brown, W. J. Eccles, and Donald P. Heldman (East Lansing/Mackinac Island, MI: Michigan State University Press/Mackinac State Historic Parks, 1994), 299–316. Widder concluded that the war strengthened British-Indian relations.

On August 26, 1779, the *Welcome* arrived at Detroit, where twenty-three-year-old, recently commissioned Lt. Alexander Harrow waited at the dock. [15] Harrow, an ambitious Scotsman with some formal education, arrived at Detroit with three years' experience under his belt commanding British boats and crews in Québec and on Lake Champlain. [16] The *Welcome*'s crew in the fall of 1779 consisted of "eight men including a Master to command, one Boatswain & Gunner." [17] Labor was in short supply on the Lakes, but high pay rates and plentiful rations attracted men to British service. The *Welcome*'s crew came from a variety of backgrounds, as suggested by their surnames: Brown, McCulloch, Finnigan, Lucien, Manuel, Dupic. Some probably came west as voyageurs, canoemen working for fur traders. Others may have been born in Michilimackinac, Detroit, or in one of the many small villages around the Lakes where Métis and Indians lived alongside each other. Perhaps a few of the crew traced their parentage to the French precursor of the liaisons De Peyster mentioned in a poem he wrote about leaving Michilimackinac:

Now to Mitchilimackinack,
We soldiers bid adieu,
And leave each squa a child on back,
Nay some are left with two. [18]

15. Harrow's commission as "Lieutenant and commander on the lakes" was dated July 7, 1778, according to Canada Parliament, *Sessional Papers, Volume 11: First Session of the Sixth Parliament of the Dominion of Canada* (Ottawa, Canada: MacLean, Roger & Co., Parliamentary Printers, 1887), 642. Some of Harrow's papers besides his 1779–1782 log are in the Burton Historical Collection of the Detroit Public Library. Another of Harrow's journals and other family newspaper clippings are in the Lehigh University Library Special Collections (see below). The Detroit Institute of Arts owns a beaver-shaped bowl that may have belonged to Harrow.

16. W. L. Jenks, "Have Lived on the Land They Now Occupy for Past 125 Years," undated printed pamphlet, likely circa 1910, "I remain: A Digital Archive of Letters, Manuscripts, and Ephemera," Lehigh University Digital Library, http://digital.lib.lehigh.edu/cdm4/remain_viewer.php?DMTHUMB=1&CISOPTR=3352&ptr=3470&CISOSTART=1&searchletters=harrow;0;0;0&view=full. Harrow is also profiled, with some inaccuracy, in Dorothy Marie Mitts, *That Noble Country: The Romance of the St. Clair River Region* (Philadelphia, PA: Dorrance & Company, 1968), 183–184.

17. "Remarks. . .," October 27, 1777, Reuben G. Thwaites, ed., *Collections of the State Historical Society of Wisconsin*, vol. XI (Madison, WI: Democrat Printing Company, State Printers, 1888), 187.

18. The poem, "A Song," continues: "When you return, my lads, take care/Their boys don't take you by the hair,/With a war whoop that shall rend the air,/And use their scalping knives": Arent Schuyler De Peyster, *Miscellanies, by an Officer*, ed. J. Watts De Peyster, vol. I, 1889, 39–40.

A mixed heritage allowed men to cross the cultural boundaries that existed in the Great Lakes long before national borders divided countries.[19] Aboard the *Welcome*, they travelled between Indian villages, British forts, and civilian trading posts as emissaries of the government.

That winter of 1779–1780, though, they spent their days north of Detroit cutting lumber in a mundane routine broken by little except bad weather and an occasional day of rest on Sundays. It was dangerous work, and over the winter five men cut themselves while working. With the closest surgeon miles away at Detroit, Harrow was careful to allow them ample recovery time, as he did with the various men who fell sick. Besides the occasional visitor, the only real event of note that winter occurred on January 28, when Harrow "punished Dupic for endeavouring to stur up a quarrel amongst the Party."[20] Whatever Dupic's complaint and punishment were, they did not deter him from remaining with the *Welcome* for another year.[21] In fact, disobedience and discipline were relatively rare aboard the *Welcome* compared to other British naval vessels.[22]

The *Welcome*'s relative disciplinary order did not extend to the region as a whole. In the summer of 1780, during a typical cargo run out of Detroit, Harrow took on board four traders, two of their wives, one child, two British soldiers, and thirteen Indians led by Musqueash.[23] An Ojibwe chief from the St. Clair River region, Musqueash regularly vis-

19. Various historians have pointed to the multi-racial and multi-ethnic nature of contemporaneous maritime work elsewhere, especially in the Atlantic World. See Paul Gilje, *Liberty on the Waterfront: American Maritime Culture in the Age of Revolution* (Philadelphia: University of Pennsylvania Press, 2004), 25.; Peter Linebaugh and Marcus Rediker, *The Many-Headed Hydra: Sailors, Slaves, Commoners, and the Hidden History of the Revolutionary Atlantic* (Boston: Beacon Press, 2000); W. Jeffrey Bolster, *Black Jacks: African American Seamen in the Age of Sail* (Cambridge: Harvard University Press, 1997); Emma Christopher, *Slave Ship Sailors and Their Captive Cargoes, 1730–1807* (Cambridge, U.K.: Cambridge University Press, 2006).
20. Alexander Harrow, "Log-Book of the Welcome, 1779–1782" n.d., Alexander Harrow Family, 1775–1930, Burton Historical Collection, Detroit Public Library. Microfilm in possession of author, January 28, 1780.
21. The last mention of Dupic in Harrow's log was on March 27, 1781.
22. See Christopher Lloyd, *The British Seaman, 1200–1860: A Social Survey* (Cranbury, NJ: Associated University Presses, Inc., 1970), 239–248, N. A. M. Rodger, *The Wooden World: An Anatomy of the Georgian Navy* (New York, NY: W. W. Norton & Company, 1996), 205–251, and Nicholas Blake, *Steering to Glory: A Day in the Life of a Ship of the Line* (London, UK/St. Paul, MN: Chatham Publishing/MBI Publishing Company, 2005), 79–80. On merchant ships, see Marcus Rediker, *Between the Devil and the Deep Blue Sea: Merchant Seamen, Pirates, and the Anglo-American Maritime World, 1700–1750* (Cambridge, U.K.: Cambridge University Press, 1987).
23. "Return . . . ." July 29, 1780, MPHS and Bartholomew, *Collections*, IX:657.

ited the *Welcome* and, along with other Indians, brought Harrow news and received rum.[24] On this particular occasion, his small band travelled north to Michilimackinac aboard the sloop.

When Harrow arrived on July 29, 1780, the new head at Michilimackinac, Lt. Gov. Patrick Sinclair, was in a fury. It was improper for Musqueash's band to be at Michilimackinac "at this advanced season of the year," he fumed.[25] An officer met Harrow's boat at the wharf and forbade him to land. Rebuffed, Harrow returned to the *Welcome* and soon after communicated with Norman McKay, master of the *Felicity*. McKay complained that, over the preceding weeks, Sinclair had repeatedly sent the vessel to Mackinac Island, "once to carry an Empty Barrell, once with a Letter & for a Load of Hay."[26] Harrow ordered McKay to Detroit, where officials could put the *Felicity* and its crew to better use.[27]

Sensitive to intrusions on his authority, Sinclair summoned Harrow back to the fort. Dare to undermine me again, Sinclair threatened, and "I'll put you in the Guard room."[28] Sinclair also accused Harrow of transporting a few supplies the previous fall without authorization.[29] Under Sinclair's orders, several officers interrogated Harrow about stores he had supposedly absconded with before allowing him to return to his sloop.[30] Before he had sailed even a few miles from Michilimackinac, an armed detachment overtook the *Welcome*, arrested Harrow, and confined him to the fort.[31] Sinclair handed over command of the *Welcome* to an underling, dispatching the sloop to Detroit, but not before reading Harrow's correspondence and refusing to allow Harrow to send the ship's log to Detroit.[32] Harrow languished under arrest at Michilimack-

---

24. Harrow mentions Musqueash, with various spellings, on September 3, 1779, and May 4 and July 10, 1780, Harrow, "Log-Book." Variant spellings are mentioned in Mitts, *That Noble Country*, 44., and in Armour and Widder, *At the Crossroads*, 117.

25. Sinclair to De Peyster, undated, and Sinclair to De Peyster, July 30, 1780, MPHS and Bartholomew, *Collections*, IX:600.

26. Harrow to Grant, July 31, 1780, Ibid., IX:601. McKay told a similar version in a letter which also demonstrates Harrow's relative education (McKay's spelling and grammar are less accomplished): McKay to Grant, July 29, 1780, Ibid., IX:606.

27. Harrow to McKay, July 30, 1780, MPHS and Bartholomew, *Collections*, IX:602–603.

28. Harrow to Grant, July 31, 1780, Ibid., IX:601.

29. These supplies amounted to three barrels of pork, three barrels of flour, and a box of candles. Harrow replied that he had only taken goods "by Receipt to the Commissary for the Vessel's use and which I had accounted for": Ibid.

30. "Questions," undated, Ibid., IX:603.

31. Harrow to Grant, July 31, 1780, and Sinclair to Harrow, July 30, 1780, Ibid., IX:602 and 605. See also the other documents Harrow attached to his letter to Grant, Ibid., IX:602–604, and Sinclair to Haldimand, August 3, 1780, Ibid., IX:572–573.

32. Sinclair to Guthrie, July 31, 1780, MPHS and Bartholomew, *Collections*, IX:605. Harrow to Bolton, August 21, 1780, Ibid., IX:606–607.

inac, hoping his expected trial might take place somewhere else, perhaps Detroit, with more impartial adjudicators.[33]

What saved Harrow from a trial, in the end, was not Sinclair's le-
niency so much as his hostility. In 1780, Sinclair also clashed with John
Askin over the British merchant's duties as deputy commissary in
charge of the King's stores at Michilimackinac, and with Capt. John
Mompesson, the new commander of British troops at the fort.[34] Meanwhile, in an attempt to calm Sinclair and secure Harrow's release,
Michilimackinac's former commander Arent Schuyler De Peyster, now
at Detroit, wrote to Governor Haldimand claiming responsibility for
the transportation of Musqueash.[35] Haldimand, equally sensitive to Sinclair's situation as a new commander and the man's bruised sense of
authority, let Sinclair decide whether to forgive or dismiss Harrow.[36]
Increasingly preoccupied with other problems, Sinclair allowed Harrow
to travel to Detroit in September, where he was almost immediately
cleared of charges and placed back in command of the *Welcome*.[37] Other
victims of Sinclair's anger were not so lucky. Samuel Robertson, the
Welcome's first civilian captain, was arrested in April 1780 for supposedly
tampering with the mail and died in Québec, still awaiting trial, two
years later.[38]

That fall, the *Welcome* helped move the Michilimackinac community
to the more defensible Mackinac Island. This work would consume the
time of Michilimackinac's residents, military and civilian, as everyone
moved their homes and businesses to the new site over the course of a
year. But as the leaves turned colors and then fell from the trees late in
1780, the crew of the *Welcome* had more immediate concerns. Winter
was coming, and the Straits of Mackinac would be no place for a
wooden sloop when the violent storms arrived and ice floes advanced
across the open water.

The winter of 1780 fatally damaged the sloop *Welcome*. On December
10, a storm carried away a large section of the Mackinac Island wharf
where the *Welcome* was moored, and the crews and soldiers from the
new fort spent most of the night and the next few days pumping out
and unloading the ship. Lacking both the necessary timber (white oak

33. MPHS and Bartholomew, *Collections*, IX:607.
34. On these clashes, see Armour and Widder, *At the Crossroads*, 135–136 and 154–156.
35. De Peyster to Haldimand, August 13, 1780, MPHS and Bartholomew, *Collections*,
IX:598.
36. Haldimand to Sinclair, August 21, 1780, Ibid., IX:573.
37. Harrow, "Log-Book." July 31, 1780 (this entry encompasses the period through September 26, 1780).
38. Armour and Widder, *At the Crossroads*, 137.

or white pine) and any experienced shipbuilders, Harrow doubted whether his crews could repair the *Welcome*.[39]

It surprised everyone when the crew was able to make the *Welcome* seaworthy again. It took weeks, but the crew and area carpenters repaired leaks, caulked places above the waterline, and built "Brush Fenders" to provide a cushion between the vessels and the dock.[40] Then, they "hove down" the *Welcome*, a process also known as careening, which tilted the sloop to one side, exposing the hull for repairs.[41] With the help of some of the soldiers, they removed the remaining ballast, washed the hold, and rigged the sloop. By late April, the ice had cleared and the ship put to sea again, albeit leaking substantially.[42]

The *Welcome* sailed for only a few months after Harrow left the sloop to take command of the *Angelica* in the summer of 1781.[43] As early as 1780, De Peyster knew the *Welcome* would soon "want a thorough overhaul," and the British government finally condemned the vessel near the end of 1781, transferring the crew to the *Angelica*.[44] A single period document listed the *Welcome* as "lost in 1781 with all her furniture and spare stores," but no other source survives to confirm or refute this.[45] Whether she was scrapped or she sank, the *Welcome*'s time on the Great Lakes ended two years before the end of the Revolution.[46]

39. Grant to Powell, March 18, 1781, MPHS, *Historical Collections*, 1892, XIX:602. In the end, however, after substantial work, both vessels returned to the Lakes in 1781: Haldimand to Powell, June 23, 1781, Ibid., XIX:641.

40. Harrow, "Log-Book." April 9, 1781.

41. Ibid., April 12 and 16, 1781. On "hove down" as synonymous with careening, see William Falconer, *An Universal Dictionary of the Marine* (London, UK: T. Cadell, 1784), s.v. "Careening."

42. Harrow, "Log-Book.", April 24, 1781.

43. Ibid., July 26–27, 1781. This page of Harrow's log is unusually faded, obscuring some minor details of the transfer.

44. De Peyster to Sinclair, May 18, 1780, MPHS and Bartholomew, *Collections*, IX:582. Grant to Powell, January 24, 1782, MPHS, ed., *Historical Collections: Collections and Researches Made by the Michigan Pioneer and Historical Society*, vol. XX, Michigan Pioneer and Historical Collections (Lansing, MI: Robert Smith & Co., State Printers and Binders, 1892), 2. The last mention of the *Welcome* in Harrow's log is on September 12, 1781, Harrow, "Log-Book."

45. "List of Vessels," 1783, MPHS, *Historical Collections*, 1895, XXIV:12.

46. At least until an interpretive reconstruction was built during the U.S. Bicentennial. After a period of ownership by the Maritime Heritage Alliance of Traverse City, Michigan, the sloop now belongs to Emmett County, Michigan. See Armour, "Askin's WELCOME," and "Welcome," *Maritime Heritage Alliance*, www.maritimeheritagealliance. org/welcome, and "Building Sloop Welcome," *Chandler Township Charlevoix County Michigan Memories*, http://chandlertownshipmichiganmemories.weebly.com/sloop-welcome.html.

But by the time the *Welcome* disappeared, she had accomplished her mission. The *Welcome* carried a variety of weapons, and Harrow occasionally sent armed scouting parties ashore to locate someone or identify landmarks, but the crew never fired a shot in anger.[47] The armed sloop failed to sooth the worries of British officers about Indian allegiance or rebel threats. And yet, no large Indian revolt ever appeared. No Americans attacked Detroit or Michilimackinac. Indeed, it was not until the 1790s, well after the end of the war, that the British finally evacuated these posts.

Amid the political history of the Revolution, the *Welcome* seems like a mere speck on Lake Huron, a simple courier of letters and passengers. But the ship forged connections between Michilimackinac, Detroit, Fort Erie, and all the scattered communities and individuals in between. The British used Lake Huron strategically, distributing provisions, ferrying troops, transporting Indians, relaying reassuring or chastising messages, and harvesting resources. The natives of the lakeshore—whether French, British, Métis, or Indian—had no reason to go to war against the British. Harrow and his crew helped maintain the prewar status quo. Sometimes the war was on their minds, but, most days, they sailed and worked without any fear of Patriot or Indian rebellion. The security of the Great Lakes worried some British authorities, but for men aboard the *Welcome* and people around Lake Huron, this was home. To many, home seemed to be becoming more British. When the time came at the end of the war to draw the borders of a new country, the Lakes became the division between the United States and British Canada.[48] The *Welcome*, as much as any other part of the Revolution on the Great Lakes, had helped solidify the British loyalty that created this border.

Acknowledgements: The author thanks Nicole Belolan, Owen White, Kelsey J.S. Ransick, Brian Jaeschke, and Keith R. Widder.

47. Harrow sent "arm'd" parties ashore on June 22, 1780, October 4 and 21, 1780, and May 11 and 12, 1781.
48. On this topic, especially relating to later periods, see John J. Bukowczyk, *Permeable Border: The Great Lakes Basin as Transnational Region, 1650–1990* (University of Pittsburgh Press, 2005).

The Stockbridge–Mohican Community in the Revolutionary War, 1775–1783

❦ BRYAN RINDFLEISCH ❧

On July 4, 1776, the authors of American independence declared to the world "that all men are created equal, [and] that they are endowed by their Creator with certain unalienable Rights." However, one of the Declaration's grievances against the English Crown was that it employed "the inhabitants of our frontiers, the *merciless Indian Savages*, whose known rule of warfare, is an undistinguished destruction of all ages, sexes and conditions." The message therein was quite clear: Native Americans were the decided enemies of independence. Such sentiments not only resonated with the revolutionary leadership, but also the general population that by and large embraced an "anti-Indian sublime," a rabidly hostile attitude toward Native peoples and communities during and particularly after the war.[1] Along with the obvious ramifications of such a statement, the founders sought to delineate the boundaries of citizenship and inclusion in the new nation, one that ultimately did not include Native Americans. As part of this, though, the revolutionaries also engaged in memory politics; meaning, they tried to whitewash, or sanitize, the narrative of rebellion by removing the agency and support of indigenous peoples who fought alongside the Americans. Instead, Native allies were lumped together with those indigenous nations that supported the British, thereby casting *all* Native peoples in the role of adversary. In the aftermath of the Revolutionary War, the United States, possessed of an insatiable hunger for indigenous lands, turned this fabricated truth into gospel truth.[2]

1. Peter Silver, *Our Savage Neighbors: How Indian War Transformed Early America* (New York: W.W. Norton & Company, 2008), xx ("anti-Indian sublime").
2. Colin Calloway, *The American Revolution in Indian Country: Crisis and Diversity in Native American Communities* (Cambridge: Cambridge University Press, 1995), xiii-xiv.

The revolutionaries' list of indigenous allies, a fluid one that changed with the circumstances of war, Native politics, and other internal and external forces, is quite striking. Foremost among those who supported the Revolution were the Stockbridge-Mohican community in New England, the Oneida and Tuscarora nations among the Iroquois, the Caughnawaga Abenaki, Micmac, and Penobscot peoples in Canada, the Catawba nation in North Carolina, towns among the Creek and Yuchi to the southeast, and others. The case of the Mohican peoples of Stockbridge, Massachusetts, illustrates that these indigenous allies defied the Declaration's dichotomy of good and bad, or civilized and savage, and paints a very complicated picture of Native communities caught up in the revolutionary events that forced them to choose sides, producing untold changes within their societies. Yet at the same time, Native Americans like the Stockbridge-Mohican continuously adapted to and navigated these transformative contexts and circumstances.

Who were the Stockbridge-Mohican? First and foremost, they *are* the "Muh-he-conneok" (Muhheakun'nuk), the "People of the Waters that are Never Still."[3] Historically, they are Mahican, Housatonic, Wappinger, Tunxis, Shawnee, and other "River Indian" (Hudson River) peoples who all congregated at the town of Stockbridge, one of several Mahican communities in New England and New York, in the mid eighteenth century.[4] Specifically, Stockbridge was a "Praying Town," a settlement of assorted Native peoples who embraced Christianity and lived in the English colonies alongside white inhabitants. Being Christian as well as residing in a "Praying Town" was both a deliberate choice (often attributed to the "Great Awakening" in the early eighteenth century) and a consequence of King Philip's War (1675–1676), therefore a mixture of indigenous agency and settler colonialism.[5] For the British, "Praying Towns" offered strategic buffers against French Canada and the inroads of Catholicism, while at the same time confining indigenous

---

3. The Stockbridge-Mohican are not to be confused with the modern Mohegan Tribe of Connecticut, but are instead the Stockbridge-Munsee Community (Band) of Mohican Indians in Wisconsin.

4. Calloway, *The American Revolution in Indian Country*, 85; Rachel Wheeler, *To Live upon Hope: Mohicans and Missionaries in the Eighteenth-Century Northeast* (Ithaca: Cornell University Press, 2008), 187; William A. Starna, *From Homeland to New Land: History of the Mahican Indians* (Lincoln: University of Nebraska Press, 2013), 175.

5. David J. Silverman, *Red Brethren: The Brothertown and Stockbridge Indians and the Problem of Race in Early America* (Ithaca: Cornell University Press, 2010), 23 (King Philip's War), 44–45 (Great Awakening); Patrick Frazier, *The Mohicans of Stockbridge* (Lincoln: University of Nebraska Press, 1994), 41 ("Praying Towns"); Calloway, *The American Revolution in Indian Country* 86 ("Praying Towns").

peoples to fixed spaces out of the way of colonial expansion. For Native Christians, these communities offered pragmatic solutions to increasingly precarious situations in the colonies. For instance, the "Praying Towns" provided a means through which the Mahican might preserve a portion of their sacred lands,[6] reconstitute their society and population through coalescence with other Native Christian groups, retain cultural identities as brokers between white and indigenous worlds, and a host of other benefits.[7] But whatever their motives, the Stockbridge time and again proved themselves staunch supporters of the British colonies, serving in militia units during King George's War, the Seven Years' War, and Pontiac's Uprising, all between 1747 and 1764.[8] In short, the Stockbridge-Mohican, and other indigenous allies along with them, were in the hearts and minds of many American colonists long before 1776.

However, the years 1764–1775 proved momentously disruptive for the Stockbridge-Mohican community. In the wake of the Seven Years' War, a flood of white settlers poured into the town and devoured thousands of acres of Mohican land, oftentimes through squatting, illegal purchases, turning Native debts into acquisitions of land, and other mechanisms of dispossession. Furthermore, the growing white majority within the community increasingly excluded Mohican members from the town council, turned colonial law and courts against them, and monitored the behavior and movement of Native residents. As John Konkapat remarked in 1763, the whites were "endeavouring not only To get all the power but our Lands too into their hands."[9] Out of this

6. At the outset of establishing the Stockbridge community, indigenous residents were promised that they would hold the lands within the town in perpetuity, so long as they allowed white families to live alongside them. Silverman, *Red Brethren,* 37.
7. As historian Rachel Wheeler suggests, this coalescence of indigenous communities at Stockbridge—Mahican, Housatonic, Wappinger, Tunxis, Shawnee, and others—fostered a distinct identity as cultural, political, economic, and religious brokers between white and Native worlds, as well as across indigenous societies and populations. In addition, Wheeler demonstrates that the amalgamation of these Native peoples at Stockbridge transformed the identity of "Mahican" into a more collective "Mohican." Wheeler, *To Life upon Hope,* 187–189.
8. The Stockbridge-Mohican were a constant presence in the New England militia and Robert Rogers' Rangers in the French & Indian War. A quick survey of the muster rolls from Massachusetts regiments and the British army from 1755–1763 shows that scores of Mohican men were involved on the front lines of the war, oftentimes in their own units, under the command of Lt. Jacob Cheeksaunkun and Capt. Jacob Naunaumphtaung. Leon Miles, "Mohican Warriors: A Documentary History, 1747–1813," Manuscript V3, Stockbridge-Munsee Library & Museum Archives, Bowler WI, pg. 2–11; Calloway, *The American Revolution in Indian Country,* 88; Frazier, *The Mohicans of Stockbridge,* 144.
9. Calloway, *The American Revolution in Indian Country,* 89 (Konkapot).

chaos evolved a deeply segregated community, where both indigenous and white inhabitants "emerged . . . with a starker sense of their differences."[10] And even when the Stockbridge-Mohican appealed to higher authorities, going so far as to plead their case in London to the Lords of Trade in 1765, both colonial and imperial administrators merely offered promises rather than answers.[11] On the eve of the Revolution, then, a greatly disillusioned Stockbridge-Mohican community seemed one of the most unlikely of allies for the Americans.[12]

Yet despite all of these experiences, the Stockbridge-Mohican overwhelmingly supported the revolutionaries, which most certainly begs the question: why? While such a decision likely involved a multitude of factors, one cannot get past the fact that the Mohican were completely surrounded by a settler community, known for its rabid opposition to the Stamp Act as well as for being a hotbed of activity for the Sons of Liberty.[13] It would take no leap of the imagination to believe that the Mohican felt enormous pressure, if not the threat of intimidation and violence, to join the revolutionary movement. Yet the Stockbridge-Mohican also saw the revolution undoubtedly as an opportunity. If they sided with the American rebels and proved their loyalty, the new nation might respect or honor their attempts to reclaim lost lands and to protect their sovereignty. In petitions to the Massachusetts legislature and Continental Congress, the Stockbridge presented their case of being "defrauded of their lands," and thereby demanded "assurances that their land rights . . . would be vindicated," to which both governments promised "to protect you to the utmost of our power."[14] Other motivations included the fact that the British occupied New England and threatened Mohican homes, ideological similarities between Mohicans struggles to preserve their autonomy and the revolutionaries' own battles for sovereignty within the empire, military service that offered wages and land bounties, and the initiative of certain individuals,

10. Wheeler, *To Live upon Hope,* 222 ("differences").

11. Frazier, *The Mohicans of Stockbridge,* 162–163 (London), 169 (promises).

12. Silverman, *Red Brethren,* 74–75 (post-1763 settlers); Frazier, *The Mohicans of Stockbridge,* 180 (debts); Wheeler, *To Live upon Hope,* 204 (courts), 227 (community segregation).

13. Frazier, *The Mohicans of Stockbridge,* 165 (Stamp Act); Silverman, *Red Brethren,* 109 ("Sons of Liberty").

14. Frazier, *The Mohicans of Stockbridge,* 204 ("vindicated," "power"); 8 March 1782, *Journals of the Continental Congress, 1774–1789, Volume XXII: January 1, 1782—August 9, 1782,* ed. Gaillard Hunt (Washington D.C.: Government Printing Office, 1914), 120 ("defrauded").

like Jehoiakim Mtohksin, who joined the revolutionary protests of their own volition.[15]

At the outset of the war, Stockbridge community leaders like Solomon Wa-haun-wan-wau-meet met with the revolutionary leadership to cement an alliance. As Solomon declared in April 1774, "Brothers: You remember when you first came over the great waters, I was great and you was very little . . . I then took you in for a friend, and kept you under my arms, so that no one might injure you." But since then, "our conditions are changed. You are become great and tall . . . and I am become small . . . Now you take care of me, and I look to you for protection." In concluding his talk, Solomon promised "Wherever you go, we will be by your sides. Our bones shall die with yours. We are determined never to be at peace with the red coats, while they are at variance with you."[16] Congressional delegates responded to Solomon that "Your engaging in this cause discovers not only your attachment to your liberties, but furnishes us with an evidence of your gratitude[,] . . . abundant proof of your fidelity[,] . . . and [we] shall depend upon your firm and steady attachment to the cause you have engaged in."[17]

It was not long before the Stockbridge-Mohican found themselves at the center of the revolutionary struggle. In the immediate aftermath of shots fired at Lexington and Concord in April 1775, dozens of the Stockbridge community joined the New England minutemen who rushed to the scene. In what became known as Battle Road, Mohican and American soldiers lined the path connecting Concord, Lexington, and Boston where they poured an incessant fire upon the British army and inflicted heavy casualties.[18] From there, the "Stockbridge Indian

15. Frazier, *The Mohicans of Stockbridge,* 193 (ideology); Starna, *From Homeland to New Land,* 193 (wages, bounties); Miles, "Mohican Warriors: A Documentary History, 1747–1813," 11–12 (Mtohksin).

16. Captain Solomon Speech to the Provincial Congress of Massachusetts, April 1774, Manuscript PPLA 17, Stockbridge-Munsee Library & Museum Archives, Bowler WI ("great waters," "great and tall"); Captain Solomon Speech at German Flats and Albany, June 17, 1775, Manuscript PPLA 17, Stockbridge-Munsee Library & Museum Archives, Bowler WI ("bones").

17. John Patterson to Jehoiakim Mtohksin, 1 April 1775, *The Life of John Patterson: Major General in the Revolutionary Army,* ed. Thomas Egleston (New York: G.P. Putnam's Sons, 1894), 38–39 ("liberties," "fidelity").

18. Eric G. Grundset, ed. *African American and American Indian Patriots of the Revolutionary War* (Washington D.C.: National Society Daughters of the American Revolution, 2001), 31 (Battle Road); Miles, "Mohican Warriors: A Documentary History, 1747–1813," 12 (Mtohksin).

Company"[19] marched to Cambridge, where thousands of militiamen besieged the British army within Boston.[20] Over the course of ten months, the Mohican built siege fortifications, patrolled the outer defenses, and conducted periodic ambushes of British forces, like on June 21 when "two Stockbridge Indians killed four British regulars."[21] Or in the exaggerated reports of Horatio Gates, "the Stockbridge Indians had ambushed a party of the Ministerial Army & Kill'd Two Officers & *Sixty* Men."[22] In one memorable instance, "some British barges sounding the waters near the mouth of the Charles River were put into a retreat by a shower of arrows that killed one redcoat and wounded three. The arrows were aimed by Stockbridges . . . who were encamped near that place."[23] And at Bunker Hill, the Stockbridge were knee-deep in the fighting to fend off the British assault, which came at the cost of one of their own, Abraham Naumanmpputaunky.[24]

The descendants of Jehoiakim Mtohksin, who relayed the following story to the missionary Cutting Marsh in 1838, fondly recalled his reckless act of bravery during the siege of Boston. At a moment when British regulars found the opportunity to occupy a watchtower in the nearby town of Charlestown, Mtohksin took it upon himself to get rid of them. Armed with "combustibles," Mtohksin successfully avoided detection and then "set fire to the [adjoining] barn," after which he "retreated with all speed . . . amidst a shower of bullets." Soon thereafter, the British-occupied "buildings with their contents were entirely consumed," which forced the British soldiers to abandon their position. When Mtohksin returned to American lines, he was received with "no small joy and surprise . . . for they expected he was killed, he having [at one point been] seen to fall amidst the fire of the enemy."[25] Although

---

19. The "Stockbridge Indian Company" consisted of two separate companies, one led by Jehoiakim Mtohksin, and the other by Solomon Uhhaunauwaunmut. Calloway, *The American Revolution in Indian Country,* 92.

20. Miles, "Mohican Warriors: A Documentary History, 1747–1813," 12–13 ("Indian Company"); Doyen Salsig, *Parole: Quebec, Countersign: Ticonderoga* (Teaneck, NJ: Farleigh Dickinson University Press, 1980), 237 ("Independent Company").

21. Richard Frothingham, *History of the Siege of Boston and of the Battles of Lexington, Concord, and Bunker Hill* (Boston: Charles C. Little and James Brown, 1851), 213. In addition, the Stockbridge on June 25, 1775 "killed more of the British guard" and the next day "Two Indians went down near Bunker Hill and killed a sentry." Andrew McFarland Davis, "The Employment of Indian Auxiliaries in the American War," *English Historical Review* Vol. 2: No. 8 (October 1887): 715.

22. Miles, "Mohican Warriors: A Documentary History, 1747–1813," 14 (Horatio Gates).

23. Miles, "Mohican Warriors: A Documentary History, 1747–1813," 14 ("barges").

24. Ibid., 14 (Abraham).

25. Ibid., 29 (Mtohksin). See also *Journals and Diaries of Rev. Cutting Marsh, Missionary to the Stockbridge (Mohican) Indians,* Wisconsin Historical Society, Madison, WI.

the story does not correlate with primary sources, it may be based on an actual event that was altered as it was recalled by successive generations.

On account of such services, the Continental Congress seized upon the Stockbridge example as evidence for the need, and imminent support, of other Native allies. Months before the signing of the Declaration, Congress resolved "That the Commander in Chief be authorised and instructed to employ in the Continental Armies a number of Indians not exceeding . . . two thousand men."[26] Although George Washington proved reluctant to enlist the Stockbridge or other Native allies at first, he eventually

Johann Von Ewald's Sketch of a Stockbridge-Mohican soldier (1778).

changed his mind and confided to Timothy Edwards, one of the Commissioners for Indian Affairs, "the expediency of engaging as many of them as you can."[27] The Stockbridge regiment soon after marched north where they joined Benedict Arnold in his stand at Valcour Bay in October 1776, as well as the defense of Fort Ticonderoga the following year.[28] During these campaigns, the Stockbridge often served as advanced scouts. In one instance, Abraham Nimham led Mohican soldiers behind enemy lines where they harassed the British army. On their return to camp, Nimham and his men met with a smaller force of Tory militia. To catch the Loyalists off guard, Nimham demanded, "will you be true to the King, and fight for him till you die?" The Tories responded "O yes!" But upon recognizing the Stockbridge as not part of their army, the Loyalists tried to backtrack, "What King do you mean? I mean *King Hancock!*" One can only imagine

26. May 25, 1776, *Journals of the Continental Congress, 1774–1789, Volume IV: January 1, 1776–June 4, 1776*, ed. Worthington Chauncey Ford (Washington D.C.: Government Printing Office, 1906), 395 ("number of Indians").

27. George Washington to Timothy Edwards, August 7, 1776, *The Writings of George Washington, Volume V: June–August 1776*, ed. Worthington Chauncey Ford (New York: G.P. Putnam's Sons, 1890), 392 ("expediency").

28. Calloway, *The American Revolution in Indian Country*, 96; Frazier, *The Mohicans of Stockbridge*, 209 (Valcour Bay); Salsig, *Parole: Quebec, Countersign: Ticonderoga*, 237 (Ticonderoga); August 9, 1777, *Pennsylvania Evening Post*, American's Historical Newspapers, Marquette University (Ticonderoga).

that Nimham smiled and retorted "we don't know kings in America yet; you must go along with us."[29]

Of even greater importance for the revolutionaries, the Stockbridge-Mohican acted on their behalf as emissaries and ambassadors to other indigenous nations. Throughout their long history, the Mohican often served as diplomatic bridges between the many people of the Hudson, Susquehanna, and Ohio Valley regions, as well as Canada.[30] As Hendrick Aupaumut asserted: "It was the business of our fathers to go around the towns of these nations to renew the agreements between them."[31] Thus the Stockbridge operated within the cultural and historical continuities of such roles. Therefore, Mohican envoys like Solomon Uhhaunauwaumut met with the headmen of the Iroquois Confederacy (Six Nations) in the early years of the war, with whom he exchanged wampum belts as well as promises of neutrality and friendship during the war.[32] Similarly, Abraham Nimham journeyed to Montreal in 1775 as the American "ambassador of peace," and appealed to Native populations like the Abenaki: "I want your Warriors to Join with me and my Warriors like Brothers and . . . help me fight [British] Regulars."[33] Meanwhile, Hendrick Aupaumut trekked westward to the Ohio River Valley where he met with the Delaware and Shawnee nations. After invoking the kinship connections between the Stockbridge, Delaware, and Shawnee people,[34] Aupaumut asked them "to rise up against the Red

29. Captain Johann Ewald, *Diary of the American War: A Hessian Journal*, trans. and ed. Joseph Tustin (New Haven: Yale University Press, 1979), 474–475 ("King Hancock").
30. Wheeler, *To Live upon Hope,* 193 (cultural, historical continuity).
31. Calloway, *The American Revolution in Indian Country,* 94–95 ("agreements").
32. Barbara Graymont, *The Iroquois in the American Revolution* (Syracuse: Syracuse University Press, 1975), 68; Calloway, *The American Revolution in Indian Country,* 93, Miles, "Mohican Warriors: A Documentary History, 1747–1813," 13. Despite Stockbridge intercessions, the Iroquois were similarly swept up by the revolution, which precipitated the Battle of Oriskany between American and Loyalist forces and also pitted Iroquois warriors on both sides of the skirmish. As a consequence, the Iroquois Six Nations erupted in civil war, with lines drawn in the sand between the Mohawk, Cayuga, and Seneca (pro-British) against the Oneida and Tuscarora (pro-American), with the Onondaga caught in the middle.
33. Graymont, *The Iroquois in the American Revolution,* 68 ("Warriors").
34. Wheeler, *To Live upon Hope,* 192 (Stockbridge-Shawnee); Stockbridge-Munsee Community, "Our History: Origin & Early Mohican History," www.mohican.com/origin-earlyhistory/ (Stockbridge-Delaware). The Stockbridge-Mohican community included several Shawnee peoples, which accounted for the kinship connections between them. For further information about the migrations and survivance patterns of the Shawnee, see Stephen Warren, *The Worlds the Shawnees Made: Migrations and Violence in Early America* (Chapel Hill: University of North Carolina Press, 2014). With the Delaware, the Stockbridge-Mohican Creation (Migration) Story establishes a centuries-old (if not

Coats that they may not do as they please with this Big Island . . . let us humble them.[35]

In the fall of 1777, the Stockbridge company requested "to be [further] employed in the service of the United States," and were thereby "referred to Major General Gates."[36] Upon arriving in upstate New York, the Mohican once again reunited with Benedict Arnold, who relied on the Stockbridge to scout and harass the British army. As German General Friedrich Adolf von Riedesel complained, "a few English soldiers, who were digging potatoes in a field 500 paces in the rear of headquarters, were suddenly surprised by the enemy, who suddenly issued from the woods and carried off the men in the very faces of their comrades. For these sallies the Americans also generally employed Indians who were called Stock bridges." Riedesel then lamented that "many soldiers disappeared in this manner."[37] Such actions by the Mohican culminated with their involvement in the Battle of Freeman's Farm, followed by the American victory at Bemis Heights that forced the surrender of Burgoyne's army. In the wake of the Saratoga campaign, the Stockbridge marched south and joined Washington's forces at Valley Forge. In June 1778 they fought at the Battle of Monmouth.[38] And the following summer, Washington personally asked the Mohican to accompany and assist his armies under the command of Major General John Sulli-

longer) relationship between the two people. During the Mohican sojourn millennia ago, they came across the Lenni Lenape (Delaware) and ever since then maintained relationships with one another.

35. Calloway, *The American Revolution in Indian Country*, 95 ("rise up").

36. October 25, 1777, *Journals of the Continental Congress, 1774–1789, Volume IX: October 3, 1777–December 31, 1777*, ed. Worthington Chauncey Ford (Washington D.C.: Government Printing Office, 1907), 840 (Gates).

37. Richard M. Ketchum, *Saratoga: Turning Point of America's Revolutionary War* (New York: Henry Holt and Company, 1997), 381 (Arnold-Stockbridge); William L. Stone, ed. and trans. *Memoirs and Letters and Journals of Major General Riedesel* (Albany: Arno Press Inc., 1969), 159 ("potatoes," "disappeared"). For instance, on September 23 the Stockbridge captured two sentries and eight other prisoners. On September 24, they took three additional prisoners. On September 26, three Hessians, one Tory, and two sailors. On September 28, two British soldiers. "Journal of Oliver Boardman of Middletown, 1777: Burgoyne's Surrender," *Collections of the Connecticut Historical Society, Volume VII* (Hartford: Massachusetts Historical Society, 1899), 226–227.

38. Ketchum, *Saratoga*, 381 (Freeman's Farm); Frazier, *The Mohicans of Stockbridge*, 227 (Monmouth).

van[39] against the Iroquois Confederacy (in what became known as the "Sullivan Expedition").[40]

However, the turning point for the Stockbridge-Mohican occurred near White Plains, New York in late 1778, at a place called Kingsbridge. Led by Abraham Nimham, the Mohican soldiers were on patrol to "annoy the enemy and prevent their Landing or making incursion into the Country," when they unexpectedly ran into a far superior force that consisted of Tarleton's dragoons, Hessian jägers, and Loyalists. The resulting skirmish was captured in vivid detail by John Graves Simcoe, commander of the Queen's Rangers. Simcoe witnessed "the Indians give a yell, and fired upon the grenadier company [of the Queen's Rangers], wounding four of them. . . . They were driven from the fences, and Lt. Col. Tarleton, with the Cavalry, got among them." Although "the Indians fought most gallantly, [and] pulled more than one of the Cavalry from their horses," the Stockbridge were eventually overwhelmed.[41] As the Hessian officer, Johann Ewald, recalled: "The Indians . . . defended themselves like brave men against all sides where they were attacked . . . however, most of the enemy were killed, partly shot dead and partly cut down by the cavalry. No Indians, especially, received quarter, including their chief called Nimham and his son."[42] In total, fourteen Mohican soldiers lost their lives at Kingsbridge, including community leaders like Nimham, a staggering blow to the Stockbridge people.[43]

39. Instructions to Major William Goodrich, June 19, 1779, *The Writings of George Washington, Volume XV: 6 May 1779–28 July 1779*, ed. John C. Fitzpatrick (Washington D.C.: Government Printing Office, 1936), 268 (Sullivan Expedition); George Washington to Major William Goodrich, July 4, 1779, *The Writings of George Washington, Vol. XV*, 367–368; George Washington to Solomon Hendricks, July 4, 1779, *The Writings of George Washington, Vol. 15*, 368–369.

40. The "Sullivan Expedition," one of the largest and deadliest invasions of Iroquoia, remains a bitter memory for the Iroquois today. The Six Nations have many reasons to still revile this military action, but none more so than the excessive violence used to wipe out entire Iroquois communities.

41. John Graves Simcoe, *Simcoe's Military Journal: A History of the Operations of a Partisan Corps, called the Queen's Rangers* (New York: Bartlett & Welford, 1844), 84–85 ("fences," "gallantly").

42. Ewald, *Diary of the American War,* 145 ("defended"). According to popular myth, Nimham, upon seeing the Loyalist dragoons descend upon them, reportedly shouted to the rest of the Stockbridge to "Fly, my people! I am old, and I can die here!" Simcoe, *Simcoe's Military Journal,* 86.

43. As General Charles Scott reported to Washington, there were "fourteen Indians . . . missing [including] Nimham his father and the whole of the officers of that Corps . . . I am in Hopes it is not so bad as it at Present appears, But I can't promise myself that." Charles Stuart to George Washington, August 31, 1778, *The Writings of George Washington, Volume XVI: July-September 1778*, ed. John C. Fitzpatrick (Washington D.C.: Government Printing Office, 1887); Frazier, *The Mohicans of Stockbridge,* 224.

Meanwhile, the Mohican families of Stockbridge similarly suffered at home, despite their services to the revolution. As early as 1777, Abraham Nimham pleaded with the Continental Congress to provide "necessary cloathing for ourselves and families . . . that we don't lieve our Wives and our Children naked."[44] Shortly thereafter, Jehoiakim Mtohksin wrote to Horatio Gates about the worsening conditions at Stockbridge, albeit thanking Gates "for your kindness in letting [our] young men come home . . . [to] help their families in gathering their harvest."[45] And in the wake of Kingsbridge, the Stockbridge appealed to the Massachusetts legislature for the "Widows [of the slain] who are now left to take care of themselves and their children; without help from their Husbands, who at this season of the year provided for their families."[46] Even when Washington himself tried to move Congress into action on behalf of the Stockbridge, little aid was ever forthcoming.[47] In particular, the white residents of Stockbridge not only neglected their indigenous counterparts, but continued to chip away at Mohican lands within the town. As Native residents demanded of the state legislature and Congress in 1782, "Brothers! What I ask is that you resign to me that land which is justly mine!" To remind the revolutionaries of their sacrifices, the petitioners invoked "Where your fathers died in battle, my fathers died by their side!"[48] But such pleas fell on deaf ears and by 1783, all Mohican land in Stockbridge was lost.[49]

While the revolutionaries reveled in the founding of a new nation according to the principles articulated in the Declaration, the renowned Mohican missionary Reverend Samson Occom remarked that the Revolution "has been the most Distructive . . . of any wars that ever happened in my Day."[50] As the Stockbridge-Mohican discovered, they were not only excluded from the new republic, but even the memory of their services were forgotten or purged from the record.[51] The only recogni-

---

44. October 1777, *Journals of the Continental Congress, 1774–1789, Volume V*, 451 ("naked").

45. Jehoiakim Mtohksin to Horatio Gates, October 22, 1777, *Horatio Gates Papers, 1726–1828*, MS 240, Series 1: Correspondence, Reel 6, New York Historical Society, New York NY ("kindness").

46. Miles, "Mohican Warriors: A Documentary History, 1747–1813," 21 ("Widows").

47. George Washington to the President of Congress, September 13, 1780, *The Writings of George Washington, Volume XX: September 6, 1780–December 20, 1780*, ed. John C. Fitzpatrick (Washington D.C.: Government Printing Office, 1938), 44–45.

48. Frazier, *The Mohicans of Stockbridge*, 235 ("battle").

49. Calloway, *The American Revolution in Indian Country*, 103 (1783).

50. Silverman, *Red Brethren*, 108 ("Distructive").

51. See David Ramsay, Mercy Otis Warren, or any other contemporary chroniclers of the Revolutionary War for evidence of such "deliberate forgetting" or "purging" of indigenous involvement with the American war effort.

tion they ever received was a "Certificate to the Muhhekunnuk Indians" from George Washington, giving "Testimony of their attachment to the United States of America during the late War," after which the Stockbridge received an "ox roast." But even this document suffered from the same narrative violence as the Declaration. Whereas Washington framed the Mohican "intention of removing their present settlement near Stockbridge" as of their own volition, the reality was that white residents forced the Mohican community out of that town, and out of the state of Massachusetts.[52] In the end, settler colonialism was the name of the game for the new American nation, and not even those indigenous peoples who bled and died for the revolution were safe from that reality.

Yet the Stockbridge-Mohican not only continued to survive these assaults upon their livelihood and sovereignty, but repeatedly adapted to and negotiated these colonial conditions. After being dispossessed of their land at Stockbridge, the Mohican drew upon their pre-existing relationships with the Oneida nation, another indigenous ally of the revolutionaries, to secure refuge among the Iroquois. And when the United States started to carve up Iroquois territory through treaties and fraudulent purchases in the late eighteenth and early nineteenth centuries, the Mohican once again improvised, this time migrating west and settling in present-day Wisconsin where they were later joined by a group of the Delaware people known as the Munsee.

Today, the Stockbridge-Munsee Community (Band) of Mohican Indians continues to navigate and adapt to their colonial circumstances and contexts within the United States. Their reservation located in Shawano County, Wisconsin, is itself a testament to a long history of survivance and acclimation to colonial conditions,[53] all despite their services rendered during the Revolution. But unlike this community's experiences during and after the war, the Stockbridge-Munsee are now a sovereign nation with an economic infrastructure all their own. Through corporate businesses such as Mohican LP Gas Company, North Star Casino, Pine Hills Golf Course & Restaurant, among others, the Stockbridge-Munsee provide extensive services to their own people and community, which include care for elders, housing, higher education and adult learning, medical and health support, insurance coverage,

52. Certificate to the Muhhekunnuk Indians, July 8, 1783, *The Writings of George Washington, Volume XXVII: June 11, 1783—November 28, 1784,* ed. John C. Fitzpatrick (Washington D.C.: Government Printing Office, 1938), 53.
53. See James W. Oberly, *A Nation of Statesmen: The Political Culture of the Stockbridge-Munsee Mohicans, 1815–1972* (Norman: University of Oklahoma Press, 2005).

family wellness, conservation, and more. The same could not be said of the Stockbridge-Mohican in 1783.[54]

The seal of the Stockbridge-Munsee nation is a testament to their innovation and reinvention as well as this community's resolve, survivance, and adaptation to the colonial worlds that they have encountered over these past four centuries. Created and designed by Edwin Martin, a Mohican member, the seal is called "Many Trails," symbolizing the "endurance, strength and hope" of the Stockbridge in the face of great violence, dispossession, and forced removal, all of which stemmed from the revolutionary era. In the words of the nation itself, the seal represents and embodies "a long suffering [but] Proud and Determined People."[55]

54. Stockbridge-Munsee Community, "Services," www.mohican.com/elderlycenter/.
55. Stockbridge-Munsee Community, "Our History: Many Trails," www.mohican.com/history/.

Colonel Tench Tilghman:
George Washington's Eyes and Ears

❀❧ JEFF DACUS ☙❀

In the Old Senate Chamber of the Maryland State House hangs a painting commissioned by the Maryland Legislature often called the "Annapolis Portrait" of George Washington by Charles Willson Peale. The moment portrayed in the work is after the surrender of the British Army at Yorktown in 1781. Two of the figures are easily recognized, Washington of course, and the Marquis De Lafayette. But the third figure, not so readily identified, is Lt. Col. Tench Tilghman. Another contemporary painting of the same event by James Peale titled "Washington and His Generals" includes the figures of Washington, Benjamin Lincoln, Comte de Rochambeau, Gen. Francois Chastellux; the remaining figure is Tilghman, though he is not a general officer. Who was he and why would he be included so conspicuously with Washington?

Tench Tilghman was born in Maryland on December 25, 1744, the son of well-todo gentry parents. His father was a member of the legislature and a well-known lawyer, his mother from an equally accomplished Maryland family that had moved to Philadelphia. His maternal grandfather sent for Tench, the oldest of six boys, in 1758 and the young man traveled to Philadelphia to attend the College and Academy of Philadelphia, later the University of Pennsylvania. One of his cousins in the town was Peggy Shippen, who would later marry Benedict Arnold.

Graduating in 1761, Tench went into business with an uncle, where he worked until committing to the colonial cause on the eve of the Revolutionary War. His first duty for the rebellious colonies was not on the battlefield but on the diplomatic front. He was chosen to accompany his uncle on a peace mission to the Six Nations with Philip Schuyler.

When the first rumblings of conflict came from the north, Tilghman joined a company of the Pennsylvania Associators (a form of militia) commanded by Captain Sharpe Delaney. Their aristocratic airs earned these soldiers the nicknames "Ladies Light Infantry" and the "Silk Stockings." The derisive names stuck. During the first campaign around New York, Tilghman's company was in the Flying Camp located in New Jersey.

As the action around New York intensified, Washington needed more staff to help manage his paperwork and he sought young men of quality backgrounds to serve as a secretary or aide.[1] Washington was familiar with the Tilghman family, having met Tench's father and uncle. Washington consulted Tilghman and the young man agreed to be part of the general's "family." In an arrangement unique among the aides, Tilghman agreed to serve as a volunteer, without rank or compensation. He told his father of the arrangement to serve Washington in a letter on October 7, 1776: "I am detained here by no particular engagements entered into with the General, so far from it, that tho' he has repeatedly told me I ought to have a Compensation for my Services, I have refused . . . I wished to serve as a Volunteer."[2]

As a volunteer aide, Tilghman served alongside Washington for the remainder of the war, riding with him in each battle and performing the task of being the general's mouthpiece as well as his eyes and ears. Like the other young members of Washington's staff, Tilghman raced about the battlefield exchanging messages, observing the action, and bringing news from various parts of the front lines. Tilghman rode next to Washington in the streets of Trenton after Christmas in 1776, and he was one of the few eyewitnesses that actually saw the confrontation between Washington and Charles Lee during the chaotic retreat before the British on June 28, 1778. The young officer shared the harsh conditions at Morristown and Valley Forge.

In camp, Tilghman performed duty as Washington's alter ego, fashioning letters from verbal outlines and placing them before the General for final approval and signature. Much of the General's correspondence is in the handwriting of Tilghman. His knowledge of French was essential to Washington when dealing with foreign officers and he became a close friend of the Marquis de Lafayette. He would serve longer than any of Washington's aides or secretaries.

1. For another look at the process of working for Washington, see J.L. Bell, "George Baylor: Spirited, Willing and Wrong for the Job," *Journal of the American Revolution,* October 12, 2015, http://allthingsliberty.com/2015/10/george-baylor-spirited-willing-andwrong-for-the-job/.
2. S. A. Harrison, *Memoir of Lieut. Col. Tench Tilghman: Secretary and Aide to Washington* (Albany: J. Munsell, 1876), 142.

In May of 1781, Washington convinced Congress that Tilghman deserved the rank and pay of a lieutenant colonel, with seniority dating to April 1, 1777. In a typical, magnanimous gesture, Tilghman refused to have his date of rank the same as that of Alexander Hamilton and Richard Kidder Meade, fellow members of Washington's "family," as they had joined the commander in chief before him.

The British were cornered at Yorktown and forced to surrender in October of 1781. As the British capitulation was finalized, Washington needed someone to carry the news of Cornwallis's surrender to Congress in Philadelphia. Tradition at the time placed a great honor on the soldier who delivered such information;[3] James Wilkinson, for example, had been given the brevet rank of brigadier general by Congress for delivering the news of the fall of British General John Burgoyne in October of 1777. Tilghman was chosen to relay the news, based on his close association with Washington and also his knowledge of the best Maryland and Pennsylvania routes to the new nation's capital.

Tilghman left on the morning of October 20 and arrived in Philadelphia at about three in the morning of the 24th. He went straight to the home of the president of Congress, Thomas McKean, on High Street. A night watchman threatened to arrest Tilghman as he pounded on the president's door but soon joined the other members of the night watch in proclaiming: "All is well and Cornwallis is taken!" This ride, along with his friendship with Washington, earned Tilghman a place in the paintings by the Peales. Congress rewarded him with a sword and a horse.

In the years after the war, Tilghman lived in Baltimore where he started a mercantile business with the help of Robert Morris. He stayed close to Washington, exchanging personal letters and news. In one note, Washington chided the young man for not notifying him of his marriage in June of 1783.[4] Tilghman served as Washington's agent in Maryland, facilitating transactions for the general. On one occasion, Washington needed plans for renovating his greenhouse and asked Tilghman to get information on the structure built at Dr. Charles Carroll's place called Mont Clare.[5] Tilghman drew a plan and gave careful details on its construction, which served as a model for Washington's own.[6] When the

3. Ibid., 42–44.
4. George Washington to Tench Tilghman, October 2, 1783, Founders Online, National Archives (http://founders.archives.gov/documents/Washington/99-01-02-11890).
5. Washington to Tilghman, August 11, 1784, *The Papers of George Washington, Confederation Series, vol. 2, July 1784– January 1785*, W.W. Abbott, ed. (Charlottesville: University Press of Virginia, 1992), 30–31.
6. Ibid.

Society of the Cincinnati, a fraternal group for former Continental Army officers, was organized, Washington had pins representing the Society made for some of the officers and sent one to Tilghman.

Tench Tilghman
(1744–1786).

Unfortunately, Tilghman would not live very long after the war ended. After delivering the news of Yorktown, he showed signs of ill health, never feeling entirely well. He became extremely sick in early 1786, dying on April 18, apparently of the effects of hepatitis.

George Washington, often portrayed by historians as "cold and formal,"[7] revealed his depth of feeling for the deceased former aide in letters to several different people. After being informed of Tilghman's, death by the man's youngest brother Thomas,[8] Washington sent a poignant reply: "As there were few men for whom I had a warmer friendship, or greater regard than for your Brother—Colonel Tilghman—when living; so, with much truth I can assure you, that, there a(re) none whose death I could more sincerely have regretted."[9]

He later sent a note to James Tilghman, the aide's father:

> Of all the numerous acquaintances of your lately deceased son, & amidst all the sorrowings that are mingled on that melancholy occasion, I may venture to assert that (excepting those of his nearest relatives) none could have felt his death with more regret than I did—No one entertained a higher opinion of his worth, or had imbibed sentiments of greater friendship for him than I had done . . . It is however a dispensation, the wisdom of which is inscrutable; and amidst your grief, there is this consolation to be drawn, that while living, no man could be more esteemed—and since dead, none more lamented.[10]

Washington placed Tilghman among the prominent of the Revolution in a letter to Thomas Jefferson:

7. Thomas Ferling, C-Span *In Depth*, July 5, 2009.
8. Thomas Ringgold Tilghman to Washington, *The Papers of George Washington, Confederation Series, vol.4, 2 April 1786–31 January 1787*, W.W. Abbott, ed. (Charlottesville: University Press of Virginia, 1995), 27.
9. Ibid., 47.
10. Ibid., 96.

You have probably heard of the death of Genl Greene before this reaches you, in which case you will, in common with your Countrymen, have regretted the loss of so great and so honest a man. Genl McDougall, who was a brave Soldier & a disinterested patriot, is also dead ... Colo. Tilghman , who was formerly of my family, died lately & left as fair as reputation as ever belonged to a human character. Thus some of the pillars of the revolution fall.[11]

The esteem that Washington held for Tilghman is obvious. The people of Maryland added their own touching and telling assessment of the former aide on the inscription on his tombstone:

In Memory of
Col. Tench Tilghman
Who died April 18, 1786
In the 42nd year of his age,
Very much lamented.
He took an early and active part
In the great contest that secured
The Independence of
The United States of America.
He was an Aide-de-Camp to
His Excellency General Washington
Commander in Chief of the American Armies,
And was honored
With his friendship and confidence,
And
He was one of those
Whose merits were distinguished
And Honorably rewarded
By the Congress
But Still more to his Praise
He was
A good man.[12]

11. Ibid., 184.
12. L. G. Shreve, *Tench Tilghman, The Life and Times of Washington's Aide-de-Camp* (Centerville, MD: Tidewater Publishers, 1982), 199–200.

Struck by Lightning!

❀ MICHAEL F. SHEEHAN ❀

Since the dawn of humanity, thunder and lightning have both terrified and awed. Protection was sought from deities like Zeus and Thor; and in later ages God and St. Barbara. By the third quarter of the eighteenth century, the Enlightenment had brought about a new sense of curiosity; reason began to replace superstition. There were experiments with Lyden Jars, and new theories on electricity. When Benjamin Franklin "tamed lightning" in 1752 in his famous kite experiment with his son, he became an Enlightenment celebrity and his lightning rod became a best seller. Despite a better understanding of lightning's power, there was still no method to lessen its damage if a lightning rod failed to work.

The American Revolution was an eight year conflict in which hundreds of thousands of soldiers and civilians carried metal implements of war; firelocks (muskets), swords, and bayonets. It was therefore inevitable that lightning would be attracted to some of these men. Here are just a few select cases regarding death or injury from lightning during the American Revolution.

In August 1776, the Continental and British armies were facing off in the environs of New York City. The Americans were dispersed throughout Manhattan and Long Island; the British occupied Staten Island and were poised to land a massive force at Gravesend on August 22. The day of the landing was clear and beautiful; the evening before, however, was anything but. Benjamin Trumbull noted in his journal that at about "8 o'clock [came] on a most terrible Storm of Thunder and Lightning. Several Houses in the City were Struck with Lightning . . . [including] a large House in w[hi]ch a Number of the Connecticut Militia. One man was killed outright and three more much hurt." It didn't stop there; in fact the lightning only became more deadly: "Several Boxes of Cartridges took fire by the Lightning . . . and blew up.

Three Officers, one Captain [Abraham Van Wyck], one Liutenant and an Ensign of Colonel MacDougall's Battalion were killed together in one Tent."[1] When the British began to land on the 22nd, many Americans saw the devastating weather of the previous evening as a bad omen of the coming campaign. They weren't wrong.

Over a year later, the energetic Massachusetts delegate to Congress and future President John Adams was named a Minister to the Court of Versailles, and ordered to join Benjamin Franklin at Passy, a Parisian suburb. In February 1778, Adams boarded the *Boston*, bound for France. Less than a month later, en route, lightning struck the vessel: "a Thunder bolt struck 3 men upon deck and wounded one of them a little by a Score upon his Shoulder." Lt. William Jennison of the Continental Marines recorded that the poor fellow who had been scorched "lived three days and died raving mad."[2]

In the late spring of 1779, the British sent a 6,000 man force with a number of vessels up the Hudson River to seize the strategic crossing of King's Ferry, where they fortified Stony and Verplanck's Points. One of the larger vessels accompanying the expedition, commanded by Capt. Andrew Sutherland, was the HMS *Vulture,* a sixteen gun sloop-of-war. Laying in Haverstraw Bay, on June 14, she was struck by lightning: " very Squally with Thunder, lightning & rain . . . The lightning struck the . . . head of the Foretopgall[an]t mast; conveyed itself down the Foretopmast & Foremast to within about 5 feet of the fore Castle Deck, rendered the mast entirely useless & wounded several men." An unknown officer at Verplanck's noted in his diary that the "*Vulture* Sloop of War . . . was struck with Lightning . . . the Foremast & Foretopmast was split in several places & three Men . . . furling the Sails were much hurt."[3]

1. Benjamin Trumbull, "Journal of the Campaign at New York, 1776–7," *Collections of the Connecticut Historical Society* (http://digitalcommons.providence.edu/cgi/viewcontent.cgi?article=1015&context=primary, accessed December 23, 2015); General Orders, June 5, 1776, Note 2, National Archives (hereafter, NA). http://founders.archives.gov/documents/Washington/03-04-02-0353
2. John Adams Diary, February 21–23, 1778, NA, http://founders.archives.gov/documents/Adams/01-02-02-0008–0009
3. Master's Log, HMS *Vulture,* June 15, 1779, ADM 52/2073, British National Archives. Though she was struck on the afternoon of June 14, the ship's log considers it the 15th, as at the time the naval day began at noon on the preceding day; i.e.: naval June 15 was land's June 14 12:00 Noon to 11:59 AM June 15. Due to the obvious confusion this caused, the Royal Navy abolished this system during the Napoleonic Wars and used local time. Carson I. A. Ritchie, "A New York Diary" in *Narratives of the Revolution in New York: A Collection of Articles from The New-York Historical Society Quarterly* (New York: New-York Historical Society, 1975), 282.

The Reverend Jacob Duché's townhouse in Philadelphia during a thunderstorm, painted by an unknown artist. Duché sided with the British when they occupied Philadelphia, and when they returned to New York City, his house was confiscated and he fled to England.

Less than two weeks later, lightning struck again. Capt. Johann Ewald, the famed Jäger officer, also at Verplanck's, noted that on June 25, "three sailors were struck dead by lightning on a ship [unknown vessel] which lay off Verplanck's Point," and that on the following day, "another stroke injured three Hessian Grenadiers of the Lengerke Battalion. The thunderstorms usually come daily and last for about four to five hours." Also in the vicinity was Capt. John Peebles of the 42nd Regiment of Foot who mentioned the same incident: "a thunder gust in the afternoon, three of the Hessian Grrs hurt with lightning."[4]

Despite the victory at Yorktown in October 1781, the war was not over and the Continental Army had to be prepared for a renewed campaign. Preparations included maintaining powder magazines, and protecting them from electricity. In June 1782, "the Officers at Kings Ferry express some apprehensions of danger to the magazine from the lightning—The quartermaster will furnish [lightning] rods for the purpose, if it meets with the approbation of the commander in chief."[5]

4. Johann Ewald, *Diary of the American War: A Hessian Journal*, Joseph P. Tustin, ed. (New Haven, CT: Yale University Press. 1979), 169; John Peebles, *John Peebles' American War: The Diary of a Scottish Grenadier, 1776–1782*, Ira D. Gruber, ed. (Mechanicsburg, PA: Stackpole Books, 1998), 272.
5. Henry Sewall to David Humphreys, July 12, 1782, NA, http://founders.archives.gov /Washington/99-01-02-08676.

After April 1783, there was at long last a cessation of hostilities between the Continental and British armies. The British prepared to evacuate; Washington and Gen. Sir Guy Carleton met in the Hudson River, and all seemed to be going well. Lightning, however, was to claim one more victim. On May 23, 1783, the Massachusetts orator and brother of Mercy Otis Warren, James Otis, Jr., stepped into the doorway of a friend's home in Andover, Massachusetts for some air during a dinner party when "he was killed . . . by a [bolt of] lightning in an instant."[6]

Although lightning casualties did not compare in number to disease and combat casualties during the war years, they were perhaps more shocking and frightening in their abruptness, and therefore more frequently noted in the diaries and journals that chronicle the war.

---

6. John Thaxter to John Adams, August 12, 1783, NA, http://founders.archives.gov/documents/Adams/06–15–02–0096.

A Series of Unfortunate Events: Chichester Cheyne's Revolutionary War, 1778–1783

❦ NICOLAS BELL-ROMERO ❦

In March 1778, George Washington, the commander-in-chief of the Continental army, was in winter quarters with his men at Valley Forge, Pennsylvania; Capt. James Cook was exploring the Pacific northwest of North America; and Voltaire, the famous French philosopher, was crowned as a poet laureate in Paris.

But Chichester Cheyne, a fifteen-year-old Virginian, gave little indication that he cared about these events as he boarded the *John*, a ship bound for New York. He had been living in Scotland for the past seven years (probably on the estate of Thomas Bruce of Arnot, a significant landowner in Scotlandwell, near Edinburgh). He was forced to return to Virginia after his father, Thomas Cheyne, died, leaving a widow, four children, and no will or guardian; a dangerous set of circumstances given that the Virginia constitution allowed for all "escheats, penalties, and forfeitures" to go to the new Commonwealth.[1]

The homecoming the teenager desired would never come. Cheyne was "unfortunately captured" by the *Marlborough*, a rebel ship, one of

---

1. Petition, Audit Office Papers Series 13, British National Archives: vol. 97, ff. 237–239. Hereafter I will set out the series, volume, and folio sections with slashes (so the last example would be: Petition, A.O. 13/97/237–239. During the eighteenth century, Scotlandwell was also a prominent home of the weaving trade (which, it can be assumed, meant Chichester's father was some sort of merchant). Thomas Bruce of Arnot (he spoke in Cheyne's defense to the Commission) is mentioned on the "roll of Freeholders . . . held at Kinross on 25th July 1811" (James Bridges, *View of The Political State of Scotland, at Michaelmas 1811; with a supplement, Exhibiting the Votes at the General Election, in 1812* [Edinburgh, 1813], 90.) For the Virginia Constitution, see Final Draft of the Virginia Constitution of 1776, June 29, in Robert A. Rutland, ed., *The Papers of George Mason*, vol. 1 (Chapel Hill: The University of North Carolina Press, 1970), 288.

the sixteen hundred privateers trawling the Atlantic Ocean in search of wealth and glory. This setback, though, was only the beginning of his ordeal. Like many of the prisoners captured by privateers during the war, Cheyne was probably confined below decks in leg-irons on board the *John*, the very ship he had set sail on in the first place. After all, cases of hostages retaking ships were an incredibly common occurrence during the period.[2]

Having been brought to Boston, Massachusetts, in chains, "he was desired by the Americans" to join them, "which on his refusing to comply"—having "always had a sturdy attachment to the Royal Crown"— "they not only stript him of all his clothes & everything else that was valuable and refused him liberty of going to his friends . . . they even compelled him to serve on B[oard] the Privateer[s] *Marlborough* & *General Mifflin* . . . [where] they treated him very harshly." He eventually served for about a year on the latter ship. That was until they captured the *Elephant*, a British armed store ship. Thrown on board the new prize along with fourteen other Americans; Cheyne suddenly decided to try his luck "with some British officers," who "had [concocted] a scheme for [using] and taking possession of the ship when they came to the British channel." But before this motley crew could act on their hastily constructed plan, a Royal Navy vessel recaptured them.[3]

Tasting freedom for the first time in over a year, Cheyne suddenly realized he had neither money nor any possibility of seeing his family. Only one option remained: join the Royal Navy and collect the meagre salary on offer. He went on to serve for two years on board a British frigate, fighting at the successful siege of Charleston, South Carolina, in

---

2. Petition, A.O. 13/97/237–239. Cheyne's capture aboard the *John* by the privateer *Marlborough* is corroborated in the Remarks for Sunday May 10th 1778, Log of Rhode Island Privateer Ship *Marlborough*, Captain George Wait Babcock, in Michael J. Crawford (with Dennis M. Conrad, E. Gordan Bowen-Hassell, and Mark L. Hayes), ed., *Naval Documents of The American Revolution*, vol. 12 (Washington, D.C.: Naval History and Heritage Command, 2013), 323. The Continental Congress issued 1,697 Letters of Marque, and around 58,400 men served on board Patriot privateers during the war (Jack Coggins, *Ships and Seamen of the American Revolution* [Mineola, New York: Dover Publications, Inc., 1969], 74). For the threat of armed takeovers on the high seas, see *Ibid.*, 68.

3. Petition, A.O. 13/97/237–239. The *General Mifflin* was originally a twelve-gun brig under the command of Captain J. Hamilton in 1776; but, when Cheyne came on board the ship in 1778, the *Mifflin* had expanded to a twenty-gun vessel under Daniel McNeil. Apparently the ship raided around France and Britain, and then engaged in a "severe action with a British privateer" which cost the lives of the English commander and twenty-two men killed or injured (see Edgar Stanton Maclay, *A History of American Privateers* [New York: Burt Franklin, 1968], 74, 88–89).

1780, where a combined naval and land attack captured the city and over five thousand rebel troops. And he had also earlier taken part in "several other expeditions in Boats up the Chesapeak in Virginia," possibly including an infamous mission on May 8, 1779, undertaken by Gen. Edward Matthew and Adm. George Collier. Together a combined fleet of thirty ships attacked Portsmouth, burned Suffolk, and destroyed more than 130 ships, three thousand hogsheads of tobacco, and other supplies worth an estimated two million pounds. This was sweet revenge for more than a year in captivity.[4]

Yet Cheyne's revolutionary journey was about to take another sharp turn. He was captured again, this time by the French, and was "carried to Martinique where he was stripped of everything, and remained a prisoner for over eight months." After this, he was pressed to serve on board the *Caton*, a French ship that saw action at the Battle of the Mona Passage on April 19, 1782. Thankfully for Cheyne, the Royal Navy under the command of Adm. Sir Samuel Hood, 1st Viscount Hood, saw off the opposition and recaptured two vessels, including the ship on which he had just served. In total, he had fought for four years with three different navies on seven different ships; but for him at least, the war was finally over.[5]

Cheyne's tale is truly an odyssey. But his experiences, and those of many others, have only recently been scrutinized. They have largely fallen through the cracks in a popular narrative that likes the frame the Loyalists—those who supported Great Britain during the American Revolutionary War (1775–1783)—as static, recalcitrant "Tories," a group of ethnic minorities, ideological Royalists, and the rich. This framework,

4. Petition, A.O. 13/97/237–239; Jim Piecuch, *Three Peoples, One King: Loyalists, Indians, and Slaves in the Revolutionary South, 1775–1782* (Columbia: University of South Carolina Press, 2008), 178–182; Michael A. McDonnell, *The Politics of War: Race, Class, and Conflict in Revolutionary Virginia* (Chapel Hill: Published for the Omohundro Institute of Early American History and Culture, Williamsburg, Virginia, by the University of North Carolina Press, 2007), 343–344. Cheyne served on the *Richmond*, a thirty-two-gun frigate.

5. Petition, A.O. 13/97/237–239. Hood was a mentor to Horatio Nelson, Britain's hero at the Battle of Trafalgar (October 21, 1805).

though, is essentially artificial. It is a product of what the "Founding Fathers"—those who led the American Revolution—wanted us to believe about their mortal enemies.[6]

Indeed, after the guns fell silent in 1783, a dominant narrative was constructed out of a conflict that had claimed between 25,000 and 36,000 American lives, a death toll that would put the Revolutionary War second only behind the American Civil War in deaths per capita. A story of unity and revolutionary fervour, orchestrated by historians including Mercy Otis Warren and David Ramsay, pushed ordinary people who opposed the Revolution to the margins. Instead, more prominent figures—including Thomas Hutchinson, the last royal governor of Massachusetts, and Banastre Tarleton, a British cavalry commander— were lambasted as "Rank Tories" who "fabricate lies to deceive and divide the American people." Even John Adams, the second president of the United States of America, entered the realm of hyperbole when he declared. "I would have hanged my own brother had he taken a part with our enemy in the contest."[7]

6. Welcome contributions to the 'rank-and-file' Loyalist literature can be found in Todd Braisted, "A Patriot-Loyalist: Playing Both Sides", *Journal of the American Revolution*, http://allthingsliberty.com/2014/04/a-patriot-loyalist-playing-both-sides/, accessed December 10, 2015; and Aaron Sullivan, "In But Not Of the Revolution: Loyalty, Liberty, and the British Occupation of Philadelphia" (Ph.D. diss., Temple University, 2014). For studies of the loyalists as a mostly elite phenomenon, see William H. Nelson, *The American Tory* (Oxford: Oxford University Press, 1961); Wallace Brown, *The Good Americans: The Loyalists in the American Revolution* (New York: William Morrow and Company Inc., 1969; and Robert M. Calhoon, *The Loyalists in Revolutionary America, 1760–1781* (New York: Harcourt Brace Jovanovich, 1973). The notion that the "Founding Fathers" were the key drivers of the narrative can be found in William Huntting Howell, "'Starving Memory': Antinarrating the American Revolution," in Michael A. McDonnell et al, eds., *Remembering the Revolution: Memory, History, and Nation Making from Independence to the Civil War* (Amherst: University of Massachusetts Press, 2013), 93.

7. For the Patriot numbers see Howard H. Peckham, ed., *The Toll of Independence: Engagements and Battle Casualties of the American Revolution* (Chicago: University of Chicago Press, 1974), 132. Even though his work focused on the American Civil War, William Blair's chapter on Confederate identity has been especially instructive (*Virginia's Private War: Feeding Body and Soul in the Confederacy, 1861–1865* [New York; Oxford: Oxford University Press, 1998], 152). For this same point with regards to the American Revolution, see Michael Kammen, *A Season of Youth: The American Revolution and the Historical Imagination* (New York: Alfred A. Knopf, 1978), 16. Mercy Otis Warren was a political writer and wife of James Warren, the President of the Massachusetts Provincial Congress and a noted Anti-Federalist (see her *History of the Rise, Progress, and Termination of the American Revolution* [Boston, 1805]). David Ramsay, a politician from South Carolina, described the Revolution thus: "a sense of common danger extinguished selfish

After two hundred years this antipathy has not completely gone away. Even though historians have known for over forty years that one-fifth of the colonial population may have remained loyal, long-standing "Tory" caricatures still dominate the secondary literature. Gordon Wood succumbed to these arguments, too, in his *Radicalism of the American Revolution* (1991): "A disproportionate number of [the Loyalists] were well-to-do gentry operating at the pinnacles of power and patronage—royal or proprietary officeholders, big overseas dry-good merchants, and rich landowners." And once this "Monarchical" culture was removed, Wood argued, a rejuvenated "Post-Revolutionary society was inevitably put together on new republican terms. The Revolution effectively weakened or severed those loyalties of the *ancien regime* that had enabled men like William Allen or James De Lancey to form their extensive webs of personal and familial influence."[8]

To some extent this interpretation is understandable. It endures because ordinary people—or the "inarticulate," as historians sometimes call them—are difficult to find in the Loyalist records, especially so in a Virginia context where seventy-five per cent of adults could not even sign their own names. All historians seem to have are the diaries and letters of elite Loyalists, who were vitriolic in their condemnation of the treasonous, dastardly, American rebels.[9]

passions . . . and local attachments and partialities were sacrificed on the altar of patriotism." (*The History of the American Revolution*, vol. 1 [Lexington, 1815], 150). Hutcheson and Tarleton were vilified following the war; for more on this point, see Bernard Bailyn, "*Thomas Hutchinson in Context*: The Ordeal *Revisited*," *American Antiquarian Society*, (October 2004), 284; and Howell, "'Starving Memory'," 93. The "Rank Tories" comment comes from the "Historical Notes of Dr. Benjamin Rush, 1777," *The Pennsylvania Magazine of History and Biography* 27 (1903): 143; and the Adams quote can be found in Wallace Brown, "The View at Two Hundred Years: The Loyalists of the American Revolution," *American Antiquarian Society* (1969): 25–47.

8. These figures, though, can only be an approximation of the number of colonists who served on the British side during the American Revolutionary War. See Paul H. Smith, "The American Loyalists: Notes on Their Organisation and Numerical Strength," *The William and Mary Quarterly* 25 (April 1968): 269. For the Gordon Wood quote, see *The Radicalism of the American Revolution* (New York: Vintage Books, 1991), 176–177.

9. For the Virginia figure, see Rhys Isaac, "Dramatising the Ideology of Revolution: Popular Mobilisation in Virginia, 1774 to 1776," *The William and Mary Quarterly* 33 (July 1976): 362. Kenneth Lockridge has found that white male literacy, outside New England, stood at or below two-thirds (the same as in England); *Literacy in Colonial New England: An Enquiry into the Social Context of Literacy in the Early Modern West* (New York: W. W. Norton & Company, 1975), 77–81.

This argument takes us back to the source of the Chichester Cheyne narrative: the Loyalist Claims Commission records. On the face of things, these memorials, depositions, and property lists only represent the biased ramblings of a rich few seeking reward. Three arguments can be made, though.[10]

First, petitions were an attempt to elevate individual heroism, loyalty, and self-sacrifice to the forefront of a narrative. This makes any general claims of loyalty to the Commission largely useless. Instead, one must look to the essential facts of a case: what role did these ordinary people play in the Revolution? What impact did they have on the results of the war? What effect did the conflict have on them?[11]

When this inquisitorial method is taken, the stories of ordinary people contained the archives start to look depressingly similar to the diaries and pension applications of war veterans on the Patriot side. Indeed, after more than thirty years of research into ordinary folk and their experiences during the Revolutionary War, it now seems that Loyalists like Chichester Cheyne and the soldier William Shoemaker were motivated by contingent factors—poverty, forced impressment, military mobilization, or sheer bad luck—to become foot soldiers and sailors in a war most wanted absolutely no part in.[12]

Second, individual memory is not as fallible as we think it is. After all, Alfred F. Young has written that George Robert Twelves Hughes, a shoemaker who participated in the Boston Tea Party (December 16, 1773), continued to astonish listeners with his memory, even at the ripe old age of ninety-three. Cheyne, in direct contrast, had only six years

---

10. The Loyalist Claims Commission was enacted in July 1783 by the British government, "to enquire into the Losses and Services of all such persons as have suffered in their Rights, Properties, and Professions . . . in consequence of their Loyalty to His Majesty, and Attachment to the British Government." John Raithby, ed., *The Statutes at Large of England and of Great Britain: From Magna Carta to the Union of the Kingdoms of Great Britain and Ireland*. Vol. 17 (London, 1811), 100. Its main job was to save the Treasury money after they spent £40,820 on pensions in 1782 for just 315 Loyalists (John Eardley Wilmot, *Historical View of the Commission for Enquiring into the Losses, Services, and Claims of the American Loyalists, at the Close of the War Between Great Britain and Her Colonies in 1783*, intr. and pref. by George Athan Billias [Boston: Gregg Press, 1972], 15–16).

11. For the three questions posed, see Alfred F. Young, "Why Write the History of Ordinary People," in *Liberty Tree: Ordinary People and the American Revolution* (New York: New York University Press, 2006), 4.

12. Historians usually refer to colonists who had no interest in the war as "disaffected." See Thomas Verenna, "Disarming the Disaffected", *Journal of the American Revolution*, http://allthingsliberty.com/2014/08/disarming-the-disaffected, accessed 10 August 2015; and Ronald Hoffman, "The 'Disaffected' in the Revolutionary South," in Alfred F. Young, ed., *The American Revolution: Explorations in the History of American Radicalism* (DeKalb: Northern Illinois University Press, 1993), 273–316.

between serving in the war and making his deposition to the Commission. He could hardly forget the trauma he experienced over this very short period of time.[13]

Third, the Claims Commission records may be filled with merchants, officeholders, and wealthy artisans; but that is hardly a function of the Loyalists themselves. Over sixty thousand refugees eventually left the United States. Of those, only 3,225 got to make a claim, and even fewer actually had a decision made on their memorials and depositions. Cheyne, for reasons unknown, never had any verdict made on his claim. Neither did Josiah Hodges, another Virginian whose property was destroyed. Having fled to London, and finding no work, he was eventually "arrested and carried into the fleet for a debt he contracted to support and maintain a helpless family," "and to render your memorialist completely miserably it pleased Providence to visit his Children with the small pox while he was a prisoner."[14]

It is clear, then, that historians should continue to examine the Commission records and the stories contained within, a task that is not just about academic equality. Ordinary people who became Loyalists fought the battles, built the fortifications, spied on the Patriots, and suffered and died in huge numbers. We know the Patriot battle casualties; but we may never know how many loyal men and women became victims of the conflict. These stories and perspectives need to be recaptured and reassessed for every single colony and state.

Once this perspective is adopted, the mist that has surrounded the Loyalist experience would dissipate. It would again be possible to regain a "sense of the tragic:" an idea that the war did not end at the parades, at the Battle of Yorktown in 1781, or even at the Treaty of Paris in 1783, but was a struggle that continued for the next twenty years as refugees from up and down the thirteen colonies attempted to find new homes. Chichester Cheyne was in exactly that situation. He returned to Britain at the age of twenty-one with no financial backers and the prospect of a lifetime on board the ships of the Royal Navy. The American Revolution gave, but in many cases it also took away.[15]

13. Alfred F. Young, *The Shoemaker and the Tea Party: Memory and the American Revolution* (Boston: Beacon Press, 1999), 10; Petition, A.O. 13/97/240.

14. Maya Jasanoff, *Liberty's Exiles: American Loyalists in the Revolutionary World* (New York: First Vintage Books, 2012), 357; Wilmot, *Historical View*, 90–91; Cheyne, Chichester in Peter Wilson Coldham, *American Migrations, 1765–1799: The Lives, Times, and Families of Colonial Americans Who Remained Loyal to the British Crown* (Baltimore: Genealogical Publishing Company, 2000), 543; Memorial, A.O. 13/96/507.

15. Michael G. Kammen, "The American Revolution as a *Crise de Conscience*: The Case of New York," in Michael G. Kammen et al, eds., *Society, Freedom, and Conscience: The American Revolution in Virginia, Massachusetts, and New York* (New York: Norton, 1976), 188; Petition, A.O. 13/97/239.

A Look at Lauzun in L'Expédition Particulière

KIM BURDICK

INTRODUCTION

Best known in this country for his role in the in the Yorktown Campaign of the American Revolution, the Duc de Lauzun (April 13, 1747–December 31, 1793) has often been dismissed as a man who loved the ladies and grumbled about Rochambeau. Lauzun deserves a much closer look. He was a dedicated and (usually) diplomatic military leader who cared deeply about his men and their mission. Rochambeau's aide-de-camp, Hans Axel von Fersen, wrote in the fall of 1780, "Opinions are divided about him. You will hear both good and harm; the first is right, the second is wrong. If people knew him, they would change their ideas and do justice to his heart."[1]

L'EXPÉDITION PARTICULIÈRE: THE YORKTOWN CAMPAIGN

On February 6, 1778, King Louis XVI of France signed the Treaty of Amity and Friendship negotiated by Benjamin Franklin, Silas Deane, and Arthur Lee. Arnold Whitridge captured the resultant enthusiasm: "To Fersen, Closen, the Berthiers, the Duc de Lauzun, and all the other gallants who had tumbled over each other to get a place in the expedition, the revolt of the English colonies in America offered the adventure of a lifetime.[2]

Thirty-one-year-old Armand Louis de Gontaut, Duc de Lauzun, was among the first to volunteer. Les Volontaires Étrangers de Lauzun was a multi-ethnic group composed of officers, infantry, artillery, workmen

---

1. Hans Axel von Fersen to his father, October 16, 1780, in *Newport, R.I., Diary and Correspondence of Count Axel Fersen* (Memphis, TN: General Books LLC).
2. Arnold Whitridge, *Rochambeau: America's Neglected Founding Father* (New York: Collier Books, 1965), 194.

and hussars. His hussars were cavalrymen used in battle for harassing enemy skirmishers, overrunning artillery positions, and pursuing fleeing troops. Due to lack of ships, half his troops and all their horses were left behind when, along with other French regiments, the Légion de Lauzun left for America on May 2, 1780.[3]

They landed in Rhode Island in July. Lauzun's Legion camped a mile in front of the rest of the French army to guard the coast.[4] He wrote, "a squadron of fourteen or fifteen men of war, commanded by Admiral Arbuthnot, come cruising in the Rhode Island channel. We were informed from New York that he had embarked a great part of the army; we expected to be attacked at any moment . . . Notwithstanding the bad condition of our troops, we toiled without ceasing at building redoubts and fortifying ourselves."[5]

On August 28, 1780, Lafayette wrote to Washington, "The extreme desire which Duke de Lauzun had of serving in this expedition made him embark with the first part of his Légion wiz three hundred hussards, hundred grenadiers, hundred chasseurs, and a company of artillery. The dress and accoutrements of the hussards make it almost impossible for them to serve a foot, and if they are not mounted, the Duke de Lauzun had rather serve in the line, than to stay with the Légion."[6]

Eventually, horses arrived from Pennsylvania. Late summer and fall were spent repairing buildings, training horses, and settling in. Rochambeau, who was old enough to have been Lauzun's father, remarked that Lauzun "rendered himself very agreeable to the Americans by his prepossessing manners, and succeeded in every transaction which he had to conclude, either with the veteran governor Trumboldt or with the other members of the legislature of the State."

A formal visit from members of the Six Nations was a social highlight of the season. Rochambeau's regiments paraded and went through their manual of arms and fired muskets and cannon. The Duc de Lauzun's hussars delighted the Indians, as did a tour of the beautiful

3. Lee Kennett, *French Forces in America* (Westport, CT: Greenwood Press, 1977), chapter 1.

4. Jean François Louis Clermont-Crèvecœur, "Journal," in *The American Campaigns of Rochambeau's Army*, edited by Howard C. Rice and Anne S. K. Brown (Princeton, N.J., Princeton University Press, 1972), 1:18.

5. Armand Louis de Gontaut Biron, Duc de Lauzun, *Memoirs of Lauzun*, translated by C.K. Scott Moncrieff (New York, NY, Brentanos, 1928), 191–193.

6. Marie Joseph Paul Yves Roch Gilbert du Moitier Lafayette, *The Letters of Lafayette to Washington*, edited by Louis Reichenthal Gottschalk (Philadelphia American Philosophical Society, 1976), 110.

ships in the harbor. In turn, the delegation entertained by performing colorful traditional tribal dances.[7]

In November, Lauzun observed: "The scarcity of forage obliged [Rochambeau] to send me to the forests of Connecticut . . . As I spoke English I was charged with an infinite number of details, boring in the extreme, but necessary. I did not leave Newport without regrets; I had formed a very pleasant circle of acquaintances there."[8]

In January 1781, Maj. Gen. Marquis de Chastellux, wrote happily of visiting Lauzun in Connecticut:

> We had fine weather all day and got to Lebanon at sunset . . . It will be easily imagined that I was not sorry to find myself in the French army, of which these Hussars formed the advanced guard, although their quarters be seventy-five miles from Newport; but there are no circumstances in which I should not be happy with M. de Lauzun. For two months I had been talking and listening; with him, I conversed, for it must be allowed that conversation is still the peculiar forte of the amiable French.
>
> The Duke de Lauzun entertained with this diversion [squirrel hunting], which is much in fashion in this country. These animals are large and have a more beautiful fur than those in Europe . . . On returning from the chase, I dined at the Duke de Lauzun's with Governor Trumbull and General Huntington.[9]

After Chastellux's visit, boredom struck. Lauzun moaned that "Siberia alone can furnish any idea of Lebanon, which consists of a few huts scattered among vast forests." One patrol of hussars, horses and all, had deserted in December. William Williams, who had turned his home over to the French officers, berated Lauzun for his troops' behavior. The winter was unseasonably cold and the legion had stolen wood, including thirty or more trees, much of Williams' fence, four or five sheep, a number of geese, and much more.[10] In February, Lauzun sent Alexander Hamilton a letter to forward to Lafayette, asking if his legion could join him. Communication was slow, but in the spring there was, finally, some positive action.

7. Richard M. Ketchum, *Victory at Yorktown* (New York, NY., Henry Holt and Co., 2004), 83.

8. Lauzun, *Memoirs*, 194–195.

9. François Jean Chastellux, *Travels in North America* (Classic Reprint, Forgotten Books ,2012), 297.

10. Williams' house was allotted to Lauzun's second-in-command, Robert Dillon. www.digplanet.com/wiki/William_Williams_House_(Lebanon,_Connecticut).

In June, the allied troops began marching south. Washington asked Rochambeau to allow Lauzun and his men to help surprise the British at Morrisania (South Bronx) with "a Coup de main" slated for July 2. They would be "joined by Colonel Sheldon with 200 horses and Foot and about 400 Infantry, both officers and men perfectly acquainted with the country." [11] The effort was in vain. Rochambeau's aide-de-camp, Baron Von Closen, explained that a deserter had forewarned their opponents of Lauzun's arrival. The event amounted to "some pistol shots fired without the loss of a man." [12] Washington sent a note to French headquarters, announcing that the mission had failed. [13]

American Henry Dearborn wrote in his journal,

> at 9 oclock in the evining the whole of our army together with the French march'd . . . & at day break were paraded before the Enemies work at King's bridg. A party of our horse, with some Militia from Connectcut, went on to Frog's Neck, (a nest of tories), & the Duke Delozen with his legion & Colonel Scammell, with a Corps of Light Infantry, went on to Morrissania, (the place of randisvoos for Delensees [DeLancey's] Infamus corps of horse thieves & murderers). a considerable number of horses, Cattle & sheep, together with about twenty of the above mentioned corps ware taken & brought off & the remeinder dispers'd, except what ware killed.[14]

On August 18, 1781, the war's theater of operations shifted from New York to Virginia. On the 19th, Count William de Deux-Ponts (not to be confused with duPont) noted, "left camp at Phillipsburg. We do not know the object of our march and are in perfect ignorance as to whether we are going against New York or whether we are going to Virginia to attack Lord Cornwallis . . . A rear-guard is essential under the present circumstances. The Count de Rochambeau formed it of the two battalions of grenadiers and chasseurs of the army and of the Légion de Lauzun. The Viscount Vioménil is Commander-in-Chief of it."[15]

11. *The Writings of George Washington*, Volume 22 (Washington, DC: Government Printing Office, 1937), 293–294.

12. Baron Ludwig Von Closen, *The Revolutionary Journal of Baron Ludwig von Closen, 1780–1783* (Chapel Hill: University of South Carolina Press, published for the Institute of Early American History and Culture at Williamsburg, 1958), 90.

13. *Diaries of George Washington*, Volume III, 1771–75, 1780–81, Donald Jackson, ed. (Charlottesville: University Press of Virginia, 1978), 390.

14. Henry Dearborn, *Revolutionary War Journals of Henry Dearborn 1775–1783*, Lloyd A. Brown and Howard H. Peckham, editors (Chicago: Caxton Club, 1939), 213.

15. William de Deux-Ponts, *My Campaigns in America: A Journal Kept by Count William de Deux-Ponts*, Samuel Abbott Green, ed. (Boston: J.K. Wiggin and Wm Parsons Lunt, 1868), 121–122.

Marching south from New Jersey, Lauzun reported:

> M. le Baron de Vioménil, whom a kick from a horse obliged to
> travel in a carriage, did not know what to make of this. He would
> indeed have been almost helpless had he been attacked. I felt that
> the greatest service that I could render him was to advance as far as
> possible towards the enemy so as to give him time to retire into the
> woods. I sent out strong patrols upon all the roads by which the eng-
> lish might come. I took fifty hussars well-mounted and went myself
> for more than ten miles along the road to Brunswick, by which they
> would most probably appear. I met two or three strong patrols of
> light troops which retired after exchanging a few pistol shots with
> my hussars. I assured myself that the English army was not on the
> march and went back to reassure the Baron de Vioménil.[16]

On September 3, the First Brigade arrived in Philadelphia. Von
Closen described the parade: "All the gilded contingent was drawn up
between the lancers and the hussars of Lauzun's Legion to salute with
all the grace possible the congress [assembled on] the balcony of the
Hall of Congress . . . All the ladies were assembled at M. de Luzerne's
residence, where they watched the army pass and were enchanted to
see such handsome men and to hear such good music. The French minister gave a dinner for 180 that day."[17]

Two days later in Chester, Pennsylvania, Lauzun witnessed Washington's relief at learning that de Grasse had anchored in the Chesapeake Bay. Lauzun commented, "I have never seen a man more
overcome with great and sincere joy than was General Washington.
We heard at the same time that Lord Cornwallis had received orders
from Sir Henry Clinton . . . to fortify himself at Yorktown."[18]

From Chester, the troops passed through Delaware to Head of Elk,
Maryland. There were not enough boats to transport everyone down
the Chesapeake. It was agreed that 1,000 men, including the Artillery
Regiment, the Grenadiers and Chasseurs of the Brigade of Bourbonne,
and the Infantry of Lauzun's Legion would sail. The rest, including
Lauzun's hussars, advanced down the road.

Arriving in Williamsburg, Virginia, Lauzun's Legion received orders
to reinforce 1,200 militiamen serving under Brig. Gen. George Weedon

16. Lauzun, *Memoirs*, 204. Vioménil was Rochambeau's second in command.
17. Von Closen, *Revolutionary Journal*, 120.
18. Lauzun, *Memoirs*, 204.

at Gloucester Courthouse.[19] Rochambeau sent artillery plus eight hundred men drawn from M. de Choisy's garrisons. Choisy, by the right of seniority, took command over both Weedon and Lauzun. Lauzun commented, "M. de Choisy is a good and gallant man, ridiculously violent, constantly in a rage, always making scenes with everyone, and entirely devoid of common sense. He began by finding fault with General Weedon and all the militia, told them they were cowards, and in five minutes had them almost as frightened of himself as of the English, which is certainly saying a good deal."[20]

The following days were busy. Count Deux-Ponts described the sights and sounds of October 2: "Rather sharp firing was heard in the morning from the other side of the river, after which Tarleton's cavalry was seen returning in a hurry and in disorder. We think that it has made a sortie from the lines of Gloucester to attack the Légion de Lauzun and we hope that it has been driven back."[21] On October 4, a woman standing outside her house told Lauzun that the British cavalry commander, Banastre Tarleton, had said he was most anxious "to shake hands with the French duke." Lauzun assured her that he had come to give Tarleton that very satisfaction.

I saw as I approached that the English cavalry outnumbered mine by three to one. I charged them without drawing rein . . . Tarleton caught sight of me, and came towards me with raised pistol. We were about to fight a duel between our lines when his horse was overthrown by one of his dragoons pursued by one of my lancers. A troop of English dragoons thrust themselves between us and covered his retreat. His horse remained in my hands . . . I charged him a third time, routed part of his cavalry and pursued him as far as the earthworks of Gloucester.[22]

Cromot du Bourg, an aide to Rochambeau, elaborated:

> The Duke de Lauzun, after charging several times at the head of his legion, was ordered by M. de Choisy to fall back and obeyed. As he was returning with his troops he saw one of the lancers of his legion at some distance engaged with two of Tarleton's dragoons. Without a word to any one, Lauzun lowered his guard and went to [the lancer's] assistance. I only knew of this incident on the 20th November from M. de Rochambeau; the modesty of M. de Lauzun had

19. Robert A. Selig, "The Duc de Lauzun and his Legion: Rochambeau's Most Troublesome, Colorful Soldiers," *The Journal of the Colonial Williamsburg Foundation* Vol. 21, No. 6 (December/January 2000), 56–63.
20. Lauzun, *Memoirs*, 205–207.
21. Deux-Ponts, *My Campaigns in America*, 137.
22. Lauzun, *Memoirs*, 208.

prevented his mentioning it, but I should feel that I was very wrong should I omit to write down in this Journal everything that relates to the Duke de Lauzun, who, in these minor actions, set the best possible example to the army.[23]

Summing up the story, Rochambeau wrote: "Tarleton happened to be thereabouts with four hundred horses and two hundred infantrymen on a foraging expedition. De Lauzun's Légion, backed by a corps of American militia, attacked him so vigorously that he was put to flight with his detachment and was obliged to put back with a severe loss."[24]

Two weeks later, Cornwallis surrendered at Yorktown. Capt. Johann Ewald, a German officer serving with the British, noted that after the British troops surrendered, every officer "was greeted by the French generals and officers with the greatest courtesy. I had the pleasure and honor of being invited to dine with the general officers, Washington, Comte de Rochambeau, Marquis de Lafayette, Duc de Lauzun, Choisy, the Princes of Deux-Ponts, and General Comte Custine. . . . One scarcely knew whether he was among his friends or foes."[25]

Rochambeau now selected Lauzun and Deux-Ponts to carry news of the capitulation to France.[26] Lauzun grumbled, "I advised him to send M. de Charlus. This would put him in the good books of M. de Castries and might perhaps secure better treatment for the army. I could not bring him to agree. He said to that I had been first in action and ought to carry the news, that M. le Comte William des Deux-Ponts had been the second, and should carry the details."[27]

Rochambeau wrote to the Comte de Ségur:

> Sir, I have the honor to send you the Duc de Lauzun who is bring-ing to the King the news of the capture of Lord Cornwallis and his corps of troops. Comte William de Deux-Ponts will bring the dupli-cate and the recommendation for Grâces. These are the two superior officers who have performed the two most distinguished feats, as you will see in the journal that will inform you of all the details.[28]

23. Marie François Joseph Maxime, Baron Cromot du Bourg, Historical Society of Pennsylvania, http://discover.hsp.org/Record/ead-Am.6360
24. Jean-Baptiste Donatien de Vimeur, comte de Rochambeau, *Memoirs of the Marshal Count de Rochambeau*, translated by M.W.E. Wright, Esq. (Paris: Belin and Co., 1838), 68.
25. Captain Johan Ewald, *Diary of the American War: A Hessian Journal,* Joseph P. Tustin, trans and ed. (New Haven, Yale University Press. 1979), 342.
26. Rochambeau, *Memoirs*, 74.
27. Lauzun, *Memoirs*, 208. Charlus, (1756–1842), second-in-command of the Saintonge Regiment, was the son of the French Minister of the Navy.
28. *The American Campaigns of Rochambeau's Army*, 63 n127.

Before leaving, Lauzun put Lt. Col. Claude Etienne Hugau in charge of his legion. Except for a February move to the settlement of Charlotte Court House where there was more fodder, that winter would prove as boring for the men as the previous winter had been.[29]

Arriving at Brest, France, on the evening of November 19, Lauzun hurried to Versailles. According to his memoirs, "My news caused great joy to the King . . . he asked me many questions and had many kind words for me.[30] Louis XVI ordered a Te Deum to be sung in the Metropolitan Church in Paris on November 27, and directed "all bourgeois and inhabitants" of the city to illuminate the front of their houses to celebrate the great victory.[31]

On May 27, 1782, Rochambeau's aide-de-camp, Axel von Fersen, wrote from Williamsburg, "We have no news as yet from M. de Lauzun; we expect some with great impatience—at least I do, and we are beginning to feel uneasy."[32] Clermont-Crevecoeur said, "Finally, a frigate arrived from France bringing us the King's bounties (graces) for the capture of York. M. de Rochambeau was awarded a governorship with a salary of 30,000 livres . . . The Baron de Vioménil was appointed governor of La Rochelle and his brother was granted a pension of 5,000 livres . . .The Duc de Lauzun was allowed to keep his legion and the Marquis de Laval was promoted brigadier.[33]

In spite of this news, there was no sign of Lauzun's return. His legion remained in the vicinity of Charlotte Courthouse, Virginia, until June 1782 when they headed back to New York and Boston with the rest of the French Army.[34] Meanwhile, back in France, Lauzun was trying to get to America. The trip was an unpleasant adventure, best described in Lauzun's own words:

> For four days [the ship] was in constant peril of being taken or dashed upon the coast . . . We anchored in the River of Nantes, our frigate greatly damaged.
>
> We then set sail from La Rochelle upon the 14th of July . . . we came into violent collision with the French frigate Ceres, she did us considerable damage. Sickness broke out among our crew . . . I had a violent fever with intense paroxysms and delirium . . . I had been ill for twelve days when we encountered by night a vessel of 74 guns

29. Gérard-Antoine Massoni, "Claude Hugau (1741–1820), Vivax Hussar," (Tarbes, no 24, 1994), 79–96.
30. Lauzun, *Memoirs*, 209.
31. Ketchum, *Victory at Yorktown*, 258.
32. Fersen, *Diary and Correspondence*, 18.
33. Clermont-Crevecoeur, "Journal," 71–72.
34. Von Closen, *Revolutionary Journal*, 216.

which we were obliged to fight. We had a score of men killed . . . A week after our battle, we arrived off the coast of America, at the mouth of the Delaware . . . at daybreak we sighted an English squadron of seven men of war bearing down upon us under full canvas. We were forced to raise anchor and enter the river without pilots . . . M. de la Touche sailed two leagues farther up the channel, then seeing that no hope remained, decided to put ashore the packages from the court, the money, and passengers.

We were put ashore about a league from the nearest habitation, without having brought away so much as a shirt a piece. I was still in a fever, I could barely stand, and I should never have been able to reach a house had it not been for a powerful negro who gave me his arm. As soon as we had put our money in a safe place, I made my way slowly towards Philadelphia . . . the French and American doctors were agreed in their opinion that I must die before the end of the autumn. The doctors had declared that it was impossible that I should think of joining the army, then M. de Rochambeau sent one of his aides-de-camp with letters for the Chevalier de la Luzerne, and wrote bidding me do everything in my power to come to camp as he had matters of the greatest importance to communicate to me. I made up my mind without consulting anyone. I mounted a horse and rode to camp, death being no worse on the road than in Philadelphia. The ride did me good. I was already much better when I arrived at Headquarters.

. . . My health returned. I wished for nothing now but letters, and we received none.[35]

That fall, Von Closen wrote, "Everyone is preparing to depart . . . We are leaving in North America the siege artillery, as well as the sick and the detachment of 400 men in Baltimore, commanded by M. de la Valette, Lieutenant Colonel of Saintonge and Brigadier. He will be subordinate of M le Duc de Lauzun who is to remain in Wilmington [Delaware] with his legion."[36]

Lauzun reported, "The inhabitants of Wilmington appear willing to deliver us by being disposed to do everything that suits us. But it will be necessary to completely build our quarters and this expense, we

35. Lauzun, *Memoirs*, 214–21.
36. Von Closen, *Revolutionary Journal*, 270.

know from the reconnaissance of M. Collot, will cost around 800 dollars." The minutes of the Trustees of Wilmington Academy show: "Duc de Lauzun, commanding officer of the King of France's troops in the service of America has fixed upon our school house as a barrack for those troops the ensuing winter." [37] Stables to hold 281 horses were built at the expense of the King of France at 8th and King Street near French Street. On December 24, 1782, more than 600 men and 281 horses arrived in Delaware, staying with Wilmington families paid to house them. Finally, on May 11, 1783, their horses sold at auction, Lauzun's Legion left for home.[38]

Ten years later, on December 31, 1793, Lauzun was guillotined. Although he had supported the French Revolution, he was accused as a nobleman sympathetic to the royalists. The story is told that his executioner interrupted Lauzun's last meal. "You don't mind if I finish my oysters?" asked Lauzun, politely offering the executioner a glass of wine. "Your business must make you thirsty." The executioner obliged and, it is said, the two men spent a pleasant half-hour together before getting on with the day's work.[39]

Special thanks to Washington-Rochambeau Revolutionary Route's Bob Selig for his many years of good and careful studies of Lauzun and the French troops of the American Revolution.

37. Manuscript folder 4, Schools, Wilmington Academy. Delaware Historical Society, Wilmington, DE.
38. Robert Selig and Daniel Griffith, *Washington-Rochambeau Revolutionary Route in the State 1781–1783* (Delaware Society Sons of the American Revolution and State of Delaware, 2003), 123–139.
39. Whitridge, *Rochambeau: America's Neglected Founding Father*, 303.

Did the First Cedar Springs Skirmish Really Happen?

❦ CONNER RUNYAN ❦

Select any narrative from the dozens of sources that tell the story of what happened on July 12, 1780, at Cedar Springs, South Carolina, and basically here is what you get:

Sometime during the night of July 12 a group of Tory militia, said to be one hundred and fifty strong, less than half a battalion, thought to be part of the command of British Maj. Patrick Ferguson, attempted a surprise attack on the Cedar Springs muster and refugee camp of the Patriot First Spartan Regiment. The Spartans, mostly members of the same Fair Forest Presbyterian Congregation,[1] had been forewarned and taken steps to protect themselves by hiding in the trees growing on a knoll behind their camp. The result was a turn-of-the-table, with those expecting to surprise being surprised, hit with a hard volley from the sixty-man Spartan Regiment. There was only one known casualty, Loyalist John White.[2] Whether White was wounded, killed outright or died

1. George Howe, *History of the Presbyterian Church of South Carolina* (Columbia, SC: Duffie & Chapman, 1870), 1:533. Howe writes, *"There was not a Tory among them."*
2. William T Graves, "McJunkin Narrative: Draper MSS, Sumter Papers 23VV153–203," *Southern Campaigns of the American Revolution* Vol 2 No 11.1 (November 2005), 40. www.southerncampaign.org/newsletter/v2n11.pdf. Learning more about John White is the key to unraveling the mysteries surrounding Cedar Springs. If indeed the skirmish did occur as currently written, he is the only known Loyalist participant and casualty, shot in the "hinder parts." He lived in the Spartan District, part of the extensive White family; was called by Patriot Major Mcjunkin "my tory" because he lived in McJunkin's militia recruitment area; was at first "non-resistant" (meaning he was a Quaker) until the British moved into Ninety Six District. But most important is that he lived near Loyalist commanders Daniel Plummer and Zacharius Gibbs. This suggests he may have been part of the Loyalist Spartan Regiment. Whatever John White did, he was never forgiven for joining the British after the fall of Charleston. John White appears on the Commander's Enemies Lists of 1783, along with such bright lights as Alexander Chesney, Adam Stedham, Thomas Fletchall, William Cunningham and John Cunningham. Who was this John White?

later remains unclear. The engagement was quick and decisive, basically over after this first volley. Neither side seemed willing to continue the fight. The Tories, with the exception of about thirty-five men who continued on to Gowen's Old Fort, disappear from the storyline. The Patriots, apparently shaken by their close call with annihilation, broke camp and moved to join Thomas Sumter.[3]

This is the die-cast narrative of First Cedar Springs. Over the next two hundred years, with minor changes here and there, it was mass produced and became entrenched as one of a dozen skirmishes and battles that took place in the summer of 1780, in the backcountry of South Carolina in and about Spartanburg. The significance of the skirmish is said to be that it was the first link in a chain of events leading to three more night time engagements—Gowen's Old Fort, Earle's Ford, and the running fight down Blackstock Road ending at Prince's Fort. All are part of the events that led to King's Mountain. Without First Cedar Springs, goes the thinking today, these links cannot be easily forged.

Today First Cedar Springs is acknowledged as a poorly documented[4] skirmish, but enough is thought to be known to include it in a driving tour of important sites as part of the Revolutionary War Trail in the Spartanburg area.[5] The skirmish is also part of the legend of a most amazing woman of the Revolution, Jane Thomas. She is thought to have made a famous sixty mile ride from the British outpost at Ninety Six to warn the men of the Spartan Regiment who were encamped at the once beautiful springs sheltered by a magnificent old Cedar.

But there is a bit of a problem: The skirmish of First Cedar Springs may never have occurred, at least not on July 12, 1780.

The skirmish must constantly be noted with care as First Cedar Springs to distinguish it from its bigger brother, Second Cedar Springs, a battle that occurred nearby in August of the same year; Second Cedar Springs is also called the Battle of Wofford's Iron Work.[6] The evidence

3. Patrick O'Kelley, *Nothing But Blood and Slaughter* (Blue House Tavern Press, 2004), 2:197; John Parker, *Parker's Guide to the Revolutionary War in South Carolina* (West Conshohocken, Pa: Infinity Publishing, 2013), 404; John Buchanan, *The Road to Guilford Courthouse,* (New York, New York: John Wiley & Sons, 1997), 112. These are but a few of the modern, and better, narratives basically telling the same story.
4. Brian Robson, Project Administrator, Battlefield Preservation Plan For Revolutionary War Battlefields in Upstate South Carolina, *"Battle of 1st Cedar Springs"* (South Carolina State Park Service: Hill Studio, 2009), 65.
5. Katherine Cann, *The American Revolution in the Spartan District* (Spartanburg, SC: Hub City Press, 2014), 140.
6. J.D. Lewis, "Wofford's Iron Works, The American Revolution in South Carolina," www.carolana.com, accessed October 16, 2016; Mary McKinney Teaster, "The Revolutionary Battle of Wofford's Iron Works," glendalesc.com/battleironworks.html, accessed October 16, 2016.

suggesting that something did happen at Cedar Springs on July 12 sits heavy on a three-legged stool. Each leg has its own set of mysteries, and does its share to add to the muddle.[7] Break one leg of this stool and all topples over.

The first mention—or stool leg—describing what might have been the skirmish appeared in 1816, in Hugh McCall's *History of Georgia*. McCall, son of patriot James McCall, wrote a narrative that is frustrating and open to more than one interpretation.[8] It is his account that causes much of the puzzle about the exact date of First Cedar Springs. McCall tells us that Col. John Jones, of Burke County, Georgia, leading his new command of thirty-five Georgia refugees, continued on to North Carolina after most of Col. Elijah Clarke's men turned back following a fording of the Savannah River. Jones asked to be guided to the loyalist camp at Gowen's Old Fort. It is well established that on the night of July 14, 1780, Colonel Jones captured the fort.[9] This date of July 14 is the register mark that gave Lyman Draper, author of *King's Mountain and Its Heroes* and the first to give a precise date for First Cedar Springs, a way to determine that the skirmish took place on July 12. Draper's work will be discussed in more detail below; of all the evidence he found for concluding when the skirmish of First Cedar Springs took place, the strongest is in this statement:

> As they passed through the disaffected country, they pretended to be a company of loyalists, engaged in the king's service; and in many instances were furnished with pilots, under that impression. When they had passed the head waters of Saluda River, one of these guides informed them, that 'a party of rebels had attacked some loyalists the preceding night, a short distance in front, and defeated them.' Jones expressed a wish to be conducted to the place, that he might join the loyalists, and have it in his power to take revenge for the blood of the king's subjects which had been selected to pursue the Americans who had retreated to the north. About eleven o'clock on the night of the 14th of July, Jones was conducted to the royal party, where about forty were collected.[10]

7. Warren Ripley, *Battleground: South Carolina in the Revolution* (Charleston, SC: The News & Courier and The Evening Post, 1983), 75.
8. Hugh McCall. *The History of Georgia, Containing Brief Sketches of the Most Remarkable Events Up to the Present Day* (Atlanta, GA: A.B. Caldwell, 1909), 2:473, https://archive.org/details/historygeorgia/ accessed March 14 2016.
9. Balfour to Cornwallis, July 17, 1780, in Ian Saberton, ed., *Cornwallis Papers* (East Sussex, England: Naval & Military Press, 2010), 1:251.
10. McCall, *History of Georgia,* 473.

Is the description above conclusive evidence that the rebel attack Jones learned about was the one at Cedar Springs? McCall could just as well be writing of Huck's Defeat, which also took place on July 12, 1780. It all depends upon where Jones was in the area McCall calls the "head water of Saluda." Cedar Springs and Brattonsville, site of Huck's Defeat, can both be considered "in front" and are separated by about forty-seven miles. News of Huck's Defeat could have reached the upper Greenville area, and Jones, within a day.[11] Interpreting the above account as a precise date for the skirmish at Cedar Springs depends on where Jones was on July 13, and what exactly is meant by "a short distance in front." How far could a good express rider, on a fast horse, with skill and luck, travel in one day? Bear in mind (with a bit of tongue in cheek) that Jane Thomas is widely believed to have made a similar ride, of sixty miles, just one day earlier.[12]

Is this leg of the stool solid or does it have a crack in it?

The second leg of our stool comes from Rev. James Hodge Saye, who recorded the recollections of his elderly grandfather-in-law. His writings were published in a number of ways, one of which is the 1837 *The Memoirs of Major Joseph McJunkin*. McJunkin was the son-in-law of Jane Thomas; consequently this narrative of First Cedar Springs also came to be called the Thomas family account.[13] It is the first three words of what Saye wrote about Jane Thomas and First Cedar Springs that are open to interpretation: "About this time. . . ."[14] Saye uses this phrase to refer to the period between the Battle of Musgrove's Mill, on August 19, 1780, and the events in September leading to the Battle of King's Mountain.

McJunkin was elderly when Saye spoke with him, and his recollections could have been faulty, something Saye talked about. But if placing the skirmish in August, and not July, was a mistake, Saye made it a second time. Saye ended his writing of the recollections of Major McJunkin by trying to clear up some misunderstanding over what took place at the Springs, noting there were "three conflicts at or near"[15] there. Saye says he knew this not only because of what the old major had told him,

11. Saberton, *Cornwallis Papers*, 200.

12. Elizabeth F. Ellet, *The Women of the American Revolution* (New York: Baker and Scribner, 1849), 253–258.

13. James Hodge Saye, "Memoirs of Major Joseph McJunkin. The Various Cedar Springs Fights," accessed March 7, 2016, sc_tories.tripod.com/battle_of_cedar_springs.htm.

14. Graves, "McJunkin Narrative: Draper MSS, Sumter Papers 23VV153–203", 40.

15. James Hodge Saye, "Memoirs of Major Joseph McJunkin. The Various Cedar Springs Fights," accessed April 26, 2016, sc_tories.tripod.com/battle_of_cedar_springs.htm.

but also from what had been written by others, or learned by Saye, in an effort to resolve what Saye saw as flaws in McJunkin's recollections. The result was that Saye relied on three additional sources: Robert Mills' 1826 *Statistics of South Carolina including a view of Its Natural, Civil, and Military History*;[16] something written by "a writer in the Magnolia for 1842,"[17] referring to J.B. O'Neall, who wrote his own version of McJunkin's life using materials given to him by Saye; and what Saye calls "local traditions"[18] These "local traditions" came from visits and correspondence Saye made with surviving Revolutionary War veterans. What these old vets told him led Saye to write one of his oddly phrased conclusions: "I have no reason to doubt that statements from local traditions in regard to these engagements are extremely liable to error and confusion."[19]

Ultimately, Saye's attempt to clarify only confounds things even more. Careful examination of these "three conflicts" leaves little doubt that two of the three "various" fights are really one and the same: Second Cedar Springs, or Wofford's Iron Works. Based solely on Saye's sources, there were not, as he stated, three conflicts, but two. Mills, in his 1826 *Statistics*, did not seem to know about First Cedar Springs. The action he described as "at the Green springs, near Berwick's iron works" [20] is an account of Second Cedar Springs. Finally, with respect to Saye's "local traditions," it is noteworthy that in the 21,151 Revolutionary War pension applications and Bounty Land Claims now online,[21] not one can clearly be identified as mentioning First Cedar Springs. Careful reading of those that talk about Cedar Springs leads to the conclusion that they describe events known to have taken place at Second Cedar Springs. If any veterans who talked or corresponded with Saye mentioned a skirmish at Cedar Springs on July 12, none said anything that can definitively be associated with it in a pension application.[22]

---

16. Robert Mills, *Statistics of South Carolina including a view of Its Natural, Civil, and Military History* (Charleston, SC: Hurlbut and Lloyd, 1826).

17. Saye, "Memoirs of Major Joseph McJunkin. The Various Cedar Springs Fights."

18. Ibid.

19. Ibid.

20. Mills, Statistics of South Carolina", 738. *"Green Springs" is an older name for Cedar Springs.*

21. William T Graves and C. Leon Harris, *Southern Campaigns Revolutionary War Pension Statements & Rosters,* revwarapps.org.

22. Graves and Harris, *Southern Campaigns Revolutionary War Pension Statements.* Use freeform search for "Cedar Springs" to duplicate the following observation: Seventeen pension applications mention "Cedar Springs." Each contain clues that suggest the veteran was speaking of Second Cedar Springs.

What is clear in Saye's attempt to clarify the muddle is his placement of First Cedar Springs in time. In another of his oddly phrased conclusions, he wrote, "The first is contained in the account given by the Thomas family. This is stated upon the authority of Major McJunkin, and was probably the last in the order of time."[23] Regardless of how many Cedar Springs fights took place, Saye is telling us First Cedar Springs was the last one, taking place after Second Cedar Springs.

The last leg of the stool is Lyman Draper, who in *King's Mountain and Its Heroes* apparently pays close attention to what Saye wrote and, as previously noted, was the first to give us the specific date of July 12, 1780.[24] In a rather perplexing way, Draper relies only on three sources to back up his statement that the skirmish "was on the twelfth day of July."[25] These sources are McCall's *Georgia,* already discussed above, Frank Moore's *Diary of the American Revolution,* and two diary entries from British Lt. Anthony Allaire, an officer in the Loyal American Regiment.

Moore's *Diary* refers to an action "at Packolet [*sic*] in the night of the 15th of July, where Colonel McDowell commanded."[26] This is Earle's Ford, not Cedar Springs. Taken alone, there is no evidence in Moore's *Diary* of a skirmish at Cedar Springs on the night of July 12.

Allaire's diary entries for the week of July 10 through July 15 leave little doubt that he was commenting on why groups of loyalist militia were moving about in the Fair Forest area, but Draper makes things ambiguous by citing only the entries for July 14 and 15.[27] entries for the week of July 10 through July 15 are ambiguous. The Loyalists from the Spartansburg area had been ordered to muster at Wofford's Old Field on July 12, resulting in groups of men, both Loyalist and Patriot, being on the move in the same small area.[28] Two days later on July 14, while this Loyalist muster continues, Allaire wrote, "Every hour news from

23. Saye, "Memoirs of Major Joseph McJunkin," *The Various Cedar Springs Fights;* Ilene Jones Cornwell, "The Various Cedar Springs Fights," Southern Campaigns of the American Revolution (SCAR), accessed March 7, 2016 Vol.2. No. 5, 1.

24. Lyman Copeland Draper, *King's Mountain and its heroes: history of the Battle of King's Mountain, October 7th, 1780, and the events which led to it* (Kessinger Legacy Reprints, undated: originally published; Cincinnati: Thomson, 1881), 73.

25. Draper, *King's Mountain,* 73n.

26. Frank Moore, *Diary of the American Revolution,* Volume II (New York, NY: Charles Scribner, 1858), 351.

27. Draper, *King's Mountain,* 500.

28. Saberton, *Cornwallis Papers,* Vol. I, 248, 289–91. One of the interesting threads woven in the Cedar Springs fabric is the relationship between Loyalist Militia Maj. Patrick Ferguson, British Col. Nesbit Balfour and Lord Cornwallis. At this point in time, Ferguson

different parts of the country of Rebel parties doing mischief."[29] This "doing mischief" is what Draper concluded was the planned British surgical strike, involving 150 loyalist militia, at First Cedar Springs. Then, in a connection difficult to make, Draper strengthened his contention that First Cedar Springs took place on July 12 because of what Allaire wrote in his diary for July 15: "Capt. [James] Dunlap had been obliged to retreat from Prince's Fort."[30]

It is possible Allaire was not referring to First Cedar Springs at all, but more likely was referring to stories told by men coming to join this Loyalist muster ordered by Balfour, four miles from Cedar Springs at

was in hot water with Cornwallis, who was fretting that Ferguson would do something rash and bring about another British debacle such as had occurred in North Carolina at Ramseur's Mill. Balfour hated Ferguson and continually undermined him. Thus, Balfour left to Ferguson to justify to Cornwallis why the lack of organization among the militia was becoming so costly. Furthermore, Balfour and Cornwallis were communicating rather nervously with one another about how best to avoid a premature conflict between roaming bands of loyalists and groups of patriots who had taken refuge in hidden camps. On July 11, Lord Cornwallis had received a letter from a rather nervous Maj. Patrick Ferguson, anxious to offer an explanation as to why the war effort in the backcountry was becoming so expensive: "I am sorry to intrude upon your time so frequently . . . At present it is evident here than many of the sufferers are casting about naturally enough to make up their losses [meaning the loyalists previously subjected to Patriot abuse until the fall of Charleston] . . . seduced into more sordid pursuits from a facility of preying upon the public." Ferguson was concerned that unless the loyalist militia were better organized, the necessary good will of backcountry settlers would be lost resulting in little chance of ". . . ever acquiring any discipline or knowledge of service." Ferguson, who was expected to bring about order in the loyalist backcountry militia, also suggested that plundering by the now-emboldened loyalists would result in the loss of the means by which Cornwallis hoped to self-finance the struggle: "slaves, horses and other property captured by the [Loyalist] militia here, with some valuable crops left by the rebels who have fled," a possible reference to the now forming Patriot refugee camps, one of which is at Cedar Springs. Balfour's solution was to order a muster Loyalist Maj. Daniel Plummer's and Maj. Zacharis Gibbs's regiment of Spartan Loyalists at Wofford's Old Field on the night of July 12. This, went the thinking of Balfour and Cornwallis, would keep everyone boxed up until the British were ready to make their move. This British strategy is at odds to the accepted historical narrative that the engagement at First Cedar Springs was an ambush, planned sixty miles away at Ninety Six, and made by 150 Loyalist militia, who managed to march those sixty miles undetected, just to surprise the Patriot Spartan Regiment at Cedar Springs. All this, if it happened, could have resulted in another Ramseur's Mill and the unraveling of British strategy in the backcountry.

29. Anthony Allaire, *Diary of Lieut. Anthony Allaire, of Ferguson's Corps, Memorandum of Occurrences During the Campaign of 1780, Month of July, 1780*, entry for July 14, 1780. www.tngenweb.org/revwar/kingsmountain/allaire1.html, accessed April 27, 2016.
30. Allaire, *Diary*, entry for July 15, 1780.

Wofford's Old Field. As each group arrived, Lieut. Allaire would have heard stories of various kinds of "rebel mischief." Had a planned ambush involving half a battalion of loyalist militia taken place during this week, in the Fair Forest area where Allaire was camped, it would have been noted in his diary. No such mention is made. It is unlikely Allaire was referring to a planned surprise attack on Thomas' regiment at First Cedar Springs.

In light of this evidence, was there a skirmish at Cedar Springs on July 12, 1780?

If the answer is "yes," based on belief in the accuracy of Draper's date, then something of a new significance for the encounter may emerge. It is quite likely it was a conflict between two Fair Forest Spartan Regiments—one Patriot and the other Loyalist. Perhaps, on the night of July 12, men journeying to join Loyalist Maj. Zacharis Gibbes's muster at nearby Wofford's Old Field stumbled across a similar Patriot muster of Col. John Thomas, Jr at Cedar Springs.

If the answer is "no," and nothing actually occurred on this date, then much work remains. Is the Second Battle of Cedar Springs really the First Battle of Cedar Springs? If so, we are left to explore with different eyes the events of July and August 1780, following the fall of Charlestown. If there had been no First Cedar Spring, would there still have been a skirmish at Gowen's Old Fort? Without Gowen's Old Fort, would Loyalist James Dunlap have rushed so recklessly to Earle's Ford? Without Earle's Ford, would the British have backed away from Prince's Fort? How we answer these questions shape our view of events leading to King's Mountain.

Clearing up this muddle that is Cedar Springs starts with "when." Can we say with conviction a skirmish took place on the night of July 12, 1780?

His Majesty's Indian Allies: Ten Notables

❀ JOSHUA SHEPHERD ❀

In many respects it was a sobering testament to Britain's mounting resolve to suppress the Revolution at all costs. "It is his Majesty's resolution," explained Lord George Germain, "that the most vigorous Effort
should be made, and every means employed that Providence has put
into His Majesty's Hands, for crushing the Rebellion." The vigorous effort to which Germain referred was the employment of Indian auxiliaries, a grim war measure adopted for the purpose of "exciting an
alarm" upon the American frontier."[1]

From the outset of the war both British and American authorities
recognized the inestimable value of forging alliances with the Indians,
or, at the very least, securing guarantees of neutrality. A number of native communities were rent by such decisions, but ultimately the majority of the tribes sided with Great Britain. Such Indian nations were
not signatories to formal alliances in the European sense, but, in elabo-
rate ceremonies often attended by British representatives, would both
figuratively and literally "take up the hatchet" on behalf of the British.
The Delaware chief Pipe later explained the ritual; the British, he said,
"put a war hatchet into my hands, saying: Take this weapon and try it
on the heads of my enemies . . . and let me afterwards know if it was
sharp and good."[2]

The tribes, whose very survival depended on the skills of a robust
warrior class, would prove to be formidable opponents. Although the

---

1. M. Shoemaker, et al, eds., *Report of the Pioneer Society of the State of Michigan* (Lansing:
Wynkoop Hallenbeck Crawford Co., 1908), 9:347. Letter, Lord George Germain to
Henry Hamilton, March 26, 1777.
2. John Heckewelder, *History, Manners, and Customs of the Indian Nations Who Once In-
habited Pennsylvania and the Neighboring States* (Philadelphia: Publication Fund of the
Historical Society of Pennsylvania, 1876), 134.

disparate Indian nations, even with British coordination, could never entirely settle intertribal rivalries and present unified opposition to the Americans, their undeniable skills at carrying out desultory guerilla actions essentially opened a devastating second front to the war. Such raids were frustratingly difficult to counter; George Washington observed that defending an extensive backcountry was "next to impossible."[3] Despite the European traditions of warfare which were generally observed by British and American troops on the eastern seaboard, the conflict on the frontier was an exceedingly brutal war of reprisal that more often than not targeted civilian populations. While serving as Virginia's governor, Thomas Jefferson nonetheless acknowledged that the backcountry fighting was an integral part of the overall war effort. "We are all embarked in one bottom," he wrote, "the Western end of which cannot swim while the Eastern sinks. I am thoroughly satisfied that nothing can keep us up but the keeping off the Indians from our Western quarter; that this cannot be done, but by pushing the war into their Country"[4]

Such an approach proved to be the only workable strategic solution. In punitive expeditions that struck native strongholds from the lake country of western New York to the mountains of North Carolina, American armies leveled Indian villages and destroyed the crops which were vital in sustaining the tribal war effort. For the nascent United States, the crippling distraction of a frontier war was sure to elicit a stern desire for national retribution. Treaty commissioners at Fort Stanwix in 1784 bluntly expressed to Iroquois chiefs the new realities of American ascendency. "You are a subdued people; you have been overcome in a war which you entered into with us, not only without provocation, but in violation of most sacred obligation. The great spirit who is at the same time the judge and avenger of perfidy, has given us victory over all our enemies."[5]

Such a stance was woefully optimistic. The Treaty of Paris, which officially put a halt to the war in 1783, had far less impact on the frontier. Although Britain would publicly maintain the peace, her tribal allies would continue to bedevil the United States with an excruciatingly costly war until 1795.

---

3. George Washington to George Clinton, September 25, 1778," Founders Online, National Archives (http://founders.archives.gov/documents/Washington/03–17–02–0118.
4. Julian P. Boyd, ed., *The Papers of Thomas Jefferson* (Princeton: Princeton University Press, 1951), 4:628. Letter, Thomas Jefferson to County Lieutenants of Berkeley and Frederick, February 16, 1781.
5. Neville B. Craig, ed., *The Olden Time: A Monthly Publication Devoted to the Preservation of Documents* (Pittsburgh: Wright & Charlton, 1848), 2:424.

JOSEPH BRANT

He was born in obscurity in the backwaters of the western frontier, but by the close of the Revolution was regarded as the most legendary Indian ally of Great Britain. His exploits as a raider elicited outrage from the highest levels. "It is in the highest degree distressing," wrote George Washington, "to have our Frontier so continually harrassed by this collection of Banditti under Brant."[6]

Possessing an extraordinarily powerful intellect and irrepressible determination, Brant was destined to distinguish himself. Born a Mohawk and christened an Anglican, Brant received formal education from the Reverend Eleazar Wheelock, the founder of Dartmouth College. He was not a hereditary chief, but rose to prominence in the Iroquois Confederacy due to his inherent ability to lead.

British patronage was likewise a factor. A favorite of Sir William Johnson, the superintendent of the Northern Indian Department, Brant enjoyed a good measure of preferment despite his relative lack of experience. During a grand tour of England beginning in 1775, he was granted an audience with King George III and reciprocated with unwavering loyalty. Brant, contrary to common misconception, was not exactly a commissioned officer in the British army (that title was bestowed through the Indian Department),[7] but nevertheless became Britain's most crucial native ally on the northern frontier.

He exceeded the expectations placed on him. At the head of a mixed bag of volunteers composed of both Indians and Loyalists, Brant struck terror into the Patriot settlements of New York and Pennsylvania. His leadership was critical at many of the larger actions in the theater, including Fort Stanwix and Oriskany. Brant likewise led a contingent during the assault on Cherry Valley during which undisciplined Seneca warriors—not under Brant's authority—perpetrated one of the most infamous massacres of the Revolution.

6. Washington to Brig. Gen. Edward Hand, November 16, 1778, Founders Online, National Archives (http://founders.archives.gov/documents/Washington/03–18–02–0167 . Washington made reference to the activities of both Joseph Brant and "Butler", presumably John Butler.

7. In April 1779 Brant was granted the somewhat hollow honorific of "Colonel of the Indians." Ernest Cruikshank, "Joseph Brant in the American Revolution," *Transactions of the Canadian Institute* (Toronto: Copp, Clark Company, 1895), 4–5:260. The following year Brant was commissioned through the Indian Department as captain of the "Northern Confederate Indians." Brant used the title but, militarily speaking, placed little stock in it, later explaining that "During the war, although I bore the commission of a captain, I never received commands as such, but acted as War Chief, which I believe was of more utility than if I had been in the other capacity." William L. Stone, *Life of Joseph Brant—Thayendanegea* (Cooperstown, New York: H. & E. Phinney, 1844), 2:408. Letter, Joseph Brant to Sir John Johnson, November, 1801.

Brant was without question the most feared of the King's Indian allies, and arguably one of the most skilled partisan commanders of the Revolutionary War. Daniel Claus, a deputy superintendent in the Indian Department, offered one of the more accurate assessments of his legacy. "In short," wrote Claus, "Mr. Brant was the dread and terror of the whole country."[8]

DRAGGING CANOE

No other name could strike such fear in the isolated settlements of America's southern backcountry, and for good reason. The Cherokee chief Dragging Canoe initially rose to prominence for opposing the accommodationist policies of tribal elders—including his own father—at the 1775 Treaty of Sycamore Shoals. Appalled that the older chiefs were willing to sell a vast tract between the Kentucky and Cumberland Rivers, a furious Dragging Canoe ominously warned Transylvania Company agents that "it was the bloody Ground, and would be dark, and difficult to settle."[9]

He made good on such threats. Despite the protests of British agents who counseled coordination with Crown forces, Dragging Canoe and the militants, who effectively seized control of tribal leadership, helped instigate a full scale war in 1776. The unacceptable depletion of Cherokee lands, Dragging Canoe asserted, was due to the bargaining of weak men that "were too old to hunt . . . but that for his part he had a great many young fellows that would support him and were determined to have their Land."[10]

Cherokee war parties struck hard at the overmountain settlements of the upper Tennessee watershed, but stirred up a hornet's nest in the process. On July 20, Dragging Canoe's party was worsted in a furious fight at Long Island of the Holston, and the chief himself was badly wounded. Punitive expeditions mounted by Virginia and the Carolinas laid waste to Cherokee country, and when tribal moderates sued for peace, Dragging Canoe led the dissidents farther west. The breakaway militants, known as the Chickamauga, incessantly attacked frontier settlements across the southeast for the rest of the war, and remained implacable opponents of American expansion into the 1790s.

8. Cruikshank, *Transactions,* 257.
9. William B. Palmer, ed., *Calendar of Virginia State Papers, and Other Manuscripts, 1652–1781* (Richmond: R.F. Walker, 1875), 1: 283. Deposition of Samuel Wilson, April 15, 1777.
10. William L. Saunders, ed., *The Colonial Records of North Carolina* (Raleigh: Josepaus Daniels, 1890), 10:764. Letter, Henry Stuart to John Stuart, August 25, 1776.

BLACKFISH

He was the bane of the Kentucky settlements. A respected war leader of the Shawnee Chillicothe band, Blackfish proved the Kentuckian's chief antagonist at the outset of the war. All through the summer of 1777 Shawnee war parties harried the settlements, but were unable to dislodge the Americans from the crude stockades in which they sought protection. That winter, Blackfish scored one of the greatest coups of the western war, capturing a party of nearly thirty Kentuckians, including the legendary frontiersman Daniel Boone.

The following September Blackfish was at it again, attempting to negotiate the surrender of Boonesborough. At a council with nine of the settlement's leading men, the chief, according to the Kentuckians, hatched an unsuccessful ruse. "Getting up," reported John Bowman, "Blackfish made a long Speech, then gave the word go."[11] Indian warriors abruptly seized the Kentuckians; in a furious tussle during which the chief was thrown to the ground, the white men miraculously escaped to the stockade, ushering in the legendary Siege of Boonesborough, which ended in failure for the Shawnee.

In the spring of 1779, an army of Kentucky militia entered the Miami Valley and attacked Blackfish's village of Chillicothe. In the ensuing battle, he received a ghastly gunshot wound that shattered his leg. Dragged to safety, the chief grimly encouraged his warriors "not to leave him but to stand their ground and all die together."[12] Blackfish lingered in considerable pain for at least a month and a half before succumbing to his wounds.

CORNPLANTER

To the people of the Six Nations he was regarded as "a chief of considerable eminence."[13] A Seneca war chief of lengthy experience, Cornplanter nonetheless urged caution when war broke out between Great Britain and the colonies, advising an Iroquois council to steer clear of a fight they had no part in. Initially advocating neutrality, Cornplanter thought it best "not to lift our hands against . . . Either Party, because they got in to Difficulty, it is nothing to us." Meddling in the Revolution,

11. James Alton James, ed., *George Rogers Clark Papers, 1771–1781* (Springfield: Illinois State Historical Library, 1912), Letter, John Bowman to George Rogers Clark, October 14, 1778.
12. "Bowman's Expedition Against Chillicothe, May-June 1779," *Ohio Archaeological and Historical Publications 19* (1910), 454–455. Account of Shawnee prisoner Joseph Jackson.
13. James E. Seaver, *A Narrative of the Life of Mrs. Mary Jemison, who was Taken by the Indians, in the Year 1755* (Canandaigua, New York: J.D. Bemis and Co., 1824), 77.

he concluded, could be costly to the Iroquois: "war is war Death is . . . Death a fight is a hard Business."[14]

Despite such reticence, Cornplanter proved to be a relentless enemy of the Americans once Iroquois involvement became all but inevitable. Regarded as one of two leading Seneca war chiefs, he commanded warriors in nearly every major clash on the New York and Pennsylvania frontier, including the battles at Oriskany and Wyoming. The raid which he helped lead against Cherry Valley in the autumn of 1778 resulted in one of the most notorious killing sprees of the Revolution.

Although present for the disastrous Iroquois defeat at Newtown, a tenacious Cornplanter continued leading raids against rebel settlements. Subsequent to the end of the war, the chief labored to lead his people through a landscape forever altered by American victory. "The great revolution amongst the White people," he wrote to George Washington, "has extended its influence to the people of my Colour: turn our faces which way we will, we find the white people cultivating the ground which our forefathers hunted over."[15]

EMISTISIGUO

For this powerful chief of the Upper Creeks, fighting was a way of life. David Truitt, the Creek agent from Britain's Southern Indian Department, made repeated diary references to Emistisiguo either preparing for war, being away at war, or having just returned from war. His preferred target was the Choctaw, a traditional tribal enemy, but when war came to the southern backcountry he just as readily turned his attention to the American rebels.

In fact, Emistisiguo had labored for years to harmonize relations with the English colonists, and British officials could consistently rely on the Creek headman to help keep the peace. His favored treatment nonetheless seems to have aggravated tribal rivalries, and the notably independent Creek bands would never throw their full weight behind the British. "The Nation is divided one part against another," Truitt reported in 1772, "in regard of the respect that has been showed to Emistisiguo."[16] At the outbreak of the war, there was no question where the chief's

14. Thomas S. Abler, ed., *Chainbreaker: The Revolutionary War Memoirs of Governor Blacksnake as told to Benjamin Williams* (Lincoln: University of Nebraska Press, 1989), 75.
15. Cornplanter to Washington, February 28, 1797, Founders Online, National Archives (http://founders.archives.gov/documents/washington/99-01-02-00367 .
16. Newton D. Mereness, ed., *Travels in the American Colonies* (New York: Macmillan, 1916), 524.

loyalties lay, and he headed war parties that struck the southern frontier from Georgia and the Carolinas into modern Tennessee; Emistisiguo likewise worked in concert with the Cherokee as well as Lt. Col. Thomas Brown's Loyalist rangers.

In June of 1782 Emistisiguo led a contingent of Creeks in an attempted link-up with British forces and, after a remarkable 500 mile journey through Patriot territory, assaulted an American camp outside of Savannah. In a confused night action in the early morning hours of June 24, the Indians gave a good accounting of themselves until they were driven off by an American counterattack. Among the dead was Emistisiguo. Brig. Gen. Anthony Wayne paid the slain chieftain a simple but fitting compliment; he was, wrote Wayne, "our greatest enemy, and principal warrior of the Creek nation."[17]

SAYENQUERAGHTA

War is perpetually a young man's undertaking, a stubborn fact which nonetheless failed to discourage the silver haired old warrior of the Seneca. Likely in his early seventies during much of the war, Sayenqueraghta, better known as Old Smoke, would act as one of the two primary war chiefs of the Six Nations.

Possessing an impressive record as a fighter that stretched back for decades, Old Smoke's support was pivotal for the British in securing an alliance with the bulk of the Iroquois Confederacy. Quebec's Governor Frederick Haldimand considered him the "King of the Senecas, and by many degrees, the most leading, and the man of the most influence in the whole of the Six Nations." Haldimand likewise warned that any overt preference of Joseph Brant could antagonize more influential war chiefs such as Old Smoke and be "productive of very dangerous consequences."[18]

Once Old Smoke openly avowed a British alliance, he proved remarkably active for his age. Often paired with his younger counterpart Cornplanter, the elder war chief led contingents of Seneca warriors in most of the major actions on the northern frontier, and was the primary Indian architect of the crushing American defeat at Wyoming in July 1778. The old warrior fought through the end of the war and died in 1786; he was, in the words of Haldimand, "brave, prudent, and perfectly attached to Government."[19]

17. H.N. Moore, *Life and Services of Gen. Anthony Wayne* (Philadelphia: John B. Perry, 1845), 157. Letter, Anthony Wayne to Nathanael Greene, June 24, 1782.
18. Horace Edwin Hayden, *The Massacre of Wyoming: The Acts of Congress for the Defense of the Wyoming Valley, Pennsylvania* (Wilkes-Barre: Wyoming Historical and Geological Society, 1895), xxii.
19. Hayden, *The Massacre of Wyoming*, xxii.

EGUSHAWA

The Ottawa chief is nearly forgotten today, but in his lifetime wielded tremendous influence over the remote tribes of modern Michigan: the Ottawa and Chippewa. British authorities had good reason to court their assistance; even the Ohio tribes regarded the warriors of their Michigan neighbors as "the wildest people."[20]

Egushawa was an unrivaled power broker among the fierce "Lake Indians." Moravian missionary David Zeisberger, who enjoyed the chief's protection, asserted that Egushawa functioned as something of a "head-chief of the Chippewa, and can call them together as often as he finds it needful, for all first comes to him, and he communicates it to the others."[21] In such a capacity, Egushawa was a key diplomatic liaison in promoting British interests in the Northwest. He was likewise an active and respected warrior, and consistently led Ottawa contingents in some of the frontier's most legendary campaigns, including the Mohawk Valley in 1777, Vincennes in 1778, and Kentucky in 1780.

Detroit's Lt. Gov. Henry Hamilton regarded Egushawa as a contemplative and determined commander, but found him most effective when espousing the cause of a British alliance. At an intertribal council in 1779 the chieftain extolled "His Majesty, the great Chief at Quebec, all His Majesty's Officers and Soldiers" as crucial allies in the preservation of tribal homelands. "We see our father was foremost," explained Egushawa, "to rise up, and come thus far to frustrate the designs of the Virginians."[22]

PIPE

No other native leader of the Revolutionary era better exemplifies the bitter fruit of a tragically squandered diplomatic opportunity. At the outset of the war the Delaware chief better known as "Captain Pipe" was a staunch advocate of neutrality, at one point scolding British agents as little more than servants who "had no power to hand the tomahawk to them; Nobody could force him neither to take it."[23]

Pipe was pushed further toward a British alliance due to the rash actions of ill-disciplined American militia. In February of 1778 an Ameri-

20. Eugene F. Bliss, ed., *Diary of David Zeisberger* (Cincinnati: Robert Clarke & Co., 1885), 1:438.

21. Bliss, *Diary of David Zeisberger*, 438.

22. John D. Barnhart, ed., *Henry Hamilton and George Rogers Clark in the American Revolution with the Unpublished Journal of Lieut. Gov. Henry Hamilton* (Crawfordsville, Indiana: R.E. Banta, 1951), 168.

23. Reuben Gold Thwaites and Louise Phelps Kellogg, eds., *Frontier Defense on the Upper Ohio, 1777–1778* (Madison: Wisconsin Historical Society, 1912), 165. Letter, David Zeisberger to Edward Hand, November 16, 1777.

can expedition out of Fort Pitt stumbled on two hunting camps of peaceful Delawares and killed a handful of noncombatants. Among the dead were members of Pipe's family. Despite the killings, Pipe assured American authorities that he intended to maintain "the friendship subsisting Between us."[24]

Ultimately the bitter realities of the war forced him to take sides, and he proved a scourge to the American backcountry. A seasoned frontier raider, Pipe likewise helped orchestrate the defeat of Colonel William Crawford's expedition in 1782, and the chief subsequently presided over Crawford's notoriously macabre death by fire.

But even after casting his lot with the British, Pipe remained embittered that he had been forced to take sides. "Father," he once addressed the commandant of Detroit, "You may, perhaps, think me a fool, for risking my life at your bidding, in a cause, too, by which I have no prospect of gaining anything; for it is your cause and not mine. It is your concern to fight the long knives;[25] you have raised a quarrel amongst yourselves, and you ought yourselves to fight it out."[26]

PLUGGY

In the opening years of the Revolution, there was no greater blight on the peace of the western frontier than, in the words of the Virginia Council, "the obstinate and wicked Disposition of the Said Indians of Pluggy's Town."[27]

Better known to the whites as "Captain Pluggy," the Mingo leader Plukkemehnotee was an inveterate enemy of the Americans at a time when many native leaders clung to a tenuous neutrality. The Mingo were, in fact, not a tribe in any conventional sense, but a heterogeneous community—largely composed of Iroquoian Seneca and Cayuga—who steered their own course. Regarded by the Americans as little more than a maverick "banditti," Pluggy's Mingo lived up to their reputation, marauding across the Virginia backcountry with a persistence that infuriated state authorities.

Plukkemehnotee's aggressiveness would be his undoing. In the winter of 1776 Pluggy led between forty and fifty warriors on a raid in Ken-

---

24. Louise Phelps Kellogg, ed., *Frontier Advance on the Upper Ohio, 1778–1779* (Madison: Wisconsin Historical Society, 1916), 187. Captain Pipe's Message, December 21, 1778.

25. The tribes generally used the expression "Long Knives" to specifically reference the Virginians.

26. Heckewelder, *History, Manners, and Customs*, 135.

27. Reuben Gold Thwaites and Louise Phelps Kellogg, *The Revolution on the Upper Ohio, 1775–1777* (Madison: Wisconsin Historical Society, 1908), 236. Orders of the Virginia Council, March 12, 1777.

tucky which was initially successful. But on December 29, the chieftain led an impetuous assault on the fortified stockade of McClelland's Station. The affair ended in a bloody repulse, and during an intense exchange of gunfire Pluggy was shot and killed.[28]

Mingo depredations would continue to nettle the Virginians. The following summer, Governor Patrick Henry wrote that "I was ever of opinion, that the severest Vengeance should be taken on Pluggy's People. The Terror of their Fate, may serve as a usefull Lesson to the Neighboring Tribes." In a blunt reflection on the brutal nature of frontier warfare, Henry concluded that "Savages must be managed by working on their Fears."[29]

Alexander McGillivray (1750–1793).

ALEXANDER MCGILLIVRAY

He was one of the Revolution's most curious enigmas. The educated and somewhat effete son of a Scottish trader, McGillivray rose to unrivaled power among a feared nation of warriors.

At the outbreak of the war McGillivray was in Charleston, where he had received an education, including studies in Greek and Latin, at the behest of his Loyalist father. By the summer of 1777 McGillivray was back among his mother's people—the Creek nation—as a commissary of Britain's Southern Indian Department. He was most effective at gathering intelligence and bolstering Britain's standing among the Creek, who were, at best, lukewarm allies of the Crown.

As a warrior he was considered something of a flop. Although he did head contingents of Creek warriors in the field, most notably in the defense of British held Pensacola, he was apparently more adept at leading from the rear. His own brother-in-law Louis Milfort considered McGillivray's penchant for avoiding battle as something of a joke. "When one has so much administrative capacity," asserted Milfort, "he does not need military virtues to be a great man."[30]

28. Thomas D. Clark, ed., *The Voice of the Frontier: John Bradford's Notes on Kentucky* (Lexington: University Press of Kentucky, 1993), 14.
29. Thwaites and Kellogg, *Frontier Defense*, 30. Letter, Patrick Henry to Edward Hand, July 27, 1777.
30. John Walton Caughey, *McGillivray of the Creeks* (Norman: University of Oklahoma Press, 1938), 4.

The Creek nation seemingly agreed with such sentiments. When the famed war chief Emistisiguo was killed at Savannah in 1782, McGillivray remarkably assumed the mantle of Creek leadership. He was likewise embittered that Crown forces had abandoned their tribal allies to the United States. While seeking a Spanish alliance, McGillivray explained that although Britain "has been compelled to withdraw its protection from us, She has no right to transfer us with their former possessions to any power whatever contrary to our Inclination and Intent."[31]

---

31. Caughey, *McGillivray of the Creeks*, 64. Letter, Alexander McGillivray to Arturo O'Neill, January 1, 1784.

The Tiger Aids the Eaglet: How India Secured America's Independence

❋ RICHARD SAMBASIVAM ❋

"No event was ever received with a more heart felt joy," Washington wrote after hearing about the official alliance between the fledgling United States and the world power France.[1] It's well established that foreign aid both before and after 1778 was crucial to America's struggle for independence: not only did the French and other European powers supply arms and ammunition to the American cause, but they also expanded the theaters of war against the British Empire. In these theaters, the conflict was complicated and amplified to the point that the British ultimately had to concede defeat in North America. Nowhere was Britain's struggle more obvious and more significant than in India.

In this theater, in which the British East Company faced off against the Kingdom of Mysore in South India, the British Empire faced challenges that might sound familiar to anyone in the modern West: an opponent under an Islamic regime, a corporation "too big to fail," and a debate over grand strategy. The British of course had a large stake in America, but it was these challenges that made British officials rethink what they wanted their empire to look like—and whether it was worth fighting for the American colonies.

A GLOBAL WAR

When France joined the war, the war took on international dimensions with significant consequences. Though France by and large contributed

---

1. George Washington, "George Washington to Continental Congress, May 1, 1778," ed. John C. Fitzpatrick, *The Writings of George Washington from the Original Manuscript Sources, 1745–1799* (Washington, D.C.: Government Printing Office, 1931), accessed March 1, 2015, https://memory.loc.gov/cgi-bin/query/r?ammem/mgw:@field(DO CID+@lit(gw110323)).

the most aid to the rebellious colonists, Spain and the Netherlands also entered the war against Britain. In addition, the League of Armed Neutrality, which included the Russian and Ottoman Empires, took a stand against Britain's hindrance of shipping. But there were even greater problems than Europe for King George to consider. There was fighting in the Caribbean and the Gulf Coast. And finally, there was India, which was not yet under the direct control of the British crown. The East India Company's forces had some successes against various kingdoms in India and held some territory on the subcontinent. But in 1780, they ran into trouble.

That year, the ruler of Mysore, Hyder Ali, decided to intervene against his rival in the region. The British had captured a French port that Hyder claimed to be under his protection. He marched thousands of troops across the Western Ghats, bound for the important British base of Fort St. George, near the port town of Madras (modern-day Chennai). From the outset the British knew to take the threat of Hyder seriously; this was actually their second war. Hyder had beaten the East India Company badly in the 1760s, and the Company had sued for peace when Madras, their only holding in South India, was threatened.[2] And now, it was threatened again.

WHO WAS AMERICA'S "ALLY"?

The city of Mysore (also known as Mysuru) lies about 150 km west of the modern-day tech hub of Bangalore (Bengaluru). By the time of Hyder's wars with the British, it had existed as a distinct kingdom for centuries. However, Hyder was a different kind of leader for Mysore. In the words of Eliza Fay, an English traveler whom he imprisoned, "having acquired by his genius and intrepidity everything that he enjoys, he makes his name both feared and respected; so that nobody chooses to quarrel with him . . . a man who can neither write nor read."[3] Though he was illiterate, Hyder earned his reputation as a military strategist. His forces pioneered the use of rockets during his first war against the British, terrifying their soldiers. The orderly, close formations typical of the era made rocket attacks particularly devastating. In response, the British eventually developed the Congreve rocket, which is famously referenced in the United States National Anthem ("and the rockets' red glare, the bombs bursting in air").

2. G. J. Bryant, *The Emergence of British Power in India, 1600–1784: A Grand Strategic Interpretation* (Woodbridge: Boydell Press, 2013), 294.
3. Eliza Fay, *Original Letters from India,* ed. E.M. Forster (New York: New York Review of Books, 2010), 137.

Hyder, as well as his son Tipu Sultan, was also problematic for his own people. He favored scorched earth policy on the land between his kingdom and the British; when the civilians living there refused to leave, he ordered them mutilated. Eliza Fay was short on kind words for him: "[Hyder] even advised his General, who is Governor of this Province, to massacre all the natives by way of quelling a rebellion which had arisen . . . In short a volume would not contain half the enormities perpetrated by this disgrace to human nature." (It's worth noting that Eliza Fay was a well-traveled woman, and had likely seen her fair share of violent rulers.)[4] Hyder was not even the legitimate ruler of Mysore; that title belonged to the Wodeyar dynasty, whose heirs were now just puppets of the regime. Hyder had served prominently in the Wodeyar king's army before usurping the throne.

It is important not to ignore the religious tension underlying opposition to Hyder Ali, a Muslim. Historically, India has been home to conflict between Hindus and Muslims, and Mysore was little different, where many Hindus resented Muslim rule. That opposition only grew after Tipu took over as ruler, when the typical punishment for rebelling Hindus was forced conversion to Islam.[5]

Like in the American theater, a quick conclusion to Hyder's war proved elusive. In 1780, Hyder defeated the British again and again; in 1781, he was more often on the retreat. Meanwhile, the French aided Hyder at sea, with a fleet led by the Admiral Pierre Andre de Suffren, and on land, with mercenaries in the Mysore army. Hyder was very much aware of the global context of his struggle; in a memo to his son, he said "the English are today all powerful in India. It is necessary to weaken them by war . . . Put the nations of Europe one against the other. It is by the aid of the French that you could conquer the British armies which are better trained than the Indian."[6]

There was awareness of a common struggle in America. The flagship of the Continental fleet that defeated a stronger British force at Delaware Bay in 1782 was named the *Hyder Ally*.[7] On top of that, there's evidence Mysore reached out to America. According to records of his correspondence, Tipu Sultan sent a letter to the Continental Congress after the Declaration of Independence, proclaiming that "every blow

4. Ibid., 116.

5. Roy Kaushik, *War, Culture, and Society in Early Modern South Asia* (New York: Routledge, 2011), 73.

6. Kaushik, *War, Culture, and Society*, 86.

7. Charles W. Goldsborough, *The United States' Naval Chronicle* (Washington, D.C.: James Wilson, 1824), 30–31, accessed March 15, 2015, https://books.google.com/books/about/The_United_States_Naval_Chronicle.html?id=a7EtAAAAYAAJ.

that is struck in the cause of American liberty throughout the world, in France, India, and elsewhere and so long as a single insolent savage tyrant remains the struggle shall continue."[8]

THE MEGACORPORATION

The same East India Company primarily responsible for the Tea Act controversial in America was now locked in a war with this Hyder Ali. The British government did not directly control the Company, but it had a great stake in its success (as evidenced, for one, by Parliament's passage of the Tea Act). Trade was of course a big motivation for the expansion and defense of European empires—twenty percent of Britain's imports in 1784 were from India.[9]

But the importance of the Company goes much deeper. In the early 1770s, the bubble in the Company's stock burst, and at the same time it had 1.5 million pounds in debt and 1 million pounds in unpaid taxes[10]— roughly a tenth of annual government revenues.[11] The Company needed a bailout; in 1773, the British crown agreed to loan it a whopping 1 million pounds. In addition, the government tried to sell off its 'liquid' assets: unsold tea, which was shipped to the American colonies. In some part, the Boston Tea Party was a response to the East India Company's bailout package.

And though Edmund Burke said the Company would "drag [the government] down into an unfathomable abyss,"[12] the government had little choice: the Company, whose profits alone contributed nearly one percent of the nation's GDP,[13] was too big to fail. The British hadn't

8. Kabir Kausir, *Secret Correspondence of Tipu Sultand* (New Delhi: Light and Life Publishers, 1980), 306.

9. H.V. Bowen, Elizabeth Mancke, and John G. Reid, *Britain's Oceanic Empire: Atlantic and Indian Ocean Worlds, c. 1550–1850* (New York: Cambridge University Press, 2012), 61.

10. William Dalrymple, "The East India Company: The original corporate raiders," *The Guardian*, March 4, 2015, accessed March 1, 2016, www.theguardian.com/world/2015/mar/04/east-india-companyoriginal-corporate-raiders.

11. B. R. Mitchell, *British Historical Statistics* (Cambridge: Cambridge University Press, 2011), 581.

12. Dalrymple, "The East India Company."

13. Nick Robins, *The Corporation That Changed the World: How the East India Company Shaped the Modern Multinational* (Ann Arbor: Pluto Press, 2006), 136. This calculation is based on a 17 percent annual profit on trade totaling 200 million pounds in the second half of the eighteenth century (Robins); national income for the United Kingdom in 1780, at 140 million pounds, is derived from "Three centuries of macroeconomic data," Bank of England, accessed March 30, 2016, www.bankofengland.co.uk/research/Pages/onebank/threecenturies.aspx.

forgotten that the spectacular collapse of the South Seas Company in the 1720s, another financial bubble, ravaged their country's economy.

So though the American colonies were important to the empire (and especially the king), the British had a lot to lose if the East India Company failed. Parliament established a board in 1773 to oversee the Company's activities in India, but it failed to keep the business from falling into even more financial trouble. From 1769 to 1784, when the second war with Mysore ended, the Company's share price tumbled 55 percent.[14] The Company's struggle to stay afloat financially and to stop Hyder Ali left the British in doubt of their future in India.

BRITAIN'S "PIVOT TO ASIA"

Just as America today assesses its role in the world, the British had to consider grand strategy. Since de Gama sailed around the Cape of Good Hope, Europeans had raced to find the fastest, most efficient ways to exploit the goods of India—and there was no easier way than directly controlling the territory. So India, as well as China, drifted closer and closer to the center of Britain's colonial vision.

Consider the economics of Britain's calculus. The raw goods to manufactured goods trade with the American colonies was profitable (North America accounted for thirty percent of English exports[15]), but it didn't compare with the potential for gains in the East. Defending America had gotten expensive, as the Seven Years' War showed, and the colonists were evidently unhappy to pay for that defense. In contrast, the colonial government in India made substantial revenue from taxes on Indians, and the goods traded, including but hardly limited to spices, were valuable. England was undergoing the agricultural and then the industrial revolutions; a growing population meant a large market in which to sell goods was not overseas but right at home. This reduced the emphasis on a market for exports, America, in favor of the source of imports, Asia.

Then there were the challenges on the battlefield. Initially, the British were overconfident in their position; in 1780, the Governor of Madras, Thomas Rumbold, left for England, assured that peace would last at least through the year. The Company was thrown off balance when Hyder started war. French involvement was a problem, too—though

14. Robins, *Corporation*, 82.
15. D.N. McCloskey and R.P. Thomas, "Overseas trade and empire 1700–1860," vol. 1 of *The Economic History of Britain, 1700–Present*, ed. Roderick Floud and D.N. McCloskey (New York: Cambridge University Press, 1981), 91.

the French had been thrown out of North America with the 1763 Treaty of Paris, they were still a threat in South Asia. The British were well aware it was French policy to maintain relations with and support any local powers opposed to the Company.[16] Whether the fear was realistic or not, surely more than one British official lost sleep over being pushed out of India by the French.

So Britain dedicated the appropriate resources. Around twenty percent of Britain's ships of the line,[17] the workhorses of its renowned navy, fought in the South Asian theater against Admiral de Suffren, a campaign the British could not even win. Importantly, the Royal Navy was also unable to prevent the French from blockading and bombarding Yorktown, which signaled the end of the American theater and ultimately ended the war. Diversion of resources to India prevented the British from making a stronger response to the French-American campaign.

But it was India that demanded Britain's attention. When word of war with Hyder reached London in 1781, it was inconvenient for the East India Company, which was in the middle of negotiations for renewing its charter with the government. For its part, the government was under public pressure over the war in America that was not going well, and the Mysore war was a reminder of the Company's incompetence. As a result, Lord North demanded a large annual payment from the Company.[18] In other words, the British government was beginning to see the need for a more direct approach to administration in India— steps toward establishing a new colony.

And that colony was especially important to the British. In the midst of the conflict with Hyder, the Fort William Council, which oversaw all British holdings in India, asserted that "the object that is at stake is the preservation of India to Great Britain and those consequent advantages which the Asiatic dominions of the State may hereafter be capac-

16. Bryant, *Emergence of British Power*, 289.
17. Jonathan Dull, *A Diplomatic History of the American Revolution* (New Haven: Yale University Press, 1985), 110; also Alfred Thayer Mahan, *The Major Operations of the Navies in the War of American Independence* (Cambridge: University Press, 1913), 200–209.
18. Robins, *Corporation*, 125.
19. "Mahratta Peace," letter from Fort William to Select Committee at Bombay, *An Authentic Copy of the Correspondence in India: Between the Country Powers and the Honourable the East-India Company's Servants*, vol. 6 (London: J. Debrett, opposite Burlington House, Piccadilly, 1787), 208, accessed March 1, 2015, https://books.google.com/books?id= PnEIAAAAQAAJ&printsec=frontcover&source=gbs_ge_summary_r &cad=0#v=one page&q&f=false.

itated to refund for the relief of the whole Empire."[19] If Britain were to push its empire to new heights in Asia, it had to prevail against Mysore. For that to happen, Britain had to end its war with France, and thus America, and abandon its control of the Thirteen Colonies.

CONCLUSION

The war in America came to a resolution of independence, but the conflict with Mysore was far from settled. When word reached Tipu Sultan that France had made peace with Britain, he decided to turn the stalemate on the battlefield into an end to hostilities in 1784. The British were humiliated but not finished—they fought two more wars with Mysore. Though he wanted to join Napoleon's French Empire, Tipu Sultan was killed by a force led by the Duke of Wellington in 1799, which effectively ended resistance to British rule in South India.

The throne was returned to the Wodeyars, who had petitioned the British for help, and they ruled (under the Raj) until Indian independence in 1947.[20] Tipu, and to a lesser extent Hyder, remains a divisive figure in modern Indian society, seen as either an early, forward-looking Indian freedom fighter or an atrocity-committing Islamic fanatic. Regardless, he and his father Hyder were consequential in America's struggle for independence, and although the British ultimately triumphed over him, by then the damage was done. America was a new, separate country.

All this is not to take away from the victory that the American colonists (and their French friends) won for themselves. The siege at Yorktown and French victories in the valuable West Indies colonies were likely at least as influential in bringing the British to the negotiating table. But if anything can be taken away from this, it's the overwhelming connectedness of the world, even over two centuries before the Internet. A rebellion that began in America led to a renewed conflict for regional hegemony in South India and shaped the future of British colonialism.

And that Second British Empire, in turn, shaped the world. G. J. Bryant notes in *The Emergence of British Power in India* that once the British established solid footing for possessions like Madras, the Empire had a strategic base to dominate trade in the East and establish new settlements in Australasia. In the nineteenth century, the British controlled all of India, the Raj, and to protect the "Crown Jewel" it would try to create buffer states in Afghanistan and Persia against Russia, and in Siam (modern Thailand) against French Indochina (Vietnam).[21]

20. Kaushik, *War, Culture, and Society*, 65.
21. Bryant, *Emergence of British Power*, 328.

One legacy of British conquest and protection of India was the Empire's meddling in the affairs of these neighboring countries. It would not be a stretch to say that in the British turning their attention in the late 1700s to India we can find some roots of the Iranian Revolution and the modern war in Afghanistan. When we understand the global nature of the American Revolution and the transformation of the British Empire, we don't just paint a more complete picture of America's origins, but of America's challenges abroad, too.

And in the late eighteenth century, it was the British Empire surveying the world map and determining what was feasible, based on the challenges of a fearsome opponent on the battlefield, a bloated but systemically important corporation, and a shift in the relative importance of regions. That whittled away support for a war in America, and the fulfillment of the Declaration of Independence is owed in at least some part to the struggle between a couple of Muslim warrior-rulers and one of history's biggest corporations, halfway around the world.

Stern Measures: Thomas Jefferson Confronts the "Hair Buyer"

JOSHUA SHEPHERD

For a high ranking British official about to be captured by Rebel forces, it was an ominous portent of future treatment. Surrounded at the frontier outpost of Fort Sackville on the Wabash River, Detroit Lt. Gov. Henry Hamilton received a less than cordial demand for surrender on the morning of February 24, 1779. In an icy message penned by American commander Lt. Col. George Rogers Clark, the outnumbered and outmatched Hamilton was bluntly warned that if he dared destroy any supplies or papers prior to capitulation "you may expect no mercy, for by Heavens you shall be treated as a Murtherer."[1]

Although captured officers could generally expect decent treatment during the Revolution, Hamilton, arguably the most reviled Briton in the trans-Appalachian west, would experience far less than the norm, and the controversy which erupted over his imprisonment was due in no small part to the very brutal nature of the war on the frontier. In June of 1777, Hamilton received orders from Lord George Germain to actively court the assistance of the region's Indians in harassing the American backcountry, or, as Germain loftily put it, to employ every means "that Providence has put into His Majesty's Hands, for crushing the Rebellion."[2] Hamilton, who claimed to be apprehensive of unleashing the horrors of an Indian war against America's civilian populace, nonetheless complied with the directive.[3]

---

1. John D. Barnhart, ed., *Henry Hamilton and George Rogers Clark in the American Revolution with the Unpublished Journal of Lieut. Gov. Henry Hamilton* (Crawfordsville, Indiana: R. E. Banta, 1951), 180. Hereinafter cited as *Hamilton Journal*.
2. Letter, Lord George Germain to Henry Hamilton, March 26, 1777, in M. Shoemaker, et al, eds., *Report of the Pioneer Society of the State of Michigan* (Lansing: Wynkoop Hallenbeck Crawford Co., 1908), 9:347.
3. Letter, Henry Hamilton to [Lord Shelburne?], April 9, 1782, in John D. Barnhart, ed., "Lieutenant Governor Henry Hamilton's Apologia", *Indiana Magazine of History*, Volume 52, Issue 4, (1956), 386.

The governor regularly supplied southbound raiding parties with supplies and ammunition, but made token gestures to soften the blow. Hamilton endeavored to attach to each war party one or more Loyalists, generally Indian Department rangers and interpreters, with orders "to attend to the behavior of the Indians, protect defenceless persons and prevent any insult or barbarity being exercised on the Prisoners."[4] Native war parties operating under Hamilton's aegis proved immensely successful, wreaking havoc on the frontier in a wide arc from Pennsylvania to Kentucky. In the first year of British-authorized raids, Hamilton reported that the tribes brought 109 prisoners into Detroit, and the governor consistently offered ransoms for such captives.[5]

Despite his attempts to operate the war with the superficial appearance of European mores, Hamilton was clearly caught up in an exceedingly nasty business which left him uneasy over the execution of his orders. From the comfortable vantage point of Whitehall, the decision to employ Indian auxiliaries was simply an essential war measure; for officers on the ground, including Hamilton, the conflict was far more complex. Clearly giving vent to a good bit of angst, Hamilton optimistically reported that he had singlehandedly moderated centuries-old tribal war practices, but confessed that attempts to alter the brutal nature of backcountry fighting was "rather to be wished than expected."[6]

The greatest point of contention that would develop over the governor's war record regarded his participation in the tribal tradition of scalping, a grim fate that fell on men, women, and children—both dead and alive. On the frontier, both sides adopted the practice as a matter of course, but the Americans were outraged that Britain and her tribal allies targeted backcountry civilians who were, ostensibly, British subjects. Warriors sent out by Hamilton were well supplied by the Indian Department; a 1778 inventory listed such items as 1,800 "scalping knives," which were clearly categorized as such.[7] War parties returning to Detroit would announce their success by shouting the "scalp yell," and were feted and resupplied by Hamilton and his subordinates.[8] Al-

4. Barnhart, "Hamilton's Apologia", 386.
5. Barnhart, "Hamilton's Apologia", 387.
6. Barnhart, "Hamilton's Apologia", 386–387.
7. A List of Goods on Hand for the Indian Department, Detroit, September 5, 1778, in Shoemaker, *Report of the Pioneer Society*, 471.
8. For a brief description of the traditional "scalp yell" as practiced by victorious war parties, see John Heckewelder, *History, Manners, and Customs of the Indian Nations Who Once Inhabited Pennsylvania and the Neighboring States* (Philadelphia: Publication Fund of the Historical Society of Pennsylvania, 1876), 216–217. For an eyewitness (if potentially biased) recollection of Hamilton receiving a war party, see Consul Wilshire Butterfield, *Leith's Narrative: A Short Biography of John Leith, With a Brief Account of His Life Among the Indians* (Cincinnati: Robert Clark & Co., 1883), 29–30.

though, in Hamilton's opinion, the tribes "have shewn a humanity hitherto unpracticed among them" toward their captives, he likewise recorded the scalps exhibited at Detroit: 129 on one occasion, 15 on another, 81 on yet another.[9]

The governor not only celebrated the taking of such grim tokens but, in a wily game of frontier diplomacy, gave them to other Indian nations in an attempt to strengthen inter-tribal cooperation. On June 17, 1778, the governor recorded that a Delaware war party "presented me with two pieces of dried meat (scalps) one of which I have given to the Chippoways, another to the Miamis."[10] All in all, Hamilton put on a cheery face regarding the prosecution of the war, telling the Indians at one council that the results "have been good, as you have succeeded in almost all your enterpizes, having taken a number of prisoners and a far greater number of scalps."[11]

Not surprisingly, Hamilton's reputation was irreparably wrecked due to distorted accounts of his activities. Rumors abounded that the governor offered hefty scalp "bounties" to Indian war parties. Such claims were a slight mischaracterization of Hamilton's actual practices, but exaggerated hearsay, which grew with the telling, served to inflame feelings against him. Readers of the *Virginia Gazette* were assured in February of 1776 "that the commanding-officer at Detroit offers them [the Indians] 10 l. for every scalp"; another source set the supposed scalp bounty at £50.[12] Daniel Sullivan, a Patriot spy who operated in the northwest and visited Detroit, passed along second hand reports that the governor "paid very high prices in Goods for the Scalps the Indians brought in."[13] By the time George Rogers Clark readied for his

---

9. Shoemaker, *Report of the Pioneer Society*, 431, 465, 477.

10. Shoemaker, *Report of the Pioneer Society*, 446. Because the governor made repeated references to American scalps in his journals and correspondence, his isolated use of the tribal euphemism "dried meat", followed by a parenthetical "scalps," is at least worthy of note. British trader Henry Hay described the macabre pairing of war trophies in detail in 1790: "I was shown this morning the Heart of the white Prisoner I mentioned the Indians killed some time ago in the Indian Country—it was quite drye, like a piece of dried venison, with a small stick run from one end of it to the other & fastened behind the fellows bundle that had killed him, with also his Scalp." Milo Quaife, ed., *Fort Wayne in 1790: The Journal of Henry Hay* (Greenfield, Indiana: William Mitchell Printing Company, 1921), 313.

11. Shoemaker, *Report of the Pioneer Society of the State of Michigan*, 445.

12. *Virginia Gazette* (Purdie), February 23, 1776, 3.

13. Daniel Sullivan's Deposition, March 20, 1778, in Reuben Gold Thwaites and Louise Phelps Kellogg, eds., *Frontier Defense on the Upper Ohio, 1777–1778* (Madison: Wisconsin Historical Society, 1912), 232.

raid against Vincennes in February of 1779, he disdainfully referred to Hamilton as "The Famous Hair Buyer General."[14]

Captured by Clark on February 25, the governor received a rude awakening. Hamilton was outraged when Clark ordered several captured officers placed in irons in retribution for their participation in Indian raids. Francois Maisonville, whom the Americans considered as particularly obnoxious, was himself the victim of a botched scalping that left him with a partly mutilated crown. Hamilton was warned "to be on my guard as there was a design of shooting me thro' the head."[15]

Greater insults awaited when Hamilton and over two dozen of his men were transferred to Virginia. Prior to setting out, Clark warned the governor that backcountry settlers would likely have little compassion on the prime instigator of Indian war, and that his life could be in danger. Hamilton and his officers were hosted in private homes along the way and treated quite hospitably; although they faced no overt threats, they endured a good measure of unpleasantness from gawkers. At Logan's Station in Kentucky, Hamilton recorded that "the people were not exceedingly well disposed to us, & we were accosted by the females especially in pretty coarse terms." All in all, the captive Britons were viewed as a set of "Infernals . . . who had each been more bloodthirsty than Herod the Tetrarch." [16] Lt. Jacob Schieffelin, a translator in the Indian Department, was indignant over the ordeal, during which, he claimed, the captives were forced to march barefoot and hungry and were "insulted by every dirty fellow as they passed through the country."[17]

Frontier families had, of course, suffered far worse, a fact which was not lost on Henry Hamilton. The governor had supplied the very war parties that were harrying the frontier, but seeing the results of their handiwork firsthand gave the governor a slightly different perspective. He was particularly struck by the cordiality of one Kentuckian whose son had been killed by Indians the previous year. Hamilton nonetheless felt that any ill manners were "very excusable" because the Kentuckians

---

14. Letter, George Rogers Clark to Patrick Henry, February 3, 1779, in James Alton James, ed., *George Rogers Clark Papers, 1771–1781* (Springfield: Illinois State Historical Library, 1912), 97.

15. Barnhart, *Hamilton Journal*, 190.

16. Barnhart, *Hamilton Journal*, 194, 196, 203. Hamilton likely made reference to Herod Antipas, the first century ruler whom the New Testament records as complicit in the executions of both Jesus Christ and John the Baptist.

17. Jacob Schieffelin, "Narrative of Gov. Henry Hamilton: Loose Notes of the Proceedings and Sufferings of Henry Hamilton," *The Magazine of American History with Notes and Queries* volume 1, (1877), 188.

"had suffered very severely from the inroads" of the Indians. Backcountry settlers, he explained, were "in hourly apprehension of attacks from the Savages, and no doubt these poor inhabitants are worthy of pity."[18]

Similar sympathy wouldn't be forthcoming for Hamilton when he reached Virginia. Before the prisoners reached the capital at Williamsburg, an American officer intercepted them with disheartening news. The Virginia Executive Council, headed by Gov. Thomas Jefferson, had opted for a conspicuous show of retribution toward Hamilton and two of his subordinates, Philip Dejean and William Lamothe. Rather than being treated as gentlemen prisoners of war, the men were to be placed in irons and confined in Williamsburg's public jail.

The council issued its orders in scathing prose generally attributed to Jefferson himself. The orders contained a lengthy remonstrance against British treatment of prisoners, which was described as "savage and unprecedented among civilized nations." The harsh treatment that would be meted out was justified on the grounds that the prisoners had "distinguished themselves personally in this line of cruel conduct" and were therefore "fit subjects to begin on with the work of retaliation." Hamilton in particular was singled out as the architect of inexcusable frontier brutality. Printed copies of his proclamations had reportedly been discovered on the bodies of slain settlers;[19] worse yet, it was asserted, Hamilton "gave standing rewards for scalps, but offered none for prisoners."[20]

In crafting the case against Hamilton, Jefferson and the council relied heavily on the testimony of John Dodge, a Connecticut Yankee turned western fur trader who had been imprisoned by the British after running afoul of authorities in Detroit. By 1779, Dodge had escaped and published his account of a truly nightmarish ordeal, grandiosely titled *An Entertaining Narrative of the Cruel and Barbarous Treatment and Extreme Sufferings of Mr. John Dodge.* Dodge claimed to have been imprisoned under the most horrific conditions: clapped in irons, thrown into a freezing and filthy dungeon, denied food and medicine, and daily threatened with execution. Dodge characterized Henry Hamilton as little more than a sadistic monster who rather enjoyed tormenting helpless

18. Barnhart, *Hamilton Journal*, 195–196.
19. "The Indians leave these on or near the bodies of the People they murder, Good encouragement." From Note 2, Washington from Brig. Gen. Edward Hand, September 15, 1777, Founders Online, National Archives (http://founders.archives.gov/documents/Washington/03–11–02–0232).
20. Order of the Virginia Council, June 16, 1779, in James, *George Rogers Clark Papers*, 338.

victims, and repeated the standard charges against the governor: that he dispatched war parties with express orders "not to spare man, woman, or child", and offered a £20 standing reward for scalps. Because Hamilton refused to pay anything for captives, claimed Dodge, the Indians were in the habit of forcing their prisoners to carry baggage to the outskirts of Detroit and then tomahawking them in sight of the city.[21]

Dodge painted a revolting picture of British brutality; unfortunately, his grasp of the truth was extraordinarily flexible. Although he claimed to have been jailed under close confinement from January to July of 1776, records seem to indicate that he was transacting real estate deals that very spring.[22] Dodge would eventually gain the reputation of a shifty frontier ne'er-do-well; in addition to slanderous scribblings, Dodge was later implicated in nefarious trading practices and cross border slave snatching. Although there were accurate bits in his *Narrative* (descriptions, for instance, of Hamilton congratulating victorious war parties), some of what Dodge wrote was wildly exaggerated or demonstrably false. In what appears to be a somewhat accurate assessment, an outraged Hamilton characterized Dodge as little more than "an unprincipled and perjured renegade."[23]

In June of 1779, however, Dodge's accusations were widely believed, and the wrath of the Old Dominion fell rather unpleasantly on Henry Hamilton. He arrived in Williamsburg on the evening June 16, and would remember the event with bitterness. His party stopped at the Governor's Palace, where Hamilton expected to be received by Jefferson himself; he would be disappointed. Jefferson refused to see the prisoners, who were unceremoniously escorted to the Williamsburg jail. Their accommodations were less than agreeable. While some captured British officers in Virginia were comfortably lodged in rented homes, Hamilton was shackled and housed in a miserable jail cell with British deserters and common criminals. Hamilton thought the space, which accommodated six men, not greater than 100 square feet, and reeking from lack of ventilation. One corner was occupied by a filthy chair used as a makeshift privy, "A kind of Throne," wrote Hamilton, "which had been of use to such miscreants as us for 60 years past, and in certain points of wind rendered the air truly Mephytic."[24]

---

21. Clarence Monroe Burton, ed., *Narrative of John Dodge During His Captivity at Detroit* (Cedar Rapids, Iowa: The Torch Press, 1909), 42.
22. Burton, *Narrative of John Dodge*, 6–7.
23. Shoemaker, *Report of the Pioneer Society of the State of Michigan*, 512.
24. Barnhart, *Hamilton Journal*, 205.

Just three days after the Virginia Council publicly issued its order, Jefferson reported the matter to George Washington with the hope that the harsh measures intended for Hamilton would meet with the commander-in-chief's "approbation."[25] Washington replied that he was in full agreement with the council, as Hamilton's policy "to excite the savages to acts of the most wanton barbarity" placed him in a separate class from common prisoners.[26]

British protests over the affair, however, quickly materialized, sparking no small controversy and a flurry of correspondence. Maj. Gen. William Phillips, who was held in Virginia subsequent to his capture at Saratoga in 1777, penned a lengthy letter to Jefferson in which he objected to Hamilton's treatment. Phillips enjoyed cordial relations with the Virginia governor and admitted that if Hamilton was actually guilty of the accusations against him he would be worthy of death. Phillips, however, refrained from speculating whether such charges "may be founded upon positive facts, be matter of hearsay, or taken from the reports of interested men." Phillips focused his arguments on the fact that Hamilton had not surrendered at discretion and should consequently be considered as a prisoner of war entitled to the civil treatment due a captured officer.[27]

Due to the kind offices of his jailer, Hamilton himself was able to acquire paper, quill, and ink even though the Virginia Council had barred him their use. Despite the unpleasant conditions of his imprisonment, Hamilton struck a very respectful tone, and rallied to the defense of his two subordinates, Dejean and Lamothe. The two men, Hamilton pointed out, had operated under his orders, and he personally assumed responsibility for their actions. "If there be any criminality in those orders Justice demands that I alone should be the sufferer. I therefore make it my request that I may suffer, alone." Hamilton expressed hope for a public trial as he was confident his character would survive "the Test of That Enquiry."[28]

Jefferson addressed such complaints in a letter to General Phillips on July 22; typically Jeffersonian, the document is a lengthy, lawyerly,

25. Jefferson to Washington, June 19, 1779, Founders Online, National Archives (http://founders.archives.gov/documents/Washington/03–21–02–0162).

26. Washington to Jefferson, July 10, 1779, Founders Online, National Archives (http://founders.archives.gov/documents/Washington/03–21–02–0343).

27. Enclosure: William Phillips to Jefferson, July 5, 1779, Founders Online, National Archives (http://founders.archives.gov/documents/Washington/03–21–02–0442–0002).

28. Hamilton to the Lieutenant Governor and Council of Virginia, July 30, 1779, Founders Online, National Archives (http://founders.archives.gov/documents/Jefferson/01–03–02–0063).

and remarkably worded polemic. Jefferson defended Hamilton's treatment on the "general principle of National retaliation" and launched into a vehement denunciation of British treatment of American prisoners of war, specifically citing the deplorable conditions on prison ships. Since American protests had gotten nowhere, wrote Jefferson, "you must excuse me for saying it is high time, by other lessons, to teach respect to the dictates of humanity."[29]

When it came to Hamilton, Jefferson clearly backed off from the worst allegations which the Virginia Council had included in its original order confining Hamilton to shackles. Gone were accusations that Hamilton had paid bounties for scalps, or that he offered no ransom for American captives. Jefferson nonetheless insisted that Hamilton was personally complicit to some of the worst atrocities of the war. Mirroring language which he had previously used in the Declaration of Independence, an incensed Jefferson explained that "The known rule of warfare with the Indian Savages is an indiscriminate butchery of men women and children. These Savages, under this well known Character, are employed by the British nation." Jefferson confessed that he was no expert on the European norms governing the treatment of prisoners, but was in no mood to quibble about Hamilton's discomfort. Regardless of what such rules of war dictated, wrote Jefferson, "I am sure that confinement, under its strictest circumstances, as a retaliation for Indian devastation and massacre, must be deemed lenity."[30]

Despite Jefferson's resolve to carry through with severe retaliatory measures, the case against Hamilton faced an unexpected reversal when General Washington abruptly, if reluctantly, changed course. After consulting with "several intelligent General Officers," Washington concluded that the entire subject was "involved in greater difficulty than I apprehended." He expressed little sympathy for Hamilton personally but confessed that "the practice of War may not justify all the measures that have been taken against him." It all rested on an unfortunate technicality; because Hamilton had signed terms of capitulation it "placed him upon a different footing from a mere prisoner at discretion." Washington's meaning was fairly clear: although Hamilton's actions merited "discrimination" from the average prisoner, it would be best if Jefferson eased up on the captured governor.[31]

---

29. Jefferson to Phillips, July 22, 1779," Founders Online, National Archives (http://founders.archives.gov/documents/Jefferson/01–03–02–0052).
30. Ibid.
31. Washington to Jefferson, August 6–10, 1779," Founders Online, National Archives (http://founders.archives.gov/documents.Washington/03–22–02–0044).

Ultimately Jefferson felt compelled to do just that. Hamilton and his fellow prisoners were released from irons, and by the first of October 1779 were offered parole. A furious and suspicious Hamilton, who felt that the parole was "artfully worded" and designed to entrap him, would have none of it. Specifically, he objected to a provision that would constrain him from saying anything to the "prejudice" the United States. Although Lamothe and Dejean accepted the terms, an intransigent Hamilton refused to budge. For another year he was held prisoner. Although he was no longer subjected to irons, the governor remained, as he put it, "under the varied tyranny of unfeeling men;" afflicted with gout, shivering beneath thin blankets, and occasionally reduced to prison rations and water. It was only from money made available by General Phillips was Hamilton able to purchase a few necessities.[32]

It was through Phillips's prodding that Hamilton finally signed a parole in October of 1780, ending a bitter personal trial that began nearly two years earlier. Initially paroled to New York City, he was officially exchanged in the spring of 1781. Hamilton penned several letters in which he attempted to vindicate himself up the chain of command, and it seems to have worked. By 1782 he was back in Canada as the lieutenant governor of Quebec; subsequent to the war he served as the governor of Bermuda and Dominica.

For over two centuries, however, American historians have vigorously endeavored to outdo each other in heaping blistering indictments on Henry Hamilton. In 1832 the governor was described as "a remorseless destroyer of the human race."[33] By 1883, frontier historian Consul Wilshire Butterfield announced that the case was closed. No further evidence was really needed, asserted Butterfield, "to fix upon the memory of Lieutenant Governor Henry Hamilton the stamp of most barbarous cruelty."[34] To the present day, some historians persist in repeating John Dodge's most damning—if distorted—accusations: that Hamilton paid generous "bounties" for American scalps but offered nothing for prisoners.

Hamilton himself feared as much. His correspondence indicates that Hamilton found the traditions of frontier warfare supremely distasteful—"a deplorable sort of war,"[35] he thought—but after assuming his

32. Barnhart, "Hamilton's Apologia", 394.
33. B.L. Rayner, *Sketches of the Life, Writings, and Opinions of Thomas Jefferson* (New York: A. Francis and W. Boardman, 1832), 188.
34. Butterfield, *Leith's Narrative*, 30.
35. Henry Bartholomew, ed., *Collections and Researches Made by the Pioneer Society of the State of Michigan* (Lansing: Wynkoop Hallenbeck Crawford Company, 1908), 10:268.

duties at Detroit, the governor, whatever his reasoning might have been, opted to take the path of least resistance. The governor made official pronouncements about the humane treatment of American civilians, but ultimately did whatever was necessary to maintain the good graces of tribal allies who waged war with an entirely different playbook. Even before his capture at Vincennes, a defensive Hamilton declared that he had simply operated under orders from London and that "I have alwaise endeavour'd to instill Humanity as much as in my power to the Indians." Such explanations may have ultimately saved the embattled governor from Thomas Jefferson's desire for "national retaliation," but failed to redeem his permanently tarnished legacy. Hamilton clearly recognized the inevitable result of his management of the Indian war out of Detroit. "I know my character has been staind," protested Hamilton, "but not deservedly."[36]

36. George Rogers Clark's Journal, February 1779, in James, *George Rogers Clark Papers*, 167–168.

Alexander Hamilton, Benedict Arnold, and a "Forgotten" *Publius*

❀ STEPHEN BRUMWELL ❀

Thanks to a critically-acclaimed and phenomenally popular Broadway musical, Alexander Hamilton has, quite literally, returned to the spotlight. The success of Lin-Manuel Miranda's *Hamilton,* a show inspired by Ron Chernow's best-selling 2004 biography *Alexander Hamilton,* has helped to rekindle interest in a man who, even when judged by the exceptional standards of the Founding Fathers, led a remarkable life.

Hamilton's career, both as an invaluable Revolutionary War *aide-de-camp* to Gen. George Washington, and as a leading Federalist politician destined to become his country's first secretary of the treasury, has been chronicled in minute detail, not simply in biographies, but through meticulous scholarly editions of his extensive writings.[1]

As these collections testify, Hamilton was a gifted, versatile and prolific writer, keen to communicate his ideas through personal letters, official reports and political essays. Given their importance in promoting the ratification of the US Constitution, particular attention has focused on Hamilton's prominent role in producing the series of articles, collectively known as *The Federalist Papers,* first published in 1787–88 in three New York newspapers: *The Independent Journal, The New-York Packet,* and *The Daily Advertiser.*

Following a convention long since adopted by political essayists in Britain and her former American colonies alike, Hamilton and his fellow authors James Madison and John Jay wrote anonymously, using pseu-

---

1. See *The Papers of Alexander Hamilton,* eds. Harold C. Syrett and Jacob E. Cooke (New York: Columbia University Press, 1961–87). All twenty seven volumes are available online via the National Archives' Founders Online website. For Hamilton's early political essays see also *The Revolutionary Writings of Alexander Hamilton,* ed. Richard B. Vernier (Indianapolis, Liberty Fund, 2008), available via the Online Library of Liberty.

donyms borrowed from the ancient world. Hamilton, who penned the majority of the eighty-five *Federalist* essays, chose the *nom-de-plume* "Publius," after one of the founders of the Roman Republic, Publius Valerius.[2]

This was not the first time that Alexander Hamilton had adopted the persona of "Publius." He'd also used it in October and November 1778, when he wrote three newspaper articles, all published in *The New-York Journal, and the General Advertiser,* attacking Maryland Congressman Samuel Chase for allegedly deploying insider knowledge in an unfair and unpatriotic—bid to monopolize the flour market.[3]

Existing scholarship maintains that it would be another nine years before Hamilton once more assumed the mantle of "Publius," yet there's compelling evidence that he resumed that identity just *two* years later in 1780, in the wake of one of the most dramatic episodes of the entire Revolutionary War, Maj. Gen. Benedict Arnold's failed attempt to betray the Hudson Valley fortress of West Point to the British.

Arnold's notorious treason was fully exposed on September 25, 1780, when he fled to New York after learning that his contact, British Army adjutant-general Maj. John André, had been captured in possession of incriminating documents. In following weeks American newspaper editors devoted many column inches to keeping their readers abreast of every twist and turn in the scarcely-credible saga, including André's trial and execution as a spy, and the public demonstrations in Philadelphia and elsewhere that culminated in ritual burnings of the hated Arnold's effigy. Besides such rolling coverage of developments, newspapers also printed letters from key players and anonymous eyewitnesses to events, along with opinion-pieces from commentators.

This proliferation of Arnold-inspired journalism included a long article that first appeared on Thursday October 12 in *The New-York Packet, and the American Advertiser.* That newspaper was an earlier incarnation of one of the trio of titles that carried the famous *Federalist* essays in 1787–88. Originally published in New York City, following the British occupation in the summer of 1776 its editor Samuel Loudon shifted his press up-state to Fishkill, a small town about ten miles northeast of the future location of West Point. It was published there between January 1777 and August 1783.[4]

---

2. For the collective use of "Publius" by Hamilton, Madison and Jay, see Daniel Walker Howe, "The Political Psychology of the Federalist," *William and Mary Quarterly* (3rd ser.), 44 (1987): 486.

3. *The Papers of Alexander Hamilton*, 1:562–63, 569, 580.

4. From November 1783 publication was resumed in New York City, with a title change to *Loudon's New-York Packet* in November 1784, shortened to *The New-York Packet* in May 1785.

The essay of October 12, 1780, which sought to exploit the wide-spread anger over Arnold's treason to revitalize the flagging and divided Patriot war-effort, was anonymous, but carried the bold, capitalized pseudonym "PUBLIUS."[5] Typical for that era, the same piece was swiftly re-published by other newspapers, making the front page of *The Pennsylvania Gazette* of October 18, 1780 ("From the New York Packet, Fishkill, October 12") and later surfacing in *The Norwich Packet, and the Weekly Advertiser* on Tuesday October 24 ("From the Fish Kill Papers").

Considering this coverage, including a conspicuous slot in one of early America's best-known newspapers, it is surprising that neither Hamilton's biographers nor the editors of his writings have noted this article, if only to eliminate it as the work of some other, less celebrated, "Publius."

That scenario must be considered, as writers who adopted pseudonyms held no monopoly over them. For example, a pseudonym employed by Hamilton in 1794, "Americanus," was used that same year by Timothy Ford, and had previously served John Stevens in 1787. Similarly, Hamilton's choice of "Phocian" in 1784 was mimicked by Fisher Ames in 1801.[6] According to William Cushing, an avid late nineteenth century student of pseudonyms, apart from Hamilton's *Federalist* collaborators, no other "Publius" was active until the late 1840s, when James De Peyster Ogden and Samuel B. Williams both wrote under that name. Even the diligent Cushing was not infallible, as he too failed to spot the presence of "Publius" in October 1780, but his comprehensive survey nonetheless underlines the point that this pseudonym was rarely used during the Revolutionary War.[7]

Aside from the possibility that this "Publius" piece is a hitherto overlooked essay by Hamilton, it is equally puzzling that the article has been

5. Unlike many newspapers of America's founding era, which survive in substantial runs and can be readily accessed online via the extremely comprehensive Readex series of "Early American Newspapers," relatively few copies of *The New-York Packet, and American Advertiser* exist from before 1783 (when the Readex coverage, in its Series 1, begins). Small clusters of original issues are scattered among several US archives. One of the strongest collections for the Revolutionary War, and particularly for 1780, is held in the New-York Historical Society, where I consulted it. As many of the Society's originals are fragile and tattered, they must be read on microfilm. A pdf of the article can be accessed at http://allthingsliberty.com/wp-content/uploads/2016/03/Publius_NY_Packet_1780_Oct_12.pdf

6. Evan Shalev, "Ancient Masks, American Fathers: Classical Pseudonyms during the American Revolution and Early Republic," in *Journal of the Early Republic*, 23 (2003): 160 note 19.

7. William Cushing, *Initials and Pseudonyms: A Dictionary of Literary Disguises* (New York: T. Y. Crowell & Co, 1885), 242 and Ibid., 2nd Series (1888), 126.

virtually ignored as a primary source by historians concerned with
Arnold and the impact of his notorious treason.[8]

Irrespective of its authorship, the essay deserves attention as a ro-
bustly-written call to arms, produced in direct response to Arnold's defection and originally published by the newspaper closest to the heart
of the drama in the Hudson Highlands. At first glance, the "Publius"
piece does not resemble Hamilton's other essays. Its style is florid, almost lurid, warning that Arnold's "horrible conspiracy . . . so narrowly
escaped" had come "within a hair's breadth" of yielding a nightmarish
scenario of burning homes, ravished womenfolk, and young men "wel-
tering in blood and carnage." Yet its sober, core message addresses
themes consistent with Hamilton's known concerns and reflected in his
writings. Appealing for "reformation in good earnest," "Publius" continued:

> let us invoke the genius of liberty to revisit us, and inspire us with
> sentiments suitable to the dignity of freemen; let us guard against
> that cursed avarice "which is as the sin of witchcraft," and has well
> nigh brought our ruin; let us contribute to the support of our army
> with cheerfulness and alacrity, not of necessity but of choice; let us
> be careful and diligent in detecting every species of villainy that may
> be practised among us, especially the dangerous and fatal practice
> of sinking the value of our currency . . . let us be very careful in choos-
> ing men of known integrity and abilities for our representatives both
> in civil and military concerns; very much indeed depends upon this.
> And above all things, let us study unanimity, which gives firmness
> and strength.

On October 12, the same day that the "Publius" piece emerged in
the *New-York Packet,* Hamilton wrote a letter from Preakness, New Jersey, to his friend Isaac Sears. While not mentioning Arnold, this flagged
up the same concerns about the prevailing "spirit of indifference to public affairs." Hamilton wrote: "It is necessary we should rouse and begin
to do our business in earnest or we shall play a losing Game. It is impossible the Contest can be much longer supported on the present footing." Voicing other familiar arguments, Hamilton wanted "a
Government with more Power . . . a Tax in kind . . . a Bank on the true

---

8. An exception is James Kirby Martin, who cited the *Pennsylvania Gazette* of October
18, 1780, in his scholarly account of Arnold's pre-treason career, *Benedict Arnold Revolutionary Hero: An American Warrior Reconsidered* (New York: New York University Press,
1977). Prof. Martin attributes the "Publius" article to an unidentified "newspaper com-
mentator." See Ibid., 8 and 437 note 18.

Principles of a Bank . . . an administration distinct from Congress and in the hands of single men under their orders." He added: "We must above all things have an Army for the war, and on an Establishment that will Interest the officers in the Service."[9]

Despite the widespread popular indignation reflected in letters, journals and public demonstrations, not even Arnold's "diabolical plot" was enough to galvanize the Revolution's supporters as "Publius" hoped. The communal rage against Arnold allowed war profiteers, or those who'd played no active role in the struggle for liberty, to offload some of their own sense of guilt upon the reviled traitor.[10] Yet there was no sudden surge of recruits for the Continental Army, no groundswell of state support for a strengthened Congress.

Alongside the bitter condemnation of Arnold, a theme highlighted by "Publius" and many other commentators was the notion that "Providence" had intervened to safeguard the liberties of America: after all, Arnold's scheme, which was widely believed to have envisaged the capture of Washington and his staff, had been within a whisker of success when baffled by André's chance encounter with a trio of "incorruptible" militiamen.

While many were optimistic that Providence would ensure the survival, and ultimate triumph, of the Patriot cause, before it did so (via the extraordinary conjunction of circumstances that permitted the decisive Yorktown campaign of October 1781) things would get much worse. The nadir came in January 1781 when exasperated Pennsylvania Continentals mutinied *en masse*, and marched on Congress for redress. Despite their anger at civilian indifference to their sufferings, such veterans maintained a loyalty to each other and to the cause they'd fought for. British attempts to exploit the unrest and encourage large-scale defections fell on deaf ears, with the mutineers spurning the "Idea of turning *Arnolds*."[11]

The factors that transformed Arnold, the hard-fighting hero of Quebec, Valcour Island, Ridgefield and Saratoga, into the most vilified turncoat in American history have inspired a substantial and steadily-growing literature. Detailed discussion of Arnold's treason lies beyond the scope of this article, but to provide context for the "Publius"

9. *The Papers of Alexander Hamilton*, 2: 472.
10. On the reaction to Arnold's treason, see especially Charles Royster, *A Revolutionary People at War: The Continental Army and American Character, 1775–1783* (Chapel Hill: University of North Carolina Press, 1979), 283–88.
11. For this disclaimer, see Gen. Anthony Wayne to Washington, Princeton, January 8, 1781, in Founders Online, National Archives http:/founders.archives.gov/documents/Washington/99-01-02-04474.

essay it is necessary to trace the twenty-three-year-old Hamilton's role in events, and to consider what he wrote, and may *possibly* have written, in response to them.[12]

On Sunday September 17, 1780, Washington set out from his head-quarters at New Bridge, New Jersey, heading for Hartford, Connecticut, where he was to confer with the French high command over joint strat-egy against the British. He was accompanied by an escort of dragoons, and his close-knit "family" of staff. Lieutenant Colonel Hamilton was present as Washington's chief aide, while his close friend, Maj. James McHenry, fulfilled that role for Maj. Gen. the Marquis de Lafayette, and Maj. Samuel Shaw acted for Brig. Gen. Henry Knox.

In Washington's absence, Arnold sought to finalize his conspiracy by fixing a face-to-face meeting with Major André, using a go-between, Joshua Hett Smith, whose precise complicity in the plot still remains unclear. This rendezvous eventually occurred at Haverstraw, in the early hours of September 22, after the major was rowed ashore from the British sloop HMS *Vulture*.

Arnold's subterfuge would, in all probability, have remained unde-tected save for two unforeseen developments. Next morning, while the *Vulture* lay off Teller's Point awaiting André's return, Col. James Liv-ingston took the unilateral decision to open fire on her from the shore with a four pounder cannon and a howitzer, inflicting enough damage to oblige the warship to temporarily fall back down the Hudson River. Instead of returning to British lines the way he'd come, André was per-suaded against his wishes to travel back to New York overland, through hostile territory. Swapping his British uniform for civilian clothes, and issued with a pass from Arnold permitting him, as "Mr John Anderson," to travel unmolested through the American lines, André set off on the afternoon of September 22 accompanied by Smith.

The major had almost reached safety when, on the morning of Sat-urday, September 23, after Smith had turned back, he was intercepted near Tarrytown by a trio of "volunteer militiamen." Taking them for Loyalists, André unwittingly revealed his own allegiance. After some deliberation, his captors searched him, discovering documents inside his stockings that suggested he was a British spy.

André, along with the papers he'd been concealing, was handed over to Lieut. Col. John Jameson of the 2nd Light Dragoons. Aware that

---

12. The brief narrative that follows draws largely upon the careful reconstructions in Carl Van Doren, *Secret History of the American Revolution* (New York: The Viking Press, 1941), 31571, and in Willard M. Wallace, *Traitorous Hero: The Life and Fortunes of Benedict Arnold* (New York: Harper and Brothers, 1954), 229–59.

Arnold had alerted his outposts to expect a "John Anderson" from New York, Jameson naively sent André to *him*, along with a letter explaining the circumstances of his capture and the discovery of the papers. When a more quick-witted officer, Maj. Benjamin Tallmadge, rode in from patrol, he badgered the reluctant Jameson into ordering André's recall. While Jameson's letter to Arnold continued on its way, the thick package of captured documents was sent to Washington, eventually joined by another letter written by none other than the retrieved André, in which he disclosed his true identity and tried to explain his predicament.

Following the summit with the French commanders, which Hamilton summarized, Washington and his entourage left Hartford on September 23. Washington was keen to inspect West Point's defenses, so the return leg of the trip followed a different route from the outward journey, passing through Fishkill on the afternoon of September 24. Soon after, Washington had a chance encounter with the French minister, the Chevalier de la Luzerne, who requested a conference, obliging him to turn back and spend the night at Fishkill.

Next morning, Monday, September 25, Washington rose early, aiming to cover the twelve or so miles to Arnold's headquarters at Robinson's House, on the east bank of the Hudson and just below West Point, before breakfast. When Washington decided upon making a short diversion to examine two redoubts, majors McHenry and Shaw were sent ahead to notify Arnold's household. Washington and his escort arrived at the Robinson House at about 10:30 AM. There, one of Arnold's own aides, Maj. David Franks, explained that while eating breakfast a short while earlier Arnold had been summoned to West Point, but expected to return in an hour. In reality, Arnold had received Jameson's notification of André's capture. An unidentified member of Washington's retinue reported: "His confusion was visible, but no person could devise the cause."[13]

After breakfasting, Washington crossed the Hudson to seek Arnold. But the commandant was not at the fort's landing, and a tour of inspection showed no sign of him. It was after 3:00 PM when Washington, with a mounting sense of unease, started back across the Hudson; nearly 4:00 PM when he reached Robinson's landing. An express rider

---

13. "Extract of a letter from a gentleman at camp . . . Robinson's House, Sept 26, 1780", in *The Pennsylvania Packet, or the General Advertiser*, October 3, 1780. Written by Major McHenry, this confirms his own and Hamilton's roles in that day's events. Also valuable is the account of another, anonymous, member of Washington's party in *The Boston Gazette*, October 16, 1780 ("Extract of a letter from a gentleman, dated Tappan, October 2, 1780")

had just delivered the damning documents forwarded by Colonel Jameson, along with André's candid letter. As Washington read on, the shocking treason was finally revealed.

As a first response, Hamilton and McHenry were sent galloping off southwards to Verplanck's Point, the eastern terminus of King's Ferry where the Hudson narrows to less than a mile, in a belated attempt to intercept the fleeing Arnold. Propelled in his personal barge by eight oarsmen, he'd long since bluffed his way down river to reach the refuge of HMS *Vulture*.

Arnold's escape was swiftly confirmed by a letter from him to Washington, delivered by a boat from the *Vulture*, and forwarded to Robinson's House by Hamilton along with a terse covering note. From Verplanck's Point, Hamilton also wrote a letter on his own initiative alerting Maj. Gen. Nathanael Greene, who commanded in Washington's absence, to the day's startling developments. It begins: "There has just been unfolded at this place a scene of the blackest treason." Later that same evening, when he was back at Robinson's House, Hamilton composed another letter to his fiancée Elizabeth Schuyler describing both the pitiful condition of Arnold's distraught wife, Margaret "Peggy" Shippen, and "the discovery of a treason of the deepest dye."[14]

Greene's general orders to his troops, issued next day from headquarters at Tappan (Orangetown), New York, include the memorable sentence: "Treason of the blackest dye was yesterday discovered." This well-turned phrase, and others that followed, would ensure that Greene's orders of September 26, 1780, became among the most influential and widely-disseminated of any issued during the Revolutionary War: they were reproduced in newspapers, and incorporated verbatim by letter writers and diarists.[15]

Given the wording, which so closely follows Hamilton's distinctive choice of vocabulary, it's tempting to detect his hand here. Although it's unlikely that Greene saw the private letter to Miss Schuyler, it is possible some now-lost note from Hamilton included further hints that subsequently colored the official orders.

Without doubt, *other* writings by Hamilton did much to shape enduring popular perceptions of Arnold's treason and its aftermath. The long, detailed and thoughtful letter that he wrote to his intimate friend

14. All given in *The Papers of Alexander Hamilton*, 2: 438–42.
15. See *The Papers of General Nathanael Greene*, ed. Richard K. Showman (Chapel Hill: University of North Carolina Press), 6: 314–15. On the impact of these orders see John A. Ruddiman, "'A record in the hands of thousands': Power and Negotiation in the Orderly Books of the Continental Army", *William and Mary Quarterly* (3rd ser.), 67 (2010):762.

and fellow aide Lt. Col. John Laurens, sent from Preakness, New Jersey, on October 11, achieved wide circulation after it was printed by newspapers in Philadelphia and elsewhere.[16]

As his letter to Laurens and another to Elizabeth Schuyler make clear, Hamilton was deeply affected by his several meetings with Arnold's collaborator, Major André. Debonair and composed in the face of impending death, André epitomized the gentlemanly code of honor that Hamilton and his brother officers in the Continental Army aspired to. Journals and letters indicate that American officers were increasingly prepared to uphold their "reputation" through dueling: tragically, both Hamilton and his beloved eldest son Philip would fall victim to such deadly "affairs of honor." Ironically, for all the accusations of greed for gold made by "Publius" and many other commentators, Benedict Arnold's belief that his own honor had been impugned by Congress and the Pennsylvania council was clearly a key motivation for his decision to defect to the British—an act widely condemned as among the most *dis*honorable in American history.

The short-lived but intense relationship between Hamilton and André provides the context for a controversial document linked to the fallout from Arnold's treason. This short letter, dated September 30, 1780, and now among the Sir Henry Clinton Papers in the William L. Clements Library at the University of Michigan, raised the possibility of trading André for Arnold. The note is signed with the abbreviation "A. B." but Clinton credited it to Alexander Hamilton, endorsing it "Hamilton Was[hington's] a[ide] de camp received after A[ndre's] death." When the editor of Washington's published *Writings*, John C. Fitzpatrick, who was well-acquainted with Hamilton's handwriting from the many letters and reports he drafted on his commander's behalf, was invited to inspect the letter in 1938, he was "completely satisfied that the original was written by Hamilton and endorsed by Sir Henry."[17]

This attribution was subsequently rejected by the editors of Hamilton's papers on the grounds that the "disguised hand" in which the note is written was not otherwise known to have been used by Hamilton, and because he had assured Elizabeth Schuyler on October 2, 1780, that

16. See for example, *The Pennsylvania Evening Post* on Saturday October 14 and Friday October 20, 1781, and *The Norwich Packet* of November 14, 1780. In these published versions, the letter was slightly edited and credited to "a gentleman at camp to his friend in Philadelphia." The full letter is in *The Papers of Alexander Hamilton*, 2:460–70.

17. Van Doren, *Secret History*, 366–67, 476, with a reproduction opposite 376. The verdict of Fitzpatrick, in a letter to Randolph G. Adams of the Clements Library dated April 18, 1938, is with the letter in the Sir Henry Clinton Papers, Vol. 124/file 34.

while it was proposed to him to suggest to André "the idea of an exchange for Arnold," he could never have acted upon it for fear of forfeiting the major's esteem.[18]

While Hamilton clearly bridled at the prospect of broaching the possibility of such a deal to André, that does not rule out his authorship of the letter. Support for this comes from the fact that Hamilton was in the perfect position to hand it over, as the next day, Sunday October 1, he accompanied Nathanael Greene to a meeting at Dobbs Ferry with British general James Robertson, who was hoping to save André's life. While the generals conferred, Robertson's *aide-de-camp*, Maj. Thomas Murray, "walked elsewhere" with Hamilton and "two other Rebel officers."[19] As Hamilton strolled with Murray he could easily have passed on the letter.

There's also the unambiguous testimony of André's close friend, Col. John Graves Simcoe of the Queen's Rangers, that Hamilton had indeed written just such a letter. In his published journal Simcoe wrote: "Amongst some letters which passed on this unfortunate event, a paper was slid in without signature, but in the handwriting of Hamilton, Washington's secretary, saying, 'that the only way to save André was to give up Arnold.'"[20] Of course, this was the one action that Clinton, who was desperate to save his adjutant, couldn't take. The gallant André went to the gallows at noon on October 2.

Returning to the enigmatic "A. B.," as is well known, Hamilton used that same abbreviation for a series of six articles entitled "The Continentalist" that were published in Loudon's *New-York Packet, and American Advertiser* between July 12, 1781 and July 4, 1782.[21]

---

18. *The Papers of Alexander Hamilton*, 2:445–46.

19. See *Historical Memoirs of William Smith, 1778–1783*, ed. W. H. W. Sabine (New York: New York Times and Arno Press, 1971), 337. See also "Paper of Intelligence transmitted by Andrew Elliot, New York. Narrative of the Capture and Execution of Major John André, 4–5 October 1780," in Benjamin F. Stevens, *Facsimiles of Manuscripts in European Archives Relating to America, 1775–1783* (25 vols., London, 1889–98), Vol. 7, Item 739.

20. John Graves Simcoe, *A Journal of the Operations of the Queen's Rangers, From the End of the Year 1777, to the Conclusion of the Late American War* (Exeter: printed for the author, 1787), Appendix [not paginated]. When Sir Henry Clinton was sent a copy of Simcoe's *Journal*, he made several comments suggesting corrections for any new edition, but did not query this point. See Howard H. Peckham, "Sir Henry Clinton's Review of Simcoe's *Journal*", in *William and Mary Quarterly* (2nd ser.), 21 (1941):361–70.

21. See *The Papers of Alexander Hamilton*, 2:649–52; 654–57; 660–65; 669–74; 3:75–82, 99–106. Acting on Washington's instructions, Hamilton had also written an article "To the New-York Packet", dated Peekskill, August 5, 1780, but which was never published. Ibid., 372–73.

Previously unrecorded, however, is the fact that "A. B." had also been used by the anonymous author of an article published in Loudon's newspaper on April 20, 1780. Written at a time when Hamilton was with Washington at Morristown, New Jersey, this essay tackled a topic close to his heart: the worsening state of his country's finances as the paper currency issued by Congress fueled rampant inflation. In particular, it criticized Congress's decision of March 18 to fix "Continental money at forty to one."[22]

If, as seems highly likely, this earlier "A. B."-initialed piece *was* written by Hamilton, it not only bolsters the case for his authorship of the disputed letter of September 30, 1780, but, by demonstrating a pre-existing connection with Samuel Loudon and his publication, likewise strengthens the argument that he also wrote the "Publius" essay published in *The New-York Packet* on October 12, 1780.

While the evidence examined here is by no means conclusive, taken together it is surely enough to prompt speculation that the substantial "Publius" article inspired by Arnold's treason is a previously-overlooked essay by the young Alexander Hamilton, written in direct response to one of the most infamous episodes in American history. As such it deserves careful scrutiny from Hamilton's growing band of admirers.

Finally, if Alexander Hamilton, the man who'd used the pseudonym "Publius" just two years earlier, who apparently had a prior connection with newspaper editor Loudon, and who most certainly was intimately involved in events following the disclosure of Arnold's plot, didn't write that impassioned appeal to his "dear Countrymen," then another, and equally intriguing, question remains: Who did?

---

22. Hamilton had addressed "the state of our currency" in an extremely long letter to an unknown recipient that his editors believe was written at Morristown sometime between December 1779 and March 1780 (*Papers of Hamilton,* 2:234–51). Like the "Publius" essay discussed above, the "A. B." article of April 20, 1780 was found on the microfilm reel of surviving issues of *The New-York Packet* held in the collections of the New-York Historical Society.

A General's Funeral:
The Burial of Enoch Poor

❦ TODD W. BRAISTED ❦

Untold thousands died during the American Revolution, some by bullets or bayonets, cannon balls or cutlasses, but the vast majority were carried away from life by the innumerable diseases present in both armies. Death came to privates as well as generals, but few accounts of their interment are as detailed as that of Brig. Gen. Enoch Poor of New Hampshire.

Born at Andover, Massachusetts in 1736, Poor joined the revolutionary forces in May 1775, and after serving as colonel of the 2nd New Hampshire Regiment was promoted to brigadier general on February 21, 1777.[1] After serving in numerous battles and campaigns in both the Northern Army and Washington's command, the summer of 1780 found this New England officer in command of one of the battalions of light infantry under Maj. Gen. the Marquis de Lafayette.

Washington, at the head of an army of 14,000 men including the light infantry, marched on August 23, 1780 from Orangetown, New York into Bergen County, New Jersey on a twofold mission: to procure food and forage for hungry soldiers and horses; and to await French troops and warships to cooperate in a final attack on the British in New York City, perhaps finally ending the war that had been raging for over five years. Enoch Poor would not live to see that outcome.

What happened to Enoch Poor the first week of September, 1780 is still unsettled. The army lay at Steenrapie, an area running south to north on the west side of the Hackensack River. Most periods accounts agree that the general died of a fever brought on by some illness. News of his illness had spread through the army. Two Pennsylvania Line sol-

---

1. Francis B. Heitman, *Historical Register of Officers of the Continental Army during the War of the Revolution* (Washington, DC: Rare Book Shop Publishing, 1914), 446.

diers, Daniel Power and Michael Logan, deserted from Fort Lee and informed the British that "General Poor was carried very ill from where the Light Infantry were but they do not know whether he be dead or not."[2] The light infantry camp alluded to was in an area of the modern day town of Oradell, still referred to as "Soldier Hill." On the clear and pleasant morning of September 9, 1780, Andrew Kettall of the 16th Massachusetts Regiment simply noted in his journal, "The Brave Genl. Poor Died."[3]

Kettall was off by a day. Poor actually passed away on September 8, 1780. Another New Englander, Elijah Fisher of the 4th Massachusetts Regiment, got the date right, but perhaps little else: "The 8th Gen. Poor Died, he received his wound by fiteing a duel with a Major. He Commanded the [Light] Infintry and belonged to New Hampshire."[4] The rumors of Enoch Poor succumbing to a wound from a duel exists to this day. To be sure, dueling occurred in the army's camp at that time. Brig. Gen. Ebenezer Huntington, writing on August 30, 1780, mentioned "four days ago a duel was fought between Lt. [Dade] Peyton and another officer, both of them of Maryland [Moyland's] Horse;[5] Peyton was killed, the other wounded. The next day a duel was fought between Baskenridge, Wm. Livingston & a Mr. [John] Stack, volunteer in the Marechosa Horse.[6] Livingston was killed, & buried the night before last at Hackensack."[7] It is entirely possible that Elijah Fisher mistook one of these duels for the cause of Poor's passing.

Washington, in his after orders of September 9, 1780, announced funeral arrangements to the army: "Brigadier General Poor will be interred tomorrow afternoon at Hackensack Church; the funeral procession will commence at four o'clock from Brower's house in front

2. Sir Henry Clinton, Information of Deserters and Others, Not Included in Private Intelligence, From October, 1780 to March 26, 1781. Emmett Collection, EM. C*, New York Public Library.

3. Journal of Andrew Kettall, entry for September 9, 1780. Collection M-804, Pension and Bounty Land Application Files, No. W13568, Andrew Kettell, Massachusetts, National Archives and Records Administration.

4. *Elijah Fisher's Journal While In The War For Independence And Continued Two Years After He Came To Maine 1775–1784* (Augusta, Maine: Badger and Manley, 1880), 39–40.

5. Moyland's was the 4th Light Dragoons.

6. The Marechaussee Corps, commanded by Capt. Bartholomew von Heer, ironically was a provost unit created to help keep discipline in the army.

7. Huntington to Col. Samuel B. Webb, Teaneck, August 30, 1780. J. Watson Webb, *Reminiscences of Gen'l Samuel B. Webb* (New York: Globe Stationary and Printing Company, 1882), 209–210.

of the Infantry."[8] Surgeon James Thacher, a comrade of Andrew Kettall in the 16th Massachusetts Regiment, left a remarkable account of General Poor's funeral the next day. It shows the somber military procession, based closely on popular European military textbooks,[9] and perhaps a level of professionalism in the Continental Army that would not have been likely earlier in the war:

> We are now lamenting the loss of Brigadier-General Poor, who died last night of putrid fever. His funeral solemnities have been attended this afternoon. The corpse was brought this morning from Paramus, and left at a house about a mile from the burying-yard at Hackensack, whence it was attended to the place of interment by the following procession: a regiment of light infantry, in uniform, with arms reversed; four field-pieces; Major Lee's regiment of light-horse; General Hand and his brigade; the major on horseback; two chaplains; the horse of the deceased, with his boots and spurs suspended from the saddle, led by a servant; the corpse borne by four serjeants, and the pall supported by six general officers. The coffin was of mahogany, and a pair of pistols and two swords, crossing each other and tied with black crape, were placed on the top. The corpse was followed by the officers of the New Hampshire brigade; the officers of the brigade of light-infantry, which the deceased had lately commanded. Other officers fell in promiscuously, and were followed by his Excellency General Washington, and other general officers. Having arrived at the burying-yard, the troops opened to the right and left, resting on their arms reversed, and the procession passed to the grave, where a short eulogy was delivered by the Rev. Mr. Evans. A band of music, with a number of drums and fifes, played a funeral dirge, the drums were muffled with black crape, and the officers in the procession wore crape round the left arm. The regiment of light-infantry were in handsome uniform, and wore in their caps long feathers of black and red. The elegant regiment of horse, commanded by Major Lee, being in complete uniform and well disciplined, exhibited a martial and noble appearance. No scene can exceed in grandeur and solemnity a military funeral. The weapons

8. General After Orders, September 9, 1780. George Washington Papers, Series 3, Continental Army Papers 1775–1783, Subseries G, General Orders, Letterbook 5, April 11, 1780 — September 5, 1781, Varick Transcripts, Library of Congress.

9. See, for example, *Regulations for the Prussian Infantry, Translated from the German Original* (London: J. Nourse, 1759), 321–327; Thomas Simes, *Military Course for the Government and Conduct of a Battalion* (London: printed for the author, 1777), 8–13; Robert Hinde, *The Discipline of the Light Horse* (London: W. Owen, 1778), 308–313.

of war reversed, and embellished with the badges of mourning, the slow and regular step of the procession, the mournful sound of the unbraced drum and deep-toned instruments, playing the melancholy dirge, the majestic mien and solemn march of the war-horse, all conspire to impress the mind with emotions which no language can describe, and which nothing but the reality can paint to the liveliest imagination. General Poor was from the state of New Hampshire. He was a true patriot, who took an early part in the cause of his country, and during his military career was respected for his talents and his bravery, and beloved for the amiable qualities of his heart. But it is a sufficient eulogy to say, that he enjoyed the confidence and esteem of Washington.[10]

Enoch Poor (1736–1780).

Long after the war had ended, and many of the high-ranking officers who had led the fight for independence had passed on, General Poor's grave had one very special visitor, one whose youth during the Revolution enabled him to survive well into the nineteenth century when many of his comrades of similar rank had long since departed. In 1825, the United States was approaching its fiftieth anniversary as a free and independent country, and one of its early heroes was returning for a tour, the Marquis de Lafayette. Amongst the places on his itinerary was Hackensack, which certainly greeted him with all the pomp and ceremony the countryside was capable of. One local resident, Nicholas P. Terhune, was an eye-witness and fifty years later sent an account of the event to the *New Jersey Republican* newspaper. Terhune's account shows what held importance to Lafayette:

> It was in the summer of '25 when he came to Hackensack in the month of June. Mr. Levi Haywood made the address on this occasion, of which I was an ear witness.
>
> The General's reply was very brief, but very much to the purpose. He said, "I recognize this place, for," pointing to the church yard, right opposite "there lies buried one of my brave generals."

10. James Thatcher, *A Military Journal During the American Revolutionary War, from 1775 to 1783* (Boston, MA: Cottons & Barnard, 1827), 212–213.

Almost immediately after, he went to the church yard accompanied by the committee among whom Robert Campbell, Esq., and Archibald Campbell, Esq., were quite conspicuous. I also remember seeing the portly form of William Halsey, Esq., of Newark, among them.

They all stood uncovered for a few moments looking at the slab which covers the remains. "That" said he, "was one of my Generals."[11]

In recent years, the Bergen County Historical Society has revived an earlier tradition of the 110–plus-year-old organization, namely, placing a wreath at General Poor's grave each Memorial Day. They believe without doubt this son of New England would approve.

11. The account is published in Kevin Wright's *The Nation's Guest—Lafayette* on the website of the Bergen County Historical Society, www.bergencountyhistory.org/Pages/lafayette.html, accessed April 21, 2016.

Top Ten Banastre Tarleton Myths

❦ JOHN KNIGHT ❦

He was arguably the greatest "anti-Hero" produced by either side during the Revolutionary War. From Washington Irving to Mel Gibson, so much has been written about the career of Banastre Tarleton that it is difficult, even today, to separate man from myth. Yet many of the most persistent and damning indictments of him are also those most easily refuted as historically exaggerated, or even quite simply, untrue. Here we look at ten of the most damaging or obstinate myths about the British Cavalry leader absolutely no contemporary called "Bloody Ban!"

I. HE MADE HIS LIVING BEFORE AND AFTER THE WAR AS A SLAVE TRADER.
Tarleton's father John certainly made his fortune from the slave trade. His three brothers were also heavily involved in both the West Indies sugar trade and the Atlantic slave trade. Banastre, however, was the only son of four to never join the family business, and being a notorious spendthrift showed little inclination for the disciplines of commerce. He was nonetheless a vociferous opponent of those who aimed at ending the slave trade in the British Empire, particularly William Wilberforce MP, whose policies he referred to as a "mistaken philanthropy."[1] After the war, Tarleton was elected as MP for Liverpool and unfailingly argued that the city's prosperity had been built on commerce, and that the slave trade in particular had been instrumental in propelling the town from struggling provincial port to Britain's second city.[2] His op-

1. R. G. Thorne, *The History of the House of Commons* (London: Boydell and Brewer 1986), 1:232, also on line at www.historyofparliamentonline.org/volume/17901820/member/tarleton-banastre-1754–1833.
2. The International Slavery Museum credits Liverpool as being responsible for employing over half the world's slave ships by 1750. www.liverpoolmuseums.org.uk/ism/srd/liverpool.aspx.

position to the Abolition movement never wavered throughout his long Parliamentary career.[3]

2. HE WAS AN ARROGANT, DETACHED, BRUTAL MARTINET.

This has been the "default" portrayal of Tarleton in American history for over two hundred years. His reputation as a ruthless thug has been almost universally accepted, and unquestioned, through popular folk tale and sober history alike. "We look in vain for any redeeming trait in his character" the nineteenth century historian C.L Hunter concluded, a judgement enduring into the twentieth century with the influential historian Christopher Ward emotively describing him as "cold hearted, vindictive and utterly ruthless."[4] As late as 1976 the author Charles Bracelen Flood felt able to go further still with a piece of doggerel psychoanalysis that concluded Tarleton was "the sort of man who needs a war to legitimise his violent and cruel impulses."[5] Mel Gibson's cinematic portrayal of a fictionalized Tarleton as a sardonic, brutal, sociopath is based largely on these and similarly unflattering histories.

Yet no contemporary who actually met Tarleton described him in such terms. That he was vain, there is no doubt, but haughty he certainly wasn't. Indeed *The Times* noted rather condescendingly that "his frankness and bonhomie make him popular among the 'lower orders' of his constituents."[6] The Comte de Revel on meeting Tarleton after his surrender at Gloucester Point described him as a young, pleasant man: "He had a most gentle and genteel face as well as elegance, a certain air of ease, and French manners."[7] That Tarleton drilled his Legion relentlessly in quiet times, and drove it hard in battle is not doubted, but he was no martinet, and it is accepted that his men greatly respected and even loved him; the Waxhaw's massacre, often blamed on Tarleton, was largely instigated by their distress on mistakenly hearing he had been killed.

An intelligent, complex, but contradictory man, perhaps the most pithy summary of Tarleton's personality came from his erstwhile lover, Mary Robinson, who in her novel "The False Friend" portrays her

---

3. Thorne, *The History of the House of Commons)*, 1:232.

4. Chistopher Ward, *The War of the American Revolution* (New York: McMillan & Co., 1952), 701.

5. Charles Bracelen Flood, *Fight and Rise Again. Perilous Times Along the Road to Independence* (New York: Dodd Meade & Co., 1976), 259.

6. Thorne, *The History of the House of Commons.*

7. Comte de Revel, *Journal particulier d'une campaign aux indies occidentals 1781–1782* (Paris: H. Charles Lavauzelle, 1898), 169. In this fascinating French language account of the war in the Indies and Chesapeake, Tarleton is referred to as "Talton."

barely disguised hero Treville as being "too polite to be religious, too witty to be learned and too handsome to be discreet."[8]

3. HE ORDERED THE WAXHAWS MASSACRE.

Tarleton's black reputation rests predominantly on his supposed actions at the Battle of Waxhaws, with "Tarleton's Quarter" becoming a rallying cry, inspiration to recruitment, and propaganda indictment against the supposed brutality of Loyalist and British forces for the rest of the war. However, much modern study has been undertaken on the battle and many previously accepted "facts" about its course have now been challenged.[9] That the British Legion continued to attack Patriot soldiers after most had sought to surrender is not disputed. However, that this butchery took place under the eyes, indeed with the complicit approval, of their commander is now widely disputed. Tarleton's horse was shot from under him, pinning him to the ground during the battle, and it is this single act that appears to have led to the subsequent confused, rudderless massacre of over one hundred Patriot soldiers, or a quarter of Colonel Buford's entire force. Tarleton himself wrote of the battle that the high American casualties were attributed to the Legion being "stimulated to a vindictive asperity not easily restrained" after Legion cavalry heard a rumor that their leader had been killed.[10] However, there is not the slightest shred of evidence that he condoned, much less ordered any such behaviour himself. Of course it could be argued that the Legion's ill-discipline, following on from similar episodes at the battle of Monck's Corner and smaller engagements, was ultimately the responsibility of its commanding officer.

4. HE AND HIS SUPERIOR, LORD CORNWALLIS, HATED EACH OTHER.

We have Mel Gibson's *The Patriot* to thank for one of the more recent myths surrounding Tarleton. In the film, Tarleton (or Tavington) is constantly rebuked by his superior Cornwallis. "Damn him! Damn that man!" his exasperated Lordship cries when Tavington disobeys yet another battle order. The entire film goes to great lengths to portray Cornwallis as regarding Tarleton with both a patrician disdain and barely concealed contempt.

8. Mary Robinson, *The False Friend* (London: Longman & Reece, 1799), 42.
9. C. Leon Harris, "Massacre at Waxhaws," Southern Campaigns of the American Revolution, May 2016, www.southerncampaign.org/2016/05/16/massacre-at-waxhaws-theevidence-from-wounds/ . This excellent forensic study of the wounds reported after the battle amongst patriot soldiers summarizes neatly the modern conflicting arguments around the "massacre" or "myth" debate.
10. Banastre Tarleton, *A history of the Campaigns of 1780 and 1781 in the Southern Provinces of North America* (London: T. Cadell, 1787), 31.

In fact Cornwallis was a mentor to Tarleton during the war, giving him his full support and an unprecedented free hand throughout the Carolinas campaign. This favored position induced much jealousy among fellow officers, who felt themselves continually overlooked for promotion. Lt. Col. John Graves Simcoe, commanding officer of the Queens Rangers, an elite Loyalist regiment, made constant complaints to Sir Henry Clinton about Cornwallis's preferences for Tarleton despite his own seniority. Cornwallis's official and private dispatches were littered with compliments showered on his Cavalry chief, many of which unquestionably strayed from military protocol. He ended one dispatch to Tarleton with the almost plaintive "I wish you could get *three* Legions and divide yourself into three parts. We can do no good without you."[11] His official report after the victory of Camden included the briefest of praise to his infantry commanders Lord Rawdon and Lt. Col. James Webster before devoting an entire paragraph to Tarleton's operations, ending with, "this action was too brilliant . . . and will highly recommend Col. Tarleton to his majesty's favour."[12]

It is true that Tarleton and Cornwallis had a severe falling out after the war when Tarleton's vainglorious military recollections attempted to shift blame onto Cornwallis for the defeats at Cowpens and Yorktown, but during the war itself they had a harmonious, constructive relationship that was akin to that of father and son.

5. HE RETURNED TO ENGLAND IN SHAME AND IGNOMINY.

Most British senior officers returned to England after the war to severe criticism from their compatriots. Sir William Howe, Sir Henry Clinton, John Burgoyne and Charles Earl Cornwallis all received varying degrees of blame and censure for the loss of the American colonies. But Tarleton was almost unique in attracting no such rebuke. Lacking any real war heroes, he was received home with universal acclaim, being feted at court and becoming an intimate friend to two future kings, George Prince of Wales and William Duke of Clarence, even sharing a mistress with the former. He was famously painted by the two greatest portrait painters of the age, Sir Joshua Reynolds and Thomas Gainsborough.

6. HE DESIGNED THE "TARLETON" HELMET.

Perhaps the most iconic headgear of the entire war, this leather helmet with a sturdy tapered peak was adorned by a fur crest and dyed feather plume. The British cavalry certainly came to refer to this dragoon head-

11. Ibid., 202.
12. Charles Marquis Cornwallis, Correspondence (London: John Murray, 1859), 494.

dress as a "Tarleton" Helmet. But it was in
use in various forms on the European continent well before the war and was in fact introduced to the British by Lt. Gen. William
Keppel in 1771. There is doubt too that Ban
even introduced it to the British Legion,
with Lord Cathcart (the regiment's original
commander and later Quartermaster General of the entire army) being it's more likely
sponsor. Regarded as the best looking headgear of the war, its attractiveness was such
that it was worn by both British and American forces and long survived the conflict,
being in common usage in the British army
until 1812 when it was replaced by the more
robust French-influenced shako.

Banastre Tarleton
(1754–1833).

7. HE RAPED AND ABUSED WOMEN DURING THE WAR.

That Tarleton was what we would now refer to as a "womaniser" there
is no conjecture. He had many mistresses, infamously bedding both the
Regency courtesan Mary Robinson and then allegedly her own daughter Maria. He seems to have adopted a sporting attitude to his conquest
of women, rakishly seducing them for a wager on more than one occasion.[13] This certainly makes the oft reported, though second-hand
quote, that he "ravished more women in America than any other man"
plausible.[14] However, portraits show Tarleton as a handsome man, with
a fine physical figure who was both charming and dashing. Most contemporary accounts by females who crossed his path attain to his gentlemanly manners and good grace, and Tarleton appears to have been
more a professional wooer of women than a dissolute brute. He also
saw members of his own British Legion hanged and flogged when they
raped and abused women, and there is absolutely no evidence that he
ever behaved with anything other than a reserved gallantry towards Patriot women in their person, though of course he was not quite so liberal
in his treatment of their property!

8. HE SLASHED THE FOREHEAD OF THE YOUNG ANDREW JACKSON.

This hoary old chestnut still turns up occasionally even in academic

13. Robert D Bass, *The Green Dragoon: the lives of Banastre Tarleton and Mary Robinson*
(London: Alvin Redman, 1957), 197.
14. Michael Pearson, *Those Damned Rebels: The American Revolution as seen through British
eyes* (Boston: Da Capo Press, 2009), 334.

studies and one can only put its longevity down to it making such a great story! Jackson, forthright and brave, a representative of the New World and new social order, encounters Tarleton his abuser, an Imperial despot, pitiless and haughty. Historical circumstances also meant that it *could* have happened. Certainly the future President, at the time already a battle-hardened thirteen year old boy, was slashed over the head by a British officer for having the temerity to refuse the demand to clean his boots.[15] It also happened at the Waxhaws, scene of Tarleton's most vicious battle, and Ban was known to be in the vicinity at the time. Unfortunately for historical conspiracy theorists, Jackson himself never named Tarleton as his tormenter, something he would surely have done, having admitted that he once saw him riding by less than one hundred yards away "and could have shot him."[16]

9. THE DISASTROUS AMERICAN WAR ENDED HIS MILITARY CAREER.

It says much about the impact Tarleton had on British military fortunes, that when the war ended he had been promoted, without purchase, from lowly cornet to lieutenant colonel in a meteoric five years. This was far from the end of his career, and he remained on active service or half pay until the end of the Napoleonic Wars, ultimately being promoted to the rank of full general in 1812. However, Ban was adept at courting influential enemies as much as he was powerful friends, and his reciprocated loathing of the Duke of Wellington may have had more than a little to do with the fact that he never commanded troops in action again after Yorktown.

10. HE WAS KNOWN TO CONTEMPORARIES AS "BLOODY BAN" OR THE "GREEN DRAGOON," AND LED "TARLETON'S RAIDERS."

The two personal monikers, the alternatingly violent and romantic caricatures by which Tarleton is now largely known, are sobriquets of pure fiction. There is no evidence that Tarleton was ever referred to by either name, though there is testimony that after Waxhaws he was known in Patriot circles as "The Butcher." Both labels appear no earlier than the 1950s, originating in the Robert Bass book *The Green Dragoon*. This was the first serious reappraisal of Tarleton's life since his death, and the nicknames simply seem to have been just too good not to have stuck.

---

15. James Patton, *The Life of Andrew Jackson* (New York: Mason Bros., 1869), 89.
16. Andrew Burstein, The Passions of Andrew Jackson (New York: Random House, 2003), 8. Tarleton is described as "a twenty-six-year old terrorist who dressed the part of a dandy in tight breeches and tall black boots and directed his men to slash and stab and spare no one."

The "Tarleton's raiders" tag occurred with increasing regularity after the American Civil War. Various Confederate partisan and guerrilla cavalry units, like Mosby's and Quantrill's, came to be named after their commanding officers, and writers began following the same fashion with the British Legion, the corps that Tarleton commanded. But the British Legion was never an irregular partisan unit, and though it carried out many daring raids, it was a mixed force of dragoon cavalry, light Infantry and small calibre artillery. Indeed, it was taken onto the British regular establishment in 1782, conferring on it official recognition of its prowess. Vain as he was, Tarleton would have been horrified at any title like "raiders" that diminished his elite regiment to the periphery of "respectable" warfare. In this final ignominy, American historians have perhaps dealt him the lowest blow of all!

How Yorktown Almost Couldn't Afford to Happen

JOHN L. SMITH JR.

Gen. George Washington, from the point of view of Americans being trapped at "York,"[1] wrote these prophetic words: "These by being upon a narrow neck of land, would be in danger of being cut off. The enemy might very easily throw up a few ships into York and James' river, as far as Queens Creek; and land a body of men there, who throwg up a few Redoubts, would intercept their retreat and oblige them to surrender at discretion."[2]

But this wasn't in connection to the famous Siege of Yorktown that we know. The words were written in 1777, four years before Yorktown. Washington was advising Brig. Gen. Thomas Nelson Jr. that he foresaw a natural trap in the plans Nelson had to base American troops at Yorktown as a way to observe British naval convoys. Washington had foreseen the situation that set itself up on the Yorktown peninsula in the spring of 1781. But in 1781, the British *would be in danger of being cut off* and the Americans could *intercept their retreat and oblige them to surrender.*

Washington, camped at Dobb's Ferry, New York, east of the Hudson River, had spent the spring and summer of 1781 concentrating on plans to attack Clinton's fully entrenched British forces within New York City. Retaking New York had been pretty much an obsession with Washington since he and the Continental Army had been badly defeated and driven out of the city in 1776. By mid-July, 1781 Washington and Maj.

---

1. Meaning York-Town, Virginia.
2. From George Washington to Brigadier General Thomas Nelson, Jr., 2 September 1777, The Papers of George Washington, Revolutionary War Series, vol. 11, 19 August 1777–25 October 1777, ed. Philander D. Chase and Edward G. Lengel. Charlottesville: University Press of Virginia, 2001, 128–130.

Gen. Comte Jean de Rochambeau were sizing up the British defenses "on the North end of York Island"[3] in preparation for the assault.

Washington was also aware that the French fleet of Admiral François de Grasse had set sail northward from Cape Francois bound for the American coast. The exact destination of the fleet, however, was still a mystery. It could be New York Harbor; it could be the Chesapeake Bay. To avoid a misunderstanding, Washington left no doubt in Admiral de Grasse's mind about a New York destination: ". . . that City and its dependencies are our primary objects."[4] In the same letter, Washington mentioned that the "relief of Virginia" could—perhaps—be a "second object" if New York somehow became impossible; but that, "I flatter myself the glory of destroying the British Squadron at New York is reserved for the King's Fleet under your command, and that of the land Force at the same place for the allied arms."

Now jump ahead to August 14 and everything had changed *radically!* Washington received word from Newport, Rhode Island that Admiral Comte de Grasse would, indeed, sail into the Chesapeake Bay, Virginia within a few weeks, complete with "between 25 & 29 Sail of the line & 3200 land Troops."[6] To Washington's credit, he wrote in his personal journal, "Matters having now come to a crisis and a decisive plan to be determined on—I was obliged . . . to give up all idea of attacking New York."[7] But things would have to happen fast. De Grasse said his fleet could only stay for two months, and then they would have to head back south to avoid hurricane season on the American east coast.

For Robert Morris, a monumental sense of panic replaced any good feelings others had of successful Yorktown plans falling into place. Just three days before, on August 11, Washington had met with "Robt. Morris Esqr. Superintendent of Finance . . . to make the consequent arrangements for [the Continental Army's] establishment and support"[8] of the New York campaign. Even with those plans, Morris had been scrambling to find the funds, materials and supplies to finance the joint American-French assault upon New York.

---

3. John Rhodehamel, ed., *George Washington—Writings*, "Journal of the Yorktown Campaign", (New York, The Library of America, 1997), 440.
4. From George Washington to François-Joseph-Paul, comte de Grasse-Tilly, 21 July 1781, Founders Online, National Archives, last modified July 12, 2016, (accessed July 27, 2016); http://founders.archives.gov/documents/Washington/99–01–02–06471.
5. Ibid.
6. Rhodehamel, *George Washington—Writings*, "Journal of the Yorktown Campaign," 451.
7. Ibid.
8. Ibid, 450.

NEW YORK'S OUT; YORKTOWN'S IN

News of the radical (and expensive) change of strategies left Morris completely rattled as to how to pay for the very long march of the armies southward to Virginia, let alone pay for any action happening once they arrived. Washington asked Morris for an estimate of the new plan's expenses. On August 21, Morris stalled on the request, saying that he needed time "to consider, to calculate."[9] At least one good thing came out of the change of objectives: the British were now so sure that New York was the object of the Franco-American attack that Cornwallis had been ordered to entrench in a Virginian seacoast port (Yorktown) and to ready half of his army to ship to New York for needed reinforcements. Cornwallis had inserted himself directly into the Patriot trap.

On August 22, Robert Morris replied to General Washington, telling him the truth. "I am sorry to inform you that I find Money Matters in as bad a Situation as possible."[10] He added that the states, which had promised to pay their fair share of expenses, had very rarely come through with those payments. All Morris could offer in this next crisis was the value of his personal credit, which even Morris himself was secretly beginning to doubt. Washington told Morris to do what he could since the American and French forces were *already* secretly moving down from New York to Philadelphia. A small diversionary force was left in New York so as not to tip off the British of their movements.

From Philadelphia, the initial plan was to transport the troops from Chester, Pennsylvania (ten miles to the southwest of Philadelphia) down to Virginia. Washington strongly reiterated that this movement of combined forces to Yorktown was *so* important, it *had* to happen. Morris assured Washington that he'd find a way to pay for it. But privately he didn't know how. The country was absolutely, completely broke.

The same day, August 22, 1781, Morris sent letters to the thirteen states—both trying to shame them and warn them:

> We are on the Eve of the most Active Operations, and should they be in anywise retarded by the want of necessary Supplies, the most unhappy Consequences may follow. Those who may be justly chargeable with Neglect, will have to Answer for it to their Country, to their Allies, to the present generation, and to all Posterity.[11]

9. Charles Rappleye, *Robert Morris, Financier of the American Revolution* (New York, Simon & Shuster, 2010), 256.
10. To George Washington from Robert Morris, 22 August 1781, Founders Online, National Archives, last modified July 12, 2016,(accessed July 28, 2016); http://founders.archives.gov/documents/Washington/99-01-02-06758.
11. From Robert Morris to The States, 22 August 1781, Founders Online, National Archives, last modified July 12, 2016, (accessed July 28, 2016); http://founders.archives.gov/documents/Washington/99-01-02-06759.

THE ARMY'S NEAR STRIKE FOR PAY

Now back in Philadelphia, Morris personally followed up his threat-letters to the states with Thomas McKeon, the president of Congress. Morris wanted to put the pressure on McKeon for the funds spelled out by The Articles of Confederation, Article VIII: "All charges of war, and all other expenses that shall be incurred for the common defense . . . shall be defrayed out of a common treasury, which shall be supplied by the several States."[12] But because there was no Articles of Confederation enforcement clause, the states gave a pittance to the national treasury, sometimes, whenever they felt like it, and only once their own state needs were taken care of. So essentially McKeon told Morris that the treasury was empty and with state debt and inflation running wild, not to expect any money in the near future . . . if ever. The proposed Bank of North America, a potential new source of credit and funds, existed only on paper.

Morris had no time and had to act. To fund the Yorktown campaign, Morris was now clutching at desperate financial straws. Based upon his good word and credit alone, Morris printed and issued Office of Finance currency backed only by Robert Morris's promise to pay. These bills, used as cash, became known as "Morris Notes" around Philadelphia. They paid a few very large and overdue Continental Army bills and kept some small immediate supplies flowing to the American and French armies on the road. (The Morris Notes that could be redeemed immediately were nicknamed "short Bobs," and the ones with a longer length of time specified were called "long Bobs"—both referring to Morris' first name of Robert).

But "Morris Notes" weren't enough, by far, to pay for the Yorktown expedition, and were only stalling tactics by Morris to buy small amounts of time. The next crisis happened when the Yorktown-bound American soldiers arrived in Philadelphia on their way to Chester, the next staging area. The revised plan was that from Chester, the combined French and American forces would march to the Head of Elk, Maryland. At that point, some would sail down the Chesapeake, some would march to Virginia. It was a hot southern summer and the heat and humidity made the soldiers tired, cranky and edgy.

To help with morale, Washington arranged for a festive fife and drum parade through the Philadelphia streets. Although cheered on by residents, the tired, hot, hungry and dirty campaigners almost choked on the dust cloud that their marching feet stirred up. And that wasn't all.

12. Barbara Silberdick Feinberg, *The Articles of Confederation, the First Constitution of the United States* (Brookfield, CT., Twenty-First Century Books, 2002), 80.

The New England soldiers in particular decided they weren't budging without getting some pay. They hadn't been paid in a year and refusing to move from the capital city until they got paid seemed to make perfect sense.

George Washington—again—turned to Robert Morris for help. On August 27, Washington pleaded,

> I must entreat you if possible to procure one months pay in specie for the detachment which I have under my command part of those troops have not been paid any thing for a very long time past, and have upon several occasions shewn marks of great discontent. . . If the whole sum cannot be obtained, a part of it will be better than none.[13]

Morris knew his own Morris Notes wouldn't appease the belligerent troops. Only "specie" (hard coins) would do, as Washington had said in his letter. Morris was down to his last angle to get some cash—he went across town to have a heart-to-heart meeting with Rochambeau at the house of the Chevalier La Luzerne (Anne-César de La Luzerne), the French Minister to the United States. After listening, Rochambeau said he was hard up for cash, too. But he passed along the rumor that supposedly Admiral de Grasse was bringing with him on his flagship *lots of Spanish silver!* The bad news was that as far as Rochambeau knew, the coins were just for French use. However he added that the person who would know more details was the treasurer of the French Special Expedition forces . . . but—unfortunately—he was on the road to Chester. The whole military plan was in motion, money or not, and Rochambeau himself said he'd be leaving for Chester within hours.

THE TWO MORRIS'S DESPERATE SILVER HUNT

Robert Morris rushed back and found one of his best friends (but no relation), Gouverneur Morris, and together the two Morris's set out on horses to hunt down the French treasurer. They weren't on the road long when they spotted another rider hurriedly riding toward them. By a fortunate twist of fate, it was a courier who'd been sent by General George Washington with an important packet of letters for "Superintendent of Finance—Robert Morris." Morris quickly opened the correspondence and sure enough, one letter in particular gave incredible, almost miraculous news! Admiral de Grasse had indeed arrived at

---

13. From George Washington to Robert Morris, 27 August 1781, Founders Online, National Archives, last modified July 12, 2016,(accessed August 1, 2016); http://founders. archives.gov/documents/Washington/99–01–02–06802.

Chesapeake Bay and with him—confirmed—were the barrels of Spanish silver!

The Morris's arrived in Chester and instead of locating the French treasurer, found Rochambeau already there. He had sailed down the Delaware River to save time and was as excited as Robert Morris was with the news of the hard coins having arrived. Morris thought a financial loan might now be authorized on the spot because of Rochambeau's presence rather than Morris having to find him. The agreement was made. Morris staved off a soldier rebellion of sorts and bought more time for Washington at Yorktown. The deal was that the French would loan Morris twenty thousand dollars in specie coin on the terms that it be repaid by October 1. The next day back in Philadelphia, Morris sent Washington an update along with copies of letters sent to Rochambeau confirming the terms of the loan,

> In Consequence of the Conversation I had the Honor to hold with your Excellency yesterday and of your Promise to supply to the United States the sum of twenty thousand Dollars for an immediate Purpose, to be replaced on the first day of October next, I have directed Mr Philip Audibert the bearer of this Letter to wait upon you. I shall be much obliged to your Excellency if you will be pleased to direct that the above Sum be paid to Mr Audibert . . . I will take Care that the money be replaced at the time agreed upon.[14]

Morris arrived back at the office only to find many other urgent requests for money. The governors of New Jersey and New York lacked the funds to get critically-needed herds of cattle down to the Continental Army. The garrison at West Point needed flour desperately and the state government said it could not help. The field army of Nathanael Greene was close to running out of food. The Virginia troops under the Marquis de Lafayette had chased Cornwallis into Yorktown and were holding them there. But Lafayette said he expected to run out of provisions very soon unless reinforcements and food made it there in time. Robert Morris privately complained within the pages of his diary, "It seems as if every person connected in Public Service entertain an opinion that I am full of money."[15]

14. To George Washington from Robert Morris, 6 September 1781, Founders Online, National Archives, last modified July 12, 2016, (accessed August 7, 2016); http://founders.archives.gov/documents/Washington/99-01-02-06904. Philip Audibert, Esq. at this time was assistant paymaster general of the Continental Army.
15. Robert Morris diary entry, 11 September 1781, *The Papers of Robert Morris II, 1781–1784: August-September 1781* (Pittsburgh, PA., University of Pittsburg Press, 1975), 244.

General Washington had departed already in advance of his army marching down to Yorktown leaving the disgruntled troops still sitting in Philadelphia insisting on being paid. Once again, luck smiled upon Morris and the French barrels of silver arrived at the Office of Finance just in time. Robert Morris instructed that John Pierce, Paymaster-General of the Continental Army, should make a spectacle showing of the specie coin when paying the sullen soldiers. So Pierce cracked open the top of one of the barrels and for grand effect, dumped the barrel on its side, letting the silver coins spill out. Crisis averted, and Morris knew word would travel quickly that soldiers were being paid in coins, not Continental dollars, certificates or vouchers.

But the crisis *wasn't* averted and Morris would get no letup.

Soon afterwards Gen. Benjamin Lincoln reported to Morris that the coins had run out prematurely and that everyone hadn't gotten paid!

The total was a little over six thousand dollars short. Lincoln warned Morris, "It will be difficult if not impossible to keep the men quiet who did not receive their pay."[16] Once again, Morris begged, borrowed and promised, based on no collateral but his good name and credit, and somehow got the money needed. He wrote to Lincoln, "I supplied the Pay Master General with Six thousand two hundred Dollars in preference of the many other demands that came on me."[17]

Although Yorktown was now financed to happen, fate told Morris the outcome of Yorktown *had* to be an allied victory. Money was gone, inflation fears made dollars near useless, and Robert Morris was at the end of his financial ropes. A Yorktown victory would mean new excitement in the international monetary arena and new offers of loans and lines of credit would likely come pouring in from foreign governments. But without a victory, well, Morris told the unvarnished truth to Joseph Reed on September 20, 1781: "The late Movements of the Army have so entirely drained me of Money, that I have been Obliged to pledge my personal Credit very deeply, in a variety of instances, besides borrowing Money from my Friends; and . . . every Shilling of my own."[18]

Yorktown had to be a victory. It was "game over" otherwise.

16. Benjamin Lincoln to Robert Morris, 8 September 1781, *The Papers of Robert Morris II, 17811784: August-September 1781* (Pittsburgh, PA., University of Pittsburg Press, 1975), 220.
17. Robert Morris to Benjamin Lincoln, 11 September 1781, ibid, 252.
18. Robert Morris to Joseph Reed, 20 September 1781, ibid, 309. Joseph Reed at the time of Yorktown was president of the Pennsylvania Supreme Executive Council. Pennsylvania had gone bankrupt the year before and it was Robert Morris who also brought it back into solvency.

How Article 7 Freed 3000 Slaves

BOB RUPPERT

The American Peace Commissioners, Benjamin Franklin, John Adams, John Jay, and Henry Laurens, signed the preliminary articles of peace in Paris with Richard Oswald, the British Commissioner, at the Hotel de York on November 30, 1782. The French Foreign Minister, Count de Vergennes, learned of the treaty and wrote to the French minister to the United States, Chevalier de la Luzerne, on December 19.[1] His letter was on the *General Washington,* the same packet vessel that brought news of the treaty to Philadelphia on March 12, 1783; the actual treaty arrived on March 24 aboard the French cutter *Triumph.*[2] Between the 12th and the 24th, la Luzerne remonstrated against the secret conduct of the American ministers to Robert R. Livingston, the Secretary for Foreign Affairs for the United States, and to sundry members of Congress, but it had little effect. On April 15, the preliminary articles of peace were approved by the Continental Congress.

There were nine articles in the treaty, eight of which were as follows:

Article 1 declared the United States to be free, sovereign, and independent;

Article 2 delineated the borders of the United States;

Article 3 permitted United States citizens to fish off all the banks of Newfoundland;

Article 4 stated that creditors were not to be impeded in the recovery of their debts;

1. Mary A. Giunta, *The Emerging Nation: A Documentary History of the Foreign Relations of the United States under the Articles of Confederation, 1780–1789* (Washington DC: National History Publication and Records Commission, 1996), 1:728–29.
2. Robert R. Livingston to George Washington, March 24, 1783," Founders Online, National Archives, http://founders.archives.gov/documents/Washington/99–01–02–109 10.

Articles 5 recommended to the states that all land and properties confiscated be returned to their rightful owners;

Article 6 recommended that there be no future confiscations or prosecution against any person or persons for their part in the war;

Article 8 stated that navigation of the Mississippi River forever would remain free;

Article 9 stated that any place or territory taken by the other side after November 30, 1782 but before the arrival of these articles in America would be restored without difficulty, or requiring any compensation.

Each of these articles fell under the direction of either the Continental Congress or the state legislatures. Article 7, however, fell under the direction of General Washington. It stated, "all hostilities both by sea and land shall . . . immediately cease; all prisoners on both sides shall be set at liberty, and his Britannick Majesty shall, with all convenient speed, and without causing any destruction, or carrying away any negroes or other property of the American inhabitants, withdraw all his armies, garrisons and fleets . . . and from every port, place and harbour within the same."[3]

On April 5, Sir Guy Carleton, who replaced Sir Henry Clinton as Commander-in-Chief of all British forces in North America, received a dispatch from Thomas Townshend, Secretary of State for the Colonies. It contained a copy of George III's Proclamation, dated February 14, declaring "a Cessation of Arms as well as by sea as by land" and "all prisoners of war are to be set at liberty."[4] The next day, Carleton declared the cessation "be published in all places under [my] command."[5] The Continental Congress approved a similar resolve six days later.

On April 14, Carleton reached out to Washington in a letter to Robert R. Livingston, the Secretary for Foreign Affairs. He wrote,

> as embarkations of persons and property are on the point of being made, I am to request that Congress would be pleased to empower any person or persons, on behalf of the United States, to be present at New York, and to assist such persons as shall be appointed by me to inspect and superintend all embarkations, which the evacuations of this place [New York] may require.[6]

3. *Journals of the Continental Congress,* April 15, 1783, 24:241–251.
4. Livingston to Washington, April 15, 1783, enclosure 1, Founders Online, National Archives, http://founders.archives.gov/documents/Washington/99–01–02–11068 .
5. Guy Carleton to Washington, April 6, 1783, Founders Online, National Archives, http://founders.archives.gov/documents/Washington/99–01–02–11002.
6. Jared Sparks, ed., *The Diplomatic Correspondence of the American Revolution* (Boston: Nathan Hale and Gray & Bowen, 1830), 11:335.

On April 15, the Continental Congress, after approving the preliminary articles, directed Washington to meet with Carleton and make all of the necessary arrangements:

> Resolved, that the Commander in Chief be, and is hereby instructed to make the proper arrangements with the Commander in Chief of the British forces for receiving possession of the posts in the United States occupied by the troops of his Britannic Majesty; and for obtaining of all negroes and other property of the inhabitants of the United States in the possession of the British forces.[7]

On the 18th, Washington issued a general order for the cessation of hostilities to commence at noon the following day;[8] on the 19th, he met with Gen. Benjamin Lincoln, the Secretary of War, to discuss the arrangements that needed to be made with Carleton regarding the delivery of the British post at New York City.[9] On the 21st he wrote to Carleton informing him that prisoners from General Burgoyne's Saratoga army and Lord Cornwallis' Yorktown army would be immediately released but because they had been "removed to the interior of the country [a] . . . far distant from New York" it was Carleton's option to have them either march "the whole distance through the Country, or to have them delivered at the nearest water which may be convenient for your ships to receive them." He also wrote, "Respecting the other subjects contained in the . . . resolution of Congress, as they may be discussed with more precision & dispatch . . . I propose a personal interview between your Excellency and myself at some convenient time and immediate place."[10]

On April 24, the Continental Congress resolved to appoint a committee to reply to Carleton's request of the 14th. The committee was made up of Alexander Hamilton, John Rutledge and Nathanial Gorham. Before the day was out they recommended the appointment of three commissioners who with their British counterparts would "inspect and superintend all embarkations" and report to Carleton "every infraction of the letter or spirit" of Article 7.[11]

---

7. *Journals of the Continental Congress,* April 15, 1783, 24:242–43.

8. General Orders, April 18, 1783, Founders Online, National Archives, http://founders. archives.gov/documents/Washington/99–01–02–11097.

9. John C. Fitzpatrick, ed., *The Writings of George Washington from the Original Manuscript Sources 1745–1799, Volume 26, January 1, 1783—June 10, 1783* (Washington DC: Government Printing Office, 1938), 342–43.

10. Ibid, 345–48.

11. *Journals of the Continental Congress,* April 24, 1783, 24:274–6.

On the same day, Carleton responded to Washington's letter of the 21st:

> Considering the quantity of tonnage necessary for the evacuation of this place, and that most part of what we have at hand is now actually employed in this business, and in the removing of incumbrances, which must be sent off previous to our departure, I am reduced to the necessity of adopting the march of those prisoners by land . . . I cannot decline the personal interview proposed by your Excellency, and purpose being in a frigate as near Tappan as may be . . . and if I hear nothing from you to occasion an alteration, I intend being up on the 5 of May.[12]

Because the "contingents of a Water passage in a frigate" prevented Carleton from arriving at Orangetown until the evening of the 5th, the two men conducted their "interview" on the 6th. Afterwards, Washington described the interview as "diffuse and desultory." The two commanders decided that the specifics on the release and forwarding of prisoners to New York City were to be handled by the Secretary of War and Carleton. On the subject of evacuating New York, Carleton explained that the quantity of transports needed to remove troops and stores, and when sufficient transports would arrive, were yet unknown, making it impossible to fix on "a determinate period within which the British would be withdrawn from the City of New York." Washington also learned that Carleton had permitted many negroes to embark and sail away ten days earlier; Carleton offered that if this was in violation of the treaty, then compensation would be demanded. Carleton justified his decision: "He conceived it could not have been the Intention of the British Government . . . to reduce themselves to the Necessity of violating their Faith to the Negroes who came into the British Lines under the Proclamation of his Predecessors."[13] Negroes had served as laborers, scouts, messengers, spies, wagon drivers, and in exceptional situations as soldiers, with the understanding that the British in return offered them protection and their freedom. Carleton also claimed that Article 7 only applied to the Negroes that came within the British lines *after* November 30.

---

12. Carleton to Washington, April 24, 1783," Founders Online, National Archives, http://founders.archives.gov/documents/Washington/99-01-02-11153.
13. Fitzpatrick, *The Writings of George Washington,* 26:402–05. Proclamations promising freedom to slaves to fled their masters and served the British cause were issued by Lord Dunmore in November 1775, by General Clinton in June 1779, and by General Leslie in June 1782.

Following the interview Washington wrote two letters, the first to Governor Benjamin Harrison of Virginia and the second to Sir Guy Carleton. He told Harrison,

> I wrote to you from Newburgh and informed you of the meeting I was to hold with Sir Guy Carleton . . . This meeting I have had . . . I have discovered enough however, in the course of the conversation . . . to convince me that the slaves which have absconded from their masters will never be restored to them.[14]

In his letter to Carleton he wrote,

> to prevent Misapprehension or misconstruction, and that I may be enabled to fulfill my Instructions with fidelity and with Candor . . . [I] propose that your Excellency . . . give me in writing Information of what measures are adopting on your part for carrying into execution . . . the evacuation of the Posts now in possession of the British troops; and also what Time it is probable those Posts may be relinquished . . . .

Concerning the embarkation that had already taken place, he continued,

> Whether this Conduct is consonant to, or how far it may be deemed an Infraction . . . is not for me to decide . . . I cannot however conceal that my opinion, is that the measure is totally different from the Letter and Spirit of the Treaty . . . I find it my Duty to signify my readiness . . . to enter into any Agreements, or take any Measures which may be deemed expedient to prevent the future carrying away any Negroes or other property of the American Inhabitants.[15]

Two days later, Washington sent the president of the Continental Congress, Elias Boudinot, copies of his communications with Carleton and wrote "I have appointed Daniel Parker, Esqr. [army contractor], Egbert Benson Esqr. [the Attorney-General for the state of New York], and Lieut. Colo. Wm. S. Smith [a former aide-de-camp and an attorney] as Commissioners on the part of the United States, to attend and inspect the Embarkations that in future may be made at N York . . . a Copy of their Appointment and Instructions . . . inclosed." [16] Boudinot had already been informed by Thomas Walke, a justice of the peace of Princess Anne County, Virginia that he, Capt. John Willoughby, Jr. a

14. Ibid., 401–02.
15. Ibid., 408–09.
16. Ibid., 410–14.

sheriff of Norfolk County, and a number of others had already been to New York and been informed by Carleton that "no slaves were to be given up who claimed the benefit of their former proclamations for liberating such Slaves as threw themselves under the protection of the British Government."[17]

On May 10, the American Commissioners arrived in New York City. On the 12th, Carleton informed Washington that he was no closer to determining "when the evacuation of this City can be completed . . . I cannot guess the quantity of shipping that will be sent me, nor the number of persons that will be forced to abandon this place." As to the Negroes that would be permitted to embark in the future, he said "an accurate register was taken of every circumstance respecting them, so as to serve as a record of the name of the original proprietor of the Negro, . . . and as a rule by which to judge of his value."[18]

The British Commissioners appointed by Carleton were Capt. Richard Armstrong, Capt. Thomas Gilfillan, Maj. Nathaniel Phillips, and Capt. Wilbur Cook. This author has been unable to discover the exact date of their appointment, but it had to occur between the meeting on May 6 and May 22 because on the latter date, Oliver Delancey, Carleton's Adjutant-General, issued orders that the commissioners were to meet at "Fraunce's Tavern every Wednesday at ten Oclock [to hear] any Person claiming property embarked, or to be embarked . . . Should any Doubts arise in Examination the circumstances of the case to be minuted down" for a possible settlement in the future.[19]

Two weeks later, the Continental Congress, having read the recent letters between Washington and Carleton, wrote to the Peace Commissioners in France:

> Resolved, That copies of the letters between the Commander-in-Chief and Sir Guy Carleton, and other papers on the subject be transmitted to the ministers plenipotentiary of these states for negotiating a peace in Europe; and that they be directed to remonstrate thereon to the Court of Great Britain, and use their utmost endeavors to take proper measures for obtaining such reparation as the nature of the case will admit.[20]

17. William T. Hutchinson and William M. E. Rachal, eds., *The Papers of James Madison, 3 May 1783—20 February 1784* (Chicago: University of Chicago Press, 1971), 5–7.
18. Carleton to Washington, May 12, 1783, Founders Online, National Archives, http://founders.archives.gov/documents/Washington/99-01-02-11252 .
19. Benjamin Quarles, *The Negro in the American Revolution* (Chapel Hill, NC: University of North Carolina Press, 1961), 167–71.
20. *Journals of the Continental Congress,* May 26, 1783, 24:364.

In the last week of May, the Commissioners in New York City submitted their first claim to Carleton. His response by way of Delancey was an omen of the difficulty the Commissioners would have submitting any claim in the future: no property was going to be delivered until it was shown to be in danger of being carried away. In a letter to Washington they stated,

> It appeared to us improbable that Sir Guy Carleton ever intended to afford Redress against his own Orders and Measures . . . We cannot forbear observing to your Excellency that in our sentiment no valuable purpose will be effected by representing, at this Juncture, violations of the Treaty—Cases where we are certain Redress will be denied, when we have it not in our power to enforce it.[21]

The commissioners were quick to discover that every negro granted the privilege of embarking had been given a signed certificate. It read

New York, April 1783
This is to certify to whomsoever it may concern that the bearer hereof
_____, a Negro restored to the British Lines in consequence of the proclamation of Sir William Howe and Sir Henry Clinton, late Commanders-in-Chief in America; and that the said Negro has hereby his Excellency's Sir Guy Carleton's permission to go to Nova Scotia or wherever else _____ may think proper.
By order of . . . . [22]

On June 2, Washington sent Carleton a copy of the May 26 Continental Congress resolution that was sent to the American commissioners in France.

One week later the American commissioners submitted another claim to Carleton and again the claim was denied, this time because a British officer produced a certificate from the commandant of New York City that the negro, previously a known slave, came within the British lines on November 2 under the sanction of Clinton's proclamation. In a letter to Washington they wrote, "We conceive it is now reduced to a certainty that all applications for the Delivery of Property will be fruitless."[23]

21. William Stephens Smith to Washington, May 30, 1783," Founders Online, National Archives, http://founders/archives.gov/documernts/Washington/99-01-02-1135.
22. James W. St. G Walker, *The Black Loyalists: The Search for a Promised Land in Nova Scotia and Sierra Leone, 1783–1870* (New York: Africana Publishing Co., 1976), 11.
23. Egbert Benson to Washington, June 14, 1783," Founders Online, National Archives, http://founders.archives.gov/documents/Washington/99-01-02-11449.

On June 10, Washington received a letter from Carleton and wrote a letter to Egbert Benson, one of the commissioners in New York, in response to their letter of May 30. Carleton, rather than being obliging as he had been, went on the offensive in his letter. He said that he understood the actions taken by Congress but,

> I have already, for my own part, referred to the King's Servants those points wherein I judged that on your side, the true intent and meaning of this treaty has not been preserved, and in particular the consideration of those impediments which have been found in the execution of the 5th and 6th Articles, even in cases where the stipulations contained therein are absolute, both in the meaning and expression, but whose effect has been opposed, both by Laws now subsisting in the different States, and by the resolves of different bodies of men, who seem to act without control.[24]

A week would pass before Washington wrote back to the American commissioners. His letter was supportive but filled with equal frustration:

> That you find Embarrassments in the Execution of your Instructions, is no more than I expected . . . It is exceedingly difficult for me . . . to give you a precise Definition or Character of the Acts which you are to represent as Infractions of the Treaty . . . As [to] your Instructions from me are given in Consequence of the Directions of Congress, and are grounded entirely on their Resolutions . . . I must be silent on the Subject; leaving it to your own good Judgment & Discretion, to execute your Commission in the best manner you can.[25]

On June 17, the Commissioners again submitted a claim to Carleton. Fourteen transports had recently departed with 173 Negroes aboard. This time they simply made a point, knowing the outcome was going to be the same:

> By the Articles of Peace His Britannic Majesty is to withdraw his Armies, Garrisons and Fleets, and [we] do not suppose any Embarkation requisite to the Evacuation of this place which is made for the purpose of removing persons who do not properly belong to the British Army, Garrison or Fleet, and if, by permitting Transports to be employed in removing persons of this description, the withdraw-

24. Carleton to Washington, June 10, 1783," Founders Online, National Archives, http://founders.archives.gov/documents/Washington/99-01-02-11422.
25. Washington to Benson, June 10, 1783, Founders Online, National Archives, http://founders/archives.gov/documents/Washington/99-01-02-11423.

ing of the British Army is delayed, [we] must view such delay as an Infraction of the Treaty.[26]

On June 23, Washington believed the American commissioners' efforts were a failure but in no way due to them. He raised the question of their recall with president of the Continental Congress, Elias Boudinot:

> Finding that merely the superintendance of Embarkation ... without the power of restraining the Property ... from being carried away, could be of little utility—having been also informed that the departure of all Negroes indiscriminately and without examination, in private Vessels is, if not publickly allowed, at least connived at ... I cannot think there will be much advantage in continuing Commissioners any longer at New York, and I take the liberty therefore to suggest whether it would not be eligible to revoke the Commission.[27]

Benson, Smith and Parker agreed to continue to meet with their counterparts until all of the British forces had evacuated the city.

The board of commissioners that met at Fraunces's Tavern heard only fourteen recorded cases; of these two were decided in favor of the slave(s), nine in favor of the owner(s), and three were referred to Brig. Gen. Samuel Birch, commanding officer in the City of New York, for a decision.[28] The inspection rolls (or registers) made by the British and American Commissioners of the Negroes show that 1,336 negro men, 914 negro women, and 750 negro children were carried away.[29] The rolls contain information such as their names, ages, former legal status, distinguishing physical characteristics, names of former owners, the circumstances under which they entered a British camp and the names and destinations of the vessels they boarded. There are two sets of rolls; the first begins April 23 and ends on July 31, the second begins on July 31 and ends on November 30. Each set was originally bound into a book. Shortly afterwards, they were combined into one book, *The Book of Negroes*. There are two versions of the book; the British copy is in the National Archives in Kew, England, the American copy is in the National Archives and Records Administration in Washington DC.

26. "Benson to Washington, June 28, 1783, Founders Online, National Archives, http://founders.archives.gov/documents/Washington/99–01–01–11473.

27. Elias Boudinot to Washington, June 23, 1783," Founders Online, National Archives, http://founders.archives.gov/documents/Washington/99–01–02–11497.

28. British Headquarters Papers, Manuscript Room, New York Public Library, Documents 3653, 5243, 5568, 7301, 7419, 7448, 7490, 7680, 8123, 8132, 9056, 9158, 9656, 9687, 10098, and 10427.

29. Benjamin Quarles, *Negro in the American Revolution*, 172.

What Do Bond Prices Tell Us About the Early Republic?

✻ RICHARD SAMBASIVAM ✻

America's early finances were, in a word, messy. The states took on enormous debt to fund the Revolutionary War while the national government chartered by the Articles of Confederation issued bonds, took out foreign loans, and even benefitted from personal gifts, all while it had no power to collect taxes. "It was the price of liberty," Hamilton wrote in his First Report on the Public Credit in 1790.[1] That same report addressed the nation's credit—during the 1780s, state debt traded at a significant discount to par, as low as $10, or ten percent their original value (a bond's face value is $100), implying that investors generally didn't expect to be paid back. Add to that the significant inflation that the nation suffered, and government bonds were certainly not a good investment.

Hamilton and the new Congress realized that strong credit was essential for the government to be able to borrow on good terms in times of war and for investment projects in their capital-scarce country. With the advent of the 1787 Constitution and Hamilton's plan for the federal government to take on states' unpaid obligations, it seemed governments at both levels would be on surer footing. As the new government began operations, how did these financial reforms play out? Today, U.S. government bonds are the safest available, the "risk-free" asset that influences interest rates around the world. But the 1780s and 1790s were a crucial period for U.S. debt, which, as the data bears out, established the nation's credit and future success.

---

1. Alexander Hamilton, "Report Relative to a Provision for the Support of Public Credit, January 9, 1790," The National Archives, accessed June 1, 2016, http://founders. archives.gov/documents/Hamilton/01–06–02–0076–0002–0001.

In Hamilton's words, a given speculator "paid what the commodity was worth in the market, and took the risks of reimbursement upon himself."[2] Bond prices ought to reflect investor sentiment towards the debt obligations of the federal government, including how likely it was the U.S. was to pay off debt as it came due. Data compiled by Sylla, Wilson, and Wright include prices recorded for a variety of securities in U.S. financial markets from 1790 to 1860, including U.S. bonds. Examining the movements in the prices of these bonds, we can see how the nation built its early credit.

ABOUT THE DATA

While data for the prices of U.S. government debt today can be found with a quick internet search, and data going back a century can be taken for granted, detailed financial data prior to the Civil War is a difficult find, especially given that U.S. financial markets were relatively undeveloped. Sylla, Wilson, and Wright painstakingly combed through periodicals from this era, such as the *New York Journal* and the *Pennsylvania Herald*, to compile reported security prices. Consequently, the dataset suffers a number of limitations, including time gaps, inconsistent reporting across markets (for example, prices reported in New York but not in Charleston), and ambiguous reporting of prices (whether they be bid, ask, midpoint, or transaction prices).[3] Naturally, these problems are worse the earlier one looks. However, the prices remain largely interpretable.

Sylla finds that early U.S. securities markets had several attributes that made them particularly modern, and advanced for what we would now call an "emerging market." The first is domestic intermarket arbitrage, or that trading across the New York, Philadelphia, and other markets took place frequently to exploit price differences—a key requirement for allocating financial capital efficiently throughout the United States. Another is that the market could price more complicated

---

2. Hamilton, "Report." The full quote: "That he is to be considered as a fair purchaser, results from this: Whatever necessity the seller may have been under, was occasioned by the government, in not making a proper provision for its debts. The buyer had no agency in it, and therefore ought not to suffer. He is not even chargeable with having taken an undue advantage. He paid what the commodity was worth in the market, and took the risks of reimbursement upon himself. He of course gave a fair equivalent, and ought to reap the benefit of his hazard; a hazard which was far from inconsiderable, and which, perhaps, turned on little less than a revolution in government."
3. Richard E. Sylla, Jack Wilson, and Robert E. Wright, "Price Quotations in Early U.S. Securities Markets, 1790–1860," Economic History Association, accessed June 1, 2016, http://eh.net/database/early-u-s-securities-prices/.

securities efficiently.[4] A third important element of this market was foreign activity, as a significant share of securities was held by Europeans.
Finally, U.S. securities were comparable to foreign securities in the eyes
of investors, even pricing competitively with British government debt.
All this to say that the early U.S. financial market was more advanced
than one might expect of a newly formed nation and that prices
recorded in this dataset likely reflect investor sentiment accurately.[5]

OUTSTANDING DEBT AND INFLATION

Two factors that bear studying before examining prices are the outstanding stock of debt, and inflation. If the outstanding stock appeared
too high, then investors might fear the government was unable to pay
off debt as it came due. While the national debt rose from $71 million
in 1790 to $83 million in 1800, there was nowhere near the explosive
growth in debt created by states and the confederation (from 0 to $71
million in fifteen years).[6] Moreover, under the new government's taxing
powers and Hamilton's funding scheme, such debt was significantly
more sustainable.

In a scenario of high inflation, investors might be turned off U.S. debt
because inflation would whittle away their returns (for example, a bond-

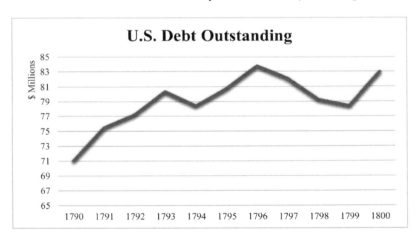

4. Specifically, a "hybrid, zero-coupon" security. Today the U.S. Treasury offers distinct
zero-coupon and coupon securities (bills vs. notes and bonds), but Hamilton came up
with a "deferred" security, with elements of both, examined later. Despite this quirk,
Sylla finds that the security is priced as one would expect.
5. Richard Sylla, "U.S. Securities Markets and the Banking System, 1790–1840," *Federal
Reserve Bank of St. Louis Review* (Federal Reserve Bank of St. Louis, 1998), 88–89.
6. "Historical Debt Outstanding—Annual 1790–1849," TreasuryDirect, accessed June 1,
2016, www.treasurydirect.gov/govt/reports/pd/histdebt/histdebt_histo1.htm.

holder who invests $100 at 3 percent would expect to get $3 a year later; an inflation rate of 3 percent would make the money worth as much as it was a year before, making the real return zero). In environments of high inflation, that return could even be negative. Therefore, it's not surprising that bond prices fell far below $100, as investors sold them at a discount to reflect that buyers would be paid in less valuable money. Fortunately, inflation began to subside by the mid-1780s and was stable until the mid-1790s.[7]

Whether the states were going to default on their debt or pay it by printing money, they weren't going to much improve their credit ratings.

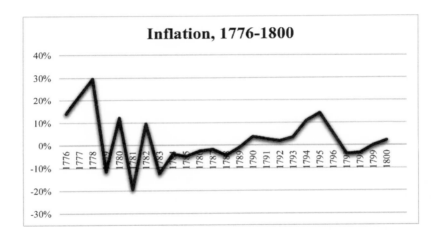

BEFORE THE CONSTITUTION

There is some data available from the Philadelphia market on debt issued by the government under the Articles of Confederation. In this data the market's growing appreciation for the plan being worked out at the Constitutional Convention becomes clear. By the end of the war, the national government had £32 million in debt outstanding, £22 million of which were in these marketable securities.[8]

The marketable securities fell into a few different categories. Continental certificates were issued for supplies and paying soldiers, didn't pay interest, and were often given to citizens in exchange for their ma-

7. Samuel H. Williamson, "The Annual Consumer Price Index for the United States, 1774–2015," MeasuringWorth, 2016, www.measuringworth.com/uscpi/.

8. John L. Smith, Jr., "How was the Revolutionary War Paid For?", *Journal of the American Revolution*, February 23, 2015, accessed June 1, 2016, https://allthingsliberty.com/2015/02/howwas-the-revolutionary-war-paid-for.

terials.[9] Perhaps unsurprisingly, in 1787 these had the lowest price, at just 10 cents on the dollar. New loan certificates were issued by the state of Pennsylvania and, because the state had taken on Continental certificates, the national government was on the hook for them.[10] Land office certificates, funded depreciated certificates, and unfunded depreciated certificates were similar.

Broadly, the trend for these instruments' prices was upward between late 1786 and October 1790, when the debt was restructured into new securities issued by the new federal government. Prices bottomed out in mid- to late-1788 as the new Constitution was ratified in June. New loan certificates, for example, traded at $30 in March 1787; at the end of this period, the price was $60, double the price. The highest price among these at the end of the period was for unfunded depreciated certificates, at $66 2/3, when it was as low as $25 in March 1787. Though still at a significant discount to par (less than $100), the general trend up is notable, and signals investors' growing comfort with the plan for a new government and its ability to pay its obligations. As Hamilton put it, buyers of the debt took on "a hazard which was far from inconsiderable, and which, perhaps, turned on little less than a revolution in government."[11]

THE BIRTH OF A MARKET

In his *Birth of a Market: The U.S. Treasury Securities Market from the Great War to the Great Depression*, Kenneth D. Garbade recounts how the

9. Ibid.
10. Hamilton, "Report."
11. Ibid.

Treasury managed the national debt in the twentieth century to establish the multitrillion dollar market at the center of world finance today—and to fund America through its great struggles during the century.[12] To get there, however, the national debt needed investor confidence and the foundation of being regularly repayment, and significant progress was made here in the decade following the Constitutional Convention.

Even the idea of an outstanding national debt was not well established in the eighteenth century; Albert Gallatin, one of Hamilton's Anti-Federalist adversaries (a statue of whom now stands in front of the Treasury Building), argued that the debt should be paid off in full and avoided in the future.[13] Hamilton, however, believing that a national debt and a central bank had allowed Britain to develop into a super-power, insisted on a different vision for American public finance (specifically, because British bonds traded freely in the market, the government was able to borrow at lower rates than its larger rival France, helping it defeat the French in the wars of the eighteenth century).[14] Hamilton's vision ultimately won out in policy, and appears to have worked out quite well.

We can examine activity in the three of the largest markets for U.S. bonds to see how this transpired: Philadelphia, at the time the country's financial center; New York, the emerging new center; and London, the financial center of the world. All three markets exhibit the same trend: reaching a peak in early 1792, and a fall in the mid-1790s that does not recover by the end of the decade.

The new Department of the Treasury reorganized the old debt examined above into three new types of issues: a bond paying 3 percent interest, a bond paying 6 percent interest, and a deferred-interest bond, that is, a bond that did not pay interest for the first 10 years and then began interest payments of 6 percent (the advantage of which is that the government does not need to factor these interest payments into the budget for a decade).[15]

Two questions bear asking: Why did bond prices climb so high at the beginning of the decade? And why did they fall by the end of the

12 Kenneth D. Garbade, *Birth of a Market: The U.S. Treasury Securities Market from the Great War to the Great Depression* (Cambridge, MA: MIT Press, 2012).

13 Edwin G. Burrows, "Gallatin, Albert," American National Biography Online, 2000, accessed June 20, 2016, www.anb.org/articles/02/02–00135.html.

14 John Steele Gordon, "Past and Present: Alexander Hamilton and the Start of the National Debt," *U.S. News & World Report*, September 18, 2008, accessed June 1, 2016, www.usnews.com/opinion/articles/2008/09/18/past-present-alexander-hamilton-and-thestart-of-the-national-debt.

15 Sylla, "U.S. Securities Markets," 88.

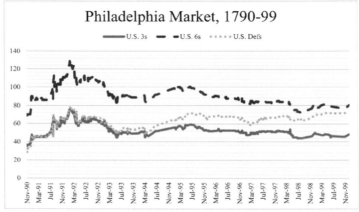

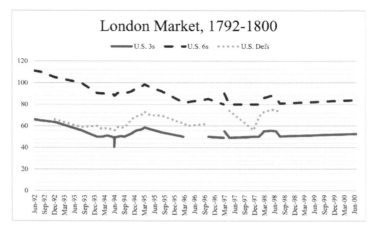

decade, not much higher than they began, and does it represent a fundamental change in the U.S. government's credit?

It's notable that the Treasury bond paying 6 percent was even trading over 100, or above par, in the 1790s, reflecting high demand for the government's 6 percent issue. This demand is in part accounted for by the First Bank of the United States; private investors owning the Bank's stock could pay for three-fourths with the issue.[16] For debt issued by a fairly new nation with a new constitution to be traded at such high prices reflects high investor confidence in that constitution—in other words, Hamilton's plan had worked. Investors now felt safe with U.S. government bonds, and had a stake in the nation's success.

So why, then, did prices fall? The answer lies likely not in doubt in the government's financial soundness but in inflation. The expansion of the money supply due to growth in the domestic banking sector and to capital inflows from Europe caused prices to rise, and to knock value off U.S. bonds. Though inflation subsided by 1800, the country would continue to struggle with inflation and volatile boom and bust cycles throughout the nineteenth century.

Although the bonds traded at significant discount to par, in no market did they trade below 40 cents on the dollar, a significant improvement from debt in the 1780s. The government had made substantial progress through its Constitutional framework, progress that is not necessarily fully reflected in this price data. For example, the debt was now sustainable, as the government collected enough revenue to cover its expenses and interest payments, and the country's new economic growth would ensure that the funding would continue for years to come.

TAKEAWAYS

The burden of the Revolutionary war debt was, through Hamilton's brilliant designs, turned into a huge positive (a "national blessing") for the United States, the effects of which can still be felt today. To date, the U.S. government has never defaulted on its debt, which is the most sought-after sovereign debt in the world. The market for this debt numbers in the trillions of dollars and greases the financial wheels of the global economy. But more important at the time of the nation's founding, the adoption and reorganization of the war debt by the federal government enabled payment of the debt, created a stake for investors both domestic and foreign, and helped develop its early financial markets. Sylla notes that other emerging-market nations might draw some lessons from the U.S. experience in attaining a sizeable, sustainable public

16. Douglas A. Edwin and Richard Sylla, *Founding Choices: American Economic Policy in the 1790s* (Chicago: University of Chicago Press, 2011), 70.

debt to both build confidence in the government as well as develop the financial sector.[17]

Of course, the success of the Revolution didn't rest only on financial factors; that entailed the development of a republican government answerable to the people, a reshaping of American society, and a group of responsible leaders. However, though these factors were minimum requirements for the success of the United States, it was Hamilton's designs and the market's confidence in the government that ensured the continuing success of the new nation.

17. Sylla, "U.S. Securities Markets," 98.

Why God is in the Declaration of Independence but not in the Constitution

❦ ANTHONY J. MINNA ❦

No country venerates its "Founding Fathers" like the United States. Academics, legislators, judges, and ordinary citizens all frequently seek to validate their opinions and policy prescriptions by identifying them with the statesmen who led America to nationhood. It is not surprising, therefore, that debates about the role of religion in the United States are infused with references to the faith of the Founding Fathers and to the two greatest documents they gave to the fledgling republic: the Declaration of Independence and the United States Constitution. People across the religious spectrum, from the most devout believers to the most committed atheists, look to these documents for support. Yet the blessings they offer are mixed. The Declaration contains several references to God, the Constitution none at all. The reasons for this variation reveal a great deal about the founding principles of the United States.

The Declaration of Independence is an apology for revolution. Support for a complete break with Great Britain was growing stronger week by week in the spring of 1776, both in the Continental Congress and in the thirteen colonies at large. On June 7, 1776, a resolution advocating independence was presented to Congress by Richard Henry Lee of the Virginia delegation. Four days later Congress appointed a committee of five delegates to draft a document explaining the historic separation it would soon be voting on.

The resulting Declaration of Independence, drafted by Thomas Jefferson and edited by his fellow delegates, contains a theory of rights that depends on a Supreme Being, not man, for its validity. The Declaration states that "all men are created equal, that they are endowed by their Creator with certain unalienable Rights, that among these are Life, Liberty and the pursuit of Happiness." It is possible to see in these words an affirmation of the Founders' religious faith, but God-given rights had less to do with theology in the summer of 1776 than they did with rebellion.

In stating that people's rights were given to them by their creator, the Continental Congress endowed those rights with a legitimacy that knows no parallel in mortal sources. What God has given to man is not enjoyed at the sufferance of any monarch or government. Liberty is the inviolable birthright of all. The right of revolution proclaimed by the Declaration flows directly from this notion of inviolability: it is to secure people's divinely endowed and unalienable rights that governments, "deriving their just powers from the consent of the governed," are established. The people consequently have the right and indeed the duty to alter or abolish a form of government that becomes tyrannical.

The Declaration contains several other references to a higher power. The introduction states that the "Laws of Nature and Nature's God" entitle the American people to a separate and equal station among the powers of the earth. In the conclusion, Congress appeals to "the Supreme Judge of the world" for the rectitude of its intentions and professes its "firm reliance on the protection of divine Providence." In each case, reference to a deity serves to validate the assertion of independence.

The genius of the Declaration is the inclusive way the divine is given expression. The appellations of God are generic. Adherents of traditional theistic sects can read the words "Nature's God," "Creator," and "Supreme Judge," and understand them to mean the god they worship. The claims made on numerous Christian websites attest to this. Yet opponents of dogma read those same words and see an embracive, non-sectarian concept of divinity. This is no small testimony to the wisdom and foresight of the Founding Fathers. All Americans could support the Revolution and independence. All can regard their rights as unalienable, their liberty as inviolable.

Unlike the Declaration of Independence, the United States Constitution contains no reference to God. At first, this may seem odd. Why did the men who drafted the Declaration invoke a Supreme Being several times, while the men who drafted the Constitution did not mention a higher power even once? Only six individuals signed both documents, so it could be hypothesized that the delegates to the Constitutional Convention that convened in Philadelphia in 1787 were a different and less religious group then the delegates to the Continental Congress, or perhaps that the delegates to the Continental Congress were savvy freethinkers cynically manipulating people's belief in God to win support for their overthrow of British rule. Neither explanation holds water. Some of the Founders were conventional Christians and some were not, but the belief in a deity implied in the Declaration was sincere and likely universal among the delegates to both the Continental Congress and the Constitutional Convention. And a belief in the possibility of divine favor was held by even some of the least religious Founders. So, again, why no invocation of God in the second major founding document?

The threefold answer lies in the stated purposes of the Constitution, its religious neutrality, and the theory of government it embodies. Whereas the Declaration explained and justified a rebellion to secure God-given rights, the Constitution is a blueprint for stable and effective republican government in a free country. The Preamble to the Constitution declares that its purposes are "to form a more perfect Union, establish Justice, insure domestic Tranquility, provide for the common defence, promote the general Welfare, and secure the Blessings of Liberty." These are wholly secular objects; religious references are extraneous in a document drafted to further them.

Eighteenth century America was religiously diverse, and by the time of the Revolution religion was widely viewed as a matter of voluntary individual choice. The Constitution acknowledged these realities and, unlike contemporary European political orders, promoted no sect and took no position whatsoever on theological issues. There is no state religion and Article VI of the Constitution provides that "no religious Test shall ever be required as a Qualification to any Office or public Trust under the United States." The First Amendment to the Constitution, ratified in 1791, provides that "Congress shall make no law respecting an establishment of religion, or prohibiting the free exercise thereof." The absence of references to a deity in the Constitution is consistent with the strict religious neutrality of the entire document.

The Constitution established a strong national government to replace the relatively feeble Confederation Congress created by the Revolutionary-era Articles of Confederation, but the Constitution is hardly a document glorifying top-down power. On the contrary, the theory of government underpinning the United States Constitution is popular sovereignty. The government derives its legitimacy from the consent of the governed, not from an assembly of elders, not from a king or a prelate, and not from a higher power. The stirring opening words of the Preamble, "We the People of the United States," make it clear both who is establishing the government and for whose benefit it exists. There is no consent required beyond the will of the people for the people to govern themselves.

This view that the Constitution is a bold assertion of popular sovereignty is often countered by pointing out how elitist some of the delegates to the Constitutional Convention were and how allegedly undemocratic the document they drafted was. Only the members of the House of Representatives were initially chosen directly by voters. Senators were to be chosen indirectly by state legislatures, and the President by electors appointed by the state legislatures.

This criticism confuses an admittedly elitist preference for government by the able with a theory of power emanating from above. The Constitution not only rejected monarchy, but all forms of hereditary privilege and arbitrary rule. It established fixed rules that delimited the powers of the governors, not the rights of the governed. It is to the citizens and the states, not to the executive, that legislators are answerable. The source of all legislative and executive power can be traced, directly or indirectly, to the people.

And in the early years of the American republic, the people in question were deeply suspicious of power. There was considerable opposition to the Constitution as initially drafted, both in the state conventions called to ratify it and among ordinary Americans. Opponents believed that a centralization of authority would lead to tyranny and argued either for outright rejection or, at a minimum, for amendments to limit the powers of the new government and safeguard liberties. In such an anti-power environment, few Americans wished to see their new rulers claim, as European rulers did, that their authority was divine in origin. In creating a political order based on popular sovereignty, the Founding Fathers thus turned prevailing European political theory on its head. In place of the divine right of monarchs, the Declaration asserted the divine rights of all men, and both the Declaration and the Constitution source the legitimacy of political rule exclusively in the consent of the governed.

The Declaration of Independence and the United States Constitution do not therefore represent competing views of the existence of a Supreme Being or its role in American political life. They are two sides of the same coin. When read together, the Declaration and Constitution tell us that the people's rights are divine in origin, sacred and unalienable, while governments are human in origin, answerable to the people and dependent entirely on their consent.

AUTHOR BIOGRAPHIES

TODD ANDRLIK

Todd Andrlik, founder and editor of *Journal of the American Revolution*, is author and editor of *Reporting the Revolutionary War: Before It Was History, It Was News* (Sourcebooks, 2012), named Best American Revolution Book of 2012 by the New York American Revolution Round Table. A full-time marketing and media professional, Andrlik has written or ghost-written thousands of published articles on various business topics. His history-related work has been featured by *Slate, Huffington Post, Boston Globe, Smithsonian, TIME*, NPR, C-SPAN, CNN, MSNBC, Mount Vernon, American Revolution Center, Fraunces Tavern Museum and more.

NICOLAS BELL-ROMERO

Nicolas Bell-Romero is currently a PhD student at the University of Cambridge in the United Kingdom. His research focuses on Loyalism during the American Revolution; and, in particular, the exclusionary languages that were used by the revolutionaries to demonize their opponents. He is also interested in the politics of memory during the Age of Revolutions, particularly the ways British intellectuals wrote about the American and French revolutions.

C. L. BRAGG

Dr. C. L. "Chip" Bragg is a practicing anesthesiologist in Thomasville, Georgia. He is the author of four books: *Distinction in Every Service: Brigadier General Marcellus A. Stovall, C.S.A.* (White Mane, 2001), the critically acclaimed *Never for Want of Powder: The Confederate Powder Works in Augusta, Georgia* (University of South Carolina Press, 2007) of which he is coauthor, *Crescent Moon Over Carolina: William Moultrie and American Liberty* (University of South Carolina Press, 2013), and *Martyr of the American Revolution: The Execution of Isaac Hayne, South Carolinian* (University of South Carolina Press, 2017). In addition, he has contributed a chapter to *Loyalty & Revolution: Essays in Honor of Robert M. Calhoon.*

TODD W. BRAISTED

Todd Braisted is an author and researcher of Loyalist military studies. His primary research and writing focus is on Loyalist military personnel, infrastructure and campaigns throughout North America. He has authored numerous journal articles and books, including *Grand Forage 1778: The Battleground Around New York City* (Westholme, 2016). He has also appeared as a guest historian on episodes of Who Do You Think You Are? (CBC) and History Detectives (PBS). He is the creator of royalprovincial.com, the largest website dedicated to Loyalist military studies. Braisted is a Fellow in the Company of Military Historians, former Honorary Vice President of the United Empire Loyalist Association of Canada, and a past-president of the Bergen County Historical Society.

Zachary Brown

Zachary Brown is a native of Toronto Ontario, and an undergraduate student studying history at Stanford University, with a concentration in the United States, under advisor Professor Richard White. His current primary research interests are the rhetoric of Anglo-Indian relations along the frontier during the Colonial and Revolutionary periods and studying the American Civil War as part of the age of nationalism. .

Stephen Brumwell

Stephen Brumwell is an award-winning writer and independent historian. His books include *Redcoats: The British Soldier and War in the Americas, 1755–1763* (Cambridge University Press, 2002); *White Devil: A True Story of War, Savagery and Vengeance in Colonial America* (Da Capo, 2005); *Paths of Glory: The Life and Death of General James Wolfe* (McGill-Queen's University Press, 2007); and *George Washington: Gentleman Warrior* (Quercus, 2013). He regularly speaks about his research in the US and UK. Stephen lives in Amsterdam, and is very grateful to the Gilder Lehrman Institute of American History for funding a short-term fellowship that supported his research in New York into Benedict Arnold's Treason.

Kim Burdick

Kim Burdick is the founder and Chairman of the American Revolution Round Table of Northern Delaware. As 2003–2009 National Project Director of the Washington-Rochambeau Revolutionary Route (now W3R-NHT), Kim coordinated a 9–state and DC effort celebrating the 225th Anniversary of the Yorktown Campaign. Advisor Emeritus to the National Trust for Historic Preservation and former Chairman of the Delaware Humanities Council, she has served as project director for some of Delaware's most innovative public history programs including the nationally-recognized June 2014 symposium entitled *George Washington: Man and Myth.*

Michael Cecere

Michael Cecere teaches U.S. History at Robert E. Lee High School in Fairfax County, Virginia, and at Northern Virginia Community College in Woodbridge, Virginia. He was recognized by the Virginia Society of the Sons of the American Revolution as their 2005 Outstanding Teacher of the Year. He is the author of thirteen books on the American Revolution, focusing primarily on the role that Virginians played in the Revolution. His latest book is *The Invasion of Virginia, 1781* part of the Journal of American Revolution Books series.

ALEX COLVIN

Alex Colvin is in his senior year at University of Houston where he is majoring in history and minoring in anthropology. His senior-level coursework involved extensive study and research in the American Revolution, under the guidance of historian James Kirby Martin. Colvin is also the charter president of the Walter Prescott Webb Historical Society (2014–2015) at the University of Houston, and is also an experienced genealogist. His work on the Clayton House was recently published by Houston History magazine.

JETT CONNER

Jett Conner is a retired political science professor, college administrator, and academic policy officer for the Colorado Department of Higher Education. He studied the political thought of the American founding period during a National Endowment for the Humanities summer fellowship at Princeton University, and previously wrote of Thomas Paine in "Tom Paine and the Genesis of American Federalism," *The Embattled Constitution: Vital Framework or Convenient Symbol*, Adolph Grundman, ed. (Malabar, Florida, Krieger Publishing Co., 1986).

JEFF DACUS

Jeff Dacus has been teaching U.S. history for 30 years and served as a U.S. Marine for 23 years, including five on active duty where he engaged in combat during Operation Desert Storm as a tank platoon sergeant. He earned his bachelor's degree in Elementary Education from Portland State University; his first master's degree in Secondary Education from Lewis and Clark College; his second master's degree in American History from University of Portland; and his third master's degree in Military History from American Military University. He is currently a middle school history teacher in Vancouver, Washington, where he lives with his wife and two daughters.

ENNIS DULING

Ennis Duling lives in East Poultney, Vermont, on land settled by a Revolutionary War veteran. Now retired, he was the communications director at Castleton State College (Castleton University). His articles and book reviews on the American Revolution have appeared in *Vermont History*. He is a graduate of Gettysburg College and serves on the boards of the Mount Independence Coalition and the Poultney Historical Society.

DANIEL N. GULLOTTA

Daniel N. Gullotta is a historian of religion, specializing in the history and scriptures of Christianity. He is currently at graduate student at Yale University Divinity School, in the Master of Arts in Religion program, with a concentration in the History of Christianity. In the 2016–17 academic year, he was the recipient of the Rev. Ben F. Wyland Scholarship. He holds a Master's Degree in Theological Studies specializing in Biblical Studies from the Australian Catholic University and a Bachelor's Degree in Theology with Honours from the University of Newcastle.

Don N. Hagist

Don N. Hagist, editor of *Journal of the American Revolution*, is an independent researcher specializing in the demographics and material culture of the British Army in the American Revolution. He maintains a blog about British common soldiers and has published a number of articles in academic journals. His books include *The Revolution's Last Men: the Soldiers Behind the Photographs* (Westholme Publishing, 2015), *British Soldiers, American War* (Westholme Publishing, 2012), *A British Soldier's Story: Roger Lamb's Narrative of the American Revolution* (Ballindalloch Press, 2004), *General Orders: Rhode Island* (Heritage Books, 2001) and *Wives, Slaves, and Servant Girls* (Westholme Publishing, 2016).

Gerald Holland

Gerald Holland presently serves as an Operations Specialist in the United States Coast Guard. Prior to joining the Coast Guard, he worked as a historical interpreter at Colonial Williamsburg. He holds a bachelor's degree in history from Christopher Newport University, a master's in military history with a concentration in the American Revolution from American Military University, and a graduate certificate in Civil War studies from American Military University.

John Knight

John Knight was educated at Warwick University where he gained a joint honours degree in American History and Politics. He was a Fine Art Valuer for a number of London-based Auction Houses including Christie's and Bonhams before changing career and taking up writing and politics full time. He is the portfolio holder for culture on Nottinghamshire County Council. A confirmed Americanophile he splits his time between homes in Nottingham, England, and Dutchess County, New York.

Nancy K. Loane

Nancy K. Loane, a former seasonal ranger at Valley Forge National Historical Park, is the author of *Following the Drum: Women at the Valley Forge Encampment* (Potomac, 2009). A Pennsylvania Commonwealth Speaker (2006-2007), she has presented over 200 lectures relating to the American Revolution throughout the country, including at the Library of Congress. A board member of the Valley Forge Park Alliance, Loane is a founding member of the American Revolution Round Table of Philadelphia and an honorary lifetime member of the Society of the Descendants of Washington's Army at Valley Forge.

James Kirby Martin

James Kirby Martin is a nationally recognized scholar of the American Revolution, well known for his writings on various aspects of American military and social history. He is the award-winning author and editor of numerous articles and books, including *Forgotten Allies: The Oneida Indians and the American Revolution*(Hill and Wang, 2006) with J. T. Glatthaar; *Benedict Arnold, Revolutionary Hero: An American Warrior Reconsidered* (New York University Press, 1997); and *A Respectable Army: The Military Origins of the Republic, 1763–1789* (3rd edition, Wiley-Blackwell, 2015) with M. E. Lender. He received his B.A. degree from Hiram College (summa cum laude) and earned his M.A. and Ph.D. degrees from the University of Wisconsin, Madison. Martin was Professor of History at Rutgers University before moving in 1980 to the University of Houston, where he currently serves as the Hugh Roy and Lillie Cranz Cullen University Professor of History.

CHRISTIAN M. MCBURNEY

Christian McBurney resides in the Washington, D.C. area and is an independent historian. He is the author of *Abductions in the American Revolution: Attempts to Kidnap George Washington, Benedict Arnold and Other Military and Civilian Leaders* (McFarland, 2016), *Spies in Revolutionary Rhode Island* (History Press, 2014), *Kidnapping the Enemy: The Special Operations to Capture Generals Charles Lee and Richard Prescott* (Westholme, 2014), and *The Rhode Island Campaign: The First French and American Operation of the Revolutionary War* (Westholme, 2011). He is also the founder and publisher of a Rhode Island history blog, at www.smallstatebighistory.com.

ANTHONY J. MINNA

Anthony J. Minna is a lawyer admitted to the bar in New York and Ontario. He holds a history degree from the University of Toronto and law degrees from the University of Toronto and the University of Brussels. He is the former CEO of UBS Trustees (Cayman) Ltd., and has worked in Canada, Liechtenstein, Switzerland, The Bahamas, and the Cayman Islands. He is currently a director of a pension plan administration company. His articles have appeared in the *Harvard Divinity Bulletin, The Bahamas Financial Review*, the *Toronto Star*, and other publications.

RON MORGAN

Since 2000, Ron has been involved with the Mount Independence Coalition, a non-profit organization dedicated to supporting the site of this critical Revolutionary War fortification on Lake Champlain in Orwell, Vermont. He has been studying, writing, and speaking about the mount and related topics whenever he has the opportunity. Ron supports his history habit by practicing law as a tax and estate planning attorney.

NEAL NUSHOLTZ

Neal Nusholtz is a graduate of Oberlin College with an A. B. in economics and a Juris Doctor from Cooley Law School. He currently practices tax law in Troy Michigan, specializing in various areas of income and estate and gift taxes and handling tax litigation in federal district and appellate courts and the United

States Tax Court, as well as administrative matters before the Internal Revenue Service. He has authored a number of articles on various aspects of tax law, including the impact of the collection of revenue on the mindset of jurists.

Jim Piecuch

Jim Piecuch earned his BA and MA degrees in history at the University of New Hampshire and his PhD at the College of William and Mary. He is an associate professor of history at Kennesaw State University. He is the author of *The Battle of Camden: A Documentary History*(History Press, 2006), *Three Peoples, One King: Loyalists, Indians, and Slaves in the Revolutionary South* (University of South Carolina Press, 2008), *"Cool Deliberate Courage": John Eager Howard in the American Revolution*, co-authored with John Beakes (Nautical & Aviation Pub, 2009), and *"The Blood Be Upon Your Head": Tarleton and the Myth of Buford's Massacre* (Southern Campaigns of the American Revolution, 2010).

Gene Procknow

Gene Procknow's research concentrations include interpreting the Revolution from a non-American perspective, better understanding the Revolution's global aspects, and Ethan Allen and the creation of Vermont. He is the author of the *Mad River Gazetteer*, which traces the naming of prominent Vermont place names to Revolutionary War patriots. Procknow authors a multidisciplinary writers blog on leadership development, poetry, and additional articles on the Revolution and Vermont at geneprock.com. He is married with two historian sons and lives in Washington, DC.

Tyler Rudd Putman

Tyler Rudd Putman is a Ph.D. candidate in the History of American Civilization Program in the Department of History at the University of Delaware. He has worked as a historical interpreter at Colonial Michilimackinac and sailed aboard the whaleship *Charles W. Morgan* and across the Atlantic aboard the *Corwith Cramer*.

Bryan Rindfleisch

Bryan Rindfleisch is an Assistant Professor at Marquette University, where he teaches courses in Colonial American and Native American history. He earned his Ph.D. degree at the University of Oklahoma. His articles have appeared in *Ethnohistory, History Compass, Graduate History Review, Wisconsin Magazine of History*, among others.

Conner Runyan

Conner Runyan was a teacher, administrator and professor for forty-one years in Alabama's public schools and universities. Now retired, he and his wife Carolyn live in Fyffe, Alabama.

Bob Ruppert

Bob Ruppert is a retired high school administrator from the greater Chicagoland area. He received his undergraduate degree from Loyola University and his graduate degree from the University of Illinois. He has been researching the American Revolution, the War for Independence and the Federal Period for more than ten years. His interest began in 1963 when he was eight years old. His parents took the whole family, by car, to Newport Beach, Virginia and a small town that was slowly being restored to its 18th century prominence— the town was Williamsburg.

RICHARD SAMBASIVAM

Richard Sambasivam is a Washington, D.C.-based public policy professional. He has conducted economic research on the U.S. economy, financial markets, and spillovers to foreign countries. He has visited South India numerous times and is currently researching the history of Mysore to learn more about geopolitics and his roots. He has an undergraduate degree in economics from UCLA.

MICHAEL J. F. SHEEHAN

Michael J. F. Sheehan holds a bachelor's degree in History from Ramapo College of New Jersey. He is the senior historian at the Stony Point Battlefield State Historic Site and is currently working on a book about the history of King's Ferry during the American Revolution. Deeply involved in the Brigade of the American Revolution since 2008, Michael has reenacted and spoken at countless historic sites and societies in New York and New Jersey, and is currently serving as a board member for Lamb's Artillery Company.

JOSHUA SHEPHERD

Joshua Shepherd, a sculptor and freelance writer, has created more than twenty public monuments. His articles, with a special focus on Revolutionary and frontier America, have appeared in publications including *MHQ: The Quarterly Journal of Military History, Military Heritage, Muzzle Blasts*, and *The Artilleryman*. He lives in rural Indiana with his wife and four children.

JOHN L. SMITH, JR.

John L. Smith, Jr. is a retired corporate communications manager for a Florida energy company. He is a state certified social sciences instructor and a former board member of the Tampa Bay History Center. Smith is a Vietnam-era veteran and holds honorable discharges from the U.S. Air Force Reserve and the U.S. Army Reserve. He graduated with a BS degree from the University of South Florida in 1989 and received an MBA from the University of Tampa. His historical work has been featured by *Knowledge Quest, National Review, CNN*, and *Smithsonian Magazine*.

ROGER SMITH

Roger Smith received his Ph.D. in Early American History and Atlantic World Studies from the University of Florida. His work received the Aschoff Fellowship Dissertation Award and the Jack and Celia Proctor Award in Southern History. He is an independent research historian with Colonial Research Associates, and has provided consultation to the AMC television series *Turn*.

ERIC STERNER

Eric Sterner is a national security and aerospace consultant in the Washington, DC area. He held senior staff positions for the Committees on Armed Services and Science in the House of Representatives and served in the Department of Defense and as NASA's Associate Deputy Administrator for Policy and Planning. He earned a Bachelor's at American University and two Master's Degrees from George Washington University. He has written for a variety of publications, ranging from academic journals to the trade and popular media.

MARY V. THOMPSON

Since 1980, Mary Thompson has worked at George Washington's Mount Vernon as a historic interpreter, curatorial assistant and registrar, research specialist, and research historian. She is currently responsible for research to support programs in all departments at Mount Vernon, with a primary focus on everyday life on the estate. She has lectured on a variety of subjects, ranging from family life and private enterprise among the slaves at Mount Vernon to funeral and mourning customs in George Washington's family. She has also authored chapters in a number of books, as well as entries in encyclopedias, and a variety of articles. She has a B.A. in History, with a minor in Folklore, from Samford University in Birmingham, Alabama, and an M.A. in History from the University of Virginia.

INDEX